Social Issues Primary Sources Collection

Immigration and Multiculturalism

Essential Primary Sources

Immigration and Multiculturalism

Essential Primary Sources

K. Lee Lerner, Brenda Wilmoth Lerner, and
Adrienne Wilmoth Lerner, Editors

GALE
CENGAGE Learning

Detroit • New York • San Francisco • New Haven, Conn • Waterville, Maine • London

Immigration and Multiculturalism: Essential Primary Sources

K. Lee Lerner, Brenda Wilmoth Lerner, and Adrienne Wilmoth Lerner, Editors

Project Editors
Dwayne D. Hayes and John McCoy

Editorial
Luann Brennan, Grant Eldridge, Anne Marie Hacht, Joshua Kondek, Andy Malonis, Mark Milne, Rebecca Parks, Mark Springer, Jennifer Stock

Permissions
Lisa Kincade, Emma Hull, Jackie Jones

Imaging and Multimedia
Dean Dauphinais, Leitha Etheridge-Sims, Lezlie Light, Michael Logusz, Dan Newell, Christine O'Bryan, Kelly A. Quin, Denay Wilding, Robyn Young

Product Design
Pamela A. Galbreath

Composition and Electronic Capture
Evi Seoud

Manufacturing
Rita Wimberley

Product Manager
Carol Nagel

LIBRARY OF CONGRESS CATALOGING-IN-PUBLICATION DATA

Immigration and multiculturalism: essential primary sources / K. Lee Lerner, Brenda Wilmoth Lerner, and Adrienne Wilmoth Lerner, editors.
  p. cm.--(Social issues primary sources collection)
  Includes bibliographical references and index.
  ISBN-10: 1-4144-0329-1 (hardcover : alk. paper)
  ISBN-13: 978-1-4144-0329-8
  1. United States--Emigration and immigration--Sources. 2. Multiculturalism--United States--Sources. I. Lerner, K. Lee. II. Lerner, Brenda Wilmoth. III. Lerner, Adrienne Wilmoth.

JV6465I4737 2007
304.80973--dc22   2006026241

This title is also available as an e-book.
ISBN-13: 978-1-4144-1265-8
ISBN-10: 1-4144-1265-7
Contact your Gale sales representative for ordering information.

Printed in the United States of America
4 5 6 7 8 9 14 13 12 11 10 09 08

Table of Contents

1   IMMIGRATION AND MIGRATION PRIOR TO 1845

4   IMMIGRATION FROM 1905-1945

5 IMMIGRATION FROM 1945 TO THE PRESENT

6 REFUGEES, ASYLEES, AND DISPLACED PERSONS

7 IMMIGRATION REFORM: THE ONGOING DEBATE

8 MULTICULTURALISM

Advisors and Contributors

While compiling this volume, the editors relied upon the expertise and contributions of the following scholars, journalists, and researchers who served as advisors and/or contributors for *Immigration and Multiculturalism: Essential Primary Sources*:

Steven Archambault (Ph.D. Candidate)
University of New Mexico
Albuquerque, New Mexico

William Arthur Atkins, M.S.
Normal, Illinois

Alicia Cafferty
University College
Dublin, Ireland

James Anthony Charles Corbett
Journalist
London, UK

Cynthia Danials, MPH
Columbia, South Carolina

Bryan Davies, J.D.
Ontario, Canada

Larry Gilman, Ph.D.
Sharon, Vermont

Amit Gupta, Ph.D.
Ahmedabad, India

Lynda Joeman
Independent Research Consultant (ex UK Home Office)
Kota Kinabalu, Sabah, Malaysia

Antoinette Johnson, MBA.
Hazel Park, MI

Alexander Ioffe, Ph.D.
Russian Academy of Sciences
Moscow, Russia

S. Layman, M.A.
Abingdon, MD

Adrienne Wilmoth Lerner (J.D. Candidate)
University of Tennessee College of Law
Knoxville, Tennessee

Pamela V. Michaels, M.A.
Forensic Psychologist
Santa Fe, New Mexico

Caryn Neumann, Ph.D.
Ohio State University
Columbus, Ohio

Mark Phillips, Ph.D.
Abilene Christian University
Abilene, Texas

Nephele Tempest
Los Angeles, California

Melanie Barton Zoltán, M.S.
Amherst, Massachusetts

Immigration and Multiculturalism: Essential Primary Sources is the product of a global group of multi-lingual scholars, researchers, and writers. The editors are grateful to Christine Jeryan, Amy Loerch Strumolo, Kate Kretschmann, John Krol and Judy Galens for their dedication and skill in copyediting both text and translations. Their efforts added significant accuracy and readability to this book. The editors also wish to acknowledge and thank Adrienne Wilmoth Lerner and Alicia Cafferty for their tenacious research efforts.

The editors gratefully acknowledge and extend thanks to Peter Gareffa, Carol Nagel, and Ellen McGeagh at Gale for their faith in the project and for their sound content advice. Special thanks go to the Gale copyright research and imaging teams for their patience, good advice, and skilled research into sometimes vexing copyright issues. The editors offer profound thanks to project managers Dwayne Hayes and John McCoy. Their clear thoughts, insights and trusted editorial judgment added significantly to the quality of *Immigration and Multiculturalism: Essential Primary Sources.*

Acknowledgements

Copyrighted excerpts in *Immigration and Multiculturalism: Essential Primary Sources* were reproduced from the following periodicals:

Economist, June 22, 2002; April 7, 2005. Copyright © 2002, 2005 The Economist Newspaper Ltd. All rights reserved. All further reproduction prohibited. www.economist.com—The Economist, December 1, 2005. Copyright © 2005 The Economist Newspaper Ltd. All rights reserved. Further reproduction prohibited. www.economist.com.—*The Guardian*, October 25, 2005. Copyright Guardian Newspapers Limited 2005. Reproduced by permission of Guardian News Service, LTD.—*Intelligence Report*, 2001. © Copyright 2001 Southern Poverty Law Center. Reproduced by permission.—*The Jewish News Weekly of Northern California*, April 19, 1996 for "Jewish Alumnus Sues Univ. of PA Over 'Water Buffalo' Incident" by Robert Leiter. Reproduced by permission of the author.—*Los Angeles Times*, March 26, 2006.Copyright © Tribune Media Services, Inc. All rights reserved. Reproduced by permission.—*Multi-Cultural Australia: United in Diversity*, 2003. Copyright © 2003 Commonwealth of Australia. Reproduced by permission.—*New York Times*, April 5, 2005; November 13, 2005; December 30, 2005. Copyright © 2005 by The New York Times Company. All reproduced by permission.— *The New York Times*, December 22, 1945; November 3, 1986. Copyright © 1945, 1986 by The New York Times Company. All reprinted with permission.—*New York Times Company*, March 16, 2006. Copyright © 2006 by The New York Times Company. Reproduced by permission.—*The News*, February 14, 1976. Reproduced by permission of Frederick News-Post and Randall Family LLC.—*Newsweek*, November 3, 2005. Copyright © 2005 Newsweek, Inc. Reproduced by permission.—*NYT*, May 26, 2005; December 16, 2005. Copyright © 2005 by The New York Times Company. All reproduced by permission.—*Poor Pat Must Emigrate*, 1845. The Historical Society of Pennsylvania, Broadsides Collection, The Balch Institute Collections. Reproduced by permission.—Reagan Signs into Law National King Holiday, *Syracuse Post Standard*, November 3, 1983. Reproduced by permission of the Associated Press.—*Washington Post*, March 18, 2006. Copyright © 2006, Washington Post. Reprinted with permission.— *What Immigrants and Refugees Need to Know about the New Tennessee Driver's License and "Certificate for Driving" Law*, June 28, 2004. Copyright © 2004 Time, Inc. All rights reserved. Reproduced by permission.

Copyrighted excerpts in *Immigration and Multiculturalism: Essential Primary Sources* were reproduced from the following books:

From *Germany for Germans: Xenophobia and Racist Violence in Germany*. Human Rights Watch (Helsinki), 1995. © Human Rights Watch 1995. Reproduced by permission.—From *Improving Education for Immigrant Students*. Northwest Regional Education Laboratory: Equity Center, 2001. Reproduced by permission.—From *Top Ten Immigration Myths and Facts*. National Immigration Forum, 2003. Reproduced by permission.—Boland, Eavan. From *An Origin Like Water: Collected Poems 1967–1987*. W. W. Norton & Company, 1987. Copyright © 1996 by Eavan Boland. All rights reserved. Used by permission of W. W. Norton & Company, Inc. In the U. K by permission of Carcanet Press Limited.—Chaudhuri, Amit. From *Granta*. Granta, 1999. Reproduced by permission of the author.—Cooke, Alistair. From *Letters From*

America: 1946–2004. Allen Lane, 2004. Copyright © 2004 The Estate of Alistair Cooke. Reproduced by permission of Penguin Books, Ltd.—Cooke, Alistair. From *Letters From America: 1946–2004.* Allen Lane, 2004. Copyright © 2004 the Estate of Alistair Cooke. All rights reserved. Reproduced by permission of Penguin Books, Ltd.—Ets, Marie Hall. From "The Trip to America" in *Rosa: The Life of an Italian Immigrant.* University of Wisconsin Press, 1999. Copyright © 1999 by University of Minnesota Press. All rights reserved. Reproduced by permission.—Hair, Penda D. From *Louder than Words.* Rockefeller Foundation, 2001. Copyright © 2001 the Rockefeller Foundation. All rights reserved. Reproduced by permission.—Hollingworth, John. From "Joseph Hollingworth to William and Nancy Rawcliff," in *The Hollingworth Letters: Technical Change in the Textile Industry.* Edited by Thomas W. Leavitt. Cambridge, MA.:M.I.T Press, 1969. Copyright © 1969 by M.I.T. Press. Reproduced by permission of The M.I.T Press, Cambridge, MA.—Powell, Enoch. From "The Annual Conference of the Rotary Club of London," in *Reflections of a Statesman: The Writings and Speeches of Enoch Powell.* Edited by Rex Collings. Bellew Publishing, 1968. Collection copyright © Enoch Powell 1991. All rights reserved. Reproduced by permission of the Estate of Enoch Powell.—Rabin, Yitzhak. From *Major Knesset Debates: 1948–1981.* University Press of America, 1993. Copyright © 1993 by University Press of America, Inc. All rights reserved. Reproduced by permission.—Santoli, Al. From *New Americans: An Oral History.* Viking, 1988. Copyright © Al Santoli, 1988. All rights reserved. Used by permission of Viking penguin, a division of Penguin Group (USA) Inc. In the U.K by permission of the author.—Somerville, Alexander. From "Longford," in *Letters from Ireland during the Famine of 1847.* Edited by K.D.M. Snell. Irish Academic Press, 1994. © K.D.M. Snell 1994. Reproduced by permission.—Thomas, Piri. From *Down These Mean Streets.* Alfred A. Knopf, 1967. Copyright © 1967 by Piri Thomas. Copyright renewed 1995 by Piri Thomas. Used by permission of Alfred A. Knopf, Inc., a division of Random House, Inc.—Yezierska, Anzia. From *Bread Givers.* Persea Books, 1975. Copyright © 1999 by Persea Books. Reproduced by permission.—Yitzak Rabin, and G. Cohen. From "Israel's Responsibility For and Policy Towards Diaspora Jewry," in *Major Knesset Debates.* Edited by Netanel Lorch. University Press of America, 1975. Copyright © 1975 by University Press of America, Inc. All rights reserved. Reproduced by permission.

Photographs and illustrations appearing in *Immigration and Multiculturalism: Essential Primary Sources* were received from the following sources:

1873 illustration from Leslie's Illustrated Magazine, photograph. © Corbis.—1933 World's Fair in Chicago, photograph. © Swim Ink 2, LLC/Corbis.—500,000 Latino workers and immigrants march in downtown Los Angeles, photograph. © Gene Blevins/LA Daily News/Corbis.—A Norwegian emigrant says good-bye, photograph. © Corbis.—A border guard on horseback escorts two Mexican illegal immigrants, photograph. © Danny Lehman/Corbis.—A close-up of a Hmong story cloth, photograph. AP Images.—A Greek family embarking on Ellis Island, photograph. © Bettmann/Corbis.—A group of Australian aborigines performs a ritual dance, photograph. © E.O. Hoppe/Corbis.—A Hmong story cloth depicting lightning and a tornado, photograph. AP Images.—A line of persons pictured at the General Post Office in New York City, photograph. © Bettmann/Corbis.—A mural showing various scenes from Irish life, photograph. STAN HONDAA/FP/Getty Images.—A painting depicting the arrival of the first prisoners at the Botany Bay penal colony, photograph. Time Life Pictures/Mansell/Time Life Pictures/Getty Images.—A poster for the Second Liberty Loan of 1917, photograph. © Swim Ink, LLC/Corbis.—A sign in Harlem, New York City, advertises Kosher Restaurant Featuring African Food, photograph. © Bettmann/Corbis.—A sketch from the Illustrated London news, photograph. © Corbis.—A student in the first and second grade class bilingual classroom, photograph. © David Butow/Corbis SABA.—A young migrant worker picks strawberries in a field, photograph. © Peter Turnley/Corbis.—A young Muslim girl marches during a rally, photograph. © Reuters/Corbis.—Aguilar, Alfonso, photograph. AP Images.—Aguirre, Eduardo and US Army Spc. Victor Alfonso Rojas, photograph. AP Images.—Amin, President Idi, photograph. AP Images.—An invitation to the inauguration of the Statue of Liberty by the president, 1886, photograph. Reproduced from the collections of the Library of Congress.—Anti-Chinese legislation cartoon, photograph. © Bettmann/Corbis.—Bartholdi, Frederic-Auguste, photograph. © Bettmann/Corbis.—Birmingham Race Riot, photograph. © Andy Warhol Foundation/Corbis.—Boatload of Haitian refugees, photograph. © Nathan Benn/Corbis.—Bok, Edward William, photograph. Getty Images.—Boys peddle bread on Mulberry Street, photograph. © Corbis.—Bramhall, Wes, photograph. © Saul Loebepaepa/Corbis.—Brown, Keith, Shelly Langlais, Command Sgt. Maj. Victor Martinez, and Army Chaplain Perry, photograph. AP Images.—Bush, President George W. poses with flag-waving new American citizens, photograph. © Reuters/Corbis.—Cartoon depicting the grim reaper arriving on a British ship, photograph. © Bettmann/Corbis.—Cartoon from the Wasp, 1885, photograph. The Library of Congress.—Cartoon of Chinese immigration, photograph. © Bettmann/Corbis.—Certificate of freedom, photograph. Australia/Hulton Archive/Getty Images.—Certificate of Indenture, photograph. Hulton Archive/Getty Images.—Chao, Elaine and President Bush, photograph. AP Images.—Chavez, Cesar, photograph. MPI/Getty Images.—Children in Bilingual Class, photograph. © Jeffry W Myers/Corbis.—Children lie on the street under a sprinkler on a hot day, photograph. © Gendreau Collection/Corbis.—Circa 1880 pamphlet encouraging westward migration to Kansas, photograph. © Bettmann/Corbis.—Composite of two bar graphs from the US Census Bureau, photograph. Adapted by Thomson Gale from data from the US Bureau of the Census. Reproduced by permission of Thomson Gale.—Crew of His Majesty's ship Guardian endeavoring to escape, photograph. Hulton Archive/Getty Images.—Cuban exiles on board a small boat, photograph. Lee Lockwood/Time Life Pictures/Getty Images.—Cuban refugees waiting for U.S. Immigration aboard shrimp boat, photograph. © Bettmann/Corbis.—De Gaulle, Charles, photograph. © Alain Nogues/Corbis/Sygma.—Displaced persons from various countries gather at a dispersal point in Ansalt, Germany, photograph. © Hulton-Deutsch Collection/Corbis.—Drawing of a slave ship, illustration. Hulton Archive/Getty Images.—East German workers, photograph. © Bettmann/Corbis.—Estonian Americans (group of people, eight men, three woman and one little girl), photograph. © UPI/Corbis-Bettmann.—Families of African American refugees, photograph. © Corbis.—Family waits to cross the border into California, photograph. © David Turnley/Corbis.—Federal agents take custody of six-year-old Cuban refugee Elian Gonzalez, photograph. © Reuters/Corbis.—Female workers examining textiles for imperfections, photograph. © Corbis-Bettmann.—Former sweatshop workers who were forced to work as garment workers, photograph. AP Images.—Funeral procession during Irish potato famine, illustration. © Hulton Getty/Liaison Agency.—Garces, Maria, photograph. AP Images.—Gefroerer, Stanislaus, photograph. Express Newspapers/Getty Images.—Gonzales, Alberto, photograph. Alex Wong/Getty Images.—Great Hall of Ellis Island, photograph. AP Images.—Grutter, Barbara, with Jennifer Gratz, photograph. AP Images.—Hamilton, Dr. Eddie photograph. AP Images.—Harper's Weekly 1869 illustration titled "Uncle Sam's Thanksgiving Dinner", photograph. The Library of Congress.—Hickok, Eugene and Jo

Lynne DeMary, photograph. AP Images.—Hines, Jason, photograph. AP Images.—Hispanic workers harvesting lettuce, photograph. © Joseph Sohm; ChromoSohm Inc./CORBIS.—Illustration depicting a colony of emigrants boarding a train, photograph. © Corbis.—Illustration of the assassination of President William McKinley, photograph. Getty Images.—Illustration shows nineteenth century hoodlums harassing a Chinese laborer, photograph .© Bettmann/Corbis.—Immigrant children being checked for disease, photograph. © Corbis-Bettmann.—Immigrant students hold a news conference, photograph. Spencer Platt/Getty Images.—Immigrants approaching the Statue of Liberty (on deck of sailing ship), painting. The Library of Congress.—Immigrants crowding the deck of the SS Prince Frederick Wilhelm, photograph. © Bettmann/Corbis.—Immigrants protest Church of Pi of Barcelona, photograph. Caser Rangel/AFP/Getty Images.—Immigration officials examine Japanese immigrants, photograph. © Corbis.—Italian immigrants (mother and three children), photograph. © Corbis-Bettmann Jewish boys wait in line to receive visas and to register in their new homeland, photograph. © Hulton-Deutsch Collection/Corbis.—Kelly, Ned, illustration. Hulton Archive/Getty Images.—King, Coretta Scott with President Ronald Reagan, photograph. © Corbis.—Lara, Aracely and Guiller mina Castellanos, photograph. AP Images.—Liberty Loan Poster, 1917, photograph. © KJ Historical/Corbis.—Madonna of the Slums memorable picture taken by Jacob Riis in a tenement, photograph. © Bettmann/Corbis.—Martinez, Guadalupe, photograph. AP Images.—Matisyahu performing in Aspen at the Belly Up, photograph. © Lynn Goldsmith/Corbis.—McCarrick, Theodore E., photograph. © Reuters/Corbis.—McKinley, William, at Pan-American Exposition, photograph.—McMullen, Thomas, photograph. David McNew/Getty Images.—Meister, Mark and Catherine with adopted children, photograph. © Dan Habib/The Concord Monitor/Corbis.—Members of the California Coali tion for Immigration Reform, photograph. AP Images.—Mexicans illegally crossing the US border, photograph. © David Turnley/Corbis.—Naturalization of foreigners, photograph. © Corbis.—Nazi Storm Troopers, photograph. © Hulton-Deutsch Collection/Corbis.—New citizens take the Oath of Allegiance, photograph. © Bettmann/Corbis.—Newly arrived Jewish exiles from Russia, illustration. © Bettmann/Corbis.—Papadopolous, Mrs. I., photograph. © Bettmann/Corbis.—People on the wharf in Christiana, Norway, photograph. © Corbis.—People pray on the eve of the 30th anniversary of the Fall of Saigon, photograph. David McNew/Getty Images.—Photo of woodcut shows anti-Irish riots in New York, photograph. © Bettmann/Corbis.—Pie chart from the US Census Bureau with the title "Foreign Born by World Region of Birth 2003", photograph. Adapted by Thomson Gale from data from the US Bureau of the Census. Reproduced by permission of Thomson Gale.—Polish and Russian passengers ride in the steerage of a ship, photograph. © Minnesota Historical Society/Corbis.—Political cartoon O'Connell, photograph. © Corbis.—Poor family in a tenement apartment, photograph. © Bettmann/Corbis.—Portraits of three native New Zealanders living near the British settlement, photograph. © Corbis.—Powell, Enoch, photograph. © Hulton-Deutsch Collection/Corbis.—Rabin, Prime Minister Yitzhak, photograph. © Bettmann/Corbis.—Red scare era cartoon originally appearing in Memphis Commercial Appeal depicting a European Anarchist sneaking up behind the Statue of Liberty with a knife and bomb, circa 1919.—Rhum, Keanu and Emily Phosy, photograph. AP Images.—Rwandan refugees arrive in Bukavu, Zaire, photograph. © Jon Jones/Sygma/Corbis.—Rwandan refugees gather at Ruzizi Bridge, photograph. © Howard Davies/Corbis.—Sanger, Marcia, photograph. AP Images.—Scandal of Mexican Illegal Immigrants, photograph. © Demaria Joe/Corbis.—Schwarzenegger, Gov. Arnold, photograph. AP Images.—Sheet music for an anti-immigrant Nativist song, photograph. MPI/Getty Images.—Sketch of a ship used to transport slaves, photograph. Hulton Archive/Getty Images.—Slave ship stowage layout, line drawing. The Library of Congress.—"Sorry" written in sky over Sydney Opera House in Sydney, Australia, photograph. A/P Images.—Springer, Dr. Bill examines Niranji Kanesalingam, photograph. © Rob Finch/The Oregonian/Corbis.—Students at Hazelton Area High School in Pennsylvania, photograph. AP Images.—Supporters of the Irish Lobby for Immigration Reform, photograph. AP Images.—Tancredo, Tom, photograph. AP Images.—Teenagers in Birmingham, Alabama, begin a segregation protest march, photograph. © Bettmann/Corbis.—Tennessee certificate for driving, photograph. AP Images.—"The Anti-Chinese Wall," political cartoon, photograph. The Library of Congress.—The Eagle Pass Border Patrol, photograph. © Shaul Schwarz/Corbis.—The house of Joseph Jenkins Roberts, photograph. © Corbis.—The Undocumented Christ, Our Lady of Refuge Catholic Church in Eagle Pass, Texas, photograph. AP Images.—The US Immigration and Naturalization Service, photograph. © Bettmann/Corbis.—The US immigration station at Angel Island, photograph. © Bettmann/Corbis.—The West Shore, a Portland, Oregon, magazine, covering the anti-Chinese riot, photograph. © Museum of History and Industry/Corbis.—Title Page for an extremely rare and early Western Colonization pamphlet from Arau, Switzerland, photograph. © Bettmann/Corbis.—Truckloads of Jewish immigrants arrive at a processing center, photograph. © Hulton-Deutsch Collection/Corbis.—Two charts from the US Census Bureau comparing educational attainment by immigrants and non-immigrants, 2003, photograph. Adapted by Thomson Gale from data from the US Bureau of the Census. Reproduced by permission of Thomson Gale.—Two Czechoslovakians women standing in front of brick wall, photograph. © Corbis/Bettmann.—Two men on the Mexican side of US/Mexico border fence, photograph. AP Images.—Ugandan Asians arrive at Stansted Airport, photograph. Keystone/Getty Images.—Uncle Sam welcomes immigrants, photograph. © Corbis.—Vaquerano, Carlos, photograph. AP Images.—Vietnamese boat people, rejected by the Malaysian authorities, photograph. © Jacques Pavlovsky/Sygma/Corbis.—World War II Propaganda Poster, photograph. © Bettmann/Corbis.—Yeperenye Festival celebrating 100 years of Australian Federation Tribes from around Australia, photograph. © John Van Hasselt/Corbis.—Young refugee from eastern Europe stand behind a chain link fence, photograph. © Jerry Cooke/Corbis.—Yun, Son Ah, photograph. AP Images.

Copyrighted excerpts in *Immigration and Multiculturalism: Essential Primary Sources* were reproduced from the following websites or other sources:

Amy [Undisclosed], "Amy's Personal Story," www.cosaonline.org/amy.html, *Coalition of Student Advocates (CoSA)*, 2002. Reproduced by permission.—Apple, R. W. Jr., "A Southern Star Rises in the Low Country," *nytimes.com*, March 15, 2006. Reproduced by permission.—"Berlusconi Warns Against Multiculturalism," *Nytimes.com*, March 28, 2006. Reproduced by permission of the Associated Press.—Bernstein, Nina, "Immigrant Victims of Abuse Are Illegally Denied Benefits, Suit Says," *New York Times*, December 13, 2005. Reproduced by permission.—Cass, Michael, "'Confederate' Will Remain in Name of Vanderbilt Dorm," *Tennessean.com*, July 12, 2005. Reproduced by permission.—Daniel B. Wood, "Discontent over Illegals in Arizona," *The Christian Science Monitor*, October 20, 2004. Reproduced by permission from *Christian Science Monitor*, (www.csmonitor.com).—Duigan, Peter, "Bilingual Education Since 1986," *Bilingual Education: A Critique*, 1992. Hoover Institution Press. Copyright © 1998 by the Board of Trustees of the Leland Stanford Junior University. Reproduced by permission of the publisher.—Ford, Richard, "Points System will Favour

Skilled Immigrant Workers," *Timesonline. co.uk*, March 8, 2006. Reproduced by permission.—Huerta, Rey, "The Most Memorable Time of Our Lives, 1968–1975," *Farmworker Movement Documentation Project*, 2003. Reproduced by permission of the author.—"Is Teaching 'La Causa' Grounds for Firing?" *Rethinking Schools*, 1998. Reproduced by permission.—Matthews, Jeffrey J., "Why Aren't Black Business Tycoons Celebrated During Black History Month?," hnn.articles/22169.html, *History News Network*, February 27, 2006. Reproduced by permission.—"McClatchy Adds 'Diversity Day' as an Annual Holiday," *PRNewswire.com*, October 7, 2003. Reproduced by permission of the McClatchy Company.—Miriam Jordan, "Immigrants Lament: Have Degree, No Job," *College Journal*, April 28, 2005. Republished with permission of Dow Jones & Company, conveyed through Copyright Clearance Center, Inc.—Ojito, Mirta, "Point of No Return," www.hispaniconline.com/magazine/2005/april/Features/ immigration.html, *Hispanic Magazine.com*, April, 2005. Reproduced by permission.—Paul Gorski, "The Language of Closet Racism: An Illustration," edchange.org/multicultural/papers/langofracism2. html, *EdChange Multicultural Pavilion Online*, 1995. © EdChange.org and Paul C. Gorski. Reproduced by permission.—Rethinking Schools Online, v. 12, 1998. © 1998 Rethinking Schools. Reproduced by permission.—Sanneh, Kelefa, "Dancehall with a Different Accent," *New York Times*, March 8, 2006. Reproduced by permission.—Smith, Nicola, "Holland Launches the Immigrant Quiz," *Times Online*, March 12, 2006. Reproduced by permission.—"Tom Tancredo's Wall," *WSJ.com Opinion Journal*, December 25, 2005. Reprinted with permission of The Wall Street Journal. Dow Jones & Company. All Rights Reserved.—"Universal Declaration of Human Rights," Articles 13–15 *http://www.un.org/Overview/rights.htm*, December 10, 1948. Reproduced by permission.

About the Set

Essential Primary Source titles are part of a ten-volume set of books in the Social Issues Primary Sources Collection designed to provide primary source documents on leading social issues of the nineteenth, twentieth, and twenty-first centuries. International in scope, each volume is devoted to one topic and will contain approximately 150 to 175 documents that will include and discuss speeches, legislation, magazine and newspaper articles, memoirs, letters, interviews, novels, essays, songs, and works of art essential to understanding the complexity of the topic.

Each entry will include standard subheads: key facts about the author; an introduction placing the piece in context; the full or excerpted document; a discussion of the significance of the document and related event; and a listing of further resources (books, periodicals, Web sites, and audio and visual media).

Each volume will contain a topic-specific introduction, topic-specific chronology of major events, an index especially prepared to coordinate with the volume topic, and approximately 150 images.

Volumes are intended to be sold individually or as a set.

THE ESSENTIAL PRIMARY SOURCE SERIES

- *Terrorism: Essential Primary Sources*
- *Medicine, Health, and Bioethics: Essential Primary Sources*
- *Environmental Issues: Essential Primary Sources*
- *Crime and Punishment: Essential Primary Sources*
- *Gender Issues and Sexuality: Essential Primary Sources*
- *Human and Civil Rights: Essential Primary Sources*
- *Government, Politics, and Protest: Essential Primary Sources*
- *Social Policy: Essential Primary Sources*
- *Immigration and Multiculturalism: Essential Primary Sources*
- *Family in Society: Essential Primary Sources*

Introduction

Immigration and Multiculturalism: Essential Primary Sources provides readings into two centuries of global changes in populations and cultures—and insights into both historical and modern political flashpoints.

Multiculturalism is a phrase used to articulate the existence, distinction, and preservation of different cultures within a larger political or social entity such as a nation, state, or society. Multiculturalism is argued to be a fundamental human right, the right to maintain culture and heritage, and this view is enshrined in the UNESCO Universal Declaration on Cultural Diversity. Akin to the human genome, the diversity of cultures is often considered a social strength, a source of robustness and capacity. Critics of multiculturalism, however, characterize cultural diversity as a social weakness. Regardless, understanding of the debate surrounding multiculturalism, its manifest joys and possible perils, is essential at a time in human history when the basis for war and terrorism is essentially and deeply rooted in a clash of cultures.

If multiculturalism reflects existing diversity, immigration describes how societies and populations evolve in term of populations. Such evolution, in turn, often alters the cultural landscape and provides the basis for the multicultural state or society.

The resources in *Immigration and Multiculturalism: Essential Primary Sources* provide ample evidence that tensions exist between the range of ideals embodied in "open immigration" and "closed border policies." The readings also provide evidence of the tensions that exist between the ideals of multiculturalism and those of assimilation. The struggles over how to define these terms, and how to put ideals into law foster contentious political debate around the world. The issues are not unique to any one nation. Many countries and societies struggle to balance progressive and tolerant policies toward immigration and multiculturalism with sometimes deeply rooted policies supporting monoculturalism.

Although the primary sources contained in *Immigration and Multiculturalism: Essential Primary Sources* are oriented toward debates taking place in Western society (mainly the United States and Europe) there is a deliberate attempt to provide a glimpse into the larger and far wider ranging global debates. The editors intend that *Immigration and Multiculturalism: Essential Primary Sources* provides readers a wide-ranging and readable collection of sources designed to stimulate interest and critical thinking, and to highlight the complexity of the issues and depth of passions related to immigration and multiculturalism debates.

K. Lee Lerner, Brenda Wilmoth Lerner, &
Adrienne Wilmoth Lerner, editors
Paris, London, and Jacksonville, FL
July, 2006

About the Entry

The primary source is the centerpiece and main focus of each entry in *Immigration and Multiculturalism: Essential Primary Sources*. In keeping with the philosophy that much of the benefit from using primary sources derives from the reader's own process of inquiry, the contextual material surrounding each entry provides access and ease of use, as well as giving the reader a springboard for delving into the primary source. Rubrics identify each section and enable the reader to navigate entries with ease.

ENTRY STRUCTURE

- Primary Source/Entry Title, Subtitle, Primary Source Type
- Key Facts—essential information about the primary source, including creator, date, source citation, and notes about the creator.
- Introduction—historical background and contributing factors for the primary source.
- Primary Source—in text, text facsimile, or image format; full or excerpted.
- Significance—importance and impact of the primary source related events.
- Further Resources—books, periodicals, websites, and audio and visual material.

NAVIGATING AN ENTRY

Entry elements are numbered and reproduced here, with an explanation of the data contained in these elements explained immediately thereafter according to the corresponding numeral.

Primary Source/Entry Title, Subtitle, Primary Source Type

[1] **Message from President of United States Favoring Repeal of the Chinese Exclusion Law**

[2]

[3] **Speech**

[1] **Primary Source/Entry Title:** The entry title is usually the primary source title. In some cases where long titles must be shortened, or more generalized topic titles are needed for clarity primary source titles are generally depicted as subtitles. Entry titles appear as catchwords at the top outer margin of each page.

[2] **Subtitle:** Some entries contain subtitles.

[3] **Primary Source Type:** The type of primary source is listed just below the title. When assigning source types, great weight was given to how the author of the primary source categorized the source.

Key Facts

[4] **Author:** Franklin Delano Roosevelt

[5] **Date:** October 11, 1943

[6] **Source:** Roosevelt, Franklin Delano. "Message to Congress Favoring Repeal of the Chinese Exclusion Law." Washington, D.C., October 11, 1943.

[7] **About the Author:** Franklin Delano Roosevelt (1882–1945) was the thirty-second President of the United States, serving from 1933 until his death in April 1945.

Roosevelt presided over two of the most difficult periods in American history, the Great Depression and World War II.

[4] **Author, Artist, or Organization:** The name of the author, artist, or organization responsible for the creation of the primary source begins the Key Facts section.

[5] **Date of Origin:** The date of origin of the primary source appears in this field and may differ from the date of publication in the source citation below it; for example, speeches are often delivered before they are published.

[6] **Source Citation:** The source citation is a full bibliographic citation, giving original publication data as well as reprint and/or online availability.

[7] **About the Author:** A brief bio of the author or originator of the primary source gives birth and death dates and a quick overview of the person's work. This rubric has been customized in some cases. If the primary source is a written document, the term "author" appears; however, if the primary source is a work of art, the term "artist" is used, showing the person's direct relationship to the primary source. For primary sources created by a group, "organization" may have been used instead of "author." Other terms may also be used to describe the creator or originator of the primary source. If an author is anonymous or unknown, a brief "About the Publication" sketch may appear.

Introduction Essay

[8] **INTRODUCTION**

The prohibitions against the immigration of Chinese persons to the United States had been a part of American law for over sixty years when President Roosevelt urged the repeal of this legislation in October 1943. The Chinese Exclusion Act of 1882 was the first of a series of laws directed at Asian immigration to the United States.

The historical focus of the Exclusion Act and its successors was economic. In response to reports of the discovery of gold in California, the first Chinese immigrants arrived in that state in 1849. Chinese laborers also formed a significant part of the workforce necessary to build the American transcontinental railroad, an engineering work completed in 1869. Following the completion of the railroad, Chinese workers were increasingly seen as a threat to the ability of the white labor force to secure jobs at a living wage.

The initial Chinese Exclusion Act was in effect for a period of ten years. This law was later extended in its scope to include most persons of Asian ancestry—Indians, Koreans, and the Japanese. In addition to the

economic impetus underlying the desire to stem Asian immigration, particularly along the West Coast of the United States, racial profiling of Asians played a role in the exclusion efforts. The Chinese and Japanese, in particular, were seen by some as a general threat to the white population of America.

In 1913, California passed the Alien Land Law to prohibit any person ineligible for American citizenship from owning property in the state. As in most areas of the United States, there was little distinction drawn between Asian groups in either legislation or public opinion. At the time, many Americans held negative attitudes towards all Asians.

American attitudes towards the Japanese and Chinese diverged as political and military events unfolded in the 1930s. Japan began a significant military build-up that culminated in the invasion of Manchuria, a region adjacent to China, in 1931. By 1937, Japan and China were engaged in a war, known as the Second Sino-Japanese War, a conflict that ultimately merged into World War II. China, a country that was also involved in a civil war between its Nationalist forces led by Chiang Kai Shek, and Communist rebels led by Mao Zedong, was now an American ally against Japanese expansionism in the Pacific region.

Proof of the new divergence in the status of the Chinese and the Japanese in the eyes of the American government was Executive Order 9066, issued by President Roosevelt in March 1942. This order mandated the construction of internment camps that would ultimately accommodate over 120,000 Japanese males. Over sixty percent of those interned in the camps were American citizens.

[8] **Introduction:** The introduction is a brief essay on the contributing factors and historical context of the primary source. Intended to promote understanding and equip the reader with essential facts to understand the context of the primary source.

To maintain ease of reference to the primary source, spellings of names and places are used in accord with their use in the primary source. Accordingly names and places may have different spellings in different articles. Whenever possible, alternative spellings are provided to provide clarity.

To the greatest extent possible we have attempted to use Arabic names instead of their Latinized versions. Where required for clarity we have included Latinized names in parentheses after the Arabic version. Alas, we could not retain some diacritical marks (e.g. bars over vowels, dots under consonants). Because there is no generally accepted rule or consensus regarding the format of translated Arabic names, we have adopted the straightforward, and we hope sensitive, policy of using names as they are used or cited in their region of origin.

[9] PRIMARY SOURCE

To the Congress of the United States:

There is now pending before the Congress legislation to permit the immigration of Chinese people into this country and to allow Chinese residents here to become American citizens. I regard this legislation as important in the cause of winning the war and of establishing a secure peace.

China is our ally. For many long years she stood alone in the fight against aggression. Today we fight at her side. She has continued her gallant struggle against very great odds.

China has understood that the strategy of victory in this World War first required the concentration of the greater part of our strength upon the European front. She has understood that the amount of supplies we could make available to her has been limited by difficulties of transportation. She knows that substantial aid will be forthcoming as soon as possible—aid not only in the form of weapons and supplies, but also in carrying out plans already made for offensive, effective action. We and our allies will aim our forces at the heart of Japan—in ever-increasing strength until the common enemy is driven from China's soil.

But China's resistance does not depend alone on guns and planes and on attacks on land, on the sea, and from the air. It is based as much in the spirit of her people and her faith in her allies. We owe it to the Chinese to strengthen that faith. One step in this direction is to wipe from the statute books those anachronisms in our law which forbid the immigration of Chinese people into this country and which bar Chinese residents from American citizenship.

Nations like individuals make mistakes. We must be big enough to acknowledge our mistakes of the past and to correct them.

By the repeal of the Chinese exclusion laws, we can correct a historic mistake and silence the distorted Japanese propaganda. The enactment of legislation now pending before the Congress would put Chinese immigrants on a parity with those from other countries. The Chinese quota would, therefore, be only about 100 immigrants a year. There can be no reasonable apprehension that any such number of immigrants will cause unemployment or provide competition in the search for jobs.

The extension of the privileges of citizenship to the relatively few Chinese residents in our country would operate as another meaningful display of friendship. It would be additional proof that we regard China not only as a partner in waging war but that we shall regard her as a partner in days of peace. While it would give the Chinese a preferred status over certain other oriental people, their great contribution to the cause of decency and freedom entitles them to such preference.

I feel confident that the Congress is in full agreement that these measures long overdue should be taken to correct an injustice to our friends. Action by the Congress now will be an earnest of our purpose to apply the policy of the good neighbor to our relations with other peoples.

Franklin D. Roosevelt.
The White House, October 1, 1943.

[9] **Primary Source:** The majority of primary sources are reproduced as plain text. The primary source may appear excerpted or in full, and may appear as text, text facsimile (photographic reproduction of the original text), image, or graphic display (such as a table, chart, or graph).

The font and leading of the primary sources are distinct from that of the context—to provide a visual clue to the change, as well as to facilitate ease of reading. As needed, the original formatting of the text is preserved in order to more accurately represent the original (screenplays, for example). In order to respect the integrity of the primary sources, content some readers may consider sensitive (for example, the use of slang, ethnic or racial slurs, etc.) is retained when deemed to be integral to understanding the source and the context of its creation.

Primary source images (whether photographs, text facsimiles, or graphic displays) are bordered with a distinctive double rule. Most images have brief captions.

The term "narrative break" appears where there is a significant amount of elided (omitted) material with the text provided (for example, excerpts from a work's first and fifth chapters, selections from a journal article abstract and summary, or dialogue from two acts of a play).

Significance Essay

[10] **SIGNIFICANCE**
The original Chinese Exclusion laws were a form of American economic protectionism. In 1943, the basis for the repeal of these laws was the removal of

an embarrassing symbol from the relations between two military and political allies.

Roosevelt hints at this fact in the course of his speech. He specifically calls the exclusion laws a mistake, one that had to be admitted for the military alliance and support the United States was extending to China to properly function. Roosevelt also obliquely acknowledges concerns regarding the economic impact of greater Chinese immigration and notes that the proposed quotas in the pending legislation will properly address this concern.

Soon after Roosevelt's address to Congress, he, British Prime Minister Winston Churchill (1874–1965), and Chinese Nationalist leader Chiang Kai-Shek (1887–1975) participated in the Cairo Conference of November 1943. In Cairo, the leaders discussed the possible post-war political alignments in the Pacific region, where all three leaders agreed that the ultimate goal in a successful war against Japan was the restoration of lands conquered by the Japanese to their former nations. The positions of China, Great Britain, and the United States in Cairo were confirmed in the publication of an official communique on December 1, 1943.

The repeal of the Chinese Exclusion Act was passed by Congress on December 17, 1943, in legislation that was also known as the Magnuson Act. While the repeal would create future immigration opportunities for tens of thousands of Chinese, the first consequence of the new law was a military one. As a result of the repeal, approximately 14,000 men of Chinese descent became immediately eligible for the American military draft.

The speed with which Roosevelt was able to initiate the desired legislative change to American immigration law was significant. Less than ten weeks passed from the time of Roosevelt's address to Congress urging the repeal of the Chinese exclusion laws to the passage of the Magnuson Act.

The American legislative action also sent a message to other nations that had constructed legislative barriers against Chinese immigration. Canada had passed its first exclusionary law against the Chinese in 1885, and like the United States, Canada had maintained its immigration restrictions with a series of amendments through the 1920s. Canada also ordered the internment of the Japanese male population on its West Coast in 1942. Canada followed the American repeal of the Chinese exclusion laws with similar legislation in 1947.

When viewed from a historical perspective, the 1943 repeal of the Chinese exclusion laws is a stepping stone in the United States to the fuller form of immigration permitted in the Immigration and Naturalization Act of 1952, where specific racial quotas were eliminated and replaced by a framework of rules based upon the applicant's country of origin. The U.S. government further modified its immigration laws with the Immigration Act of 1965.

The great irony of the 1943 legislation and the motivation of Roosevelt to ensure strong relations with his Chinese military ally came after World War II ended in 1945. In 1946, a full scale civil war erupted in China; by 1949, the Communists of Mao Zedong had taken control of the country, driving the Nationalists of Chiang Kai-Shek onto the island of Taiwan. By 1950, the new Chinese government and its army were a de facto enemy of the United States in the Korean War (1950–1953), since China was allied with North Korea against South Korea, the United States, and various allied nations. Since 1949, the United States has continued to support the Nationalist government in Taiwan in the face of significant Chinese governmental pressure to renounce this tie.

[10] **Significance:** The significance discusses the importance and impact of the primary source and the event it describes.

Further Resources

[11] **FURTHER RESOURCES**
Books

Dower, John W. *War without Mercy: Race and Power in the Pacific War*. New York: Pantheon, 1987.

Tucker, Nancy Bernkoft, ed. *China Confidential: American Diplomats and Sino-American Relations 1945–1996*. New York: Columbia University Press, 2001.

Periodicals

Ma, Xiaohua. "A Democracy at War: The American Campaign to Repeal Chinese Exclusion in 1943." *Japanese Journal of American Studies* 9 (1998): 121–142.

[11] **Further Resources:** A brief list of resources categorized as Books, Periodicals, Web sites, and Audio and Visual Media provides a stepping stone to further study.

SECONDARY SOURCE CITATION FORMATS (HOW TO CITE ARTICLES AND SOURCES)

Alternative forms of citations exist and examples of how to cite articles from this book are provided below:

APA Style

Books: Dublin, Thomas, ed. (1993). *Immigrant Voices: New Lives in America, 1773–1986*. Urbana: University of

Illinois Press. Excerpted in K. Lee Lerner and Brenda Wilmoth Lerner, eds., (2006) *Immigration and Multiculturalism: Essential Primary Sources*, Farmington Hills, Mich.: Thomson Gale.

Periodicals: Eldershaw, Philip S. (September 1909). "The Exclusion of Asiatic Immigrants in Australia." *The Annals of the American Academy of Political and Social Science* 34 : 190–203.Excerpted in K. Lee Lerner and Brenda Wilmoth Lerner, eds., (2006) *Immigration and Multiculturalism: Essential Primary Sources*, Farmington Hills, Mich.: Thomson Gale.

Web sites: *Coalition of Student Advocates*. "Amy's Story." Retrieved from http://www.cosaonline.org/amy.html. Excerpted in K. Lee Lerner and Brenda Wilmoth Lerner, eds., (2006) *Immigration and Multiculturalism: Essential Primary Sources*, Farmington Hills, Mich.: Thomson Gale.

Chicago Style

Books: Dublin, Thomas, ed. *Immigrant Voices: New Lives in America, 1773–1986*. Urbana: University of Illinois Press, 1993. Excerpted in K. Lee Lerner and Brenda Wilmoth Lerner, eds., *Immigration and Multiculturalism: Essential Primary Sources*, Farmington Hills, Mich.: Thomson Gale, 2006.

Periodicals: Eldershaw, Philip S. "The Exclusion of Asiatic Immigrants in Australia." *The Annals of the American Academy of Political and Social Science* 34 (September 1909): 190–203. Excerpted in K. Lee Lerner and Brenda Wilmoth Lerner, eds., *Immigration and Multiculturalism: Essential Primary Sources*, Farmington Hills, Mich.: Thomson Gale, 2006.

Web sites: *Coalition of Student Advocates*. "Amy's Story." <http://www.cosaonline.org/amy.html> (accessed July 1, 2006). Excerpted in K. Lee Lerner and Brenda Wilmoth Lerner, eds., *Immigration and Multiculturalism: Essential Primary Sources*, Farmington Hills, Mich.: Thomson Gale, 2006.

MLA Style

Books: Dublin, Thomas, ed. *Immigrant Voices: New Lives in America, 1773–1986*, Urbana: University

of Illinois Press, 1993. Excerpted in K. Lee Lerner and Brenda Wilmoth Lerner, eds., *Immigration and Multiculturalism: Essential Primary Sources*, Farmington Hills, Mich.: Thomson Gale, 2006.

Periodicals: Eldershaw, Philip S. "The Exclusion of Asiatic Immigrants in Australia." *The Annals of the American Academy of Political and Social Science*, 34, September 1909: 190–203. Excerpted in K. Lee Lerner and Brenda Wilmoth Lerner, eds., *Immigration and Multiculturalism: Essential Primary Sources*, Farmington Hills, Mich.: Thomson Gale, 2006.

Web sites: "Amy's Story." *Coalition of Student Advocates*. 1 July, 2006. <http://www.cosaonline.org/amy.html> Excerpted in K. Lee Lerner and Brenda Wilmoth Lerner, eds., *Immigration and Multiculturalism: Essential Primary Sources*, Farmington Hills, Mich.: Thomson Gale, 2006.

Turabian Style

Books: Dublin, Thomas, ed. *Immigrant Voices: New Lives in America, 1773–1986* (Urbana: University of Illinois Press, 1993). Excerpted in K. Lee Lerner and Brenda Wilmoth Lerner, eds., *Immigration and Multiculturalism: Essential Primary Sources* (Farmington Hills, Mich.: Thomson Gale, 2006).

Periodicals: Eldershaw, Philip S. "The Exclusion of Asiatic Immigrants in Australia." *The Annals of the American Academy of Political and Social Science* 34 (September 1909): 190–203. Excerpted in K. Lee Lerner and Brenda Wilmoth Lerner, eds., *Immigration and Multiculturalism: Essential Primary Sources* (Farmington Hills, Mich.: Thomson Gale, 2006).

Web sites: *Coalition of Student Advocates*. "Amy's Story." available from http://www.cosaonline.org/amy.html; accessed 1 July, 2006. Excerpted in K. Lee Lerner and Brenda Wilmoth Lerner, eds., *Immigration and Multiculturalism: Essential Primary Sources* (Farmington Hills, Mich.: Thomson Gale, 2006).

Using Primary Sources

The definition of what constitutes a primary source is often the subject of scholarly debate and interpretation. Although primary sources come from a wide spectrum of resources, they are united by the fact that they individually provide insight into the historical *milieu* (context and environment) during which they were produced. Primary sources include materials such as newspaper articles, press dispatches, autobiographies, essays, letters, diaries, speeches, song lyrics, posters, works of art—and in the twenty-first century, web logs—that offer direct, first-hand insight or witness to events of their day.

Categories of primary sources include:

- Documents containing firsthand accounts of historic events by witnesses and participants. This category includes diary or journal entries, letters, email, newspaper articles, interviews, memoirs, and testimony in legal proceedings.
- Documents or works representing the official views of both government leaders and leaders of terrorist organizations. These include primary sources such as policy statements, speeches, interviews, press releases, government reports, and legislation.
- Works of art, including (but certainly not limited to) photographs, poems, and songs, including advertisements and reviews of those works that help establish an understanding of the cultural milieu (the cultural environment with regard to attitudes and perceptions of events).
- Secondary sources. In some cases, secondary sources or tertiary sources may be treated as primary sources. In some cases articles and sources are created many years after an event. Ordinarily, a historical retrospective published after the initial event is not be considered a primary source. If, however, a resource contains statement or recollections of participants or witnesses to the original event, the source may be considered primary with regard to those statements and recollections.

ANALYSIS OF PRIMARY SOURCES

The material collected in this volume is not intended to provide a comprehensive overview of a topic or event. Rather, the primary sources are intended to generate interest and lay a foundation for further inquiry and study.

In order to properly analyze a primary source, readers should remain skeptical and develop probing questions about the source. As in reading a chemistry or algebra textbook, historical documents require readers to analyze them carefully and extract specific information. However, readers must also read "beyond the text" to garner larger clues about the social impact of the primary source.

In addition to providing information about their topics, primary sources may also supply a wealth of insight into their creator's viewpoint. For example, when reading a news article about an outbreak of disease, consider whether the reporter's words also indicate something about his or her origin, bias (an irrational disposition in favor of someone or something), prejudices (an irrational disposition against someone or something), or intended audience.

Students should remember that primary sources often contain information later proven to be false, or contain viewpoints and terms unacceptable to future generations. It is important to view the primary source within the historical and social context existing at its creation. If for example, a newspaper article is written within hours or days of an event, later developments may reveal some assertions in the original article as false or misleading.

TEST NEW CONCLUSIONS AND IDEAS

Whatever opinion or working hypothesis the reader forms, it is critical that they then test that hypothesis against other facts and sources related to the incident. For example, it might be wrong to conclude that factual mistakes are deliberate unless evidence can be produced of a pattern and practice of such mistakes with an intent to promote a false idea.

The difference between sound reasoning and preposterous conspiracy theories (or the birth of urban legends) lies in the willingness to test new ideas against other sources, rather than rest on one piece of evidence such as a single primary source that may contain errors. Sound reasoning requires that arguments and assertions guard against argument fallacies that utilize the following:

- false dilemmas (only two choices are given when in fact there are three or more options)
- arguments from ignorance (*argumentum ad ignorantiam*; because something is not known to be true, it is assumed to be false)
- possibilist fallacies (a favorite among conspiracy theorists who attempt to demonstrate that a factual statement is true or false by establishing the possibility of its truth or falsity. An argument

where "it could be" is usually followed by an unearned "therefore, it is.")
- slippery slope arguments or fallacies (a series of increasingly dramatic consequences is drawn from an initial fact or idea)
- begging the question (the truth of the conclusion is assumed by the premises)
- straw man arguments (the arguer mischaracterizes an argument or theory and then attacks the merits of their own false representations)
- appeals to pity or force (the argument attempts to persuade people to agree by sympathy or force)
- prejudicial language (values or moral judgments are attached to certain arguments or facts)
- personal attacks (*ad hominem*; an attack on a person's character or circumstances)
- anecdotal or testimonial evidence (stories that are unsupported by impartial facts or data that is not reproducible)
- *post hoc* (after the fact) fallacies (because one thing follows another, it is held to cause the other)
- the fallacy of the appeal to authority (the argument rests upon the credentials of a person, not the evidence).

Despite the fact that some primary sources can contain false information or lead readers to false conclusions based on the "facts" presented, they remain an invaluable resource regarding past events. Primary sources allow readers and researchers to come as close as possible to understanding the perceptions and context of events and thus, to more fully appreciate how and why misconceptions occur.

Chronology

So that the events in this volume may be placed in a larger historical context, the following is a general chronology of important historical and social events along with specific events related to the subject of this volume.

1772: England outlaws slavery.

1775: James Watt invents the steam engine. The invention marks the start of the Industrial Revolution.

1776: Declaration of Independence proclaims American colonies' independence from the British Empire.

1781: The thirteenth state ratifies the Articles of Confederation, creating the United States.

1785: *The Daily Universal Register*, later known as *The Times* (London), publishes its first issue.

1786: The United States establishes first Native American reservation.

1786: Britain establishes its first colony in Southeast Asia, beginning an age of European colonial expansion in Asia.

1787: The Constitutional Convention in Philadelphia adopts the U.S. Constitution.

1787: The Society for the Abolition of the Slave Trade is established in Britain.

1789: First nationwide election in the United States.

1789: Citizens of Paris storm the Bastille prison. The event ignites the French Revolution.

1789: Declaration of the Rights of Man is issued in France.

1790: The federal government established residency requirements for naturalization.

1790: First U.S. census is taken.

1791: The states ratify the Bill of Rights, the first ten amendments to the U.S. Constitution.

1793: Louis XVI, King of France, is guillotined by revolutionaries.

1793: "Reign of Terror" begins in France. Almost 40,000 people face execution.

1794: The French Republic abolishes slavery.

1796: Edward Jenner administers the first vaccination for smallpox.

1798: Irish tenant farmers rebel against British landowners in the Irish Rebellion.

1798: The United States enacts the Alien and Sedition Acts making it a federal crime to "write, publish, or utter false or malicious statements" about the United States government.

1800–1849

1800: World population reaches one billion.

1801: Union of Great Britain and Ireland.

1803: Napoleonic Wars begin. Napoleon's army conquers much of Europe before Napoleon is defeated at Waterloo in 1815.

1803: The United States pays France $15 million for the Louisiana Territory extending from the Mississippi River to the Rocky Mountains.

1808: The importation of slaves is outlawed in the United States, but the institution of African slavery continues until 1864.

1812: The North American War of 1812 between the United States and the United Kingdom of Great Britain and Ireland. The war lasts until the beginning of 1815.

1814: The Congress of Vienna redraws the map of Europe after the defeat of Napoleon.

1819: Congress mandates immigration reports.

1819: South American colonial revolutions begin when Columbia declares its independence from Spain in 1819.

1820: Temperance movement begins in United States.

1821: Mexico declares independence from Spain.

1821: Jean-Louis Prévost (1790–1850), Swiss physician, jointly publishes a paper with French chemist Jean-Baptiste-Andr, Dumas (1800–1884), which demonstrates for the first time that spermatozoa originate in tissues of the male sex glands. In 1824 they also give the first detailed account of the segmentation of a frog's egg.

1822: American Colonization Society advocates the repatriation of freed African slaves to the Colony of Liberia.

1822: Jean-François Champollion (1790–1832), French historian and linguist, deciphers Egyptian hieroglyphics using the Rosetta Stone. He is the first to realize that some of the signs are alphabetic, some syllabic, and some determinative (standing for a whole idea or object previously expressed).

1822: William Church (c.1778–1863), American-English inventor, patents a machine that sets type. Patented in Boston, his machine consists of a keyboard on which each key releases a piece of letter type that is stored in channels in a magazine.

1829: Lambert-Adolphe-Jacques Quetelet (1796–1874), Belgian statistician and astronomer, gives the first statistical breakdown of a national census. He correlates death with age, sex, occupation, and economic status in the Belgian census.

1830: Indian Removal Act forces the removal of Native Americans living in the eastern part of the United States.

1831: Charles Robert Darwin began his historic voyage on the H.M.S. *Beagle* (1831–1836). His observations during the voyage lead to his theory of evolution by means of natural selection.

1832: The advent of the telegraph.

1833: A washboard is patented in the United States. This simple wooden-framed device has a corrugated rectangular surface that is used for scrubbing clothes clean.

1835: Rubber nipples are introduced for infant nursing bottles.

1836: Johann Nikolaus von Dreyse (1787–1867), German inventor, patents the "needle" rifle with a bolt breech-loading mechanism. This gun is loaded through the rear of the barrel.

1838: More than 15,000 Cherokee Indians are forced to march from Georgia to present-day Oklahoma on the "Trail of Tears."

1838: Samuel Finley Breese Morse (1791–1872) and Alfred Vail (1807–1859) unveil their telegraph system.

1839: Theodore Schwann (1810–1882), German physiologist, extends the theory of cells from plants to animals. He states in his book, *Mikroscopische Untersuchungen*, that all living things are made up of cells, each of which contains certain essential components. He also coins the term "metabolism" to describe the overall chemical changes that take place in living tissue.

1840: John William Draper (1811–1882), American chemist, takes a daguerreotype portrait of his sister, Dorothy. This is the oldest surviving photograph of a person.

1840: Pierre-Charles-Alexandre Louis (1787–1872), French physician, pioneers medical statistics, being the first to compile systematically records of diseases and treatments.

1841: Horace Greeley (1811–1872), American editor and publisher, founds the *New York Tribune*, which eventually becomes the *Herald Tribune* after a merger in 1924.

1842: John Benne Lawes (1814–1900), English agriculturalist, patents a process for treating phosphate rock with sulfuric acid to produce superphosphate. He also opens the first fertilizer factory this year, thus beginning the artificial fertilizer industry.

1842: Samuel Finley Breese Morse (1791–1872), American artist and inventor, lays the first underwater telegraph cable in New York Harbor. It fails due to a lack of proper insulation materials.

1842: The first shipment of milk by rail in the United States is successfully accomplished.

1844: Robert Chambers (1802–1871), Scottish publisher, publishes anonymously his *Vestiges of the Natural History of Creation*. This best-selling book offers a sweeping view of evolution and although incorrect in many specifics, it does pave the way for Darwin's theory by familiarizing the public with evolutionary concepts.

1845: The potato famine begins in Ireland. Crop failures and high rents on tenant farms cause a three-year famine. Millions of Irish immigrate to flee starvation.

1846: Mexican War begins as U.S. attempts to expand its territory in the Southwest.

1846: Oliver Wendall Holmes (1809–1894), American author and physician, first suggests the use of the terms "anaesthesia" and "anaesthetic" in a letter to William Thomas Green Morton (1819–1868), American dentist.

1847: Claude-Felix-Abel-Niepce de Saint-Victor (1805–1870) of France first uses light sensitive materials on glass for photographs. He coats a glass plate with albumen containing iodide of potassium which, after drying, is coated with aceto-silver nitrate, washed in distilled water, and exposed.

1847: John Collins Warren (1778–1856), American surgeon, introduces ether ancsthesia for general surgery. It is soon taken up worldwide as an essential part of surgery.

1847: Richard March Hoe (1812–1886), American inventor and manufacturer, patents what proves to be the first successful rotary printing press. He discards the old flatbed press and places the type on a revolving cylinder. This revolutionary system is first used by the *Philadelphia Public Ledger* this same year, and it produces 8,000 sheets per hour printed on one side.

1848: Karl Marx publishes *The Communist Manifesto*.

1848: Delegates at the Seneca Falls Convention on Woman Rights advocate equal property and voting rights for women.

1848: Series of political conflicts and violent revolts erupt in several European nations. The conflicts are collectively known as the Revolution of 1848.

1848: A group of six New York newspapers form an association or news agency to share telegraph costs. It is later called the Associated Press.

1848: The first large-scale department store opens in the United States. The Marble Dry Goods Palace in New York occupies an entire city block.

1849: Gold fever sparks mass immigration to the United States from China.

1849: First woman to receive a medical degree in the United States is Elizabeth Blackwell (1821–1910). She graduates this year from Geneva College (now a part of Syracuse University) in New York.

1849: John Snow (1813–1858), English physician, first states the theory that cholera is a water-borne disease and that it is usually contracted by drinking. During a cholera epidemic in London in 1854, Snow breaks the handle of the Broad Street Pump, thereby shutting down what he

considered to be the main public source of the epidemic.

1850–1899

1850: Fugitive Slave Act passed in the United States.

1851: James Harrison, Scottish-Australian inventor, builds the first vapor-compression refrigerating machinery to be used in a brewery.

1851: James T. King of the United States invents a washing machine that uses a rotating cylinder. It is hand-powered and made for home use.

1852: Harriet Beecher Stowe's novel *Uncle Tom's Cabin* is published. It becomes one of the most influential works to stir anti-slavery sentiments.

1854: Crimean War begins between Russia and allied forces of Great Britain, Sardinia, France, and the Ottoman Empire.

1854: Violent conflicts erupt between pro-and anti-slavery settlers in Kansas Territory. The "Bleeding Kansas" violence lasts five years.

1854: Florence Nightingale (1823–1910), English nurse, takes charge of a barracks hospital when the Crimean War breaks out. Through dedication and hard work, she goes on to create a female nursing service and a nursing school at St. Thomas' Hospital (1860). Her compassion and common sense approach to nursing set new standards and create a new era in the history of the sick and wounded.

1854: Cyrus West Field (1819–1892), American financier, forms the New York, Newfoundland and London telegraph Company and proposes to lay a transatlantic telegraph cable.

1855: Alfred Russel Wallace (1823–1913), English naturalist, publishes his paper "On The Law Which Has Regulated the Introduction of New Species." Although this is written before Wallace conceives of the notion of natural selection, it shows him in the process of anticipating Darwin.

1856: *Illustrated London News* becomes the first periodical to include regular color plates.

1857: Supreme Court of the United States decision in *Dred Scott v. Sanford* holds that slaves are not citizens and that Congress cannot prohibit slavery in the individual states.

1857: The Indian Mutiny revolt against British colonial rule in India begins.

1858: The transatlantic cable is first opened with an exchange of greetings between English Queen Victoria (1819–1901) and U. S. President James

Buchanan (1791–1868). Several weeks later, a telegraph operator applies too much voltage and ruins the cable connection.

1858: Mary Anna Elson (1833–1884), German-American physician, is the first Jewish woman to graduate from the Women's Medical College of Philadelphia. She practices in Philadelphia and later in Indiana.

1859: Charles Robert Darwin (1809–1882), English naturalist, publishes his landmark work *On the Origin of Species by Means of Natural Selection*. This classic of science establishes the mechanism of natural selection of favorable, inherited traits or variations as the mechanism of his theory of evolution.

1859: Ferdinand Carr, (1824–1900), French inventor, introduces a refrigeration machine that uses ammonia as a refrigerant and water as the absorbent. This method becomes widely adopted.

1860: Repression in Poland sparks immigration to America.

1860: The U. S. Congress institutes the U. S. Government Printing Office in Washington, D. C.

1861: The Civil War begins in the United States.

1861: The popular press begins in England with the publication of the *Daily Telegraph*.

1862: The American Homestead Act allows any male over the age of twenty-one and the head of a family to claim up to 160 acres of land and improve it within five years or to purchase the land at a small fee.

1864: The United States legalizes importation of contract laborers.

1864: U.S. President Abraham Lincoln issues the Emancipation Proclamation, freeing the slaved in Union-occupied lands.

1865: The Civil War ends with the surrender of the secession states. The United States is reunified.

1865: President Lincoln is assassinated by John Wilkes Booth.

1865: The Thirteenth and Tourteenth Amendments to the U.S. Constitution are ratified. The Thirteenth Amendment outlaws slavery; the Fourteenth Amendment declares all persons born or naturalized in the United States as U.S. citizens and extends equal protection under the law.

1867: Britain grants Canada home rule.

1868: The Fourteenth Amendment of the Constitution endows African Americans with citizenship.

1869: Japanese laborers start to arrive *en masse* in Hawaii.

1869: The first transcontinental railroad across the United States is completed.

1870: The Franco-Prussian War (1870–1871) begins.

1871: The era of New Imperialism, or "empire for empire's sake," starts a multinational competition for colonies in Africa, Asia, and the Middle East.

1871: Charles Robert Darwin (1809–1882), English naturalist, publishes his *The Descent of Man, and Selection in Relation to Sex*. This work extends his theory of evolution by applying it to humans.

1874: Thomas Alva Edison (1847–1931), American inventor, perfects his quadruplex telegraph. It is able to transmit two messages over one telegraph line or four messages in each direction over two wires.

1875: Robert Augustus Chesebrough (1837–1933), American manufacturer, first introduces petrolatum, which becomes known by its product name of Vaseline. This smooth, semisolid blend of mineral oil with waxes crystallized from petroleum becomes useful as a lubricant, carrier, and waterproofing agent in many products.

1876: Alexander Bell files for a patent for the telephone.

1876: Robert Koch (1843–1910), German bacteriologist, is able to cultivate the anthrax bacteria in culture outside the body. He then studies its life cycle and learns how to defeat it. During the next six years, Koch isolates the tubercle bacillus and discovers the cause of cholera.

1876: The American Library Association is founded in Philadelphia, Pennsylvania by American librarian, Melvil Dewey (1851–1931), the founder of the decimal system of library classification.

1877: Reconstruction, the period of rebuilding and reunification following the U.S. Civil War, ends.

1879: Albert Ludwig Siegmund Neisser (1855–1916), German dermatologist, discovers gonococcus, the pus-producing bacterium that causes gonorrhea.

1879: John Shaw Billings (1838–1913), American surgeon, and Robert Fletcher (1823–1912) of England issue the first volume of *Index Medicus*. This massive medical bibliography is initially arranged by author and subject and continues today.

1880: Difficult conditions in Italy spur start of mass immigration to America.

1880: Louis Pasteur (1822–1895), French chemist, first isolates and describes both streptococcus and staphylococcus (both in puerperal septicemia).

1882: Russian poverty and oppression spurs immigration to the United States.

1882: The Chinese Exclusion Act of 1882 temporarily halts immigration of Chinese laborers.

1883: *Journal of the American Medical Association* is first published.

1884: International conference is held at Washington, D. C., at which Greenwich, England, is chosen as the common prime meridian for the entire world.

1885: The United States bans the importation of contract laborers.

1885: Karl Benz invents an automobile in Germany.

1885: Edouard van Beneden (1846–1910), Belgian cytologist, proves that chromosomes persist between cell divisions. He makes the first chromosome count and discovers that each species has a fixed number of chromosomes. He also discovers that in the formation of sex cells, the division of chromosomes during one of the cell divisions was not preceded by a doubling.

1885: James Leonard Corning (1855–1923), American surgeon, is the first to use cocaine as a spinal anesthetic.

1885: Louis Pasteur (1822–1895), French chemist, inoculates a boy, Joseph Meister, against rabies. He had been bitten by a mad dog and the treatment saves his life. This is the first case of Pasteur's use of an attenuated germ on a human being.

1886: Richard von Krafft-Ebing (1840–1902), German neurologist, publishes his landmark case history study of sexual abnormalities, *Psychopathia Sexualis*, and helps found the scientific consideration of human sexuality.

1887: The Dawes Act passed.

1887: Theodor Boveri observes the reduction division during meiosis in *Ascaris* and confirmed August Weismann's predictions of chromosome reduction during the formation of the sex cells.

1888: First incubator for infants in the United States is built by William C. Deming.

1888: Heinrich Wilhelm Gottfried Waldeyer-Hartz (1836–1921), German anatomist, first introduces the word "chromosomes."

1889: Oklahoma land rush begins for white settlers.

1889: Francis Galton (1822–1911), English anthropologist, culminates his work on inheritance and variation with his book *Natural Inheritance*. It influences Karl Pearson and begins the science of biometrics or the statistical analysis of biological observations and phenomena.

1889: Pasteur Institute first opens in Paris.

1889: Richard Altmann (1852–1900), German histologist, isolates and names nucleic acid.

1890: The U.S. Census Bureau announces that the American frontier is closed.

1890: Herman Hollerith (1860–1929), American inventor, puts his electric sorting and tabulating machines to work on the U. S. Census. He wins this contract after a trial "run-off" with two other rival systems and his system performs in one year what would have taken eight years of hand tabulating. This marks the beginning of modern data processing.

1891: Maximilian Franz Joseph Wolf (1863–1932), German astronomer, adapts photography to the study of asteroids and demonstrates that stars appear as points in photographs while asteroids show up as short streaks. He makes the first discovery of an asteroid from photographs and during his lifetime discovers over 500 asteroids in this manner.

1891: Hermann Henking (1858–1942), German zoologist, describes sex chromosomes and autosomes.

1892: Ellis Island becomes chief immigration station of the eastern United States.

1893: Panic of 1893 triggers a three-year economic depression in the United States.

1893: Sigmund Freud (1856–1939), Austrian psychiatrist, describes paralysis originating from purely mental conditions and distinguishes it from that of organic origin.

1894: Thomas Alva Edison (1847–1931), American inventor, first displays his peep-show Kinetoscopes in New York. These demonstrations serve to stimulate research on the screen projection of motion pictures as well as entertain.

1895: John Cox is the first U. S. physician to use x-rays as an adjunct to surgery.

1896: Landmark Supreme Court of the United States decision, *Plessy v. Ferguson*, upholds racial segregation.

1896: Edmund Beecher Wilson (1856–1939), American zoologist, publishes his major work, *The Cell in Development and Heredity* in which he connects chromosomes and sex determination. He also correctly states that chromosomes affect and determine other inherited characteristics as well.

1897: Guglielmo Marconi (1874–1937), Italian electrical engineer, exchanges wireless messages across 3.5 miles of water in England.

1897: Havelock Ellis (1859–1939), English physician, publishes the first of his seven-volume work *Studies in the Psychology of Sex*. This contributes to the more open discussion of human sexuality and supports sex education.

1898: *USS Maine* sinks in harbor in Havana, Cuba; Spanish-American War begins.

1900–1949

1900: In Puerto Rico the Jones Act grants U.S. citizenship to residents.

1901: Guglielmo Marconi (1874–1937), Italian electrical engineer, successfully sends a radio signal from England to Newfoundland. This is the first transatlantic telegraphic radio transmission and is considered by most as the day radio is invented.

1902: Clarence Erwin McClung (1870–1946), American zoologist, isolates the "x" or sex chromosome which is combined with a "y" chromosome in the male, as compared to two "x" chromosomes in the female.

1902: Ernest H. Starling (1866–1927) and William M. Bayliss (1860–1924), both English physiologists, isolate and discover the first hormone (secretin, found in the duodenum). Starling also first suggests a name for all substances discharged into the blood by a particular organ, and it is "hormones" from the Greek word meaning to "rouse to activity."

1902: The Horn & Hardart Baking Company of Philadelphia, Pennsylvania creates an early automat that offers food for a "nickel in a slot."

1903: Wright brothers make first successful flight of a controlled, powered airplane that is heavier than air.

1903: *The Great Train Robbery*, the first modern movie, debuts.

1903: Walter S. Sutton (1876–1916) of the United States writes a short paper in which he states the chromosome theory of inheritance. This important idea that the hereditary factors are located in the chromosomes is also offered independently by Theodor Boveri (1862–1915) of Germany.

1904: Russo-Japanese War (1904–1905): Japan gains territory on the Asian mainland and becomes a world power.

1904: First radical operation for prostate cancer is performed by the American urologist, Hugh Hampton Young (1870–1945).

1904: Ivan Petrovich Pavlov (1849–1936), Russian physiologist, is awarded the Nobel Prize for Physiology or Medicine for his work establishing that the nervous system plays a part in controlling digestion and by helping to found gastroenterology.

1905: Albert Einstein (1879–1955), German-Swiss-American physicist, uses Planck's theory to develop a quantum theory of light which explains the photoelectric effect. He suggests that light has a dual, wave-particle quality.

1905: Fritz Richard Schaudinn (1871–1906), German zoologist, discovers *Spirocheta pallida*, the organism or parasite causing syphilis. His discovery of this almost invisible parasite is due to his consummate technique and staining methods.

1905: Albert Einstein (1879–1955), German-Swiss-American physicist, submits his first paper on the special theory of relativity titled "Zur Elektrodynamik bewegter Korpen." It states that the speed of light is constant for all conditions and that time is relative or passes at different rates for objects in constant relative motion. This is a fundamentally new and revolutionary way to look at the universe and it soon replaces the old Newtonian system.

1905: Albert Einstein (1879–1955), German-Swiss-American physicist, publishes his second paper on relativity in which he includes his famous equation stating the relationship between mass and energy: $E = mc2$. In this equation, E is energy, m is mass, and c is the velocity of light. This contains the revolutionary concept that mass and energy are only different aspects of the same phenomenon.

1905: Hermann Walter Nernst (1864–1941), German physical chemist, announces his discovery of the third law of thermodynamics. He finds that entropy change approaches zero at a temperature of absolute zero, and deduces from this the impossibility of attaining absolute zero.

1905: Alfred Binet (1857–1911), French psychologist, devises the first of a series of tests (1905–1911) that make him the "father of intelligence testing."

1905: Edmund Beecher Wilson (1856–1939), American zoologist and Nettie M. Stevens independently discover the connection between chromosomes and sex determination. They are the first to note the X chromosome and Y chromosomes.

1905: Robert Koch (1843–1910), German bacteriologist, is awarded the Nobel Prize for Physiology or Medicine for his investigations and discoveries in relation to tuberculosis. He is one of the founders of the science of bacteriology.

1906: Marie Sklodowska Curie (1867–1934), Polish-French chemist, assumes her husband Pierre's professorship at the Sorbonne after he is killed in a traffic accident. She becomes the first woman ever to teach there.

1907: The United States and Japan agree to limit Japanese immigration to the United States.

1907: Alva T. Fisher of the United States designs the first electric washing machine. Manufactured by the Hurley Machine Corporation, it is the first washing machine that does not require an operator to crank a handle to perform the washing action.

1907: Boris Rosing, a lecturer at the Technological Institute, St. Petersburg, Russia, first introduces the idea of using a cathode ray tube as a means of reproducing a television picture. Known as "Rosing's Apparatus," he names it the "electric eye." Although this system uses an electronic receiver, it still has a mechanical camera.

1907: Clemens Peter Pirquet von Cesenatico (1874–1929), Austrian physician, and Bela Schick, Austrian pediatrician, introduce the notion and term "allergy."

1907: The first powdered soap for home use is called "Persil" and is sold by Henkel & Co. in Germany.

1908: A. A. Campbell-Swinton of England first suggests the use of a cathode ray tube as both the transmitter (camera) and receiver. This is the first description of the modern, all-electronic television system.

1909: Phoebus Aaron Theodore Levene (1869–1940), Russian-American chemist, discovers the chemical distinction between DNA (deoxyribonucleic acid) and RNA (ribonucleic acid).

1910: Charles-Jules-Henri Nicolle (1866–1936), French bacteriologist, discovers the viral origin of influenza.

1910: Harvey Cushing (1869–1939), American surgeon, and his team present the first experimental evidence of the link between the anterior pituitary and the reproductive organs.

1911: Mexican laborers are exempt from immigrant "head tax."

1912: The value of wireless at sea is demonstrated during the *S.S. Titanic* disaster as those who get to lifeboats are saved by rescuing vessels.

1913: California's Alien Land Law declares that aliens not eligible for citizenship are ineligible to own certain types of farm property.

1913: Alfred Henry Sturtevant (1891–1970), American geneticist, produces the first chromosome map, showing five sex-linked genes.

1914: Assassination of Archduke Franz Ferdinand of Austria-Hungary and his wife Sophie; World War I begins.

1914: Panama Canal is completed.

1914: The beginning of the massacre of 1.5 million Armenians by the Turkish government, later known as the Armenian Genocide.

1914: John Broadus Watson (1878–1958), American psychologist, launches his theory of behaviorism. This approach, which says that brain activity comprises responses to external stimuli, restricts psychology to the objective, experimental study of human behavior or human responses to stimuli.

1915: U.S. Supreme Court delivers *Ozawa v. United States* ruling that declares first-generation Japanese ineligible for naturalization.

1915: German U-boats sink the British passenger steamer *RMS Lusitania*.

1916: Easter Rising in Ireland begins fight for Irish independence.

1917: The United States enters World War I, declaring war on Germany.

1917: The United States enters World War I and anti-German sentiment grows. Names are changed to sound less Germanic.

1917: The Russian Revolution begins as Bolsheviks overthrow the Russian monarchy.

1918: World War I ends.

1918: The Great Flu; nearly twenty million perish during the two-year pandemic.

1918: The Red Terror in Russia: Thousands of political dissidents are tried and imprisoned; five million die of famine as Communists collectivize agriculture and transform the Soviet economy."

1919: The ratification of the Nineteenth Amendment to the U.S. constitution gives women the right to vote.

1919: Mahatma Gandhi initiates satyagraha (truth force) campaigns, beginning his nonviolent resistance movement against British rule in India.

1920: Red Scare (1920–1922) in the United States leads to the arrest, trial, and imprisonment of suspected communist, socialist, and anarchist "radicals."

1920: KDKA, a Pittsburgh Westinghouse station, transmits the first commercial radio broadcast.

1922: Twenty-six of Ireland's counties gain independence; the remaining six become Northern Ireland and remain under British rule.

1922: Mussolini forms Fascist government in Italy.

1922: The British Broadcasting Company (BBC) is formed.

1922: The first canned baby food is manufactured in the United States by Harold H. Clapp of New York.

1923: Max Wertheimer (1880–1943), German psychologist, publishes *Untersuchungen zur Lehre der Gestalt*, which first originates the concept of Gestalt psychology. This school of psychological thought attempts to examine the total, structured forms of mental experience.

1924: Immigration Act of 1924 establishes fixed quotas of national origin and eliminates Far East immigration.

1925: Geneva Protocol, signed by sixteen nations, outlaws the use of poisonous gas as an agent of warfare.

1925: The Scopes Monkey Trial (July 10-25) in Tennessee debate the state's ban on the teaching of evolution.

1927: Charles Lindbergh makes the first solo nonstop transatlantic flight.

1927: Lemuel Clyde McGee, American biochemist, first obtains an active extract of the male sex hormone from bull testicles.

1927: Selmar Aschheim and Bernhardt Zondek, both German physicians, devise a pregnancy test in which the subject's urine is injected subcutaneously in immature female mice. A positive reaction is marked by congestion and hemorrhages of the ovaries in the mice.

1928: Alexander Fleming discovers penicillin.

1929: The United States establishes annual immigration quotas

1929: Black Tuesday. The U.S. stock market crashes, beginning the Great Depression.

1929: Adolf Friedrich Johann Butenandt (1903–1994), German chemist, isolates the first of the sex hormones, estrone. He obtains this female sex hormone from the urine of pregnant women.

1929: Casimir Funk, Polish biochemist, and Harrow obtain active male hormone from male urine.

1929: Edward Adelbert Doisy (1893–1986), American biochemist, first isolates estrone from the urine of pregnant women.

1930: Ronald Aylmer Fisher (1890–1962), English biologist, publishes *The Genetical Theory of Natural Selection* which, together with Sewall Wright's *Mendelian Populations* (1931), lays the mathematical foundations of population genetics.

1930: Rubber condoms made of a thin latex are introduced.

1932: Hattie Wyatt Caraway of Arkansas is the first woman elected to the U.S. Senate.

1932: Nazis capture 230 seats in the German Reichstag during national elections.

1932: Werner Karl Heisenberg (1901–1976), German physicist, wins the Nobel Prize for Physics for the creation of quantum mechanics, the application of which has led to the discovery of the allotropic forms of hydrogen.

1932: RCA (Radio Corporation of America) makes experimental television broadcasts from the Empire State Building in New York.

1933: Adolf Hitler named German chancellor.

1933: President Franklin D. Roosevelt announces the New Deal, a plan to revitalize the U.S. economy and provide relief during the Great Depression. The U.S. unemployment rate reaches twenty-five percent.

1933: U. S. President Franklin Delano Roosevelt (1882–1945) makes the first of his "fireside chats" to the American people. He is the first national leader to use the radio medium comfortably and regularly to explain his programs and to garner popular support.

1933: Christopher Howard Andrewes, English pathologist, Wilson Smith (1897–1965), English bacteriologist and virologist, and Patrick Playfair Laidlaw (1881–1940), English physician, demonstrate the viral nature of the human influenza agent by transmitting it to a ferret and then transferring the virus onto a suitable culture medium.

1934: George W. Beadle, working with Boris Ephrussi, in collaboration with A. Kuhn and A. Butenandt, worked out the biochemical genetics of eye-pigment synthesis in *Drosophila* and *Ephestia*, respectively.

1934: John Marrack begins a series of studies that leads to the formation of the hypothesis governing the association between an antigen and the corresponding antibody.

1935: Germany's Nuremburg Laws codify discrimination and denaturalization of the nation's Jews.

1935: Antonio Caetano de Abreu Freire Egas Moniz (1874–1955), Portuguese surgeon, performs the first lobotomy. This operation which severs the patient's prefrontal lobes of the brain opens a new field called psychosurgery. It is usually employed as a last resort and eventually is done away with once tranquilizers and other mind-affecting drugs are discovered.

1935: K. David and associates first isolate a pure crystalline hormone from testicular material and name it testosterone.

1936: Herbert McLean Evans (1882–1971), American anatomist and embryologist, and his group first isolate the interstitial cell stimulating hormone (ICSH). Also called luteinizing hormone, it is concerned with the regulation of the activity of the gonads or sex glands, and is produced by the pituitary gland.

1938: Anti-Jewish riots across Germany. The destruction and looting of Jewish-owned businesses is know as *Kristalnacht*, "Night of the Broken Glass." political and geographical union of Germany and Austria proclaimed. Munich Pact—Britain, France, and Italy agree to let Germany partition Czechoslovakia.

1938: Mass hysteria among American radio listeners is caused by a dramatic reenactment of H. G. Wells' (1866–1946) novel, *War of the Worlds*. American actor, writer, and director, George Orson Welles, (1915–1985) leads many to believe that a "gas raid from Mars" is actually happening.

1939: U.S. declares its neutrality in World War II.

1939: Germany invades Poland. Britain, France, and Russia go to war against Germany.

1939: The Holocaust (Shoah) begins in German-occupied Europe. Jews are removed from their homes and relocated to ghettos or concentration camps. The *Einsatzgruppen*, or mobile killing squads, begin the execution of one million Jews, Poles, Russians, Gypsies, and others.

1939: Television debuts at the World's Fair.

1940: George Wells Beadle, American geneticist, and Edward Lawrie Tatum (1909–1975), American biochemist, establish the formula "One gene = one enzyme." This discovery that each gene supervises the production of only one enzyme lays the foundation for the DNA discoveries to come.

1940: Ernest Chain and E.P. Abraham detail the inactivation of penicillin by a substance produced by *Escherichia coli*. This is the first bacterial compound known to produce resistance to an antibacterial agent.

1941: The U.S. Naval base at Pearl Harbor, Hawaii is bombed by Japanese Air Force. Soon after, the United States enters World War II, declaring war on Germany and Japan.

1941: Japanese-Americans are incarcerated on grounds of national security.

1941: The first Nazi death camp, Chelmno, opens. Victims, mainly Jews, are executed by carbon monoxide poisoning in specially designed killing vans.

1942: Executive Order 9066 orders the internment of Japanese immigrants and Japanese-American citizens for the duration of World War II.

1942: Enrico Fermi (1901–1954), Italian-American physicist, heads a Manhattan Project team at the University of Chicago that produces the first controlled chain reaction in an atomic pile of uranium and graphite. With this first self-sustaining chain reaction, the atomic age begins.

1943: The Magnuson Act repeals the Chinese Exclusion Act of 1882.

1943: Penicillin is first used on a large scale by the U. S. Army in the North African campaigns. Data obtained from these studies show that early expectations for the new drug are correct, and the groundwork is laid for the massive introduction of penicillin into civilian medical practice after the war.

1945: The War Bride Act and the G.I. Fiancées Act are enacted.

1945: The United States admits immigrants based on the fact that they are fleeing persecution from their native lands.

1945: Auschwitz death camp is liberated by allied forces.

1945: World War II and the Holocaust end in Europe.

1945: Atomic bombings of Hiroshima and Nagasaki; Japan surrenders on August 15.

1945: Trials of Nazi War criminals begin in Nuremberg, Germany.

1945: United Nations is established.

1945: Displaced Persons (DP) camps established throughout Europe to aid Holocaust survivors. In the three years following the end of World

War II, many DPs immigrate to Israel and the United States.

1945: First atomic bomb is detonated by the United States near Almagordo, New Mexico. The experimental bomb generates an explosive power equivalent to between fifteen and twenty thousand tons of TNT.

1945: RCA Victor first offers vinyl plastic records to the public.

1945: United States destroys the Japanese city of Hiroshima with a nuclear fission bomb based on uranium-235. Three days later a plutonium-based bomb destroys the city of Nagasaki. Japan surrenders on August 14 and World War II ends. This is the first use of nuclear power as a weapon.

1946: John von Neumann (1903–1957), Hungarian-American mathematician, begins work at the Institute for Advanced Study at Princeton, New Jersey to establish a digital computer project. He is soon joined by Julian Bigelow, American engineer, and American mathematician, Herman Heine Goldstein.

1948: Gandhi assassinated in New Delhi.

1948: Soviets blockade Berlin. The United States and Great Britain begin airlift of fuel, food and necessities to West Berlin. The event, the first conflict of the Cold War, became known as the Berlin Airlift (June 26-Sept 30, 1949).

1948: United Nations issues the Universal Declaration of Human Rights.

1948: Israel is established as an independent nation.

1948: American zoologist and student of sexual behavior, Alfred C. Kinsey (1894–1956) first publishes his *Sexual Behavior in the Human Male*.

1949: South Africa codifies apartheid.

1949: Soviets test their first atomic device.

1950–1999

1950: President Truman commits U.S. troops to aid anti-Communist forces on the Korean Peninsula. The Korean War lasts from 1950–1953.

1951: First successful oral contraceptive drug is introduced. Gregory Pincus (1903–1967), American biologist, discovers a synthetic hormone that renders a woman infertile without altering her capacity for sexual pleasure. It soon is marketed in pill form and effects a social revolution with its ability to divorce the sex act from the consequences of impregnation.

1952: U.S. Immigration and Nationality Act enacted

1952: First hydrogen bomb is detonated by the United States on an atoll in the Marshall Islands.

1953: Francis Harry Compton Crick, English biochemist, and James Dewey Watson, American biochemist, work out the double-helix or double spiral DNA model. This model explains how it is able to transmit heredity in living organisms.

1954: The Supreme Court delivers *Brown v. Topeka Board of Education* decision that "separate but equal" doctrine is unconstitutional.

1954: Sen. Joseph R. McCarthy begins hearings of the House Un-American Activities Committee, publicly accusing military officials, politicians, media, and others of Communist involvement.

1954: The first frozen TV dinners become available in the United States.

1955: Emmett Till, age fourteen, is brutally murdered for allegedly whistling at a white woman. The event galvanizes the civil rights movement.

1955: Rosa Parks refuses to give up her seat on a Montgomery, Alabama, bus to a white passenger, defying segregation.

1955: Warsaw Pact solidifies relationship between the Soviet Union and its communist satellite nations in Eastern Europe.

1955: Chlorpromazine and lithium are first used to treat psychiatric disorders.

1957: President Eisenhower sends federal troops to Central High School in Little Rock, Arkansas, to enforce integration.

1957: Soviet Union launches the first satellite, Sputnik, into space. The Space Race between the USSR and the United States begins.

1958: Explorer I, first American satellite, is launched.

1959: Cuban revolution prompts mass immigration to the United States.

1960: African American students in North Carolina begin a sit-in at a segregated Woolworth's lunch counter; the sit-in spread throughout the South.

1961: Soviet Cosmonaut Yuri Gagarin becomes first human in space.

1961: Berlin Wall is built.

1961: Bay of Pigs Invasion: the United States sponsors an overthrow of Cuba's socialist government but fails.

1962: *Silent Spring* published; environmental movement begins.

1962: Cuban Missile Crisis occurs.

1963: Rev. Martin Luther King Jr., delivers his "I Have a Dream" speech at a civil rights march on Washington, D.C.

1963: The United States and the Soviet Union establish a direct telephone link called the "hot line" between the White House and the Kremlin. It is intended to permit the leaders of both countries to be able to speak directly and immediately to each other in times of crisis.

1964: U.S. President Lyndon Johnson announces ambitious social reform programs known as the Great Society.

1964: Congress approves Gulf of Tonkin resolution.

1964: President Johnson signs the Civil Rights Act of 1964.

1965: U.S. Immigration Act passed.

1965: March to Selma: state troopers and local police fight a crowd of peaceful civil rights demonstrators, including the Rev. Martin Luther King Jr., as the group attempted to cross a bridge into the city of Selma.

1965: First U.S. combat troops arrive in South Vietnam.

1965: Voting Rights Act prohibits discriminatory voting practices in the United States.

1965: Watts Riots: 35 people are killed and 883 injured in six days of riots in Los Angeles.

1965: François Jacob, French biologist, André-Michael Lwoff, French microbiologist, and Jacques-Lucien Monod, French biochemist, are awarded the Nobel Prize for Physiology or Medicine for their discoveries concerning genetic control of enzyme and virus synthesis.

1965: Geoffrey Harris, British anatomist, shows that sexuality is built into the hypothalamus.

1966: U.S. Cuban Refugee Act enacted.

1966: Betty Friedan and other leaders of the feminist movement found the National Organization for Women (NOW).

1966: Choh Hao Li, Chinese-American chemist and endocrinologist, describes the structure of human growth hormone and first synthesizes it (1966–1971).

1967: The new fertility drug clomiphene is introduced. Although it can result in multiple births, it proves very successful in increasing a woman's chances of getting pregnant.

1968: Rev. Martin Luther King Jr., is assassinated in Memphis, Tennessee.

1968: Cesar Chavez leads a national boycott of California table grape growers, which becomes known as "La Causa."

1969: Stonewall Riots in New York City spark the gay rights movement.

1969: The United States successfully lands a manned mission, Apollo 11, on the moon.

1970: Four anti-war demonstrators are killed when the National Guard fires into the crowd of protesters at Kent State University.

1972: Arab terrorists massacre Israeli athletes at Olympic Games in Munich, Germany.

1973: *Roe v. Wade*: Landmark Supreme Court decision legalizes abortion on demand during the first trimester of pregnancy.

1973: The American Psychiatric Association removes the classification of homosexuality as a mental disorder.

1973: Last U.S. troops exit Vietnam.

1974: U.S. President Richard Nixon resigns as a result of the Watergate scandal.

1975: As the South Vietnamese government surrenders to North Vietnam, the U.S. Embassy and remaining military and civilian personnel are evacuated.

1976: Steve Jobs and Steve Wozniak invent personal computer.

1977: Earliest known AIDS (Acquired Immuno-deficiency Syndrome) victims in the United States are two homosexual men in New York who are diagnosed as suffering from Kaposi's sarcoma.

1978: Congress passes the Pregnancy Discrimination Act, stating that individuals in the workforce cannot face discrimination "because of or on the basis of pregnancy, childbirth, or related medical conditions."

1979: Three Mile Island nuclear reactor in Pennsylvania suffers a near meltdown.

1979: Iran hostage crisis begins when Iranian students storm the U.S. embassy in Teheran. They hold sixty-six people hostage who are not released until 1981, after 444 days in captivity.

1980: U.S. Refugee Act enacted.

1980: 130,000 Cuban refugees flee to the United States during the Mariel Boatlift (April 4 -October 31).

1980: President Carter announces that U.S. athletes will boycott Summer Olympics in Moscow to protest Soviet involvement in Afghanistan (Jan. 20).

1981: Sandra Day O'Connor is sworn in as the first woman justice on the Supreme Court of the United States.

1981: Urban riots breakout in several British cities, protesting lack of opportunity for minorities and police brutality.

1981: AIDS identified.

1982: Deadline for ratification of the Equal Rights Amendment to the Constitution; without the necessary votes the amendment failed.

1982: New surgical technique for prostate cancer that does not result in impotency is developed by Patrick Walsh.

1984: Steen A. Willadsen successfully clones sheep.

1986: The Immigration Reform and Control Act (IRCA) offers legalized status to aliens residing in the United States illegally since 1982.

1986: U.S. space shuttle Challenger explodes seventy-three seconds after liftoff.

1986: Chernobyl nuclear disaster in the Soviet Union contaminates large swath of Eastern Europe with radioactive fallout. The disaster is the worst nuclear accident to date.

1987: U.S. President Ronald Reagan challenges Soviet leader Mikhail Gorbachev to open Eastern Europe and the Soviet Union to political and economic reform.

1988: Civil Liberties Act provides compensation and apology to Japanese American survivors of WWII internment camps.

1988: Henry A. Erlich of the United States and colleagues develop a method for identifying an individual from the DNA in a single hair.

1989: Fall of the Berlin Wall.

1989: Tiananmen Square protest in Beijing, China.

1989: Oil tanker Exxon Valdez runs aground in Prince William Sound, spilling more than 10 million gallons of oil (March 24).

1989: The Internet revolution begins with the invention of the World Wide Web.

1989: Tim Berners-Lee invents the World Wide Web while working at CERN.

1990: *The Simpsons*, an animated satirical look at the imperfect, ideal American family, debuts on television and becomes an instant hit.

1990: Human Genome Project begins in the United States with the selection of six institutions to do the work.

1990: The U.S. Census includes question about gay couples and families.

1991: Soviet Union dissolves.

1991: Persian Gulf War (January 16 -February 28): The United States leads "Operation Desert Storm" to push Iraqi occupying forces out of Kuwait.

1991: The sex of a mouse is changed at the embryo stage.

1991: U.S. FDA (Food and Drug Administration) announces it will speed up its process for approving drugs. This change in procedure is due to the protests of AIDS activists.

1992: U.S. and Russian leaders formally declare an end to the Cold War.

1992: L.A. Riots: The acquittal of four white police officers charged with police brutality in the beating of black motorist Rodney King sparks days of widespread rioting in Los Angeles.

1992: WHO (World Health Organization) predicts that by the year 2000, thhirty to forty million people will be infected with the AIDS-causing HIV. A Harvard University group argues that the number could reach more than 100 million.

1993: A terrorist bomb explodes in basement parking garage of World Trade Center, killing six.

1993: Software companies introduce programs making the Internet easier to use, and several on-line information services open gateways into this "network of networks," making its popularity explode.

1993: After analyzing the family trees of gay men and the DNA of pairs of homosexual brothers, biochemists at the United States National Cancer Institute reported that at least one gene related to homosexuality resides on the X chromosome, which is inherited from the mother.

1993: U.S. military adopts the "Don't Ask, Don't Tell" policy, permitting gay individuals to serve in the military only if they do not disclose their homosexuality and do not engage in homosexual acts.; military recruiters and personnel are barred from inquiring about an individual's sexuality.

1993: The federal Family and Medical Leave Act is enacted, allowing workers to take unpaid leave due to illness or to care for a newborn or sick family member.

1994: First all-race elections in South Africa; Nelson Mandela elected President.

1996: Federal Defense of Marriage Act (DOMA) enacted; states permitted to enact legislation refusing to honor same-sex marriages entered into in another state.

1998: Terrorist attacks on U.S. embassies in Kenya and Tanzania.

1998: House of Representatives votes to impeach President William Jefferson Clinton. The Senate acquits President Clinton two months later.

1998: Torture and murder of gay college student Matthew Shepherd.

1999: NATO forces in former Yugoslavia attempt to end mass killings of ethnic Albanians by Serbian forces in Kosovo.

2000–

2000: The United Nations adopts the Millennium Declaration that results setting eight goals (known as the Millennium Development Goals), which "promote poverty reduction, education, maternal health, gender equality, and aim at combating child mortality, AIDS and other diseases" by the year 2015.

2001: Terrorists attacks on the World Trade Center in New York and the Pentagon in Washington, D.C. killing 2,752.

2001: Controversial Patriot Act passed in the United States.

2001: United States and coalition forces begin War on Terror by invading Afghanistan (Operation Enduring Freedom), overthrowing the nation's Islamist Taliban regime in December of 2001.

2002: Slobodan Milosevic begins his war crimes trial at the UN International Criminal Tribunal on charges of genocide and crimes against humanity. He is the first head of state to stand trial in an international war-crimes court, but died before the trial concluded.

2002: After United States and coalition forces depose Islamist Taliban regime in Afghanistan, girls are allowed to return to school and women's rights are partially restored in areas controlled by U.S. and coalition forces.

2002: The International Olympic Committee suspends gender verification procedures for the Olympics in Sydney, Australia citing potential harm to "women athletes born with relatively rare genetic abnormalities that affect development of the gonads or the expression of secondary sexual characteristics."

2002: The agricultural chemical atrazine, used in weed control, is thought to be partially responsible for the dramatic global decline in amphibians, as it is found to disturb male frog sex hormones, altering their gonads.

2003: U.S. space shuttle Columbia breaks apart upon re-entry, killing all seven crew members.

2003: Supreme Court of the United States strikes down sodomy laws in the landmark decision, *Lawrence v. Texas*

2003: United States and coalition forces invade Iraq.

2003: The United States declares an end to major combat operations in Iraq. As of June 2006, U.S. fighting forces remain engaged in Iraq.

2003: American troops capture Iraq's former leader, Saddam Hussein.

2003: Canada recognizes same-sex marriages throughout the country.

2003: November 18, the Massachusetts Supreme Judicial court rules denying same-sex couples marriage rights violates the state constitution, legalizing same-sex marriages.

2004: Islamist terrorist bombing of commuter rail network in Madrid, Spain.

2004: Jason West, mayor of New Paltz, New York, defies state law and performs same-sex weddings. Later charged with twenty-four misdemeanor counts of performing illegal marriages, he was cleared of all charges in 2005.

2004: The California state supreme court, in a 5-2 decision, voids nearly 4,000 same-sex marriages performed in San Francisco earlier that year.

2005: U.S. House bill passes Border Protection, Antiterrorism, and Illegal Immigration Control Act (HR 4437) proposing building a fence along portions of the U.S.-Mexico border and other anti-immigration measures.

2005: U.S. House bill proposes making the provision of humanitarian assistance a felony.

2005: Islamist terrorist bombings in London: Bombs simultaneously detonate in the Underground and on a city bus.

2006: U.S. Senate passes Comprehensive Immigration Reform Act that would impose penalties on employers of illegal immigrants but that also would allow illegal immigrants who have lived in the United States for more than five years the opportunity to apply for U.S. citizenship after paying fines and taxes. Congressional leaders enter talks to try to reach compromise with House bills that would make compromise measures law.

2006: Massive rallies and protests spread across the United States both in support and opposition to proposed immigration legislation.

1 Immigration and Migration Prior to 1845

Immigration and Migration Prior to 1845

From 1750 to 1845, emigrants to the United States predominantly came from the nations of Western Europe. Before the American Revolution, most were from Great Britain—then composed of England, Scotland, Wales, Ulster, and Ireland. By 1790, Germans were the second largest immigrant group in the United States. Revolution, warfare, crop failures, economic instability, and religious and political persecution fueled immigration to the Americas from 1790 to 1845. Whether fleeing revolution in France or following economic opportunity from the ports of Holland to the streets of New York, immigration to the fledgling United States boomed bringing. From 1812 to 1850, nearly five million immigrants arrived in the United States.

This chapter features a range of sources from informational pamphlets for newly arrived immigrants to immigrant narratives. Also included is a brief survey of the first attempts to address immigration through U.S. law and policy.

While many emigrated voluntarily, many more individuals were forced to migrate to Europe and the New World. This chapter covers the zenith, and the eventual curtailment, of the trans-Atlantic African slave trade. No accurate records exist that document the number of African slaves brought to the Americas; many historians estimate between ten and fifteen million. "Plan of a Slave Ship's Hold" illustrates one of the many horrors of the slave trade, the dreaded Middle Passage across the Atlantic that claimed over three million lives.

Convicts and prisoners also became forced migrants during this period. Some English convicts were sentenced to penal colonies in Australia (as in "The Arrival of Prisoners at Botany Bay Penal Colony"); others were given the option of prison in England or exile to convict colonies abroad. Some convicts were given the option of indentured servitude as an alternative to prison. "Freedom from Indenture or Prison in Australia" features the reward for those who survived their tenure, freedom papers noting the fulfillment of the indenture and repayment of passage. In exchange for paid passage abroad, thousands of emigrants also signed voluntary contracts of indenture.

Plan of a Slave Ship's Hold

Illustration

By: Anonymous

Date: c. 1750

Source: The Library of Congress.

About the Artist: This image is part of the collection at the Library of Congress, the national library of the United States and the largest library in the world.

INTRODUCTION

It is estimated that between 1540 and 1850, fifteen million Africans were packed tightly into ships and transported to be slaves in the Americas. Profit-maximizing slave merchants overloaded their boats with would-be slaves, chaining them together by their hands and feet. The journey usually took 60-90 days, but sometimes a trip would last up to four months. Many slaves died from diseases such as dysentery and smallpox. Some committed suicide by refusing to eat, and others were crippled for life as a result of the cramped conditions. Only half of those slaves transported actually became effective slaves in the Americas. Even with the death rate, traders made a decent profit, as one slave bought in Africa was worth three times the amount in the Americas.

The human cargo was typically put into the hull of the ship, which was divided into several makeshift decks or shelves. The space between each was very limited. In an extreme case, it was reported that people were packed onto a deck which only had eighteen inches between the floor and ceiling. Such conditions made it very difficult for the slaves to sit up, or even move around to change their position. During times of rough seas, the people had difficulty keeping their balance. It was not uncommon for the slaves to be

A sketch of a ship used to transport slaves in the 1750s illustrates how slaves were kept beneath the main deck. PHOTO BY HULTON ARCHIVE/ GETTY IMAGES.

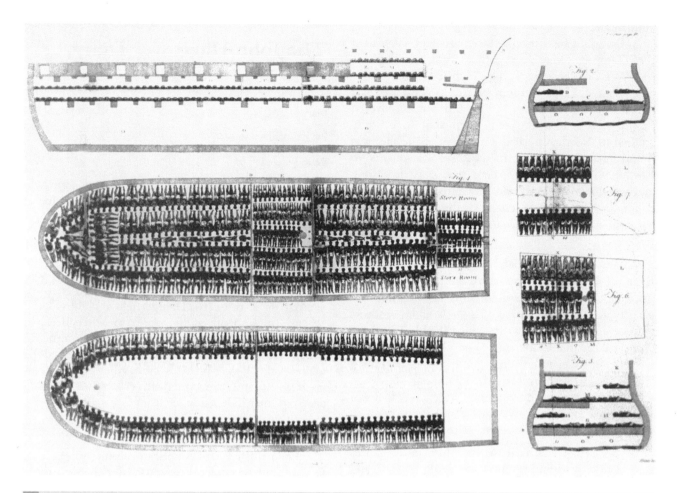

PRIMARY SOURCE

Plan of a Slave Ship's Hold: A drawing of the British slave ship *Brookes* demonstrates how enslaved Africans were packed into the ship's holds for transportation to market. THE LIBRARY OF CONGRESS.

trapped, injured, and even smothered to death under a pile of bodies tossed around as a ship rocked. Men, women and children were often put in separate areas. It was not uncommon for owners to exceed the capacity for which their ships were designed. A British House of Commons committee heard a case in which 600 slaves were packed onto a ship designed for 451 people.

The slaves sold to the Americas would often be gathered in the interior of the African continent, and were then brought to the western and northern coasts of Africa to wait for merchant ships coming from Europe. Would be slaves were often kidnapped by other Africans, some were criminals or owed debt to a village chief. In return for slaves and other goods such as ivory, gold, and pepper, African traders and chiefs would be given European farm products, weapons, textiles, alcohol, and brass. Some of the most notorious points of departure for slave ships were the Slave Coast, which included present day Benin, Togo, and western Nigeria; the Gold Coast, which is present day Ghana; and present day Ivory Coast. The ships would sail west with the slaves to the Caribbean Islands, South America, and the southern United States. There they would trade the Africans and other goods for sugar, tobacco, wood, cotton, and other items highly valued in Europe. This route, beginning and ending in Europe, was often called the Triangular Trade Route. The segment of the route from Africa to the Americas was called the Middle Passage.

PRIMARY SOURCE

PLAN OF A SLAVE SHIP'S HOLD
    See primary source image.

SIGNIFICANCE

Historians have used a slave merchant ship called the Henrietta Marie to gather information about the design of slave ships. The Henrietta Marie, considered a typical slave-trading vessel, sank off the coast of Florida in the early 1700s, and was discovered in the 1970s. It is the only such ship to be fully studied in North America. The name of the ship was found on its bell, and matched to documents in Europe. The Henrietta Marie was sixty feet long and weighed 120 tons, and its center mast was fifty feet tall. Archeologists consider the ship important for understanding an important part of the slave trade era.

Slaves and slave boat operators who recounted their experience on the ships spoke of violence, unclean conditions, terrible smells, and stagnant air. In acts of desperation, slaves would purposely suffocate one another to free up valuable breathing space in the tight quarters. The slaves were given very little to eat and drink, and those who died would be tossed overboard. Whipping, beatings, and other forms of punishment were used to force the human cargo onto the ships, and keep order on the ships in case the slaves tried to revolt.

The British Parliament and the United States passed bills prohibiting the slave trade in 1807 and 1808. Although this did not end slave trading within the countries, it did outlaw overseas transportation of slaves. Following the passage of these laws, the United States and Britain patrolled the seas off the coast of Africa, stopping and inspecting suspected slave vessels, and confiscating ships upon the discovery of slaves. These slaves would then be transported back to ports in Africa, and set free.

FURTHER RESOURCES

Books

Dow, George F. *Slave Ships and Slaving*. Salem, Mass.: Marine Research Society, 1927.

Klein, Herbert S. *The Atlantic Slave Trade*. Cambridge, U.K.: Cambridge University Press, 1999.

Calonius, Erik. *The Wanderer: The Last American Slave Ship and the Conspiracy That Set Its Sails*. New York: St. Martin's Press, 2006.

Canot, Theodore. *Adventures of an African Slaver; Being a True Account of the Life of Captain Theodore Canot, Trader in Gold, Ivory & Slaves on the coast of Guinea*. Garden City, N.Y.: Garden City Pub. Co, 1928.

The John Harrower Diary, 1773–1776

Diary

By: John Harrower

Date: 1773–1776

Source: Dublin, Thomas, ed. *Immigrant Voices: New Lives in America, 1773–1986*. Urbana: University of Illinois Press, 1993.

About the Author: John Harrower was a Scottish immigrant who arrived in America in 1774 as an indentured servant. After his arrival, his contract was sold to Colonel William Daingerfield, and Harrower worked as a tutor to Daingerfield's children and other local students at his plantation, Belvidera, in Fredericksburg, Virginia. Harrower kept a journal in which he recorded both details of everyday life and the major events taking place as the revolutionary movement grew and the American colonies eventually declared their independence from Great Britain.

INTRODUCTION

The British North American colonies were established in the seventeenth century; over the next three hundred years they absorbed a great wave of emigrants from Europe. Most came to escape poverty and unemployment caused by rapid population increases combined with the social and economic upheavals that were destroying traditional rural societies and occupations. Although the English formed the majority of the earliest settlers, in the eighteenth century Scottish and Scots-Irish formed the largest group; by 1790 there were around 260,000 people of Scottish birth or descent in the new United States.

John Harrower had originally left the Scottish Highlands to seek work in London, but was unsuccessful, and accepted instead a four-year appointment as an indentured schoolmaster. At this time, many poor Europeans who could not pay their own fares to the New World readily accepted posts as indentured servants, some going to work there as manual laborers, others as clerks, bookkeepers or storekeepers, and some, like John Harrower, as schoolteachers. Merchants and businessmen often used the indenture system to recruit and train young men who would eventually assist them in running their enterprises.

Within Britain, agents representing the colonies, such as the Virginia or Massachusetts Bay Companies, actively promoted the opportunities available there.

Under the indenture arrangement, the employer normally paid the emigrants' fares and living expenses in return for a specified number of years' service. After that time, the servants would usually be given their freedom and sometimes a piece of land on which to settle. As many as half the settlers living in the colonies south of New England came to America under this system, given the high demand for labor in the colonies and the scarcity of employment in Britain at the time. Many indentured servants later became very successful businessmen themselves.

The primary source included here retains the original spellings and grammatical choices of the author.

▉ PRIMARY SOURCE

The John Harrower Diary, 1773–1776

Thursday, 28th. This morning I recd. from Benjamin Edge by the hand of his daughter two Dollars, one half and one Quarter Dollar being in all sixteen shillings and Sixpence in part payment for teaching his son and daughter. Same day I seed a Compy. of 70 Men belonging to one of the Regiments of Regullars raised here for the defence of the rights and liberties of this Colly. in particular and of North America in Generall. They were on their March to Williamsburg.

Thursday, October 12th. Company here last night Vizt. Old Mrs. Waller, her son and his wife and at school here Mr. Heely Schoolmaster and Mr. Brooks Carpenter and they wt. Mr. Frazer and myself played whist and danced until 12 Oclock, Mr. Heely and Fidle and dancing. We drank one bottle of rum in time. Mr. Frazer verry sick after they went home.

Munday, sixteenth. This morning 3 men went to work to break, swingle and heckle flax and one woman to spin in order to make course linnen for shirts to the [slave], This being the first of the kind that was made on the plantation. And before this year there has been little or no linnen made in the Colony.

Tuesday, seventteenth. Two women spinning wool on the bigg wheel and one woman spinning flax on the little wheel all designed for the Nigers.

Munday, 23d. One Frieday last I lent to Miss Lucy one pair of my shoes to spin with. This day General Washingtons Lady dined here, As did her son and Daugt in Law, Mrs. Spotswood, Mrs. Campbell, Mrs. Dansie, Miss Washington and Miss Dandrige, They being all of the highest Rank and fortunes of any in this Colony.

Saturday, 28th. Last night came here to school Mr. Heely and Thos. Brooks in order to spend the evening. . . .

Thursday, November 9th. Upon Thursday 2d Inst. there was a Camp Marked out close at the back of the school

for a Batallion of 500 private men besides officers and they imediatly began to erect tents for the same. . . .

Sunday, 12th. this day a great number of company from Toun and Country to see the Camp four of which (Gentlemen) paid me a visite which put me to 1/3 expence for a bottle of rum. at noon by Accident one of the Captains tents was set on fire and all consumed but none of the things of any Accot. Lost.

Munday, 13th. This forenoon the Col. sent a waggon Load of Turnups and Pitatoes to the Camp as a present for all the men.

Tuesday, 14th. All the minute-men in the Camp employed learning their exercise.

Wednesday, 15th. This morning I drank a small dram of rum made thick with brown suggar for the cold, it being the first dram I have drunk since I lived on the Plantation.

Thursday, sixteenth. The soldiers at muster.

Friday, seventteenth. The soldiers at D., and I left of going into the Nursery and taking charge of the children out of school.

Wednesday, 29th. This day the camp was brocke up and the whole Batallion dismissed. . . .

Saturday, December 2d. At noon went to Toun and seed two Companys of regulars from the Ohio among which was one real Indian. he was of a Yelow couler short bod faced and rather flat nosed, and long course black [hair] quite streight. he spoke verry good english. I staid in Toun all night and slept at Mr. Andersons; I bought from Mr. Porter a black Silk Handkerchief at 5/ [5 shillings]

Sunday, 3d. After breackfast I went and found out Miss Mollly White and left with her cloth to make me two winter Stocks and a stock to make them b. Dined in Toun, came home in the afternoon. . . .

Wednesday, January 10th, 1776. This day we hade the Confirmation of Norfolk being reduced to ashes by the Men of War and British Troops under Command of Lord Dunmore. It was the Largest Toun in the Collony and a place of great Trade, it being situated a little within the Capes. Seerall Women and Childn. are killed.

Saturday, 13th. After 12 O Clock I went six Miles into the Forrest to one Daniel Dempsies to see if they wou'd spin three pound of Cotton to run 7 yds per lb., 2/3 of it belonging to Miss Lucy Gaines for a goun and 1/3 belonging to myself for Vestcoats, which they agd. to do if I carried the cotton there on Saturdy. 27th Inst. . . .

Munday, 15th. Miss Lucy spinning my croop of Cotton at night after her work is done; to make me a pair of gloves.

Wednesday, seventteenth. This evening Miss Lucy came to school with Mr. Frazer and me, and finished my croop of Cotton by winding it, after its being doubled and twisted the whole consisting of two ounces.

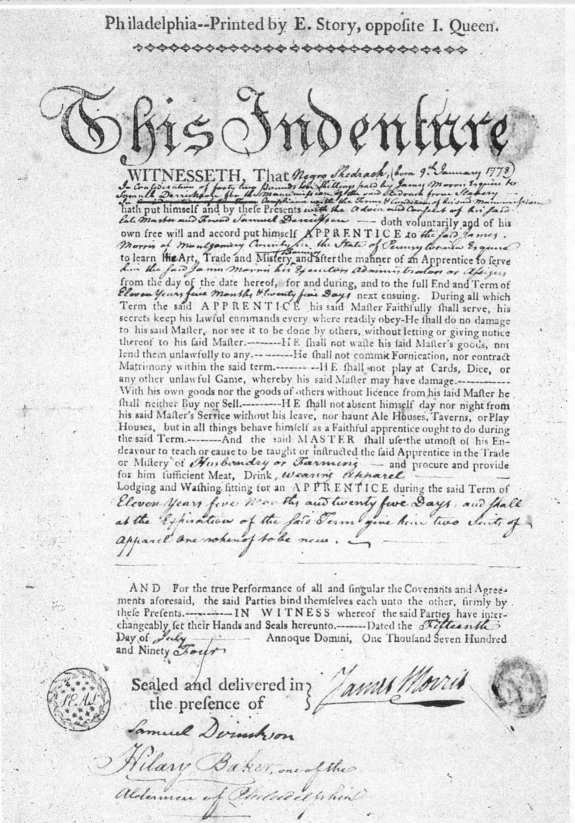

A Certificate of Indenture from 1794. It describes the terms of a contract under which Shadrach, a former slave, is indentured to serve a Pennsylvania farmer named James Morris for eleven years and five months, during which time Morris will teach him the business of farming. HULTON ARCHIVE/GETTY IMAGES.

Tuesday, 23ᵈ. This day I entred Edwin into the Latin Gramer.

Saturday, 27ᵗʰ. After 12 pm I went to the forrest to the house of Daniel Dempsies and carried with me three pound of pick'd Cotton two of which belongs to Miss Lucy Gaines and one to me, which his wife has agreed to spin to run 8 Yds. Per lb., I paing her five shillings per lb. for spinning it and it is to be done by the end of May next.

Tuesday, March 5ᵗʰ. This morning Bathurest Daingerfield got don reading through the bible and the Newtestament, and began to learn to write 15 Ult. I gave them Holyday this Afternoon.

Saturday, April twentieth. At noon I asked the Col. for a bottle of rum as I expected two Countrymen to se me tomorrow, which he verry cheerfully gave and desired me to ask him for one any time I wanted it and told me to take them to the Howse to dinner with me. in the afternoon he, his Lady, and Daughter went over the river to Mr. Jones's in King George County.

Tuesday, 23ᵈ. At noon rode to Town, got the Newspapers and settled with Mr. Porter for teaching his two sons 12 Mos. when he verry genteely allowed me 6 for them, besides a present of two silk vests and two pair of Nankeen Breeches last summer and a Gallon of rum at Christenmass, both the and Mrs. Porter being extreamly well satisfied with what I hade don to them.

Wednesday, 24ᵗʰ. General Muster of all the County Malitia in Town today. at Breackfast the Col. desired me to go and see it if I pleased, But being in town yesterday I chose to stay to day with my boys.

Sunday, 28ᵗʰ. this day came here to pay me a visit Mr. Reid from Mansfield and Mr. Scott from Toun and dined with me in the great house by the Colos. order, and after we hade spent the afternoon verry agreeably together they returned home in the evening.

Sunday, May, 5ᵗʰ. Early this morning I went to Mr. McCalley's and entred his oldest son (about 8 years of age) to writting, stayed there all day and rode his horse home in the evening. The Colo. went to Newport and dinned there.

Tuesday, 7ᵗʰ. Billie ended reading through his Bible.

Thursday, 9ᵗʰ. After dinner I tok the boys with me to Massaponacks Briges to see 56 prisoners that were taken at the late battle in North Carolina, among them was a great many 'Emigrants from Scotland who were all officers. I talked with several of them from Ross Shr. and the Isle of Sky.

Freiday, seventteenth. Gen. Fast by order of the Congress. I went to Church in Toun but no sarmon. dined at Mr. McAlleys and came home in the evening. The Colo. and his lady at Mount Ch.

Munday, 27ᵗʰ. At 9 am I went to Mr. McAlleys and staid teaching his Son and sister untill dark and then rode home bringing with me 1 1/2 Yd. Linen for summer breeches. . . .

Saturday, [June] 8ᵗʰ. At noon I went to Mrs. Bataile's and entred two of her Daughters to writting, Vis. Miss Sallie and Miss Betty and continoued teaching them until night, when I agreed to attend them every Saturday afternoon and every other Sunday from this date until 8ᵗʰ June 1777 (If it please God to spare me) for four pound Virginia currancy.

Sunday, 9ᵗʰ. After breackfast I rode to Mr. McAlleys and teach'd his son to write untill 4 pm and then came home in the evening.

Freiday, 14ᵗʰ. At noon went to Jn. McDearmons and had 6 Yd. stript Cotton warped for 2 Veastcoats and two handkerchiefs all prepared at my own expence.

Wednesday, nineteenth. At noon went to snow creek and the boys and dined at the spring on Barbaque and fish. At 5 pm I went to Mrs. Bataile and teac'd until 1/2 an hour past 7.

Wednesday, 20ᵗʰ. At 5 pm I went to Mr. Decks and had a short Coat cut out of cotton cloth wove Jeans. I bought the cotton and paid for spinning it at the rate of 2/6 [2 shillings and six pence] per lb. and one shilling per Yd. for weaving.

Sunday, July 7ᵗʰ. This morning I rode to Mansfield and breackfast with Mr. Reid and stayed and dined with him and in the afternoon he and I rode to see the Rowgallies that was building where we met with Mr. Anderson and Jacob Whitely and went to Town with them to Whitelys where we Joyned in Comp. with Mr. Wright and one Mr. Bruce from King George. about 11 pm we brock up and every one went to his own home as I did.

Wednesday, 10ᵗʰ. At 6 pm went to Mrs. Battaile's and teach'd untill sunset and then return'd home and soon after heard a great many guns fired towards Toun. about 12 pm the colo. Despatched Anthy. Frazer there to see what was the cause of [it] who returned, and informed him that there was great rejoicings in Toun on Accot. of the Congress having declared the 13 United Colonys of North America Independent of the Crown of great Britain.

Thursday, 25ᵗʰ. I imployed this morng. and forenoon getting Lead off Snowcreek house.

SIGNIFICANCE

John Harrower's diary provides a personal record of key events in American history. He left a fascinating account of these developments, along with more mundane descriptions of everyday life for an indentured immigrant on the plantation, such as his students' progress, and the spinning and weaving of materials to make clothes, particularly for the black slaves who worked on the plantation.

In 1775, when Harrower arrived in America, the colonies were already preparing for war with Great Britain. Tensions had increased during the previous decade, as Britain tried to impose greater control over the colonies and introduced a series of taxes and duties on imported goods. Many colonists resented being taxed so heavily when they were not even represented in the British Parliament. The revolutionary movement grew in strength, and the Continental Congress convened to build up munitions and mobilize troops in preparation for war.

The soldiers were known as the Minutemen, because they were prepared to fight on a minute's notice. Harrower describes a camp of these troops near the plantation. He also recounts the shelling and virtual destruction of the town of Norfolk on the orders of the British Governor Lord Dunmore, in a desperate attempt to control the colonists' rebellion, after the British troops had suffered a major defeat in the Battle of the Great Bridge.

On June 7, 1776, the Second Continental Congress passed a resolution agreeing that the colonies should declare their independence from Great Britain. Harrower's diary entry for July 10 of that year records in a somewhat understated way the celebrations that were being held following the adoption of the Declaration of Independence on July 4. The recording of such momentous events interspersed between entries about daily affairs brings history to life very effectively. Although John Harrower was healthy when his diary ended in 1776, he died suddenly in 1777, never able to realize his dream of bringing his Scottish wife to join him in America.

FURTHER RESOURCES
Books

Brock, William Ranulf, *Scotus Americanus: A Survey of the Sources for Links between Scotland and America in the Eighteenth Century.* Edinburgh: Edinburgh University Press, 1982.

Dublin, Thomas, ed. *Immigrant Voices: New Lives in America, 1773–1986.* University of Illinois Press, 1993.

Riley, Edward Miles, ed. *The Journal of John Harrower: an indentured servant in the Colony of Virginia, 1773–1776.* Williamsburg, VA: Colonial Williamsburg Foundation, 1963.

Web sites

U.S. Department of State: Outline of U.S. History. "Chapter 3: The Road to Independence." November 2005 <http://usinfo.state.gov/products/pubs/histryotln/road.htm> (accessed July 17, 2006).

The Arrival of Prisoners at Botany Bay Penal Colony

Illustration

By: Anonymous

Date: January 26, 1788

Source: Photo by Time Life Pictures/Mansell/Time Life Pictures/Getty Images.

About the Artist: This image is part of the collection at Getty Images, a worldwide provider of visual content materials to such communications groups as advertisers, broadcasters, designers, magazines, new media organizations, newspapers, and producers. The photograph came from Time Life Pictures. The name of the illustrator is not known.

INTRODUCTION

Botany Bay is an inlet of the Tasman Sea in eastern Australia, near the city of Sydney, New South Wales. Near the bay are the facilities for the Kingsford Smith International Airport. Botany Bay National Park and the Towra Point Nature Reserve are also located at Botany Bay. In 1770, the inlet (which was initially called Stingray Bay) was the landing site of British explorer and navigator James Cook (1728–1779) and his ship, the *HMS Endeavour.* Captain Cook's landing is generally considered the beginning of England's exploration and eventual colonization of Australia. The name Botany Bay was given to the bay in reference to the abundance of plant life (as in botany, the scientific study of plants) that was discovered by Cook's crew.

In 1788, British naval officer Arthur Phillip (1738–1814) captained another English fleet consisting of eleven ships into Botany Bay to establish a penal colony for England and its colonies. Finding a better site north of Botany Bay, and with a French expedition in fast pursuit, Phillip sailed to Sydney Cove (an area now called New South Wales). About 780 prisoners were delivered to the site. Two more fleets of ships with convicts arrived in 1790 and 1791. From 1788 to 1823, the site at New South Wales was officially recognized as an English penal colony. It consisted of convicts (who were called transportees), marines, and wives of the marines. Although never built at Botany Bay, the Australian penal colony at Sydney Cove was popularly referred to as Botany Bay by the people of England.

During this time, Phillip, who was now the colony's governor, established a system where all convicts were worked according to their abilities to help develop the British colony. They worked as carpenters, cattlemen, farmers, nurses, servants, and at other necessary occupations. The prisoners constructed public facilities such as bridges, buildings, hospitals, and roads, and worked at various occupations for free settlers and landowners.

About 162,000 male and female prisoners were sent to Botany Bay between 1788 and 1868, the last year that convicts were sent there. Most prisoners at Botany Bay were from England, Ireland, or Scotland, but some were from other colonies of England such as Canada, India, New Zealand, Hong Kong, and the countries of the Caribbean Sea. Many prisoners were sent to Botany Bay for such crimes as desertion, insubordination and mutiny (in the case of soldiers), and larceny and robbery (for the general population). People convicted of crimes were often sent to Botany Bay in order to reduce the population of England, as a way to deal with increasing poverty, and to purge the country of its most undesirable citizens.

By 1868, the English population of Australia stood at about one million. By this time, the population of the country was large enough so that the island country could sustain itself without the introduction of additional convicts.

PRIMARY SOURCE

The Arrival of Prisoners at Botany Bay Penal Colony: A painting depicting the arrival of the first prisoners at the Botany Bay penal colony, Port Jackson, Australia. The day has become a holiday, designated the National Day of Australia. PHOTO BY TIME LIFE PICTURES/ MANSELL/TIME LIFE PICTURES/GETTY IMAGES.

THE ARRIVAL OF PRISONERS AT BOTANY BAY PENAL COLONY

See primary source image.

SIGNIFICANCE

The Industrial Revolution began in England in the middle part of the eighteenth century. It greatly strengthened many sectors of the English economy. However, it hurt the rural areas when young workers left to pursue the enormous monetary opportunities available in urban factories. Even the industrializing cities of England did not have enough jobs for all the potential job seekers. For example, between 1750 and 1770, the city of London doubled in population. By the end of the century, England had large numbers of able-bodied but unemployed people concentrated in its largest cities. With this condition growing, crime became an increasing problem in England.

Most historians contend that the English government sent prisoners to Botany Bay as a way to deal with overpopulation, poverty, and an overcrowding prison population in England. The costs of transporting convicts to Australia were considered less than the cost of continuing to deal with them on English soil. Other historians state that convicts were sent to Botany Bay in order to provide the inexpensive labor needed to establish a colony in Australia. A colony in Australia would provide England with a naval base, enhance overseas trade, and provide flax and timber products (which were both important to England's economy).

Due to the lack of equipment and materials sent with the prisoners onboard the ships and the small number of skilled workers (such as bricklayers and carpenters) included among the convicts, it is generally considered that the Botany Bay Penal Colony was

Part of the crew of the H.M.S. *Guardian* endeavouring to escape after the ship struck an iceberg on the way to the penal colony at Botany Bay, Australia. PHOTO BY HULTON ARCHIVE/GETTY IMAGES.

established to reduce the unwanted and undesired criminal population from England and its colonies. For whatever reason, removing prisoners from England and its colonies to the remote island of Australia was a good way to solve the growing problem of criminals on English lands.

In the twenty-first century, Australia is the sixth largest nation by area after Russia, Canada, China, the United States, and Brazil, but the smallest continent on Earth. Though it is a large country, Australia has a small population, with just over twenty million residents as of 2005. About ninety-two percent of its citizens live in urban areas such as its largest cities of Sydney, Melbourne, and Brisbane. Since the last quarter of the eighteenth century when it was first colonized with thousands of English convicts, immigration has been an important contribution for the population of Australia. Since the end of World War II (1939–1945), over six million people from about two hundred countries have arrived in Australia. Some of the countries providing the most immigrants include Canada, China, England, India, Ireland, New Zealand, Scotland, Serbia and Montenegro (formerly Yugoslavia), South Africa, and the United States. Over one-fourth of all people in Australia were born outside of the country.

Australia's early history involved receiving many criminals from England and its colonies. Since then the federal government of Australia has evolved into a stable and successful parliamentary democracy, one of the many forms of governments around the world where people live free and are represented by elected government officials. Many of its practices are modeled from English and North American examples of government. Australia's system of government is based on democratic traditions such as religious acceptance and tolerance, freedom of choice, and freedom of association.

FURTHER RESOURCES

Books

Eldershaw, M. Barnard. *Phillip of Australia*. Sydney, Australia: Augus & Robertson, 1972.

Gillen, Mollie. *The Search for John Small: First Fleet*. North Sydney, Australia: Library of Australia History, 1985.

Mackay, David. *A Place of Exile: European Settlement of New South Wales*. Melbourne, Australia: Oxford University Press, 1985.

Molony, John. *The Penguin Bicentennial History of Australia: The Story of 200 Years*. Ringwood, Victoria, Australia: Penguin Books, 1988.

Periodicals

Abbott, Graham. "The Excepted Cost of the Botany Bay Scheme." *Journal of the Royal Historical Society* 81 (1995): Part 2.

Web sites

Cameron Riley, Hawkesbury Historical Society. "The 1804 Australian Rebellion and Battle of Vinegar Hill." November 2003. <http://www.hawkesburyhistory.org.au/articles/Battle_of_Vinegar.html> (accessed June 28, 2006).

The City of Botany Bay. "The History of Botany Bay." <http://www.botanybay.nsw.gov.au/city/history.htm> (accessed June 28, 2006).

Australian Government Culture and Recreation Portal. "European Discovery and the Colonisation of Australia." <http://www.cultureandrecreation.gov.au/articles/australianhistory> (accessed June 28, 2006).

Act of March 26, 1790

Legislation

By: U.S. Congress

Date: March 26, 1790

Source: "Act of March 26, 1790." First United States Congress.

About the Author: The First United States Congress met March 4, 1789–March 3, 1791. Congress is the legislative body of the United States Government made up of two chambers, the Senate and House of Representatives.

INTRODUCTION

The United States Congress passed the Act of March 26, 1790, to dictate when and how a resident of the United States could become a citizen. Citizenship afforded a person to participate fully in society and in the democratic process as a voter. According to the Act, residents could become naturalized citizens after living in the United States for a minimum of two years. Only free people could become citizens; the Act did not grant citizenship to slaves, indentured servants, Native Americans, and most women, as these persons were considered dependent upon other citizens. The Act put forth the regulations for naturalization, but the courts were given the responsibility of carrying out the naturalization process.

An illustration from *Leslie's Illustrated Weekly* depicting foreigners gathering at Tammany Hall, New York City, for naturalization. © CORBIS.

The Act required those desiring citizenship to prove they posessed good moral character and loyalty to the country; the two-year period of residency in the country was intended as proof of loyalty. One of the residency years had to occur in the state where the applicant would apply for citizenship. A Petition of Naturalization could be filed in any court within the applicant's jurisdiction. Once the court was convinced of the applicant's good moral character, the applicant would take an oath of allegiance to support to the United States Constitution. Carrying out these procedures would lead to full citizenship.

After the United States gained its independence from England, the colonial leaders were eager to institute their own rules and regulations regarding citizenship. In the Declaration of Independence, the colonists stated that rules set by England's King George III had obstructed the immigration of new citizens, and prevented the naturalization of residents already in the colonies. The colonists claimed that these policies minimized the potential for growth and development. Following independence, each state drafted its own rules for state citizenship in accordance with the

Articles of Confederation. The rules and procedures for gaining citizenship under the Articles were inconsistent and sometimes contradictory from state to state. When the United States Constitution replaced the Articles of Confederation in 1789, Congress was given the authority to govern citizenship. The Act of March 26, 1790, standardized the naturalization regulations.

PRIMARY SOURCE

Section 1. *Be it enacted by the Senate and House of Representatives of the United States of America in Congress assembled*, That any alien, being a free white person, who shall have resided within the limits and under the jurisdiction of the United Stares, for the term of two years, may be admitted to become a citizen thereof, on application to any common law court of record, in any one of the states wherein he shall have resided for the term of one year at least, and making proof to the satisfaction of such court, that he is a person of good character, and taking the oath or affirmation prescribed by law, to support the constitution of the United States, which oath or affirmation such court shall administer; and the clerk of such court shall record such application, and the proceeding thereon; and thereupon such person shall be considered as a citizen of the United States. And the children of such persons so naturalized, dwelling within the United States, being under the age of twenty-one years at the time of such naturalization, shall also be considered as citizens of the United States. And the children of citizens of the United States, that may be born beyond sea, or out of the limits of the United States, shall be considered as natural born citizens: *Provided*, That the right of citizenship shall not descend to persons whose fathers have never been resident in the United States: *Provided also*, That no person heretofore prescribed by any state, shall be admitted a citizen as aforesaid, except by an act of the legislature of the state in which such person was proscribed.

Approved, March 26, 1790.

SIGNIFICANCE

As a reaction to changes in political thought and circumstances, Congress has amended the 1790 Act many times. The Act of 1795 extended the residency requirement to five years, and made it mandatory for immigrants to state their naturalization intentions at least three years before their official application. Later acts made it illegal for citizens from countries the United States was at war with to go through the naturalization process. The Act of February 10, 1855, allowed immigrant women to become citizens without naturalization, as long as a woman's husband was a citizen. A law in 1907 stated that women born in the United States would lose their citizenship upon marrying a non-citizen. Women's citizenship was separated from that of their husbands in 1922. African-Americans were allowed to gain citizenship after the Civil War. Native Americans were granted citizenship in 1924, with the Indian Citizenship Act.

In the 1900s, naturalization procedures had an increasing lack of uniformity around the United States. Courts would charge different fees, and used different forms to record naturalization. Also, depending on the court, there would be different interpretations of some of the naturalization requirements, such as what was meant by having good moral character. Investigation into the matter by a special Presidential unit also found that fraud was occurring during naturalization court hearings. A 1906 law created the Bureau of Immigration and Naturalization in the Department of Commerce and Labor to supervise naturalization procedures, and store naturalization documents. The Bureau also systemized naturalization procedures that included standardized fee schedules and standardized forms. This Bureau was a predecessor of the modern Immigration and Naturalization Service (INS).

Modern naturalization requirements include variations of the original Act of 1790, although the principles of naturalization remain. Immigrants must have a lengthy period of continuous legal residence in the United States, and still must prove good moral character. Modern applicants must be able to read, write, and speak English. Also, to become a citizen, one must have knowledge of United States history and government, agree with the principles of the Constitution, and have a positive outlook about the United States.

FURTHER RESOURCES

Books

Glenn, Evelyn N. *Unequal Freedom: How Race and Gender Shaped American Citizenship and Labor*. Cambridge, MA: Harvard University Press, 2002.

Kerber, Linda K. *No Constitutional Right to be Ladies: Women and the Obligations of Citizenship*. New York: Hill and Wang, 1998.

Kettner, James H. *The Development of American Citizenship, 1608–1870*. Chapel Hill: University of North Carolina Press, 1978.

LeMay, Michael, and Elliott R. Barkan, eds. *U.S. Immigration and Naturalization Laws and Issues: A Documentary History*. Westport, CT: Greenwood Press, 1999.

Web site

United States Department of Homeland Security. "United States Citizenship and Immigration Services." June 23, 2006 <http://www.uscis.gov/graphics/index.htm> (accessed June 28, 2006).

Alien Act of 1798

Legislation

By: The Fifth Congress of the United States

Date: June 25, 1798

Source: "Alien Act of 1798." Fifth United States Congress.

About the Author: Speaker of the House of Representatives Jonathan Dayton (1760–1824) and Thomas Jefferson (1743–1826), U.S. vice president and president of the Senate, were the two leaders of the Fifth

U.S. Congress. Dayton was elected to the House of Representatives (1791–1799) and was the Speaker of the House of Representatives for the Fourth and Fifth Congresses. He was also elected to the U.S. Senate (1799—1805). Thomas Jefferson was elected the third president of the United States (1801–1809).

INTRODUCTION

In 1798, John Adams (1735–1826), of the Federalist Party, became the second President of the United States and Thomas Jefferson, of the Democratic-Republican Party (or Jeffersonian Party), became the vice-president. The Federalists, led by Adams and Alexander Hamilton, were composed mostly of wealthy, propertied-class businessmen. They were concerned about the country's security (and their own properties), thought most citizens were irresponsible, and did not like criticism from the opposing party. The Jeffersonian party, led by Jefferson and James Madison, consisted primarily of poor farmers, craftspeople, and immigrants. They prized the country's liberty, felt the country's power should rest with individuals, and were suspicious of the Federalists. They were often called anti-federalists because of their open and frequently bitter disagreements with the Federalists.

The two parties vehemently disagreed about the country's relationship with France. The United States had temporarily resolved its differences with England, arousing the anger of French leaders (who provided the U.S. with aid during the Revolutionary War and were enemies of England). After French diplomats threatened the United States, the Federalists wanted to declare war on France, while the Jeffersonians wanted to remain at peace. With talks of war and rumors of French invasion running rampant throughout the country, many Federalists felt they could better protect the United States from foreign invaders—while weakening the Jeffersonians—if they enacted the Alien and Sedition Acts.

Federalist members of Congress proposed four laws to make the United States more secure from foreign spies and domestic traitors. On July 14, 1798, President Adams signed into law the Alien Act along with three other acts within the Alien and Sedition Acts.

PRIMARY SOURCE

SECTION 1. Be it enacted by the Senate and the House of Representatives of the United States of America in Congress assembled, That it shall be lawful for the President of the United States at any time during the continuance of this act, to order all such aliens as he shall judge dangerous to the peace and safety of the United States, or shall have reasonable grounds to suspect are concerned in any treasonable or secret machinations against the government thereof, to depart out of the territory of the United States, within such time as shall be expressed in such order, which order shall be served on such alien by delivering him a copy thereof, or leaving the same at his usual abode, and returned to the office of the Secretary of State, by the marshal or other person to whom the same shall be directed. And in case any alien, so ordered to depart, shall be found at large within the United States after the time limited in such order for his departure, and not having obtained a license from the President to reside therein, or having obtained such license shall not have conformed thereto, every such alien shall, on conviction thereof, be imprisoned for a term not exceeding three years, and shall never after be admitted to become a citizen of the United States. Provided always, and be it further enacted, that if any alien so ordered to depart shall prove to the satisfaction of the President, by evidence to be taken before such person or persons as the President shall direct, who are for that purpose hereby authorized to administer oaths, that no injury or danger to the United States will arise from suffering such alien to reside therein, the President may grant a license to such alien to remain within the United States for such time as he shall judge proper, and at such place as he may designate. And the President may also require of such alien to enter into a bond to the United States, in such penal sum as he may direct, with one or more sufficient sureties to the satisfaction of the person authorized by the President to take the same, conditioned for the good behavior of such alien during his residence in the United States, and not violating his license, which license the President may revoke, whenever he shall think proper.

SEC. 2. And be it further enacted, That it shall be lawful for the President of the United States, whenever he may deem it necessary for the public safety, to order to be removed out of the territory thereof, any alien who may or shall be in prison in pursuance of this act; and to cause to be arrested and sent out of the United States such of those aliens as shall have been ordered to depart therefrom and shall not have obtained a license as aforesaid, in all cases where, in the opinion of the President, the public safety requires a speedy removal. And if any alien so removed or sent out of the United States by the President shall voluntarily return thereto, unless by permission of the President of the United States, such alien on conviction thereof, shall be imprisoned so long as, in the opinion of the President, the public safety may require.

SEC. 3. And be it further enacted, That every master or commander of any ship or vessel which shall come into any port of the United States after the first day of July next, shall immediately on his arrival make report in writing to the collector or other chief officer of the customs of such port, of all aliens, if any, on board his vessel, specifying their names, age, the place of nativity, the country from which they shall have come, the nation to which they belong and owe allegiance, their occupation and a description of their persons, as far as he shall be informed thereof, and on failure, every such master and commander shall forfeit and pay three hundred dollars, for the payment whereof on default of such master or commander, such vessel shall also be holden, and may by such collector or other officer of the customs be detained. And it shall be the duty of such collector or other officer of the customs, forthwith to transmit to the office of the department of state true copies of all such returns.

SEC. 4. And be it further enacted, That the circuit and district courts of the United States, shall respectively have cognizance of all crimes and offences against this act. And all marshals and other officers of the United States are required to execute all precepts and orders of the President of the United States issued in pursuance or by virtue of this act.

SEC. 5. And be it further enacted, That it shall be lawful for any alien who may be ordered to be removed from the United States, by virtue of this act, to take with him such part of his goods, chattels, or other property, as he may find convenient; and all property left in the United States by any alien, who may be removed, as aforesaid, shall be, and remain subject to his order and disposal, in the same manner as if this act had not been passed.

SEC. 6. And be it further enacted, That this act shall continue and be in force for and during the term of two years from the passing thereof.

Jonathan Dayton, Speaker of the House of Representatives.

TH. Jefferson, Vice President of the United States and President of the Senate.

I Certify that this Act did originate in the Senate.

Attest, Sam. A. Otis, Secretary

APPROVED, June 25, 1798.

John Adams
President of the United States.

SIGNIFICANCE

The Alien Act of 1798—officially, An Act Concerning Aliens, and sometimes also called the Alien Friends Act—authorized the president to detain, arrest, deport, or imprison any alien that was considered dangerous to the country, whether during peace or war. The law had the potential to authorize the removal of large numbers of immigrants, though it never resulted in the deportation of any aliens and was in effect for only two years.

Besides the Alien Act, the Alien and Sedition Acts also contained three other acts. First, the Alien Enemies Act (An Act Respecting Alien Enemies) authorized the president, once war had been declared, to deport or imprison any male citizen associated with a country fighting against the United States. This law could potentially have led to the removal of 25,000 French-American citizens. No person was deported under this law, however, because the country did not go to war. Second, the Naturalization Act (An Act to Establish a Uniform Rule of Naturalization) increased residency requirements from five years to fourteen years for immigrants seeking citizenship. Since immigrants generally joined the Jeffersonian Party, lengthening the citizenship time would have impeded the growth of the Jeffersonians and strengthened the power of the Federalists. Third, the Sedition Act (An Act for the Punishment of Certain Crimes against the United States) outlawed conspiracies and made it a crime to publish "false, scandalous, and malicious writing" against the government or its officials. In reality, any Jeffersonian who spoke against Federalists—especially the Adams administration—were likely targets.

Although the Federalists stated publicly that these acts were intended to increase national security, for all intents and purposes the laws were enacted to control dissent, to silence opposing views, and to increase Federalist power. The laws were enacted specifically to eliminate criticisms levied against the Adams administration and the Federalists by Thomas Jefferson and the Jeffersonians.

The four laws limited the right of free speech and dissent in the United States. In particular, the Jeffersonians felt that the Alien Act was unconstitutional because it violated the Bill of Rights (the first ten amendments to the Constitution). Consequently, the Jeffersonians drafted the Kentucky and Virginia Resolutions, which sought elimination of the Alien Act at the state level. In the resolutions, the authors accused Congress of exceeding its powers. They also declared the Alien and Sedition Acts void.

At the same time, Federalist members organized an alien list for deportation. Prominent Jeffersonian newspaper editors and publishers and U.S. Congressman Matthew Lyon (a Jeffersonian from Vermont) were on the list. Lyon was indicted for intentionally criticizing President Adams. He was found guilty by a Federalist judge, spent four months in jail, and was re-elected to office from his jail cell.

Aliens line up to obtain specimen forms outside the General Post Office in New York City, 1940. The forms list questions they will have to answer when they are registered and fingerprinted under the Alien Registration Act of 1940. © BETTMANN/CORBIS.

Thirteen more indictments were brought under the acts, with some people being brought to trial.

During these years, the acts provoked a debate between Federalist and Jeffersonian politicians over freedom of speech and the press. Of note, James Madison (1751–1836), who became the fourth U.S. president, wrote an exceptionally skillful argument against the acts.

The acts expired at the end of John Adams's presidency, which occurred on March 3, 1801. Thomas Jefferson was elected the third U.S. president and members of the Jeffersonian Party were elected to a majority in the Congress. Jefferson stopped prosecutions under the acts, and he arranged for those affected by these laws to be compensated or apologized to by

members of Congress. During Jefferson's two terms as president, he developed new definitions of freedom of speech and freedom of the press, which are in effect in the United States today. Throughout the nineteenth and twentieth centuries, Alien and Sedition Acts were known as the first attack on basic American civil liberties.

In the twenty-first century, parallels have been drawn between the Alien and Sedition Acts of 1798 and the USA PATRIOT Act of 2001 (short for Uniting and Strengthening America by Providing Appropriate Tools Required to Intercept and Obstruct Terrorism). After the September 11, 2001 attacks on the United States, the PATRIOT Act has increased the power of the federal government to gather domestic intelligence and restrict the activities of potentially dangerous citizens. Many organizations and individuals find a connection between the Alien and Sedition Acts, especially the Alien Act, and the PATRIOT Act with regards to limiting civil liberties for the sake of security in the pursuit of domestic and international terrorism. Others see the additional security restrictions as necessary in a time of war on terrorism.

FURTHER RESOURCES

Books

Rudanko, Martti Juhani. *James Madison and Freedom of Speech: Major Debates in the Early Republic.* Dallas, TX: University Press of America, 2004.

Smith, James Morton. *Freedom's Fetters: The Alien and Sedition Laws and American Civil Liberties.* Ithaca, NY: Cornell University Press, 1966.

Web sites

The University of Oklahoma College of Law. "The Sedition Act of 1798." <http://www.law.ou.edu/ushistory/sedact.shtml> (accessed June 26, 2006).

The White House. "John Adams." <http://www.whitehouse.gov/history/presidents/ja2.html> (accessed June 26, 2006).

The White House. "Thomas Jefferson." <http://www.whitehouse.gov/history/presidents/tj3.html> (accessed June 26, 2006).

The Avalon Project at Yale Law School. "An Act Respecting Alien Enemies." <http://www.yale.edu/lawweb/avalon/statutes/alien.htm> (accessed June 26, 2006).

Alien Enemy Act

Legislation

By: John Adams

Date: July 6, 1798

Source: Adams, John. "Alien Enemy Act." *Statutes at Large.* Boston: Little, Brown, 1798.

About the Author: John Adams (1735–1826) served as the second President of the United States from 1797 to 1801. A conservative who belonged to the Federalist Party, Adams spent his presidency wrestling with the problems associated with creating a new nation.

INTRODUCTION

When France signed the Treaty of Amity with the United States in 1778, it officially became the first friend of the fledgling nation. This friendship did not last for long. By 1798, relations with France had deteriorated to the point that an undeclared Quasi-War had begun. President John Adams, concerned about protecting the U.S. from French saboteurs and spies, pushed the Alien Enemy Act through Congress.

The Alien Enemy Act is generally regarded as one of the Alien and Sedition Acts passed in 1798. All of the acts arose in response to the same concerns. The beginning of the French Revolution initiated a generation of warfare between France and Great Britain. The fighting placed all neutral nations, especially the U.S., in a precarious position. As war escalated in Europe, both France and Britain violated U.S. neutrality rights by seizing American ships and sailors. Americans viewed this as an insult to their national honor and a threat to their sovereignty. However, the young nation was far too weak to do much about the situation. Federalists argued that the U.S. should link itself with Britain because of a shared culture and the stability of the English government. Democratic-Republicans (the forerunners to the modern Democratic Party) argued that the U.S. should move closer to France because France had supported the U.S. during the Revolutionary War and had a similar democratic government. In 1798, the U.S began a Quasi-War with France. This undeclared war took place strictly at sea.

In the midst of war, Congress passed a series of legislative acts, including the Alien Enemy Act, in response to a request from Adams. In practice, the act was transparently partisan. It was used to punish Democratic-Republicans, whom Federalists could barely distinguish from traitors. It was an era when the idea of loyal dissent had not yet become established. Democratic-Republicans for their part also resorted to scandalous lies and misrepresentations. The Federalists, however, controlled the machinery of government; Democratic-Republicans were the ones jailed and deported, although very few were prosecuted. When Democratic-Republican Thomas Jefferson beat Adams in the 1800 election, he let all of the Alien and Sedition Acts quietly expire.

PRIMARY SOURCE

Section 1. *Be it enacted by the Senate and House of Representatives of the United States of America in Congress assembled,* That whenever there shall be a declared war between the United States and any foreign nation or government, or any invasion or predatory incursion shall be perpetrated, attempted, or threatened against the territory of the United States, by any foreign nation or government, and the President of the United States shall make public proclamation of the event, all natives, citizens, denizens, or subjects of the hostile nation or government, being males of the age of fourteen years and upwards, who shall be within the United States, and not actually naturalized, shall be liable to be apprehended, restrained, secured and removed, as alien enemies. And the President of the United States shall be, and he is hereby authorized, in any event, as aforesaid, by his proclamation thereof, or other public act, to direct the conduct to be observed, on the part of the United States, towards the aliens who shall become liable, as aforesaid; the manner and degree of the restraint to which they shall be subject, and in what cases, and upon what security their residence shall be permitted, and to provide for the removal of those, who, not being permitted to reside within the United States, shall refuse or neglect to depart therefrom; and to establish any other regulations which shall be found necessary in the premises and for the public safety: Provided, that aliens resident within the United States, who shall become liable as enemies, in the manner aforesaid, and who shall not be chargeable with actual hostility, or other crime against the public safety, shall be allowed, for the recovery, disposal, and removal of their goods and effects, and for their departure, the full time which is, or shall be stipulated by any treaty, where any shall have been between the United States, and the hostile nation or government, of which they shall be natives, citizens, denizens or subjects: and where no such treaty shall have existed, the President of the United States may ascertain and declare such reasonable time as may be consistent with the public safety, and according to the dictates of humanity and national hospitality.

Sec. 2. *And be it further enacted*, That after any proclamation shall be made as aforesaid, it shall be the duty of the several courts of the United States, and of each state, having criminal jurisdiction, and of the several judges and justices of the courts of the United States, and they shall be, and are hereby respectively, authorized upon complaint, against any alien or alien enemies, as aforesaid who shall be resident and at large within such jurisdiction or district, to the danger of the public peace or safety, and contrary to the tenor or intent of such proclamation, or other regulations which the President of the United States shall and may establish in the premises, to cause such alien or aliens to be duly apprehended and convened before such court, judge, or justice; and after a full examination and hearing on such complaint, and sufficient cause therefore appearing, shall and may order such alien or aliens to be removed out the territory of the United States, or to give sureties of their good behavior, or they be otherwise restrained, conformably to the proclamation or regulations which shall and may be established as aforesaid, and may imprison, or otherwise secure such alien or aliens, until the order which shall and may be made, as aforesaid, shall be performed.

Sec. 3. *And be it further enacted*, That it shall be the duty of the marshal of the district in which any alien enemy shall be apprehended, who by the President of the United States, or by order of any court, judge or justice, as aforesaid, shall be required to depart, and to be removed, as aforesaid, to provide therefore, and to execute such order, by himself or his deputy, or other discreet person or persons to be employed by him, causing a removal of such alien out of the territory of the United States; and for such removal the marshal shall have the warrant of the President of the United States, or of the court, judge or justice ordering the same, as the case may be.

Approved, July 6, 1798

SIGNIFICANCE

The Quasi-War ended with the Treaty of Mortefontaine in 1800. However, relations between the two countries remained poor. Jefferson, Adams' successor, prepared for war when France closed New Orleans to American trade in 1802. When Napoleon suddenly decided to sell Louisiana to the U.S., the 1803 Louisiana Purchase removed the French presence from North America and dramatically reduced tensions with the United States. The respite proved to be brief. As France battled with Great Britain in the Napoleonic Wars, both sides seized American ships and shipping. The U.S. responded with a series of legislative restrictions, including the 1807 Embargo Act, which stopped trade with both countries. Only the defeat of Napoleon ended American tensions with France. By the mid-nineteenth century, both countries were firm allies.

In times of war, some Americans argue that constitutionally guaranteed freedoms need to be suspended to preserve national security. Statutes similar to the Alien Enemy Act have remained in force throughout most of U.S. history and have been used in many declared wars. Enemy aliens were interned in subsequent wars, including the War of 1812, World War I, and most notably, World War II. After the internment of Japanese Americans in the 1940s, such imprisonment fell deeply into disfavor as an abuse of civil liberties. Although there have been occasional calls to jail perceived national enemies, such as Muslims in the 1990s, no national public official has publicly voiced support for such measures. Any official who does advocate such measures is likely to come under heavy attack for trampling the freedoms enshrined by the Constitution.

FURTHER RESOURCES

Books

McCullough, David G. *John Adams*. New York: Simon and Schuster, 2001.

Smith, James M. *Freedom's Letters: The Alien and Sedition Laws and American Civil Liberties*. Ithaca, N.Y.: Cornell University Press, 1966.

Vidal, Gore. *Inventing a Nation: Washington, Adams, Jefferson*. New Haven, Conn.: Yale University Press, 2003.

Explanations and Sample Contracts for German-Speaking Emigrants Wishing to Purchase Land in America

Photograph

By: Anonymous

Date: 1804

Source: © Bettmann/Corbis.

About the Photographer: Photograph residing in the Bettmann Archives of Corbis Corporation, an image group headquartered in Seattle, with a worldwide archive of over seventy million images.

INTRODUCTION

The extraordinary increase in immigration to the United States in the early decades of the nineteenth century was one of the wonders of the age. The huge scale of the movement and its seeming inexhaustibility captured the public imagination on both sides of the Atlantic Ocean. In these years, the overwhelming majority of immigrants to the United States came from northern and western Europe. After Great Britain, Germany provided the most newcomers with Switzerland also sending large numbers of German-speakers to the New World.

The first wave of German immigrants had arrived in the eighteenth century. From the start, many Americans were prejudiced against these newcomers. The Germans were regarded as especially resistant to assimilation, mostly because they maintained separate communities with a visibly different culture. Settling

Erläuterungen über die Unternehmung eines Land-Ankaufs in den vereinigten Staaten von Nord-Amerika und über den daherigen Contract vom 1ten May 1804.

Mangel an Zeit, um alle Fragen schriftlich zu beantworten, die uns in Betreff des übernommenen Kaufes von Ländereyen in den vereinigten Staaten von Nord-Amerika gemacht werden, nöthigt uns, diese Beantwortung samt einigen Bemerkungen und einem Prospectus der Unternehmung drucken zu laßen. Wir bemerken daher was folget:

1. Da unser Contract durch Leute und für Leute gemacht worden, welche die Lage der Dinge in Amerika, so wie die Art, wie solche Unternehmungen gemacht werden müßen, kennen, so war es anfänglich unnöthig, einen Prospectus beyzufügen; übrigens werden dieselben sonst mehrentheils nicht nur zum Unterricht, sondern mehr oder weniger dazu gemacht, um zur Theilnahme zu bereden. So geneigt wir in ersterer Rücksicht dazu gewesen wären, so hielt uns jedoch die zweyte Rücksicht davon ab. Bey der Überzeugung, die wir haben, wie

PRIMARY SOURCE

Explanations and Sample Contracts for German-Speaking Emigrants Wishing to Purchase Land in America: Title page from a rare and early Western Colonization pamphlet from Arau, Switzerland, 1804. It explains the procedure for buying land in the United States, with an explanation of an accompanying contract to be signed by emigrants. © BETTMANN/ CORBIS.

in the Pennsylvania German region, these immigrants were densely concentrated in a way that reinforced the influence of conservative German churches and the German language.

By 1800, the rise of a commercial agricultural economy weakened German insularity and forced them to begin assimilating. German-Americans increasingly were coming into contact with neighboring English and Scots-Irish settlements. The diminishing use of the German language in favor of English is one clear sign of the acculturation process set off by

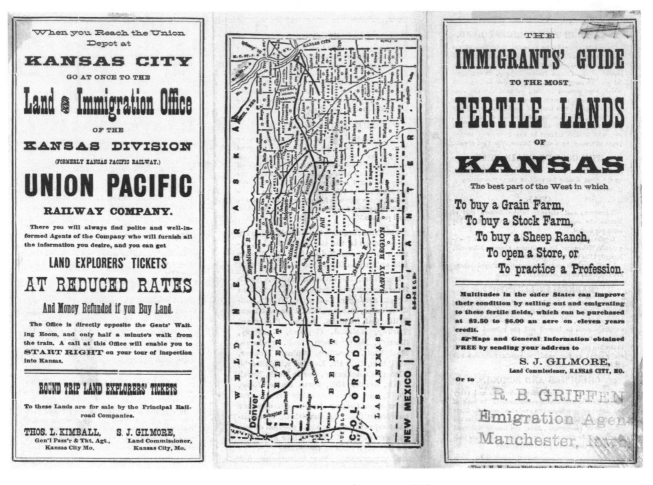

Pamphlet encouraging westward migration to Kansas, including a map of the state, 1880. © BETTMANN/CORBIS.

the need to do business with outsiders. Most of the German-language newspapers in the United States shut down their presses by 1815. At the same time, the German churches gradually stopped holding services in German. By 1820, the majority of German-Americans were second or third generation and had assimilated into American society.

PRIMARY SOURCE

EXPLANATIONS AND SAMPLE CONTRACTS FOR GERMAN-SPEAKING EMIGRANTS WISHING TO PURCHASE LAND IN AMERICA

See primary source image.

SIGNIFICANCE

After a brief lull, German immigrants again began pouring into the United States beginning in

the 1820s. This mass exodus from the Old World would continue until World War I halted most civilian transport ships. The new immigrants spread into the major cities of the Northeast and then across the plains of the Midwest. German institutions of all sorts grew dramatically. The great array of German organizations that flourished encouraged a misconception that the immigrants were forming structures to avoid assimilating into American culture.

The issue of assimilation has been frequently raised in the history of Germans in America. While eighteenth century Anglo-Americans complained about the refusal of Germans to blend into broader American society, nineteenth century native-born Americans took action to combat the perceived effects of such resistance to American social and political values. Nativists organized the Know Nothings in the 1850s as part of an anti-immigrant wave that swept through the United States in the decade prior to the Civil War. In response, Germans huddled within the fortresses of their churches, clubs, mutual aid societies, and rural communities. This German resistance to acculturation and involvement in the larger society persisted until World War I when anti-German sentiments left much of German-America in ruins.

FURTHER RESOURCES

Books

Gordon, Milton M. *Assimilation in American Life: The Role of Race, Religion, and National Origin.* New York: Oxford University Press, 1964.

Kazal, Russell M. *Becoming Old Stock: The Paradox of German-American Identity.* Princeton, N.J.: Princeton University Press, 2004.

Trommler, Frank, and Joseph McVeigh, editors. *America and the Germans: An Assessment of a Three-Hundred Year History.* Philadelphia: University of Pennsylvania Press, 1985.

Steerage Act

Legislation

By: U.S. Congress

Date: March 2, 1819

Source: "Steerage Act." *Statutes-at-Large.* 3, 488. New York: Little Brown, 1819.

About the Author: The U.S. Congress is responsible, among other things, for the regulation of commerce. It passes laws that cover ships bringing people and goods into the country.

INTRODUCTION

Immigrants had trickled into North America until the early decades of the nineteenth century when mass migration began. Floods of newcomers from Europe took advantage of improvements in transportation to immigrate to the United States. Many of the immigrants were steerage passengers, who historically paid the lowest fares for the poorest shipboard placements. To protect such people, Congress instituted the first of a series of Steerage Acts in 1819.

The transportation revolution in the early nineteenth century was brought about in part by an unprecedented expansion of transatlantic commerce. The most striking new development was the rise of the North American timber trade. As early as 1820, more

than 1000 vessels were employed annually in carrying North American timber to the British Isles. This number doubled within twenty years. Simultaneously, there was an astonishing increase in the amount of tonnage engaged in transporting American staple products, particularly cotton, to Europe. On the eastward voyage across the Atlantic, the ships were generally fully laden. When returning to the United States, much of the cargo space was unoccupied.

With space available for passengers, merchants and shipowners came to look to emigrants to provide part of the return freight. In a short time, the emigrant trade became a highly organized and lucrative branch of transatlantic commerce. Competition dropped the price of steerage passage, prompting more people to immigrate to the United States to improve their circumstances. Travel remained uncomfortable, however, with people often stuffed into any available space on tiny brigs for a journey that typically took four to eight weeks.

▮ PRIMARY SOURCE

Chap. XLVI.—*An Act regulating passenger ships and vessels. (a)*

SEC.1. *Be it enacted by the Senate and House of Representatives of the United States of America, in Congress assembled,* That if the master or other person on board of any ship or vessel, owned in the whole or in part by a citizen or citizens of the United States, or the territories thereof, or by a subject or subjects, citizen or citizens, of any foreign country, shall, after the first day of January next, take on board of such ship or vessel, at any foreign port or place, or shall bring or convey into the United States, or the territories thereof, from any foreign port of place; or shall carry, convey, or transport, from the United [States] or the territories thereof, to any foreign port or place, a greater number of passengers than two for every five tons of such ship or vessel, according to the custom-house measurement, every such master, or other person so offending, and the owner or owners of such ship or vessels, shall severally forfeit and pay to the United States, the sum of one hundred and fifty dollars, for each and every passenger so taken on board of such ship or vessel over and above the aforesaid number of two to every five tons of such ship or vessel; to be recovered by suit, in any circuit or district court of the United States, where the said vessel may arrive, or where the owner or owners aforesaid may reside: *Provided, nevertheless,* That nothing in this act shall be taken to apply to the complement of men usually and ordinarily employed in navigating such ship or vessel.

SEC.2. *And be it further enacted,* That if the number of passengers so taken on board of any ship or vessel as aforesaid, or conveyed or brought into the United States,

Polish and Russian passengers ride in the steerage of a ship heading to America from Europe in the early 1900s. © MINNESOTA HISTORICAL SOCIETY/CORBIS.

or transported therefrom as aforesaid, shall exceed the said proportion of two to every five tons of such ship or vessel by the number of twenty passengers, in the whole, every such ship or vessel shall be deemed and taken to be forfeited to the United States, and shall be prosecuted and distributed in the same manner in which the forfeitures and penalties are recovered and distributed under the provisions of the act entitled "An act to regulate the collection of duties on imports and tonnage."

SEC. 3. *And be it further enacted*, That every ship or vessel bound on a voyage from the United States to any port on the continent of Europe, at the time of leaving the last port whence such ship or vessel shall sail, shall have on board, well secured under deck, at least sixty gallons of water, one hundred pounds of salted provisions, one gallon of vinegar, and one hundred pounds of wholesome ship bread, for each and every passenger on board such ship or vessel, over and above such other provisions, stores, and live stock as may be put on board by such master or passenger for their use, or that of the crew of such ship or vessel; and in like proportion for a shorter or longer voyage; and if the passengers on board of such ship or vessel in which the proportion of provisions herein directed shall not have been provided, shall at any time be put on short allowance, in water, flesh, vinegar, or bread, during any voyage aforesaid, the master and owner of such ship or vessel shall severally pay to each and every passenger who shall have been put on short allowance as aforesaid, the sum of three dollars for each and every day they may have been on such short allowance; to be recovered in the same manner as seamen's wages are, or may be, recovered.

SEC. 4. *And be it further enacted*, That the captain or master of any ship or vessel arriving in the United States, or any of the territories thereof, from any foreign place whatever, at the same time that he delivers a manifest of the cargo, and, if there be no cargo, then at the time of making report or entry of the ship or vessel, pursuant to the existing laws of the United States, shall also deliver and report, to the collector of the district in which such ship or vessel shall arrive, a list or manifest of all the passengers taken on board of the said ship or vessel at any foreign port or place; in which list or manifest it shall be the duty of the said master to designate, particularly, the age, sex, and occupation, of the said passengers, respectively, the country to which they severally belong, and that of which it is their intention to become inhabitants; and shall further set forth whether any, and what number, have died on the voyage; which report and manifest shall be sworn to by the said master, in the same manner as is directed by the existing laws of the United States, in relation to the manifest of the cargo, and that the refusal or neglect of the master aforesaid, to comply with the provision of this section, shall incur the same penalties, disabilities, and forfeitures, as are at present provided for a refusal or neglect to report and deliver a manifest of the cargo aforesaid.

SEC. 5. *And be it further enacted*, That each and every collector of the customs, to whom such manifest or list of passengers as aforesaid shall be delivered, shall, quarter yearly, return copies thereof to the Secretary of State of the United States, by whom statements of the same shall be laid before Congress at each and every session.

APPROVED, March 2, 1819.

SIGNIFICANCE

The 1819 Steerage Act did not do much to improve the safety and comfort of steerage passengers. Continuing problems prompted Congress to pass the Steerage Passenger Act in 1882 to establish accommodation requirements for people traveling in steerage. The 1882 law was repealed in 1983. In 1995, at the recommendation of the Coast Guard, Congress abolished all of the steerage regulations enacted in the nineteenth century. The rules were deemed unnecessary or obsolete because they covered vessels and equipment that were no longer operating.

While steerage passengers no longer arrive in the United States, many Americans are descended from ancestors who immigrated in this manner. For Irish fleeing the potato famine, for Jews escaping pogroms in Russia, for Italians seeking a better life, steerage offered the only affordable means of passage. For generations of immigrants, it was the only way to come to America.

FURTHER RESOURCES

Books

Gowdey, David. *Before the Wind: True Stories about Sailing.* Camden, Maine: International Marine, 1994.

LaGumina, Salvatore J. *From Steerage to Suburb: Long Island Italians.* New York: Center for Migration Studies, 1988.

Rossi, Renzo. *A History of Powered Ships.* San Diego: Blackbird Press, 2005.

The Hollingworth Family Letters, 1827–1830

Letter

By: Joseph Hollingworth

Date: 1827–1830

Source: Dublin, Thomas, ed. *Immigrant Voices: New Lives in America, 1773–1986.* University of Illinois Press, 1993.

About the Author: Joseph Hollingworth was one member of the Hollingworth family who emigrated from England to America in the 1820s. They were skilled textile workers and hoped to find better opportunities for employment in the New World. They were all successful in finding jobs on arrival and settled in New York, Connecticut, and Massachusetts, working in the rapidly expanding textiles industry there. Their letters to family members in England provide an account of their journey to America and their experiences of living and working there.

INTRODUCTION

The Hollingworth letters were written by members of the Hollingworth family who emigrated from England to America in the early nineteenth century to

Female employees inspect fabric for defects prior to shipment at a Boston textile mill, 1912. © CORBIS-BETTMANN. REPRODUCED BY PERMISSION.

work in the textile factories there. This letter, written by one of the family of brothers to his relatives back in England, gives a very personal and humorous account of his voyage and of his reunion with familiar people upon his arrival.

In 1820, around 8,000 immigrants entered the country, a number that increased steadily during the decade to around 23,000 in 1830. Immigration swelled into a massive wave later in the century, with numbers rising sharply in the 1850s, when around 400,000 immigrants arrived per year.

During the early years of the nineteenth century, various categories of English immigrants came to America, their migration being related largely to the British Industrial Revolution and the development of new employment opportunities in the expanding American textiles industry. The majority of immigrants at that time were farmers and agricultural workers, as well as traditional artisans and craftsmen, who had been displaced due to the industrialization of the

English economy. However, significant numbers of industrial workers—such as the Hollingworth brothers who had experience in the English textiles industry—also migrated to America at this time, and may even have formed the majority of immigrants from the late 1820s onwards.

Since jobs for skilled textiles workers were likely to have been readily available in England at this time, the brothers probably migrated by choice rather than necessity, and may even have been encouraged to move to America by the owner of a mill there or by relatives who had already emigrated. Joseph Hollingworth's mention of other family members that he met on arrival in America indicates the existence of an extended family network already based there; this type of chain migration within families was fairly common at that time.

The draw for many British immigrants was the establishment of large mechanized textile mills that used manufacturing techniques originally invented in

England, an industry that was expanding to meet the enormous demand for the cloth in America, particularly after the 1809 embargo on imports from England. Immigrants, particularly those who had experience working in British textile mills, were an important source of labor. In some areas, especially Philadelphia, which developed into the largest textile-producing center in the United States, it was more common for textiles to be manufactured in small shops or home based operations using more traditional spinning and weaving techniques, but these relied equally heavily on skilled English immigrants.

Although the United States was still largely rural at this time, most immigrants settled in urban areas. By 1850, more than thirty-six percent of immigrants were living in places that had more than 10,000 residents, compared to only nine percent of the male native born population. Half of all immigrants lived in New York, Pennsylvania, and Ohio, although specific patterns of settlement depended largely on the employment opportunities available for workers with particular skills and experience. For example, knitters settled mainly in the Philadelphia region, silk workers in Paterson, New Jersey; cotton textile workers in Fall River, Massachusetts; and steel workers in Pittsburgh.

■ PRIMARY SOURCE

Joseph Hollingworth to William and Nancy Rawcliff
South Leicester. Tuesday Morning May 20th, 1828

Dear Uncle and Dear Aunt,

I'm very glad to say
That your kind letter I received
On the fifteenth day of May.

It was Dated March 25th. We was [sic] short of provision on board the ship or at least it was not the right sort. We had plenty of buisquit; enough for 3 voyages. We cold not eat it. I believe I ate as much of it myself as all the rest. I contrived to pound it in a bag (made of sail cloth for the purpose) and made it into Pudings [sic]. That was the only way we could eat it. We bought 20 lb. of flour in addition to what we had when you left. Some of our provision was good, but we had some not fit to eat. We ate the good first and we had finished a great part in the first 4 weeks. Our potatoes would have lasted out pretty well had it not been for a set of dishonest rascals. I mean the paddys. We had nearly 1 third stolen, but it will take to [sic] much of my time and paper to give you every particular relating to this circumstance. Sufice it to say that should you ever come to America or have to buy provision for any body that is coming O Beware of Becket! That Infernal wrech [sic] who when he could subsist no longer by riding his own

country-men in Irland [sic] came over to Liverpool to impose on my Honest Countrymen who are flying from the wrath to come and going to seek an asylum in a country where that Villanous [sic] Becket would be brought to Justice. The most appropriate punishment that could be inflicted on that imposter would be to confine him in the Middle of the Atlantic Ocean in old *Isaac Hicks* [the ship on which the Hollingworths sailed to America] and feed him on his own Biskit [sic] and stinking water but to conclude, O Beware of Becket.

I saw Joseph Hirst when I was at Poughkeepsie. He was a Spiner [sic] at Wadsworth's Factory. He was the only man that I have seen wear Breeches in America. I had no particular conversation with him. He asked me some Questions and I answered them. I have forgot what they were. My Mother told him that his Wife was badly situated that she wanted to come to America and soon. By what he said then and by what another person told me, on whose word I can rely, I got to understand that he has no intention for sending for his wife. May Hollingworth knew her Grandfather when she first saw him here. She did not know me at first but when I began to ask her about the Oldfield she could recolect both you and your Daughter Mary-Ann. She says if Aunt Nancy was here she would say "Thank you mam" and give her a cent for the frock. She goes to school and seldom failes[sic] to bring home a ticket for reward of … I don't know what reason Jack-o-Micks has to give such a bad account of America. I dare say he'll not find a Factory in England where the workmen will subscribe him Mony [sic] to send him back to America. I would scorn say anything about such a Black-Gard as Haddock for I don't calculate of fighting him with my hands but should not mind doing it with my tong provided he would not tell so many Infernal lies. William Perken knows very little about America or the American Manufactory. He only came from New York to this place and I believe took the same rout [sic] back-again. 'Tis true that they work on sundays here. Bro' Jbz. has to work every 2 or 3 sundays in the factory repairing machiniry [sic] and doing such work as can not be conveniently done on other days. Bro. James is a spiner and he was ordered by the Bos spiner one sunday afternoon in the Church while attending Devine Service to go spin that evening soon as the church service ended, but he neither woad [sic] nor did obey. I had to go to enter the second sunday after I began work and was ordered to go again but I did not obey and I have not been on a sunday since. The Factory system is the caus [sic] of this.

I hate to see a factory stand
In any part of the k[n]own land
To me it talks of wickedness

Of Families that's in destress
Of Tyrany and much extortion
And of slavery a portion
I wish that I no more might see
Another woollen Factory.

John says he will write you in a few weeks. Jbz. says he would write again but that he has told you all he knows, he has nothing to wright [*sic*], you must excuse him. My Mother was a little sea sick on our voyage but it cured her leg. Sister H[annah] was never sick at all but she could not walk when we landed. Mother likes country "vary weel" but she got disapointed [*sic*] she has got more work than ever [in] this a land of labour. Sister H. knew her Father as soon as she saw him. He took her into his arms and she would not leave him for several hours. On the 2nd of March Miss Hollingworth was brought to bed of an Anglo-yankee. The Black Cloth which you sent Capt Barnet came here in Febry. It was 12 yds long. You must write when you get this and tell me how you get along with regard to your soar [*sic*] hole and other matters relating to that concern and you oblige your Inteligent[*sic*]

Joseph Hollingworth. . . .

P.S. When you this letter have reciev'd
Its contents read an all believ'd
Then put it in your Chest
Don't let each Busibody view
What I have writ tho' all is true
They would begin to Jest.

—J.H. . . .

SIGNIFICANCE

Early nineteenth-century migration from England to America played an important role in the industrialization of the United States, providing not only a cheap labor force, but one that brought many workers with valuable skills. At the same time, it provided a safety valve for Great Britain during its Industrial Revolution, when many agricultural and traditional craft workers were being displaced and faced declining opportunities to make a living in Britain.

Although England never experienced the mass emigration that Ireland did in the mid-1800s, large numbers of British immigrants did come to America throughout the nineteenth and into the early decades of the twentieth century. By bringing industrial and manufacturing expertise from Britain, they had a significant and lasting impact on American society and culture.

FURTHER RESOURCES
Books

Erickson, Charlotte. *Leaving England: Essays on British Emigration in the Nineteenth Century.* Ithaca, NY: Cornell University Press, 1994.

Ferrie, Joseph P. *Yankeys Now: Immigrants in the Antebellum United States, 1840–1860.* New York: Oxford University Press, 1999.

Leavitt, Thomas W. *Hollingworth Letters: Technical Change in the Textile Industry 1826–1937.* Cambridge, MA: MIT Press/ Society for the History of Technology, 1969.

Freedom from Indenture or Prison in Australia

Certificate

By: Anonymous

Date: June 5, 1838

Source: "Freedom from Indenture or Prison in Australia," June 5, 1838. Photo by Hulton Archive/ Getty Images.

About the Author: The Hulton Archives are a collection of significant historical documents maintained by Getty Images, a worldwide provider of visual content materials to such communications groups as advertisers, broadcasters, designers, magazines, new media organizations, newspapers and producers. The document is in the standard form employed by New South Wales correctional authorities in 1838.

INTRODUCTION

The history of the transportation of convicted criminals by Britain to its Australian colonies commencing in 1788 is an integral part of the history of Australia. When Captain James Cook first explored the Australian coast in 1770, he reported to his English political masters of the agricultural potential of the region. The first significant economic benefit that England directed to Australia was the establishment of a penal colony in the district that Cook had named New South Wales. The modern Australian city of Sydney is today the capital of the state of New South Wales.

The decision by Britain to export a significant percentage of its criminal population was motivated by a number of factors. The first was that of rampant overcrowding in English and Irish prisons; for offences that did not call for an automatic imposition of the death penalty, transportation to far-off

Australia (a term synonymous with deportation) was an attractive and economical alternative. The second benefit gained by British authorities was the usually permanent removal of an undesirable lower-class strata of its citizens.

The third benefit gained by the imposition of a transportation sentence to Australia was the provision of free labor in the new Australian colonies. The typical sentences imposed in English and Irish courts as the alternative to imprisonment was a period of seven to fourteen years in the colony, where the convicted person would be required to work for no income to the satisfaction of the colonial authorities.

The rigors of the transportation sentence began with the sea voyage to Australia. The passage from England would typically take between six and eight months, including necessary stoppages for repairs and reprovisioning. It was not uncommon for the convicted passengers to succumb to scurvy, a disease caused by a vitamin-C deficiency, or dysentery, an often fatal intestinal infection.

The type of service that a convict would be required to perform in Australia depended upon the severity of the crime committed and the skills possessed by the convict. The two general categories of penal service were government labor and the labor provided to a private landowner. Much of the government service was carried out under armed guard in a fashion similar to the chain gangs common in parts of North America during the twentieth century. The work directed by private landowners was primarily that of agricultural labor.

The successful conclusion of the sentence was marked by the issuance of a *Certificate of Freedom*, documentary confirmation that the sentence had been served. Where a sentence was partially served to the satisfaction of the authorities, a probationary document, better known in the Australian colonies as the "ticket-of-leave," might be issued, permitting the holder some liberties as to where they could be employed. Once a Certificate of Freedom was issued, the convicted criminal generally had no restrictions upon their liberty, except that in most cases the holder was prohibited from returning to England.

The Australian population became an intermingling of British convicts and immigrant settlers when the first free settlement began in the colonies in 1793. By 1850, British authorities had transported over 150,000 convicts to New South Wales. Virtually all of the transported persons were from the British Isles, with six males transported for every female. Given the relative populations of England and Ireland during the period of transportation, a disproportionate number of Irish persons were sent to New South Wales.

PRIMARY SOURCE

FREEDOM FROM INDENTURE OR PRISON IN AUSTRALIA
See primary source image.

SIGNIFICANCE

The penal colonies of Australia played a pivotal role in the establishment of the modern Australian population, as an overwhelming majority of the ticket-of-leave and Certificate of Freedom convicts remained in Australia at the conclusion of their sentences to settle, farm, and to raise families.

The modern traits of the Australian national character are ones that can be traced to the establishment of the Australian penal colonies. It is not surprising that the remnants of a decided anti-British feeling in the country would persist to this day, given that the forced transportation of over 150,000 people to Australia was carried out by Britain against its own citizens. It is significant that this sentiment has persisted notwithstanding Australia's formal political connection to Britain through its Commonwealth membership.

An early example of this attitude is found in the installation in the Australian public consciousness of the outlaw Ned Kelly as an Australian national folk hero. The story of Kelly, the son of an Irish ticket-of-leave man and the killer of a number of police officers in a spree of lawlessness near Melbourne until his shooting by the authorities in 1880, springs directly from the convict heritage of Australia.

The 1838 Certificate of Freedom depicted here was the culmination of what by modern standards would constitute a harsh criminal penalty—transportation to a far-off, primitive, and often inhospitable place, where labor was demanded over a seven-year period with no remuneration. For most convicts, the prospect of life anew in Australia was a reasonable alternative to the life of the under classes they had left behind in London, Manchester, or Dublin. While alleviating a problem of prison overcrowding in Britain, the authorities inadvertently stimulated the growth of an Australian population that would become largely homogeneous and capable of developing a definable national spirit and outlook in a relatively short period of time. The last British convicts were transported to the western coast of Australia in 1868, and Australia was declared an independent nation in 1901.

PRIMARY SOURCE

Freedom from Indenture or Prison in Australia: This certificate of freedom (commonly referred to as a ticket-of-leave) demonstrates that an Irish convict, Francis Neill, has completed his seven years of obligatory labor in the penal colony of New South Wales, Australia, and is now restored to conditional freedom, June 5, 1838. PHOTO BY HULTON ARCHIVE/GETTY IMAGES.

The notion of freedom as guaranteed by the Certificate was a most valuable commodity given the legal basis upon which the lesser ticket-of-leave could be revoked by the penal authorities. Australian records confirm that tickets-of-leave were frequently "deprived," as the Australian authorities described their surrender by the holder, returning the convict to his initial convict status in the colony. The seemingly trivial breaches of the peace that included insubordination, a suspicion of having stolen money, and for

This 1880 illustration shows bushranger Ned Kelly, the notorious Australian outlaw, in the gun battle with police that resulted in his capture and execution. Kelly is wearing his famous armor and helmet. PHOTO BY HULTON ARCHIVE/GETTY IMAGES.

being present in a public house (tavern) after hours were all legal bases for the loss of a ticket-of-leave. The ticket-of-leave was intended by the colonial authorities as a rehabilitative tool.

A further unintended significance of the Certificate of Freedom was that unlike other cultures, where a criminal record would be a lifelong stigma, given the nature of the developing Australian society and the large numbers of persons in similar circumstances, the stigma of a criminal sentence was not the same impediment to future progress.

Certificates of Freedom would issue to those convicts who had served the standard sentences of seven, ten, or fourteen years; convicts serving a life sentence could be granted a pardon, but not a Certificate of Freedom.

The importance of the issuances of Certificates of Freedom to Australian convicts is evidenced today in the comprehensive records maintained by the State Records of New South Wales. The index of the Certificate of Freedoms extends from 1823, when New South Wales was converted from a penal colony to a formal colony of the British Empire, to 1869, when the last Certificate was issued. Over 40,000 Certificates are on record in New South Wales alone.

FURTHER RESOURCES

Books

Maxwell-Stewart, Hamish and Cassandra Pybus. *American Citizens, British Slaves: Yankee Political Prisoners in an Australian Penal Colony 1839–1850.* Melbourne, Australia: Melbourne University Press, 2002.

Neal, David. *The Rule of Law in a Penal Colony: Law and Politics in Early New South Wales.* Cambridge, U.K.: Cambridge University Press, 1992.

Web sites

National Archives of Ireland. "Transportation of Irish Convicts to Australia (1791–1853)." <http://www.nationalarchives.ie/topics/transportation/transp1.htm> (accessed June 19, 2006).

State Records Office of Western Australia. "Convict Records." <http://www.sro.wa.gov.au/collection/convict.asp> (accessed June 19, 2006).

2 Immigration from 1845-1870

Immigration from 1845–1870

In 1845, the potato crop failed in Ireland. An estimated 500,000–1,000,000 Irish died of starvation. Millions emigrated from Ireland, fleeing not only famine but also oppressive tenancy and inheritance laws. The crisis in Ireland sparked a great wave of immigration to the United States. Many of those who fled the Great Famine immigrated to the United States, England, Canada, and Australia. The mass of Irish migration left an indelible mark on Irish culture in Ireland and abroad.

The story of these Irish immigrants is captured in this chapter through letter, song, and poem. The lyrics of "Poor Pat Must Emigrate" recount the tale of troubles in Ireland that forced many sons to search for work abroad. "No Irish Need Apply" laments discrimination faced by Irish immigrants, though historians debate whether employment ads including the phrase "No Irish Need Apply" were a common occurrence or a cultural myth. "Mise Eire," a recent work describing the difficulty of women making the passage across the Atlantic, demonstrates how the memory of Great Famine-era emigration continues to shape Irish culture.

The mass immigration of Irish also sparked an anti-immigrant backlash. In the United States, anti-Irish violence erupted in New York and Boston. The Know-Nothings, a political party advocating anti-immigrant and anti-Catholic policy directed against the Irish, reached their brief zenith. Some Irish-Americans responded in-kind, becoming one of the most organized political forces in New York and Boston during the nineteenth century.

The Irish were not the only immigrants to arrive in the United States from 1845 to 1870. Many German political dissidents sought refuge in the United States after a series of failed democratic revolutions in 1848. The passage of the Homestead Act encouraged immigration and naturalization by promising a free 160 acres of land on the frontier. As depicted in "Departure of a Colony of Emigrants at Train Station," German and Scandinavian immigrants played a key role in settling the American west through the establishment of farming colonies and towns.

Finally, this chapter also highlights non-European emigration. The "California 'Anti-Coolie' Act of 1862" discusses the strong anti-immigrant sentiment surrounding the arrival of the first wave of Chinese immigrants to the west coast. At the height of the slavery debate, some abolitionists advocated African American emigration from the United States to Liberia, an African nation established as a haven for former slaves. "Liberia" and "The Home of the Colored Race" discuss the promotion of Black emigration and the motivations of its champions.

"Poor Pat Must Emigrate"

Song lyrics

By: Anonymous

Date: 1847

Source: *The Historical Society of Pennsylvania* "Irish Immigrant Ballads." <http://www.hsp.org/default.aspx?id=580> (accessed June 29, 2006).

About the Author: The Historical Society of Pennsylvania was founded in 1924 and is one of the United States' oldest historical societies. It has a vast collection of printed, manuscript, and graphic items relating to Pennsylvania and the surrounding region, and is a center for the study of immigrants and ethnic groups in the United States. The song's composer is not known.

INTRODUCTION

The words of this ballad, written by a mid-nineteenth century Irish immigrant to the United States, express the sentiments of those who were forced by poverty and famine to leave Ireland at this time. The words highlight the political factors that were thought to have exacerbated Ireland's problems.

During the late eighteenth and early nineteenth centuries, the population of Ireland had been expanding very rapidly but the country was still predominantly rural, lacking the large-scale industrial development that had supported population growth in England. The potato was the staple food crop for the Irish people, many of whom were poor farmers forced to pay high rents for their farms and properties to rich landowners. When they could not pay, they were often evicted from their homes and their possessions taken by the landlord.

Disaster struck when the whole potato crop was blighted by disease in 1845, and a potato famine spread throughout the country during the following year. To make matters worse, the harvest failed again in 1848. Tens of thousands of people died from starvation, or from the many diseases which spread among a population weakened by hunger, including a cholera epidemic in 1948. Skibbereen, mentioned in this ballad, was one of the areas worst hit, where there were so many victims that they were thrown into mass graves without proper burial.

Although the potato famine was a natural disaster, many Irish, especially the Catholics, blamed the British government for their plight. Ireland had effectively been a colony of Great Britain since it was invaded by the Normans in 1169, and it was formally made part of Great Britain under the Act of Union in 1801. This act was passed by Britain in response to the threat of Irish Republican movements inspired by the French Revolution, in particular the United Irishmen, who staged the Irish Rebellion of 1798, an uprising against the British Army which claimed around thirty thousand lives before it was suppressed by the British. The movement had attracted members of the Presbyterian community and the Catholic majority, both of which had been discriminated against by the Protestant Irish Parliament, who had banned, for example, their formal involvement in politics and ownership of land. The "Dan" referred to in this ballad was Daniel O'Connell, a leading Irish politician of the time, who led the Catholic community in a powerful political campaign for Catholic emancipation and for Irish independence. The lyrics also make reference to the fact that Irish troops fought alongside the British to put down the Indian Rebellion in 1857.

Many Irish felt that the British government did not do enough to help them during the famine. The ruling Whig Party at that time followed a laissez-faire ideology and believed that government should not interfere in trade and the free market. They thought it should be left to private merchants to import food for the Irish population while the government would establish work schemes to enable people to earn money to buy the food; however, pay rates under the schemes were inadequate to support a family.

Although the Irish had been immigrating to the United States since the early nineteenth century, the numbers peaked during the famine years, as people fled the severe poverty of Ireland. Many women and children as well as men emigrated, traveling in appallingly overcrowded and unsanitary conditions in so-called "coffin ships," in which many died from disease or hunger before reaching their destination. Many had their passage paid by relatives already in America, while others had to pay their own fares or received help from charities. Overall, it has been estimated that 1.5 million people emigrated from Ireland to the United States between 1845 and 1855, the majority settling in the cities of New York, Boston, Chicago,

An 1848 political cartoon portrays Daniel O'Connell, an Irish leader, admonishing Irish emigrants that went to the United States. Conditions in Ireland are portrayed as oppresive and cruel, whereas life in America looks idyllic. An Irish immigrant to America replies that he is satisfied where he is. © CORBIS.

Philadelphia, and Baltimore. Tens of thousands more immigrated to other countries such as England, Australia, and Canada.

On arrival in America the emigrants found work in the cities, mainly working as unskilled laborers in construction and industry, or as domestic servants. Whole Irish communities developed, establishing their own schools, churches, hospitals, and Irish associations.

The Fenians, referred to at the end of the ballad, were a revolutionary movement created in 1848, the leaders of which went to America to try to encourage Irish emigrants to support a new uprising against the British. The movement attracted many supporters among the Irish community in America, but the movement was unsuccessful in their attempts to overthrow the British government in Ireland.

■ PRIMARY SOURCE

Fare you well poor Erin's Isle, I now must leave you for awhile;
The rents and taxes are so high I can no longer stay.

From Dublin's quay I sailed away and landed here but yesterday; Me shoes,
and breeches and shirts now are all that's in my kit
I have dropped in to tell you now the sights I have seen before I go,
Of the ups and downs in Ireland since the year of ninety-eight;
But if that Nation had its own, her noble sons might stay at home,
But since fortune has it otherwise, poor Pat must emigrate.

The divil a word I would say at all, although our wages are but small,
If they left us in our cabins, where our fathers drew their breath,
When they call upon rent-day, and the divil a cent you have to pay.
They will drive you from your house and home, to beg and starve to death
What kind of treatment, boys, is that, to give an honest Irish Pat?
To drive his family to the road to beg or starve for meat;
But I stood up with heart and hand, and sold my little spot of land;
That is the reason why I left and had to emigrate.

Such sights as that I've often seen, but I saw worse
    in Skibbareen,
In forty-eight (that time is no more when famine it was
    great),
I saw fathers, boys, and girls with rosy cheeks and
    silken curls
All a-missing and starving for a mouthful of food to eat.
When they died in Skibbareen, no shroud or coffins
    were to be seen;
But patiently reconciling themselves to their horrid fate,
They were thrown in graves by wholesale which cause
    many an Irish heart to wail
And caused many a boy and girl to be most glad to
    emigrate.

Where is the nation or the land that reared such men as
    Paddy's land?
Where is the man more noble than he they call poor
    Irish Pat?
We have fought for England's Queen and beat her
    foes wherever seen;
We have taken the town of Delhi—if you please come
    tell me that,
We have pursued the Indian chief, and Nenah Sahib,
    that cursed thief,
Who skivered babes and mothers, and left them in their
    gore.
But why should we be so oppressed in the land of St.
    Patrick blessed.
The land from which we have the best, poor Paddy
    must emigrate.

There is not a son from Paddy's land but respects the
    memory of Dan,
Who fought and struggled hard to part the poor and
    plundered country
He advocated Ireland's rights, with all his strength and
    might,
And was but poorly recompensed for all his toil and pains.
He told us to be in no haste, and in him for to place our
    trust,
And he would not desert us, or leave us to our fate,
But death to him no favor showed, from the beggar
    to the throne;
Since they took our liberator poor Pat must
    emigrate.

With spirits bright and purses light, my boys we can no
    longer stay,
For the shamrock is immediately bound for America,
For there is bread and work, which I cannot get in
    Donegal,
I told the truth, by great St. Ruth, believe me what I say,
Good-night my boys, with hand and heart, all you who
    take Ireland's part,
I can no longer stay at home, for fear of being too late,
If ever again I see this land, I hope it will be with a Fenian
    band;
So God be with old Ireland, poor Pat must emigrate.

SIGNIFICANCE

The mass emigration from Ireland in the mid-nineteenth century left the country in a severe state of population decline, which it would not recover from until well into the twentieth century, and which affected its economic progress for many decades. However, the longer-term impact of the famine and mass emigration did bring about land reform in Ireland, as the remaining farmers were gradually able to add to and consolidate their holdings, while the landlords lost much of their power.

The mass migration from Ireland also had a lasting influence on the ethnic and national compositions of the major American cities where many of the emigrants settled, with the Irish accounting for up to twenty percent of the population of some American cities by the mid–1850s. In 1850 alone, an estimated 370,000 immigrants entered the United States from Ireland and other European countries, the highest rate of immigration in America's history. The surge in numbers gave rise to concern about the impact of immigration on the native-born population, and eventually resulted in the passing of laws in the late nineteenth century and early twentieth century that banned certain categories of immigrants. Until the passing of the Immigration Act of 1924, however, these were very limited and high levels of immigration continued to boost America's population.

FURTHER RESOURCES
Books

Dudley-Edwards, R. and Desmond T. Williams. *The Great Famine: Studies in Irish History, 1845–52.* New York: New York University Press, 1957.

Ferrie, Joseph P. *Yankeys Now: Immigrants in the Antebellum United States, 1840–1860.* New York: Oxford University Press, 1999.

Gallman, Matthew J. *Receiving Erin's Children: Philadelphia, Liverpool, and the Irish Famine Migration, 1845–1855.* Chapel Hill, N.C.: University of North Carolina Press, 2000.

Mulrooney, Margaret M. *Fleeing the Famine: North America and Irish Refugees, 1845–1851.* Westport, Conn.: Praeger, 2003.

Nowlan, Kevin B., and Maurice R. O'Connell. *Daniel O'Connell, Portrait of a Radical.* New York: Fordham University Press, 1985.

Potter, George W. *To the Golden Door: The Story of the Irish in Ireland and America.* Boston: Little Brown, 1960.

Web sites

Irish History Online. <http://www.irishhistoryonline.ie> (accessed June 29, 2006).

"Mise Eire"

Poem

By: Eavan Boland

Date: 1987

Source: "Mise Eire." In *The Journey*, Eavan Boland. Manchester, U.K.: Carcanet Press, 1987.

About the Author: Eavan Boland, award-winning Irish poet and writer, was born in Dublin, Ireland. Educated in New York, London, and Dublin, she has taught at Trinity College, University College Dublin, and Bowdoin College.

INTRODUCTION

By the 1950s, a century after Ireland's great potato famine (1845–1849), fifty-seven percent of Irish emigrants were women. Some women and girls, disconnected from families that could not feed them, were driven to survival measures such as prostitution or working long hours in poor conditions for little pay. Poverty and famine, although undeniably the major forces in the relocation of millions from the twenty-six counties of Ireland, was not the only important stimuli that encouraged women to leave their island country.

During this great emigration, Ireland was under both external and internal rule. On the one hand, the country was conducted by the colonial rule of England, and on the other, Ireland was ruled socially through its national religion, Catholicism. This combination of authority led many women to feel a distinct paralysis under an increasingly patriarchal society. Amidst the male-dominated social revolutions and caste system of the nation's religion, women and issues facing women were often dismissed, even in terms of their established traditional roles as mother and wife, let alone progressive movements.

British and Irish landlords and poor land conditions due to the famine left remaining harvestable land an especially valuable commodity. Families often strived to keep land through inheritance or the opportune marriage of a daughter, thus resulting in many arranged marriages for the sake of land consolidation. After the prim Victorian era, countries progressing through sexual revolutions such as the United States and England were enticing prospects for women who desired simple freedoms such as marrying for love and finding work in thriving cities.

Eavan Boland, Irish poet and feminist, wrote her poem "Mise Eire", meaning "I am Ireland" to illuminate the female Irish emigrants on their journey from their homeland in hopes of finding opportunity abroad. No longer oppressed, the Irish woman narrator finds her voice in a new found freedom.

PRIMARY SOURCE

I won't go back to it—
my nation displaced
into old dactyls,
oaths made
by the animal tallows
of the candle—
land of the Gulf Stream,
the small farm,
the scalded memory,
the songs
that bandage up the history,
the words
that make a rhythm of the crime
where time is time past.
A palsy of regrets.
No. I won't go back.
My roots are brutal:
I am the woman—
a sloven's mix
of silk at the wrists,
a sort of dove-strut
in the precincts of the garrison—
who practices
the quick frictions,
the rictus of delight
and gets cambric for it,
rice-colored silks.
I am the woman
in the gansy-coat
on board the *Mary Belle*,
in the huddling cold,
holding her half-dead baby to her
as the wind shifts east
and north over the dirty
water of the wharf
mingling the immigrant
guttural with the vowels
of homesickness who neither
knows nor cares that
a new language
is a kind of scar
and heals after a while
into a passable imitation
of what went before.

SIGNIFICANCE

Boland's opening line of her poem "I won't go back to it—" is one of defiance and self-exile. The lines that follow characterize the women of Ireland, who feel they have no other choice but to leave its shores to find greater opportunity, escaping their rigid traditional roles. Between 1840 and 1895, almost one million Irish women immigrated to the United States.

Boland's poem refers to the "scar" of a new language to be learned for the immigrant, however, the English language was also forced upon Irish society by their English rulers during this time. Although English was used in schools and in governing Ireland, the Irish Gaelic language was very much alive among the Irish community and was responsible for the rhythm and rhyme of their traditional poetry. In modern times, the 2003 Official Languages Act was passed in Ireland, mandating that all official communications be published in both official languages of Ireland, English and Irish Gaelic.

Boland's "Mise Eire" is the second poem to be written under its title. Padraig Pearse (1879–1916), nationalist, writer, poet, and political activist known for his participation as a leader of the 1916 Easter Rising, wrote the original poem entitled "Mise Eire" in 1912, which would later inspire Boland to write her version. Originally written in Irish Gaelic, Pearse's poem refers to Irish mythology, the Old Woman of Beare, fabled to be the oldest woman ever to live. From a poem dating to the ninth or tenth century bearing the title of her name, Beare is painted with a life as strong an unyielding as the ocean. Famous for her seven periods of youth, always outliving her male counterpart, it can be recognized that she is a symbol of the strong Irish everywoman. Boland seems to take inspiration from this aspect of Pearse's original "Mise Eire," humanizing her with characteristics relevant to women during the time of the potato famine, the time of revolution, and nationalism—the time of mass Irish emigration.

FURTHER RESOURCES

Web sites

Irish Culture and Customs. "Padraic Pearse." <http://www.irishcultureandcustoms.com/Poetry/PadraicPearse.html> (accessed July 15, 2006).

Library of Congress. "American Memory; Immigration...Irish." <http://memory.loc.gov/learn/features/immig/irish.html> (accessed June 10, 2006).

Norton Poets Online. "Eavan Boland." <http://www.wwnorton.com/trade/external/nortonpoets/bolande.htm> (accessed July 15, 2006).

The Longford Letter

Book excerpt

By: Alexander Somerville

Date: March 5, 1847

Source: Somerville, A. *Letters from Ireland during the Famine of 1847.* Edited by K. D. M. Snell. Dublin: Irish Academic Press, 1995.

About the Author: Alexander Somerville (1811–1885), was a British journalist who traveled throughout Ireland in the 1840s writing newspaper reports on the famine there for the *Manchester Examiner.*

INTRODUCTION

This article by English journalist Alexander Somerville attacks the Irish gentry—and especially those landlord members of the Repeal Association—for their part in the Irish famine of the 1840s. At this time, Ireland was a predominantly rural country with a rapidly growing population. Most people were poor tenant farmers or agricultural workers who rented their land and homes from rich landlords. For the majority of the population, the potato was the main source of food. In 1845, the potato crop failed for the first time, followed by even worse failures in the succeeding four years. The result was a widespread famine that killed over a million people through starvation and disease, and forced around one and a half million to leave Ireland for England or America.

Although the famine was sparked by potato crop failures, many other factors contributed to the scale of the disaster. Because Ireland was part of Great Britain, the British government was blamed for not sending more food and help to Ireland. The Liberal government that came to power in 1846 believed that free trade and the market would resolve the problems and restricted its assistance to loans and establishing work programs.

In response to the crop failure many landlords sold their grain to merchants in England to offset their own losses, instead of retaining it for consumption within Ireland. Livestock that could have been used to feed the Irish population were also exported. At the same time, cheap cornmeal was imported to feed the peasant families, but this provided very little nutrition and did not help to solve the problems of starvation and the many diseases which rapidly spread among a malnourished population.

An illustration from an 1847 edition of the *Illustrated London News* depicts the funeral procession of a victim of Ireland's Great Famine, in Skibbereen, Cork County. © HULTON GETTY/LIAISON AGENCY. REPRODUCED BY PERMISSION.

Somerville's commentary about the "natural order" of things is rich in sarcasm as he reflects on the causes of the famine. First, he makes reference to the theory of Thomas Malthus, who believed that population size would always be kept in check, since any rapid population increase would ultimately outrun the available food supply, and famine would be the result. Somerville adds to this, however, the view that agriculture will always be insufficient to feed the population when the crops are appropriated for profit by an exploitative landlord class, reducing any incentive for the agricultural workers to work harder and produce more. He also argues that famine is inevitable in a purely agricultural economy, since there are no non-rural communities to buy the produce, and, because people tend to have big families to help work the land, when crops fail there is not enough to feed everyone.

In 1840, a Repeal Association had been formed by Daniel O'Connell, a leading Irish politician who believed that independence from Britain was necessary for Ireland to solve its problems. O'Connell's Repeal Association, which campaigned for repeal of the 1801 Act of Union, gained support mainly from the poor Catholic peasant population, as well as some radicals and intellectuals. In 1843, a landowner and politician called William Smith O'Brien joined the Repeal Association, but broke away three years later to form the Young Ireland movement, a more radical group who stressed the cultural differences between Ireland and England, and advocated violence against the British government. This movement gained political influence in Ireland in 1847 and 1848, hindering relations between Ireland and England and reducing the level of assistance and charity provided to the Irish population.

PRIMARY SOURCE

Mr John O'Connell, M.P. for Kilkenny, has written a letter from London to the Repeal Association, which is reprinted in most of the Irish newspapers. It may possibly attract no attention in England, nor may this notice of it attract attention in Ireland; but the subject is profoundly important; and, as the member for Kilkenny has the temerity to provoke a discussion on such a subject—that of the generosity of the English public to the Irish people in this present season of distress—I shall not shrink from telling him, respectfully yet firmly, that his letter to the Repeal Association now circulated throughout Ireland is a most unfounded and unworthy libel upon the English people. And more, that of all the gentry in Ireland, the repeal members of parliament, so far as I have yet seen their estates and the starving people on their estates, (and I have already visited a considerable number of them,) are the gentry least entitled to accuse the English public of apathy or hardheartedness....

I can prove to Mr John O'Connell, and to all whom it may concern, by reference to Irish estates one by one, to farms upon those estates one by one, and by reference to the charity given or *wages paid for actual labour now performed,* giving the names of the proprietors and middlemen one by one, whose reputation is involved in the question, that, whatever the state of liberality may be now arrived at by the government, public opinion and public generosity in England are far in advance of public opinion and public generosity in Ireland.

Some Irish gentlemen may be too poor to have much to give away in the present emergency; but the poorest of them might give something. The greatness of the necessity seems to be, for them, an excuse for doing nothing at all—literally nothing at all. Moreover, they might pay wages sufficient to keep their work-people out of the public soup-kitchens, and in a condition able to work. I shall here relate a case I witnessed the other day; I might relate twenty such seen within a week.

Seven men were in a field which measured three acres, and which had just been sown with oats. They were employed in breaking the clods of earth, in clearing the furrows for letting off top water, and in otherwise finishing the sowing of the oats. It was about four in the afternoon when I saw them. They appeared to me to work very indifferently; the whole seven were doing less than one man's work. I watched them for some time, while they did not see me, consequently they could not be enacting a part before a stranger. I was soon convinced that the men were, some of them, leaning on their implements of work, and others staggering among the clods, from sheer weakness and hunger. I concluded this to be the case from the frequency of such signs. One of the men, after I had watched them some time, crawled through a gap in the hedge, came out upon the road on his hand and knees, and then tried to rise, and got up bit by bit as a feeble old man might be supposed to do. He succeeded in getting upon his feet at last, and moved slowly away, with tottering steps, towards the village, in a miserable hovel of which was his home.

I thought I would speak to the feeble old man, and followed and came up with him. He was not an old man. He was under forty years of age; was tall and sinewy, and had all the appearances of what would have been a strong man if there had been flesh on his body. But he bowed down, his cheeks were sunken, and his skin sallow-coloured, as if death were already within him. His eyes glared upon me fearfully; and his skinny skeleton hands clutched the handle of the shovel upon which he supported himself while he stood to speak to me, as it were the last grasp of life.

"It is the hunger, your honour; nothing but the hunger," he said in a feeble voice: "I stayed at the work till I could stay no longer. I am fainting now with the hunger. I must go home to lie down. There is six children and my wife and myself. We had nothing all yesterday, (which was Sunday,) and this morning we had only a handful of yellow meal among us all, made into stirabout, before I came out to work—nothing more and nothing since. Sure this hunger will be the death of all of us. God have mercy upon me and my poor family."

I saw the poor man at home and his poor family, and truly might he say, "God have mercy!" They were skeletons all of them, with skin on the bones and life within the skin. A mother skeleton and baby skeleton; a tall boy skeleton who had no work to do; who could now do nothing but eat, and had nothing to eat. Four female children skeletons, and the tall father skeleton, not able to work to get food for them, and not able to get enough of food when he did work for them. Their only food was what his wages of 10d. [10 pence] per day would procure of "yellow meal"—the meal of the Indian corn. The price of that was 3s. [3 shilings] per stone of 16lb. This gave for the eight persons 26lb. 10oz. of meal for seven days; being about seven ounces and a half per day for each person. No self-control could make such persons distribute such a starvation measure of food over seven days equally. Their natural cravings made them eat it up at once, or in one, or three days at most, leaving the other days blank, making the pangs of hunger worse still.

But in this calculation I am supposing all the wages to go for meal. I believe none of it was expended on anything else, not even salt, save fuel: fuel in this village must all be purchased by such people; they are not allowed to go to the bogs to cut it for themselves. Nor is this the season to go to the bogs, if they were allowed. The fuel required to keep the household fire merely burning, hardly sufficient to give warmth to eight persons sitting around it, to say nothing of half-naked persons, would cost at least sixpence per day. Wherefore, no fuel was used by this family, nor by other working families, but what was required to boil the meal into stirabout.

Now this was one of the best paid men on the estate; all have not such large families as him, but all have as low wages; all have to pay the same price for food and fuel; all have to pay house rent. . . .

It is said to be "in the natural order of things for a population to *suffer from* a diminution of food, and to sink in wretchedness and suffering in proportion to the increase in their numbers and the decrease in the supply of their food; ultimately, if the diminution of food becomes excessive and of long duration, to die and diminish with it." It is in the natural order of things for human beings to die if they do not obtain sustenance for their bodies, just as it is in the natural order of things for agriculture to languish and fail to produce food for a great population when idle, dissolute, and improvident proprietary classes exact, and compulsorily extract, from the cultivators all their capital, the improving cultivator only being a mark for the landlord's cupidity. It is in the natural order of things for the tenant farmers of Ireland to be oppressed and degraded and made bad farmers when their political uses are deemed of higher importance by the landlords than their agricultural uses. It is in the natural order of things for the oppressed tenantry to listen to those who are continually telling them of their oppression, and promising them a blissful change by some one mighty action which cannot be performed, and which would be as worthless if performed as another moon would be in the sky to give them moonshine of their own. It is in the natural order of things, at least Irish things, for the people to be deluded.

It would be in the natural order of things for an Irish parliament of Irish landlords to legislate for themselves and against their tenantry and the great body of the people. Cruel as the political Protestant landlords have been in persecuting the Catholic tenantry for their religion and their adherence to repeal politics, they are exceeded in cruelty by landlords of the repeal party—the very vultures of a heartless, ignorant, haughty, and selfish class of men.

It is in the natural order of things for agriculture to be profitless without a manufacturing and trading population to purchase and consume the agricultural produce. It is in the natural order of things for an exclusively agricultural population to be always liable to famine; for it is in the natural order of things for such a population to overstock the land with itself, having no other outlet for the younger branches of families, until they become so numerous and so poor that they cannot afford to cultivate the land: they eat up their seed, their stock, their implements, and consume their own strength. . . .

SIGNIFICANCE

Alexander Somerville's graphic accounts of the suffering of the Irish during the famine, published in the British press, would probably have helped to raise public awareness of the appalling conditions in Ireland and may have increased the level of private charity, as well as government assistance that was extended to the Irish population. His interpretation of the problem, with its emphasis on the culpability of the Irish gentry rather than the British government would have been influenced no doubt by his own English nationality and perhaps his political beliefs; others have argued that the British government was largely responsible for the severity of the disaster by failing to provide adequate assistance. The government had even commissioned a study of Ireland in 1843 that highlighted the vulnerability of Ireland's agricultural economy, yet no steps were taken to address the problem.

As a result of the famine, the population of Ireland was reduced by more than two million between 1845 and 1851, as a result of death and emigration. The effects of this hampered economic progress in Ireland for many decades. The mass exodus from Ireland created substantial Irish communities overseas, especially in the United States, and these later contributed support and assistance to the Irish movement for Home Rule.

FURTHER RESOURCES
Books
Somerville, A. *Letters from Ireland during the Famine of 1847.* Edited by K. D. M. Snell. Dublin: Irish Academic Press, 1995.

Cronin, Mike. *A History of Ireland.* New York: Palgrave, 2001.

Periodicals
Harrison Jennifer. "William Smith O'Brien and the Young Ireland Rebellion of 1848." *Australian Journal of Politics and History.* 50 (March 2004).

Web sites
Irish History Online. "Welcome to Irish History Online." <http://www.irishhistoryonline.ie/> (accessed June 23, 2006).

North Bank of Waitera

Illustration

By: Anonymous

Date: c. 1850

Source: © Corbis.

About the Artist: This image originally appeared in *The Illustrated Daily News,* a publication that has provided a pictorial record and commentary on domestic and international events since its first printing in 1842. The image is part of the collection of the Corbis Corporation.

INTRODUCTION

Captain James Cook was the first European to arrive in New Zealand. Staying for six months in New Zealand in 1769, Cook often interacted with the indigenous peoples, the Maoris, and at the time of his exploration of the territory, there were approximately 100,000 Maoris in New Zealand. Despite Cook's positive experiences with the Maori, the remote land gained the reputation of being inhabited by bloodthirsty savages and surrounded by treacherous coasts.

As a result, immigration to New Zealand was slow. The first immigrants came from across the Tasman Sea from Australia, which had been established as a British penal colony in 1788. By 1820, the non-Maori people inhabiting New Zealand consisted of whalers, merchants, and missionaries. Those of European descent were referred to as *Pakeha* by the Maori.

The Pakeha population numbered approximately 2,000 by 1839, most of whom emigrated from Britain. The situation in nineteenth century Britain compelled many people to immigrate to the colonies. The population in Britain rose from sixteen million in 1801 to twenty-six million, and the industrial and agricultural revolution displaced many workers. However, disincentives for immigration to New Zealand discouraged many from moving. The long, expensive journey, the presence of closer, more established colonies, as well as the proximity of New Zealand to the penal colony of

Australia kept immigration into New Zealand slow until 1840.

In 1840, British Captain William Hodson and forty-five Maori chiefs signed the Treaty of Waitangi. This treaty granted British citizenship to those residing on the island and established the principle that the Maori could only sell their land to the government. Also in 1840, the New Zealand Company was established to settle the new colony. The New Zealand Company, created by Edward Gibbon, was based on the philosophy that the problems created by the population explosion in Britain could be fixed by exporting a portion of its population. As a result, Gibbon designed a plan to facilitate large migrations of Britons to New Zealand. The New Zealand Company used advertisements and propaganda in books and pamphlets to create the vision that New Zealand was the "Britain of the South," a fertile land

FEB. 8, 1851.]   THE ILLUSTRATED LONDON NEWS.   109

S K E T C H E S   I N   N E W   Z E A L A N D.

NORTH BANK OF WAITERA RIVER, NEAR NEW PLYMOUTH.

PRIMARY SOURCE

North Bank of Waitera: A sketch from the *Illustrated London News*, 1853, shows a settlement on the North Bank of the Waitera River in New Zealand. Illustrations like these were aimed at attracting emigrants from Europe. © CORBIS.

without the economic hardships occurring in Europe. The company offered free passage to craftsmen, builders, blacksmiths, and gardeners, and promised investors one hundred acres of farmland and one acre of town land. As a result, the Pakeha population rose from 2,000 in 1839 to 28,000 in 1852.

There were three types of settlers immigrating to New Zealand: those families offered free passage from companies like the New Zealand Company, those individuals crossing the Tasman Sea from Australia, and military settlers. In 1854, the New Zealand provincial government was tasked with immigration. As a result, the government began using advertisements and propaganda similar to the New Zealand Company to facilitate immigration. The government once again offered free passage to laborers, brick masons, and single women. In the Auckland region, land grants were offered as incentives for immigration.

PRIMARY SOURCE

NORTH BANK OF WAITERA
See primary source image.

SIGNIFICANCE

The initial introduction of Europeans to the Maori allowed for trade between the two peoples. Europeans educated Maori by teaching them how to read and write, as well as teaching the Maori more efficient agricultural techniques. The introduction of firearms, often given as payment to the Maori, began to facilitate greater tribal conflicts.

The Treaty of Waitangi eventually became the focus of contention, as the Maori began to lose more of their land to the Pakeha. The Maori language version of the treaty expressed that the British were granted *kawanatanga*, or the right to maintain order and make laws. The Maori would, however, retain *rangatiratanga*, or sovereignty. In addition, the Maori law, or *ture*, asserts that the land is owned by the community and that property could not be sold without the consent of the entire tribe. As land ownership was a foreign concept, Maori scholars suggest that the tribesmen that signed treaties to sell land believed that they were agreeing to allow the Pakeha use of the land, thereby explaining why land was often sold to many parties.

In 1860, British troops tried to remove Te Ataiwa tribes people from the land at Waitera, which was purchased from Te Teira, the nephew of the Te Ataiwa chief, Te Rangitake (also referred to as Wiremu Kingi, his Christian name). Although the sale was disputed, the government ordered 350 troops to enforce the removal of the tribe. The Te Ataiwa were reinforced by other Maori tribes and continued to resist until 1872.

In 1973, February 6th was designated Waitangi Day. This led to a series of protests by Maori activists, including a 30,000-person march to Wellington. This protest led to the 1975 Treaty of Waitangi Act and the creation of the Waitangi Tribunal. The tribunal was tasked with reviewing land claims that, as the result of an additional act in 1985, go back as far as 1840. This includes challenges to confiscations, title grants, and interests in rivers, lakes, and mined resources.

TAMATI.   TAMATI'S WIFE.   TAHANA HONI.

Portraits of three native New Zealanders living near the British settlement at New Plymouth, New Zealand colony. © CORBIS.

FURTHER RESOURCES

Periodicals

Mydans, Seth. "The Maori Rights Furor: A Question of Ancestry." *New York Times*. October 29, 1985.

Slavicek, Louise Chipley. "The Maori and the Pakeha." *Faces*. January 1, 2001.

Web sites

New Zealand Government. "History of Immigration." <http://www.teara.govt.nz/NewZealanders/NewZealandPeoples/HistoryOfImmigration/2/e> (accessed June 15, 2006).

Liberia

Magazine article excerpt

By: Anonymous

Date: July 1851

Source: Anonymous. "Liberia." *Living Age* 30 (July 1851): 261–263.

About the Author: The *Living Age* (also known as *Littell's Living Age*) was a general readership publication that excerpted selections from English and American newspapers and magazines. The *Living Age* was published from 1844 through 1941.

INTRODUCTION

The idea to develop a separate nation on the continent of Africa for slaves from the American South came about in the mid–1810s. Attitudes in the southern United States were firmly pro-slavery, while northerners had yet to develop a strong abolitionist movement. Some former slaves lived as free men and women in the northern United States, and some states prohibited slavery, but employment and housing could be difficult matters for these freed slaves. In 1815 Paul Cuffee (1759–1817), an African American businessman, financed a voyage for African Americans to settle in Sierra Leone. Cuffee believed that prejudice against slaves and former slaves was too great in the United States; for former slaves and free blacks to rise to their highest potential, in Cuffee's opinion, they would have to live in a nation where African American self-determination and self-governance prevailed.

Cuffee's vision included not only the settlement, or "repatriation," of slaves in Africa, but also the exchange of information and skills between former slaves and those on the African continent; former slaves could teach Africans the skills learned while

enslaved, such as horsemanship, iron work, farming techniques, and woodworking. Cuffee died in 1817 without having realized the establishment of his imagined nation. Inspired by Cuffee's idea, a group of white southern men formed the American Colonization Society (ACS) in 1816. Freed African Americans were excluded from membership. The first president of ACS was former U.S. president James Monroe.

Robery Finley, a Presbyterian minister and founder of ACS, worked toward the establishment of an African colony for freed American slaves. By 1820 the colony of Liberia had been founded. ACS helped to create Liberia but did not pay for slaves to be freed for immigration to the new colony; ACS members lobbied Congress and state legislatures, however, to provide funds for existing freed slaves to emigrate.

As divisions between the North and South in the United States intensified throughout the late 1840s and 1850s, and as abolitionism rose as a force in the industrialized North—with growing support from women as well as men—Liberia became a point of interest for southerners wishing to export freed slaves from their states, and for fugitive slaves wishing to find safe harbor away from slave bounty hunters. Some states created their own settlements in Liberia, such as Maryland's Cape Palmas. Slave states used such settlements in combination with legislature-approved transportation funds to export freed blacks.

By 1847 Liberia was home to more than 10,000 freed blacks. The ACS had controlled the colony, but Liberians declared their independence on July 26,1847, with the Liberian Declaration of Independence. Liberians noted abuses by the U.S. government and requested formal recognition from other independent nations. Britain recognized Liberia's independence in 1848, as did France; Liberia's first president, J. J. Roberts, worked to secure international recognition for the emerging country.

PRIMARY SOURCE

The new republic of Liberia is one of the notable features of our singularly progressive age. It is one of the things which the people of the eighteenth could have least expected to be produced by the nineteenth century. Yet it is probably enough that many not unintelligent persons in England never even heard of its name.

Liberia is a free negro Christian state, enjoying republican institutions, on the coast of Africa. Situated between the fourth and eighth degree of north latitude, it occupies about 500 miles of what is called the Guinea coast—a country wonderfully rich in natural productions, but heretofore blighted by the accursed slave-trade. The proper citizens of Liberia are said to be little over 7000; but they have a quarter of a million of the native population under their protection. They are distributed through a chain of well-built towns, surrounded by well-cultivated fields, they have ports and shipping, custom-houses, a president, and a national flag. Churches and schools everywhere give pleasing token of civilization. The people in general seem to be animated by a good spirit. On the whole, Liberia is a thriving settlement, and its destiny appears to be one of no mean character.

The efforts to put down the African slave-trade by a blockade have, it is well known, been signally unsuccessful. Britain's share in it costs about three quarters of a million per annum; and the money is spent not merely in vain, but to the increase of the inhumanities meant to be extinguished. Under the powerful temptations held out by the sugar-trade of Brazil, more slaves are now exported from Africa than ever—the only effect of the blockade being to cause the trade to be conducted under much more cruel circumstances than formerly. While this costly and mischievous mockery has been going on, a humble and almost unnoticed association of emancipated negroes from the United States has been doing *real work*, by quietly planting itself along the African coast, and causing, wherever it set its foot, the slave-trade to disappear. Strange to say, it has done this, not as a primary object, but as one only secondary and incidental to a process of colonization, the prompting causes of which were of a different, and, as some might think, partly inconsistent nature.

The situation of the free negroes in the United States is well known to be an unpleasant one. They have neither the political nor social privileges of other citizens; and though matters were put formally to rights in this respect, it is to all appearance hopeless that the colored should ever be admitted to a true fellowship with the white people. In these circumstances the man of African blood is like a small tree under the shade of a great one. His whole nature is dwarfed; his best aspirations are checked. The results are not over-comfortable for the white man either. Some American citizens, seeing and deploring these evils, were induced, about five-and-thirty years ago, to form themselves into a society, which should promote the return of emancipated negroes to their own quarter of the globe, where it was thought they might be able, to some extent, to introduce the intelligence, religion and usages of civilized communities among their heightened brethren, and form the most effective of battalions for the repression of the slave-trade—their constitutions being able to endure climatic influences under which the whites are sure to sink. The result has been this republic of Liberia. The whole movement has, we believe, from first to last, been regarded with jealousy, if not hostility, by the abolition party, who saw in it only the dislike of white for black, and shut their eyes to the religious and philanthropic

objects, which were in reality alone capable of being promoted to any considerable extent; for of course a serious diminution of the colored population of America by such means is not to be expected. We do not profess to know how far this was a reasonable feeling on the part of the worthy men who are standing up for negro rights in America; but assuredly, whatever were the motives of the Colonization Society, the consequences of their acts are such as to give them no small ground for triumph. For anything that we can see, their settling of Liberia has been the most unexceptional good movement against slavery that has ever taken place. Perhaps it has not been the worse, but rather the better, of that infusion of the wisdom of this world, which has discommended it so much to the abolitionist. . . .

SIGNIFICANCE

Liberia and the export of freed slaves for resettlement created a difficult situation for some abolitionists. Many southern slave owners supported Liberia as an alternative to abolition; if freed blacks could be sent away to Liberia, the owners theorized, then the tension between slave states and non-slave states might lessen, and the need for abolition would decrease as slave owners could point to Liberia as a middle ground in the slavery argument.

Some abolitionists, such as William Lloyd Garrison, disagreed with the American Colonization Society and the concept of Liberia as a colony for freed slaves, while other prominent American figures such as Henry Clay supported ACS and its goals. By the 1840s abolitionists viewed Liberia as a possible threat to full emancipation of slaves.

In 1862 U.S. president Abraham Lincoln (1809–1865) extended official recognition to Liberia; Lincoln supported the repatriation of freed slaves to the African nation. There were more than four million slaves in the southern United States, and Lincoln viewed resettlement in Liberia, or similar colonies, as a potentially positive option for freed slaves. After his assassination in 1865, the idea, not popular with Congress or the new administration, was dropped.

Once the Civil War ended in the United States, the flow of free blacks across the Atlantic from North America to Africa ended. Malaria and yellow fever had plagued the earlier settlers in Liberia, thinning their numbers and forcing some to question whether their new lives in Africa were worse than the lives as slaves they'd left behind in the United States. Liberia remained populated, however, and grew throughout the end of the nineteenth century. After achieving independence,

President Joseph Jenkins Roberts' house in Monrovia, Liberia, in the 1870s, shortly after Liberia became the first African colony to gain its independence. © CORBIS.

Liberia became the only free republic in Africa, providing an example to other African colonies in the twentieth century as other colonies slowly became independent nations.

Liberia's promise in the 1820s represented different goals to different people: for white slavery supporters, Liberia meant gradualism, for abolitionists a threat to emancipation, and for freed blacks a chance at a new life, away from American society and prejudice. By the 1970s Liberia faced internal struggles, and from 1989 through 2004 the nation experienced civil war and extreme violence. In 2005 Liberia once again gained a unique place in history books by electing Ellen Johnson-Sirleaf to the presidency, the first democratically elected woman to lead an African nation.

FURTHER RESOURCES
Books
Jeffrey, Julie Roy. *Great Silent Army of Abolitionism: Ordinary Women in the Antislavery Movement*. Chapel Hill: University of North Carolina Press, 1998.

Levitt, Jeremy. *The Evolution of Deadly Conflict in Liberia: From 'Paternaltarianism' to State Collapse*. Durham, N.C.: Carolina Academic Press, 2005.

Mayer, Henry. *All on Fire: William Lloyd Garrison and the Abolition of Slavery*. New York: St. Martin's Press, 2000.

Tsesis, Alexander. *The Thirteenth Amendment and American Freedom: A Legal History*. New York: New York University Press, 2004.

The Know-Nothing and American Crusader

Pamphlet

By: Anonymous

Date: July 15, 1854

Source: *The Know-Nothing and American Crusader*. The Nativist Press, 1854.

About the Author: *The Know-Nothing and American Crusader* was a pamphlet published by the America Party in the mid–1850s in the eastern United States. The America Party was closely associated with a political movement known as the "Know-Nothings." Both groups advocated the promotion of the interests of native-born Americans over those of foreigners.

INTRODUCTION

Nativism is the term that defined the political philosophy of the Know-Nothings, a political movement that arose in the late 1840s and early 1850s in the United States. Nativism was defined as a general support for all aspects of American culture and society that were the product of native-born Americans as opposed to those attributable to foreign influences. George Washington was the oft-cited hero to many in the nativist movement.

The American Party was the formal political organization that was the product of the Know-Nothing movement. The American Party was formed in the wake of the collapse of the Whigs, the party that arose in opposition to Andrew Jackson and the Democratic Party in 1832. The Whigs took their name from the British party that opposed a strong monarchy; the American Whigs championed the powers of Congress over those of the presidency. The Whig party attracted notables such as Daniel Webster and Abraham Lincoln to their banner. By 1850, the Whigs were divided over the most incendiary issue in American politics of that era, the extension of slavery into the new western states of the Union. The slave question foreshadowed the secession of the southern states and the subsequent Civil War that began in 1861.

The nativist element of the Whig party became the core of the Know-Nothings, an organization that took its name from its semi-secret practices; if a member was approached by anyone and asked about their political affiliation, the member was expected to reply that they "know nothing."

The Know-Nothing and American Crusader was published by the American Party in the period leading up to the 1856 presidential election. The publication was ceaseless in its attacks upon any element perceived as undermining a pure, native-born American social, cultural, or political identity.

The Know-Nothings were a strident and forceful outlet for a mixture of xenophobic and racist sentiments during their period of national political prominence. In addition to promoting nativist American interests, the Know-Nothings demonized the pope as a highly dangerous and un-American force. The Catholic population of the United States, particularly in the northeastern cities of New York and Boston, had risen significantly due to Irish immigration precipitated by a series of famines in Ireland in the mid–1840s.

In the period between 1850 and 1854, the Know-Nothings won control of a number of state legislatures and city councils on the eastern seaboard of the nation. The mayor elected in San Francisco in 1854 was also a Know-Nothing member. Just as it seemed that the Know-Nothings were poised to become a national political force, the movement found itself divided over the slave issue. The 1856 presidential election, where the incumbent Millard Fillmore ran under the American Party banner, was the last significant exposure of the Know-Nothing policies on a national scale, as Fillmore was resoundingly defeated. The anti-slavery elements of the Know-Nothings migrated to the newly constituted Republican Party, leading to the election of Abraham Lincoln in 1860.

Sheet music for an anti-immigrant Nativist song proclaims "Citizen Know-Nothing" as "Uncle Sam's Youngest Son." PHOTO BY MPI/GETTY IMAGES.

■ PRIMARY SOURCE

THE KNOW-NOTHING: AND AMERICAN CRUSADER
15 July 1854

American Platforms

1. —Repeal of all Naturalization Laws.
2. —None but NATIVE AMERICANS for Office.
3. —A pure American Common School System.
4. —War to the hilt, on Romanism.
5. —Opposition, first and last, to the formation of Military Companies composed of foreigners.
6. —The advocacy of a sound, healthy, and safe Nationality.
7. —Hostility to all Papal Influences, in whatever form, and under whatever name.
8. —American Institutions and American Sentiments.
9. —More stringent and effective Emigration Laws.
10. —The amplest Protection to Protestant Interests.
11. —The doctrines of the revered WASHINGTON and his compatriots.
12. —The sending back of all Foreign Paupers landed on our shores.
13. —The formation of Societies to protect all American Interests.
14. —Eternal enmity to all who attempts to carry out the principles of a foreign Church or State.
15. —Our Country, our whole Country, and nothing but our country.
16. —And finally,—American Laws and American Legislation, and Death to all Foreign Influences, whether in high places or low!

Naturalization Laws

This is our point: ENTIRE AND UNCONDITIONAL REPEAL.

Nothing short of this must be advocated or listened to by Native Americans. Half and half doctrines are fatal. Milk-and-water compromises will never do. We must plant ourselves on solid, massive, immovable ground. 'REPEAL' must be written in gigantic letters on all our banners. It is what we owe to our country to do. There is no dodging the issue. *The Naturalization Laws must be repealed.*

Some one—some man who lacks patriotism, nationality, and all that is great and good as an American—asks, perhaps, why? We answer,

1st. Because we cannot preserve our nationality without it. When the hordes of other lands are permitted to come here, as is the case daily; when ignorance, poverty, crime is allowed to land upon our shores and be transformed, hardly without ceremony, and with no time to learn the nature of our institutions, into what is called the 'American' citizens—when these things are done, it is time that good

men lifted their arms and sounded their voices against the abomination.

2nd. Because it is *unjust to the Republic.* No man has a *right* to perform an act of injustice to a nation. We care not whether the offense is defined in a written law, or not. There is a right and a wrong in this as in other matters. Every man of intelligence must understand it. Making *citizens* of such *stuff* as too often seeks our land is an injustice, the grossness of which can hardly be described. It should no longer be tolerated. The laws which permit the crime should at once be abolished.

3rd. Because it is every day weakening the strength, and destroying the character of the country. America can only be America by keeping it American. Its halls of legislation must reflect American sentiment, uttered by American tongues. There is no avoiding this position. Americans must fill our offices, great and small. To do this we must cut off all change of foreigners getting such. How? By repealing Naturalization Laws—by saying to foreigners, 'Gentlemen, you are welcome to live in our country if you conduct yourself in a worthy manner, but you must have no offices. This is *our* land. We own it. We mean to take care of it. If you don't like things as you find them, you can leave. We only *demand* in this country what we should expect in yours.'

4th. Because these laws have already produced an immense amount of evil, political, social, moral and religious. Had we never had Naturalization laws—and no country should ever have them—our country would have possessed a hundred-fold the strength, efficiency, political pursuits and symmetrical stature it now does. It has been the deadliest, most sad and ruinous course that has ever afflicted the nation. It has opened the flood-gates of poison, and through its moral and political St. Lawrences, Aroostooks, Potomacs, Ohios, Mississippis and Rio Grandes is spreading disease and death in every direction. Never, never can this be stopped—never can the nation become healthy and strong—until the *means* which permits this greatest and most gigantic of misfortunes is done away with. The stream at the fountain must be made pure, or the branches will run pollution.

5th. Because it is an immense *wrong* to have such laws. Even allowing that the tide of emigration to this country was made up mostly of intelligent, decent, patriotic men and women, the case would not be changed. To grant such full citizenship—to clothe them with the full power of the American—would be a gross wrong, a violation of all common sense and common justice. How much more is the case when ignorance, crime, poverty, all manner of baseness—when traitors, ruffians, moral, political, civil *murderers*—are granted this same citizenship, which is done by the fifties and hundreds every day in this city of Boston, and in almost every part of the land. The first path that is trodden from the ship's deck is often to the office where this legalized crime, in the shape of Naturalization, is performed. Do any wonder why Americans desire these enormities to be abolished? Do any wonder why a just patriotism and a lofty principle execrates the monsters who are engaged in this crime?

6th. Because we are false to the Republic if we fail to effect this repeal. We must either go for it, and be on the side of the Republic, or go against it and oppose the Republic. The point is clear as sunlight. No man can sustain the present Naturalization laws and be a friend of the Republic. It is an impossible thing. It is only by still more Americanizing America—Americanizing its sentiment, institutions, genius, native masses—that our mission and destiny can be achieved. Depend upon it that the initial step to this is a THOROUGH, UNCONDITIONAL REPEAL OF ALL NATURALIZATION LAWS.

SIGNIFICANCE

If the importance of the Know-Nothing movement is gauged simply by the number of years in which it occupied a prominent place on the American political stage, the Know-Nothings would be regarded as a mere blip on the long and intricate continuum that is the history of the United States. Instead, the Know-Nothings are an important component in the evolution of American attitudes towards both immigration and the development of American party politics.

The fears articulated by the Know-Nothings regarding the undermining of American society by immigration was founded upon the weight of numbers that is evidenced by census data. Between 1820 and 1845, immigration to the United States had ranged between 10,000 and 100,000 persons per year. In the period between 1845 and 1854, the time frame in which the Know-Nothings rose to national prominence, 2.9 million people immigrated to the United States, with 1.2 million Irish and over one million German settlers constituting the two largest immigrant populations. Most of these persons were Catholics. The introduction of such a large number of persons into the predominately Protestant and relatively settled American population was the primary impetus to the Know-Nothing movement. John F. Kennedy observed in his 1958 book *Immigration in America* that the Irish were the only immigrant group to precipitate the formation of an American political party to oppose them.

A corollary theme to the Know-Nothing attack on immigration was the stated belief that the Papacy, as the spiritual leadership of the worldwide Catholic Church, was the institution to which these new immigrants would pledge ultimate loyalty, and not the government of the United States. The Know-Nothings believed that allegiance to the United States was impossible for such immigrants, and that they should be barred from settling in America. Such was the stridency of the Know-Nothings in their nativist approach that Abraham Lincoln was quoted as saying during the 1856 national election that if the Know-Nothings were to obtain control of the American government, the Declaration of Independence would be amended to read, "All men are created equal except for Negroes, foreigners and Catholics."

Nativism is a significant movement in American history because its rigid, uncompromising exclusionism is the polar opposite to the modern concept of multiculturalism, with its implicit encouragement of racial and ethnic tolerance. In many respects, multiculturalism is used to celebrate the differences between peoples.

The sentiments of the Know-Nothings as expressed in their publication of July 15, 1854, were repeated in various forms when Asian immigration to the west coast of the United States became more prolific after the California gold rush of 1849 and the demand for construction workers to build the transcontinental railway completed in 1869. The political battles that took place in the 1870s and 1880s over the exclusion of the Chinese and later the Japanese from immigration to the United States were as vitriolic and as determined as any waged by the Know-Nothings. It is significant that the Chinese Exclusion Act of 1882, which barred the immigration of the Chinese and later extended to other Asiatic races, was of the type that the Know-Nothings had emphatically endorsed in 1854.

The prominence of the parochial schools in American education is a direct result of the Anti-Catholic sentiments expressed by the Know-Nothings. Faced by repeated attacks, the American Catholic church established its own schools as a means of ensuring that Catholic education would be preserved. The parochial schools have endured throughout the United States to the present day.

The echoes of the Know-Nothing nativist campaigns resonated in American politics as late as the 1960 presidential campaign, when the Catholicism of Democratic candidate John F. Kennedy was a significant political issue.

FURTHER RESOURCES

Books

Anbinder, Tyler. *Nativism and Slavery: The Northern Know Nothings and the Politics of the 1850s.* New York: Oxford University Press, 1994.

Voss-Hubbard, Mark. *Beyond Party: Cultures of Anti-partisanship in Northern Politics before the Civil War.* Baltimore, Md.: Johns Hopkins University Press, 2002.

Web sites

PBS.org. "Freedom: A History of Us." 2002. <http://www.pbs.org/wnet/historyofus/web08/segment5.html> (accessed June 20, 2006).

United States Bureau of the Census. "Historical Statistics of the Foreign Born Population of the United States, 1850–1990." <http://www.census.gov/population/www/documentation/twps0029/twps0029.html> (accessed June 20, 2006).

The Home of the Colored Race

Magazine article

By: Anonymous

Date: January 1857

Source: "The Home of the Colored Race." *Littell's Living Age* 52 (1857): 306.

About the Author: The author of this short article is unknown.

INTRODUCTION

By the 1800s, the United States was starkly divided between slave and free states. In the South, slavery remained a fact of daily life, and slaves were frequently punished or killed for trying to cross the Mason-Dixon Line. But even in the free North, assimilation of freed slaves was creating tensions. With few skills and little education, free blacks frequently found themselves living in abject poverty with little hope of improvement.

Northern politicians of various political philosophies criticized the state of black affairs. Liberals denounced the deplorable living conditions of most blacks, while conservatives warned that a growing black underclass might threaten the domestic stability of the nation. Robert Finley, a minister from New Jersey, was convinced that the history of slavery in America made assimilation into American society virtually impossible for freed slaves. Consequently, Finley proposed returning freed slaves to their historical homelands. To advance this cause, he founded the

American Colonization Society (ACS), a charitable organization intended to provide funds and support for returning former slaves to Africa. The Society would become a model for numerous other such organizations.

Black Americans were divided on the plan; many preferred to remain in the United States and exercise their rights as Americans, working to free the remaining slaves. Others wished to leave America and begin anew, and volunteers for the voyage to Africa were plentiful. With funding from numerous supporters and the U.S. Congress, the ACS launched its first voyage to Africa in 1816. Landing in Sierra Leone, the immigrants began constructing a settlement; within weeks, one-fourth had died of disease. In addition, the African residents of the land resisted the first settlers as well as those who arrived on later ships.

In 1821, officials of the American Colonization Society concluded that a more hospitable location was needed for the settlement. After a survey trip, the group succeeded in purchasing approximately 100 square miles (260 square kilometers) of territory along the Atlantic coast. In 1824, the primary city of Christopolis was renamed Monrovia, after U.S. President James Monroe, and the colony as a whole was christened Liberia, which means Land of Freedom. Other colonization societies formed in the United States, and the population of the region grew.

PRIMARY SOURCE

In the course of an interesting article on the commerce of Western Africa, showing its steady advance of late years, and the excellent basis it affords for a much greater increase, the New York Journal of Commerce remarks:

> "Not less certain is it that emigration will follow in the footsteps of commerce; and from present indications it is not difficult to conceive that the Western coast of Africa may yet become to the free blacks of the United States as attractive as California has been to the whites."

This idea must have occurred to many persons who have devoted attention to the rise and progress of Liberia. The admirable manner in which the settlement of the country goes on; the extension of the Republican authority over large numbers of natives and a wide expanse of territory; the prosperity of agricultural industry; the order, good government, and capacity for improvement manifested, must, in the end, present such a picture as will remove all the prejudices of the free blacks in the United States. Already the number of colored persons desirous of emigrating thither exceeds the capacity of the vessels engaged to convey them. Every one who goes out and does well, sends back such tidings by letter as must induce kindred and friends to try the same experiment. All the progress and prosperity of Liberia are reflected back upon the United States, and produce such an effect upon the colored population here as to increase the emigration.—*Colonization Herald.*

SIGNIFICANCE

Tensions continued to simmer between the residents of the new settlement and their governing representatives from the Colonization Society, which eventually granted them much greater self-rule. In 1846, the residents of Liberia voted to become an independent nation. In 1847, the colony ratified a Declaration of Independence from the United States. The following year, a constitution was adopted and Joseph Jenkins was elected the first president.

Despite its origins among oppressed former slaves, the Republic of Liberia was surprisingly slow in recognizing the rights of native residents within its own borders. During the early 1800s, an international commission found that the nation exploited native workers, and not until 1846 were indigenous residents granted the right to vote.

Through the twentieth century, Liberia struggled to rule itself, and the struggling country frequently found itself pulled into disputes between neighboring countries. Civilian governmental control was punctuated with totalitarian rule. In 1980, Samuel Doe assassinated the sitting president and took control of the country. In 1986, a new constitution was adopted, though Doe remained in power. In 1989, Doe was ousted from power by Charles Taylor, resulting in fourteen years of civil war and an estimated 150,000 deaths. Taylor's rule ended in 2003 when he was exiled to Nigeria.

African Americans from Arkansas gathered at Mount Olivet Baptist Chapel in New York City, while they await transportation to Liberia, 1880. © CORBIS.

United Nations troops entered Liberia following Taylor's ouster and established a transitional government along with a comprehensive disarmament program. In 2005, new elections were held and Ellen Johnson-Sirleaf was chosen as the nation's new president, making her Africa's first female chief executive.

The Republic of Liberia was conceived as a new beginning for freed slaves. While fleeing the United States did liberate the immigrants from the prejudice of white Americans, it also deprived them of the benefits of the nation's educational, financial, and industrial institutions. The former slaves' lack of education ill-equipped them to found a new nation, and the nation of Liberia today far more closely resembles its war-torn neighbors on the African continent than the home country of its founders. In most measurable respects, life in Liberia remains difficult, and its citizens enjoy a far lower standard of living than African Americans in the United States.

FURTHER RESOURCES

Books

Clegg, Claude A., III. *The Price of Liberty: African Americans and the Making of Liberia*. Charlotte, N.C.: University of North Carolina Press, 2003.

McPherson, J. H. T. *History of Liberia*. Kieler, Mont.: Kessinger Publishing, 2004.

Pham, John-Peter. *Boston Liberia: Portrait of a Failed State*. New York: Reed Press, 2004.

Periodicals

Bush, Laura. "Africa's First Female President." *Time* 167 (2006): 54.

Lloyd, Robert. "Rebuilding the Liberian State." *Current History* 105 (2006): 229–233.

Wolters, Raymond. "The Travail of Liberia." *Diplomatic History* 30 (2006): 307–310.

Web sites

BBC News. "Country Profile: Liberia." <http://news.bbc.co.uk/1/hi/world/africa/country_profiles/1043500.stm> (accessed June 7, 2006).

The Carter Center. "There's Hope in Liberia's History: An Op-Ed by Jimmy Carter." July 13, 2003 <http://www.cartercenter.org/doc1366.htm> (accessed June 7, 2006).

University of Pennsylvania. African Studies Center. "Liberia Page." <http://www.africa.upenn.edu/Country_Specific/Liberia.html> (accessed June 7, 2006).

The Integration of Aborigines in Van Diemen's Land

Report

By: W. Tweedie

Date: May 1860

Source: "The Integration of Aborigines in Van Diemen's Land." *Proceedings of the Twenty-Third Annual Meeting of the Aboriginal Protection Society*.

About the Author: W. Tweedie belonged to the Aboriginal Protection Society, one of the first efforts to protect the original inhabitants of Australia from extermination.

INTRODUCTION

The settlement of Australia in the early nineteenth century brought conflict with the indigenous people, known as Aborigines, who had inhabited the continent for at least 40,000 years. When the Aborigines had been removed as a military threat, philanthropists and missionaries began to advocate for their protection. These charitable activities focused on Aborigines in such areas as Van Diemen's Land, present-day Tasmania.

The first Europeans to settle on Van Diemen's Land were British convicts, military men, and free settlers who arrived in September 1803. To colonize the area, the British granted 100 acres, tools, and livestock to individuals who planned to farm. Despite instructions from the British Colonial Office to try to get along with the natives, the colonizers quickly entered a state of war with the Aborigines.

The problem between the whites and the indigenous people did not simply involve a struggle over land. The British had believed for centuries that the world should be made as Anglo-Saxon as possible. Englishness implied superiority; the Aborigines were an irrelevance. While some English regarded the Aborigines with uneasy interest, others tried to kill them. Many settlers believed that the destruction of the Aborigines was as inevitable as British colonial success.

The Aboriginal Protection Society was the most important of several organizations that formed in the nineteenth century to advocate for the indigenous people of Australia. Founded in 1836, it argued that rapid assimilation and incorporation into the developing mainstream was in the best interests of the indigenous cultures. The society lobbied extensively for the

A group of Australian aborigines perform a ritual dance. © E.O. HOPPÉ/CORBIS.

protection of government reserves, health and education services, and a more respectful approach by British colonial authorities to the Aborigines.

PRIMARY SOURCE

... Some recent information respecting the remnant of the Tasmanian race has been given by a gentleman, whose benevolent interest induced him to pay them a visit of observation and inquiry. It will be in the recollection of some members of this Society, that a few years ago the natives of Van Dieman's Land were, as far as possible, collected from all parts of the island, and removed to a small island called Hinder's Island, situated not far from the coast: this retreat was devoted to them and their keepers, and their number amounted to about fifty persons. They have since been brought back again to Van Dieman's Land, and are at present reduced to eleven persons, of whom more are females than males, and all of middle or declining age, but they are chiefly of the latter description. They live in small ill-kept tenements, and, except their keeper, they are apart from the other inhabitants, but they are not far from convicts, with whom they have injurious intercourse.

They are exposed to the temptation of ardent spirits, and are induced to part with articles of clothing, with which they are furnished. Except that one man, of good natural abilities, is engaged as a postman, and that two or three others are occasionally taken on whaling voyages, they seem to have no employment. Deprived of the religious instruction which they once received, and had begun to appreciate, they are in a truly deplorable condition. Destitute of physical and moral comfort and consolation, they are depressed below the zero of hope, and are consequently void of all energy. It is well known that such was not the state of the happy Tasmanians, when they were first seen by Europeans, and is it fair or right to point to the remnant of a race whom we have rendered abject and all but extinct, and say, it is the ordination of Providence to get rid of such a people, to make room for ourselves who are so much better?

SIGNIFICANCE

Wherever Europeans historically settled, indigenous peoples often faced a brutal onslaught. Van

Diemen's Land was no exception. In an island such as Tasmania, there was no interior to push natives into as whites took the land. Instead, the Aborigines were slaughtered. Upon European arrival, there were 3,000 to 4,000 Aborigines in Van Diemen's Land. By 1830, only about 300 were left and most of the usable land in Tasmania had been placed in European hands.

Racial harmony has not been achieved with the descendents of the original settlers. At the start of the millennium, Aborigines make up about two percent of the population of Australia. They suffer appalling housing, health, and medical disadvantages. The Aboriginal and Torres Straits Islanders Commission funds programs designed to correct the two centuries of disadvantages. Its creation reflects the desire of present-day whites in Tasmania to ammend for the actions of their ancestors.

FURTHER RESOURCES
Books

Morgan, Sharon. *Land Settlement in Early Tasmania: Creating an Antipodean England.* Cambridge, UK: Cambridge University Press, 1992.

Robson, Lloyd. *A History of Tasmania.* Melbourne, Australia: Oxford University Press, 1983.

"No Irish Need Apply"

Song lyrics

By: Kathleen O'Neil

Date: 1862

Source: O'Neil, Kathleen. "No Irish Need Apply." J. H. Johnson, 1862.

About the Author: Kathleen O'Neil, also known as "Kitty," was a young dancer and singer. Born in 1852, she was approximately ten years old when she began to sing "No Irish Need Apply." The song is also credited to John F. Poole; the final stanza is believed to have been added by O'Neil. O'Neil went on to perform as a dancer in music halls from New York to San Francisco.

INTRODUCTION

The largest wave of Irish immigrants to the United States began in the 1840s; between 1846 and 1854, more than two million Irish people immigrated to the United States. Irish immigrants were largely pushed out of their homeland by the potato blight, a disease that destroyed the potato crop in Ireland.

Potatoes constituted a significant part of the diet for Ireland's poor, as well as income for numerous potato farmers. The blight, a fungus that ripped through the potato crop, began in 1846; within five years, between 500,000 and one million people had died of starvation.

Given the choice between starvation at home and leaving for the United States, two million chose to emigrate. Most were poor farmers and their children. By 1850, more than one-fourth of the population in cities such as New York, Toronto, Chicago, Boston, and Baltimore was Irish. At the time of the great migration, U.S. population stood at approximately twenty-three million, with the majority being Protestant. The primarily Catholic Irish immigrants increased the U.S. population by nearly ten percent, just seventy years after American independence.

The English government sent ship after ship of Irish immigrants to Canada, but many Irish—angry with the English government for its role in the famine—landed in Canada and migrated into the United States. The English government discouraged Irish citizens from immigrating to England, where anti-Catholic sentiment ran high. Protestant Irish, however, had a slightly easier time in England. In general, the poorest of Irish citizens who left their country went to England, unable to afford the fare to Canada, the United States, or even Scotland or Wales. In 1847, the city of Liverpool was overwhelmed by more than 300,000 Irish; although many men had been seasonal migrants to England for the harvest, this time wives and children made the journey as well.

Those Irish citizens who did move to England and who settled in London faced discrimination in housing and employment. Malnourished, poor, and often ill, the new immigrants seeking jobs were offered lower wages and poor working conditions; at times, they were denied employment altogether, being told that "No Irish Need Apply." This popular song from the 1860s, sung in taverns and halls, tells the story of such discrimination.

■ PRIMARY SOURCE

I'm a simple Irish girl, and I'm looking for a place
I've felt the grip of poverty, but sure that's no disgrace
'twill be long before I get one, tho' indeed it's hard I try
For I read in each advertisement, "No Irish need apply."
Alas! for my poor country, which I never will deny
How they insult us when they write, "No Irish need apply."
Now I wonder what's the reason that the fortune-favored few

Should throw on us that dirty slur, and treat us as they
   do
Sure they all know Paddy's heart is warm, and willing is
   his hand
They rule us, yet we may not earn a living in their
   land. . . .
Ah! but now I'm in the land of the "Glorious and Free,"
And proud I am to own it, a country dear to me
I can see by your kind faces, that you will not deny
A place in your hearts for Kathleen, where "All Irish may
   apply."
Then long may the Union flourish, and ever may it be
A pattern to the world, and the "Home of Liberty!"

SIGNIFICANCE

While London newspapers carried advertisements advising Irish people not to apply, according to historian Richard J. Jensen the anti-Irish attitude was less prevalent in the United States: "In the entire file of the *New York Times* from 1851 to 1923, there are two NINA [No Irish Need Apply] ads for men, one of which is for a teenager. Computer searches of classified help wanted ads in the daily editions of other online newspapers before 1923 such as the *Brooklyn Eagle*, the *Washington Post*, and the *Chicago Tribune* show that NINA ads for men were extremely rare—fewer than two per decade." While many advertisements for female positions stated "Protestants Only," Jensen finds few instances in the United States of "No Irish Need Apply" ads, and in fact points to the last stanza of this song as evidence that life for the Irish was far better in the United States than in England.

In England, where the NINA attitude was more prevalent, Protestant Irish persons experienced far less discrimination than did the Catholic Irish. The "Protestant Only" advertisements were intended to exclude Irish Catholics, and the deep divisions within Ireland between Protestants and Catholics were exacerbated by the famine and outflow of Irish citizens to other countries. In addition, the poor Irish

A woodcut illustration shows anti-Irish riots in New York City, July 12, 1871. © BETTMANN/CORBIS.

immigrants after 1846 were malnourished, ill, and unable to handle hard manual labor in their first year or two after emigrating; unlike previous Irish immigrants, these victims of the blight entered England not as strong contributors to the labor market but as weak, sick people in need of help. The English viewed the Irish as disgusting for their habits and for the dirty, crowded conditions they were willing to live in; attitudes from the middle and upper class were elitist and condescending, while working-class British men and women feared labor-market competition from immigrants willing to work for nearly any wage to support their families.

Most jobs assumed by the Irish immigrants were either unskilled labor, temporary farm labor, or domestic work. "Bridgets," Irish girls who worked as kitchen and cleaning servants in households, were common throughout England and the United States, and while the prevailing opinion of Irish female household labor was that they performed adequately, some ladies of the home refused to hire Irish Catholic girls for fear of a perceived moral corruption or negative influence on the children of the household. This was rare—perhaps one in ten women held this opinion, according to Jensen—but helped to feed the NINA concept.

At that time, poverty was viewed by the British middle and upper classes as a reflection on the poor person's morality; the influx of poor Irish citizens into England only served to reinforce negative stereotypes about the Irish. Upper- and middle-class Brits feared that the Irish would overwhelm the charity system, and the rise in street crime, begging, and street children only added to English resentment and prejudice. The "No Irish Need Apply" attitude limited the types of jobs available for Irish immigrants escaping the famine and shaped their experiences in their adopted homelands.

FURTHER RESOURCES

Books

Foster, R. F. *The Oxford History of Ireland*. New York: Oxford University Press, 2001.

Ignatiev, Noel. *How the Irish Became White*. New York: Routledge, 1996.

Roediger, David R. *Working Toward Whiteness: How America's Immigrants Become White: The Strange Journey from Ellis Island to the Suburbs*. New York: Basic Books, 2005.

Periodicals

Jensen, Richard J. "'No Irish Need Apply:' A Myth of Victimization." *Journal of Social History* 36 (2002): 405–429.

California "Anti-Coolie" Act of 1862

Legislation

By: State of California

Date: April 26, 1862

Source: California "Anti-Coolie" Act of 1862. State of California.

About the Author: The "Anti-Coolie" Act of 1862 was passed by the state legislature of California and signed by Governor Leland Stanford.

INTRODUCTION

California was the site for the largest concentration of Chinese immigrants to the United States from the early 1850s through the end of the nineteenth century. Drawn to the Gold Rush, Chinese immigrants from Canton, aware of the United States through American Christian missionaries, immigrated to the west coast of the United States to work in gold mines; the Chinese referred to America as *Gam Saan*, or "Gold Mountain." By 1851 more than 25,000 Chinese immigrants were settled on the west coast, with the goal of spending as little as possible, saving their money, and returning home to China to live well.

Once in California after surviving the ocean voyage, Chinese immigrants seemed alien to white Americans with their basket hats made of woven bamboo, fur-lined coats, knee-length trousers, Chinese accents (when they spoke any English), different facial features, and completely different culture. In mining towns small supportive industries, such as stores, brothels, and taverns, relied on miners' expenditures; Chinese immigrants often brought their own rice and food with them, and spent very little if any on vices. Business owners viewed their frugality with contempt, and as the gold dried up, Chinese immigrants faced harsher discrimination by being forced to work older mines, accept lower wages than white counterparts, and began to experience racial violence from white Americans.

The "coolies," a term for an unskilled Chinese or Asian immigrant that is derived from a Hindi word but later became an ethnic slur, worked on the transcontinental railroad as mining jobs disappeared. Paid less than other workers, Chinese workers were found by railroad crew supervisors to be hard-working and dependable. At the same time, white workers were

THE WEST SHORE

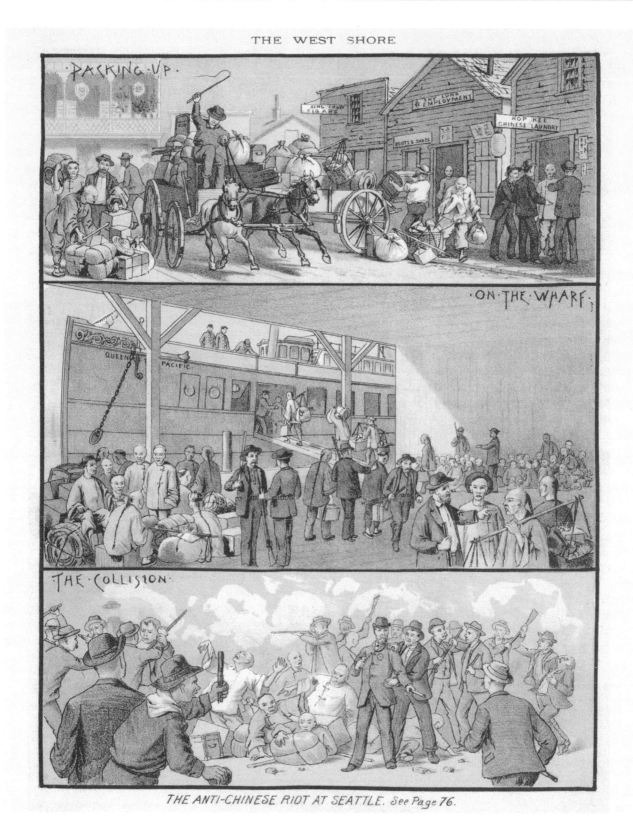

The West Shore, a Portland, Oregon, magazine, depicts Seattle's March 1886 anti-Chinese riot. © MUSEUM OF HISTORY AND INDUSTRY/CORBIS.

threatened by the Chinese, and alarmed at their growing numbers. An 1850 Miner's Foreign Tax Law in California had charged non-native miners an extra tax, and in 1862 the California legislature passed a similar measure, the "Anti-Coolie" Act.

PRIMARY SOURCE

An Act To Protect Free White Labor Against Competition With Chinese Coolie Labor, And To Discourage The Immigration Of The Chinese Into The State Of California April 26, 1862

The People of the State of California, represented in Senate and Assembly, do enact as follows:

SECTION 1. There is hereby levied on each person, male and female, of the Mongolian race, of the age of eighteen years and upwards, residing in this State, except such as shall, under laws now existing, or which may hereafter be enacted, take out licenses to work in the mines, or to prosecute some kind of business, a monthly capitation tax of two dollars and fifty cents, which tax shall be known as the Chinese Police Tax; provided, That all Mongolians exclusively engaged in the production and manufacture of the following articles shall be exempt from the provisions of this Act, viz: sugar, rice, coffee, tea . . .

SECTION 4. The Collector shall collect the Chinese police tax, provided for in this Act, from all person refusing to pay such tax, and sell the same at public auction, by giving notice by proclamation one hour previous to such sale; and shall deliver the property, together with a bill of sale thereof, to the person agreeing to pay, and paying, the highest thereof, which delivery and bill of sale shall transfer to such person a good and sufficient title to the property. And after deducting the tax and necessary expenses incurred by reason of such refusal, seizure, and sale of property, the Collector shall return the surplus of the proceeds of the sale, if any, to the person whose property was sold; provided, That should any person, liable to pay the tax imposed in this Act, in any county in this State, escape into any other County, with the intention to evade the payment of such tax, then, and in that event, it shall be lawful for the Collector, when he shall collect Chinese police taxes, as provided for in this section, shall deliver to each of the persons paying such taxes a police tax receipt, with the blanks properly filled; provided, further, That any Mongolian, or Mongolians, may pay the above named tax to the County Treasurer, who is hereby authorized to receipt for the same in the same manner as the Collector. And any Mongolian, so paying said tax to the Treasurer of the County, if paid monthly, shall be entitled to a reduction of twenty percent of said tax. And if paid in advance for the year next ensuing, such Mongolian, or Mongolians, shall be entitled to a reduction of thirty-three

and one third percent on said tax. But in all cases where the County Treasurer receipts for said tax yearly in advance, he shall do it by issuing for each month separately; and any Mongolian who shall exhibit a County Treasurer's receipt, as above provided, to the Collector for the month for which said receipt was given.

SECTION 5. Any person charged with the collection of Chinese police taxes, who shall give any receipt other than the one prescribed in this Act, or receive money for such taxes without giving the necessary receipt therefor, or who shall insert more than one name in any receipt, shall be guilty of a felony, and, upon conviction thereof, shall be fined in a sum not exceeding one thousand dollars, and be imprisoned in the State Prison for a period not exceeding one year.

SECTION 6. Any Tax Collector who shall sell, or cause to be sold, any police tax receipt, with the date of the sale left blank, or which shall not be dated and signed, and blanks filled with ink, by the Controller, Auditor, and Tax Collector, and any person who shall make any alteration, or cause the same to be made, in any police tax receipt, shall be deemed guilty of a felony, and, on conviction thereof, shall be fined in a sum not exceeding one thousand dollars, and imprisoned in the State prison for a period not exceeding 2 years; and the police tax receipt so sold, with blank date, or which shall not be signed and dated, and blanks filled with ink, as aforesaid, or which shall have been altered, shall be received in evidence in any Court of competent jurisdiction.

SECTION 7. Any person or company who shall hire persons liable to pay the Chinese police tax shall be held responsible for the payment of the tax due from each person so hired; and no employer shall be released from this liability on the ground that the employee in indebted to him (the employer), and the Collector may proceed against any such employer in the same manner as he might against the original party owing the taxes. The Collector shall have power to require any person or company believed to be indebted to, or to have any money, gold dust, or property of any kind, belonging to any person liable for police taxes, or in which such person is interested, in his or their possession, or under his or their control, to answer, under oath, as to such indebtedness, or the possession of such money, gold dust, or other property. In case a party is indebted, or has possession or control of any moneys, gold dust, or other property, as aforesaid, of such person liable for police taxes, he may collect from such party the amount of such taxes, and may require the delivery of such money, gold dust, or other property, as aforesaid; and in all cases the receipt of the Collector to said party shall be a complete bar to any demand made against said party, or his legal representatives, for the amounts of money, gold dust, or property, embraced therein.

SECTION 8. The Collector shall receive for his service, in collecting police taxes, twenty percent of all moneys which he shall collect from persons owing such taxes. All of the residue, after deducting the percentage of the Collector, forty percent shall be paid into the County Treasury, for the use of the State, forty percent into the general County Fund, for the use of the County, and the remaining twenty percent into the School Fund, for the benefit of schools within the County; provided, That in counties where the Tax Collector receives a specific salary, he shall not be required to pay the percentage allowed for collecting the police tax into the County Treasury, but shall be allowed to retain the same for his own use and benefit; provided, That where he shall collect the police tax by Deputy, the percentage shall go to the Deputy . . .

SECTION 10. It is hereby made the duty of the various officers charged with the execution of the provisions of this Act, to carry out said provisions by themselves of Deputies; and for the faithful performance of their said duties in the premises, they shall be liable on their official bonds, respectively. The Treasurer of the respective counties shall make their statements and settlements under this Act with the Controller of State, at the same time and in the same manner they make their settlements under the general Revenue Act.

SECTION 11. This Act shall take effect and be in force from and after the first day of May, next ensuing.

SIGNIFICANCE

The 1862 law taxed all Chinese immigrant workers who were from the "Mongolian" race, adding a $2.50 work permit fee per month to Chinese immigrants. As work on the Central Pacific Railroad heated up in San Francisco, and labor was needed for laying track, the work permit tax was an onerous financial burden, but did not prevent Chinese laborers from finding work.

As Chinese immigration picked up in the 1850s and 1860s on the west coast, Irish immigration increased dramatically on the east coast; in the 1840s Irish immigrants comprised more than half of all immigrants to the United States, and between 1820 and 1930 more than 4.5 million Irish immigrated to the United States. Chinese and Irish immigrants worked side by side on the railroads; once the transcontinental railroad was completed in 1869, railroad development continued, but the United States and Europe entered into an economic depression that, combined with the end of the Civil War and issues with Reconstruction, led to

severe unemployment in the United States. Prejudice turned to violence against Chinese immigrants in California, Denver, and Oregon in the 1870s.

In 1882 the U.S. Congress passed the Chinese Exclusion Act, signed by President Chester A. Arthur. The act placed severe limits on Chinese immigration, limiting legal immigration to 100 Chinese immigrants per year. The act stripped Chinese immigrants of the right to bring Chinese wives to the United States, and later versions of the law removed their right to act as a witness at a trial. The 1882 law, the first piece of immigration legislation in the United States to target a specific immigrant group, set the tone for the next sixty years for Chinese immigrants. California's "Anti-Coolie" of twenty years earlier was the first of such legislation aimed at curtailing Chinese immigration in the United States, though certainly not the last law of its kind.

FURTHER RESOURCES
Books

Gyory, Andrew. *Closing the Gate: Race, Politics, and the Chinese Exclusion Act.* Chapel Hill: University of North Carolina Press, 1998.

Lee, Erika. *At America's Gates: Chinese Immigration during the Exclusion Era, 1882–1943.* Chapel Hill: University of North Carolina Press, 2003.

Wong, K. Scott, and Sucheng Chan, eds. *Claiming America: Constructing Chinese American Identities during the Exclusion Era.* Philadelphia: Temple University Press, 1998.

Web sites

Central Pacific Railroad Photographic History Museum. "Chinese-American Contribution to Transcontinental Railroad." <http://cprr.org/Museum/Chinese.html> (accessed June 25, 2006).

National Archives and Records Administration. "Chinese Immigration and the Chinese in the United States." <http://www.archives.gov/locations/finding aids/chinese-immigration.html> (accessed June 25, 2006).

Uncle Sam's Thanksgiving Dinner

Illustration

By: Thomas Nast

Date: November 21, 1869

Source: Nast, Thomas. "Uncle Sam's Thanksgiving Dinner." *Harper's Weekly* (November 21, 1869). Courtest of the Library of Congress.

About the Illustrator: American political illustrator and cartoonist Thomas Nast (1840–1902) was considered one of the best political cartoonists of the nineteenth century. Nast illustrated the majority of his work—approximately 2,200 cartoons between the years 1859 and 1896—while with Harper & Brothers, who published such periodicals as *Harper's Weekly*. During this time Nast created or popularized such figures as the current characterizations of Santa Claus, Uncle Sam, the donkey representing the Democratic Party, and the elephant representing the Republican Party.

INTRODUCTION

In 1817, brothers James and John Harper began a small printing business in New York City. Two more Harper brothers, Fletcher and Joseph, joined the business later. By 1825, Harper & Brothers had become the largest book-publishing company in the United States. In 1850, the brothers began publishing *Harper's Monthly*, which featured articles from established and well-known authors. Based on its success, the company in 1857 began *Harper's Weekly*. Expanding the business as circulation increased, Thomas Nast joined the company in 1862 as its cartoonist. Nast developed a unique style that frequently used embellishment of the physical characteristics of his subjects.

At around the time Nast joined Harper & Brothers, the popular nickname and symbol used to personify the United States was changing from Brother Jonathan to Uncle Sam. Brother Jonathan was the clever Yankee character that appeared initially in the late-eighteenth-century play *The Contrast*. It is generally considered that Uncle Sam originated from the initials U.S., which first appeared on military supply containers, such as barrels of meat, during the War of 1812. Folklore holds that soldiers joked that the initials stood for Uncle Samuel Wilson, a meat

PRIMARY SOURCE

Uncle Sam's Thanksgiving Dinner: Featured in an 1869 edition of *Harper's Weekly*, this illustration criticizes anti-immigrant sentiments by portraying people of all racial and ethnic backgrounds gathered for Thanksgiving dinner served by Uncle Sam. THE LIBRARY OF CONGRESS.

supplier for the military. Later, around 1832, cartoon caricatures of a stars-and-stripes clad Uncle Sam figure appeared in political cartoons. In both figures (Brother Jonathan and Uncle Sam), the short-bearded man generally wore a top hat, a coat with tails, and striped pants.

PRIMARY SOURCE

UNCLE SAM'S THANKSGIVING DINNER
See primary source image.

SIGNIFICANCE

The Reconstruction era (1865–1877) of the United States—the period of time after the Civil War (1861–1865)—was a time dedicated to rebuilding the country and to concentrating on the equal rights and citizenship of all Americans. For example, the Fourteenth Amendment to the U.S. Constitution, which was ratified in July 1868, protected the rights of Southern blacks and restricted the political power of former Confederates. Later, in 1869, the Fifteen Amendment

was ratified, which stated that U.S. citizens could not be denied the right to vote due to "race, color or previous condition of servitude."

Showing the patriotic idealism popular during these times, Thomas Nast is often credited with creating, in part, the popular image of Uncle Sam. The initials U.S. and the likeness of Uncle Sam have grown to represent the moral values within the United States. The image frequently was associated with military recruiting posters showing a likeness of Uncle Sam saying "I Want YOU for U.S. Army."

The illustration "Uncle Sam's Thanksgiving Dinner" was Nast's first drawing of the Uncle Sam character, which appeared in the November 20, 1869 edition of *Harper's Weekly*. In the picture, Uncle Sam is shown standing while carving the Thanksgiving turkey. Although Uncle Sam is not wearing his now-familiar top hat and striped pants, Nast drew the illustration to imply images of freedom, equality, and unity—images still associated with Uncle Sam today. Nast wrote out in the lower left-hand corner of the illustration the words "Come One, Come All," and in the lower right-hand corner the words "Free and Equal." He used these phrases to show that all the men and women of different

Uncle Sam welcomes immigrants into a structure marked "U.S. Ark of Refuge". A sign in front advertises the benefits of immigrating to the United States, such as "No compulsory military service." © CORBIS.

races and backgrounds—such as Chinese, Indian, White, and Black—were equal while sitting at the dinner table of Uncle Sam.

With the portraits of U.S. Presidents George Washington, Abraham Lincoln, and Ulysses S. Grant in the background, Nast's illustration played an important role in developing the popular image of Uncle Sam. Consequently, Nast helped to solidify some of the principles from which the nation is founded: that all people are equal and free in the United States. Nast's image of Uncle Sam evolved over the years into the image that is now popular in twenty-first century America. However, though the image of Uncle Sam has changed over time, his message remained the same with respect to the country's goals and objectives.

On September 15, 1961, the eighty-seventh U.S. Congress adopted the figure of Uncle Sam as a national symbol of the country. Uncle Sam, along with the Statue of Liberty, are generally considered the two most recognizable representations of the United States. In addition, based on the popularity of the Uncle Sam recruiting posters, other countries promoted their own patriotic characters, such as England's Lord Kitchener.

FURTHER RESOURCES

Books

Keller, Morton. *The Art and Politics of Thomas Nast*. New York: Oxford University Press, 1968.

Ketchum, Alton. *Uncle Sam: The Man and the Legend*. New York: Hill and Wang, 1959.

Nast, Thomas. *Thomas Nast's Christmas Drawings*. New York: Dover Publications, 1978.

Paine, Albert Bigelow. *Thomas Nast: His Period and his Pictures*. Gloucester, Mass.: P. Smith, 1967.

Web sites

The National Archives. "Constitution of the United States: Amendments 11–27." <http://www.archives.gov/national-archives-experience/charters/constitution_amendments_11-27.html> (accessed June 28, 2006).

ThomasNast.com. "The World of Thomas Nast." <http://www.thomasnast.com> (accessed June 28, 2006).

Departure of a Colony of Emigrants at Train Station

Illustration

By: Anonymous

Date: 1869

Source: © Corbis.

About the Artist: The artist is unknown. This image is part of the collection of the Corbis Corporation, headquartered in Seattle. Corbis maintains a worldwide archive of more than seventy million images.

INTRODUCTION

Since the first settlements on the Atlantic coast, Americans had been moving westward in search of better opportunities. To many, it was their god-given or manifest destiny to fill up the land between the Atlantic and Pacific Oceans. They viewed Americans as chosen people who had divine blessing to multiply and to push out the Native Americans. Many whites would eventually prosper in the West but survival in a such a challenging environment proved to be quite difficult and a good number of people failed.

By the 1840s, American settlers had reached the Missouri River. From there, until they reached the West Coast, pioneers had to cross plains, mountains, and deserts. Many, however, found other ways to reach California and Oregon. Pioneers with enough money to do so traveled by sailing ship around South America, while others sailed to Panama, traveled on foot or by horse across the Isthmus, and then sailed up the Pacific coast. (The Panama Canal was not yet built). The Great Plains of the West, also known as the Great American Desert, were strewn with the wrecks of wagons, the bones of cows and oxen, and the graves of the unlucky.

On the eve of the Civil War in 1865, approximately 175,000 white Americans and a sprinkling of blacks were in the future states of Montana, Arizona, Utah, Nevada, Wyoming, New Mexico, Idaho, and Colorado. Except for the 25,000 Mormons who settled in Utah, almost all of them moved around frequently like the Native American inhabitants. Most settlement of the American west came after the Civil War, aided by the construction of railroads that speeded and eased travel. Immigrants could board a train and spend a couple of days traveling safely to their destination instead of devoting months to a risky trip.

■ PRIMARY SOURCE

DEPARTURE OF A COLONY OF EMIGRANTS AT TRAIN STATION

See primary source image.

PRIMARY SOURCE

Departure of a Colony of Emigrants at Train Station: Illustration depicting a colony of immigrants boarding a train heading for Colorado, at a Chicago & St. Louis railroad station, August 24, 1869. © CORBIS.

SIGNIFICANCE

In 1890, the U.S. Census announced the end of the frontier as a clear dividing line between settled and undeveloped areas. The frontier no longer existed. The availability of free land and influence of the frontier had played a major role in American history from the founding of the colonies. The West had been a place where emigrants could start anew. An era had closed. In short order, the western territories became states.

Colorado, the destination of many emigrants, became as settled as the rest of the nation. Its growth in the years since World War II has been typical of the states in the Mountain West. The state grew by 156 percent from 1950 to 1992, with much of this growth occurring after 1970. Most of the change came from interstate migration, drawn to Colorado for employment and the attractiveness of its environment. Up until the mid–1990s, Colorado's immigrant population remained small

and politically inconsequential. This changed by the start of the twenty-first century with Mexican immigrants in particular becoming much more of a political concern. Along with other Mountain West states, Colorado is experiencing a boom in Latino immigration that has the potential to significantly shape the state's future.

FURTHER RESOURCES
Books

Abbott, Carl, Stephen J. Leonard, and Thomas J. Noel. *Colorado: A History of the Centennial State*. Boulder: University Press of Colorado, 2001.

Casper, Scott E., and Lucinda M. Long. *Moving Stories: Migration and the American West, 1850–2000*. Reno: University of Nevada Press, 2001.

Gimpel, James G. *Separate Destinations: Migration, Immigration, and the Politics of Places*. Ann Arbor: University of Michigan Press, 1999.

Naturalization Act of 1870

Legislation

By: United States Congress

Date: July 14, 1870

Source: United States Congress. "Naturalization Act of 1870." *Statutes at Large*. Boston: Little Brown, 1870.

About the Author: The Congress of the United States was established by Article 1 of the United States Constitution of 1787. It is the legislative arm of the U.S. federal government.

INTRODUCTION

Naturalization policy, which governs the way that foreigners may obtain U.S. citizenship, is considered so important that it is mentioned in the first article of the Constitution. The founding fathers did not list the rules for obtaining citizenship, preferring to leave that obligation to Congress. Through the years, Congress has passed a series of Naturalization Acts, including the Naturalization Act of 1870.

In the colonial era, naturalization laws were passed with the intent of encouraging immigration. Desperate for workers, colonial assemblies realized that the best way to get foreigners to come to the New World was to offer them equal privileges. By the early national period, Americans were becoming a bit less welcoming. The first Naturalization Act, passed in 1790, required from immigrants only a two-year period of residency before they could acquire citizenship. During the following decade, Americans came increasingly to question the liberality of such a policy. The groups of political refugees who came to America and the fear of aliens created by the Quasi-War with France made Americans consider stronger naturalization requirements.

Despite the presence of a strong nativist movement in the United States in the 1850s, naturalization was not addressed again until 1868, when the Fourteenth Amendment to the Constitution made the former slaves who had been born in the United States into citizens. The change gave blacks access to the courts and Constitutional protections as well as the right to own land and to enter certain professions. In 1870, Congress expanded the list of those eligible for naturalization to include all white persons and persons of African descent. Congress specifically rejected a proposal by

Aliens arriving in the United States are screened at Ellis Island, New York City, in 1950. © BETTMANN/CORBIS.

Senator Charles Sumner of Massachusetts to open naturalization to all. Asians remained ineligible for naturalization. (In this era, Latinos were not considered.)

■ PRIMARY SOURCE

An Act to amend the Naturalization Laws and to punish Crimes against the same, and for other Purposes.

Be it enacted by the Senate and House of Representatives of the United States of America in Congress assembled, That in all cases where any oath, affirmation, or affidavit shall be made or taken under or by virtue of any act or law relating to the naturalization of aliens, or in any proceedings under such acts or laws, and any person or persons taking or making such oath, affirmation, or affidavit, shall knowingly swear or affirm falsely, the same shall be deemed and taken to be perjury, and the person or persons guilty thereof shall upon conviction thereof be sentenced to imprisonment for a term not exceeding five years and not less than one year, and to a fine not exceeding one thousand dollars.

And be it further enacted, That if any person applying to be admitted a citizen, or appearing as a witness for any such person, shall knowingly personate any other person than himself, or falsely appear in the name of a deceased person, or in an assumed or fictitious name, or if any person shall falsely make, forge, or counterfeit any oath, affirmation, notice, affidavit, certificate, order, record, signature, or other instrument, paper, or proceeding required or authorized by any law or act relating to or providing for the naturalization of aliens; or shall utter, sell, dispose of, or use as true or genuine, or for any unlawful purpose, any false, forged, ante-dated, or counterfeit oath, affirmation, notice, certificate, order, record, signature, instrument, paper, or proceeding as aforesaid; or sell or dispose of to any person other than the person for whom it was originally issued, any certificate of citizenship, or certificate showing any person to be admitted a citizen;

... every person so offending shall be deemed and adjudged guilty of felony, and, on conviction thereof, shall be sentenced to be imprisoned and kept at hard labor for a period not less than one year nor more than five years, or be fined in a sum not less than three hundred dollars nor more than one thousand dollars, or both such punishments may be imposed, in the discretion of the court.

And be it further enacted, That the naturalization laws are hereby extended to aliens of African nativity and to persons of African descent.

Approved, July 14, 1870.

■

SIGNIFICANCE

The naturalization laws were the basis for later restrictions upon immigration, including the notorious Chinese Exclusion Act of 1882. The Naturalization Act of 1790 introduced race by limiting the acquisition of citizenship by naturalization to "free white persons." The Naturalization Act of 1870 expanded the privilege to all blacks. Once the issue of race had been introduced as a part of immigration policy, it was a simple step to use race as a justification for excluding would-be immigrants from the United States. Accordingly, in response to public pressure, Congress approved a series of exclusionary immigration laws in the years following 1882.

During World War II, these race-based restrictions became a great national embarrassment, chiefly because we were united with the Chinese, the Indians, and the Filipinos to defeat the Japanese. The administration of President Franklin D. Roosevelt openly worried that the Chinese Exclusion Act would hurt the war effort in Asia. Discriminating against immigrants from our allies was poor foreign policy and foreign policy dictated a change in domestic policy. In 1943, the right of naturalization was extended to the Chinese. In 1946, it was extended to the Filipinos and Indians. In 1952, naturalization was extended to members of all ethnic and racial groups. For the first time, naturalization became color blind.

FURTHER RESOURCES
Books

Hutchinson, E. P. *Legislative History of American Immigration Policy, 1798–1965*. Philadelphia: University of Pennsylvania Press, 1981.

The Immigration Reader: America in a Multidisciplinary Perspective, edited by David Jacobson. Malden, Mass.: Blackwell Publishing, 1998.

Jones, Maldwyn Allen. *American Immigration*. Chicago: University of Chicago Press, 1960.

3

Immigration from 1870-1905

Immigration from 1870–1905

Over fourteen million immigrants arrived in the United States between 1870 and 1905. In the 1870s and early 1880s, the majority of European immigrants to the United States came from Ireland, Britain, and Germany. By 1890, New York City alone had a German population equal to that of Hamburg, Germany. The demographics of immigration then underwent a dramatic shift. By 1900, most who arrived in the United States emigrated from southern and eastern Europe.

The first residence of many European immigrants was New York City, especially in the Five Points district and surrounding areas. The busy neighborhoods garnered an exaggerated reputation for violence and vice, partially stemming from prejudiced ethnic stereotypes and negative public opinion about some immigrant groups. The tenements were at once an arena for hope and despair, abuse and opportunity, poverty and possibility; they were both flourishing and crumbling. The population of these neighborhoods changed with the tide of immigration. Blocks once populated by recent immigrants from Ireland or Germany became Italian, Russian, and Jewish ethnic enclaves. Several articles in this chapter chronicle the stories of these nineteenth-century immigrant neighborhoods and their inhabitants. "Italian Life in New York," "From Russia to the Lower East Side in the 1890s," and the "The English Lesson" convey immigrant and outside perceptions of these communities. "The Mixed Crowd," is an excerpt from social reformer Jacob Riis's influential *How the Other Half Lives*, the work of essays and photographs that stirred public outcry against the squalor, abuses, and poverty of tenements. In response, the city razed the notorious slums.

Immigration was not limited to the East coast, nor were all immigrants Europeans. Included in this chapter is also a look at non-Western immigration. While railroad and mining companies relied on inexpensive Chinese labor, Chinese immigrant populations on the West coast faced increasing discrimination. The Chinese Exclusion Act of 1882, included in this chapter, severely restricted immigration, curtailing the ability for Chinese to immigrate with their families and excluding those permitted entry from becoming citizens. "Is it Right for a Chinaman to Jeopard a White Man's Dinner?" illustrates the racist and economically motivated underpinnings of anti-Chinese laws.

Ellis Island and the Statue of Liberty, two U.S. landmarks associated with immigration, were constructed in this period. Ellis Island attained its greatest fame during the period of mass immigration beginning in 1905 and is thus profiled in the next chapter. While Ellis Island was from its creation a landmark of immigration, the Statue of Liberty was not originally intended for such a role. A poem enshrined on the statue's pedestal best captures—and debatably created—the statue's role as a welcoming beacon for immigrants. In the United States, the words form an indelible part of the national consciousness as a nation of immigrants, "Give me your tired, your poor/Your huddled masses yearning to breathe free." The full text of Emma Lazarus's poem, "The New Colossus," is the heart of this chapter and this volume.

The Emigrants' Dangers

Magazine article

By: Harper's Weekly

Date: August 2, 1873

Source: *Harper's Weekly*, August 2, 1873

About the Author: *Harper's Weekly* was established in 1850 as a magazine of fiction, essays, and cultural and political commentary.

INTRODUCTION

Passage to the New World always brought hazards. Emigrants were put on grossly overcrowded ships and often housed in the same area as cargo. Captains and crews had little incentive to protect the health of passengers, with deaths at sea common. In the nineteenth century, a dramatic increase in immigration led to more publicity of the dangers faced onboard ships.

Advances in overseas transportation made emigration to the New World cheaper than ever before in the early decades of the nineteenth century. The Atlantic crossing, however, remained filled with dangers. Until the Civil War in the 1860s, the immigrant trade was virtually monopolized by sailing vessels, resulting in a crossing that still took at least four weeks, and often far longer. Transport ships remained primarily freight carriers that were quickly converted for passenger carrying on the westward journey. Steerage quarters were cramped and poorly ventilated, sanitary arrangements were crude, and cooking facilities completely inadequate. At every stage of the journey, the emigrant was swindled, imposed upon, and poorly treated by dishonest passenger brokers, lodging house keepers, and unscrupulous ship captains. Women additionally suffered sexual harassment. As one traveler reported, everything was disagreeable.

The ship *City of Washington*, the subject of the *Harper's Weekly* essay, sank off the coast of Nova Scotia without any loss of life. Built in 1855 at Glasgow, the steamship left Liverpool for New York on June 24, 1873. On the afternoon of July 5, the ship struck the reefs off Newfoundland, Canada. It was enveloped in a thick fog at the time and the captain had neglected to take soundings to identify hidden rocks. He lost his license for a year. The passengers and crew, amounting to 576 persons, escaped in life boats.

Sailing through thick fogs and over an unknown sea at the rate of twelve miles an hour, dashing forward into the jaws of death, landing with a sudden shock upon a Nova Scotian reef, escaping only by a miracle from total destruction, is the fate which the foreign lines of steamers offer to their throngs of helpless passengers. If the *City of Washington* had swerved only a few feet from her providential path, the horrors of her disaster would have outdone all that was told of the fate of the *Atlantic*. It is possible that no one in the dim and misty surf would have been able to reach the shore. All must have gone down together. Happily the friendly rock bore up the ship. Her officers attempted to drag her back and sink her, with all the crew, in the deep water behind. They were prevented. The lives at least of the great company of travelers were saved. Yet they were saved only, apparently, to show the continued inhumanity of the steamer's officials. No effort, we are told by Colonel Parnell, was made to soften the sufferings of the three hundred and fifty immigrants, men, women, children, who were thrown upon the barren coast, and who for days and nights were left without shelter, fire, and almost food. On the bleak rocks and sands they remained shivering, wet, and famished in the misty rain, yet thankful that life at least had been spared them in spite of the cruel negligence of the steamer's officers.

Indeed, the characteristics of this unprecedented voyage seem to verge upon the extreme of madness. For seven days, we are told, the steamer pressed on at a rapid rate in the midst of a thick fog. She was in the centre of a crowded pathway, where ships were to be looked for incessantly. Even on our narrow rivers and bays, when a fog prevails, it is usual for steamers to move with constant caution, to sound an incessant alarm, and to watch with extraordinary diligence the approach to the shore. No Hudson River steamer or ferry-boat would neglect to secure itself by the most natural precautions. Yet of these nothing was provided in the *City of Washington*. She was hurried on in spite of warnings and remonstrances, of rock weeds that told of the nearing reef, of the total ignorance of her officers as to her position and her danger; and it was only when she had struck with a sharp crash that guns were fired, steam-whistles sounded, bells rung, and that the officers came to know that their perilous voyage had reached its natural end. Yet not even then, until the voices of Swanberg and Fergusson sounded hopefully in the misty night, does there seem to have been any proper effort made to save the passengers. But for these two heroes, for all that appears, the *City of Washington* might have swung unrelieved on her friendly rock until she parted in the sea.

Immigrants crowd the deck of the S.S. Prince Frederick Wilhelm, July 24, 1915. © BETTMANN/CORBIS.

The same incompetence on the part of the officers seems to have marked the wrecks of the *Atlantic* and the *City of Washington*. Both were emigrant steamers. Both seem to have been committed to the charge of men who were unfit for any trust; and that the throng of emigrants who perished in the *Atlantic* was not rivaled in the later disaster is due to no precaution on the part of the owners of the steamer. The remedy for these inexcusable events lies, in great part, with the emigrants themselves. They should carefully avoid patronizing all lines of travel where

their interests are not provided for, and their lives and comfort secured; they should warn their friends in Europe of the dangers that await them, and show to the companies, who make immense sums from the host of immigration, that they are resolved to have a proper return for their money.

Yet the failures and the discomforts, the needless disasters and ceaseless inhumanity, on the part of foreign ships and ship-owners, show that the ocean travel should no longer be left in their hands. To the immigrant an

American line of steamers is an absolute need. On the European steamer he is too often looked upon as a serf, and treated with European inhumanity. The moment he touches an American deck he is free. That an American line of steamers, conducted with discretion and liberality, might engross a large share of this gainful traffic we are quite confident; and that the American ship-owner and the American government are better fitted than the foreign to watch over the interests of our future citizens no one can doubt, or that the immigrant, from the moment he leaves his native shore, should be under the protection of the country where rests his hope of freedom and of peace.

SIGNIFICANCE

In 1873, at the request of the U.S. Senate and in response to disasters such as the *City of Washington* wreck, a team of Treasury officials investigated steerage conditions. They concluded, after inspecting thirty ships, that much of the abuse of passengers and poor living conditions was part of the past. They commended the present conditions of the ships. Along with many Americans, the officials believed that any problems were rare and the fault of European authorities. In reality, the Europeans had stronger regulations than the Americans, but all of the standards remained fairly low. Governments were reluctant to insist on anything because any increase in costs might stop either emigration or immigration.

By the first decades of the twentieth century, conditions for emigrants had improved considerably. The change was due to advances in epidemiology that stopped outbreaks of diseases from wiping out passengers as well as improvements in shipbuilding and navigation. Abuses remained, however, because of a lack of law enforcement. Illegal immigrants have been especially at risk of predatory captains and abusive crews.

FURTHER RESOURCES
Books

Friedland, Klaus, ed. *Maritime Aspects of Migration*. Cologne, Germany: Bohlau, 1989.

LaGumina, Salvatore J. *From Steerage to Suburb: Long Island Italians*. New York: Center for Migration Studies, 1988.

Rossi, Renzo. *A History of Powered Ships*. San Diego, Calif.: Blackbird Press, 2005.

Arrival of Mennonite Emigrants

Illustration

By: Anonymous

Date: September 6, 1873

Source: © Corbis.

About the Artist: This image was featured in *Leslie's Illustrated Magazine*, which was published from 1855 to 1922. One of the most popular magazines of its day, the periodical was begun by Frank Leslie. It printed serial fiction as well as news accounts and features. The artist is unknown. The image is part of the collection held by the Corbis Corporation.

INTRODUCTION

The Mennonites, descended from Swiss and Dutch Anabaptists, believed in a form of Christianity that did not include participation in military service or in government. For resisting government service and challenging government control of Christianity, they were persecuted. To escape, numbers of Mennonites migrated to other parts of Europe and eventually to the United States, typically settling in the West and Midwest.

The Mennonites are Anabaptists. The left wing of the Protestant Reformation, Anabaptists argued that only adults could make a free choice about religious faith, baptism, and entry into the Christian community. They took the Gospel literally and favored a return to a voluntary church that they considered existed among the earliest Christians. The Anabaptist belief that only a few people would experience an inner light necessary for membership in the church put the sect in direct opposition to the notion that the Christian community and the Christian state were identical. Additionally, they refused all public offices and would not serve in the armed forces. Absolute pacifism and opposition to state-run churches logically led to the separation of church and state and, ultimately, the complete secularization of society. Accordingly, the Anabaptists were viciously attacked in their homelands of Switzerland and Germany. They were banished or sometimes executed by burning, beating, or drowning.

In the late eighteenth century, Catherine the Great of Russia offered Mennonite settlers 165 acres

An 1873 illustration from Leslie's Illustrated Magazine portrays the arrival of Mennonites expelled from Russia in New York City. They are on their way to settle in the Dakotas. © CORBIS.

of farm land per family, plus religious freedom and a guarantee that they would never have to serve in the Russian military. Catherine offered immigrants the opportunity to live in settlements where they could control their own education and local government. Beginning in 1789, Dutch Mennonites living in Prussia began settling in Russia. They prospered, but in 1871, the Russian government rescinded the exemption of Mennonites from military service. Canada and the U.S. both invited the Russian Mennonites to farm their plains. Both governments offered free land, religious freedom, and the right to control the education of their children. Canada also offered military exemption. From 1874 to 1890, about 10,000 Russian Mennonites settled in the Midwest and Great Plains states with another 8,000 settling in Manitoba, Canada.

ARRIVAL OF MENNONITE EMIGRANTS
See primary source image.

SIGNIFICANCE

In subsequent migrations of Mennonites, most immigrants went to Canada, Paraguay, or Brazil, because these countries were perceived as more welcoming than the U.S. Most of the Russian Mennonites who settled in the U.S. were more urban and progressive than the Swiss-German Mennonites who had established the older settlements in Pennsylvania and the Midwest. However, by the late twentieth century, most of these differences had disappeared.

Mennonite gradually became more of a religious categorization than a cultural description. While their Amish cousins have remained distinctly separate from American society, Mennonites have largely assimilated.

FURTHER RESOURCES

Books

Hostetler, John. *Amish Society*. Baltimore: Johns Hopkins University Press, 1993.

Loewen, Harry and Steven Nolt. *Through Fire and Water: An Overview of Mennonite History*. Scottsdale, PA: Herald Press, 1996.

Loewen, Royden. *Hidden Worlds: Revisiting the Mennonite Migrants of the 1870s*. Winnipeg, Manitoba: University of Manitoba Press, 2001.

Italian Life in New York

Magazine article

By: Charlotte Adams

Date: April 1881

Source: Adams, Charlotte. "Italian Life in New York." *Harper's New Monthly* (April 1881).

About the Author: Charlotte Adams was a regular contributor to *Harper's New Monthly Magazine*, which began in 1850 as a publisher of fiction, essays, and cultural and political commentary.

INTRODUCTION

Although an Italian named Christopher Columbus discovered America, only thirty thousand Italians came to North America before 1870. Most of the migrants were northern Italians. Large-scale migration from Italy south of Rome and from Sicily began only after 1880. By the time Italian immigration dropped dramatically in 1920, four million Italians had arrived in the United States. From no other ethnic group have so many come so fast.

Most Italian immigrants were males. Over time, greater gender balance developed in many communities, but in some cities, the percentage of female Italian immigrants remained below forty percent as late as 1920. Most of the immigrants were unskilled peasants. In the U.S., they chiefly worked as laborers in railroad and road construction as well as the building trades. With the largest "Little Italy" in the U.S. located in New York City, many used New York as a

base from which they migrated for seasonal work in surrounding areas. A minority worked in agriculture in California, where they established the wine industry.

Once established in the U.S., immigrants tried to recreate the life that they had known in Italy. For many, this included the development of institutions that literally spoke their language. Almost all Italian immigrants were Catholic and they strongly supported parish churches. The first Italian-language newspaper, *Progresso Italo-Americano*, appeared in 1879. By the mid–1920s, it had a nationwide circulation of 120,000 and remained in existence until 1988. Italians refused to adopt the food habits of Anglo-Americans, famously refusing to feed their children oats because that is what the horses ate. Some of the immigrants opened fresh pasta shops, while others started Italian bakeries, restaurants, and pizzerias. The Italian grocery was a common feature of urban life in the Northeast until the development of large supermarkets after World War II.

PRIMARY SOURCE

The fact that Italian immigration is constantly on the increase in New York makes it expedient to consider both the condition and status of these future citizens of the republic. The higher walks of American life, in art, science, commerce, literature, and society, have, as is well known, long included many talented and charming Italians; but an article under the above title must necessarily deal with the subject in its lower and more recent aspect. During the year 1879 seven thousand two hundred Italian immigrants were landed at this port, one-third of which number remained in the city, and there are now over twenty thousand Italians scattered among the population of New York. The more recently arrived herd together in colonies, such as those in Baxter and Mott streets, in Eleventh Street, in Yorkville, and in Hoboken. Many of the most important industries of the city are in the hands of Italians as employers and employed, such as the manufacture of macaroni, of objects of art, confectionery, artificial flowers; and Italian workmen may be found everywhere mingled with those of other nationalities. It is no uncommon thing to see at noon some swarthy Italian, engaged on a building in process of erection, resting and dining from his tin kettle, while his brown-skinned wife sits by his side, brave in her gold earrings and beads, with a red flower in her hair, all of which at home were kept for feast days. But here in America increased wages make every day a feast day in the matter of food and raiment; and why, indeed, should not the architectural principle of beauty supplementing necessity be applied even to the daily round of hod-carrying? Teresa from the Ligurian mountains

Boys peddle bread on Mulberry Street in an Italian American neighborhood, New York City, 1900. © CORBIS.

is certainly a more picturesque object than Bridget from Cork, and quite as worthy of incorporation in our new civilization. She is a better wife and mother, and under equal circumstances far outstrips the latter in that improvement of her condition evoked by the activity of the New World. Her children attend the public schools, and develop very early an amount of energy and initiative which, added to the quick intuition of Italian blood, makes them valuable factors in the population. That the Italians are an idle and thriftless people is a superstition which time will remove from the American mind. A little kindly guidance and teaching can mould them into almost any form. . . .

In the second generation many Italians easily pass for Americans, and prefer to do so, since a most unjust and unwarranted prejudice against Italians exists in many quarters, and interferes with their success in their trades and callings. It is much to be regretted that the sins of a few turbulent and quarrelsome Neapolitans and Calabrians should be visited upon the heads of their quiet, gentle,

and hard-working compatriots. All Italians are proud and high-spirited, but yield easily to kindness, and are only defiant and revengeful when ill-treated.

SIGNIFICANCE

Despite their numbers, Italians remained a marginalized and poverty-stricken group well into the twentieth century. Prejudice against the new Catholic immigrants with the strange cultural habits limited their opportunities for advancement. The voices of tolerance were generally ignored. Italian immigration was greatly curtailed by the Immigration Act of 1924. The law, one of the Quota Acts, intentionally discriminated against immigrants from eastern and southern Europe.

Not until Italian Americans returned from fighting in World War II with a new sense of pride were they fully integrated into American society. By this point, most Italian emigrants chose to move to Argentina or Australia. For a few years after the Immigration Act of 1965, Italians were the most numerous immigrant group admitted to the U.S., but few have come since then.

FURTHER RESOURCES
Books

Gabaccia, Donna R. *From Sicily to Elizabeth Street: Housing and Social Change among Italian Immigrants, 1880–1930.* Albany, N.Y.: State University Press of New York, 1984.

Mangione, Jerre and Ben Morreale. *La Storia: Five Centuries of the Italian American Experience.* New York: Harper Collins, 1992.

Salomone, Frank A. *Italians in Rochester, New York, 1900–1940.* Lewiston, N.Y.: Edwin Mellen Press, 2000.

Chinese Exclusion Act 1882

Legislation

By: United States Congress

Date: May 6, 1882

Source: "Chinese Exclusion Act." 22 Stat. 58, U.S. Congress, 1882.

About the Author: The Forty-seventh United States Congress passed the Chinese Exclusion Act in 1882; ten years later the Fifty-second Congress renewed the act's provisions and strengthened Chinese immigration laws with the Geary Act. In 1902 the restrictions on Chinese immigration were made permanent, though repealed some forty years later.

INTRODUCTION

Chinese relations with the United States stretched back to the 1784 trade expedition in which the ship the *Empress of China* brought American cotton and furs to China and returned with Chinese silk and spices, all with a handsome profit for the merchants involved. Over the next century, Chinese-U.S. diplomatic relations centered around trade and immigration.

Early Christian missionary activity in China stretches back to the early 1800s for American and British missionaries; their forays into the Canton (Guangdong) region helped to deliver news of the United States and its culture to China. After the Opium War (1839–1842) and Britain's forced opening of trade with China, the United States worked to

negotiate the Wangxia Treaty, which gave the U.S. unilateral trade rights and helped Americans to enter the illegal opium trade.

By the early 1850s, news of the Gold Rush in California reached China. Some of the earlier immigrants were from Canton, where missionaries had helped native Chinese to conceptualize the U.S. and to understand more about U.S. culture. The 1850 foreign Miner's Tax Law, passed in California, was the first in a series of state and federal laws designed to discriminate directly against the Chinese. By charging an additional tax for foreign miners, authorities targeted Chinese miners for their differences while helping native-born miners. The Chinese miners called the U.S. *Gam Saan*, or "Gold Mountain," although many white and native-born miners forced Chinese immigrants to work older (and more depleted) mines, or paid lower wages for Chinese laborers. Throughout the 1850s, the U.S. government restricted naturalization for immigrants of non-white status, placing Chinese immigrants in limbo.

By the 1860s, a substantial number of Chinese immigrants worked as railroad construction laborers; after the Civil War, and in the early 1870s when an economic depression affected the U.S., Chinese laborers were viewed by poor whites and former slaves as interlopers who took jobs away from native-born Americans. Anti-Chinese sentiment increased dramatically throughout the 1870s, as incidents of mob violence against Chinese immigrants in Colorado, California, and Washington demonstrated increasing prejudice. An 1877 report from the Joint Special Committee to Investigate Chinese Immigration documented native beliefs that Chinese workers took American jobs, that Chinese immigrants were unable to support and function in a democracy, and that the Chinese refused to learn English. By the early 1880s, Congress was prepared to curb Chinese immigration in spite of diplomatic relations with China in which the Chinese government expressed disapproval of these actions. In 1882, Congress passed The Chinese Exclusion Act.

■ **PRIMARY SOURCE**

CHINESE EXCLUSION ACT

An Act to execute certain treaty stipulations relating to Chinese
Whereas in the opinion of the Government of the United States the coming of Chinese laborers to this country endangers the good order of certain localities within the territory thereof: Therefore,

A cartoon critical of the Chinese Exclusion Act of 1882 depicts the United States building a wall against Chinese immigration—using bricks of jealousy and non-reciprocity and "congressional mortar"—at the same time that China is tearing down a wall against trade with the United States. THE LIBRARY OF CONGRESS.

Be it enacted by the Senate and House of Representatives of the United States of America in Congress assembled, That from and after the expiration of ninety days next after the passage of this act, and until the expiration of ten years next after the passage of this act, the coming of Chinese laborers to the United States be, and the same is hereby, suspended; and during such suspension it shall not be lawful for any Chinese laborer to come, or having so come after the expiration of said ninety days to remain within the United States.

SEC. 2. That the master of any vessel who shall knowingly bring within the United States on such vessel, and land or permit to be landed, any Chinese laborer, from any foreign port or place, shall be deemed guilty of a misdemeanor, and on conviction thereof shall be punished by a fine of not more than five hundred dollars for each and every such Chinese laborer so brought, and maybe also imprisoned for a term not exceeding one year.

SEC. 3. That the two foregoing sections shall not apply to Chinese laborers who were in the United States on the seventeenth day of November, eighteen hundred and eighty, or who shall have come into the same before the expiration of ninety days next after the passage of this act, and who shall produce to such master before going on board such vessel, and shall produce to the collector of the port in the United States at which such vessel shall arrive, the evidence hereinafter in this act required of his being one of the laborers in this section mentioned; nor shall the two foregoing sections apply to the case of any master whose vessel, being bound to a port not within the United States, shall come within the jurisdiction of the United States by reason of being in distress or in stress of weather, or touching at any port of the United States on its voyage to any foreign port or place: Provided, That all Chinese laborers brought on such vessel shall depart with the vessel on leaving port.

SEC. 4. That for the purpose of properly identifying Chinese laborers who were in the United States on the seventeenth day of November eighteen hundred and eighty, or who shall have come into the same before the expiration of ninety days next after the passage of this act, and in order to furnish them with the proper evidence of their right to go from and come to the United States of their free will and accord, as provided by the treaty between the United States and China dated November seventeenth, eighteen hundred and eighty, the collector of customs of the district from which any such Chinese laborer shall depart from the United States shall, in person or by deputy, go on board each vessel having on board any such Chinese laborers and cleared or about to sail from his district for a foreign port, and on such vessel make a list of all such Chinese laborers, which shall be entered in registry-books to be kept for that purpose, in which shall be stated the name, age, occupation, last place of residence, physical marks of peculiarities, and all facts necessary for the identification of each of such Chinese laborers, which books shall be safely kept in the custom-house; and every such Chinese laborer so departing from the United States shall be entitled to, and shall receive, free of any charge or cost upon application therefor, from the collector or his deputy, at the time such list is taken, a certificate, signed by the collector or his deputy and attested by his seal of office, in such form as the Secretary of the Treasury shall prescribe, which certificate shall contain a statement of the name, age, occupation, last place of residence, personal description, and facts of identification of the Chinese laborer to whom the certificate is issued, corresponding with the said list and registry in all particulars. In case any Chinese laborer after having received such certificate shall leave such vessel before her departure he shall deliver his certificate to the master of the vessel, and if such Chinese laborer shall fail to return to such vessel before her departure from port the certificate shall be delivered by the master to the collector of customs for cancellation. The certificate herein provided for shall entitle the Chinese laborer to whom the same is issued to return to and re-enter the United States upon producing and delivering the same to the collector of customs of the district at which such Chinese laborer shall seek to re-enter; and upon delivery of such certificate by such Chinese laborer to the collector of customs at the time of re-entry in the United States said collector shall cause the same to be filed in the custom-house and duly canceled.

SEC. 5. That any Chinese laborer mentioned in section four of this act being in the United States, and desiring to depart from the United States by land, shall have the right to demand and receive, free of charge or cost, a certificate of identification similar to that provided for in section four of this act to be issued to such Chinese laborers as may desire to leave the United States by water; and it is hereby made the duty of the collector of customs of the district next adjoining the foreign country to which said Chinese laborer desires to go to issue such certificate, free of charge or cost, upon application by such Chinese laborer, and to enter the same upon registry-books to be kept by him for the purpose, as provided for in section four of this act.

SEC. 6. That in order to the faithful execution of articles one and two of the treaty in this act before mentioned, every Chinese person other than a laborer who may be entitled by said treaty and this act to come within the United States, and who shall be about to come to the United States, shall be identified as so entitled by the Chinese Government in each case, such identity to be evidenced by a certificate issued under the authority of said government, which certificate shall be in the English language or (if not in the English language) accompanied by a translation into English, stating such right to come, and which certificate shall state the name, title or official rank, if any, the age, height, and all physical peculiarities, former and present occupation or profession, and place of residence in China of the person to whom the certificate is issued and that such person is entitled, conformably to the treaty in this act mentioned to come within the United States. Such certificate shall be prima-facie evidence of the fact set forth therein, and shall be produced to the collector of customs, or his deputy, of the port in the district in the United States at which the person named therein shall arrive.

SEC. 7. That any person who shall knowingly and falsely alter or substitute any name for the name written in such certificate or forge any such certificate, or knowingly utter any forged or fraudulent certificate, or falsely personate any person named in any such certificate, shall be deemed guilty of a misdemeanor; and upon conviction thereof shall be fined in a sum not exceeding one thousand dollars, and imprisoned in a penitentiary for a term of not more than five years.

SEC. 8. That the master of any vessel arriving in the United States from any foreign port or place shall, at the same time he delivers a manifest of the cargo, and if there be no cargo, then at the time of making a report of the entry of the vessel pursuant to law, in addition to the other matter required to be reported, and before landing, or permitting to land, any Chinese passengers, deliver and report to the collector of customs of the district in which such vessels shall have arrived a separate list of all Chinese passengers taken on board his vessel at any foreign port or place, and all such passengers on board the vessel at that time. Such list shall show the names of such passengers (and if accredited officers of the Chinese Government traveling on the business of that government, or their servants, with a note of such facts), and the names and other particulars, as shown by their respective certificates; and such list shall be sworn to by the master in the manner required by law in relation to the manifest of the cargo. Any willful refusal or neglect of any such master to comply with the provisions of this section shall incur the same penalties and forfeiture as are provided for a refusal or neglect to report and deliver a manifest of the cargo.

SEC. 9. That before any Chinese passengers are landed from any such line vessel, the collector, or his deputy, shall proceed to examine such passenger, comparing the certificate with the list and with the passengers; and no passenger shall be allowed to land in the United States from such vessel in violation of law.

SEC. 10. That every vessel whose master shall knowingly violate any of the provisions of this act shall be deemed forfeited to the United States, and shall be liable to seizure and condemnation in any district of the United States into which such vessel may enter or in which she may be found.

SEC. 11. That any person who shall knowingly bring into or cause to be brought into the United States by land, or who shall knowingly aid or abet the same, or aid or abet the landing in the United States from any vessel of any Chinese person not lawfully entitled to enter the United States, shall be deemed guilty of a misdemeanor, and shall, on conviction thereof, be fined in a sum not exceeding one thousand dollars, and imprisoned for a term not exceeding one year.

SEC. 12. That no Chinese person shall be permitted to enter the United States by land without producing to the proper officer of customs the certificate in this act required of Chinese persons seeking to land from a vessel. And any Chinese person found unlawfully within the United States shall be caused to be removed therefrom to the country from whence he came, by direction of the President of the United States, and at the cost of the United States, after being brought before some justice, judge, or commissioner of a court of the United States and found to be one not lawfully entitled to be or remain in the United States.

SEC. 13. That this act shall not apply to diplomatic and other officers of the Chinese Government traveling upon the business of that government, whose credentials shall be taken as equivalent to the certificate in this act mentioned, and shall exempt them and their body and household servants from the provisions of this act as to other Chinese persons.

SEC. 14. That hereafter no State court or court of the United States shall admit Chinese to citizenship; and all laws in conflict with this act are hereby repealed.

SEC. 15. That the words "Chinese laborers," wherever used in this act shall be construed to mean both skilled and unskilled laborers and Chinese employed in mining.

Approved, May 6, 1882.

SIGNIFICANCE

The Chinese Exclusion Act revised laws from 1880 restricting Chinese immigration and ended the provisions of the 1868 Burlingame Treaty. Under the Chinese Exclusion Act, laborers were barred from entering the country for ten years, and Chinese immigrants were prevented from becoming naturalized citizens. The act—the first piece of federal legislation that singled out one immigrant group—dictated Chinese immigration for the next sixty years.

As a result of the act, Chinese immigration dropped from nearly 40,000 per year to less than one hundred legal Chinese immigrants per year. Later revisions prohibited Chinese workers who had left the United States to visit China from re-entering the country and restricted the ability to bring spouses from China to the U.S.

In 1892, despite vocal opposition from Chinese business organizations, missionary groups, and some native-born supporters of Chinese immigrant rights, the Exclusion Act was renewed. The new version was called the Geary Act, and in addition to the provisions of the Exclusion Act, the Geary Act stripped Chinese immigrants of the right to post bail or to act as a witness in court.

The Chinese government, angered by the restrictions but hopeful for U.S. aid in foreign relations with Russia as well as trade, criticized the act but did nothing to stop it. Congregationalist missionaries, represented by the American Missionary Association, feared retaliation against Americans in China when the 1882 act was up for renewal.

Small Chinese immigrant communities continued in spite of the act; "Chinatowns" helped maintain a sense of Chinese community in major cities such as San Francisco, though birth rates declined as the population—largely male—aged, and Chinese brides were not permitted to enter the country. The 1924 immigration law restricted legal immigration to no more than one hundred Chinese per year, and in 1943 the Magnuson Act repealed the strictest provisions of the 1882 Exclusion Act. The Immigration Act of 1965 finally placed Chinese immigrants on equal status with immigrants from other parts of the world seeking residency in the U.S.

FURTHER RESOURCES
Books

Claiming America: Constructing Chinese Identities During the Exclusion Era, edited by K. Scott Wong and Sucheng Chan. Philadelphia: Temple University Press, 1998.

Gyory, Andrew. *Closing the Gate: Race, Politics, and the Chinese Exclusion Act.* Chapel Hill, N.C.: University of North Carolina Press, 1998.

Lee, Erika. *At America's Gates: Chinese Immigration During the Exclusion Era, 1882–1943.* Chapel Hill, N.C.: University of North Carolina Press, 2003.

Web sites

National Archives and Records Administration. "Chinese Immigration and the Chinese in the United States." <http://www.archives.gov/locations/finding-aids/chinese-immigration.html> (accessed June 26, 2006).

Rosa Cavalleri: From Northern Italy to Chicago, 1884–1926

Book excerpt

By: Marie Hall Ets

Date: 1970

Source: Ets, Marie Hall. *Rosa: The Life of an Italian Immigrant.* Madison: University of Wisconsin Press, 1970.

About the Author: Marie Hall Ets was born in Wisconsin in 1895. She was best known as a writer and illustrator of children's books and won many awards for her work. In 1918, she became a social worker in a settlement home in Chicago, where she met Rosa Cavalleri. Rosa told her many stories of her early life in an Italian village and of her arrival in America in 1884. Ets published these stories in 1970 as *Rosa, the Life of an Italian Immigrant.*

INTRODUCTION

This is an excerpt from the biography of Rosa Cavelleri, an Italian immigrant who arrived in America at the height of European immigration in the late nineteenth century, when she was eighteen years old. Born in a silk-making village in Lombardy, Rosa was an orphan who was brought up by various foster parents. At the age of sixteen, she was married off to a brutal older man called Santino. Shortly after their wedding, Santino joined a work gang who went to America for work in the Missouri iron mines. He soon sent a ticket for Rosa to join him there so that she could keep house for him and the other miners. She reluctantly left Italy in 1884 with other young women who were going to join husbands or fiancés in the United States.

Although the early waves of European immigration to the United States had been from western and northern Europe, by 1890 immigrants from these areas were equaled in number by southern and eastern Europeans, especially Italians, Greeks, and Eastern European Jews. Within a few years, they accounted for two-thirds of all immigrants to the United States. While economic stability in northern Europe was reducing emigration, in the south and east a number of factors contributed to its increase. These included, for example, the displacement of rural people as a result of industrialization, unemployment, poverty, high taxation, and compulsory military service.

In Italy, labor migration to nearby countries was already commonplace. In the mid-nineteenth century, America became a viable alternative with the development of the steamship, which greatly shortened journeys. In addition, many steamship companies competed against each other to offer cheap fares. With high levels of poverty and unemployment in Italy, many Italians took advantage of the opportunity to find employment and a better life in America.

Often men emigrated first, with their wives and other family members joining them later, when the men had saved up enough money to pay for their fares. However, many single Italian women also immigrated to America, either to join their fiancés there, or to live with relatives. One factor that affected women's migration from Italy was their parents' increasing difficulty in providing a dowry, which in some areas of the country was expected to consist of a house, land, or furnishings. Between 1881 and 1890, around a fifth of Italian immigrants to the United States were women, but this percentage increased to thirty-nine percent between 1921 and 1930. Family networks also brought many Italians to America, forming the bases of Italian communities that developed in New York and other cities.

The Italian government also encouraged labor migration to the United States. Officially, men who were liable for military service were banned from emigrating. However, this policy was not effectively enforced, due partly to the weak authority of the newly established government in a country only recently unified, and partly because the money emigrants sent back to Italian families helped the Italian economy. Over time, the government introduced measures to facilitate migration, introducing a literacy program in 1901 to help migrants pass the tests being proposed as a condition of entry to the United States and recommending the establishment of employment offices for Italian immigrants in New York, to help them secure jobs there.

At the time of Rosa Cavelleri's emigration, Castle Garden was the main immigrant processing center for the steerage-class immigrants to the eastern United States. It was already very rundown, and immigrants were often exploited by the many concessionaires based there who charged exorbitant prices for food and transport. In 1892, Castle Garden was closed and replaced by the much more welcoming, architecturally grand Ellis Island immigration station. This was operated by the federal government and had a much higher standard of facilities.

Rose Cavalleri eventually managed to escape from her abusive husband and worked for more than forty years as a cook and cleaner at the Chicago Commons Settlement, where she met Marie Hall Ets.

PRIMARY SOURCE

The Trip to America The day came when we had to go and everyone was in the square saying good-bye. I had my Francesco in my arms. I was kissing his lips and kissing his cheeks and kissing his eyes. Maybe I would never see him again! It wasn't fair! He was my baby! Why should Mamma Lena keep him? But then Pep was calling and Mamma Lena took Francesco away and Zia Teresa was helping me onto the bus and handing up the bundles.

"But Rosa, don't be so sad!" It was the other Rosa and Zia Maria in the station in Milan, kissing me good-bye and patting my shoulder. "It is wonderful to go to America even if you don't want to go to Santino. You will get smart in America. And in America you will not be so poor."

Then Paris and we were being crowded into a train for Havre. We were so crowded we couldn't move, but my paesani were just laughing. "Who cares?" they laughed. "On our way to America! On our way to be millionaires!"

Day after day in Havre we were leaving the lodging house and standing down on the docks waiting for a ship to take us. But always the ship was full before it came our turn. "O Madonna!" I prayed. "Don't ever let there be room! Don't ever let there be room!"

But here, on the sixth day we came on. We were almost the last ones. There was just one young French girl after us. She was with her mother and her sister, but when the mother and sister tried to follow, the marinaro at the gate said, "No more! Come on the next boat!" And that poor family was screaming and crying. But the marinaro wouldn't let the girl off and wouldn't let the mother and sister on. He said, "You'll meet in New York. Meet in New York."

All us poor people had to go down through hole to the bottom of the ship. There was a big dark room down there with rows of wooden shelves all around where we were

going to sleep—the Italian, the German, the Polish, the Swedes, the French—every kind. And in that time the third class on the boat was not like now. The girls and women and the men had to sleep all together in the same room. The men and girls had to sleep even in the same bed with only those little half-boards up between to keep us from rolling together. But I was lucky. I had two girls sleeping next to me. When the dinner bell rang we were all standing in line holding the tin plates we had to buy in Havre, waiting for soup and bread.

"Oh, I'm so scared!" Emilia kept saying and she kept looking at the little picture she carried in her blouse. "I'm so scared!"

"Don't be scared, Emilia," I told her. "That young man looks nice in his picture."

"But I don't know him," she said. "I was only seven years old when he went away."

"Look at me," said the comical Francesca with her crooked teeth. "I'm going to marry a man I've never seen in my life. And he's not Lombardo—he's Toscano. But I'm not afraid."

Of course Francesca was not afraid "Crazy Francesca" they called her at the silk mill. She was so happy she was going to America and going to get married that she didn't care who the man was.

On the fourth day a terrible storm came. The sky grew black and the ocean came over the deck. Sailors started running everywhere, fastening this and fastening that and giving orders. Us poor people had to go below and that little door to the deck was fastened down. We had no light and no air and everyone got sick where we were. We were like rats trapped in a hole, holding onto the posts and onto the iron frames to keep from rolling around. Why had I worried about Santino? We were never going to come to America after all! We were going to the bottom of the sea!

But after three days the ship stopped rolling. That door to the deck was opened and some sailors came down and carried out two who had died and others too sick to walk. Me and all my paesani climbed out without help and stood in line at the wash-house, breathing fresh air and filling our basins with water. Then we were out on the narrow deck washing ourselves and our clothes—some of us women and girls standing like a wall around the others so the men couldn't see us.

Another time there was fog—so much fog that we couldn't see the masts and we couldn't see the ocean. The engine stopped and the sails were tied down and a horn that shook the whole boat started blowing. All day and all night that horn was blowing. No one could sleep so no one went to bed. One man had a concertina and the ones who knew how to dance were dancing to entertain the others. Me, I was the best one. There was no one there to scold me and tell me what to do so I danced with all my *paesani* who knew how. Then I even danced with some of the Polish and the French. We were like floating on a cloud in the middle of nowhere and when I was dancing I forgot for a little while that I was the wife of Santino going to him in America. But on the third day the fog left, the sails came out, the engine started, and the ship was going again. . . .

Then one day we could see land! Me and my *paesani* stood and watched the hills and the land come nearer. Other poor people, dressed in their best clothes and loaded down with bundles, crowded around. *America!* The country where everyone could find work! Where wages were so high no one had to go hungry! Where all men were free and equal and where even the poor could own land! But now we were so near it seemed too much to believe. Everyone stood silent—like in prayer. Big sea gulls landed on the deck and screamed and flew away.

Then we were entering the harbor. The land came so near we could almost reach out and touch it. "Look!" said one of the *paesani*. "Green grass and green trees and white sand—just like in the old country!" The others laughed—loud, not regular laughs—so that Pep wouldn't know that they too had expected things to be different. When we came through that narrow place and into the real harbor everyone was holding their breath. Me too. There were boats going everywhere—all sizes and all kinds. There were smoke chimneys smoking and white sails and flags waving and new paint shining. Some boats had bands playing on their decks and all of them were tooting their horns to us and leaving white trails in the water behind them.

"There!" said Pep, raising his hand in greeting. "There it is! *New York!*" . . .

"Look," said Pep. "Brooklyn Bridge! Just opened this year with fireworks and everything."

"And there's Castle Garden."

"Castle Garden! Castle Garden was the gate to the new land. Everyone wanted to see. But the ship was being pulled off to one side—away from the strange round building.

"Don't get scared," said Pep. "We go just to the pier up the river. Then a government boat brings us back."

Doctors had come on the ship and ordered us inside to examine our eyes and our vaccinations. One old man who couldn't talk and two girls with sore eyes were being sent back to the old country. "O Madonna, make them send me back too!" I prayed. "Don't make me go to Santino!"

About two hours later me and my *paesani* were back at Castle Garden on a government boat, bumping the dock and following Pep across a boardwalk and leaving our bundles with some officers. I wanted to hold onto my bottles of oil—they might get broken—but the officers

made me leave those too. Then one by one we went through a narrow door into Castle Garden. The inside was a big, dark room full of dust, with fingers of light coming down from the ceiling. That room was already crowded with poor people from earlier boats sitting on benches and on railings and on the floor. And to one side were a few old tables where food was being sold. Down the center between two railings high-up men were sitting on stools at high desks. And we had to walk in line between those two railings and pass them.

"What is your name? Where do you come from? Where are you going?"

Those men knew all the languages and could tell just by looking what country we come from.

After Pep, it was my turn.

"Cristoforo, Rosa. From Lombardy. To the iron mine in Missouri."

Emilia was holding me by the skirt, so I stayed a little behind to help her. "Gruffiano, Emilia. From San Paola. What *signore?* You don't know San Paola?"

"She's from Lombardy too," I said. "But she's going to stay in New York." . . .

"Get your baggage and come back. Wait by the visitors' door—there at the left. Your name will be called. All right. Move on!"

There were two other decks—one for railroad tickets and one for American money—but we *Lombardi* had ours already so we went back for our bundles.

We *Lombardi* put down our bundles and sat on the floor near the visitors' door. At last after all the new immigrants had been checked, an officer at the door started calling the names. "Gruffiano, Emilia" was the first one.

"Presente! Presente!" shouted Pep jumping to his feet and waving his hands. But Emilia was so scared I had to pull her up and drag her along after him.

At the door the officer called the name again and let us pass. Then here came up a young man. He was dressed—O Madonna!—like the president of the Untied States! White gloves and a cane and a diamond pin in his tie. Emilia tried to run away but Pep pulled her back. *"Non e vero! Non e vero!* It's not true!" she kept saying.

"But it *is* true!" the young man laughed. "Look at me, Emilia! Don't you remember Carlo who used to play the *tromba* in San Paola when you were a little girl?" And he pulled her out from behind us and took her in his arms and kissed her. (In America a man can kiss the girl he is going to marry!) "But I never thought you would come like this," he said, holding her of a little and looking at her headkerchief and full skirt. "I'm afraid to look. Did you come in the wooden soles too?"

"No," said Emilia, speaking to him for the first time. "My mother bought me real shoes to come to America!" And she was lifting her feet to show him.

"She looks just the same as when she was seven years old," the young man said to Pep, and he was happy and laughing. 'But I'm going to take her up Broad Street and buy her some American clothes before I take her home."

I was glad for Emilia that she was gong to marry that nice young man, but why couldn't something like this ever happen to me?

Other visitors were called. Some families separated at Havre found each other again and were happy. But that nice young French girl, she was there all alone—nobody could find her mother and her sister. I don't think they ever found each other again.

When the gate was opened men wearing badges came running in, going to the different people. One dressed-up man with a cane waxed mustache came to us. "*Buon giorno, paesani! Benvenuto!* Welcome to America! Welcome to the new country!" He was speaking Italian and English too and putting out his hand to shake hands with Pep. We other *paesani* looked on in wonder. A high man like that shaking hands with the poor! This was America for sure!

An Italian emigrant and her children arrive at Ellis Island in 1905.
© CORBIS-BETTMANN. REPRODUCED BY PERMISSION.

SIGNIFICANCE

Although most Italian immigrants had been agricultural workers from rural areas of Italy, once in America the majority stayed in the New York and New Jersey area and adapted to an urban lifestyle. They formed distinctive Italian communities within which there was further residential segregation among immigrants from different regions of Italy, reflecting the Italian tendency to associate themselves with an individual town or locality rather than their country. Most were housed in the tenements of lower Manhattan.

Some of the men secured jobs in construction and public service works and were involved in building, for example, the subway system and the New York sewer system. For the majority of Italian immigrants, life in America was harsh and did not offer the freedom from poverty and unemployment that they had expected. Italian women generally had to work to supplement the family income and gradually they dominated the hand-sewing and other non-mechanized jobs in the garment industry, working either in factories or in their homes while looking after children.

Although many Italian immigrants intended their stay in America to be a temporary one, and they did indeed return in higher numbers to their home country than other immigrant groups, it is estimated that around three-quarters of all Italian immigrants settled permanently in the United States. Unlike other immigrant groups, who gradually moved into mixed-immigrant communities, Italians have tended to remain within their "Little Italy" ethnic clusters. They also remain geographically concentrated within particular areas of the United States, especially the northeast and California.

Levels of emigration from Italy to America declined sharply from the 1920s onwards as a result of the quota system on immigration from different countries introduced under the 1924 Immigration Act; the majority of Italian-Americans in the United States today are the descendants of earlier immigrants.

FURTHER RESOURCES
Books

Bogen, Elizabeth. *Immigration in New York*. New York: Praeger Publishers, 1987.

Dublin, Thomas, ed. *Immigrant Voices: New Lives in America, 1773–1986*. Urbana: University of Illinois Press, 1993.

Ets, Marie Hall. *Rosa: The Life of an Italian Immigrant.* Madison: University of Wisconsin Press, 1999.

Friedman-Kasaba, Kathie. *Memories of Migration: Gender, Ethnicity, and Work in the Lives of Jewish and Italian Women in New York, 1870–1924.* Albany: State University of New York Press, 1996.

Web sites

Department of Translation Studies, University of Tampere. "Italian Immigration to the United States." January 2000 <http://www.uta.fi/FAST/US2/PAPS/db-italy.html> (accessed July 22, 2006).

Is It Right for a Chinaman to Jeopard a White Man's Dinner?

Editorial cartoon

By: T. Walter

Date: July–December 1885

Source: Walter, T. "Is It Right for a Chinaman to Jeopard a White Man's Dinner?" [back cover] *The Wasp* 15 (July–December 1885). Courtesy of the Library of Congress.

About the Artist: Little is known of the career of T. Walter, the artist who created the 1885 cartoon published in *The Wasp. The Wasp* was a San Francisco satirical magazine published between 1876 and 1928. Its often graphic and topical cartoons were a mainstay of the publication.

INTRODUCTION

In 1885, the city of San Francisco was at the epicenter of the debate that then raged concerning the position of Chinese immigrants in California society. Chinese laborers, known as "coolies," first began to arrive in significant numbers on the West Coast of the United States in the late 1840s, following reports of gold being discovered in California. Significant numbers of Chinese men worked on the construction of the American transcontinental railroad until its completion in 1869. The perception that grew into a belief on the part of the white majority in California into the 1870s was that the Chinese workers had taken away employment from the white laboring population.

In 1882, the federal government passed the Chinese Exclusion Act, a law that prohibited the immigration of Chinese persons for a period of ten years. The law was subsequently extended both in duration and to widen the immigrant population affected to include Japanese and Indian peoples.

In the vanguard of the media attacks upon the Chinese workforce in San Francisco was *The Wasp*, a magazine founded in 1876. The magazine regularly published both editorial cartoons and opinion articles that attacked the Chinese population in very blunt terms. *The Wasp* characterized the Chinese as not simply an economic issue in California, but as a threat to the stability and the social fabric of American society.

In the 1885 cartoon depicted here, the artist employed a number of symbols to convey his anti-Chinese theme. The Chinese figure is shown as a grasping, fearsome-looking individual, a threat to the white family seated at the dinner table awaiting the meal to be served to them by the goddess representing California. The artist has positioned California as barring the Chinese man from getting any closer to the table and the family, an image consistent with the function of the Exclusion Act.

The Wasp routinely depicted the Chinese through voracious and predatory symbols. "In the Clutches of the Chinese Tiger" (1885) is a multiple panel cartoon where the tiny tabby cat fed by a white family grows into a marauding beast. In 1897, *The Wasp* described the "heathen Chinee" and their lifestyle as being anti-American.

There were few journalistic influences to counter these sentiments in the latter portion of the nineteenth century in California. Journals such as *Harper's Weekly* were relatively balanced in their views in contrast to the invective of *The Wasp*, but even Harper's published a number of articles suggesting that in the 1880s in California, the Chinese workforce had crowded out an army of white labor.

PRIMARY SOURCE

IS IT RIGHT FOR A CHINAMAN TO JEOPARD A WHITE MAN'S DINNER?

See primary source image.

SIGNIFICANCE

The 1882 Chinese Exclusion Act was a far-reaching and influential piece of legislation. It created an absolute bar to Chinese immigration to the United States for a period of ten years. However, from the perspective of the publishers of *The Wasp* and their large constituency in California, the Act did not address the continuing negative impact of the existing Chinese workforce on the ability of white laborers to

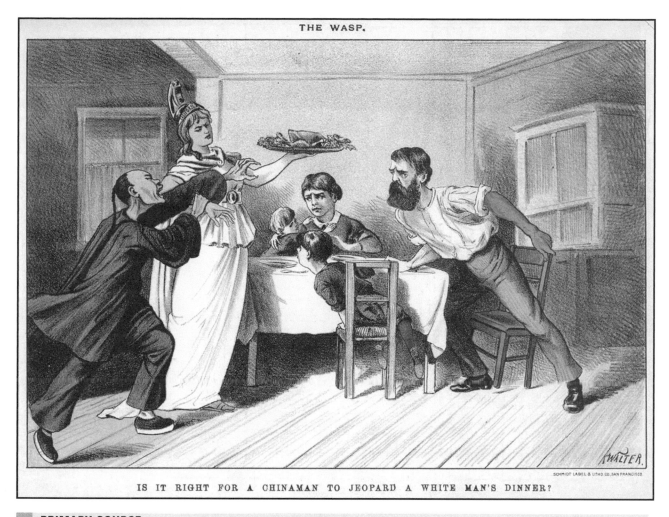

THE WASP.

IS IT RIGHT FOR A CHINAMAN TO JEOPARD A WHITE MAN'S DINNER?

■ **PRIMARY SOURCE**

Is It Right for a Chinaman to Jeopard a White Man's Dinner?: This cartoon from an 1885 edition of *The Wasp* reflects anti-Chinese prejudices common in America at the time. Fears that Chinese immigrants would take jobs and livelihoods away from native born Americans are depicted by a caricatured Chinese man stealing the dinner of a white family. THE LIBRARY OF CONGRESS.

succeed in the California economy of 1885. For the publishers of *The Wasp* and others, the best policy was the removal of the Chinese entirely from the state of California.

Chinese laborers often took jobs that were seen as menial or otherwise beneath the dignity of the predominately white population. This willingness to do jobs shunned by other laborers allowed Chinese workers to become established and successful in California and other western states. Industries such as domestic cleaning, cooking, and clothing manufacture had a significant Chinese workforce in California into the 1880s.

The sentiment of journals such as *The Wasp* did not so much stir public opinion as it reflected the majority view of the California population. The chief example of that anti-Chinese sentiment, the Chinese Exclusion Act, represents a turning point in the history of American attitudes towards immigration. Until 1882, the United States had permitted any race or ethnic group to immigrate. The Exclusion Act began a long period of American social policy during which significant immigration limits were placed upon Chinese, Japanese, Southeast Asian, and other minority groups.

When the Chinese Exclusion Act expired in 1892, it was extended for another ten years by the Geary Act. This act placed additional restrictions on Chinese residents of the United States by requiring them to register and obtain a certificate of residence. Without this

A cartoon caricatures Chinese immigrants to the United States circa 1880. © BETTMANN/CORBIS.

certificate, any Chinese person residing in the United States could be deported. The state of California placed its own restrictions on the Japanese community in 1909. There was little lessening in the antipathy felt towards the Asian communities generally in California as World War II approached. Thus, the internment of Japanese and Japanese-americans during World War II occurred against a backdrop of over sixty years of various limitations directed against Asian people.

The designation of the Chinese as outsiders to mainstream California society was the chief stimulus

in the creation of the San Francisco Chinatown in the 1880s. Chinatown became an enclave of Chinese culture that has remained vibrant to the present day.

In the midst of the significant anti-Chinese sentiment in San Francisco, a seminal immigration case was decided by the United States Supreme Court. In 1898, Wong Ark Kim, a twenty-two-year-old man born in San Francisco to Chinese parents, brought an action for a declaration that he was entitled to the full benefit of American citizenship. American government authorities had sought to deny Wong's re-entry into the United States when he returned from a trip to China. The Supreme Court ruled that notwithstanding the provisions of the Chinese Exclusion Act, the Fourteenth Amendment guarantees of equality applied to Wong because he was born in the United States. There are modern implications to this precedent, since the prospect remains that individuals may illegally enter the United States to ensure that their child is born in the United States. Such children will automatically be entitled to both American citizenship and the collateral benefits of public education and health care.

FURTHER RESOURCES

Books

Kwong, Peter. *Forbidden Workers: Chinese Immigrants and American Labor.* New York: New Press, 1998.

Lee, Erika. *At America's Gates: Chinese Immigration During the Exclusion Era.* Chapel Hill, N.C.: University of North Carolina Press, 2003.

Web sites

Brechin, Gray. "The Wasp: Stinging Editorials and Political Cartoons." *Bancroftiana,* Fall 2002. <http://bancroft.berkeley.edu/events/bancroftiana/121/wasp.html> (accessed June 5, 2006).

Library of Congress/American Memory. "The Chinese in California 1850–1925." <http://memory.loc.gov/ammem/award99/cubhtml/cichome.html> (accessed June 5, 2006).

PBS. "Becoming American: The Chinese Experience." <http://www.pbs.org/becominganamerican/> (accessed June 5, 2006).

Invitation to the Inauguration of the Statue of Liberty by the President

Photograph

By: Anonymous

Date: October 28, 1886

Source: The White House. "Invitation to the Inauguration of the Statue of Liberty by the President." William Maxwell Evarts Papers, Library of Congress.

About the Photographer: The White House, as the official home of the current President of the United States, is responsible for issuing invitations to official state functions on his behalf. William Maxwell Evarts

(1818–1901) was the U.S. Secretary of State from 1876 to 1880 and a U.S. Senator from New York from 1885 to 1891. His voluminous correspondence and other papers are held in the Manuscript and Prints and Photographs Divisions of the Library of Congress.

INTRODUCTION

The Statue of Liberty was officially inaugurated on October 28, 1886. A gift to the United States from the people of France, the statue commemorates the relationship between the two nations that began during the American Revolution, and honors the countries' shared commitment to liberty and democracy. Designed by Frederic Auguste Bartholdi, the statue was intended to be completed in time for the centennial celebration of the signing of the Declaration of Independence in 1776, however financial difficulties slowed the process, both in France where the statue was to be built, and in America, where money needed to be raised to build the pedestal for the completed statue. Ultimately, the statue was completed in France in 1884, and the pedestal in New York in April 1886, allowing for the inauguration that October, with President Grover Cleveland presiding.

PRIMARY SOURCE

INVITATION TO THE INAUGURATION OF THE STATUE OF LIBERTY BY THE PRESIDENT

See primary source image.

SIGNIFICANCE

The Statue of Liberty, or Lady Liberty, was officially named "Statue of Liberty Enlightening the World." She holds a torch in one hand over her head, and in her other arm a tablet with July 4, 1776 inscribed in Roman numerals to mark the date that the Declaration of Independence was signed. Her crown has seven spikes, to represent the seven continents and the seven seas, and the chains beneath one of her feet are meant to represent newly acquired freedom. Not including the pedestal, the statue stands 151 feet high to the top of the torch, and weighs more than 150 tons. The pedestal adds an additional 154 feet and 27,000 tons to the monument. While the statue was designed by Bartholdi, the internal steel skeleton was engineered by Alexandre Gustave Eiffel, the man responsible for the Eiffel Tower in Paris. It consists of thin copper plates attached to wooden forms, which were then attached to the metal frame. For the trip to the United States, the statue was divided into three

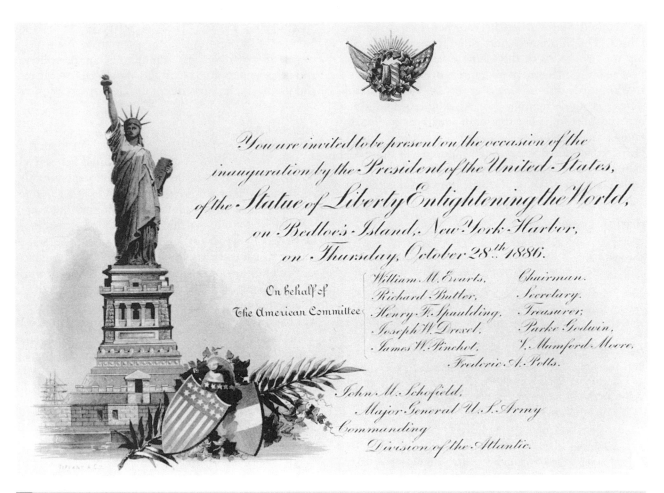

You are invited to be present on the occasion of the inauguration by the President of the United States, of the Statue of Liberty Enlightening the World, on Bedloe's Island, New York Harbor, on Thursday, October 28th 1886.

On behalf of The American Committee

William M. Evarts, Chairman.
Richard Butler, Secretary.
Henry F. Spaulding, Treasurer.
Joseph W. Drexel, Parke Godwin,
James W. Pinchot, V. Mumford Moore,
Frederic A. Potts.

John M. Schofield,
Major-General U.S. Army
Commanding
Division of the Atlantic.

PRIMARY SOURCE

Invitation to the Inauguration of the Statue of Liberty by the President: A photograph of an original invitation to the inauguration of the Statue of Liberty. REPRODUCED FROM THE COLLECTIONS OF THE LIBRARY OF CONGRESS.

hundred-fifty pieces and shipped in more than two hundred crates, then reassembled on the pedestal. The statue sits on what was once Bedloe's Island, until the nickname "Liberty Island" became so popular that it was made official in 1956. Visitors may visit a museum about the statue's history within the pedestal, and climb a spiral staircase inside the statue to an observation deck in the crown.

Although the Statue of Liberty eventually became a popular New York tourist destination, its origins are rooted in the beliefs of the nation: democracy, freedom, and opportunity. These beliefs were the reason so many immigrants risked long journeys by boat to come to the United States in the late nineteenth and early twentieth centuries, and the Statue of Liberty became the ultimate symbol of freedom to those immigrants when they first arrived in New York's harbor.

The inauguration speeches held in 1886 made no mention of immigration in relation to the statue, but they did focus on the idea of liberty, which was the foundation of the Declaration of Independence in the United States, and of the French Revolution, as well. However, Emma Lazarus, who wrote the poem "The New Colossus" that appears on a bronze plaque on the interior of the statue, recognized that the placement of the monument would be symbolic for immigrants. Her poem calls out to the world to send their poor and homeless, the struggling masses, promising that America will give them the chance to start a new life. The statue might have been intended as a representation of the friendship between France and America, but Lady Liberty provided a beacon and a welcome to every ship entering the New York harbor, and for an immigrant, would have been their first glimpse of the new country they planned to make their home.

Frederic-Auguste Bartholdi, creator of the Statue of Liberty, explains the inner construction of the statue's hand to a visitor. © BETTMANN/ CORBIS.

As air travel became more popular and immigration patterns shifted so that people were migrating from other parts of the world, the Statue of Liberty ceased to be the first indication that an immigrant had reached America. However, the statue itself remains iconic around the world, representing the freedom and democracy America promises its citizens, and the opportunities that Americans have to change their situation in life. Immigrants continue to consider the statue as a symbol of all the things they came to the United States to achieve and attain, and citizens consider it representative of the democratic principles on which the nation was founded. When accepting the statue from France on behalf of all Americans, President Grover Cleveland promised that the United States would continue to be the home of liberty. That concept was echoed and elaborated upon in 1986 during the centennial celebration of the statue,

when President Ronald Reagan reminded his audience that Lady Liberty, coming as she did from France, was an immigrant herself.

FURTHER RESOURCES

Books

Merriman, Eve. *Emma Lazarus Rediscovered*. New York: Biblio Press, 1999.

Provoyeur, Paul, and June Ellen Hargrove, eds. *Liberty: Th French-American Statue in Art and History*. New York: Perennial Library, 1986.

Weinbaum, Paul Owen. *Statue of Liberty: The Story Behind the Scenery*. Las Vegas: K.C. Publishing, 1988.

Web sites

Great Buildings.com. "The Statue of Liberty." 2006 <http://www.greatbuildings.com/buildings/Statue_of_Liberty.html> (accessed June 24, 2006).

Library of Congress. "A Century of Immigration: 1820–1934." September 7, 2005 <http://www.loc.gov/exhibits/haventohome/haven-century.html> (accessed June 24, 2006).

Statue of Liberty-Ellis Island Foundation, Inc. "Statue History." <http://www.statueofliberty.org/Statue_History.html> (accessed June 24, 2006).

University of Texas: Reagan Archive. "Remarks at the Opening Ceremonies of the Statue of Liberty Centennial Celebration in New York, New York" July 3, 1986 <http://www.reagan.utexas.edu/archives/speeches/1986/70386d.htm> (accessed June 24, 2006).

The New Colossus

Book

By: Emma Lazarus

Date: 1883

Source: Lazarus, Emma. "The New Colossus" in *100 Greatest Poems by Women.* The Ecco Press, 1995.

About the Author: Emma Lazarus (1849–1887) was one of the earliest successful Jewish American authors. She was born in New York City and became part of the elite literary circle of her time. In addition to writing her own poetry, she translated the works of other authors, particularly the poems of German Jewish poet Heinrich Heine. Lazarus became increasingly involved in speaking out for Jewish rights and against anti-Semitism in her later years, prompted in part by the plight of Russian Jews who were being killed in pogroms, and was one of the first people to voice the idea of a Jewish homeland years prior to the start of the Zionist movement.

INTRODUCTION

Emma Lazarus's poem, "The New Colossus," was written in 1883, and included as a donation in an arts auction that was intended to raise capital in order to finance the construction of a pedestal for the Statue of Liberty. Lazarus was hesitant to participate in the project at first, but later agreed when she learned what an important image the statue would project for new immigrants just arriving by boat in New York harbor. The poem was later inscribed on a bronze plaque and mounted inside of the pedestal itself, and Lazarus's words helped to cement the statue's role as the first sign that immigrants had reached the end of their journey to America.

PRIMARY SOURCE

Not like the brazen giant of Greek fame
With conquering limbs astride from land to land;
Here at our sea-washed, sunset gates shall stand
A mighty woman with a torch, whose flame
Is the imprisoned lightning, and her name
Mother of Exiles. From her beacon-hand
Glows world-wide welcome; her mild eyes command
The air-bridged harbor that twin cities frame,
"Keep, ancient lands, your storied pomp!" cries she
With silent lips. "Give me your tired, your poor,
Your huddled masses yearning to breathe free,
The wretched refuse of your teeming shore,
Send these, the homeless, tempest-tossed to me,
I lift my lamp beside the golden door!"

SIGNIFICANCE

Immigration to the United States increased dramatically during the nineteenth century, due to a combination of the improved speed and safety of travel methods, and the political and economic situations in much of Europe. From the late 1880s on, the first indication that most immigrants had that they were nearing shore was the Statue of Liberty. The statue itself, sculpted by Frederic Auguste Bartholdi, was a gift from the French government for America's centennial in 1876, to honor both France's and the United States' dedication to the idea and promise of liberty. Although the statue technically had no direct correlation to immigration, and no mention of immigration was made during the dedication ceremony, Emma Lazarus recognized that the placement of the statue made it a sort of symbolic guardian of the entrance to the nation, as well as a representation of all the things America stood for, and which immigrants sought out when they decided to risk the trip across the ocean. When writing her poem, "The New Colossus," Lazarus attempted to capture this spirit in her words, uniting the hopes and fears of the immigrants with the welcoming sentiment of the Statue of Liberty.

The opening phrase of Lazarus's poem, as well as the title itself, reference the Colossus of Rhodes, a giant statue of the Greek god Helios, the daily bearer of the sun, which was erected on the island of Rhodes between 290 and 283 B.C. The original statue was approximately the same height as the Statue of Liberty, and also stood positioned at the entrance to a harbor. The Colossus of Rhodes is considered one of the Seven Wonders of the Ancient World. In citing the similarity between the Colossus and the Statue of Liberty, Lazarus drew a comparison between the old world and the new one, and everything they each stood

Immigrants to the United States sail past the recently finished Statue of Liberty. THE LIBRARY OF CONGRESS.

for in the eyes of the people migrating from Europe to America. While the Colossus of Rhodes was the sun bearer, shining brightly over the harbor at Rhodes, the Statue of Liberty held the torch to light the way for the immigrants entering the United States. She offered them democracy, freedom, and a wealth of opportunities to recreate their lives. Many immigrants fled from persecution, due to religion and economic class, poverty, famine, and servitude. They were often the lowest members of society in their homelands, barely able to scrape together the fare to pay for the voyage. Those who were slightly better off were still searching for a better life, away from the political whims of royalty and the harsh working conditions that never allowed them to improve their situation. Lazarus calls these immigrants tired, poor, and wretched; she refers to them as refuse and homeless. While the tone can be considered harsh, it still offers hope. There is a door to the new world, an entrance through New York harbor, and the Statue of Liberty holds the light to shine the way.

Though born in the United States, Emma Lazarus became passionately involved in the plight of immigrants, and in the mistreatment of people in other parts of the world. She spoke actively for Jewish rights, despite having been raised very much without religion, and incorporated Jewish and immigrant themes into her writing even before she became an activist. She used her popularity as a poet to get her message across to as broad an audience as possible, speaking out against anti-Semitism and the use of stereotypes that encouraged people to continue in their prejudiced thinking against Jews. Although the words of "The New Colossus" can easily be applied to the majority of European immigrants coming to America through Ellis Island in the late eighteenth and early nineteenth centuries, it is possible to see how Lazarus could have been applying them to a very specific portion of the immigrant population: the people suffering from brutal persecution that Lazarus could have experienced herself had she been born in a different part of the world.

FURTHER RESOURCES
Books

Merriman, Eve. *Emma Lazarus Rediscovered*. New York: Biblio Press, 1999.

Weinbaum, Paul Owen. *Statue of Liberty: The Story Behind the Scenery*. Haddonfield, NJ: K.C. Publishing, 1988.

Web sites

Jewish Women's Archive. "Exhibit: Women of Valour: Emma Lazarus." 2006 <http://www.jwa.org/exhibits/wov/lazarus/el12.html> (accessed June 20, 2006).

U.S. State Department. "The New Colossus." <http://usinfo.state.gov/usa/infousa/facts/democrac/63.htm> (accessed June 22, 2006).

The Mixed Crowd

Book excerpt

By: Jacob A. Riis

Date: 1890

Source: Riis, Jacob A. "The Mixed Crowd." In *How the Other Half Lives.* New York: Charles Scribner's Sons, 1890.

About the Author: Jacob Riis was a Danish immigrant and photojournalist who documented the New York slums. He was also a reformer for New York slums and schools.

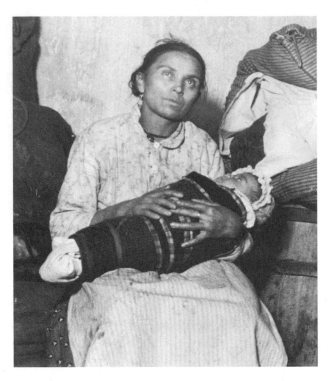

A picture taken by Jacob Riis titled "Madonna of the Slums," in New York, New York, 1890. © BETTMANN/CORBIS.

INTRODUCTION

In 1864, a group of concerned citizens took a survey of New York and found that 495,592 people lived in tenements—more than half the population. By the 1860s, the population of New York exploded with the influx of immigrants into the city. Buildings were erected, en masse, to accommodate large numbers of these families. Hundreds of these buildings were constructed, mostly in Manhattan, on the Lower East Side and in southern Manhattan. By the year 1900, nearly all of New York City's residents lived in tenements. Tenements were the first multiple dwellings and were built primarily for poor immigrant families.

The first tenements were erected on 25-foot-wide (7.6-meter-wide) lots. Usually they were constructed with four apartments per floor, with three rooms per apartment. There were no extras—no running water, light, or ventilation. The largest apartments were no more than 325 square feet (30 square meters). There was no privacy—one often had to walk through a bedroom to access another room. About twenty to twenty-two families lived in one building; this contributed to crowding and poor conditions. There were no building codes or requirements. In 1867, the first tenement law was passed with the aim of improving sanitation and ventilation. In 1879, a new law requiring a window in each room of newly constructed tenements was passed. In response, dumbbell tenements were built so that interior rooms could include windows opening onto ventilation shafts. These dumbbell-shaped buildings proved to be worse than the older, unregulated tenements. In 1901, in response to the failure of dumbbell tenements, another law was passed that required every room to have a window that looked out onto a street, yard, or courtyard. This law also made it difficult for investors to build on 25-foot lots.

Conditions eventually improved for some due to the introduction of model tenements, east river houses, and later union housing. The first model tenement was built by Alfred Tredway White, a successful businessman and member of the Unitarian Church. He constructed buildings for the working poor—people that worked hard but simply could not afford decent housing. In order to qualify for this housing, families must have two parents, show proof of employment, and not have social problems such as alcoholism. In contrast to earlier tenements, these apartments had running water, cross-ventilation, and windows that faced a street or large courtyard. They also had baths in the basement (a luxury in a time when most poor people had no access to bathing facilities). Model tenements were also constructed to house solely African-American families. In addition, East River houses were built primarily for families caring for a loved one with tuberculosis.

As time progressed into the early and mid-twentieth century, more housing was introduced in response to these problems. Citizens debated whether housing was the responsibility of the private individual or the government. In response, union, government, and federal housing was constructed from the 1920s through the 1930s.

New York housing reform spurred the development of improved residential housing for its diverse population. The first tenement studies were conducted by several groups and individuals, including an activist from the Council of Hygiene and Public Health in 1864 and Jacob A. Riis in 1890. Jacob Riis was a Danish immigrant and reporter who documented the New York slums in two works, *How the Other Half Lives* and *Battle with the Slums*. The famous *How the Other Half Lives* inspired public compassion and solidified Riis as an accomplished photojournalist, reporter, and reformer.

PRIMARY SOURCE

WHEN once I asked the agent of a notorious Fourth Ward alley how many people might be living in it I was told: One hundred and forty families, one hundred Irish, thirty-eight Italian, and two that spoke the German tongue. Barring the agent herself, there was not a native-born individual in the court. The answer was characteristic of the cosmopolitan character of lower New York, very nearly so of the whole of it, wherever it runs to alleys and courts. One may find for the asking an Italian, a German, French, African, Spanish, Bohemian, Russian, Scandinavian, Jewish, and Chinese colony. Even the Arab, who peddles "holy earth" from the Battery as a direct importation from Jerusalem, has his exclusive preserves at the lower end of Washington Street. The one thing you shall vainly ask for in the chief city of America is a distinctively American community. There is none; certainly not among the tenements. Where have they gone to, the old inhabitants? I put the question to one who might fairly be presumed to be of the number, since I had found him sighing for the "good old days" when the legend "no Irish need apply" was familiar in the advertising columns of the newspapers. He looked at me with a puzzled air. "I don't know," he said. "I wish I did. Some went to California in '49, some to the war and never came back. The rest, I expect, have gone to heaven, or somewhere. I don't see them 'round here."

Whatever the merit of the good man's conjectures, his eyes did not deceive him. They are not here. In their place has come this queer conglomerate mass of heterogeneous elements, ever striving and working like whiskey and water in one glass, and with the like result: final union and a prevailing taint of whiskey. The once unwelcome Irishman has been followed in his turn by the Italian, the Russian Jew, and the Chinaman, and has himself taken a hand at opposition, quite as bitter and quite as ineffectual, against these later hordes. Wherever these have gone they have crowded him out, possessing the block, the street, the ward with their denser swarms. But the Irishman's revenge is complete. Victorious in defeat over his recent as over his more ancient foe, the one who opposed his coming no less than the one who drove him out, he dictates to both their politics, and, secure in possession of the offices, returns the native his greeting with interest, while collecting the rents of the Italian whose house he has bought with the profits of his saloon. As a landlord he is picturesquely autocratic. An amusing instance of his methods came under my notice while writing these lines. An inspector of the Health Department found an Italian family paying a man with a Celtic name twenty-five dollars a month for three small rooms in a ramshackle rear tenement—more than twice what they were worth—and expressed his astonishment to the tenant, an ignorant Sicilian laborer. He replied that he had once asked the landlord to reduce the rent, but he would not do it.

"Well! What did he say?" asked the inspector. "'damma, man!' he said: 'if you speaka thata way to me, I fira you and your things in the streeta.'" And the frightened Italian paid the rent. In justice to the Irish landlord it must be said that like an apt pupil he was merely showing forth the result of the schooling he had received, re-enacting, in his own way, the scheme of the tenements. It is only his frankness that shocks. The Irishman does not naturally take kindly to tenement life, though with characteristic versatility he adapts himself to its conditions at once. It does violence, nevertheless, to the best that is in him, and for that very reason of all who come within its sphere soonest corrupts him. The result is a sediment, the product of more than a generation in the city's slums, that, as distinguished from the large body of his class, justly ranks at the foot of tenement dwellers, the so-called "low Irish."

It is not to be assumed, of course, that the whole body of the population living in the tenements, of which New Yorkers are in the habit of speaking vaguely as "the poor," or even the larger part of it, is to be classed as vicious or as poor in the sense of verging on beggary.

New York's wage-earners have no other place to live, more is the pity. They are truly poor for having no better homes; waxing poorer in purse as the exorbitant rents to which they are tied, as ever was serf to soil, keep rising. The wonder is that they are not all corrupted, and speedily, by their surroundings If, on the contrary, there be a steady working up, if not out of the slough, the fact is a powerful argument for the optimist's belief that the world is, after all, growing better, not worse, and would go far toward disarming apprehension, were it not for the steadier growth of the sediment of the slums and its constant menace. Such an impulse toward better things there certainly is. The German rag-picker of thirty years ago, quite as low in the scale as his Italian successor, is the thrifty tradesman or prosperous farmer of to-day.

The Italian scavenger of our time is fast graduating into exclusive control of the corner fruit-stands, while his black-eyed boy monopolizes the boot-blacking industry in which a few years ago he was an intruder. The Irish hod-carrier in the second generation has become a brick-layer, if not the Alderman of his ward, while the Chinese coolie is in almost exclusive possession of the laundry business. The reason is obvious. The poorest immigrant comes here with the purpose and ambition to better himself and, given half a chance, might be reasonably expected to make the most of it. To the false plea that he prefers the squalid homes in which his kind are housed there could be no better answer. The truth is, his half chance has too long been wanting, and for the bad result he has been unjustly blamed.

As emigration from east to west follows the latitude, so does the foreign influx in New York distribute itself along certain well-defined lines that waver and break only under the stronger pressure of a more gregarious race or the encroachments of inexorable business. A feeling of dependence upon mutual effort, natural to strangers in a strange land, unacquainted with its language and customs, sufficiently accounts for this.

The Irishman is the true cosmopolitan immigrant. Allpervading, he shares his lodging with perfect impartiality with the Italian, the Greek, and the "Dutchman," yielding only to sheer force of numbers, and objects equally to them all. A map of the city, colored to designate nationalities, would show more stripes than on the skin of a zebra, and more colors than any rainbow. The city on such a map would fall into two great halves, green for the Irish prevailing in the West Side tenement districts, and blue for the Germans on the East Side. But intermingled with these ground colors would be an odd variety of tints that would give the whole the appearance of an extraordinary crazy-quilt. From down in the Sixth Ward, upon the site of the old Collect Pond that in the days of the fathers drained the hills which are no more, the red of the Italian would be seen forcing its way northward along the line of Mulberry Street to the quarter of the French purple on Bleecker Street and South Fifth Avenue, to lose itself and reappear, after a lapse of miles, in the "Little Italy" of Harlem, east of Second Avenue. Dashes of red, sharply defined, would be seen strung through the Annexed District, northward to the city line. On the West Side the red would be seen overrunning the old Africa of Thompson Street, pushing the black of the negro rapidly uptown, against querulous but unavailing protests, occupying his home, his church, his trade and all, with merciless impartiality. There is a church in Mulberry Street that has stood for two generations as a sort of milestone of these migrations. Built orginally for the worship of staid New Yorkers of the "old stock," it was engulfed by the colored tide, when the draft-riots drove the negroes out of reach of Cherry Street and the Five Points. Within the past decade the advance wave of the Italian onset reached it, and today the arms of United Italy adorn its front. The negroes have made a stand at several points along Seventh and Eighth Avenues; but their main body, still pursued by the Italian foe, is on the march yet, and the black mark will be found overshadowing today many blocks on the East Side, with One Hundredth Street as the centre, where colonies of them have settled recently.

Hardly less aggressive than the Italian, the Russian and Polish Jew, having overrun the district between Rivington and Division Streets, east of the Bowery, to the point of suffocation, is filling the tenements of the old Seventh Ward to the river front, and disputing with the Italian every foot of available space in the back alleys of Mulberry Street. The two races, differing hopelessly in much, have this in common: they carry their slums with them wherever they go, if allowed to do it. Little Italy already rivals its parent, the "Bend," in foulness. Other nationalities that begin at the bottom make a fresh start when crowded up the ladder. Happily both are manageable, the one by rabbinical, the other by the civil law. Between the dull gray of the Jew, his favorite color, and the Italian red, would be seen squeezed in on the map a sharp streak of yellow, marking the narrow boundaries of Chinatown. Dovetailed in with the German population, the poor but thrifty Bohemian might be picked out by the sombre hue of his life as of his philosophy, struggling against heavy odds in the big human bee-hives of the East Side. Colonies of his people extend northward, with long lapses of space, from below the Cooper Institute more than three miles. The Bohemian is the only foreigner with any considerable representation in the city who counts no wealthy man of his race, none who has not to work hard for a living, or has got beyond the reach of the tenement.

Down near the Battery the West Side emerald would be soiled by a dirty stain, spreading rapidly like a splash of ink on a sheet of blotting paper, headquarters of the Arab tribe, that in a single year has swelled from the original dozen to twelve hundred, intent, every mother's son, on trade and barter. Dots and dashes of color here and there would show where the Finnish sailors worship their djumala (God), the Greek pedlars the ancient name of their race, and the Swiss the goddess of thrift. And so on to the end of the long register, all toiling together in the galling fetters of the tenement. Were the question raised who makes the most of life thus mortgaged, who resists most stubbornly its levelling tendency—knows how to drag even the barracks upward a part of the way at least toward the ideal plane of the home—the palm must be unhesitatingly awarded the Teuton. The Italian and the poor Jew rise only by compulsion. The Chinaman does not rise at all; here, as at home, he simply remains stationary. The Irishman's genius runs to public affairs rather than domestic life; wherever he is mustered in force the saloon is the gorgeous centre of political activity. The German struggles vainly to learn his trick; his Teutonic wit is too heavy, and the political ladder he raises from his saloon usually too short or too clumsy to reach the desired goal. The best part of his life is lived at home, and he makes himself a home independent of the surroundings, giving the lie to the saying, unhappily become a maxim of social truth, that pauperism and drunkenness naturally grow in the

tenements. He makes the most of his tenement, and it should be added that whenever and as soon as he can save up money enough, he gets out and never crosses the threshold of one again.

Note 1. The Sheriff Street Colony of rag-pickers, long since gone, is an instance in point. The thrifty Germans saved up money during years of hard work in squalor and apparently wretched poverty to buy a township in a Western State, and the whole colony moved out there in a body. There need be no doubt about their thriving there.

SIGNIFICANCE

Tenements were not only the center of family life for millions of poor immigrants; they were often turned into garment shops. Families turned their apartments into shops where they took on contract work for large manufacturers. Living conditions were

This 1880s photo by Jacob Riis shows a poor family in their tenement building apartment in New York City. © BETTMANN/CORBIS.

terrible—the combination of poor ventilation, crowding, moist air, and dust contributed to diseases such as tuberculosis and silicosis.

The slums became the center of national debate about work, family, and the role of immigrants in America. As of 2006, immigrants from thirty-six nations reside in the Lower East Side of Manhattan. At least thirty-six percent of the residents are foreign-born, and sixty percent speak a language other than English. Immigrants residing in America today continue to face the same challenges as their predecessors, including class bias, housing abuse, racism, and language barriers.

Initiatives such as Teaching English through History (provided by the Lower East Side Tenement Museum) and Immigrant Resource Guide (provided by the *New York Times* and St. Martin's Press) seek to address these issues and provide a dialogue to encourage public awareness.

FURTHER RESOURCES

Books

Hopkinson, Deborah. *Shutting Out the Sky: Life in the Tenements of New York, 1880–1924.* New York: Orchard, 2003.

Riis, Jacob A. *The Making of an American.* Honolulu, Hawaii: University Press of the Pacific, 2003.

Web sites

Columbia University Digital Knowledge Ventures. "The Architecture and Development of New York City: Living Together." <http://nycarchitecture.columbia.edu> (accessed June 28, 2006).

Tenement Museum. <http://www.thirteen.org/tenement/eagle.html> (accessed June 28, 2006).

From Russia to the Lower East Side in the 1890s

Essay

By: Rose Gollup Cohen

Date: 1918

Source: Reprinted in *Immigrant Voices: New Lives in America, 1773–1986.* Dublin, Thomas, ed. Urbana: University of Illinois Press, 1993.

About the Author: Rose Gollup Cohen (1880–1925) was a Jewish Russian immigrant who arrived in America

in 1892 at the age of twelve to join her father who had settled there a year earlier. She lived in a poor Jewish community on New York's Lower East Side and initially worked as a seamstress in a sweatshop. She began writing her autobiography *Out of the Shadow* soon after she arrived in the United States; it was published in 1918. She continued to write and to publish short stories until her death in 1925.

INTRODUCTION

This is an autobiographical account of a Russian Jewish immigrant's arrival and first experiences of living in America. Rose Gollup Cohen arrived in New York in 1892 as a young girl of twelve years old to join her father who was already living there. The family could not afford to migrate to America together, so Rose's father went first and saved up to pay the fares of his wife and children. Rose's mother reportedly joined them a year later.

Rose's emigration to America was part of a massive wave of Jewish immigration between 1881 and 1914. It was estimated that around two million Eastern European Jews entered the United States at this time. The main reason for the large-scale emigration of Jews from Eastern Europe was the economic and social persecution they were facing at that time, but other contributing factors were population pressures and the growing industrialization which was threatening traditional Jewish communities and livelihoods.

In the nineteenth century the majority of Russian Jews lived in the Pale of Settlement, an area adjacent to Poland that was under the control of Russia and Austria-Hungary. The region was very densely populated, partly due to rapid population growth among the Jewish population at this time and also because of the Russian laws that restricted their residence to this area. It became very difficult for Jews to make a living, because their traditional occupations as middlemen were largely dependent on an agricultural economy, and also because they were banned from working in many of the new sectors of the industrialized economy. As a result, many Jewish families in Russia fell into poverty in the late nineteenth century.

These factors created pressure for migration, but the large scale mass emigration that did occur was sparked off by the violent riots and pogroms against Jewish people that occurred after the assassination of Tsar Alexander II in 1881, for which the Jews were used as scapegoats, and by the May Laws brought in the following year, which imposed even narrower restrictions on Jewish residence and economic activity.

Although Jews had increasingly been moving out of Russia since the 1870s, most of the earlier migrants

Jewish refugees from Russia that have recently arrived in New York City, leaving Castle Garden on their way to emigrants' quarters on Ward's Island. © BETTMANN/CORBIS. REPRODUCED BY PERMISSION.

settled in European cities such as Berlin and Warsaw. From the 1880s onwards, however, the United States became the most popular destination, and more than eighty percent of all emigrants at this time settled there, mostly in the New York area. Chain migration was very important, with emigrants joining friends who already lived in America. As a result, a very large community of Eastern European Jews developed in New York's Lower East Side, where Rose Gollup Cohen went to live. As noted by Rose and in other sources, the area was almost exclusively Jewish, with Yiddish signs and clothing to be seen everywhere. This area reportedly became the most densely populated urban neighborhood in the world by the early twentieth century. However, despite the retention of some aspects of their Jewish culture, many Jewish immigrants were keen to assimilate into American society and soon adopted American styles of clothing, dropping some of their traditional customs, such as the

wearing of long beards by the men and of wigs by married women. This was encouraged by the Jewish community leaders who established programs to help new immigrants integrate into their new country. Rose's autobiography traces her own transition from being shocked at the western appearance of her father when she first arrives in America, to persuading her mother to adopt American clothing when she came to join them a year later.

On arrival in New York, most Jewish immigrants, including young girls such as Rose, had to go out to work, many of them in the garment industries and sewing trades which were dominated by Jewish entrepreneurs. Despite Rose's tender age, it was normal in Jewish society for women and girls to be employed outside the home, and many were trained in skills such as sewing and knitting when very young. Young girls were in demand for lower-skilled occupations in the garment trade, as they were often good workers and could be paid less than men.

PRIMARY SOURCE

... From Castle Garden we drove to our new home in a market wagon filled with immigrant's bedding. Father tucked us in among the bundles, climbed up beside the driver himself and we rattled off over the cobbled stone pavement, with the noon sun beating down on our heads.

As we drove along I looked about in bewilderment. My thoughts were chasing each other. I felt a thrill: "am I really in America at last?" But the next moment it would be checked and I felt a little disappointed, a little homesick. Father was so changed. I hardly expected to find him in his black long tailed coat in which he left home. But of course yet with his same full grown bead and earlocks. Now instead I saw a young man with a closely cut beard and no sign of earlocks. As I looked at him I could scarcely believe my eyes. Father had been the most pious Jew in our neighbourhood. I wondered was it true then as Mindle said that "in America one at once became a libertine?"

Father's face was radiantly happy. Every now and then he would look over his shoulder and smile. But he soon guessed what troubled me for after a while he began to talk in a quiet, reassuring manner. He told me he would take me to his own shop and teach me part of his own trade. He was a men's coat finisher. He made me understand that if we worked steadily and lived economically we should soon have money to send for those at home. "Next year at this time," he smiled, "you yourself may be on the way to Castle Garden to fetch mother and the children." So I too smiled at the happy prospect, wiped some tears away and resolved to work hard.

From Mrs. Felesberg we learned at once the more serious side of life in America. Mrs. Felesberg was the woman with whom we were rooming. A door from our room opened into her tiny bedroom and then led into the only other room where she sat a great part of the day finishing pants which she brought in big bundles from a shop, and rocking the cradle with one foot. She always made us draw our chairs quite close to her and she spoke in a whisper scarcely ever lifting her weak peering eyes from her work. When she asked us how were liked America, and we spoke of it with praise, she smiled a queer smile. "Life here is not all that it appears to the 'green horn,'" she said. She told us that her husband was a presser on coats and earned twelve dollars when he worked a full week. Aunt Masha thought twelve dollars a good deal. Again Mrs. Felesberg smiled. "No doubt it would be," she said, "where you used to live. You had your own house, and most of the food came from the garden. Here you will have to pay for everything; the rent!" she sighed, "for the light, for every potato, every grain of barley. You see these three rooms, including yours? Would they be too much for my family of five?" We had to admit they would not. "And even from these," she said, "I have to rent one out."

Perhaps it was due to these talks that I soon noticed how late my father worked. When he went away in the morning it was still dark, and when he came home at night the lights in the halls were out. It was after ten o'clock. I thought that if mother and the children were here they would scarcely see him.

One night when he came home and as he sat at the table eating his rice soup, which he and Aunt Masha had taught me to cook, I sat down on the cot and asked timidly, knowing that he was impatient of questions, "Father, does everybody in America live like this? Go to work early, come home late, eat and go to sleep? And the next day again work, eat, and sleep? Will I have to do that too? Always?"

Father looked thoughtful and ate two or three mouthfuls before he answered. "No," he said smiling. "You will get married."

So, almost a week passed and though life was so interesting, still no matter where I went, what I saw, mother and home were always present in my mind. Often in the happiest moments a pain would rise in my throat and my eyes burned with the tears held back. At these moments I would manage to be near Aunt Masha so that I could lean against her, touch her dress

On the following day father came home at noon and took me along to the shop where he worked. We climbed the dark, narrow stairs of a tenement house on Monroe Street and came into a bright room filled with noise. I saw about five or six men and a girl. The men turned and looked at us when we passed. I felt scared and stumbled. One man asked in surprise:

"Avrom, is this your daughter? Why, she is only a little girl!"

My father smiled. "Yes," he said, "but wait till you see her sew."

He placed me on a high stool opposite the girl, laid a pile of pocket flaps on the little narrow table between us, and showed me how to baste.

All afternoon I sat on my high stool, a little away from the table, my knees crossed tailor fashion, basting flaps. As I worked I watched the things which I could see by just raising my eyes a little. I saw that the girl, who was called Atta, was very pretty.

A big man stood at a big table, examining, brushing and folding coats. There was a window over his table through which the sun came streaming in, showing millions of specks of dust dancing over the table and circling over his head. He often puffed out his cheeks and blew the dust from him with a great gust so that I could feel his breath at our table.

The machines going at full speed drowned everything in their noise. But when they stopped for a moment I caught the clink of a scissors laid hastily on a table, a short question and answer exchanged, and the pounding of a heavy iron from the back of the room. Sometimes the machines stopped for a whole minute. Then the men looked about and talked. I was always glad when the machines started off again. I felt safer in their noise.

Late in the afternoon a woman came into the shop. She sat down next to Atta and began to sew on buttons. Father, who sat next to me, whispered, "This is Mrs. Nelson, the wife of the big man, our boss. She is a real American."

She, too, was pretty. Her complexion was fair and delicate like a child's. Her upper lip was always covered with shining drops of perspiration. I could not help looking at it all the time.

When she had worked a few minutes she asked father in a very imperfect Yiddish: "Well, Mr ———, have you given your daughter an American name?"

"Not yet," father answered. "What would you call her? Her Yiddish name is Rahel."

"Rahel, Rahel," Mrs. Nelson repeated to herself, thoughtfully, winding the thread around a button; "let me see." The machines were going slowly and the men looked interested.

I was surprised at the interest every one showed. Later I understood the reason. The slightest cause for interruption was welcome, it broke the monotony of the long day.

Mrs. Nelson turned to me: "Don't let them call you Rachel. Every loafer who sees a Jewish girl shouts 'Rachel' after her. And on Cherry Street where you live there are many saloons and many loafers. How would you like Ruth for a name?"

I said I should like to be called Ruth

I liked my work and learned it easily, and father was pleased with me. As soon as I knew how to baste pocket-flaps he began to teach me how to baste the coat edges. This was hard work. The double ply of overcoat cloth stitched in with canvas and tape made a very stiff edge. My fingers often stiffened with pain as I rolled and basted the edges. Sometimes a needle or two would break before I could do one coat. Then father would offer to finish the edge for me. But if he gave me my choice I never let him. At these moments I wanted so to master the thing myself that I felt my whole body trembling with the desire. And with my habit of personifying things, I used to bend over

the coat on my lap, force the obstinate and squeaking needle, wet with perspiration, in and out of the clothe and whisper with determination: "No, you shall not get the best of me!" When I succeeded I was so happy that father, who often watched me with a smile, would say, "Rachel, your face is shining. Now rest a while." He always told me to rest after I did well. I loved these moments. I would push my stool closer to the wall near which I sat, lean my back against it, and look about the shop

Father began to strain all his energy to save the money to send for mother and the children. In the shop one morning I realised that he had been leaving out of his breakfast the tiny glass of brandy for two cents and was eating just the roll. So I too made my sacrifice. When as usual he gave me the apple and the roll, I took the roll but refused the apple. And he did not urge me. When a cold grey day at the end of November found him in his light tan suit quite worn and me in my thin calico frock, now washed out to a tan colour, we went to a second-hand clothing store on Division Street and he bought me a fuzzy brown coat reaching a little below my waist, for fifty cents, and for himself a thin threadbare overcoat. And now were ready for the winter.

About the same time that the bitter cold came father told me one night that he had found work for me in a shop where he knew the presser. I lay awake long that night. I was eager to begin life on my own responsibility but was also afraid. We rose earlier than usual that morning for father had to take me to the shop and not be over late for his own work. I wrapped my thimble and scissors, with a piece of bread for breakfast, in a bit of newspaper, carefully stuck two needles into the lapel of my coat and we started.

The shop was on Pelem Street, a shop district one block long and just wide enough for two ordinary sized wagons to pass each other. We stopped at the door where I noticed at once a brown shining porcelain knob and a half rubbed off number seven. Father looked at his watch and at me.

SIGNIFICANCE

Unlike many other immigrants to America in the late nineteenth century who migrated mainly for economic reasons, the Eastern European Jews mainly left their homes to escape persecution, and were therefore more likely to regard their move as a permanent one. This is likely to have been one factor contributing to their very successful integration into American society, as well as the fact that many Jewish immigrants were more likely than other groups to arrive with some resources in which to start up businesses.

Jewish immigrants became, arguably, the most successful ethnic group of immigrants that has ever entered America. Over the following decades, they became upwardly mobile at a time when it was very unusual in American society to move from the working classes into the middle classes.

Further major waves of Jewish immigration continued in the early decades of the twentieth century, with thousands of new immigrants arriving every year. This might have threatened the economic and social well-being of the established Jewish community in New York, where unemployment was already very high, had not the Industrial Removal Office, part of the Jewish Agricultural and Industrial Aid Society, promoted and assisted the dispersion of Jews from the area to other parts of the United States. Over two decades, the IRO helped 80,000 Jewish people to move to around 1,000 towns and cities throughout the United States where many continued the Jewish tradition of entrepreneurship and contributed to the demographic, cultural, and economic profile of many parts of the country.

Some historians have noted that the mass migration of Jews from some areas of Eastern Europe in the late nineteenth century played a significant role in preserving the Jewish population, as Jewish immigrants to the United States escaped the looming Holocaust during World War II (1939–1945).

FURTHER RESOURCES
Books

Cohen, Rose. *Out of the Shadow: A Russian Jewish Girlhood on the Lower East Side*. Ithaca, N.Y.: Cornell University Press, 1993.

Dublin, Thomas, ed. *Immigrant Voices: New Lives in America, 1773–1986*. Urbana: University of Illinois Press, 1993.

Glazier, Jack. *Dispersing the Ghetto: The Relocation of Jewish Immigrants across America*. Ithaca, N.Y.: Cornell University Press , 1998.

Godley, Andrew. *Jewish Immigrant Entrepreneurship in New York and London, 1880–1914: Enterprise and Culture*. New York: Palgrave, 2001.

Joseph, Samuel. *Jewish Immigration to the United States from 1881 to 1910*. New York: Columbia University Press, 1914.

Rockaway, Robert A. *Words of the Uprooted: Jewish Immigrants in Early Twentieth-Century America*. Ithaca, N.Y.: Cornell University Press, 1998.

Weinberg, Sydney Stahl. *The World of Our Mothers: The Lives of Jewish Immigrant Women*. Chapel Hill: University of North Carolina Press, 1988.

The Chinese Exclusion Bill

Magazine article

By: Anonymous

Date: January 1892

Source: Anonymous. "The Chinese Exclusion Bill." *The American Missionary*. 44 (January 1892): 143

About the Author: *The American Missionary* was a publication from the American Missionary Association. The journal, published from 1846 through 1934, highlighted missionary work, religious issues, and racial issues regarding missionary outreach from the Congregationalist Church.

INTRODUCTION

The 1882 Chinese Exclusion Act was the first piece of U.S. immigration legislation aimed at immigrants from a particular country. While trade with China extended back to the eighteenth century, substantial Chinese presence in the United States did not develop until the early 1850s, when the Gold Rush in California and increased development across the western United States led to the influx of Chinese miners, prospectors, and businessmen seeking gold or merchant opportunities. While many of the Chinese immigrants faced severe discrimination from white settlers, prospectors, fellow merchants and later mine owners, hundreds and later thousands of Chinese immigrants made the West Coast their permanent home.

By the 1850s and 1860s, Chinese immigrants flocked to parts of Latin America (notably Peru) for mining opportunities, and to the United States to work as laborers on the development of the railroad throughout the western territories. In the U.S., Chinese immigrants were easily targeted for discrimination because of their distinct features and accents; they were paid lower wages than white counterparts, and were the victims of violence during low employment opportunities or times of supply scarcity. Chinese settlers nonetheless persisted in their work, often bringing relatives, wives, and children to the U.S. once they'd saved enough money to do so.

Throughout the 1870s, nativism—discrimination against immigrants of any kind by native-born citizens—led to a series of reports and policies aimed at reducing Chinese employment, relocation, and later immigration into the U.S. An 1871 riot in Los Angeles led to the targeted killings of twenty Chinese immigrants. An 1877 report from the Joint Special

Committee to Investigate Chinese Immigration stated that: "The American race is progressive and in favor of a responsible representative government. The Mongolian race seems to have no desire for progress, and to have no conception of representative and free institutions. While conditions should be favorable to the growth and occupancy of our Pacific possessions by our own people, the Chinese have advantages, which will put them far in advance in this race for possession. They can subsist where the American would starve. They can work for wages, which will not furnish the barest necessities of life to an American. They make their way in California as they have in the islands of the sea, not by superior force or virtue, or even industry, although they are, as a rule, industrious, but by revolting characteristics, and by dispensing with what have become necessities in modern civilization. To compete with them and excel them the American must come down to their level, or below them; must work so cheaply that the Chinese cannot compete with him, for in the contest for subsistence he that can subsist upon the least will last the longest." Anti-Chinese sentiment ran high at the beginning of the 1880s.

In 1882, Congress passed the Chinese Exclusion Act, which placed severe restrictions on Chinese immigration into the U.S. Religious groups, such as the American Missionary Association, feared that the act would cause problems with relations between the U.S. and China, restricting missionary activity throughout Asia. In 1892, Congress considered the renewal of the act. The following editorial expresses the views of the predominant Congregationalist missionary association in the U.S.

PRIMARY SOURCE

Undoubtedly this nation must throw some limitations in immigration to its shores. We cannot safely make this land the dumping-ground for the pauper and criminal classes of the old continents. But, in making such limitations, we must be guided by fairness and justice to all concerned. We must discriminate against character and not against races or nations. And especially we must not violate treaty obligations, nor cripple trade with the great nations of the old world, nor raise up such a sense of indignation as will exclude missionaries from heathen lands. We fear that all these objections lie against the bill recently passed in the House of Representatives excluding Chinese from our shores.

SIGNIFICANCE

Chinese immigration eastward included the West Coast of the United States and the island nation of Hawaii as well; by 1884, long before Hawaii became part of the United States, Chinese immigrants constituted more than twenty percent of the population of Hawaii, working as laborers on sugar plantations. As in the U.S. mainland, Chinese immigrants were paid lower wages and viewed as a threat to local workers; the 1882 Chinese Exclusion Act had placed missionary workers in the U.S., Hawaii, and China in a difficult position, and the prospect of its renewal concerned missionaries.

Christian missionary outreach into China from the United States had begun in the early decades of the 1800s, with British and American missionaries working their way through Canton (Guangdong), China. The long history of Christian missionary activity was highly restricted, but these early Christian mission efforts linked directly with Chinese immigration during the Gold Rush in the early 1850s, as the first Chinese immigrants were from Guangdong, having heard of the United States through mission efforts. The 1882 Chinese Exclusion Act threatened mission workers with the potential of deteriorating foreign relations between the U.S. and China. In addition, in 1903, Hawaii imposed restrictions of Chinese immigrants that were similar to the provisions of the Chinese Exclusion Act.

In effect, the 1882 law halted legal Chinese immigration; by 1887, only ten Chinese immigrants had been permitted to enter the U.S. with proper documentation, down from 40,000 in 1882. In 1878, China had established an embassy in Washington D.C. and a consulate office in San Francisco; the Chinese government worked to negotiate with the U.S. on a series of acts and treaties, and strongly opposed the 1882 act. In 1885, a mob of 400 white men attacked Chinese immigrants in Colorado, killing one Chinese person and injuring others. In Tacoma, Washington, anti-Chinese sentiment reached a zenith when all Chinese immigrants were forced out of the city by railroad into Portland. As news of these violent events and others reached China, American missionaries feared local anti-American sentiment and worried about retaliatory violence.

In 1892, the Exclusion Bill, which became the Geary Act, reaffirmed the 1882 act and required all legal Chinese immigrants to carry a certificate of proof of legal residence, a requirement placed on no other immigrant group in the U.S. Chinese immigrants could not post bail or appear as a witness in court; the Geary Act applied to Chinese immigrants only.

The fear of miscegenation, which motivated the Asiatic Exclusion League and other organizations to support anti-Chinese legislation during the 1870's and 1880's, finds sympathetic expression in this 1877 cartoon. © BETTMANN/CORBIS.

By the 1940s, Chinese presence in the U.S. had dropped by nearly half; the 1945 Magnuson Act replaced the Chinese Exclusion Act, and set the limit of Chinese immigrants at 105 per year. A post-World War II "war brides" provision allowed more than 6,000 Chinese women to enter the country, though Chinese immigrants would not receive equal treatment under the law until the Immigration Act of 1965.

FURTHER RESOURCES

Books

Gyory, Andrew. *Closing the Gate: Race, Politics, and the Chinese Exclusion Act.* University of North Carolina Press, 1998.

Lee, Erika. *At America's Gates: Chinese Immigration During the Exclusion Era, 1882–1943.* University of North Carolina Press, 2003.

Wong, K. Scott (ed.) and Sucheng Chan. *Claiming America: Constructing Chinese Identities During the Exclusion Era.* Philadelphia, Pennsylvania: Temple University Press, 1998.

Web sites

Central Pacific railroad Photographic History Museum. "Report of the Joint Special Committee to Investigate Chinese Immigration." <http://cprr.org/Museum/Chinese_Immigration.html> (accessed June 11, 2006).

Cornell University: Making of America Archives. "The American Missionary." <http://cdl.library.cornell.edu/moa/browse.journals/amis.html> (accessed June 11, 2006).

National Archives and Records Administration. "Chinese Immigration and the Chinese in the United States." <http://www.archives.gov/locations/finding-aids/chinese-immigration.html> (accessed June 11, 2006).

Shall Immigration be Suspended?

Magazine article

By: W. E. Chandler

Date: January 1893

Source: Chandler, W. E. "Shall Immigration Be Suspended." *North American Review* 156 (1893): 1–8.

About the Author: The *North American Review* is one of America's oldest literary magazines, published from 1815 until 1940 and from 1968 to the present. In the early 1800s, the journal was considered the country's leading literary publication. W. E. Chandler was the Chairman of the U.S. Senate Committee on Immigration.

INTRODUCTION

Daily life was far more hazardous before the development of antibiotic drugs. A minor cut or infection carried the risk of serious complications, and minor illnesses were potentially fatal. Diseases such as pneumonia, which today threatens primarily the elderly, posed a significant risk even for healthy young adults. The threat of pneumonia and other infections, combined with a limited understanding of disease transmission made the possibility of an epidemic even more terrifying.

Cholera, a bacterial infection of the intestines, is rare in developed countries today, but, in the 1800s, the disease was fairly common in Europe and North America. Cholera is generally spread when healthy individuals ingest food or water contaminated with feces from an infected person. Prior to the widespread adoption of water purification and sewage treatment, human waste frequently found its way into water and food supplies, where the bacteria multiplied and spread. For this reason, cholera often appeared without warning, caused widespread infection, and then receded. Causing severe vomiting and diarrhea, cholera killed forty to sixty percent of its victims, usually from dehydration and often within twenty-four to forty-eight hours of infection.

The World's Fair, scheduled for 1893 in Chicago, was seen as a fitting end to what had been a glorious century for the United States. Millions of Americans were expected to travel by train to the Midwest, where they could marvel at exhibits of technology and commerce, including wonders of architecture, a seventy-foot-high tower of light bulbs, and an eleven-ton block of cheese. Many more were expected to arrive from overseas to experience this grand showcase of American and world progress. Years of planning and millions of dollars were invested in the showcase event, which had been secured for Chicago after a fierce and sometimes bitter battle with Saint Louis, Washington, D. C., and New York City.

In 1892, cholera raged through Europe. In the cramped and unsanitary conditions below decks on most ocean vessels, disease spread quickly, and the United States began requiring inspections of all vessels leaving Europe. Ships carrying cholera victims were required to fly a yellow flag signaling infection, and arriving ships were quarantined for twenty days as a precaution. With American sentiment toward immigrants already negative, Europe's cholera epidemic led to a drastic reduction in immigration. As the date for the Columbia Exposition approached, American officials faced a serious question. Should immigration be halted entirely in order to protect the United States

Cartoon depicting the grim reaper arriving on a British ship, draped with a cloth labeled "cholera." © BETTMANN/CORBIS.

from the epidemic and the Exposition from bad press and a potential financial loss?

PRIMARY SOURCE

Opportunities come to nations as well as to individuals, and they must not be neglected. A republic especially should be prompt to seize its opportunity; for, while a monarchy or despotism can act on the impulse of one ruler or a few rulers, many minds must concur to put a republic in motion. When the people, or their representatives in the legislature, are ready, there should be no delay or hesitation, or the opportunity may pass.

The United States is now offered an opportunity to make a wise initial movement towards the restriction of immigration, some of whose existing evils an almost universal feeling demands should be immediately checked. A concurrence of imperative reasons favors the suspension of all immigration for the year 1893, during which period

suitable conditions for its resumption may be fixed and promulgated.

. . .

There is already a virtual suspension which may be easily prolonged.

The cholera of 1892 has almost stopped immigration. It will not be resumed in full proportions before the spring of 1893. This cessation should be prolonged by law until new conditions are matured under which immigration for settlement in the United States may be resumed. The interest and anxiety manifested during the last few years by the American people concerning the enormous inroads of inferior immigrants have been supplemented by the outbreak of cholera in Europe, by its presence in the harbor of New York, and its advent into the city itself. The evil was limited and the danger averted, only by the virtual suppression of immigration from certain countries. It will be the highest wisdom to take advantage of this fortuitous circumstance to continue the suspension until a new policy can be adopted by the United States covering the whole subject of immigration into its territory.

II.

The cholera again threatens us, and can only be averted by the suspension of immigration.

Not only will it be wise on general grounds to take advantage of the suspension of immigration which the cholera of 1892 has caused, to continue the same for 1893, but there is no other safe method of averting an invasion of cholera in the coming year. The most eminent authorities assert that the suspension of all immigration is the best way to keep out the cholera. Many believe that it is the only reasonably sure method.

It is not believed that the cholera germs are now here, although it is possible that they are. There will be another outbreak of cholera in Europe; indeed it has already appeared there. If it comes to this country, it will be brought with the immigrants in the steerages of the steamships. There is no serious danger from cabin passengers coming as visitors.

If there is no suspension of immigration it will be indispensable to secure the adoption and observance of the most rigid precautions and rules in the European ports, for a period before the sailings of emigrant vessels, and the maintenance of strict regulations during the voyages. For this strictness we must depend upon foreign officials and the officers of the steamship companies and not upon ourselves. No one believes that we can prescribe and enforce upon foreign governments and the steamship officers such measures as will keep the cholera from coming here. It will sail into our ports and overtax all the resources of our quarantine and health authorities, and will alarm and distress our whole people, even if it does not widely break into our borders and ravage our homes. If we allow immigration we are largely at the mercy of foreigners. If we suspend it our lives are in our own hands. In suspension alone is there any certainty of safety.

III.

Protection to the World's Fair requires the suspension.

The Columbian Exposition at Chicago can only be protected from cholera, and made a success so far as foreign visitors are concerned, by the proposed suspension of immigration. We are inviting, and we very much desire, European visitors to the World's Fair. They will not come in the same steamships with swarms of immigrants, nor will they come even in steamships bringing no steerage passengers if they are to encounter the immigrants upon the docks of the steamship companies. Two currents, one of cabin passengers coming as visitors, and

one of immigrants, will not cross the ocean side by side. One or the other will stop, and that one should be the current of immigrants.

It is certain that there is to be some cholera in Europe. If there is also to be cholera in the Untied States, Europeans will not come here. If, however, it can be made tolerably certain, as it can, by the suspension of immigration, that there will be no cholera in the United States, foreigners will come here in large numbers. It will be the safest place for them to visit, indeed it will be the only place in the world which they can visit where they will be reasonably sure to avoid cholera.

The success of the World's Fair may be possible even without many foreign visitors. But such success will not be possible with any considerable amount of cholera in the Untied States. With cholera existing anywhere in this country Chicago will be the last place to which Americans will go. They will stay at home or flee to the mountains; they will not go to the city of Chicago. The case seems too clear for argument. It is an absolutely imperative necessity for the welfare of the Columbian Exposition, either as a resort for Americans alone or for Americans and foreigners as well, that European immigration shall be suspended. It is unfortunate for the Exposition that it is to be held during the second of a series of cholera years, but the misfortune exists. The failure of the Fair can be averted by simply asking immigrants who wish to come for settlement to delay their departure for one year.

SIGNIFICANCE

While the direct impact of Senator Chandler's recommendation is unknown, immigration continued to rise in the decade following his appeal, jumping from 3.7 million in the 1890s to 8.8 million the following decade. The feared American cholera epidemic never materialized.

As U.S. officials wrestled with the cholera question in the 1800s, evidence already pointed toward the disease's cause. In 1854, a severe cholera outbreak hit the London neighborhood of Soho. Within a few days, more than 100 people had died and most residents of the affected area soon fled. Ten days after the outbreak, the death toll had climbed to 500, and most of those who died lived within a relatively small area. John Snow, a physician living nearby, believed that cholera was spread not by air, as was popularly believed, but by contaminated water. When the Soho outbreak began, Snow quickly began interviewing residents of the area. His investigation led him to theorize that a single water source was the origin of the outbreak. After mapping the outbreak, he found himself at its epicenter, a public water pump on Broad Street. Microscopically examining a water sample, Snow observed small white objects. He quickly reported his suspicions to the local authorities.

Snow's theories were considered outlandish at the time, but with few other alternatives the authorities agreed to remove the handle of the suspected pump as an experiment. Soon after, the cholera epidemic subsided. While Snow had identified the cause of the outbreak, city officials remained skeptical of his water-borne illness theory. Despite encouragement from Snow and others, Soho continued to employ open cesspools, many of which leaked.

While cholera has been largely controlled, other diseases continue to present the threat of an epidemic. In 2003, an influenza virus known as H5N1 began spreading through Asia. Limited almost entirely to birds, the so-called bird flu led to the slaughter of millions of infected or exposed animals. As the virus spread to Africa and Europe, public health officials became increasingly concerned that the virus might mutate and infect humans. If that were to occur, modern transportation methods could quickly spread the disease, making it much more difficult to contain. Numerous government agencies have drawn up contingency plans to deal with such a scenario.

FURTHER RESOURCES

Books

Barry, John M. *The Great Influenza: The Epic Story of the Deadliest Plague in History.* New York: Penguin Books, 2004.

McPherson, J. H. T. *The Cholera Years: The United States in 1832, 1849, and 1866.* Chicago: University of Chicago Press, 1987.

Summers, Judith. *Soho: A History of London's Most Colourful Neighborhoods.* London: Bloomsbury, 1989.

Periodicals

Keller, C. C., et al. "The 'Americanisation' of Migrants: Evidence for the Contribution of Ethnicity, Social Deprivation, Lifestyle and Life-Course Processes to the Mid–20th Century Coronary Heart Disease Epidemic in the U.S." *Social Science and Medicine* 63 (2006): 465–484.

Schwartz, James Z. "A Melancholy and Trying Season: Cholera and the Conflict over Cultural Boundaries in Early Michigan." *Journal of the Early Republic* 26 (2006): 95–116.

Sepulveda, Jaime, et al. "Cholera in Mexico: The Paradoxical Benefits of the Last Pandemic." *International Journal of Infectious Diseases* 10 (2006): 4–13.

Web sites

Illinois Institute of Technology. "World's Columbian Exposition of 1893." <http://columbus.gl.iit.edu/> (accessed June 12, 2006).

UCLA Department of Epidemiology. "John Snow." <http://www.ph.ucla.edu/epi/snow.html> (accessed June 12, 2006).

U.S. Centers for Disease Control and Prevention. "Cholera." <http://www.cdc.gov/ncidod/dbmd/diseaseinfo/cholera_g.htm> (accessed June 12, 2006).

The Census and Immigration

Newspaper article

By: Henry C. Lodge

Date: 1893

Source: Lodge, Henry Cabot. "The Census and Immigration." *The Century*, 1893.

About the Author: Henry Cabot Lodge (1850–1924) was a noted historian and politician in the early twentieth century. He was the chairman of the Senate Foreign Relations Committee and opposed U.S. participation in the League of Nations.

INTRODUCTION

American history has been marked by periods of anti-immigrant sentiment. In many ways, the story of immigrants is associated with the history of racism. Immigrants have experienced social exclusion due to their heritage and language differences. During times of economic hardship, immigrants have been blamed for lack of jobs, decreased property values, and crime. Immigrants have been subjected to deculturalization (the stripping away of one's heritage to replace it with a new culture) and Americanization, a movement in the early 1900s to assimilate immigrants and non-English speakers, especially school children, into the dominant Anglo-American Protestant culture.

The history of American immigration can be divided into four waves. During the first wave of immigration, from 1840 to 1880, more than ten million immigrants, primarily Irish and German, came to the United States. Most of these immigrants arrived due to massive crop failures during the Irish potato famine and the German depression. The sentiment among American citizens varied from neutral to hostile, except during the American Civil War (1861–1865), when citizenship was used as an incentive to recruit

Irish and German immigrants into the Union Army. This first wave of voluntary immigrants witnessed a country at odds in political agendas and racial and social doctrines. The Civil War, in large part a fight to end slavery and to gain economic control of the South, divided America. In the ensuing decades, public policy became increasingly anti-immigrant.

The second wave of immigration was expedited by the introduction of railroads and steamships and by the industrial revolution. More than thirty-seven million immigrants came to America between 1880 and 1920. The majority came from southern and eastern Europe as well as from Germany, Ireland, the Netherlands, and Scandinavia. Orthodox Christians, Catholics, and Jews arrived from Russia, Austria, Hungary, Poland, the Balkan and Baltic nations, and Greece. In lesser numbers others arrived from Armenia, Lebanon, Syria, Spain, Portugal, Japan, Korea, the Caribbean, and the West Indies.

The first Naturalization Act, signed into law by George Washington in 1795, restricted citizenship to free whites living in the United States who renounced their allegiance to their former country. In 1891, the Bureau of Immigration was created to enforce immigration policies. Immigration stations were constructed to process arriving immigrants and weed out undesirables. The most well-known of these stations was at New York's Ellis Island. In addition to criminals, contract laborers, prostitutes, and disabled persons, Chinese immigrants were often singled out during screening. The Chinese immigrant population peaked after the 1849 gold rush in California, and resistance to further Chinese immigrants was growing. Hostility and discrimination eventually led to the first federal exclusion legislation in 1882, aimed at Chinese laborers. Contract labor laws were also exclusionary, as they prevented immigrants entry to the United States to work under a contract that had been made prior to their arrival.

In addition to anti-immigration laws, small groups formed aimed at protecting the country against the immigrant population. One group in particular, the Know Nothing Party, came about in the 1850s. This group sought to use government connections to preserve a native society by restricting immigration and changing citizenship requirements. Such political groups created and promoted ethnic stereotypes that persist in American culture today.

■ PRIMARY SOURCE

Expressed in percentages of the total white population in the United States, the division is as follows:

Native parentage . . . . .62 percent
Foreign parentage . . . . .21 "
Foreign-born. . . . . .17 "
Foreign birth and parentage . . .38 "

The proportion of undesirable elements in these divisions can be shown in part by a comparison of these percentages with those of like divisions in the criminal and pauper classes. An examination of the statistics of criminals, juvenile delinquents, and paupers ought to disclose the same proportions in birth and parentage as the total population, provided our immigration is equal in character to the inhabitants of the United States who have been here for one or more generations. The result of such an examination, however, is widely and even alarmingly different, as the following figures prove.

Of the convicts in penitentiaries, 48 percent are of native parentage, while 52 percent, are of foreign birth and parentage; or, in other words, while persons of foreign birth and parentage furnish a little more than one third of the total white population of the country, they furnish more than half of the criminals.

Of juvenile delinquents, 39 percent are of native parentage, and 61 percent, of foreign birth or parentage. That is to say, persons of foreign birth or parentage are a little more than one third of our population, and yet they furnish nearly two thirds of our juvenile delinquents, the inmates of reformatories.

Of the paupers in almshouses, 41 percent are of native parentage, and 59 percent of foreign birth or parentage. Again it will be noticed that while persons of foreign birth or parentage furnish only one third of the population, they supply nearly two thirds of the paupers in almshouses. In this last case, however, it is proper to go a little more into detail. Of the 59 percent, of paupers of foreign birth or parentage only 8 percent, are born in this country, while 51 percent are foreign-born. These last figures are startling. The foreign-born constitute only 17 percent of our total white population,—in round numbers about a sixth,— and yet they furnish *over half of all the paupers in almshouses throughout the country.* This fact of itself certainly shows that an immigration which supplies more than half the inmates of our almshouses might, to say the least, be sifted with great advantage.

The census of 1890 unfortunately has no statistics in regard to the defective classes, so that we are unable to get any light from it upon the physical conditions of our immigrants during the past ten years. The census of 1880, on the other hand, although it gave full statistics of the defective as well as of the delinquent classes, did not classify the population or the criminal, delinquent, and pauper classes according to parentage, but merely divided them into native- and foreign-born. It is therefore possible to make comparisons only between the foreign-born of

1880 and the foreign-born of 1890 in the criminal, delinquent, and pauper classes. Even these limited comparisons, however, are well worth making, and are very suggestive.

In 1880, the foreign-born furnished 15.4 percent of the total white population, while of criminals (classified in 1880 as prisoners, and including both convicts in penitentiaries and prisoners in county jails) they furnished 30 percent; of paupers in almshouses they supplied 38 percent; and of juvenile delinquents, 10 percent.

The following table gives the comparison between these percentages and those of 1890 in the same classes:

	1880	1890
Percentage of foreign-born to total white population	15.4	17
Prisoners in penitentiaries and county jails	30	28
Paupers in almshouses	38	51
Juvenile delinquents	10	14.5

It will be seen from this comparison that the percentage of criminals of foreign birth has fallen off slightly in the last ten years, owing probably to the improvements in immigrant legislation and the better enforcement of the immigration laws, which have taken effect, so far as they have had any effect at all, almost exclusively against criminals. The number of juvenile delinquents of foreign birth, on the other hand, has increased somewhat (four and a half per cent) since 1880. In these two classes, therefore, there has been, comparatively speaking, no marked change of percentages; but when we come to paupers in almshouses we find a very different result. While the percentage of our foreign-born inhabitants to the total white population has increased only about two per cent, the number of paupers of foreign birth in our almshouses has increased thirteen per cent, from 1880 to 1890. This fact shows in the most unanswerable way that the immigration to this country has deteriorated very decidedly during the last ten years, and that the race changes which have begun in that period have been accompanied by a far greater change in the general quality of the immigrants.

There seems to be little need of comment upon these facts and figures, which speak for themselves only too plainly. Something certainly ought to be done, and at once, to restrict, or at least to sift, thoroughly an immigration which furnishes more than half our paupers, while it supplies only one sixth of our total white population. The undesirable proportion thus disclosed is too dangerously large....

There can be no reasonable doubt, moreover, judging from these facts, that if we had the means of comparison, it would appear that the defective classes, the insane, and the physically disabled among the immigrants had increased during the last decade in like ration with the paupers.

These are facts which may well give us pause, and they disclose conditions which, if continued, will have graver and worse effects upon our people and our future welfare than all other public questions now engaging public attention would have together....

Whatever may be said on the general question of foreign immigration, it is beyond question that it is not only our right but our plain, imperative, and very immediate duty to protect ourselves against the immigration of criminals, and also against this steadily swelling stream of pauperism which fills our almshouses, places upon our taxpayers burdens which should be borne by other nations, and introduces among us an ever-increasing element of deterioration in the general quality of our citizenship. More legislation is needed, and needed at once, to exclude, if nothing more, the criminal and pauper classes now being thrust upon us in large numbers by Europe. We should not, in my opinion, think for a moment of stopping there, but at the point where we are confronted with pauperism, disease, and crime we ought certainly to make a beginning in the work of restriction.

SIGNIFICANCE

A rise in isolationism and racism occurred during World War I (1915–1918). In turn, the Immigration Act of 1917 was passed, excluding even more foreign-born persons from entering the United States. In 1921, Congress devised a quota system for immigrants. The National Origins Act of 1924 reduced the quotas even further for immigrants deemed less desirable (namely Russian Jews and those from Italy). However, the Displaced Persons Acts of 1948 and 1950 and the Refugee Relief Act eased immigration restrictions, designed to help people escaping from persecution in post-World War II Europe. This legislation allowed for the admission of over 500,000 immigrants and signaled a turn in immigration policy.

Immigration policies following World War II varied. The Immigration and Nationality Act of 1952 (also known as the McCarran-Walter Act) incorporated most existing laws on immigration. It also abolished the Asiatic Barred Zone which had banned Asian immigrants since 1917. Due to labor shortages, the Emergency Labor Program (also known as the Bracero Program) was passed. This allowed Mexican laborers, braceros, to enter the United States to replace American workers who were at war. Many

New York City police load undocumented immigrants from Mexico into a van. Deaf and mute, the immigrants were being held against their will in a Queens home and exploited as slave labor. 1997. © DEMARIA JOE/CORBIS SYGMA.

remained in the country illegally, and in response to this Operation Wetback was enacted in 1954 to locate and return undocumented workers to Mexico. As a result, millions of Mexican workers were deported. This program was cancelled in 1964.

The Immigration and Nationality Act in 1965 signaled major changes in immigration law. A number of refugees and undocumented workers were expected to arrive in the United States in the coming decades. Quotas were abolished and annual limits in visas were created. The Vietnam War sparked the Refugee Act of 1980 to accommodate Vietnamese refugees. Then, the Immigration Reform and Control Act of 1986 gave legal residency status to more than 2.7 million undocumented immigrants. This law also prohibited discrimination based on national origin and race.

The lastest waves in U.S. immigration history were from 1960 to 1995, and from 1996 to the present.

The impact of immigration on America has been analyzed and debated since the 1800s. Following public sentiment, laws and regulations have oscillated between tolerance during times of prosperity to hostility and xenophobia during economic downturns. The United States is a nation of immigrants, and immigrants continue to contribute to society by working and creating jobs, and as active participants in the community.

FURTHER RESOURCES
Periodicals

The Congress of the United States, Congressional Budget Office. "The Role of Immigrants in the U.S. Labor Market." *Congressional Budget Office Report* (November 2005).

Ohlemacher, Stephen. "U.S. Population to Hit 300 Million in 2006." Associated Press. (June 25, 2006).

Romero, Victor. "Race, Immigration, and the Department of Homeland Security." *St. John's Journal of Legal Commentary* 19 (2004): 51–58.

Web sites

American Immigration Law Foundation. "America's Heritage:
A History of U.S. Immigration." March 29, 2006.
<http://www.ailf.org/exhibit> (accessed June 26, 2006).

Immigration and Naturalization

Magazine article excerpt

By: H. Sidney Everett

Date: March 1895

Source: Everett, H. Sidney. "Immigration and Naturalization." *Atlantic Monthly.* (March 1895): 75, 351–354.

About the Author: *The Atlantic Monthly* began publication
in 1857 in Boston as a monthly literary and cultural
magazine. By 1895, it also included articles on political
science and foreign affairs. It remained in publication
as of 2006.

INTRODUCTION

The United States has accepted more immigrants
than any other country in the world and has accommodated more ethnic groups than any other nation. Its
strength rests upon its transplanted population of
mixed ethnic ancestry. Yet Americans in every generation have warned of the dangers of unrestricted
immigration.

A century of mass migration brought 38 million
people to American shores from 1820 to 1920. These
immigrants came chiefly from Germany, Italy, Ireland,
Russia, England, and Hungary. Smaller fractions of
the influx came from Asia, the Middle East, the
Caribbean, and Latin America. By contrast, other
English-speaking immigration countries, such as
Australia and Canada, drew their settlers almost
wholly from other English-speaking nations. Latin
American countries also showed a narrow spectrum
of national diversity limited chiefly to Iberian and
Italian origins.

Legislation enacted by Congress both shaped and
reflected the changing demographic pattern of U.S.
immigration. Immigration policy was in a constant
state of evolution. National policy depended on the
shifting characteristics of immigrants as well as a
changing vision of the agenda for national
development.

Two Czech immigrants pose for a photo at Ellis Island, New York,
in 1920. © CORBIS/BETTMANN. REPRODUCED BY PERMISSION.

PRIMARY SOURCE

...In 1893, 440,783 immigrants arrived, a decrease of
141,044 as compared with the year 1892, during which
581,827 arrived; and the decrease in the following year
was 152,763 as compared with 1893; or a total decrease in
the two years of 293,807 immigrants, which is more than
the total number of arrivals for the year ending June 30,
1894.

The decrease in 1893 was largely caused by quarantine regulations against cholera, and in 1894 was largely
attributable to business depression and diminished
demand for labor; but with all this allowance, the decrease
must be greatly due to strict inspection, prompt deportation of the prohibited classes, and the conviction on the
part of both immigrants and transportation agencies that
our immigration laws have been, and will continue to be,
faithfully and rigorously executed. The double system of
inspection before sailing and after arrival will doubtless
become more effective with practice and experience,
and may be aided further by some changes in the law.
The number of undesirable immigrants will continue to

decrease, and those who are allowed to remain will prove to be a more desirable class of citizens for amalgamation with our population. As regards the competition with foreign labor, we find also that in 1892 out of 581,827 immigrants only 932 alien contract laborers were returned; in 1893, out of 440,783 immigrants 516 were returned; and in 1894, out of 288,020 immigrants 2369 were returned; thus providing the increasing benefit of the law to the working classes of the United States. . . .

Each of the States and Territories should also be urged to conform its laws of local citizenship to the requirements of the national law; and at any rate, no alien who is not fully naturalized should be allowed to sit on a jury, or to vote for President of the United States, for a member of Congress, or for any judicial official. As long as aliens are allowed to live among us with all the rights and privileges of native citizens, and States and Territories are allowed to decide who are citizens, and when and how they can vote, the provision of the Constitution that Congress has power to establish a uniform rule of naturalization would seem to be a farce, and our country will continue to be subjected to all the present abuses of the franchise, and to the dishonest and wasteful mismanagement of our municipal affairs which makes us a by-word among nations, and a mortification to the better elements of our population. . . .

H. Sidney Everett

SIGNIFICANCE

By 1920, the United States no longer sought immigrants to fill its factories and work its farms. Many Americans argued that too many of the wrong kinds of immigrants were entering the country. They wanted immigration restrictions. In 1921 and 1924, Congress passed immigration acts that imposed quotas. This legislation not only deliberately reduced immigration but also intentionally discriminated against immigrants from eastern and southern Europe.

American immigration policy began to become more tolerant during World War II. In 1943, the Chinese Exclusion Act was repealed and Chinese were made eligible for naturalization. Removal of the restrictions on the Filipinos and Indians soon followed. In 1948, the quota system for Europeans was temporarily broken as a Displaced Persons Act was passed to admit victims of the war. The Immigration Act of 1952 eliminated all racial and ethnic bars to naturalization but kept most of the quota system. Not until 1965 did the United States welcome all immigrants from all places. The Immigration Act of 1965 ended the quota system and made immigration truly global in its reach. Most legislation passed since then has focused on problems related to illegal immigration, without changing either the composition or the volume of immigration.

FURTHER RESOURCES
Books

Daniels, Roger. *Guarding the Golden Door: American Immigration Policy and Immigrants since 1882.* New York: Oxford University Press, 1996.

Dinnerstein, Leonard, Roger, L. Nichols, and David M. Reimers. *Natives and Strangers: A Multicultural History of Americans.* New York: Oxford University Press, 1996.

Friedland, Klaus, ed. *Maritime Aspects of Migration.* Cologne, Germany: Bohlau, 1989.

The Assassination of McKinley at the Pan-American Exposition In Buffalo

Illustration

By: T. Dart Walker

Date: 1901

Source: Getty Images

About the Artist: T. Dart Walker (1869–1914) was a well known American artist who specialized in political subjects and themes. His work was frequently published in journals such as *Harper's Weekly* and *The Graphic.* This image is found in the archive maintained by Getty Images, a worldwide provider of visual content materials to such communications groups as advertisers, broadcasters, designers, magazines, new media organizations, newspapers and producers.

INTRODUCTION

The second presidential term of William McKinley began in 1901, buoyed by a surge of economic prosperity across the United States. The city of Buffalo, New York, is today a center of regional importance to western New York State. In 1901, it was of sufficient national prominence and influence to stage the second Pan-American Exposition, a six month long celebration of American technological and economic might. Known as the 'Queen City', Buffalo's prosperity was derived in part from its role as a busy port and a terminus of the Erie Canal that ran from the Hudson River to Lake Erie.

McKinley waged a previous hotly contested 1896 presidential campaign against the charismatic populist candidate William Jennings Bryan. McKinley's re-election in 1900 was a virtual landslide, aided by his vice presidential nominee and Spanish-American war hero Theodore Roosevelt.

The upswing in American prosperity had not raised the fortunes of all American citizens at the turn of the twentieth century. A number of disaffected persons turned to radical politics, including anarchism, socialism, and other philosophies that advocated direct action against the wealthy and the powerful interests in America. The organized labor movement's most prominent symbol was the American Federation of Labor (AFL), headed by Samuel Gompers (1850–1924). The AFL was perceived as too complacent in its views and not sufficiently radical by more militant forces in America. Anarchists such as Emma Goldman (1869–1940) developed a following among these activist-minded persons.

Anarchists were blamed by many conservative Americans for many social ills. For example, they were said to be chiefly responsible for the tragedy that occurred at the Haymarket Labor riot in 1886 in Chicago, where a bomb thrown by an alleged anarchist killed eight police officers. Largely regarded as a foreign import into American society, anarchism had attracted Leon Czolgosz to its cause in the early 1890s. Czolgosz was American-born to Polish immigrant parents, and he had never enjoyed any employment success, working in a series of low wage jobs until 1901. After both hearing Emma Goldman speak and meeting her briefly in May 1901, also encouraged by the murder of King Umberto in Italy at the hands of anarchists in 1900, Czolgosz resolved that he would assassinate President McKinley at the Pan-American Exposition to strike a blow for all oppressed American persons.

PRIMARY SOURCE

The Assassination of McKinley at the Pan-American Exposition in Buffalo: An illustration by T. Dart Walker depicts the assassination of President William McKinley by Leon Czolgosz. GETTY IMAGES.

Czolgosz managed to exploit a weak security presence guarding McKinley at an official greeting session arranged at the Buffalo Exposition on September 6, 1901. After waiting in the line of well wishers that had formed to shake the President's hand, Czolgosz was able to approach the president and as McKinley's hand was proffered, Czolgosz fired two shots into McKinley's stomach from a revolver he had hidden under a handkerchief.

PRIMARY SOURCE

THE ASSASSINATION OF MCKINLEY AT THE PAN-AMRECIAN EXPOSITION IN BUFFALO

See primary source image.

SIGNIFICANCE

There were a number of significant outcomes that flowed from the assassination of William McKinley. The most prominent of these was the creation of an understanding in the collective mind of the American public that the anarchism espoused by Czolgosz as his rationale for shooting the President of the United States was a dangerous political philosophy that had to be eradicated. The United States Congress passed the *Alien Immigration Act* in 1903 as a partial response to the perceived threat of the anarchist movement. The Act excluded a wide variety of persons from admission to the United States, including the mentally ill, paupers, persons carrying contagious diseases and convicted felons. The definition of the excluded classes extended to anarchists, or "persons who believe in or advocate the overthrow by violence of the government of the United States". The statute also provided for the deportation of all existing American residents who espoused such causes.

Emma Goldman, whose speech in May 1901 inspired Czolgosz to formulate his plan to assassinate McKinley, was arrested in the aftermath of the shooting as an alleged co-conspirator in the plot; there was no evidence to connect her to the actions of Czolgosz, and she was released nine days later. Goldman published a letter in the aftermath of Czolgosz's arrest and execution that is notable for both its stridency concerning the oppressive power of the forces in America represented by President McKinley and its lack of sympathy for the death of the president. Goldman was ultimately deported from the United States to Russia in 1917 under the same legislation inspired by the McKinley assassination.

The speed with which Czolgosz was tried and executed is remarkable by modern standards.

President William McKinley poses for a photo upon arriving at a reception for the Pan-American Exposition in Buffalo, New York, September 6, 1901. McKinley was fatally shot later that evening. PUBLIC DOMAIN.

Arrested at the scene, Czolgosz escaped a certain death at the hands of a mob that had assembled on the Buffalo Exposition grounds when the local police kept these rioters from attacking Czolgosz. His trial commenced nine days later; Czolgosz offered no meaningful defense, and he stated to the court that he had done his duty in killing McKinley; Czolgosz held himself out as a martyr to the cause of anarchy in the United States. No appeal was filed upon his conviction, and no defense of either insanity or other mental instability was offered. His death on October 29, 1901 was by means of the new form of capital punishment, electrocution.

The assassination of President McKinley was the third shooting of an American president in thirty-six years, following on the murders of Abraham Lincoln in 1865 and James Garfield in 1881. McKinley had been protected at the Buffalo Exposition by a combined force of Pinkerton Detectives, soldiers, and local police officers. As a subsequent review of the presidential security procedures revealed how lax the protection had been to permit Czolgosz his relatively unobstructed access to McKinley, Congress established a permanent Secret Service detail for the protection of all presidents in 1903.

The shooting of McKinley is also significant for the resulting elevation of the Vice President Theodore Roosevelt to the American presidency in 1901. Roosevelt would remain in office until 1909; the notable achievements of his presidency included greater regulation of big business and consumer protection, the construction of the Panama Canal, and his receipt of the Nobel Peace Prize in 1906. Roosevelt was himself shot in a failed assassination attempt when he ran for the presidency in 1912.

FURTHER RESOURCES

Books

Phillips, Kevin. *William McKinley*. New York; Times Books, 2003.

Rauchway, Eric. *Murdering McKinley; The Making of Theodore Roosevelt*. New York; Hill and Wang, 2003.

Web sites

University of Buffalo. "McKinley Assassination." 2004 <http://www.ublib.buffalo.edu/libraries/exhibits/panam/law/assassination.html> (accessed June 13, 2006).

University of California at Berkeley. "Emma Goldman." June 2003 <http://www.sunrite.berkeley.edu/Goldman/Exhibition/assassination.html> (accessed).

The English Lesson

Book excerpt

By: Anzia Yezierska

Date: 1925

Source: Yezierska, Anzia. *Bread Givers: A Struggle between a Father of the Old World and a Daughter of the New*. New York: G. Braziller, 1975.

Mrs. I. Papadopolous, a Greek immigrant to the United States, struggles against her poor eyesight while studying in an English class for the foreign born in New York City, 1940. © BETTMANN/ CORBIS. REPRODUCED BY PERMISSION.

About the Author: Anzia Yezierska (1885?–1970) is the best known writer of fiction about the struggles of immigrant Jewish women in America in the late nineteenth and early twentieth centuries. The Polish-born Yezierska arrived with her family in the United States in the 1890s.

INTRODUCTION

A Polish immigrant with Russian roots, Anzia Yezierska came to America in the peak era of Jewish immigration. While immigrants have always struggled with the differences between the values of their home countries and their newly-adopted country, Yezierska was the first fiction writer to explore the special impact of immigration upon women.

When the Yeziersky family came to America in 1890, immigration officers gave them new easy-to-spell names. Yezierska, the youngest of nine children, became Hattie Mayer. The family moved to a dark, airless, tenement apartment that looked out at the blank wall of the next house. When Yezierska's teen-aged sisters went to work sewing shirtwaists in a sweatshop, Anzia learned the English language and American ways in public school. This bit of learning gave her the critical, rebellious eye that she cast on the lot of women in Jewish immigrant families. As Yezierska noted, her mother ended her long day at a terrible job by fighting for food from pushcarts while her father was a Hebrew scholar and dreamer who was always too much in the air to come down to such thoughts as bread and rent. This subject of the brutal life of Jewish immigrants would lead her to write many short stories and her best known work, *Bread Givers*, in 1925.

In the 1920s, Yezierska became a celebrity. Newspapers frequently retold the tale of how she had risen from New York's Lower East Side ghetto to literary stardom. With the advent of the Great Depression of the 1930s, Yezierska lost both her audience and her money. She continued to write, however, and received awards from the National Institute of Arts and Letters in 1965 in recognition of her distinction as a writer. Following Yezierska's death in 1970, she was discovered by feminists and social historians. *Bread Givers* has since become a standard text in history and women's studies courses.

▮ PRIMARY SOURCE

Not one of the teachers around me had kept the glamour. They were just peddling their little bit of education for a living, the same as any pushcart peddler.

But no. There was one in this school who was what I had dreamed a teacher to be—the principal, Mr. Hugo Seelig. He had kept that living thing, that flame, that I used to worship as a child. And yet he had none of the aloof dignity of a superior. He was just plain human. When he entered a classroom sunlight filled the place.

How had he created that big spirit around him? What a long way I had to go yet before I could become so wholly absorbed in my work as he. The youngest, dirtiest child in the lowest grade he treated with the same courtesy and serious attention as he gave to the head of the department.

One of Mr. Seelig's special hobbies was English pronunciation, and since I was new to the work, he would come in sometimes to see how I was getting on. My children used to murder the language as I did when I was a child of Hester Street. And I wanted to give them that better speech that the teachers in college had tried to knock into me.

Sometimes my task seemed almost hopeless. There was Aby Zuker, the brightest eleven-year-old boy in my class of fifty. He had the neighbourhood habit of ending almost every sentence with "ain't it." For his special home work I had given him a sentence with the words "isn't it" to be written a hundred times.

The next morning eh brought it back and with a shining face declared, "I got it all right now, Teacher! Ain't' it?"

"Oh, Aby!" I cried. "And you want to be a lawyer! Don't you know the judges will laugh you out of court if you plead your case with 'ain't it'?

Poor Aby! His little fingers scratched his mop of red curls in puzzlement. From his drooping figure I turned, laughing, to the class.

"Now, children, let's see how perfectly we can pronounce the words we went over yesterday."

On the board, I wrote, s-i-n-g.

"Aby! Pronounce this word."

"Sing-gha," said Aby.

"Sing," I corrected.

"Sing-gha," came from Aby again.

"Rosy Stein! You can do better. Show our lawyer how to speak. Make a sentence with the word 'sing.'"

"I he boids sing-gha."

"Rosy, say bird."

"Boid," repeated small Rosy with great distinctness. "Boid."

"Wrong still," I laughed. "Children, how do you pronounce this?" And I wrote hastily on the board, OIL.

"Earl," cried the class, triumphantly.

"You know how to make the right sounds for these words, but you put them in the opposite places." And I began to drill them in pronunciation. In the middle of the chorus, I heard a little chuckle. I turned to see Mr. Seelig himself, who had quietly entered the room and stood enjoying the performance. I returned his smile and went right on.

"You try it again, Rosy. The birds sing-gg."

"Sing," corrected Mr. Seelig, softly.

There it was. I was slipping back into the vernacular myself. In my embarrassment, I tried again and failed. He watched me as I blundered on. The next moment he was close beside me, the tips of his cool fingers on my throat. "Keep those muscles still until you have stopped. Now say it again," he commanded. And I turned pupil myself and pronounced the word correctly....

▮

SIGNIFICANCE

Foreign-born women, more than men, have experienced sharp tensions between the traditions of the

Old World and American expectations of individualism and freedom. Most immigrant women, like their fathers and husbands, welcomed the challenges and opportunities of a dynamic American economy. Yet, like men, they showed some hesitance about accepting unchanged the personal freedoms to be had in the U.S. However, women were expected to be the guardians of cultural identity. To many, they were the heart of a culture. Immigrant women and their daughters were markers of the line dividing Americans from outsiders. As a result, they found their lives subjected to intensive scrutiny both from other immigrants and from Americans.

By 2000, about seven million Americans possessed Jewish heritage. Many of their ancestors immigrated during the peak of immigration from 1880 to 1914. Like Yezierska, most of them settled in New York City, making the area into one of the largest Jewish settlements in the world in the present-day. More Jews live in the United States than in any other country, including Israel. The American community of Jews is different from the Old World communities in that the tradition of separation of church and state in the United States meant that no national laws discriminating against Jews ever existed. Individuals did discriminate against Jews in housing and employment, however. Some of the best universities, including Yale and Princeton, had quotas that limited the number of Jews who would be admitted. Yet the constitutional protection against religious discrimination prompted Jews to see the United States as a land of freedom. In the 1930s, some of the most distinguished scientists in the world, including Albert Einstein, fled the Nazis for the United States. This migration of intellectuals helped make the United States into a world power.

FURTHER RESOURCES
Books

Diner, Hasia. *Jews in America*. New York: Oxford University Press, 1999.

Gabaccia, Donna. *From the Other Side: Women, Gender, and Immigrant Life in the U.S., 1820–1990*. Bloomington: Indiana University Press, 1994.

Henriksen, Louise Levitas. *Anzia Yezierska: A Writer's Life*. New Brunswick, N.J.: Rutgers University Press, 1988.

4 | Immigration from 1905-1945

Immigration from 1905–1945

While the exact division of chapters by year in this volume is somewhat arbitrary, the chapter divisions do track ebbs, flows, and waves of immigration to the United States. Although 1905–1945 was a critical period in U.S. history, it witnessed a dramatic reduction in immigration from its zenith in the period from 1905–1914, to a brief nadir during World War I (1915–1918) and the early years of the Great Depression in the 1930s.

Between 1905 and 1914, an average of one million immigrants per year landed in the United States. Two-thirds of those individuals emigrated from eastern, southern, and central Europe. The outbreak of World War I in Europe in the summer of 1914 suddenly halted the era of mass emigration. From 1915 until 1945, two world wars, pandemic influenza, a global depression, and increasingly restrictive quota laws limited immigration to the United States.

Ellis Island remains an enduring symbol of the mass-immigration era. For millions of European immigrants, Ellis Island, New York, was their gateway to the United States. "Processing Immigrant Arrivals at Ellis Island" is a glimpse at the process of immigration and one of the iconic images of the immigration station itself. On the other side of the American continent, Angel Island, California, processed immigrants from Asia. The two stations differed in their handling of immigrants and their overall philosophy. More frequently detained and deported, Asian immigrants were subjected to restrictive immigration and employment laws as well as limitations on their general liberties. The Angel Island experience is captured here in a photograph of the station and the poetry of immigrants detained on the island.

The era of mass immigration was also the era of the melting pot, the idea that the United States was a crucible in which the amalgamation of immigrant cultures was a critical social force. Of special interest in this chapter is the article "The Melting-Pot" featuring an excerpt from Israel Zangwill's play, the presumed spark of popular use of the metaphor to describe the effects of European immigration on U.S. society. Other articles such as "Good Metal in Our Melting Pot, Says Miss Wald," "Materials of the New Race," and "What I Owe to America" further elaborate and debate the melting-pot theory and ideas of European immigrant assimilation.

This chapter ends with the rise of institutionalized anti-Semitism in Nazi Germany and World War II years. The internment of Japanese-Americans and Japanese immigrants during World War II was among the darkest episodes in American history. Wartime alliances, however, benefited Chinese immigrants, long victims of discrimination and legal restrictions. Included here is a presidential message urging repeal of the laws that excluded Chinese immigrants.

The Exclusion of Asiatic Immigrants in Australia

Journal article

By: Philip S. Eldershaw

Date: September 1909

Source: Eldershaw, Philip S. "The Exclusion of Asiatic Immigrants in Australia." *The Annals of the American Academy of Political and Social Science* 34 (September 1909): 190–203.

About the Author: Philip S. Eldershaw was a political science professor in the early twentieth century.

INTRODUCTION

In the nineteenth century and for much of the twentieth century, Australia rejected immigrants from non-European nations for permanent residence.

This policy of White Australia reflected the idea that Asians and Africans were inferior to Europeans. For the young nation of Australia to succeed, it needed immigrants from the advanced nations of Europe. White Australia became a severe national embarrassment in latter twentieth century and came to an official end in 1966.

A trickle of Indian and Chinese laborers who entered the Australian colonies in the late 1830s and in the 1840s constituted the first nonwhite immigrants to set foot on the continent. There were too few of them to scare white Australians. This situation changed in the 1850s when the discovery of gold in Victoria and New South Wales brought shipload after shipload of Chinese into Australia. The Asians were deeply resented by the white gold miners. In response, the state governments passed laws that restricted Chinese immigration.

Australia moved from a British colony to a commonwealth in 1901. In that same year, the government passed the Immigration Restriction Act. This

An apology to Australia's aboriginal people is written in the sky over the Sydney Opera House on May 28, 2000, as part of the reconcilliation event Corroboree 2000. AP/WIDE WORLD PHOTOS.

legislation, which officially established the White Australia policy, prevented the immigration of any nonwhites. Asians who were British subjects were also specifically banned. The law immediately caused great diplomatic embarrassment for Australia as the Japanese particularly objected to its racial bias. The vast majority of Australians, however, welcomed it. In 1966, a revision of immigration restriction laws permitted persons with appropriate qualifications and their family members to enter Australia.

▉ PRIMARY SOURCE

In the history of the Australian colonies, now forming the Australian Commonwealth, the frequent recurrence of legislation directed against Asiatic immigrants is impressive. To quote one example, no sooner did the colony of Victoria obtain responsible government in 1855 than a restriction act was passed, imposing duties on the masters of vessels bringing Chinese to Victorian ports. This is typical of the attitude of all six colonies on the subject. Intermittently restrictive legislation continued till 1890, when public opinion seems to have subsided, to awaken again, with renewed apprehension, in the twentieth century—chiefly owing, be it said, to Japan's prominence in the East, dating from her entry into the family of nations in 1899. It is by no means difficult to realize the cause of this uneasiness.

Within a few days' steam of the northern shores lie the densely populated eastern countries, which demand expansion as a result of economic and other social forces. There are three whose inhabitants are represented in our alien population (which does not, however, exceed 5 per cent of the total). These are India, China, and Japan, which together have a population of 715,000,000 people....

It is only of recent years that the true position of affairs has been apprehended by the mass of the people; this tardy recognition being mainly due to the isolation of Australia from world politics.

But even from the first, hidden under economic and other reasons, there has been an instinctive idea that to allow Asiatics to obtain a footing on the continent would be fatal. Twelve thousand miles from the parent and, at present, protecting state, the full recognition of the problem or rather the crisis has been seen in late years in the feverish desire for the desirable immigrant,—the white who is quickly naturalized under laws suitable to the situation in which we find ourselves....

Reasons for Legislation

The reasons for such drastic legislation fall naturally into three groups. (1) Physiological, (2) Economic, (3) Political, chiefly from the aspect of defence.

1. *Physiological.* With the examples of the two Americas before our eyes no other object lesson is needed to impress the Australian mind with the undesirable result of a land inhabited by people of two different colors. The mixture of one European nation with another may have a tendency for good, the faults of one species may be corrected by the infusion of foreign blood, and the result of such alliances may be virile and progressive. But in every case the outcome of the union between European and Asiatic or European and African has been a generation with the faults of both and the virtues of neither. If ever a great body of aliens become domiciled in Australia, either to the north or south, two conceivable results might happen. The two elements might coalesce, as in the case of the hybrid communities in South America with fatal results to the individuality and energy which is the birthright of the pure white race. Or they would not coalesce as in the case of the negro and white population of the United States of America. In this case the problem of reconciling two antagonistic races to live in peace and fellowship is one which strains the best statesmanship. Even under the best rule occasional outbreaks would and do occur. Neither of these alternatives commends itself to a community whose alien population does not exceed at present 5 per cent of the total. Hence it is that every effort is made backed up by public opinion to administer the restriction acts as strictly as possible.

In all great cities the miserable mongrel springing from white and yellow seen, and even now in the slums of Sydney, Melbourne and Brisbane he can be found, though but one in fifty of the small Asiatic population has a white mate. It is in the south, however, that there is cause for alarm. The north of Queensland, and the whole of the northern territory of South Australia have but a very sparse population of whites, a vast and for the most part fertile territory, and a dangerous proximity to Asiatic neighbors. There the physiological problem has manifested itself. There also to some extent the aboriginal native of Australia enters as a factor. Elsewhere, however, he may be ignored as an element in the nation's problems owing to his fast diminishing numbers. Every healthy community has the power of absorbing a certain number of these undesirable crosses, and apparently that is what is happening to the few half-breed children in the segregated aboriginal camps.

But the beginning of a hybrid race with all the vices and physical infirmities of the eastern coolie race is visible in the far northern corner of the continent, having its origin in the time before the immigration restriction acts. The Malay, Filipino and Japanese have crossed with Australian aboriginals. White half-castes have bred with Chinese, Malays and Manilamen, until the low type of humanity which results is dignified by the name of mongrel. But all these considerations have been rather instinctive and innate, than explicit in prompting anti-Asiatic legislation. Those most emphasized have been reasons of economic and of political expediency.

2. *Economic.* This phase of the question of Asiatic immigration is viewed with peculiar interest by Australian statesmen. Their fear of the lowering of the standard of living is perhaps more acute than that of the statesmen of other countries by reason of peculiar natural circumstances.

In the first place with an area of 2,975,000 square miles the density of Australian population is only 1.46 persons per square mile, in comparison with Japan with a density of population of 266.84, British India with a density of 2213.27 and China with a density of 101.36. Such figures show that an unrestricted inflow of Asiatic labor would be fatal to Australian industrial interests. Secondly, not only the rate of remuneration of labor in Australia is high—as it should be in any new country, but the prosperity of the wage-earners has been increased by legislative experiments of a socialistic tendency in some of the states at least. Under systems of compulsory arbitration in industrial disputes, and of wages boards where employers and employees confer together under the impartial presidents to regulate powers and conditions of work, strikes of any length or importance have almost ceased, and the interests of the wage-earning class are being carefully safeguarded.

Thus an inflow of cheap labor must be most carefully guarded against. A good deal has been said, however, in favor of colored labor being utilized in the tropical parts of Australia, which include more than two-fifths of the continent. But it is particularly for the cane-growing districts of Queensland and the northern territory of South Australia that colored labor has been advocated. It would seem, however, that labor of this description is not indispensable. By the Pacific Islanders laborers' act, 1901, the gradual deportation of Polynesians was ordered. At the same time a bonus was paid on white-grown sugar. As a result the production of sugar in the commonwealth has grown and white labor is replacing the colored with no disastrous effect to the farmer.

It would seem that in tropical Australia there is no absolute need of colored labor—save in the pearl fisheries on the northern coasts, which only produce about 3,000,000 worth of shell annually. Thus the general policy of the commonwealth seems justified. The careful regard paid to the retention of a high standard of living is seen in the contract immigrants act, 1905, which applies even to white labor. This act, in substance, provides that where immigrants enter Australia under contract, this contract must be in writing, and its terms approved by the minister for external affairs. The contract must not be made with intention to affect any industrial dispute; and remuneration of the contract immigrant is to be as high as the current wage. The penalty for abrogation of provisions of the act is 5 [dollars] to the contract immigrant and 20 [dollars] for the employer.

3. *Defence.* This aspect of the question is a vital one. The need of an adequate system of defence was a principal factor in the movements which led to the foundation of the commonwealth. Australia, by reasons of her geographical position, has in the past been outside the center of world politics. But there is every reason to believe that in the future the Pacific Ocean will be an important sphere of international activity and rivalry. . . .

Northern Australia lies within a few days' journey from the East. Asiatic nations must expand, and Australia, little developed, scantily populated, presents a natural field.

From the nation most in need of new territory for growth, of new fields for commercial development and which can best support its claims by arms—Japan—Australia is secured by the Anglo-Japanese treaty of 1906. But when this expires, when Manchuria ceases to satisfy her, the crisis of the commonwealth will come. At present Australia has a land force, including permanent, militia and volunteer arms of 26,000 only, although in a few years a general cadet system supported by the proposed conscription scheme will multiply this force many times. Lines of communication overland between the East and West, North and South do not yet exist, and the isolation of outposts of local defence would be fatal should a struggle occur in the next decade. When these circumstances are considered the policy of excluding Asiatics is justified by Australia's extreme needs. Any immigration that would tend to weaken the unity of a nation small in numbers, holding a territory of vast extent must be prevented. . . .

No expense is grudged to keep unsullied the policy, and more than a policy, the ideal of a "White Australia." This, as has been shown, is not a passing ebullition of feeling. It may be not inaptly described as the Monroe doctrine of Australia, only it should be borne in mind that we are acting with reference to Eastern Asiatic peoples only. The Australian continent is not a subject for future colonization and further than that not even for present immigration on the part of eastern races. Any attempt in derogation of this doctrine would be viewed with grave apprehension by Australia, under the aegis of the British empire, and resented as an unfriendly act. This is true even though at present a great part of the continent is far from adequately occupied.

SIGNIFICANCE

The White Australia policy not only stopped virtually all migration from China but also severely limited new immigration from other non-European countries. Places such as Lebanon were just beginning to send emigrants to Australia and this migration came to a virtual halt. However, communities of non-whites had already been established in Australia. These communities remained in existence and were reinforced by migration later in the twentieth century. Additionally, White Australia permitted special entry to a small number of non-Europeans to set up import-export businesses. The flow of non-Europeans into Australia never completely stopped.

By the 1990s, there were significant numbers of settlers from Lebanon, Taiwan, Malaysia, China, Hong Kong, India, and Korea in the large cities of Australia. Conservatives such as Pauline Hanson from the One Nation political party charged that such people did not assimilate and posed a significant threat to Australia's national culture. One Nation had some success in the state of Queensland, but never became a wide force. By 2000, the idea of a multicultural Australia had gained broad acceptance throughout the nation.

FURTHER RESOURCES

Books

Burnley, Ian H. *The Impact of Immigration on Australia: A Demographic Approach*. South Melbourne, Australia: Oxford University Press, 2001.

Jayasuriya, Laksiri, and Kee Pookong. *The Asianisation of Australia?: Some Facts about the Myths*. Carlton South, Australia: Melbourne University Press, 1999.

London, H. I. *Non-White Immigration and the "White Australia" Policy*. New York: New York University Policy, 1970.

The Melting Pot

Play

By: Israel Zangwill

Date: 1909

Source: Zangwill, Israel. *Melting Pot, Drama in Four Acts*. New York: The Macmillan Company, 1909.

About the Author: Israel Zangwill (1864–1926) was an Anglo-Jewish writer and political activist, born in London. He began his career as a teacher in the Jewish Free School in London's East End, then became a writer and journalist. His most famous works include the novel *Children of the Ghetto*, published in 1892, and *The Melting Pot*, which achieved great success in the United States. He founded the Jewish Territorialist Organization, with the aim of establishing a homeland for the Jewish people.

INTRODUCTION

The Melting Pot is a play by Israel Zangwill that opened in Washington in 1908, at the height of European immigration to the United States. It has been estimated that between 1890 and 1920 some eighteen million immigrants from Ireland, Germany, Italy, Eastern Europe, and other countries entered and settled in the United States.

Zangwill's play was closely based on William Shakespeare's *Romeo and Juliet*, and was set in New York City, the home of many new U.S. immigrants. It told the story of David, a recent Jewish immigrant from Russia, who fell in love with a Christian Greek-Orthodox Russian girl and was able to overcome racial prejudice between their respective communities in America. In this excerpt, David reflects emotionally on how immigrants from diverse races and nationalities were merging into one American race and describes America metaphorically as a "melting pot." The concept of the melting pot as applied to American society is believed to have originated in the works of the writer Hector St. Jean de Crevecoeur (1735–1813), but Zangwill's play first brought the concept into popular use.

The "Melting Pot" theory, later known as "cultural assimilation," assumed that immigrants would lose their own separate cultural and religious identities, take on the ways and characteristics of the dominant host society, and weaken their links with their own native cultures.

Even at the time that Zangwill's play opened in Washington, many opposed the idea that America was a melting pot into which immigrants from different races and cultures could seamlessly assimilate, or that they would want to lose their own ethnic and cultural identities and become American. Some of the established Americans at the time were also uncomfortable with the idea of welcoming and integrating many new groups of immigrants into American society.

Indeed, there was considerable prejudice and discrimination in America in the late nineteenth and early twentieth centuries towards various nonwhite immigrants and ethnic minorities such as the Chinese and African Americans, but also towards

A sign in Harlem, New York City, advertises "Kosher Restaurant Featuring African Cuisine," 1973. © BETTMANN/CORBIS.

European immigrants including the Jews and the Irish. In the case of most European immigrants, however, a high degree of assimilation into existing American society did occur, and the society in turn was undoubtedly influenced by the distinctive cultural features of these groups. This indicates that there may have been some merit in the idea of a cultural melting pot, but that at best the mixing was limited to groups that were already racially or culturally similar.

Some decades later, in the 1960s, a publication by Nathan Glazer and Sen. Daniel Patrick Moynihan entitled *Beyond the Melting Pot* argued that even white immigrant groups retained their own ethnic identities and continued to be largely segregated within their own communities, while sharing a national 'American' culture. Other authors have argued that America never really had a history of welcoming immigrants in the way that the melting pot concept suggests, pointing out that immigration has always been tightly controlled, especially in relation to certain races and nationalities.

PRIMARY SOURCE

DAVID *[Opens it eagerly, then smiles broadly with pleasure.]* Oh, Miss Revendal! Isn't that great! To play again at your Settlement. I *am* getting famous.

VERA But we can't offer you a fee.

MENDEL *[Quickly sotto voce to VERA]* Thank you!

DAVID A fee! I'd pay a fee to see all those happy immigrants you gather together—Dutchmen and Greeks, Poles and Norwegians, Welsh and Armenians. If you only had Jews, it would be as good as going to Ellis Island.

VERA *[Smiling]* What a strange taste! Who on earth wants to go to Ellis Island?

DAVID Oh, I love going to Ellis Island to watch the ships coming in from Europe, and to think that all those weary, sea-tossed wanderers are feeling what *I* felt when America first stretched out her great mother-hand to *me*!

VERA *[Softly]* Were you very happy?

DAVID It was heaven. You must remember that all my life I had heard of America—everybody in our town had friends there or was going there or got money orders from there. The earliest game I played at was selling off my toy furniture and setting up in America. All my life America was waiting, beckoning, shining—the place where God would wipe away tears from off all faces. *[He ends in a half-sob.]*

MENDEL *[Rises, as in terror]* Now, now, David, don't get excited. *[Approaches him.]*

DAVID To think that the same great torch of liberty which threw its light across all the broad seas and lands into my little garret in Russia, is shining also for all those other weeping millions of Europe, shining wherever men hunger and are oppressed—

MENDEL *[Soothingly]* Yes, yes, David. *[Laying hand on his shoulder]* Now sit down and—

DAVID *[Unheeding]* Shining over the starving villages of Italy and Ireland, over the swarming stony cities of Poland and Galicia, over the ruined farms of Roumania, over the shambles of Russia—

MENDEL *[Pleadingly]* David!

DAVID Oh, Miss Revendal, when I look at our Statue of Liberty, I just seem to hear the voice of America crying: "Come unto me all ye that labour and are heavy laden and I will give you rest—rest————" *[He is now almost sobbing.]*

MENDEL Don't talk any more—you know it is bad for you.

DAVID But Miss Revendal asked—and I want to explain to her what America means to me.

MENDEL You can explain it in your American symphony.

VERA *[Eagerly—to DAVID]* You compose?

DAVID *[Embarrassed]* Oh, uncle, why did you talk of—? Uncle always—my music is so thin and tinkling. When I am *writing* my American symphony, it seems like thunder crashing though a forest full of bird songs. But next day—oh, next day! *[He laughs dolefully and turns away]*

VERA So your music finds inspiration in America?

DAVID Yes—in the seething of the Crucible.

VERA The Crucible? I don't understand!

DAVID Not understand! You, the Spirit of the Settlement! *[He rises and crosses to her and leans over the table, facing her.]* Not understand that America is God's Crucible, the great Melting-Pot where all the races of Europe are melting and re-forming! Here you stand, good folk, think I, when I see them at Ellis Island, here you stand *[Graphically illustrating it on the table]* in your fifty groups, with your fifty languages and histories, and your fifty blood hatreds and rivalries. But you

won't be long like that, brothers, for these are the fires of God you've come to—these are the fires of God. A fig for your feuds and vendettas! Germans and Frenchmen, Irishmen and Englishmen, Jews and Russians—into the Crucible with you all! God is making the American.

MENDEL I should have thought the American was made already ——eighty millions of him.

DAVID Eighty millions! *[He smiles toward VERA in good-humoured derision.]* Eighty millions! Over a continent! Why, that cockleshell of a Britain has forty millions! No, uncle, the real American has not yet arrived. He is only in the Crucible, I tell you—he will be the fusion of all races, perhaps the coming superman.

SIGNIFICANCE

Recent waves of immigration to the United States have been mainly from the countries of Latin America, Asia, and the Middle East—countries that are racially, linguistically, and culturally very different to the United States. These immigrants are therefore less likely to become part of the American melting pot in the same way as the earlier waves of immigrants from Europe. Moreover, the policy emphasis in the United States has shifted from encouraging the full assimilation of immigrant groups to promoting a degree of multi-culturalism, for example, by introducing bilingual and bicultural educational programs in schools.

It has been predicted by demographers that the non-white percentage of the population will increase dramatically over the next few decades as a result of family reunification policies and natural increase, and that by 2050 around twenty-five percent of the American population will be Hispanic, twelve percent black and three percent Asian. In certain states, including California, Nevada, Texas, and New Jersey, non-white people are soon expected to be in the majority. Already, there is considerable ethnic segregation both geographically and economically, with many new immigrants concentrated in low-skilled or unskilled work and living in disadvantaged areas. It seems likely that the trend will be for increased multi-culturalism rather than assimilation, but the nature of the segregation that is occurring presents major social and economic challenges for the United States. At the same time, it can be argued that different ethnic groups are losing aspects of their cultural identities and being "Americanized" through the very strong influence of the media, especially television, which transcends ethnic and racial boundaries.

FURTHER RESOURCES

Books

Glazer, Nathan, and Daniel P. Moynihan. *Beyond the Melting Pot, Second Edition: The Negroes, Puerto Ricans, Jews, Italians, and Irish of New York City.* Cambridge, Mass.: The MIT Press, 1970.

Sollors Werner. *Beyond Ethnicity: Consent and Descent in American Culture.* Oxford and New York: Oxford University Press, 1986.

Periodicals

Burkhead, Paul. "Stirring the Pot: Immigrant and Refugee Challenges to the United States and the World." *Journal of International Affairs* 47 (1994).

Szuberla, Guy. "Zangwill's 'the Melting Pot' Plays Chicago." *MELUS.* 20 (3) (1995): 3–20.

Wortham, Anne. "The Melting Pot—Part I: Are We There Yet?" *World and I* 16 (9) (September 1, 2001).

Web site

Washingtonpost.com. "The Myth of the Melting Pot." February 22, 1998 <http://www.washingtonpost.com/wp-srv/national/longterm/meltingpot/melt0222.htm> (accessed July 14, 2006).

Good Metal in Our Melting Pot, Says Miss Wald

Newspaper article

By: Edward Marshall

Date: November 16, 1913

Source: Marshall, Edward. "Good Metal in Our Melting Pot, Says Miss Wald." *New York Times*, November 16, 1913.

About the Author: Edward Marshall was a writer for the *New York Times* in the 1910s, writing on immigration, drug policy, and other issues for the newspaper.

INTRODUCTION

During the period 1881–1884 Russian pogroms—targeted attacks against Jewish people—ravaged Russia, Ukraine, Poland, and Monrovia after the assassination of the Russian leader Tsar Alexander II. The killer was assumed to be Jewish, and the ensuing riots and mob violence spread throughout the Russian empire. The new tsar, Alexander III, wrongly accused the Jewish people of instigating the riots and cracked down on Jews in a series of strident laws restricting Jewish citizens' rights. Russian Jews fled Eastern Europe, and immigration to the United States increased dramatically. These Eastern European Jewish immigrants spoke Yiddish and were Ashkenazi Jews—of German descent—in sharp contrast to many Jewish citizens in the United States, who were Sephardic Jews, descended from Iberian ancestors.

Another wave of pogroms in 1903–1906 left thousands dead from mob violence, and a new group of immigrants reached the United States, settling in large cities such as New York, Cleveland, and Boston, cities with established Jewish neighborhoods. By 1924, more than two million Jews from Eastern Europe had entered the United States, all within a forty-year span.

The impact on American society was dramatic. The new immigrants were largely poor, observant in their religion, and came from rural backgrounds. Thrust into overcrowded city tenements and low-paying wage labor in factories, the Russian Jews changed New York City and alarmed Progressive Era social workers and reformers with their extensive needs.

Eastern European immigration and the Progressive Era are inexorably intertwined in U.S. history; social reformers such as Jane Addams of Hull House and Lillian Wald of Henry Street settlement house looked at the new immigrants with a mixture of compassion, determination, and social science analysis. Part of a group of well-educated women who worked to professionalize and legitimize human service work, women such as Addams and Wald viewed poverty, crime, disease, and poor education not as the product of character flaws, but of social conditions. By changing society—through government initiative, private efforts, or individually with education—such social problems could, in the opinion of Progressive Era reformers, be resolved.

Settlement houses provided new immigrants with shelter, food, social activities, "Americanization," English language classes, and other support. Over time, while prejudice against Jewish immigrants from white Anglo-Saxon citizens persisted, the Eastern European Jewish immigrants gradually became better assimilated into U.S. society.

Lillian Wald, interviewed in a newspaper article from 1913, expressed the opinion of many reformers who worked with Russian immigrants.

■ PRIMARY SOURCE

Russian Intellectual Hunger

"The effect of years of revolution upon the many Russian girls among them is to give them a solidarity which the American working girl does not possess at all. They have a

Students at Hazelton Area High School dance to meringue between classes, Pennsylvania, September 20, 2005. All are recent immigrants from Latin America. AP IMAGES.

definite vision of a better society in which opportunity for real life will be made possible: their intellectual hunger is as extraordinary as their love of beauty."

"Life to them is incomplete that offers nothing but hard, grinding, soul-stultifying labor, insufficiently recompensed to put better things within their reach. That they are willing to struggle to attain what they seek is evidenced by the attendance of hordes of them at night school four nights a week after a hard day's work. They must know, of course, that this will sap vitality and make them old before their time; but, however small it may be, they demand something of the glory and beauty of life."

"The divine discontent, the enthusiasm, the hope and the vision of the Russian Jewish girl and woman immigrant have been and are a vastly valuable contribution to America in general and the American labor movement in particular."

"Even the Italian working women, who are notably kept under the guidance and control of their men, whether fathers, brother, or husbands, are beginning now to feel this elevating influence of Jewish women workers."

"The contemptuous attitude of the American people toward the immigrant has cost the nation much. An illustration of it lies in New York's experience with midwives. Although it was demonstrable that 50,000 childbirths every year were attended by midwives and that midwives attended at not less than 98 percent of all Italian births, it was not until 1911 that a definite public plan for the training of midwives in city hospitals was taken up."

"Thus, through many years, midwives, untrained, unsupervised, were permitted to commit their crimes of viciousness or ignorance unchecked, uneducated. Our native population did not suffer, for it did not employ midwives."

"We must find no defense for our indifference in the fact that foreigners are exploited mainly by their own people. That argument was used by those opposed to or lukewarm in regard to the recent admirable campaign against white slavers. The American public through this moral indifference has condoned too many grave offenses. Why can we forget that in to-day's raw immigrant is really hidden tomorrow's citizen, enfranchised and powerful?

For our own sake we should protect and educate newcomers."

"To many foreigners indolence in justice, which condones violations of the laws, failures to meet contracts, and that deplorable sort of thing, have come to constitute 'the American way.' Whose fault is this? Not theirs!"

"An interesting aspect of the immigration problem is political assimilation. The Jewish immigrant, with his tradition of persecution, is naturally interested in movements of protest against exploitation and tyranny. You will find him in sympathy, especially the young immigrant, with the Socialist and other radical movements. But the Jewish immigrant adapts himself to our political life; he soon becomes, like the American, a political opportunist."

"His Americanization makes him more conservative, but always in sympathy with independent and progressive political tendencies. The east side has followed progressive, independent leadership, irrespective of party affiliations. The Jewish immigrant responds to an idealistic appeal, especially when that appeal is in favor of freedom from political dependence. The Americanized Jewish immigrant is not closely attached to the machine. He becomes an independent voter. When he moves from his first way-station into quarters that indicate growing prosperity it means increasing political independence."

"The east side is independent in political revivals. But the Bronx is independent normally. The recent election returns will show how strongly anti-Tammany was the vote in those Jewish districts which had been believed to have been captured by Tammany."

I asked Miss Wald to summarize, in some degree, the changes she had seen on the east side during the score of years through which she has watched it.

"Standards of living are definitely higher here than they were twenty years ago," she answered, "in spite of its increased cost. It was once said that if an east side building was provided with bathtubs the tenants would keep coal in them. I never quite subscribed to that."

"My belief has found notable corroboration in the fact that no municipal bath in the world has so great a patronage as ours on the east side, in proportion to the population which it is designed to serve."

"There have been improvements in the quality of the material coming to us. From Russia, for example, we are getting a much more open-minded class than once came to us from there."

"Perhaps because they emigrated rapidly and in large groups at first, virtually stripping their country of their class, Russian immigration now may show fewer splendid individuals from highly intellectual circles than it at first did. These early coming individuals constituted a notable intellectual circle. There were Gordin, the playwright; Abe Kahn

of The Jewish Vorwarts, and many scientific men and physicians."

"But the general level of our Russian immigration is far higher than it was some years ago."

Vicious Conditions Here

"Frequent recent statements to the discredit of the Jews of the east side indicate only the demoralization of our own conditions; prove the fact that these have now become so vicious that they can break down even the fine traditions of the Jew. That we should influence for evil the class of immigration which is so notably more susceptible to good than evil is tragic."

"The reduction in infant mortality in the tenements, so notable of late, could never have been wrought had we not had a fine physical foundation on which to work."

"And intellectually the east side is capable of anything. The standing of the east side youngsters in the schools attests that. The results among tenement house mothers of the work of the milk stations prove that. At our station we have not found a mother who could not be educated, or who did not want to be. Last year we had an infant mortality of but one-half of one per cent."

"It is my strong conviction that most immigrants who have gone wrong have fallen, first, because of the environment into which we blindly thrust them; second, because our treatment of them does not dignify, does not even recognize, the personality of the individual."

"The American is arrogant. To him an immigrant is a 'dago' or a 'sheeny.' That does great harm."

SIGNIFICANCE

By the mid 1910s, anti-immigrant sentiment in urban centers had caused problems for immigrants—especially Jewish immigrants. Many Jewish immigrants, as the article notes, supported more progressive political causes and held left-of-center political positions, supporting unions, Socialism, and at times Communism. The United States appealed to Eastern European Jews for a number of reasons: freedom of political thought, economic opportunity, and the lack of registration requirements present in many European countries for Jewish residents. At the same time, nativism increased in urban centers.

Wald's comments on midwives and the tendency for immigrants to be victimized by their own countrymen are reflected in this passage:

> We must find no defense for our indifference in the fact that foreigners are exploited mainly by their own people. That argument was used by those opposed to or lukewarm in regard to the recent

admirable campaign against white slavers. The American public through this moral indifference has condoned too many grave offenses. Why can we forget that in to-day's raw immigrant is really hidden tomorrow's citizen, enfranchised and powerful? For our own sake we should protect and educate newcomers.

The "Americanization" movement was a strong element in progressive reform thought; social services, education, and proper moral guidance, reformers believed, could help to make immigrants an important part of U.S. society, but more importantly, molded immigrants into a more conventional form that fit into the progressive era's ideal of scientific management and orderly society. At the same time, many Jews were suspicious of offers for assistance from Christians—Protestants in particular—for fear that acceptance of such offers was contingent upon conversion, or that the support had strings attached.

Wald's portrayal of Russian immigrant women as hardworking, devoted to school and work, and a "valuable contribution to America in general and the American labor movement in particular" was a calculated attempt to sway white citizens toward immigration support. By linking Russian Jewish immigrants to the labor movement, Wald tried to use "good" immigrants to bridge the issues of immigration and labor. More than ninety percent of all Russian Jews who left their home countries settled into the United States; absorbing all those workers into the labor force was a painstaking process, coinciding with massive industrial development and strong union coalescence.

The "red scare" of the late 1910s and early 1920s hurt immigrants from all backgrounds, but had a particularly strong impact on Jewish immigrants. The wrongful arrest, conviction, and execution of Italian immigrants Sacco and Vanzetti; the American Protection League that gained 250,000 Americans in its membership, all prepared to report anti-American activities to the federal government; and the Palmer Raids that resulted in activist Emma Goldman's deportation—each fed into an insecurity concerning Jewish immigration and assimilation into American society at a time of great upheaval and adaptation in the American economic and social structure.

FURTHER RESOURCES
Books
Chambers, John Whiteclay. *The Tyranny of Change: America in the Progressive Era, 1890–1920.* New York: St. Martin's Press, 2000.

Friedman-Kasaba, Kathie. *Memories of Migration: Gender, Ethnicity, and Work in the Lives of Jewish and Italian Women in New York, 1870–1924.* Albany: State University of New York Press, 1996.

Hindus, Milton. *The Jewish East Side, 1881–1924.* New Brunswick, N.J.: Transaction Publishers, 1996.

Wald, Lillian. *The House on Henry Street.* New York: Henry Holt and Company, 1915.

Your Duty—Buy United States Government Bonds

2nd Liberty Loan of 1917

Poster

By: U.S. Treasury

Date: 1917

Source: © Swim Ink, LLC/Corbis.

About the Artist: The artist who composed this poster is unknown. The image is part of the collection of the Corbis Corporation, headquartered in Seattle, with a worldwide archive of over seventy million images.

INTRODUCTION
From 1914 to 1918, the nations of the world spent an estimated $185 billion fighting the Great War, better known today as World War I. Another $150 billion was probably spent as well, making the total cost of the conflict more than $300 billion. From its entry in 1917 to the war's conclusion the following year, the United States incurred an estimated $23 billion in direct costs. Given that total federal receipts for 1917 were only $1 billion, the U.S. Congress and the president needed to quickly boost revenue to underwrite the war.

As in the Civil War, Congress first expanded the federal income tax, doubling the rate from one percent to two percent and lowering the threshold at which individuals began paying. Taxpayers fortunate enough to earn $1 million or more were taxed at a rate of fifty percent, a rate later raised to seventy-seven percent. Federal revenues quadrupled, rising to $4 billion in 1918, due largely to these tax changes.

Anticipating climbing war costs, Congress also passed the Emergency Loan Act of 1917. This action raised war capital by authorizing the treasury to issue $5 billion in war bonds. These bonds, dubbed Liberty Bonds, carried an interest rate of 3.5 percent. By purchasing a bond, citizens were loaning the government money to prosecute the war in return for repayment after the war ended.

Liberty Bonds were among the most heavily marketed financial products of the early twentieth century. Massive rallies were held to promote bond sales. Celebrities lent their names and their time to the sales effort, and civilian volunteers traveled the country promoting the cause. Colorful posters depicted the suffering of enlisted men and the threat to children and homes, urging Americans to help defeat the enemy by buying bonds. As war costs mounted, another $4 billion in Liberty Bonds were issued later that year, followed by $9 billion more in 1918.

■ PRIMARY SOURCE

YOUR DUTY—BUY UNITED STATES GOVERNMENT BONDS
See primary source image.

SIGNIFICANCE

While warfare is generally incited by ideology, it is supported with money. In the simplest economic analysis, the Allies won World War I due to their deeper pockets. Whereas the Allies spent $126 billion during the war, the four Central Powers were able to invest less than half that amount. This enormous financial advantage ultimately proved insurmountable.

In the years since World War I, the costs of warfare have spiraled upward. World War II was significantly more expensive than World War I. The total cost is difficult to accurately estimate due to the war's immense scope. The United States is generally acknowledged to have invested more than $341 billion, or more than the total direct cost to all combatants of World War I. Germany's expenditures in World War II also exceeded the combined cost of World War I, spending an estimated $272 billion, while the Soviet Union and Great Britain each spent more than $100 billion. Estimates of the total cost of the war range from $1 trillion upward.

Later conflicts have not reached the massive scope of World War II, however, war continues to be an expensive undertaking. In colloquial terms, governments often must make a choice between guns and butter, meaning that government resources spent on the military are not available to carry out domestic programs. During the two World Wars, the nation was willing to make this sacrifice in the name of winning a massive conflict. Later wars have been fought on

■ PRIMARY SOURCE

Your Duty—Buy United States Government Bonds: A poster for the Second Liberty Loan of 1917 war bonds. Designed to stir patriotic feeling in recent arrivals, it shows immigrants on the deck of a ship looking at the Statue of Liberty as they arrive in America. © SWIM INK, LLC/CORBIS.

a more limited scale, forcing presidents to weigh spending options and make difficult choices.

The involvement of the United States in the Korean War was relatively limited and cost an estimated $20 billion, minimizing its financial impact at home. But the Vietnam War dragged on for years and became increasingly costly. President Lyndon Johnson's administration was committed to a massive expansion of federal social programs, an effort he labeled The Great Society. Johnson believed he could battle poverty at home and Communists in Southeast Asia simultaneously. However, the rising cost of the Vietnam conflict, which eventually topped $140 billion, drained funds from domestic initiatives, hamstringing his efforts.

The financial cost of the Cold War, a fifty-year nuclear standoff between the United States and the

REMEMBER!
THE FLAG OF LIBERTY
SUPPORT IT!

BUY
U.S.Government Bonds
3rd. LIBERTY LOAN

A 1917 poster featuring images of immigration to the United States encourages Americans to support the war effort and buy government bonds. © K.J. HISTORICAL/CORBIS.

Soviet Union is harder to quantify. Throughout this period, the United States consistently spent five to ten percent of its Gross National Product on defense. An analysis by the CATO Institute places total U.S. military expenditures from 1948 to 1986 at $6.3 trillion. Following the fall of the Soviet Union, the former Cold War adversaries have each incurred billions of dollars per year in clean-up costs related to nuclear weapons production.

As he left office in 1961, President Eisenhower, a former military officer, warned of the dangers of a growing military-industrial complex, as the United States had, for the first time in its history, developed industrial firms dedicated solely to military production. Eisenhower feared that the influence of these firms would lead to rising military expenditures, and along with them the incentive to employ military force more frequently.

In 2005, New York governor George Pataki proposed the issuance of state-backed Liberty Bonds.

These tax-free bonds would help fund the redevelopment of the area destroyed in the terrorist attacks of September 11, 2001.

FURTHER RESOURCES

Books

Blum, John Morton. *V Was for Victory. Politics and American Culture during World War II*. New York: Harcourt Brace Jovanovich, 1976.

Hackemer, Kurt. *The U.S. Navy and the Origins of the Military Industrial Complex, 1847–1883*. Washington, D.C.: Naval Institute Press, 2001.

O'Neill, William L. *A Democracy at War. America's Fight at Home and Abroad in World War II*. New York: The Free Press, 1993.

Periodicals

Bagli, Charles V. "Pataki Offers Liberty Bonds to Keep Tower On Schedule." *New York Times* 155 (2005): B3.

Taliaferro, Jeffrey W. "Power Politics and the Balance of Risk: Hypotheses on Great Power Intervention in the Periphery." *Political Psychology* 25 (2004): 177–211.

Whitney, J. D. "Insurance Oil for War Waters." *Nation* 106 (1918): 162–164.

Web sites

Brigham Young University. "The World War I Document Archive." <http://www.lib.byu.edu/~rdh/wwi/> (accessed June 8, 2006).

PBS. "The Great War and the Shaping of the 20th Century." <http://www.pbs.org/greatwar/> (accessed June 7, 2006).

University of Houston: Digital History. "A Chronology of World War I." <http://www.digitalhistory.uh.edu/historyonline/ww1_chron.cfm> (accessed June 8, 2006).

Come Unto Me, Ye Opprest!

Editorial cartoon

By: James Pinckney Alley

Date: July 5, 1919

Source: Alley, James Pinckney. "Come Unto Me, Ye Opprest!" *Literary Digest* (reprinted from the *Commercial Appeal*), July 5, 1919.

About the Author: James P. Alley (1885–1934) was an editorial cartoonist for the Memphis newspaper *Commercial Appeal* between the years of 1916 and 1934. He is best known as the creator of "Hambone," a popular, nationally syndicated cartoon.

INTRODUCTION

During World War I, Americans had grown accustomed to the suppression of dissent. With the war's end, the intolerance that had been directed mainly against those suspected of sympathizing with Germany came to cover a wider range of people. Foreigners, Catholics, Jews, blacks, radicals, and strikers all came under assault for being un-American. Foreigners, the main source of membership for the new American Communist Party, and the various anarchist groups, were particularly disliked.

The new wave of fear found a scapegoat in the Bolshevik Revolution in Russia and the threat of worldwide revolution against capitalism. However, the number of communists in the United States never exceeded one percent of the population, and most were intellectuals rather than workers. But political radicals, the overwhelming majority of whom were foreign-born immigrants from southern and eastern Europe, attracted considerable comment from both politicians and newspaper writers. These new immigrants had such different ideas and customs from the old immigrants of northern and western Europe that they were disturbing to many of the native-born. Worsening the climate, violence in labor relations right after the war deepened concern about public safety. Bomb scares turned that concern into panic.

In 1919 and 1920, news of bombs filled headlines. A time bomb was discovered in a package addressed to the mayor of Seattle. Another bomb blew off the hands of a Georgia senator's house servant. No less than thirty-six bombs addressed to such prominent people as financier J. P. Morgan and oil magnate John D. Rockefeller were discovered in various post offices. A bomb exploded in front of the Washington home of the attorney general, and in September 1920, a bomb exploded on Wall Street that killed thirty-eight and wounded hundreds of people. To many Americans, including the editorial cartoonist Alley, it seemed as if immigrants were coming to American shores with the intent of blowing up the United States.

PRIMARY SOURCE

COME UNTO ME, YE OPPREST!

See primary source image.

SIGNIFICANCE

In response to the bomb scares, Attorney General A. Mitchell Palmer encouraged fears of imminent revolution. Palmer, who had presidential

"COME UNTO ME, YE OPPREST!"

PRIMARY SOURCE

Come Unto Me, Ye Opprest!: This cartoon from 1919 depicts immigrants from southern and eastern Europe as dangerous, bomb-throwing radicals intent upon destroying the United States. Many Americans held such views during the Red Scare after World War I. PUBLIC DOMAIN.

aspirations, apparently viewed the Red Scare as a key to higher office. He claimed to see Reds almost everywhere that he looked and he proceeded to hunt them down. On January 1, 1920, Palmer ordered simultaneous raids on every Bolshevik cell in the country. In about a week, more than four thousand people were arrested and their property confiscated. Friends who visited the jailed were also jailed on grounds of having sympathy for revolutionaries. Though supposedly armed to the teeth, the thousands of radicals yielded a total of three pistols and no explosives. The raids were followed by the eventual deportation of 556 aliens convicted of no crime. Vigilantism spread across the nation but the Red Scare quickly waned.

The fear of immigrant radicals led to a decline in the Americanization movement as the United States turned its attention from resident aliens to the question of immigration restriction. Since the enactment of the literacy test in 1917, questions of immigration policy had remained on the back burner. However, the end of the war permitted the resumption of large-scale European immigration that coincided with a sharp economic downturn in 1920 and the Red Scare. The agitation for restriction only quieted down with the adoption of laws that reduced immigration to a trickle. An era of isolationism had begun that would only end with the entrance of the United States into World War II.

FURTHER RESOURCES

Books

Keene, Jennifer D. *The U.S. and the First War*. New York: Longman, 2000.

Morgan, Ted. *Reds: McCarthyism in Twentieth-Century America*. New York: Random House, 2004.

Schmidt, Regin. *Red Scare: FBI and the Origins of Anticommunism in the U.S., 1919–1943*. Copenhagen: University of Copenhagen, 2000.

Processing Immigrant Arrivals at Ellis Island

Photograph

By: Anonymous

Date: 1920

Source: AP/Wide World Photos.

About the Author: The Associated Press (AP) is a worldwide news agency based in New York.

INTRODUCTION

The official United States immigration facilities located on Ellis Island received more than 12 million immigrants between 1892 and 1954. Ellis Island lies near the Statue of Liberty in the New York Harbor, near the mouth of the Hudson River. Ellis Island was used to register immigrants, and also to screen out those who had contagious diseases or legal problems that would be a burden to society. Inspection at Ellis Island was primarily for the poorer immigrants arriving as third-class passengers aboard steamships, the most common mode of arrival during this time period. Passengers in first and second-class were briefly screened on board the ships, and only had to stop through Ellis Island if they had obvious problems with their health or paperwork.

Medical exams and legal inspections took place in a large room on Ellis Island called the Great Hall. Immigrants reported the Great Hall to be a vociferous place, with the sounds of many different

languages echoing throughout the Hall's high ceilings. The arrivals were herded through metal guardrails, lining up alphabetically and according to nationality. It was in the Great Hall where immigrants would learn if they were free to enter the United States, or whether they would have to stay on Ellis Island for further inspection. Approximately one to two percent of arrivals were told they had to return to their country of origin. For immigrants whose documents were in order, the check-in process would last between two and five hours. Doctors from the United States Public Health Service looked quickly over the arrivals for obvious medical problems, including anemia and goiter. Each arrival was required to fill out a questionnaire while still on board the ship, which would then be reviewed by legal inspectors with the Bureau of Immigration.

The Federal Government opened the Ellis Island facility as a response to the large influx of immigrants that overwhelmed the New York State immigration center at Castle Garden in the 1880s. Originally the Ellis Island structures were built of pinewood, but five years after opening a fire completely destroyed the buildings along with millions of immigration records dating back to 1855. The facility was promptly rebuilt under the condition that all buildings be fireproof. Due to unexpected increases in immigrants between 1900 and 1915, masons and carpenters struggled to keep up with the need for larger hospital buildings, dormitories, contagious disease wards, and kitchens.

PRIMARY SOURCE

PROCESSING IMMIGRANT ARRIVALS AT ELLIS ISLAND
See primary source image.

SIGNIFICANCE

As immigrants flooded into the United States during the late 1800s and early 1900s, there was belief among some politicians that immigration should be restricted. Such legislation came in 1882 with the Chinese Exclusion Act, and then the first Immigration Act that forbade the entrance of criminals into the United States. Later, the Alien Contract Labor Laws restricted the entrance of immigrants who had arranged labor contracts prior to their arrival. The government also enacted a requirement that immigrants must pass a literacy test before entering the United States. Despite these first laws, the flow of immigrants did not start to decrease until

Processing Immigrant Arrivals at Ellis Island: Hundreds of immigrants sit in the Great Hall of Ellis Island in New York City as they await processing procedures to begin for their possible entrance into the United States. AP/WIDE WORLD PHOTOS.

the passage of the Quota Laws in 1921, and the National Origins Act of 1924. These laws attempted to reduce the large number of immigrants from countries such as Poland and Italy, in eastern and southern Europe, as they were considered inferior to those who came from the more traditional immigrant countries in western and northern Europe.

As the United States began opening embassies throughout the world in the 1920s, the need for Ellis Island faded. Embassies allowed would-be immigrants to apply for U.S. visas and undergo medical exams in their own countries. After 1924, people stopping through Ellis Island were only immigrants whose paperwork had problems, as well as people displaced by war and other events. Before being closed, Ellis Island was used during World War II for detaining merchant seamen from enemy countries. President Lyndon Johnson made Ellis Island part of the Statue of Liberty National Monument in 1965. The facilities later underwent restoration, and were opened to the public as a museum in 1990.

The agency responsible for determining the legal status of immigrants at Ellis Island, the United States Public Health Service and the Bureau of Immigration, later became the Immigration and Naturalization Service (INS). As part of the United States Department of Homeland Security, the INS was re-structured in 2003, creating the Bureau of Citizenship and

Immigrant children are examined by a New York City health officer after arriving in the city from Ellis Island, 1911. © CORBIS-BETTMANN. REPRODUCED BY PERMISSION.

Immigration Services, Bureau of Immigrations and Customs Enforcement, and the Bureau of Customs and Border Protection.

FURTHER RESOURCES
Books

Brownstone, David M., Irene M. Franck, and Douglass Brownstone. *Island of Hope, Island of Tears*. New York: Metro Books, 2003.

Moreno, Barry. *Ellis Island*. Charleston, S.C.: Arcadia Publishing, 2003.

Wilkes, Stephen. *Ellis Island: Ghosts of Freedom*. New York: W.W. Norton & Company, 2006.

Periodicals

"Cabin Passengers to Be Inspected Too." *New York Times* (November 1, 1905): 6.

"Crowding Ellis Island." *New York Times* (April 13, 1902): 3.

Web sites

United States Homeland Security. "U.S. Citizenship and Immigration Services." June 23, 2006 <http://www.uscis.gov/graphics/index.htm> (accessed June 26, 2006).

The Materials of the New Race

Book excerpt

By: Margaret Sanger

Date: 1920

Source: Sanger, Margaret. *Woman and the New Race.* New York: Bretano's, 1920.

About the Author: Margaret Sanger (1879–1966) was a nurse who fought for public access to information on contraception in the early part of the twentieth century. Her efforts to disseminate birth control information led to her repeated arrest for violating the Comstock Law in the United States. She helped to found Planned Parenthood, an organization that helps provide health and gynecological care for women in the United States.

INTRODUCTION

The forces of urbanization, industrialization, and immigration combined in the early decades of the twentieth century to create social conditions for families in inner cities that were, at times, unbearable and deadly. With infant mortality rates as high as twenty percent for children under the age of five, reformers such as Lillian Wald of Henry Street, Jane Addams of Hull House, and Florence Kelley fought to change the social and policy conditions that fed into child mortality and poverty.

Margaret Sanger was a middle class, married woman with three children, one of whom died in childhood. She began working as a nurse in the Lower East Side of New York City in the early 1900s; as part of the Progressive Era reform movement, Sanger represented the well-educated, white middle class women who sought to help poor, immigrant, and minority women to assimilate into American culture and to fight against infectious disease, poverty, and high rates of child mortality.

Sanger viewed the lack of family planning options for families to be the single greatest social problems facing all families—upper, middle, and lower class. If families could not choose the timing and the pacing of their children, she argued, then they could not reduce or eliminate the social conditions that fed into the cycles of poverty, disease, and neglect so readily apparent in tenements and slums in the inner cities.

In addition, Sanger argued that when poor women were forced to work in factories and experience eight, ten, twelve, or more pregnancies in their lifetime, the nutritional and health toll on their bodies was so great

Margaret Sanger. AP/WIDE WORLD PHOTOS. REPRODUCED BY PERMISSION.

that the next generation experienced a negative impact; in Sanger's words, "In the United States, some 300,000 children under one year of age die each twelve months. Approximately ninety percent of these deaths are directly or indirectly due to malnutrition, to other diseased conditions resulting from poverty, or to excessive childbearing by the mother."

In the following essay, from her book *Woman and the New Race*, Sanger focuses on the experience of the poorest sectors in American society, their affect on the culture, and the development of a "new race."

PRIMARY SOURCE

Each of us has an ideal of what the American of the future should be. We have been told times without number that out of the mixture of stocks, the intermingling of ideas and aspirations, there is to come a race greater than any which has contributed to the population of the United States. What is the basis for this hope that is so generally indulged in? If the hope is founded upon realities, how may it be realized? To understand the difficulties and the obstacles to

be overcome before the dream of a greater race in America can be attained, is to understand something of the task before the women who shall give birth to that race.

What material is there for a greater American race? What elements make up our present millions? Where do they live? How do they live? In what direction does our national civilization bend their ideals? What is the effect of the "melting pot" upon the foreigner, once he begins to "melt?"

Are we now producing a freer, juster, more intelligent, more idealistic, creative people out of the varied ingredients here?

Before we can answer these questions, we must consider briefly the races which have contributed to American population.

Among our more than 100,000,000 population are Negroes, Indians, Chinese and other colored people to the number of 11,000,000. There are also 14,500,000 persons of foreign birth. Besides these there are 14,000,000 children of foreign-born parents and 6,500,000 persons whose fathers or mothers were born on foreign soil, making a total of 46,000,000 people of foreign stock. Fifty percent of our population is of the native white strain.

Of the foreign stock in the United States, the last general census, compiled in 1910, shows that 25.7 percent was German, fourteen percent was Irish, 8.5 percent was Russian or Finnish, 7.2 was English, 6.5 percent Italian and 6.2 percent Austrian. The Abstract of the same census points out several significant facts. The Western European strains in this country are represented by a majority of native-born children of foreign-born or mixed parentage. This is because the immigration from those sources has been checked. On the other hand, immigration from Southern and Eastern Europe, including Russia and Finland, increased 175.4 percent from 1900 to 1910. During that period, the slums of Europe dumped their submerged inhabitants into America at a rate almost double that of the preceding decade, and the flow was still increasing at the time the census was taken. So it is more than likely that when the next census is taken it will be found that following 1910 there was an even greater flow from Spain, Italy, Hungary, Austria, Russia, Finland, and other countries where the iron hand of economic and political tyrannies had crushed great populations into ignorance and want. These peoples have not been in the United States long enough to produce great families. The census of 1920 will in all probability tell a story of a greater and more serious problem than did the last. . . .

That these foreigners who have come in hordes have brought with them their ignorance of hygiene and modern ways of living and that they are handicapped by religious superstitions is only too true. But they also bring in their hearts a desire for freedom from all the tyrannies that afflict the earth. They would not be here if they did not bear within them the hardihood of pioneers, a courage of no mean order. They have the simple faith that in America they will find equality, liberty and an opportunity for a decent livelihood. And they have something else. The cell plasms of these peoples are freighted with the potentialities of the best in Old World civilization. They come from lands rich in the traditions of courage, of art, music, letters, science and philosophy. Americans no longer consider themselves cultured unless they have journeyed to these lands to find access to the treasures created by men and women of this same blood. The immigrant brings the possibilities of all these things to our shores, but where is the opportunity to reproduce in the New World the cultures of the old?

What opportunities have we given to these peoples to enrich our civilization? We have greeted them as "a lot of ignorant foreigners," we have shouted at, bustled and kicked them. Our industries have taken advantage of their ignorance of the country's ways to take their toil in mills and mines and factories at starvation wages. We have herded them into slums to become diseased, to become social burdens or to die. We have huddled them together like rabbits to multiply their numbers and their misery. Instead of saying that we Americanize them, we should confess that we animalize them. The only freedom we seem to have given them is the freedom to make heavier and more secure their chains. What hope is there for racial progress in this human material, treated more carelessly and brutally than the cheapest factory product?

Nor are all our social handicaps bound up in the immigrant.

There were in the United States, when the Federal Industrial Relations Committee finished its work in 1915, several million migratory workers, most of them white, many of them married but separated from their families, who were compelled, like themselves, to struggle with dire want.

There were in 1910 more than 2,353,000 tenant farmers, two-thirds of whom lived and worked under the terrible conditions which the Industrial Relations Commission's report showed to prevail in the South and Southwest. These tenant farmers, as the report showed, were always in want, and were compelled by the very terms of the prevailing tenant contracts to produce children who must go to the fields and do the work of adults. The census proved that this tenancy was on the increase, the number of tenants in all but the New England and Middle Atlantic States having increased approximately thirty percent from 1900 to 1910.

Moreover, there were in the United States in 1910, 5,516,163 illiterates. Of these 1,378,884 were of pure native white stock. In some states in the South as much as twenty-nine percent of the population is illiterate, many of these, of course, being Negroes.

There is still another factor to be considered—a factor which because of its great scope is more ominous than any yet mentioned. This is the underpaid mass of workers in the United States—workers whose low wages are forcing them deeper into want each day. Let Senator Borah, not a radical nor even a reformer, but a leader of the Republican party, tell the story. "Fifty-seven percent of the families in the United States have incomes of $800 or less," said he in a speech before the Senate, August 24, 1917. "Seventy percent of the families of our country have incomes of $1,000 or less. Tell me how a man so situated can have shelter for his family; how he can provide food and clothing. He is an industrial peon. His home is scant and pinched beyond the power of language to tell. He sees his wife and children on the ragged edge of hunger from week to week and month to month. If sickness comes, he faces suicide or crime. He cannot educate his children; he cannot fit them for citizenship; he cannot even fit them as soldiers to die for their country.

"It is the tragedy of our whole national life—how these people live in such times as these. We have not yet gathered the fruits of such an industrial condition in this country. We have been saved thus far by reason of the newness of our national life, our vast public lands now almost exhausted, our great natural resources now fast being seized and held, but the hour of reckoning will come."

Senator Borah was thinking, doubtless, of open revolution, of bloodshed and the destruction of property. In a far more terrible sense, the reckoning which he has referred to is already upon us. The ills we suffer as the result of the conditions now prevailing in the United States are appalling in their sum. . . .

A few scattered statistics lack the power to reflect the broken lives of overworked fathers, the ceaseless, increasing pain of overburdened mothers and the agony of childhood fighting its way against the handicaps of ill health, insufficient food, inadequate training and stifling toil.

Can we expect to remedy this situation by dismissing the problem of the submerged native elements with legislative palliatives or treating it with careless scorn? Do we better it by driving out of the immigrant's heart the dream of liberty that brought him to our shores? Do we solve the problem by giving him, instead of an opportunity to develop his own culture, low wages, a home in the slums and those pseudo-patriotic preachments which constitute our machine-made "Americanization?"

Every detail of this sordid situation means a problem that must be solved before we can even clear the way for a greater race in America. Nor is there any hope of solving any of these problems if we continue to attack them in the usual way.

Men have sentimentalized about them and legislated upon them. They have denounced them and they have applied reforms. But it has all been ridiculously, cruelly futile.

This is the condition of things for which those stand who demand more and more children. Each child born under such conditions but makes them worse—each child in its own person suffers the consequence of the intensified evils.

If we are to develop in America a new race with a racial soul, we must keep the birth rate within the scope of our ability to understand as well as to educate. We must not encourage reproduction beyond our capacity to assimilate our numbers so as to make the coming generation into such physically fit, mentally capable, socially alert individuals as are the ideal of a democracy.

The intelligence of a people is of slow evolutional development—it lags far behind the reproductive ability. It is far too slow to cope with conditions created by an increasing population, unless that increase is carefully regulated.

We must, therefore, not permit an increase in population that we are not prepared to care for to the best advantage—that we are not prepared to do justice to, educationally and economically. We must popularize birth control thinking. We must not leave it haphazardly to be the privilege of the already privileged. We must put this means of freedom and growth into the hands of the masses.

We must set motherhood free. We must give the foreign and submerged mother knowledge that will enable her to prevent bringing to birth children she does not want. We know that in each of these submerged and semi-submerged elements of the population there are rich factors of racial culture. Motherhood is the channel through which these cultures flow. Motherhood, when free to choose the father, free to choose the time and the number of children who shall result from the union, automatically works in wondrous ways. It refuses to bring forth weaklings; refuses to bring forth slaves; refuses to bear children who must live under the conditions described. It withholds the unfit, brings forth the fit; brings few children into homes where there is not sufficient to provide for them. Instinctively it avoids all those things which multiply racial handicaps. Under such circumstances we can hope that the "melting pot" will refine. We shall see that it will save the precious metals of racial culture, fused into an amalgam of physical perfection, mental strength and spiritual progress. Such an American race, containing the best of all racial elements, could give to the world a vision and a leadership beyond our present imagination.

SIGNIFICANCE

Sanger's attitude toward the new immigrants—largely from southern and eastern Europe and mainly Jewish—reflected the beliefs of many Progressive Era reformers of her time. Americans regarded the new immigrants—who were mostly poor and uneducated, fleeing anti-Jewish pogroms and prejudice—as the cause of the squalor in the slums of the inner city.

Progressive Era reformers, however, viewed immigrants as ignorant, but educable. Through programs at settlement houses where immigrants could learn English, American customs, and basic home economics and household skills, progressive era reformers believed that these new immigrants could assimilate into American culture, changing the shape of society. Sanger found that whether a family was "native" or "immigrant" meant little if they were poor; the lack of birth control options coupled with the need for many poor mothers to work sixty to eighty hours a week in factories with poor working conditions led to the premature death of the mother, children with health problems, and the ongoing cycle forcing older children into the factories without benefit of ever receiving an education. Birth control, Sanger asserted, would give men and women control over their bodies, their families, and their personal circumstances.

The "new race" Sanger envisions incorporates the best of native and immigrant traits. Some modern critics have accused Sanger of espousing eugenics as a positive force in society; Sanger did promote voluntary sterilization, immigration restrictions against diseased or "enfeebled" immigrants, and strict controls on criminals, drug addicts, and some people with mental challenges. At the same time, her work in making birth control available to all women focused on universal access, to help families to accomplish the peace and progress that they, and progressive reformers, sought in society.

FURTHER RESOURCES
Books
Chambers, John Whiteclay. *The Tyranny of Change: America in the Progressive Era, 1890–1920*. New York: St. Martin's Press, 2000.

Friedman-Kasaba, Kathie. *Memories of Migration: Gender, Ethnicity, and Work in the Lives of Jewish and Italian*

Women in New York, 1870–1924. Albany, NY: State University of New York Press, 1996.

Sanger, Margaret. *The Autobiography of Margaret Sanger.* Mineola, NY: Dover Publications, 2004.

———. *The Selected papers of Margaret Sanger.* Champaign, IL: University of Illinois Press, 2002.

Wald, Lillian. *The House on Henry Street.* New York: Henry Holt and Company, 1915.

What I Owe to America

Book excerpt

By: Edward Bok

Date: 1921

Source: Bok, Edward. *The Americanization of Edward Bok*, Chapter 39. New York: Charles Scribner's Sons, 1921.

About the Author: Edward Bok (1863–1930), a Dutch immigrant to the United States, was the editor of the *Ladies' Home Journal* for thirty years.

INTRODUCTION

The editor and author Edward Bok came to America from the Netherlands in 1870 and quickly went from rags to riches. He demonstrated that an immigrant with no money and little formal education could succeed in the United States through hard work. Bok emphasized this notion through his writings.

Bok was born in Helder, Netherlands, in 1863, and settled in New York City upon his arrival in the United States in 1870. In 1876, he became an office boy for Western Union Telegraph. Later, he worked as a stenographer taking dictation at publisher Henry Holt and, later, for publisher Charles Scribner's Sons. In 1886, he founded the Bok Syndicate Press, which marketed a variety of feature articles to newspapers throughout the country. The syndicated "Bok page" was unique in that it featured articles by women writer's on women's interests. The success of this enterprise attracted the attention of publisher Cyrus Curtis, who invited Bok to become editor of his *Ladies' Home Journal.*

Bok spent thirty years at *Ladies' Home Journal*, becoming one of the most respected journalists in the nation. He introduced many innovations that later became standard in the field, including the advice-to-readers format, the polling of readers, and

correspondence columns. Bok always emphasized that there was no such thing as luck. Immigrants could only succeed as he had done, through hard work, thrift, and absolute honesty. He was convinced that the business elite of the Gilded Age, such as John D. Rockefeller, owed their position to superior talent and he romanticized their achievements in the pages of his magazine. During the final years of his life, Bok devoted his energies to philanthropy. His autobiography, *The Americanization of Edward Bok*, won the Pulitzer Prize in 1921. "What I Owe to America" is its concluding chapter.

PRIMARY SOURCE

WHATEVER shortcomings I may have found during my fifty-year period of Americanization; however America may have failed to help my transition from a foreigner into an American, I owe to her the most priceless gift that any nation can offer, and that is opportunity.

As the world stands to-day, no nation offers opportunity in the degree that America does to the foreign-born. Russia may, in the future, as I like to believe she will, prove a second United States of America in this respect. She has the same limitless area; her people the same potentialities. But, as things are to-day, the United States offers, as does no other nation, a limitless opportunity: here a man can go as far as his abilities will carry him. It may be that the foreign-born, as in my own case, must hold on to some of the ideals and ideas of the land of his birth; it may be that he must develop and mould his character by overcoming the habits resulting from national shortcomings. But into the best that the foreign-born can retain, America can graft such a wealth of inspiration, so high a national idealism, so great an opportunity for the highest endeavor, as to make him the fortunate man of the earth to-day.

He can go where he will: no traditions hamper him; no limitations are set except those within himself. The larger the area he chooses in which to work, the larger the vision he demonstrates, the more eager the people are to give support to his undertakings if they are convinced that he has their best welfare as his goal. There is no public confidence equal to that of the American public, once it is obtained. It is fickle, of course, as are all publics, but fickle only toward the man who cannot maintain an achieved success.

A man in America cannot complacently lean back upon victories won, as he can in the older European countries, and depend upon the glamour of the past to sustain him or the momentum of success to carry him. Probably the most alert public in the world, it requires of its leaders that they be alert. Its appetite for variety is insatiable, but its appreciation, when given, is fullhanded and whole-hearted. The American public never holds back from the man to whom it gives; it never bestows in a niggardly way; it gives all or nothing.

What is not generally understood of the American people is their wonderful idealism. Nothing so completely surprises the foreign-born as the discovery of this trait in the American character. The impression is current in European countries—perhaps less generally since the war—that America is given over solely to a worship of the American dollar. While between nations as between individuals, comparisons are valueless, it may not be amiss to say, from personal knowledge, that the Dutch worship the gulden infinitely more than do the Americans the dollar.

I do not claim that the American is always conscious of this idealism; often he is not. But let a great convulsion touching moral questions occur, and the result always shows how close to the surface is his idealism. And the fact that so frequently he puts over it a thick veneer of materialism does not affect its quality. The truest approach, the only approach in fact, to the American character is, as Viscount Bryce has so well said, through its idealism.

It is this quality which gives the truest inspiration to the foreign-born in his endeavor to serve the people of his adopted country. He is mentally sluggish, indeed, who does not discover that America will make good with him if he makes good with her.

But he must play fair. It is essentially the straight game that the true American plays, and he insists that you shall play it too. Evidence there is, of course, to the contrary in American life, experiences that seem to give ground for the belief that the man succeeds who is not scrupulous in playing his cards. But never is this true in the long run. Sooner or later—sometimes, unfortunately, later than sooner—the public discovers the trickery. In no other country in the world is the moral conception so clear and true as in America, and no people will give a larger and more permanent reward to the man whose effort for that public has its roots in honor and truth.

"The sky is the limit" to the foreign-born who comes to America endowed with honest endeavor, ceaseless industry, and the ability to carry through. In any honest endeavor, the way is wide open to the will to succeed. Every path beckons, every vista invites, every talent is called forth, and every efficient effort finds its due reward. In no land is the way so clear and so free.

How good an American has the process of Americanization made me? That I cannot say. Who can

say that of himself? But when I look around me at the American-born I have come to know as my close friends, I wonder whether, after all, the foreign-born does not make in some sense a better American—whether he is not able to get a truer perspective; whether his is not the deeper desire to see America greater; whether he is not less content to let its faulty institutions be as they are; whether in seeing faults more clearly he does not make a more decided effort to have America reach those ideals or those fundamentals of his own land which he feels are in his nature, and the best of which he is anxious to graft into the character of his adopted land?

It is naturally with a feeling of deep satisfaction that I remember two Presidents of the United States considered me a sufficiently typical American to wish to send me to my native land as the accredited minister of my adopted country. And yet when I analyze the reasons for my choice in both these instances, I derive a deeper satisfaction from the fact that my strong desire to work in America for America led me to ask to be permitted to remain here.

It is this strong impulse that my Americanization has made the driving power of my life. And I ask no greater privilege than to be allowed to live to see my potential America become actual: the America that I like to think of as the America of Abraham Lincoln and of Theodore Roosevelt—not faultless, but less faulty. It is a part in trying to shape that America, and an opportunity to work in that America when it comes, that I ask in return for what I owe to her. A greater privilege no man could have.

SIGNIFICANCE

Congress passed the Immigration Act of 1921 in the same year that *The Americanization of Edward Bok* was published. The legislation established annual quotas for each country outside of the Western Hemisphere. Three years later, Congress refined this legislation to severely limit immigration from eastern and southern European countries. Bok's book, although popular and well-respected, did not significantly change American attitudes toward immigration. While northern European Protestants, such as Bok, remained welcome, the golden door was slammed in the faces of all others.

Dutch immigrants were among the first to settle on American shores. They established a settlement in the Albany, New York, area in 1619—only a few years after British colonies founded Jamestown. After the colonial era, the peak years of Dutch immigration to the United States were 1830 to 1857, 1880 to 1893, 1900 to 1914, and 1945 to 1965. Most immigrants settled in rural areas of New York, Michigan, and

Edward Bok. GETTY IMAGES.

Wisconsin. Prior to World War II, the Dutch government neither hindered nor encouraged emigration. After the war, which left the Netherlands devastated, the Netherlands' governent wanted people to leave, but immigration has remained small in comparison to other groups such as the Irish and Germans. Many of the Dutch immigrants matched Bok in initiative and drive. Dutch-American successes include Presidents Theodore and Franklin Roosevelt as well as their cousin, Eleanor Roosevelt; President Martin Van Buren; and millionaire railroad entrepreneur Cornelius Vanderbilt.

FURTHER RESOURCES
Books

Krabbendam, Hans. *The Model Man: A Life of Edward William Bok, 1863–1930*. Amsterdam: Rodep, 2001.

Steinberg, Salme. *Reformer in the Marketplace: Edward W. Bok and the Ladies' Home Journal*. Baton Rouge: Louisiana State University, 1979.

Emigrant Woman Saying Goodbye

Photograph

By: Keystone View Company

Date: 1922

Source: © Corbis.

About the Author: The Key stone View Company was founded in 1892 by B. L. Singley in Meadville, Pennsylvania. By the 1920s, the company was the largest publisher of stereographs, three-dimensional photographs. This image is now held in the collection maintained by the Corbis Corporation.

INTRODUCTION

The Norwegians were one of the first groups to immigrate to the United States in significant numbers. Norwegian migration to North America began on July 1, 1825, when the "Norwegian Mayflower," the sloop *Restauration* sailed from Stavanger, Norway, to New York City with fifty-two passengers. About 850,000 Norwegians followed in the next hundred years. Unlike many immigrants, the Norwegians so quickly assimilated that they attracted comparatively little attention.

Only Ireland suffered the loss of more young men and women proportionally than Norway during the peak years of European immigration. A scenic country in the North Atlantic, Norway has more beauty than natural resources. With only three percent of its 125,000 square miles of land suitable for cultivation, Norwegians historically relied upon agriculture, timber, and fish for sustenance until shipping and shipbuilding injected new life into the economy in the late nineteenth century. However, the industrial revolution was never strong enough to stem the tide of Norwegian emigration. Sons and daughters left for permanent residence in the United States after reading handbooks, travel guides, and letters from other Norwegians who had already emigrated.

Several American states vied for Norwegian immigrants. Wisconsin, Minnesota, and Iowa all had commissioners of immigration for a few decades. However, most Norwegians settled in the Brooklyn borough of New York City or in Minnesota. They came chiefly for economic opportunity. By 1850, an absolute majority of Norway's rural population owned no land and there were few urban employment

People wave goodbye to passengers on the *S.S. Angelo* departing from Christiana, Norway, in 1905. They are immigrating to the United States. © CORBIS.

opportunities. In Minnesota, they could farm. In New York, Norwegian sailors knew that American ship owners paid better wages than the Scandinavians. Some Norwegians were pulled to the Uinted States by cultural, political, or religious concerns. Universal manhood suffrage and prospects for women's rights in the New World offered exciting possibilities for the future. Others appreciated the absence of an official class system and the opportunity to practice their religion under less restrictive rules.

PRIMARY SOURCE

EMIGRANT WOMAN SAYING GOODBYE

See primary source image.

SIGNIFICANCE

A quota system that took effect in 1924 led to a sharp decline in Norwegian immigration to the United States Although favored by the law, Scandinavians failed to emigrate as they had in former years. The major period of Norwegian immigration thus ended by

PRIMARY SOURCE

Emigrant Woman Saying Goodbye: A Norwegian emigrant says good-bye while preparing for a journey to America, 1922. © CORBIS.

1930. There was a flurry of activity in the years after World War II, when nearly 50,000 Norwegians immigrated between 1945 and 1970, but relatively few have come after that. By the millennium, about four million Americans had Norwegian ancestry in contrast to the forty million who claim an Irish background and the ten million who descend from French ancestors.

Despite their small numbers, Norwegians developed a strong culture in the United States They published about 800 Norwegian-American newspapers and magazines, most of which were printed in Dano-Norwegian, a language that Danes could also read. The Norwegians also founded colleges, including highly regarded St. Olaf's in Northfield, Minnesota, in 1874. Almost all Norwegians are Protestant, and in the United States the immigrants contributed to the many Lutheran synods. Perhaps the greatest impact of the Norwegians has been economic, as they helped the north central states prosper and New York City expand its reputation as a world-class shipping center.

FURTHER RESOURCES

Books

Andersen, Arlow W. *The Norwegian-Americans*. Boston: Twayne, 1975.

Blegen, Theodore C. *Norwegian Migration to America, 1825–1860*. Northfield, MN: The Norwegian-American Historical Association, 1931.

Web sites

Library of Congress. "Norwegian-American Immigration and Local History." June 28, 2005 <http://www.loc.gov/rr/genealogy/bib_guid/norway.html> (accessed June 13, 2006).

High Lights on the Chinese Exclusion and Expulsion

Letter

By: Oliver P. Stidger

Date: September 1924

Source: Stidger, Oliver P. *High Lights on the Chinese Exclusion and Expulsion*. Chinese Chamber of Commerce, San Francisco, California, September 1924.

About the Author: Oliver P. Stidger was the attorney for the San Francisco Chinese Chamber of Commerce, an organization that promoted Chinese businesses.

INTRODUCTION

Trade between the United States and China began in 1784 with the successful docking of the ship *Empress of China*; the Americans delivered cotton and fur and returned with silks, spices, and porcelain. The successful trade, netting a high profit for the merchants, led to an opening of Chinese-U.S. trade relations into the nineteenth century.

The Opium War in the late 1830s and early 1840s opened China further to European goods and trade. In 1844, American diplomats negotiated the Wangxia Treaty, which allowed for U.S. access to trade with China and for involvement in the illegal opium trade. For the next few decades, Chinese immigrants entered the United States, spurred by the Gold Rush in the early 1850s. Chinese settlement on the west coast of the United States, particularly in San Francisco, led to the development of small "Chinatowns" where Chinese immigrants clustered, opening businesses to serve both Chinese and native-born American customers. The 1868 Burlingame Treaty gave immigrants from each country most-favored-nation status in protection and immigration rights.

By the 1870s, anti-Chinese sentiment grew in the west, fueled by unemployment, racism, and anger over employers' preference for lower-paid Chinese workers. Violence, initiated by white mobs, led to deaths in Los Angeles and Colorado, with other incidents in Washington, Oregon, and throughout California. In 1882, despite the Chinese government's opposition and opposition from Chinese diplomats stationed in Washington, D.C., in the embassy opened there in 1878, the United States passed the Chinese Exclusion Act of 1882. The first piece of legislation aimed at a particular immigrant group, the 1882 law severely restricted Chinese immigration, limited labor opportunities, and worked to weaken Chinatowns and Chinese businesses. Within ten years the law was renewed and tightened. The resulting Geary Act of 1892 limited legal rights in court and in the criminal law system as well.

An 1884, United States Supreme Court decision, *Heong v. United States*, placed limits on Chinese laborers' ability to bring Chinese spouses to the United States. The 1888 Scott Act barred even those Chinese with proper documentation from returning to the United States after visiting China. The result drastically lowered the number of Chinese immigrants who remained in the United States.

This illustration shows nineteenth-century hoodlums harassing a Chinese laborer on a street corner in San Francisco. © BETTMANN/CORBIS.

By the early twentieth century, the Chinese Exclusion Act, now the Geary Act, was a firm component in the U.S. immigration policy toward China. Renewed in 1902 indefinitely, the Geary Act continued to restrict Chinese immigration. By 1905, Chinese citizens in China, most notably in Guangdong Province, but also in most major Chinese cities, began a boycott of American goods to protest the restrictions. In spite of such limitations, Chinese immigrants continued to trickle in to the United States, and the remaining Chinese community grew over time through marriages and births. By 1924, organizations such as the Chinese Chamber of Commerce gained strength and issued public statements to call attention to the various immigration laws that restricted the Chinese.

■ **PRIMARY SOURCE**

The Officers and Members of the Chinese Chamber of Commerce of San Francisco respectfully direct your attention to the following letter received from our attorney, O.P. Stidger, Esquire, and request that you consider the injustice pointed out and do all within your power to relieve the intolerable conditions enforced upon the Chinese mercantile interests of this country—by securing a Congressional amendment to the Immigration Law of 1924.

The fact that we are restricted by the Immigration Law of 1924, in addition to being subjected to the harshness of the various treaties and exclusion laws since 1844, makes it impossible for us to continue in upbuilding and maintaining friendly business relations with our brother merchants in the Orient. This intolerable and deplorable condition can only be remedied by the co-operation and assistance of those who believe that the future of San Francisco and the whole Pacific Coast lies within its trade with the Orient.

With these thoughts in mind we ask for your hearty co-operation.

Respectfully,

The Chinese Chamber of Commerce of San Francisco.

By
President.

By
Secretary.

September, 1924.

SIGNIFICANCE

The Immigration Law of 1924 completely overhauled the immigration system in the United States. In 1921 a temporary quota system had been instituted; the 1924 law made it permanent. Before 1924, more than 350,000 people were permitted into the United States as immigrants each year; the 1924 law cut that number to 164,000 with an ultimate goal of 154,000. The law permitted two percent of the current population of immigrants from a particular country to enter, based on 1890 census figures. With nearly eight years of enforcement of the Chinese Exclusion Act depressing the number of Chinese immigrants, the number of Chinese permitted to enter the country legally (the allowed two percent) came to one hundred people allowed per year under the 1924 immigration law.

As the letter from the Chinese Chamber of Commerce notes, the severe restrictions imposed by the 1924 law inhibited business growth, immigration, and trade. The brief letter highlights trade and commerce as victims of the 1924 law as it

stood, and suggests an amendment to change the Chinese quota and to help smooth trade difficulties with China. Unlike Europeans, Africans, or other Asians negatively affected by the new law, Chinese immigration restrictions had stretched back for forty-two years; the four decades had created conditions that limited Chinese immigrant development in the United States, and the Chinese Chamber of Commerce's appeal used simple economics and profit to work toward a change in U.S. policy.

By 1924, industrial development in the United States—aided by wartime industry during World War I—had fueled economic growth. By alluding directly to the 1924 law's negative impact on west coast economic development and trade relations with China and other Asian nations restricted by the immigration overhaul, the Chinese Chamber of Commerce attempted to appeal to the nation's industrial interests.

A series of U.S. Supreme Court decisions in 1925 and 1927, *Chang Chan et al. v. John D. Nagle*, *Cheung Sumchee v. Nagle*, and *Weedin v. Chin Bow* set limits on Chinese immigrants wishing to bring wives to the United States from China and interpreted the 1924 immigration law in light of Chinese interests. The Chinese Chamber of Commerce's appeal did not result in an amendment to the 1924 law lifting restrictions. For the next nineteen years, Chinese immigration was virtually eliminated, until the 1943 Magnuson Act lifted the Geary Act's restrictions. By 1965, a new immigration law gave the Chinese equal footing with other immigrants, eighty-three years after the 1882 Chinese Exclusion Act.

FURTHER RESOURCES
Books

Gyory, Andrew. *Closing the Gate: Race, Politics, and the Chinese Exclusion Act*. Chapel Hill: University of North Carolina Press, 1998.

Lee, Erika. *At America's Gates: Chinese Immigration During the Exclusion Era, 1882–1943*. Chapel Hill: University of North Carolina Press, 2003.

Wong, K. Scott, and Sucheng Chan, eds. *Claiming America: Constructing Chinese Identities During the Exclusion Era*. Philadelphia, Pennsylvania: Temple University Press, 1998.

Web sites

National Archives and Records Administration. "Chinese Immigration and the Chinese in the United States." <http://www.archives.gov/locations/finding-aids/chinese-immigration.html> (accessed June 11, 2006).

Germany's Anti-Jewish Campaign

Magazine article

By: Sidney B. Fay

Date: May 1933

Source: Fay, Sidney B. "Germany's Anti-Jewish Campaign." *Current History* (May 1933): 142–145

About the Author: Sidney B. Fay (1876–1967), educated in Germany, was a historian specializing in eighteenth-century Prussia. He wrote about the origins of World War II and served as the president of the American Historical Association in the 1940s.

INTRODUCTION

Persecution of Jews dates back to medieval times. It was not a creation of Germany in the 1930s and 1940s, although the Nazis took anti-Semitism to extremes. Nazi harassment of Jews prompted some to emigrate but many did not take the opportunity to flee in time to avoid the Holocaust.

The Nazi regime of Adolf Hitler was founded on a hierarchical notion of races. Among its principles was the belief that one race, the Jews, was irredeemably evil and so dangerous as to be potentially deadly to the German race. In consequence, all the power at the disposal of the state and all the energies of society had to be directed toward the elimination of this threat.

As soon as the Nazis took control of Germany in 1933, they began to harass the Jews. One of the first acts of the Third Reich was to expel Jews from public employment. There were exceptions, for those who were only partly Jewish, those who were war veterans, and for those married to Aryans (people of northern European descent). In 1935, these people were forced out of office too. The restrictions against Jews increased throughout the entire Nazi period. The Nuremberg Laws of 1935 deprived Jews of full citizenship and prohibited sexual relations with Aryans. Eventually, Jews were banned from using public transportation, from library reading rooms, from public parks, from the streets bordering on public parks, from restaurants, and from theaters. They were confined to their homes after 9 P.M. and forced to wear yellow stars to identify themselves as Jews. In 1936, Jews were forced to give up their telephones. In 1940, Jews were limited to one hour of shopping, between three and four in the afternoon.

Some Jews, especially academics and professionals in fields or with qualifications that would be welcomed in other countries, fled from Germany. Only a minority of Jews were able to get out of Germany, though. While women often read the writing on the wall, many Jewish men wanted to stand firm in the face of harassment. The possibility of emigration for those Jews who remained after 1935 was restricted by a series of ever more stringent decrees. Emigration was eventually banned entirely on October 23, 1941. In that same year, the Germans began to construct death camps on occupied territory in Poland. Stripped of their position as human beings, Jews were then systematically killed, either outright or as a result or hard labor and starvation rations in concentration camps or grotesque medical experiments. The goal of eliminating all Jews was called the "Final Solution" by the Nazis, and the resulting murder of millions came to be known as the Holocaust.

PRIMARY SOURCE

In the rise of the Hitler party to power in Germany his spokesmen continually uttered dire threats as to what it would do to the Jews if once it controlled the government To appeal to racial and religious animosities was an easy way of getting votes. The Nazis capitalized all sorts of hatred against the Jews. They revived the medieval religious prejudice against a downtrodden people. They urged that Jews, because they were not "Nordic" or "Aryan," were not good Germans. Jews were accused of not being patriotic because of their economic and other affiliations with people of their own race in other countries. The Nazis declared that many of the great banks, newspapers and department stores in Germany were controlled by Jews, who sucked up the money of the poor people in the interests of international Jewry, that the leading war profiteers had been Jews, and that Jews had far more than their share, on the basis of populations, of the positions in the professions, especially in law and in medicine.

With this long preparation of propaganda dinned into the ears of the Nazis at their mass meetings, it is not surprising that the Hitler victory in the Reichstag elections, with its natural feeling of exultation and excitement, should have led to a widespread series of outrageous attacks upon Jews by undisciplined Nazis. It is not necessary to suppose that the attacks were deliberately ordered by Hitler or his immediate agents. It is true, however, that in the first days after the election Nazi brown shirts picketed Jewish stores and in some cases broke windows or caused the stores to close, while the government and police took no steps to prevent such injustice. It also appears to be true that innumerable little groups of unauthorized armed Nazis for two or three days carried on a regular campaign calculated to terrorize the Jewish

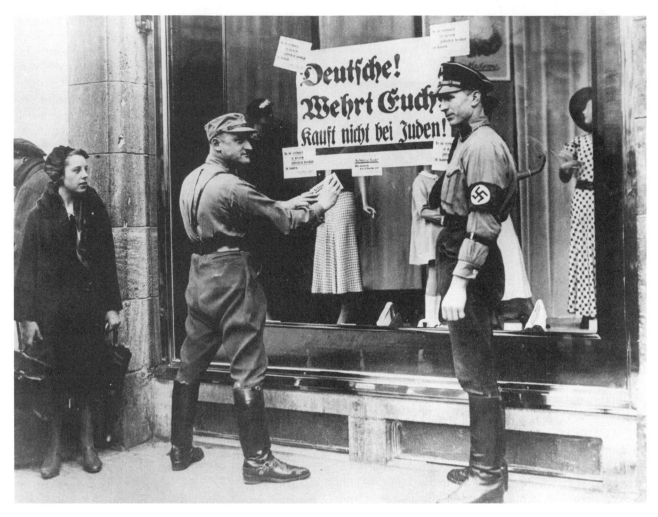

Nazi stormtroopers post anti-Jewish signs on a Berlin shop during an anti-Jewish campaign, 1933. © HULTON-DEUTSCH COLLECTION/CORBIS.

population. Jews in cafes were beaten up. Jewish houses were broken into at night and their inmates dragged out and maltreated. Under the influence of this terror many Jews fled abroad.

Naturally enough the stories told by those who fled were greatly exaggerated. Sensationalist newspapers abroad magnified the horrors with tales of eyes gouged out and Jews murdered at the gates of Jewish cemeteries. Fear, credulity and racial and religious hatred combined to produce stories of "atrocities" such as were once alleged to have been practiced by the Germans in Belgium and France during the World War. How much truth there was in the stories of Nazi outrages against the Jews it is impossible at this time to ascertain. Granting, however, that most of the stories were much exaggerated, there can be no doubt that where there was so much smoke there was some fire. Even Hermann Goering, who is one of the most ruthless of the Nazi leaders, in denouncing the barrage of "foreign defamation," admitted that the national

revolution accomplished by Nazis had been marked by "unavoidable" blemishes in the form of irresponsible acts of lawlessness. Such an admission by him means as much.

The reports of outrages against Jews in Germany quickly stirred up a feeling of indignation and a wave of protest from Jews abroad, especially in Great Britain and the United States. Jewish societies urged their governments to protest to the German Government. They urged retaliation in the form of a movement to boycott German goods. At first sight these protests seemed to have a beneficial effect in touching a sensitive spot in the Nazi government's armor. Its official spokesmen were profuse in indignantly denying most of the charges as being grossly exaggerated and as manufactured simply to discredit the new National government which had come into power. Hitler announced that strict orders had been given to the Nazi organizations that there should be no more such acts of violence; that no one should act against individual rights except upon orders issued from above.

And editorial in the *Frankfurter Zeitung* summed up the situation in an editorial on March 23, saying:

"Just as the outside world has failed, with the fewest exceptions, to form a true conception of the German state of mind since the war—otherwise the policy pursued toward Germany would have been the opposite of what it was—just as it has completely misunderstood the German youth, so now it has interpreted the recent overturn under the distortion of preconceived opinions and thus misunderstood it.

"Excesses there have been, but to generalize such bad isolated cases into a general picture of Germany does not express the truth. This also applies to the Jewish problem. The un-bridled anti-Semitism of National Socialism during the period of agitation is fraught with danger of sudden explosions and appeared indeed to create a threatening situation for German Jews after the overturn. From the demands raised in the outside world—not only in Jewish but also in Christian circles—for succor for German Jews by international action, one would infer that pogroms were the order of the day in Germany.

"We should fail in our journalistic duty if we did not state emphatically that such generalizations do not correspond to the situation in Germany. Since assuming power, the men in authority, at all events, have refrained from anti-Semitic utterances, and it should be remembered that Hermann Goering has assured the Central Jewish Federation that all Jewish citizens loyal to the government would have the protection of the law for person and property.

"Just as one must emphasize that this 'revolution' has been a bloodless one, so the idea that there are any pogroms in Germany must be repudiated. Those circles outside Germany that are propagandizing for international action for the protection of German Jews should, therefore, be made to understand that their activity, however well intentioned, misses the mark.

"National Socialist anti-Semitism is an internal German problem. The intervention of non-German circles distorts the whole question, implies a supererogatory vote of non-confidence in German public opinion, and puts the burden just on those German Jews who, through birth, speech, education and disposition, have felt and still feel themselves united with the German State."

Nevertheless, in spite of this hint from the *Frankfurter Zeitung* that protests from abroad would hurt the German Jews whom it was intended to help, in spite of telegrams from numerous German Jewish organizations that the stories of the anti-Semitic attacks were greatly exaggerated and that they did not welcome foreign interference in the question, in spite of a report from the United States

Department of State gathered from its Consuls in Germany indicating "that whereas there was for a short time considerable physical mistreatment of Jews, this phase may be considered terminated," the foreign campaign of protest increased in vehemence, culminating in a gigantic mass meeting in Madison Square Garden in New York on March 27. And the dangers from such a foreign agitation began to be more apparent than the benefits which had appeared at first sight. . . .

The National Socialist party's proclamation of a boycott against Jewish stores and business establishments was announced from the Nazi Brown House at Munich on March 28. It was declared to be the answer of nationally minded Germany—"tolerated but not supported by the government"—to the demonstrations of protest in Great Britain, and the United States. The boycott, it was announced, would start universally throughout Germany on Saturday, April 1, at 10 A.M., and would continue until lifted by the party management. It was to be "a measure of defense against the lies and defamation of hair-raising perversity being loosed against Germany" from abroad. The details of the execution of the boycott were carefully laid down in eleven articles, the wording of which suggested that Dr. Goebbels may have had a hand in it.

According to these eleven articles, committees of action were to be formed in every local group and organization of the National Socialist party. These committees were to carry out a systematic boycott against Jewish business establishments, goods, physicians and lawyers. The committees were to be responsible for not having the boycott hit the innocent, but were to see to it that it hit the guilty all the harder. They must popularize the boycott through propaganda and public enlightenment and watch the newspapers carefully to see that they participated in the intelligence campaign of the German people against Jewish atrocity propaganda abroad. Newspapers not doing so were to be removed from every house and no German business concern was to advertise in such papers. The committees must be formed in the smallest peasant villages in order to hit Jewish tradesmen in the rural districts.

"The committees shall also take care," the boycott plan read, "that every German having connections abroad shall use these for disseminating the truth—by letter, telegraph and telephone—that quiet and order may reign in Germany; that the German people has no more ardent wish than peaceably to do its work and live in peace with the outside world, and that it conducts its fight against Jewish atrocity propaganda as a purely defensive measure. The committees are responsible for having the whole campaign run off in complete orderliness and with the strictest discipline. Do not hurt a hair on a Jew's head. We shall settle this drive by the mere weight of these measures."

Though the boycott program was the work of the Nazi party organization and not of the Hitler government, and though it was not to begin until April 1, it was broadcast over the government-controlled radio on March 29 and at once began to go into effect in may places. Nazi pickets placed themselves in front of Jewish stores so effectively that many had to close. The municipal authorities of Berlin and many other cities announced that they would buy no supplies except from Nazi-Nationalist business institutions. Later statements by the government limited the boycott to only April 1, with the threat that it would be resumed if foreign agitation did not cease. It soon became clear that because of pressure upon the Cabinet, both from without and within, the boycott would not be repeated. The fate of the Jews of Germany, however, continued to distress the world. Such was the situation when these lines were written. For the outcome we must wait until the record is continued in next months' issue of this magazine.

SIGNIFICANCE

When World War II ended, only a small fragment of Europe's six million Jews had survived. Many of the survivors sought to emigrate to Palestine, a protectorate of Great Britain. Through the war, the British government had limited emigration to Palestine. After the war, the British continued to tightly restrict Jewish emigration. In response, illegal immigration was organized by Zionist underground sources. The foundation of the state of Israel in 1948 brought an open door policy on Jewish immigration to the former Palestine.

Many of the Jews who sought to remain in continental Europe changed their minds after the Kielce progrom in Poland in 1946 and other episodes of anti-Semitism. Of the remaining Jewish Displaced Persons in Europe, about 40,000 emigrated to North America, Australia, and Latin America while only 2000 Jewish survivors of the Holocaust gained admission to Britain. Migration has been one of the constants in Jewish history as the Jews react to the other constant of anti-Semitism.

FURTHER RESOURCES
Books

Breitman, Richard, and Alan M. Kraut. *American Refugee Policy and European Jewry, 1933–1945*. Bloomington: Indiana University Press, 1987.

Dawidowicz, Lucy. *The War Against the Jews, 1933–1945*. London: Weidenfeld and Nicolson, 1975.

Wyman, David S. *Paper Walls: America and the Refugee Crisis, 1938–1941*. Amherst: University of Massachusetts Press, 1968.

Zucker, Bat-Ami. *In Search of Refuge: Jews and US Consuls in Nazi Germany, 1933–1941*. London: Vallentine Mitchell, 2001.

Angel Island

Photograph

By: Anonymous

Date: February 22, 1935

Source: © Bettmann/Corbis.

About the Photographer: The Corbis Corporation is a worldwide provider of visual content materials based in Seattle, Washington. The name of the photographer is not known.

INTRODUCTION

Angel Island is located in the San Francisco Bay on the west coast of the United States. At various times from about 1863 to 1910, Angel Island was used for such functions as discharge depot, infantry garrison, and military camp. Beginning in 1910, Angel Island became the headquarters of the Angel Island Immigration Station, which processed about 175,000 Asian immigrants entering into the United States from China and then later from other countries such as the Philippines, Korea, and Japan. It served in a similar capacity to Ellis Island, which was used primarily by European immigrants. Angel Island was often referred to as The Ellis Island of the West.

In the mid–1800s, the United States favored the immigration of Chinese into its western lands. They worked at many low-paying menial jobs such as clearing swampland, developing fisheries and hatcheries, and building railroads that were crisscrossing the country. By 1880, about 100,000 Chinese lived in the United States. However, when the economy failed in the 1870s, the Chinese people were widely accused of helping to degrade economic conditions by working for low wages that other groups would not accept. Anti-Chinese sentiment eventually led to a series of local, state, and national laws to restrict Asian immigration, especially from China. One such law was the Chinese Exclusion Act of 1882, which limited immigration due to nationality and race. It specifically prohibited Chinese laborers from immigrating to the United States unless family members were already established in the country. Other laws followed as peoples from other Asian countries followed the Chinese into the country.

In order to control and regulate Asian immigration into the west coast of the United States, immigration officials opened an immigration facility on Angel Island in 1910. It was more like a detention center than a facilty to wlecome immigrants to the United States. Officials nicknamed it The Guardian of the Western Gate.

Passengers on ships were separated by nationality and financial status. Those with higher-class tickets, such as immigrants from Australia, Canada, Mexico, New Zealand, various countries in Central and South America, Portugal, and Russia, were quickly processed and allowed to enter the United States. The rest of the immigrants—primarily Chinese and other Asians but also people from elsewhere who did not meet financial or health requirements—were ferried to Angel Island, where they were isolated from people on the mainland. The immigrants were given medical examinations for various ailments such as communicable diseases and parasitic infections. If they failed the tests, hospitalization (at their own expense) or deportation was the result. Because laws only allowed for certain exempt classes of people (such as clergy, diplomats, merchants, students, and teachers) to enter the United States, thousands of Chinese bought false identification that described them as children of exempt classes or children of U.S. citizens. To expose such fraud, immigration officials implemented strenuous interrogations that often caused processing delays of months or years. The immigrants were forced to wait in detention facilities, a condition likened to prison with almost inedible food and unsanitary conditions.

In 1940, a fire burned down the administration building. The processing of immigrants was ended on Angel Island and transferred to San Francisco.

PRIMARY SOURCE

ANGEL ISLAND
See primary source image.

PRIMARY SOURCE

Angel Island: A view of Angel Island in San Fancisco Bay, 1935. Angel Island was the primary processing center for immigrants arriving at the west coast of the United States in the early twentieth century. © BETTMANN/CORBIS.

SIGNIFICANCE

Because the Chinese Exclusion Act of 1882 and other anti-immigration laws involved restrictions for entrance into the country, many immigrants were detained for up to two years. Many detainees felt anger and hostility—some committed suicide—with the injustices inflicted upon them by the United States, a new country they hoped would lead them to a better life.

Complaints about the terrible conditions inside Angel Island and the discrimination imposed onto the Asian people finally forced the United States to repeal the Chinese Exclusion Act in November 1943. The law was also repealed because China was now an U.S. ally in World War II. By this time, the Immigration Station was used as prisoner-of-war processing center. After the war, the facility was abandoned. Even though the processing of immigration had improved, in the 1950s only one hundred or so Chinese were allowed to legally enter the United States each year. By the 1960s, new immigration laws were in place to give Chinese and other Asian immigrants equal access to the country.

In 1963, Angel Island became a California state park. California park ranger Alexander Weiss found poetry beneath layers of paint on the walls of the barracks and dormitories. Chinese immigrants detained at Angel Island had written the poems, many of which were carved into wooden walls and contained historical references and symbolic expressions. Aspirations, anger, sadness, and other emotions filled the poems. Weiss contacted Dr. George Araki of San Francisco State College to verify the historic importance of the poems and photographer Mak Takahashi to document them. As a result, Weiss and Paul Chow (as a representative of Bay Area Asian Americans) helped to form the Angel Island Immigration Station Historical Advisory Committee (AIISHAC) to preserve the station. Money was raised to establish a museum to restore and preserve the barracks and dormitories where the poems had been written.

In the 1970s, leaders of the Chinese-American population in the United States successfully lobbied the state of California to designate the Angel Island Immigration Station as a state landmark. In 1997, the National Park Service declared Angel Island Immigration Station a National Historic Landmark. The National Trust and the White House Millennium Council, in 1999, included the Angel Island Immigration Station as one of its ongoing projects. In March 2000, bond referendum Proposition 12 allocated $15 million to restore the Immigration Station.

As of 2006, the AIISHAC hopes to develop the Angel Island Immigration Station into a research and study center for Pacific Rim immigration while preserving the history of the site for future generations. Different races, immigration laws and practices, and the history of the United States came together at Angel Island in the early twentieth century. Wrongs inflicted upon a race of people and complicated lessons learned will now be remembered due to efforts to save Angel Island.

FURTHER RESOURCES

Books

Lai, Him Mark, Genny Lim, and Judy Yung. *Poetry and History of Chinese Immigrants on Angel Island, 1910–1940*. Seattle, Wash.: University of Washington Press, 1999.

Periodicals

Lai, Him Mark. "The Chinese Experience at Angel Island." *East West Chinese American Journal* (February 1976).

Web sites

Angel Island Association. "Angel Island State Park." <http://www.angelisland.org> (accessed June 29, 2006).

Angel Island Immigration Station Foundation (AIISF). <http://www.aiisf.org> (accessed June 29, 2006).

Lum, Lydia. *Angel Island: Immigrant Journeys of Chinese-Americans*. <http://www.angel-island.com> (accessed June 29, 2006).

Modern American Poetry. "Angel Island: Guardian of the Western Gate." <http://www.english.uiuc.edu/maps/poets/a_f/angel/natale.htm> (accessed June 29, 2006).

PBS.org. "Online News Hour: Angel Island." September 5, 2000. <http://www.pbs.org/newshour/bb/entertainment/july-dec00/Angel_8-5.html> (accessed June 29, 2006).

Puerto Rican or Negro?

Growing Up in East Harlem during WW II

Book excerpt

By: Piri Thomas

Date: 1993

Source: Dublin, Thomas, ed. *Immigrant Voices: New Lives in America, 1773–1986*. Urbana: University of Illinois Press, 1993.

Immigration officials examine Japanese immigrants aboard the ship Shimyo Maru, at Angel Island, California, 1931. © CORBIS.

About the Author: Piri Thomas, originally called Juan Pedro Tomás was born in New York City's Spanish Harlem in 1928, of Puerto Rican and Cuban parents. He struggled to overcome the background of street crime, drugs and gang warefare that he had grown up with, and became an author, poet and journalist. In 1967, he published his autobiography "Down these Mean Streets," which became a bestseller. He continues to write as well lecture worldwide on racism and social justice issues.

INTRODUCTION

This extract describes the experiences of a young Puerto Rican boy living in New York during World War II, including racial prejudice from other immigrant children in his mixed-race neighborhood.

Puerto Ricans have been one of the main groups of immigrants to the United States since the nineteenth century, with the vast majority settling in New York. However, there were many other groups of immigrants in New York in the early and mid-twentieth century, resulting in frequent racial tensions between the different groups, especially when difficult economic conditions led to high rates of unemployment and competition for jobs. At a more basic level of prejudice, color differences created suspicion and resentment, even among the children of immigrant families.

The majority of immigrants from Puerto Rico to the American mainland have been economic migrants seeking to escape poverty and unemployment in Puerto Rico. When the United States acquired

Puerto Rico as a colony as a result of the Spanish-American War in 1898, the numbers of migrants to the mainland increased. They were attracted by the availability of jobs in the United States, the positive reports of life there from earlier Puerto Rican migrants, and the availability of cheap efficient transport links between the island and the mainland. Puerto Rican immigration was further boosted by the 1924 Immigration Act, which severely curtailed the number of European immigrants to the United States and led to an expansion of job opportunities especially for unskilled workers. Although the depression years reduced these opportunities and migration slowed down, by the 1940s the American economy was booming and the government initiated formal labor recruitment policies to bring workers to the United States from Puerto Rico. Between 1947 and 1949, a yearly average of 32,000 individuals migrated, mostly taking jobs in the garment and needle-trade industries.

The vast majority of Puerto Rican immigrants arrived in New York and settled in the city. By 1920, approximately 7,400, or sixty-two percent, of all Puerto Rican immigrants lived in New York, and by 1940 this had risen to 61,500, or eighty-five percent. They often created communities close to

Children playing under a sprinkler on 103rd Street, in the Spanish Harlem district of New York City, 1948. © GENDREAU COLLECTION/ CORBIS. REPRODUCED BY PERMISSION.

their workplaces that became almost exclusively Puerto Rican in ethnicity, language and culture. During the inter-war period, East and South-Central Harlem, previously the home of large Italian and Jewish communities, became the largest Puerto Rican neighborhood in New York, known as "El Barrio." Puerto Ricans were concentrated particularly between 90th Street and 116th Street between First and Fifth Avenues, and 110th Street and 125th Street between Fifth and Manhattan Avenues.

From the outset of their settlement in large numbers in the United States, Puerto Ricans experienced much racial prejudice and discrimination, largely because they did not fit the traditional racial stereotypes of white and black. Most were of mixed racial origin and were brown-skinned, having intermarried extensively with the Spanish colonial settlers during early generations, and they faced discrimination not only from the American-born white population, but from European immigrants such as the Italians. When a major wave of West Indian immigration to New York began in the early 1940s, many whites associated the Puerto Ricans with this group. Largely as a result of the personal and institutional racism they faced, Puerto Ricans became concentrated in the lowest-skilled, poorest-paid jobs, faced high levels of unemployment in times of economic downturn, and were segregated into disadvantaged areas with poor social conditions. During the Great Depression, many Puerto Ricans, such as the author's father, were employed in unskilled manual jobs by the Works Progress Administration, one of the New Deal agencies established to provide work and income to the unemployed. It was disbanded in 1943 when the economy had improved and full employment was achieved.

PRIMARY SOURCE

Alien Turf

Sometimes you don't fit in. Like if you're a Puerto Rican on an Italian block. After my new baby brother, Ricardo, died of some kind of germs, Poppa moved us from 111th Street to Italian turf on 114th Street between Second and Third Avenue. I guess Poppa wanted to get Momma away from the hard memories of the old pad.

I sure missed 111th Street, where everybody acted, walked, and talked like me. But on 114th Street everything went all right for a while. There were a few dirty looks from the spaghetti-an'-sauce cats, but no big sweat. Till that one day I was on my way home from school and almost had reached my stoop when someone called: "hey, you dirty [expletives deleted]."

The words hit my ears and almost made me curse Poppa at the same time. I turned around real slow and found my face pushing in the finger of an Italian kid about my age. He had five or six of his friends with him.

"Hey, you," he said. "What nationality are ya?"

I looked at him and wondered which nationality to pick. And one of his friends said, "Ah, Rocky, he's black enuff to be a [expletive deleted]. Ain't that what you is, kid?"

My voice was almost shy in its anger. "I'm Puerto Rican," I said. "I was born here." I wanted to shout it, but it came out like a whisper.

"Right here inna street?" Rocky sneered. "Ya mean right here inna middle of da street?"

They all laughed.

I hated them. I shook my head slowly from side to side. "Uh-uh," I said softly. "I was born inna hospital—inna bed."

"Umm, *paisan*—born inna hospital—inna bed." Rocky said.

I didn't like Rocky Italiano's voice. "Inna hospital," I whispered, and all the time my eyes were trying to cut down the long distance from this trouble to my stoop. But it was no good; I was hemmed in by Rocky's friends. I couldn't help thinking about kids getting wasted for moving into a block belonging to other people.

"What hospital, *paisan*?" Bad Rocky pushed.

"Harlem Hospital," I answered wishing like all hell that it was 5 o'clock instead of just 3 o'clock, 'cause Poppa came home at 5. I looked around for some friendly faces belonging to grown-up people, but the elders were all busy yakking away in Italian. I couldn't help thinking how much like Spanish it sounded. [expletive deleted] that should make us something like relatives.

"Harlem Hospital?" said a voice. "I knew he was a [expletive deleted]."

"Yeah," said another voice from an expert on color. "That's the hospital where all them black bastards get born at."

I dug three Italian elders looking at us from across the street, and I felt saved. But that went out the window when they just smiled and went on talking. I couldn't decide whether they had smiled because this new whatever-he-was was gonna get his [expletive deleted] kicked or because they were pleased that their kids were welcoming a new kid to their country. And older man nodded his head at Rocky, who smiled back. I wondered if that was a signal for my funeral to begin.

"Ain't that right, kid?" Rocky pressed. "Ain't that where all black people get born?"

I dug some of Rocky's boys grinding and pushing and punching closed fists against open hands. I figured they were looking to shake me up, so I straightened up my humble voice and made like proud. "There's all kinds of people born there. Colored people, Puerto Ricans like me, an';—even spaghetti-benders like you."

"That's a dirty [expletive deleted] lie"—*bash*, I felt Rocky's fist smack into my mouth—"you dirty [expletives deleted]."

I got dizzy and more dizzy when fists started to fly from everywhere and only toward me. I swung back, *splat, bish*—my fist hit some face and I wished I hadn't, cause then I started getting kicked.

I heard people yelling in Italian and English and I wondered if maybe it was 'cause I hadn't fought fair in having hit that one guy. But it wasn't. The voices were trying to help me.

"Whas'sa matta, you no-good kids, leeva da kid alone," a man said. I looked through a swelling eye and dug some Italians pushing their kids off me with slaps. One even kicked a kid in the [expletive deleted]. I could have loved them if I didn't hate them so [expletive deleted] much.

"You all right, kiddo?" asked the man.

"Where you live, boy?" said another one.

"Is the *bambino* hurt?" asked a woman.

I didn't look at any of them. I felt dizzy. I didn't want to open my mouth to talk, 'cause I was fighting to keep from puking up. I just hoped my face was cool-looking. I walked away from that group of strangers. I reached my stoop and started to climb the steps.

"Hey, spic," came a shout from across the street. I started to turn to the voice and changed my mind. "Spic" wasn't my name. I knew that voice, though. It was Rocky's. "We'll see ya again, [expletive deleted]" he said.

I wanted to do something tough, like spitting in their direction. But you gotta have spit in your mouth in order to spit, and my mouth was hurt dry. I just stood there with my back to them.

"Hey, your old man just better be the janitor in that [expletive deleted] building."

Another voice added, "Hey, you got any pretty sisters? We might let ya stay ona block."

Another voice mocked, "Aw, fer Chrissake, where ya ever hear of one of them black broads being pretty?"

I heard the laughter. I turned around and looked at them. Rocky made some kind of dirty sign by putting his left hand in the crook of his right arm while twisting his closed fist in the air. . . .

All I could think of was how I'd like to kill each of them two or three times. I found some spit in my mouth and splattered it in their direction and went inside.

Momma was cooking, and the smell of rice and beans was beating the smell of Parmesan cheese from the other apartments. I let myself into our new pad. I tried to walk fast past Momma so I could wash up, but she saw me.

"My God, Piri, what happened?" she cried.

"Just a little fight in school, Momma. You know how it is, Momma, I'm new in school an';..." I made myself laugh. Then I made myself say, "But Moms, I whipped the living—outta two guys, and' one was bigger'n me."

"*Bendito*, Piri, I raise this family in Christian way. Not to fight. Christ says to turn the other cheek."

"Sure, Momma." I smiled and went and showered, feeling sore at Poppa for bringing us into spaghetti country. I felt my face with easy fingers and though about all the running back and forth from school that was in store for me.

I sat down to dinner and listened to Momma talk about Christian living without really hearing her. All I could think of was that I hadda go out in that street again. I made up my mind to go out right after I finished eating. I had to, shook up or not; cats like me had to show heart.

"Be back, Moms," I said after dinner, "I'm going out on the stoop." I got halfway to the stoop and turned and went back to our apartment. I knocked.

"Who is it?" Momma asked.

"Me Momma."

She opened the door. "*Que pasa?*" she asked.

"Nothing Momma, I just forgot something," I said. I went into the bedroom and fiddled around and finally copped a funny book and walked out the door again. But this time I made sure the switch on the lock was open, just in case I had to get back real quick. I walked out on that stoop as cool as could be, feeling braver with the lock open.

There was no sign of Rocky and his killers. After awhile I saw Poppa coming down the street. He walked like beat tired. Poppa hated his pick-and-shovel job with the WPA. He couldn't even hear the name WPA without getting a fever. *Funny*, I thought, *Poppa's the same like me, a stone Puerto Rican, and nobody in this block even pays him a mind. Maybe older people get along better'n us kids.*

Poppa was climbing the stoop. "Hi, Poppa," I said.

"How's it going, son? Hey, you sure look a little lumped up. What happened?"

I looked at Poppa and started to talk it outta me all at once and stopped, 'cause I heard my voice start to sound scared, and that was no good.

"Slow down, son," Poppa said. "Take it easy." He sat down on the stoop and made a motion for me to do the same. He listened and I talked. I gained confidence. I went from a tone of being shook up by the Italians to a tone of being a better fighter than Joe Louis and Pedro Montanez lumped together, with Kid Chocolate thrown in for extra.

"So that's what happened," I concluded. "And it looks like only the beginning. Man, I ain't scared, Poppa, but like there's nothin' but Italianos on this block and there's no me's like me except me an' our family."

Poppa looked tight. He shook his head from side to side and mumbled something about another Puerto Rican family that lived a coupla doors down from us.

I thought *What good would that do me, unless they prayed over my dead body in Spanish*? But I said, "Man! That's great. Before ya know it, there'll be a whole bunch of us moving in, huh?"

Poppa grunted something and got up. "Staying out here, son?"

"Yeah, Poppa, for a little while longer."

From that day on I grew eyes all over my head. Anytime I hit that street for anything, I looked straight ahead, behind me, and from side to side, all at the same time. Sometimes I ran into Rocky and his boys—that cat was never without his boys—but they never made a move to snag me. They just grinned at me like a bunch of hungry alley cats that could get to their mouse anytime they wanted.

SIGNIFICANCE

Puerto Ricans are still one of the main ethnic groups in the United States, with an estimated 3.4 million in the country in 2000. They remain concentrated in the northeastern United States, mainly in New York and New Jersey. However, they were dispersed in the 1940s and 1950s from East and south-central Harlem to other areas of the city, partly as a result of major slum clearance programs. By the 1950s, the traditional European immigrant enclaves had also lost their distinctiveness, and there were more ethnically-mixed residential communities in New York.

Over time, the socio-economic circumstances of Puerto Ricans have improved, partly due to affirmative action programs that gave Puerto Ricans the opportunity to improve their educational performance and increased their employment opportunities. However, they continue to have among the highest unemployment and poverty rates of all ethnic minority groups and are over-represented in low-skilled and unskilled jobs.

FURTHER RESOURCES

Books

Sánchez Korrol, Virginia E. *From Colonia to Community: The History of Puerto Ricans in New York City, 1917–1948.* Westport, Conn.: Greenwood Press, 1983.

Pérez Y Gonzìlez, María E. *Puerto Ricans in the United States.* Westport, Conn.: Greenwood Press, 2000.

Padilla, Elena. *Up from Puerto Rico.* New York: Columbia University Press, 1958.

Periodical

Grosfoguel, Ramon. "Puerto Ricans in the USA: A Comparative Approach." *Journal of Ethnic and Migration Studies* 25 (2) (1999): 233–249.

Message from President of United States Favoring Repeal of the Chinese Exclusion Law

Speech

By: Franklin Delano Roosevelt

Date: October 11, 1943

Source: Roosevelt, Franklin Delano. "Message to Congress Favoring Repeal of the Chinese Exclusion Law." Washington, D.C., October 11, 1943.

About the Author: Franklin Delano Roosevelt (1882–1945) was the thirty-second President of the United States, serving from 1933 until his death in April 1945. Roosevelt presided over two of the most difficult periods in American history, the Great Depression and World War II.

INTRODUCTION

The prohibitions against the immigration of Chinese persons to the United States had been a part of American law for over sixty years when President Roosevelt urged the repeal of this legislation in October 1943. The Chinese Exclusion Act of 1882 was the first of a series of laws directed at Asian immigration to the United States.

The historical focus of the Exclusion Act and its successors was economic. In response to reports of the discovery of gold in California, the first Chinese immigrants arrived in that state in 1849. Chinese laborers also formed a significant part of the workforce necessary to build the American transcontinental railroad, an engineering work completed in 1869. Following the completion of the railroad, Chinese workers were increasingly seen as a threat to the ability of the white labor force to secure jobs at a living wage.

The initial Chinese Exclusion Act was in effect for a period of ten years. This law was later extended in its scope to include most persons of Asian ancestry—Indians, Koreans, and the Japanese. In addition to the economic impetus underlying the desire to stem Asian immigration, particularly along the West Coast of the United States, racial profiling of Asians played a role in the exclusion efforts. The Chinese and Japanese, in particular, were seen by some as a general threat to the white population of America.

In 1913, California passed the Alien Land Law to prohibit any person ineligible for American citizenship from owning property in the state. As in most areas of the United States, there was little distinction drawn between Asian groups in either legislation or public opinion. At the time, many Americans held negative attitudes towards all Asians.

American attitudes towards the Japanese and Chinese diverged as political and military events unfolded in the 1930s. Japan began a significant military build-up that culminated in the invasion of Manchuria, a region adjacent to China, in 1931. By 1937, Japan and China were engaged in a war, known as the Second Sino-Japanese War, a conflict that ultimately merged into World War II. China, a country that was also involved in a civil war between its Nationalist forces led by Chiang Kai Shek and Communist rebels led by Mao Zedong, was now an American ally against Japanese expansionism in the Pacific region.

Proof of the new divergence in the status of the Chinese and the Japanese in the eyes of the American government was Executive Order 9066, issued by President Roosevelt in March 1942. This order mandated the construction of internment camps that would ultimately accommodate over 120,000 Japanese. Over sixty percent of those interned in the camps were American citizens.

▪ PRIMARY SOURCE

To the Congress of the United States:

There is now pending before the Congress legislation to permit the immigration of Chinese people into this country and to allow Chinese residents here to become American

A poster calling for aid for China, an ally of the United States during World War II. © BETTMANN/CORBIS.

citizens. I regard this legislation as important in the cause of winning the war and of establishing a secure peace.

China is our ally. For many long years she stood alone in the fight against aggression. Today we fight at her side. She has continued her gallant struggle against very great odds.

China has understood that the strategy of victory in this World War first required the concentration of the greater part of our strength upon the European front. She has understood that the amount of supplies we could make available to her has been limited by difficulties of transportation. She knows that substantial aid will be forthcoming as soon as possible—aid not only in the form of weapons and supplies, but also in carrying out plans already made for offensive, effective action. We and our allies will aim our forces at the heart of Japan—in ever-increasing strength until the common enemy is driven from China's soil.

But China's resistance does not depend alone on guns and planes and on attacks on land, on the sea, and from the air. It is based as much in the spirit of her people and her faith in her allies. We owe it to the Chinese to strengthen that faith. One step in this direction is to wipe from the statute books those anachronisms in our law which forbid the immigration of Chinese people into this country and which bar Chinese residents from American citizenship.

Nations like individuals make mistakes. We must be big enough to acknowledge our mistakes of the past and to correct them.

By the repeal of the Chinese exclusion laws, we can correct a historic mistake and silence the distorted Japanese propaganda. The enactment of legislation now pending before the Congress would put Chinese immigrants on a parity with those from other countries. The Chinese quota would, therefore, be only about 100 immigrants a year. There can be no reasonable apprehension that any such number of immigrants will cause unemployment or provide competition in the search for jobs.

The extension of the privileges of citizenship to the relatively few Chinese residents in our country would operate as another meaningful display of friendship. It would be additional proof that we regard China not only as a partner in waging war but that we shall regard her as a partner in days of peace. While it would give the Chinese a preferred status over certain other oriental people, their great contribution to the cause of decency and freedom entitles them to such preference.

I feel confident that the Congress is in full agreement that these measures long overdue should be taken to correct an injustice to our friends. Action by the Congress now will be an earnest of our purpose to apply the policy of the good neighbor to our relations with other peoples.

Franklin D. Roosevelt.
The White House, October 1, 1943.

SIGNIFICANCE

The original Chinese Exclusion laws were a form of American economic protectionism. In 1943, the basis for the repeal of these laws was the removal of an embarrassing symbol from the relations between two military and political allies.

Roosevelt hints at this fact in the course of his speech. He specifically calls the exclusion laws a mistake, one that had to be admitted for the military alliance and support the United States was extending to China to properly function. Roosevelt also obliquely acknowledges concerns regarding the economic impact of greater Chinese immigration and notes that the proposed quotas in the pending legislation will properly address this concern.

Soon after Roosevelt's address to Congress, he, British Prime Minister Winston Churchill (1874–1965), and Chinese Nationalist leader Chiang Kai-Shek (1887–1975) participated in the Cairo Conference of November 1943. In Cairo, the leaders discussed the possible post-war political alignments in the Pacific region, where all three leaders agreed that the ultimate goal in a successful war against Japan was the restoration of lands conquered by the Japanese to their former nations. The positions of China, Great Britain, and the United States in Cairo were confirmed in the publication of an official communique on December 1, 1943.

The repeal of the Chinese Exclusion Act was passed by Congress on December 17, 1943, in legislation that was also known as the Magnuson Act. While the repeal would create future immigration opportunities for tens of thousands of Chinese, the first consequence of the new law was a military one. As a result of the repeal, approximately 14,000 men of Chinese descent became immediately eligible for the American military draft.

The speed with which Roosevelt was able to initiate the desired legislative change to American immigration law was significant. Less than ten weeks passed from the time of Roosevelt's address to Congress urging the repeal of the Chinese exclusion laws to the passage of the Magnuson Act.

The American legislative action also sent a message to other nations that had constructed legislative barriers against Chinese immigration. Canada had passed its first exclusionary law against the Chinese in 1885, and like the United States, Canada had maintained its immigration restrictions with a series of amendments through the 1920s.

Canada also ordered the internment of the Japanese male population on its West Coast in 1942. Canada followed the American repeal of the Chinese exclusion laws with similar legislation in 1947.

When viewed from a historical perspective, the 1943 repeal of the Chinese exclusion laws is a stepping stone in the United States to the fuller form of immigration permitted in the Immigration and Naturalization Act of 1952, where specific racial quotas were eliminated and replaced by a framework of rules based upon the applicant's country of origin. The U.S. government further modified its immigration laws with the Immigration Act of 1965.

The great irony of the 1943 legislation and the motivation of Roosevelt to ensure strong relations with his Chinese military ally came after World War II ended in 1945. In 1946, a full scale civil war erupted in China; by 1949, the Communists of Mao Zedong had taken control of the country, driving the Nationalists of Chiang Kai-Shek onto the island of Taiwan. By 1950, the new Chinese government and its army were a de facto enemy of the United States in the Korean War (1950–1953), since China was allied with North Korea against South Korea, the United States, and various allied nations. Since 1949, the United States has continued to support the Nationalist government in Taiwan in the face of significant Chinese governmental pressure to renounce this tie.

FURTHER RESOURCES

Books

Dower, John W. *War without Mercy: Race and Power in the Pacific War*. New York: Pantheon, 1987.

Tucker, Nancy Bernkoft, editor. *China Confidential: American Diplomats and Sino-American Relations 1945–1996*. New York: Columbia University Press, 2001.

Periodicals

Ma, Xiaohua. "A Democracy at War: The American Campaign to Repeal Chinese Exclusion in 1943." *Japanese Journal of American Studies* 9 (1998): 121–142.

Web sites

U.S. Citizenship and Immigration Services. "This Month in Immigration History: December 1943." <http://www.uscis.gov/graphics/aboutus/history/dec43.htm> (accessed June 12, 2006).

New Jewish Immigrants Await Processing in Haifa, Palestine

Photograph

By: Anonymous

Date: c. 1945

Source: Hulton-Deutsch Collection

About the Photographer: The Hulton-Deutsch collection is managed by Corbis, a photo-repository company that provides photographs and video imagry, along with licensing services, to advertisers, publishers, film-makers, and marketers.

INTRODUCTION

Following episodes of anti-Semitism throughout Europe in the latter decades of the nineteenth century, the idea of establishing a Jewish homeland gained popularity among Jews. The movement to create a Jewish state in Palestine became know as Zionism. In France, the Dreyfus affair, during which a Jewish army captain was convicted of treason based on forged evidence, highlighted the institutionalized anti-Semitism and influenced writers such as Leon Pinsker (1821–1891) and Theodore Herzl (1860–1904). In 1986, Herzl published *Der Judenstaat* (*The State of the Jews*), which argued that the condition of the Diaspora, or Jews residing throughout the world, would continue to deteriorate unless they create a national homeland. Under Herzl's leadership, the first Zionist Congress met in August 1897 in Basle and determined the goal of Zionism to be the establishment of a Jewish national homeland. As such, the Zionist movement established itself as an international organization with a structure and institutions, including the Zionist General Council and the Zionist Executive. The Third Congress passed the first constitution for the organization in 1899. After Herzl's death, Chaim Weizmann (1874–1952) led the Zionist movement and met with British leaders in the hopes to gain British support for a homeland. By 1907, Weizmann had visited Palestine and concluded that the region should be the colonized by the Jews. As such, a trickle of immigrants began to move into the region.

During this time, Western powers viewed Palestine as a region that lacked a unified national settlement. The approximately 200,000 Arabs there were identified based on common language rather than national identity and resided in the region but lacked a formal government structure. As World War I began to spread to European colonies, Britain negotiated agreements with both Arabs and the Jews who resided in the Middle East. In 1917, with the Balfour declaration, the British acknowledged sympathy for Zionist goals and their intent to sponsor a national home for the Jews. As the Allied powers defeated Germany and Turkey, Britain occupied much of the Middle East, allowing it to become the dominant power in the region. The League of Nations granted Britain a Mandate for Palestine at the San Remo Conference in 1922, whereby the region would be administered by British forces. As a provision under the Mandate for Palestine granted to Britain, an agency was created to represent the Jewish people and aid in the establishment of a Jewish homeland. The Zionist Organization established by Herzl was initially tasked as this agency. In 1929, the Jewish Agency for Palestine was created under the League of Nations Mandate for Palestine as an element of the World Zionist Organization in building a homeland for Jews. Meanwhile, Jews began to immigrate in larger numbers to Palestine. During the period 1919–1931 the Jewish segment grew from 8 to 177 percent of the total population as their numbers increased from 60,000 to 175,000.

In 1933, Adolf Hitler began to implement his policies to eradicate the Jews. During this period, Arabs became increasingly resistant to the increase in Jewish immigrants to Palestine. The British negotiated with both the Jewish and Arab populations in order to create alliances against Germany. As a stipulation of the agreement with the Arabs, the British established a blockade, preventing further immigration of Jews to the region. The White Paper of 1939, published by the British government after a series of conflicts that resulted in the deaths of Britons, Jews and Arabs, marked a change in Britain's policy toward the Jewish homeland. The White Paper announced that Britain sought an independent Palestinian state, governed by Jews and Arabs who shared authority. As World War II came to an end, approximately 250,000 Jews had become displaced as a result of the conflict. Many displaced were widows and orphans of victims of the Holocaust. These refugees were housed in displaced person camps in the Allied zones of Germany, Austria, and Italy. The refugees had no homes to which to return, and few countries were willing to allow immigration into their country. In 1945, U.S. special envoy Earl Harrison created a report for President Harry Truman calling for a mass evacuation of Jews from Europe to Palestine. The British rejected this as an option, and other nations were slow to amend their immigration policies to allow for immigration.

New Jewish Immigrants Await Processing in Haifa, Palestine: Truckloads of Jewish immigrants arrrive at a processing center near Haifa, Palestine, 1945. © HULTON-DEUTSCH COLLECTION/CORBIS.

NEW JEWISH IMMIGRANTS AWAIT PROCESSING IN HAIFA, PALESTINE

See primary source image.

SIGNIFICANCE

In July 1945, an organized movement to assist in the illegal immigration from Eastern Europe to Palestine began. Brischa (Hebrew for "escape") was organized by the Aliyah Bet organization and sought to transfer those displaced Jewish persons to Palestine. The exodus was led by soldiers from the Jewish Brigade who routed immigrants through Poland into the U.S. zone in Germany. Once there, clandestine ships awaited to make the passage to their new homes. Although many of the transport ships reached their destination, some ships were captured and their passengers interred. In July 1947, the *Exodus 1947* was stopped by British forces. When the passengers and crew refused to surrender, the British opened fire on the vessel. Worldwide publicity of the event led to support for the Jewish cause. Until 1948, approximately 100,000 Jews successfully crossed the British Blockade to relocate to Palestine as a result of the Brischa.

The Jewish inhabitants of the region declared their independence and the statehood of Israel following the 1948 termination of the Mandate

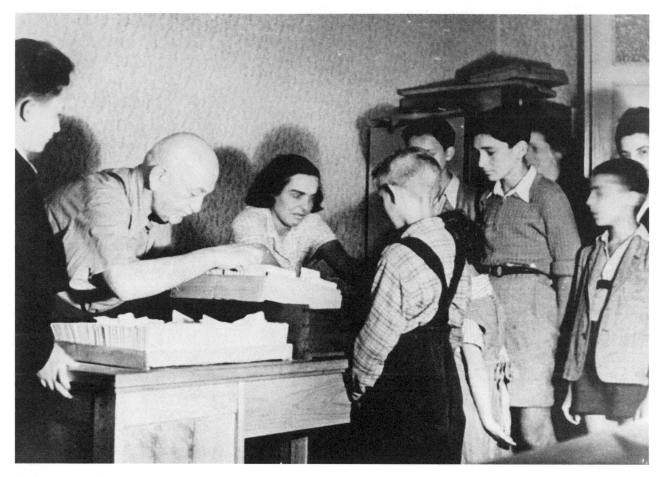

Jewish boys wait in line to receive visas and register in their new home, Palestine, 1945. © HULTON-DEUTSCH COLLECTION/CORBIS.

for Palestine by the United Nations Resolution 181. Surrounding Arab nations rejected the state of Israel while western powers and the Soviet Union acknowledged the new country. Shortly after the British left the newly formed state, several Arab nations, including Egypt, Syria, Iraq, Lebanon, Jordan, and Saudi Arabia, declared war on Israel. Invasions by Egyptian, Syrian, and Jordanian forces began the Israeli War of Independence. The armistice for this war, signed in 1949, partitioned more land to Israel than originally agreed to by the United Nations resolution.

FURTHER RESOURCES

Books

Brenner, Michael. *Zionism: A Brief History*. Princeton, N.J.: Markus Weiner Publishers, 2003.

Sacher, Howard M. *A History of Israel*. New York: Alfred Knopf, 1979.

Periodicals

Bennis, Phyllis. "The United Nations and Palestine: Partition and its Aftermath." *Arab Studies Quarterly* (June 22, 1997).

Ovendale, Ritchie. "The Origins of the Arab-Israeli Conflict." *Historian* (January 1, 2002).

Web sites

Library of Congress. "Israel Country Study." <http://countrystudies.us/israel/88.htm> (accessed June 15, 2006).

United States Holocaust Memorial Museum. "Emigration." <http://www.ushmm.org/museum/exhibit/online/dp//emigrate.htm> (accessed June 15, 2006).

5 Immigration from 1945 to the Present

Immigration from 1945 to the Present

After World War II in 1945, the demographics and character of immigration to the United States again shifted. Larger numbers of immigrants came to the United States from Mexico, Central America, and the Caribbean. Populous Latino communities flourished far from the border states. The repeal of discriminatory exclusion laws and the extension of citizenship privileges fueled a dramatic increase in immigration from Asia.

The legal structure governing immigration also transformed during this period. Modifying the quota system that had governed legal immigration to the United States for nearly a century, legislators established a tiered visa system that sought immigrants with special skills, professions, or research interests. Special allowances were made for unskilled and limitedly skilled workers, especially migrant agricultural workers. A supplemental lottery system was introduced to diversify immigration. While no less controversial than their predecessors, these laws shaped the development of immigration over the last half of the twentieth and early twenty-first centuries. The articles "Amnesty—Who is Eligible?" and "Your Rights and Responsibilities as a Permanent Resident" discuss some of these issues. More current debates on immigration reform are featured in a subsequent chapter.

A significant portion of immigration during the period covered in this chapter involved refugees, asylum seekers, and displaced persons. From the emigration of victims of the Holocaust after World War II, to the flight of victims of more recent human rights abuses, these groups are discussed in the chapter *Refugees, Asylees, and Displaced Persons*.

Many of the articles in this chapter discuss immigration as it relates to economic and social policy. However, immigration is the result of deeply personal decisions and sacrifices made by millions of individuals. Whether spurned by war, famine, economic circumstance, concerns of personal safety, a desire for liberty, or want for a better life, immigration is not simply an economic or demographic phenomenon. "Top Ten Immigration Myths and Facts" responds to some arguments advanced by critics of both legal and illegal immigration. "15 Years on the Bottom Rung" chronicles the everyday struggles of undocumented immigrants to the United States. Finally, the inclusion of the Universal Declaration of Human Rights, Articles 13–15 is a deliberate reminder that immigration issues often converge with human rights concerns.

Universal Declaration of Human Rights, Articles 13–15

Declaration

By: United Nations

Date: December 10, 1948

Source: United Nations. *Universal Declaration of Human Rights, Articles 13–15*. New York: United Nations, 1948.

About the Author: The United Nations (UN), founded in 1945, is the premier international organization worldwide. The UN has agencies that address topics ranging from population to human rights to world health, in addition to working on international relations between various signators.

INTRODUCTION

The creation of the United Nations in 1945 and the 1948 Universal Declaration of Human Rights brought the issue of human rights and basic recognition of humanity as an international political issue to the attention of world leaders. As the world attempted to rebuild and heal from the ravages of World War II, issues such as sexual slavery in Japan; the treatment of displaced persons and refugees unable or unwilling to return to their home countries; and fascism in Spain and Italy compelled diplomats to create a basic set of written rights, modeled on constitutions and other documents of government, to codify basic expectations of human dignity and treatment by governments.

In June 1946, the United Nations created the UN Commission on Human Rights (UNCHR), chaired by Eleanor Roosevelt (1884–1962), which would oversee human rights issues in member nations. Coupled with the 1948 Universal Declaration of Human Rights, the commission would use the document as a guide for monitoring human rights abuses, reporting to the UN, and for facilitating greater expression of rights for all citizens of member nations.

Articles 13, 14, and 15 of the Declaration of Human Rights specifically address internal and external migration and national identity. World War II displaced millions of people throughout Western Europe, Eastern Europe, Russia, Asia, and northern Africa. New borders were drawn and redrawn throughout the war and after; prisoners of war struggled to find their way home, while non-combatants found their villages destroyed, and needed shelter, communities, and jobs. The 1948 creation of the state of Israel led to mass migrations of Jewish people to the new state—and the displacement of Palestinians who had occupied that territory before Israel's borders were drawn.

The UN's inclusion of Articles 13, 14, and 15 in the Declaration of Human Rights was an acknowledgement not only of the contemporaneous immigration and emigration issues in the late 1940s, but of future international migration issues.

▉ PRIMARY SOURCE

Universal Declaration of Human Rights: Nationality and Freedom of Movement

Article 13.

(1) Everyone has the right to freedom of movement and residence within the borders of each state.
(2) Everyone has the right to leave any country, including his own, and to return to his country.

Article 14.

(1) Everyone has the right to seek and to enjoy in other countries asylum from persecution.
(2) This right may not be invoked in the case of prosecutions genuinely arising from non-political crimes or from acts contrary to the purposes and principles of the United Nations.

Article 15.

(1) Everyone has the right to a nationality.
(2) No one shall be arbitrarily deprived of his nationality nor denied the right to change his nationality.

SIGNIFICANCE

The right to move within one's own country and to leave it, as defined in Article 13, was violated during the Cold War by various member nations. Subjects under the Soviet Union could be prosecuted for defecting, while the United States made travel to communist Cuba illegal. In 1967, the United States Supreme Court determined in the case *United States v. Laub* that the United States could not prosecute U.S. citizens who chose to violate travel bans. In 1977, President Jimmy Carter lifted all travel restrictions, but in 1982 President Ronald Reagan imposed currency controls on U.S. dollars spent on travel, lodging, food, and items in Cuba. Some legal experts interpret such travel restrictions as a violation of civil liberties and of Article 13 of the Universal Declaration of Human Rights.

The 1951 Convention relating to the Status of Refugees defined the term refugee, placed the United Nations in the position of assisting with

U.S. Attorney General Alberto Gonzales speaks during a naturalization ceremony at the National Archives, on Bill of Rights Day, December 15, 2005 in Washington, D.C. PHOT BY ALEX WONG/GETTY IMAGES.

international issues related to political asylum, and detailed housing, employment, and other necessary life aspects for persons designated as refugees living in member states. However, Article 14 of the Declaration of Human Rights is limited with respect to refugee status; While it recognizes a person's right to request asylum and to accept it, it imposes no obligation on member states to extend such asylum.

Article 15 recognizes the right of all persons to a nationality; no country can strip nationality from a person "arbitrarily" or without cause, and no person can be deprived of the right to change his or her nationality at will. Again, however, the UN Declaration of Human Rights does not obligate member states to offer nationality to any person who requests it; Ireland, for instance, is not obligated by Article 13 to grant citizenship to someone from Senegal simply because the Senegalese person asked for it. At the same time, a native-born Irish person cannot lose his or her nationality simply because the Irish government decided to do so without cause.

With immigration a huge political issue in the United States, Europe, and other parts of the world in the early years of the twenty-first century, Articles 13–15 define and recognize rights concerning internal migration, civil liberties, asylum, and nationality, but leave open the question of immigration rights for non-asylum purposes. As policymakers and international law experts debate such issues, the Universal Declaration of Human Rights remains a guide—though not a treaty—for framing basic questions of movement, identity, and humanity.

FURTHER RESOURCES
Books

Donnelly, Jack. *Universal Human Rights in Theory and Practice*. Ithaca, New York: Cornell University Press, 2002.

Ishay, Micheline. *The History of Human Rights: From Ancient Times to the Globalization Era*. Berkeley: University of California Press, 2004.

Steiner, Henry, and Philip Alston. *International Human Rights in Context: Law, Politics, Morals.* Oxford: Oxford University Press, 2000.

Web site

United Nations. "Human Rights." <http://www.un.org/rights/> (accessed June 11, 2006).

Oyama v. California

California's Alien Land Law

Legal decision

By: Frederick Vinson

Date: January 19, 1948

Source: *Oyama v. California.* 332 U.S. 633 (1948).

About the Author: The Supreme Court of the United States, the nation's highest court, is comprised of eight justices and one chief justice. In 1948, the associate justices were Wiley B. Rutledge, Frank Murphy, Robert H. Jackson, Harold Burton, Felix Frankfurter, Hugo L. Black, Stanley Reed, and William O. Douglas. Chief Justice Frederick Moore Vinson (1890–1953) authored the majority ruling in the Supreme Court decision of *Oyama v. California.* His opinion was endorsed by the five other justices that constituted the majority of the Supreme Court in the Oyama case.

INTRODUCTION

The California Alien Land Law that was the subject of the constitutional challenge advanced in *Oyama v. California* had its philosophical roots in the more general prohibitions first enacted against Asians in the United States in the late 1800s. The Chinese Exclusion Act of 1882 was extended to include Japanese and Indian persons by the federal government in 1892. The state of California had emphatically supported the enactment of the Chinese Exclusion Act and its successors out of prejudice against the large Asian population that had developed along the West Coast, particularly in the San Francisco area.

The white population's distrust of the Asian immigrants living in California had its basis in racism and economics. Many in the white population believed that the Chinese workforce had both driven down wages for general laborers as well as caused unemployment among the white workforce. With the arrival of Japanese farmers in California in significant numbers by 1900, many white landowners grew concerned that

the Japanese agricultural expertise on small farm plots would render white farmers less competitive.

The Alien Land Law was first passed in 1913 by the California legislature and subsequently broadened in 1920. The law prohibited anyone who was ineligible for American citizenship from owning land in California. The federal Exclusion Acts had defined such ineligibility in a broad fashion—those of Caucasian or African descent were eligible for citizenship, but members of virtually every other racial background were not.

The facts that gave rise to the Oyama case represent the most common device employed by Japanese farmers to avoid the effect of the Alien Land Law. Since a Japanese-born adult farmer was prohibited by law from holding legal title to land in California, title would typically be taken in the name of a child of the farmer who had been born in the United States. Birth created an absolute right to citizenship on the part of the child, making them eligible within the meaning of the Alien Land Law to hold title to the subject property. A corresponding trust agreement would be held by the ineligible parent, creating a well understood property law distinction between the child's paper title and the parent's beneficial or substantive title.

The initial application that led to the Supreme Court case was advanced by Fred Oyama, who was then sixteen years old. In Oyama, the state of California relied upon a failure on the part of the land holders to file requisite reports under the Alien Land Law as a basis to seize the property. A contributing factor in the failure of Oyama to file the necessary documentation was his internment in 1942 as a consequence of the war with Japan. The trial court ruled that the actions of the Oyamas to obtain and to maintain title to the farm property were a subterfuge, rendering the purchase transactions void and vesting the title to the property in the state.

The trial decision was appealed to the Supreme Court of California, where the trial decision was upheld. Oyama brought an application for *certiorari* to the U.S. Supreme Court; certiorari is a request for legal relief where a higher court is requested to review a lower court proceeding on the basis that the lower court ruling was the subject of an irregularity.

◼ PRIMARY SOURCE

Mr. Chief Justice VINSON delivered the opinion of the Court.

Petitioners challenge the constitutionality of California's Alien Land Law as it has been applied in this case to effect an escheat of two small parcels of agricultural land. One of the petitioners is Fred Oyama, a minor American citizen in whose name title was taken. The other is his father and guardian, Kajiro Oyama, a Japanese citizen not eligible for naturalization, who paid the purchase price.

Petitioners press three attacks on the Alien Land Law as it has been applied in this case: first, that it deprives Fred Oyama of the equal protection of the laws and of his privileges as an American citizen; secondly, that it denies Kajiro Oyama equal protection of the laws; and, thirdly, that it contravenes the due process clause by sanctioning a taking of property after expiration of the applicable limitations period. Proper foundation for these claims has been laid in the proceedings below.

In approaching cases, such as this one, in which federal constitutional rights are asserted, it is incumbent on us to inquire not merely whether those rights have been denied in express terms, but also whether they have been denied in substance and effect. We must review independently both the legal issues and those factual matters with which they are commingled.

In broad outline, the Alien Land Law forbids aliens ineligible for American citizenship to acquire, own, occupy, lease, or transfer agricultural land. It also provides that any property acquired in violation of the statute shall escheat as of the date of acquisition and that the same result shall follow any transfer made with 'intent to prevent, evade or avoid' escheat.

In addition, that intent is presumed, prima facie, whenever an ineligible alien pays the consideration for a transfer to a citizen or eligible alien.

The first of the two parcels in question, consisting of six acres of agricultural land in southern California, was purchased in 1934, when Fred Oyama was six years old. Kajiro Oyama paid the $4,000 consideration, and the seller executed a deed to Fred. The deed was duly recorded.

Some six months later, the father petitioned the Superior Court for San Diego County to be appointed Fred's guardian, stating that Fred owned the six acres. After a hearing, the court found the allegations of the petition true and Kajiro Oyama 'a competent and proper person' to be appointed Fred's guardian. The appointment was then ordered, and the father posted the necessary bond.

In 1936 and again in 1937, the father as guardian sought permission to borrow $4,000, payable in six months, for the purpose of financing the next season's crops and to mortgage the six-acre parcel as security. In each case notice of the petition and date for hearing was published in a newspaper, the court then approved the borrowing as advantageous to Fred Oyama's estate, and the father posted a bond for $8,000. So far as appears from the

record, both loans were obtained, used for the benefit of the estate, and repaid on maturity.

The second parcel, an adjoining two acres, was acquired in 1937, when Fred was nine years old. It was sold by the guardian of another minor, and the court supervising that guardianship confirmed the sale 'to Fred Oyama' as highest bidder at a publicly advertised sale. A copy of the court's order was recorded. Fred's father again paid the purchase price, $1,500.

From the time of the two transfers until the date of trial, however, Kajiro Oyama did not file the annual reports which the Alien Land Law requires of all guardians of agricultural land belonging to minor children of ineligible aliens.

In 1942, Fred and his family were evacuated from the Pacific Coast along with all other persons of Japanese descent. And in 1944, when Fred was sixteen and still forbidden to return home, the State filed a petition to declare an escheat of the two parcels on the ground that the conveyances in 1934 and 1937 had been with intent to violate and evade the Alien Land Law. At the trial the only witness, other than a court official testifying to records showing the facts set forth above, was one John Kurfurst, who had been left in charge of the land at the time of the evacuation. He testified that the Oyama family once lived on the land but had not occupied it for several years before the evacuation. After the evacuation, Kurfurst and those to whom he rented the property drew checks to Fred Oyama for the rentals (less expenses), and Kurfurst transmitted them to Fred Oyama through the War Relocation Authority. The canceled checks were returned endorsed 'Fred Oyama,' and no evidence was offered to prove that the signatures were not by the son. Moreover, the receipts issued by the War Relocation Authority for the funds transmitted by Kurfurst were for the account of Fred Oyama, and Kurfurst identified a letter signed 'Fred Oyama' directing him to turn the property over to a local bank for management.

On direct examination by the State's Attorney, however, Kurfurst also testified that he knew the father as 'Fred,' but he added that he had never heard the father refer to himself by that name. In addition, he testified on cross-examination that he had once heard the father say, 'some day the boy will have a good piece of property because that is going to be valuable.' He also admitted that he knew 'the father was running the boy's business' and that 'the property belonged to the boy and to June Kushino' (Fred's cousin, an American citizen). Kurfurst further acknowledged that in a letter he had written about the property and had headed 're: Fred Yoshihiro Oyama and June Kushino' he meant by 'Fred Yoshihiro Oyama' the boy, not the father. He also understood a letter written to him by the War Relocation Authority 're: Fred Oyama' to refer to the boy.

From this evidence the trial court found as facts that the father had had the beneficial use of the land and that the transfers were subterfuges effected with intent to prevent, evade or avoid escheat. Accordingly, the court entered its conclusion of law that the parcels had vested in the State as of the date of the attempted transfers in 1934 and 1937.

The trial court filed no written opinion but indicated orally that its findings were based primarily on four inferences: (1) the statutory presumption that any conveyance is with 'intent to prevent, evade or avoid' escheat if an ineligible alien pays the consideration; (2) an inference of similar intent from the mere fact that the conveyances ran to a minor child; (3) an inference of lack of bona fides at the time of the original transactions from the fact that the father thereafter failed to file annual guardianship reports; and (4) an inference from the father's failure to testify that his testimony would have been adverse to his son's cause. No countervailing inference was warranted by the exhibits in Fred's name, the judge said, 'because there are many instances where there is little in a name.'

In holding the trial court's findings of intent fully justified by the evidence, the Supreme Court of California pointed to the same four inferences. It also ruled that California could constitutionally exclude ineligible aliens from any interest in agricultural land, and that Fred Oyama was deprived of no constitutional guarantees since the land had passed to the State without ever vesting in him.

We agree with petitioners' first contention, that the Alien Land Law, as applied in this case, deprives Fred Oyama of the equal protection of California's laws and of his privileges as an American citizen. In our view of the case, the State has discriminated against Fred Oyama; the discrimination is based solely on his parents' country of origin; and there is absent the compelling justification which would be needed to sustain discrimination of that nature.

By federal statute, enacted before the Fourteenth Amendment but vindicated by it, the states must accord to all citizens the right to take and hold real property. California, of course, recognizes both this right and the fact that infancy does not incapacitate a minor from holding realty. It is also established under California law that ineligible aliens may arrange gifts of agricultural land to their citizen children. Likewise, when a minor citizen does become the owner of agricultural land, by gift or otherwise, his father may be appointed guardian of the estate, whether the father be a citizen, an eligible alien, or an ineligible alien. And, once appointed, a guardian is entitled to have custody of the estate and to manage and husband it for the ward's benefit. To that extent Fred

Oyama is ostensibly on a par with minors of different lineage.

At this point, however, the road forks. The California law points in one direction for minor citizens like Fred Oyama, whose parents cannot be naturalized, and in another for all other children—for minor citizens whose parents are either citizens or eligible aliens, and even for minors who are themselves aliens though eligible for naturalization. In the first place, for most minors California has the customary rule that where a parent pays for a conveyance to his child there is a presumption that a gift is intended; there is no presumption of a resulting trust, no presumption that the minor takes the land for the benefit of his parent. When a gift is thus presumed and the deed is recorded in the child's name, the recording suffices for delivery, and, absent evidence that the gift is disadvantageous, acceptance is also presumed. Thus the burden of proving that there was in fact no completed bona fide gift falls to him who would attack its validity. Fred Oyama, on the other hand, faced at the outset the necessity of overcoming a statutory presumption that conveyances financed by his father and recorded in Fred's name were not gifts at all. Something very akin to a resulting trust was presumed and, at least prima facie, Fred was presumed to hold title for the benefit of his parent.

In the second place, when it came to rebutting this statutory presumption, Fred Oyama ran into other obstacles which, so far as we can ascertain, do not beset the path of most minor donees in California.

Thus the California courts said that the very fact that the transfer put the land beyond the father's power to deal with it directly—to deed it away, to borrow money on it, and to make free disposition of it in any other way—showed that the transfer was not complete, that it was merely colorable. The fact that the father attached no strings to the transfer was taken to indicate that he meant, in effect, to acquire the beneficial ownership himself. The California law purports to permit citizen sons to take gifts of agricultural land from their fathers, regardless of the fathers' nationality. Yet, as indicated by this case, if the father is ineligible for citizenship, facts which would usually be considered indicia of the son's ownership are used to make that ownership suspect; if the father is not an ineligible alien, however, the same facts would be evidence that a completed gift was intended.

Furthermore, Fred Oyama had to counter evidence that his father was remiss in his duties as guardian. Acts subsequent to a transfer may, of course, be relevant to indicate a transferor's intent at the time of the transfer. In this case the trial court itself had reservations as to the evidentiary value of the father's omissions; with these we agree, especially because there was some reason to believe reports were not required of him until 1943, and he had been excluded from the state from 1942 on. More important to the issue of equal protection, however, our attention has been called to no other case in which the penalty for a guardian's derelictions has fallen on any one but the guardian. At any time the court supervising the guardianship could have demanded the annual accounts and, if appropriate, could have removed Kajiro Oyama as guardian; severe punishment could also have been meted out. The whole theory of guardianships is to protect the ward during his period of incapacity to protect himself. In Fred Oyama's case, however, the father's deeds were visited on the son; the ward became the guarantor of his guardian's conduct.

The cumulative effect, we believe, was clearly to discriminate againt Fred Oyama. He was saddled with an onerous burden of proof which need not be borne by California children generally. The statutory presumption and the two ancillary inferences, which would not be used against most children, were given such probative value as to prevail in the face of a deed entered in the public records, four court orders recognizing Fred Oyama as the owner of the land, several newspaper notices to the same effect, and testimony that business transactions regarding the land were generally understood to be on his behalf. In short, Fred Oyama lost his gift, irretrievably and without compensation, solely because of the extraordinary obstacles which the State set before him. The only basis for this discrimination against an American citizen, moreover, was the fact that his father was Japanese and not American, Russian, Chinese, or English. But for that fact alone, Fred Oyama, now a little over a year from majority, would be the undisputed owner of the eight acres in question.

The State argues that racial descent is not the basis for whatever discrimination has taken place. The argument is that the same statutory presumption of fraud would apply alike to any person taking agricultural land paid for by Kajiro Oyama, whether the recipient was Fred Oyama or a stranger of entirely different ancestry. We do not know how realistic it is to suppose that Kajiro Oyama would attempt gifts of land to others than his close relatives. But in any event, the State's argument ignores the fact that the generally applicable California law treats conveyances to the transferor's children differently from conveyances to strangers. Whenever a Chinese or English parent, to take an example, pays a third party to deed land to a stranger, a resulting trust is presumed to arise, and the stranger is presumed to hold the land for the benefit of the person paying the consideration; when the Alien Land Law applies a similar presumption to a like transfer by Kajiro Oyama to a stranger, it appears merely to reiterate the generally applicable law of resulting trusts. When, on the other hand, the same Chinese or English father uses his own funds to buy land in his citizen son's name, an indefeasible title is presumed to vest in the boy; but when Kajiro Oyama arranges a similar transfer to Fred Oyama, the Alien Land Law interposes a presumption just to the contrary. Thus, as between the citizen children of a Chinese or English father and the citizen children of a Japanese father, there is discrimination; as between strangers taking from the same transferors, there appears to be none.

It is for this reason that Cockrill v. California, 1925, 268 U.S. 258, does not support the State's position. In that case an ineligible alien paid for land and had title put in a stranger's name, and this Court affirmed a decision upholding the statutory presumption of the Alien Land Law as there applied.

There remains the question of whether discrimination between citizens on the basis of their racial descent, as revealed in this case, is justifiable. Here we start with the proposition that only the most exceptional circumstances can excuse discrimination on that basis in the face of the equal protection clause and a federal statute giving all citizens the right to own land. In Hirabayashi v. United States this Court sustained a war measure which involved restrictions against citizens of Japanese descent. But the Court recognized that, as a general rule, 'distinctions between citizens solely because of their ancestry are by their very nature odious to a free people whose institutions are founded upon the doctrine of equality.' 1943, 320 U.S. 81, 100, 1385. The only justification urged upon us by the State is that the discrimination is necessary to prevent evasion of the Alien Land Law's prohibition against the ownership of agricultural land by ineligible aliens. This reasoning presupposes the validity of that prohibition, a premise which we deem it unnecessary and therefore inappropriate to reexamine in this case. But assuming, for purposes of argument only, that the basic prohibition is constitutional, it does not follow that there is no constitutional limit to the means which may be used to enforce it. In the light most favorable to the State, this case presents a conflict between the State's right to formulate a policy of landholding within its bounds and the right of American citizens to own land anywhere in the United States. When these two rights clash, the rights of a citizen may not be subordinated merely because of his father's country of origin.

Since the view we take of petitioners' first contention requires reversal of the decision below, we do not reach their other contentions: that the Alien Land Law denies ineligible aliens the equal protection of the laws, and that failure to apply any limitations period to escheat actions under that law takes property without due process of law.

Reversed.

SIGNIFICANCE

The U.S. Supreme Court decision in *Oyama v. California* was rendered less than three years after the American victory over Japan in World War II, a conflict in which anti-Japanese feeling ran very high throughout the United States. The circumstances that led the state of California to initiate a seizure of the Oyama holdings related, in part, to the internment of the male Japanese population in California that had commenced in 1942. The Supreme Court ruling as reflected in both the majority and minority reasons for judgment is noteworthy in its absence of any reference to the recent and horrible conflict between the United States and Japan. Only the applicable legal principles are discussed, and this judicial focus gives the Oyama decision a particular clarity.

The majority position is one that would be advanced in numerous other post-war decisions of the Supreme Court, namely that the right of an individual to equality before the law pursuant to the Fourteenth Amendment is a constitutional guarantee that usually triumphs over the ability of a state or other legally constituted local body to control its own processes. The court did not question the power of the state of California to determine how land would be owned within its jurisdiction, but the Supreme Court majority determined that the racial definitions tied to ownership by the state were a violation of the equality guaranteed to Fred Oyama, an American-born person. As the majority emphasized, the transaction that was the subject of the legal action would have been legal in California if Fred Oyama were of almost any other racial origin except Japanese.

The American Civil Liberties Union (ACLU) represented Oyama at the Supreme Court. Founded in 1920, the ACLU was established as a national legal advocacy organization to advance the protection of individual civil liberties in a wide range of circumstances. The ACLU was counsel in a number of cases dealing with Japanese rights of property and citizenship that arose in the aftermath of World War II, of which the Oyama case was the most noteworthy.

One of the lawyers who appeared on behalf of Oyama before the Supreme Court is also a significant figure beyond the scope of the appeal proceeding. The ACLU approached prominent Washington lawyer Dean Acheson (1893–1971) to act as one of the counsels to argue the case. Acheson's participation in this appeal is significant on a number of levels, since Acheson was one of the most influential Democratic political figures of the post-war era.

Acheson worked as Under Secretary of State from 1945 to 1947, and he was subsequently appointed Secretary of State in the Truman administration in 1949, serving in that post until 1953. Acheson was also a valued advisor in the Kennedy administration from 1961 to 1963. The securing of Acheson's services by the ACLU was a clear message to any observer that the issues at stake in the Oyama case should be considered as significant and deserving of attention.

The approach adopted by the majority of the Supreme Court in *Oyama v. California* towards the California Alien Land Law in 1948 was echoed in later judicial decisions dealing with race and the ability to own land. The most prominent examples are found in those cases where a challenge was made to the legality of a deed that contained a restrictive covenant. Restrictive covenants are a legal condition forming a part of the title to property where the title holder agrees that they will not take certain actions with respect to their property. Restrictive covenants were often created to prevent the conveyance of property to a designated class or classes of persons, with a goal of keeping such persons from owning property in a particular neighborhood.

Between 1900 and 1945 in various regions of the United States, restrictive covenants were commonly used to exclude persons of black, Jewish or other ethnicities from owning both residential and commercial properties. In May 1948, the U.S. Supreme Court ruled in the case of *Shelley v. Kramer* that such restrictive covenants were subject to the provisions of the Fourteenth Amendment. The Oyama decision was specifically cited by the Supreme Court as a basis for the principle that the use of a restrictive covenant to exclude certain racial or ethnic groups from owning land in a particular location was a violation of the prospective purchaser's property rights.

FURTHER RESOURCES

Books

Daniels, Roger. *Politics of Prejudice: The Anti-Japanese Movement in California.* Berkeley, Calif.: University of California Press, 1999.

Hirobe, Izumi. *Japanese Pride, American Prejudice.* Stanford, Calif.: Stanford University Press, 2001.

Web sites

Brown, Jay M. "When Military Necessity Overrides Constitutional Guarantees: The Treatment of Japanese Americans During World War II." *Yale-New Haven Teachers Institute.* <http://www.yale.edu/ynhti/curriculum/units/1982/3/82.03.01.x.html> (accessed June 7, 2006).

Report on Testing of Children of Migratory Agricultural Workers in the Waupun Area

Report

By: Governor's Commission on Human Rights, Wisconsin

Date: August 4, 1950

Source: *Wisconsin Historical Society.* "Turning Points in Wisconsin History." <http://content.wisconsinhistory.org/cdm4/> (accessed July 10, 2006).

About the Author: The Governor's Commission on Human Rights, Wisconsin, was an educational program initiated in 1945 "to disseminate information and to attempt by means of discussion as well as other proper means to educate the people of the state to a greater understanding, appreciation and practice of tolerance, to the end that Wisconsin will be a better place in which to live." The commission was established in response to outbursts of anti-Semitism and racial prejudice during the Second World War.

INTRODUCTION

During the 1940s and 1950s, educational programs were introduced for the children of migrant farm workers in a number of American states. The agricultural sector in the United States has depended heavily on migrant labor since the late nineteenth century, and there was a big increase in the numbers of migrant farm workers after World War II (1939–1945). Most of these were either non-English-speaking Mexican migrants or African Americans from the southern states. Many of them traveled in family groups, moving frequently from place to place to

Deputy Secretary of Education Eugene Hickok presents a grant to Virginia Superintendent of Schools Jo Lynne DeMary in 2004. It will be used to fund a program for educating the children of migrant workers, some of whom are standing in the background. AP IMAGES.

meet the demands of the planting and harvesting seasons for different crops. They were typically very poor, receiving low and intermittent earnings, and the children were often required to contribute to the family income, by working in the fields.

Under these circumstances it was very difficult for the children of migrant farm workers to attend school regularly, and some received little or no schooling at all, particularly if their parents put little value on education. Those who did attend school typically did so for only part of the school year, and they would often attend many different schools over time as their family migrated between different locations. Studies found that the majority of migrant children fell behind on school work and often had to repeat grades, while many dropped out of the school system completely by the age of thirteen or fourteen and became full-time farm workers. A study carried out in San Antonio in the 1960s found that only six percent of the children of migrant farm worker families completed high school, and thirty percent received a maximum of three years of schooling.

In order to address this problem, the federal government provided funding for educational programs that would account for the special needs of migrant children, and studies like this 1950 report in Wisconsin were conducted to evaluate their learning ability. Many summer schools in particular were established across the country; migrant children were encouraged to attend such schools between their seasonal agricultural work. Some of the programs were developed with the objective of promoting ethnic and racial tolerance through education at a time when the nonwhite immigrant population of the United States was increasing rapidly.

▮ PRIMARY SOURCE

Statement of Problem:

To attempt to determine the educability in relation to mental capacity of children of Spanish-speaking migrant agricultural workers in the Waupun area.

Subjects:

The group of children tested was composed of six boys and seven girls, ranging in age from five to thirteen years, and having virtually no formal education. At the time of the testing these children were receiving schooling in English under the joint auspices of the Community Council on Human Relations of Waupun, and the Governor's Commission on Human Rights. They were children of Spanish-speaking migrant agricultural workers employed at that time in the Waupun area.

Selection of Tests Used:

The problem of selecting suitable measurement instruments was complicated by several factors: a) a distinct language handicap, the children for the most part had but a few weeks' formal instruction in English and used Spanish exclusively in their social group; b) a literacy handicap, these children were virtually illiterate in both English and Spanish at the beginning of their summer schooling; c) a cultural handicap was also present in that the experiential background of this group was different from that of the American white groups used to standardize most existing tests.

It can be seen then that the subjects as a group were such that no measurement instrument designed for a white, English-speaking population would be wholly adequate. However it was felt that certain portions of the Wechsler Intelligence Scale for Children and the Goodenough "Draw-A-Man" Test would tend to minimize the importance of verbal and language factors inherent in most tests. Two instruments were used in hopes that one would in part serve as a check on the other, and that a fuller evaluation could be made.

The tasks involved in these tests were:

I. Wechsler Intelligence Scale for Children—Performance Scale

a) Picture Completion: Here the task was recognition of the important missing part of pictures of familiar objects. This was an attempt to measure the individual's ability to differentiate between essential and unessential details in these pictures.

b) Picture Arrangement: Arrangement of cut-out pictures in a sensible, logical sequence was the task here. This, the test author claims, is a kind of measure of social intelligence.

c) Block Design: This is the arrangement of multicolored blocks in a pattern. What is probably measured here is performance in planning an approach and arranging colored blocks to reproduce a fixed geometric pattern.

d) Object Assembly: this is a type of jig-saw puzzle in which the task is to assemble the parts as quickly as possible. This purports to measure whole-part relationships in a problem-solving situation.

e) Coding: Here the subject must associate and insert signs (such as plus marks, dashes, circles, etc.) with geometric patterns according to a coded relationship—i.e., a dash goes with a triangle, a circle with a cross, etc. This is a speed test. It attempts to measure memory and, to a limited extent, learning.

f) Mazes: The subject must trace a path through a maze and find the exit without making more than a certain limited number of mistakes within a time limit. This is claimed to be a measure of planning in problem solving.

II. The Goodenough Draw-A-Man Test

This task is to draw a man. The attempt is scored on the basis of completeness of detail, realistic approach, coordination of line, as well as content—i.e., clothing, correct number of fingers, eyebrows, etc. The author of this test believes that the child draws what he knows. This test should have a more universal application with non-English groups than the Wechsler Scale and was used as an additional measure.

Observed Behavior During Testing:

Each child was tested individually and spent about 45 minutes with the two examiners. In conjunction with the psychological examination each child was interviewed by one of the workers in an attempt to get as full a picture of the operating level of the individual as possible. Whenever the child was obviously unable to comprehend directions in English, the teacher was called in to supplement the directions in Spanish.

As far as it was able to determine, none of the children had ever been tested before. However, without exception, each entered the examination situation with enthusiasm, and the workers felt that each child was trying as hard as he could in solving the tasks set before him. This enthusiasm together with a serious attitude, a persistence of effort, and attempts to try even the most difficult of the tasks was marked for the group as a whole.

Some group peculiarities in comparison with excepted performance of white groups were noted. In the Picture Completion sub-test many of the group missed easier items introduced early in the test such as missing button holes on a full-dress suit coat or a missing spade in a seven of spades playing card, but correctly answered harder items toward the end of the test such as a missing spur on a rooster and the missing cleft hoof of a cow. This type of performance can probably be laid to differences in background of this group with the standardization group.

The group as a whole did better than their own sub-test average on the Coding and Mazes parts. The former has some aspects of the learning situation in that the earlier the subject "learns" the code the faster he can finish the test and gain a higher score. The Maze sub-test scores for the group indicated some ability to solve problems calling for planning in execution. The children seemed to enjoy these two sub-tests as well as any other.

Results of Testing-Interpretations:

In the opinion of both of the examiners the children as a group seemed to be within the normal range of mental capacity found in school children as a whole. It is very difficult to compare them with exactness in terms of Intelligence Quotient with the white, English-speaking group on whom the scales were developed. Therefore no attempt will be made to evaluate each child on this basis.

However both examiners felt that the group was definitely educable in terms of mental capacity. This potential capacity for education was demonstrated throughout the contact with the child in a number of ways:

1—Observation of the group during the testing situation—in their mode of attacking the tasks, in their attitudes, and in their relative success as measured by the standardized scoring procedures led the examiners to believe that probably none of the group was to be classified as "feeble-minded." It was felt on the basis of the testing results that their range of mental capacity would differ little from that found in many rural classrooms throughout the state.

2—The behavior of the group during the testing was indicative of strong motivation to succeed. When asked in the interview what one thing they would like to do if they had a month of free time, several of them answered that they would like to study and learn to read and write in English above all.

3—Their adaptiveness to a learning situation was seen in some measure by their ability to adjust quickly to the newness of a testing situation, by their perseverance in pursuing the tasks set before them, and by their learning as measured in several of the sub-tests themselves.

4—Accepting them at their present level of apparent achievement, classroom instruction which would be individualized enough to meet their specific needs and interests. This is not to say that these children are to be taught with the same techniques and methods which the average boy and girl are taught in Wisconsin's schools.

Recommendations:

1—Further individual testing after some mastery of English has been achieved might prove fruitful in a further attempt to gain more definite estimates of individual intellectual capacity.

2—Coordinated cooperative efforts utilizing the resources of the United States Office of Education and the State Departments of Public Instruction of Texas, New Mexico, Colorado, Arizona, and California might point to more suitable measurement devices for dealing with the Spanish-American minority.

3—Grade placement as it is normally viewed is very difficult with a group such as this. The ungraded, one-room school has much to offer the particular needs of this group. Transition from Spanish to English must be gradual. After acculturalization and achievement of minimum fluency in English and minimum achievement in reading has been attained, a more meaningful grade placement might be attempted with the aid of standardized achievement batteries.

4—Because of the peculiar socio-economic position of the families of these children and their migratory character during their residence in Wisconsin, consideration of a type of travel-school or traveling faculty might help in arriving at the answer for this particular educational problem.

5—A careful follow-up plan for keeping in touch with these children throughout the year would be highly desirable as an aid in a careful child study plan which in the long run would enable the educational planning for this type of child to be more meaningful.

Conclusions:

1—The group tested seemed in the opinion of the examiners to be educable.

2—Because of the specific handicaps to learning of members of this group, special educational facilities must be made available within the normal classroom structure.

3—One very important other consideration in planning the education of this group is the socio-economic position it holds in our society. Education then becomes one part of the total adjustment process of this minority group.

SIGNIFICANCE

When the Wisconsin report was published, intelligence tests were ill-designed to measure the educational ability of ethnic minority groups, especially non-English-speaking migrants. Even though this study attempted to minimize the impact of language difficulties, the measuring instruments used were culturally biased towards the native white population and often underestimated the ability of other ethnic or language groups.

Once in school, migrant farm worker children were often found to be highly motivated learners who achieved results quickly. For example, a 1956 Colorado study found that migrant children gained an average of five-and-a-half months' education in a single seven-week session. That study concluded that it was a lack of regular school attendance due to their itinerant lifestyles that contributed to the educational difficulties of migrant children, not inability. Other studies found that language barriers and the lack of interest in education among parents also had a negative impact on the educational attainment of migrant farm worker children.

In 1967, under an amendment to Title I of the Elementary and Secondary Education Act of 1965, funding was provided for the recruitment of bilingual teachers and the renting of classrooms for migrant children's educational programs, and a computerized record-keeping system, the Migrant Student Record

Transfer System (MSRTS), was established with the aim of centralizing the school records of migrant children from all over the United States. This system achieved limited success, but there was still much discontinuity in the education of migrant children, and it proved difficult to keep comprehensive records.

There continue to be low levels of schooling and educational attainment among the children of migrant farm workers, due largely to their geographical mobility and the pressures of poverty. A 1980s study found that seventy-six percent of migrant children sampled failed to complete high school. The same study found, however, that those children who did attend school for a reasonable length of time without too much disruption were more likely to move into non-farm-work jobs by the time they reached the age of eighteen or twenty. Education therefore offers an important route to upward mobility and an escape from the poverty of migrant farm work for these children.

FURTHER RESOURCES

Books

Duncan, Cynthia M., ed. *Rural Poverty in America.* New York: Auburn House, 1992.

Shotwell, Louisa R. *The Harvesters: The Story of the Migrant People.* New York: Octagon Books, 1979.

Taylor, Ronald B. *Sweatshops in the Sun: Child Labor on the Farm.* Boston: Beacon Press, 1973.

Web sites

Wisconsin Historical Society. "Turning Points in Wisconsin History." <http://content.wisconsinhistory.org/cdm4/> (accessed July 10, 2006).

Naturalization Oath of Allegiance to the United States

Oath

By: U.S. Congress

Date: 1952

Source: U.S. Congress. "Naturalization Oath of Allegiance to the United States."

About the Author: The U.S. Congress is responsible, according to the Constitution, for establishing a uniform rule of naturalization.

INTRODUCTION

Naturalization is the process of acquiring the nationality of a country. As a nation built on immigration, the United States has struggled more with naturalization than any other country in the world.

The problem of naturalization was one of the first ones addressed by the new nation. The framers of the Constitution gave Congress the responsibility for determining citizenship and, in 1790, Congress established rules for naturalization. The law, reformed several times in the next few years, provided that aliens who had resided in the United States for a period of time could be naturalized along with their children. Only aliens of European and African descent were eligible for citizenship, blocking those with any Asian blood from pursuing naturalization. The ban on Asian citizenship was later upheld by the Supreme Court in several cases that denied naturalization to those of Japanese, Korean, Indian, Afghanistan, and Filipino descent. The Court ruled that Mexicans and Arabs were white persons and thus, eligible for citizenship.

To help straighten out the confusion surrounding immigration laws and improve foreign relations with Asian countries, President Theodore Roosevelt proposed a revision of the immigration laws in 1905. The revision required only that an alien be literate in a language and that he intend to reside permanently in the United States. This legislation has remained the foundation of naturalization policy.

PRIMARY SOURCE

Naturalization Oath of Allegiance to the United States of America

"I hereby declare, on oath, that I absolutely and entirely renounce and abjure all allegiance and fidelity to any foreign prince, potentate, state or sovereignty, of whom

During Naturalization Day, new citizens take the Oath of Allegiance in the Court of the Eastern District of New York, 1924. © BETTMANN/ CORBIS.

or which I have heretofore been a subject or citizen; that I will support and defend the Constitution and laws of the United States of America against all enemies, foreign and domestic; that I will bear true faith and allegiance to the same; that I will bear arms on behalf of the United States when required by the law; that I will perform noncombatant service in the armed forces of the United States when required by the law; that I will perform work of national importance under civilian direction when required by the law; and that I take this obligation freely without any mental reservation or purpose of evasion; so help me God."

SIGNIFICANCE

Historically, immigrants are more likely to naturalize the longer that they have lived in the United States. Among the foreign-born population in 2000, 80.4 percent of those who had entered the country before 1970 were citizens. Only 8.9 percent of those who had entered after 1990 had been naturalized. Overall, the percentage of foreign-born residents who are American citizens has declined steadily since 1970. The drop is attributed to several factors including a flood of new immigrants who have not been residents long enough to qualify for citizenship and the rise in migrant workers who tend to return home. Additionally, the United States admits a great number of nonimmigrants such as students and temporary workers, who are not eligible to naturalize.

However, the number of naturalization applications has skyrocketed in response to political threats to deny public benefits to immigrants. The success of Proposition 187 in California, federal immigration and welfare reforms in 1996, and laws that increased the threat of deportation for criminal aliens pushed many immigrants to safeguard their rights by naturalizing. Adding to the push, ethnic advocacy groups have been encouraging immigrants to naturalize by helping them with the process. The ongoing threat of immigration reform is likely to continue to encourage immigrants to naturalize.

FURTHER RESOURCES
Books

Gardner, Martha. *The Qualities of a Citizen: Women, Immigration, and Citizenship, 1870–1965*. Princeton, N.J.: Princeton University Press, 2005.

Gimpel, James G., and James R. Edwards, Jr. *The Congressional Politics of Immigration Reform*. Needham Heights, Mass: Allyn and Bacon, 1999.

Enoch Powell on the Immigration Crisis

Book excerpt

By: Enoch Powell

Date: November 16, 1968

Source: Powell, Enoch, and Rex Collings. *Reflections of a Statesman: The Selected Writings and Speeches of Enoch Powell*. London: Bellew Publishing, 1992.

About the Author: Enoch Powell (1912–1998) was a Conservative Party Minister of Parliament (MP) in Great Britain between 1950 and 1974, and subsequently an Ulster Unionist MP. He held controversial, extreme right-wing views on issues such as race and immigration, and on the United Kingdom's entry into the European Union.

INTRODUCTION

This speech was given by the British Conservative MP Enoch Powell in November 1968, as a follow-up to his controversial "Rivers of Blood" speech made in Birmingham earlier that year, in which he had warned about the adverse consequences of further immigration on the United Kingdom. As a result, Powell was dismissed from the Shadow Cabinet for expressing racist views.

Powell's 1968 speeches were a response to the rapidly increasing immigration into Britain from its former colonies during the 1950s and 1960s. Up until 1962, New Commonwealth immigrants from the West Indies, India, and Pakistan were allowed to enter and settle freely in the United Kingdom, having acquired the status of full British citizens under the 1948 British Nationality Act. During the post-war years, both European and New Commonwealth immigrants had been encouraged to come to Britain by both Labour and Conservative Governments, in order to help solve a labor shortage problem, especially in the textiles and steel industries. The numbers of immigrants from the New Commonwealth increased from an estimated 2,000 in 1953 to around 58,000 in 1960, and to 231,000 during eighteen months between January 1961 and July 1962.

In recognition that the numbers were spiraling out of control, in 1962 the Conservative Government of the time passed the Commonwealth Immigrants Act, which required Commonwealth citizens to obtain labor vouchers in order to enter the United Kingdom and reduced the number of immigrant workers from

Right wing conservative politician Enoch Powell speaks at Islington Town Hall. © HULTON-DEUTSCH COLLECTION/CORBIS.

approximately 50,000 during the first six months of operation of the scheme, to around 13,000 for the entire year 1965. However, the Act also allowed entry of the family dependants of immigrant workers. This reduced its impact on overall numbers of immigrants to the United Kingdom and had the effect of increasing levels of permanent settlements, because families were more likely to stay in the United Kingdom than single migrant workers. The majority of immigrants settled in London, Birmingham, and other main cities, and some city neighborhoods became heavily populated with specific ethnic groups, leading Powell to emphasize, in his "Rivers of Blood" speech, the threat to the native white British population of immigrants taking over their communities.

By the late 1960s, racial tension was increasing, and in 1968 riots broke out in the Notting Hill area of London between West Indian immigrants and groups of right-wing locals. The Labour Government then in power introduced a Race Relations Bill intended to ensure equality of opportunity in British society and to address the increasing problems of racism and discrimination.

Enoch Powell and his extreme right-wing followers were opposed to this policy strategy, which favored the integration of immigrants, and put forward their own radical proposals to control immigration to Britain and to reduce the number of immigrants in the country. Particularly radical were the proposals to stop allowing dependents to join immigrants already in the country and to implement an assisted repatriation scheme for those who decided to return to their home countries.

PRIMARY SOURCE

Seven months ago I made a speech in Birmingham which attracted some considerable attention. I discussed in it the present and prospective consequences of the immigration of Commonwealth citizens into this country during the last fifteen years which took place because, until 1962, this country, alone of all the nations in the world, had no definition of its own people, so that for all purposes an Englishman born in Birmingham and a tribesman from the North-West Frontier were indistinguishable in the law of the United Kingdom. It was a subject on which I had spoken and written on a number of occasions over the preceding months and years. The immediate occasion was the imminent Second Reading of the Government's Race Relations Bill, which the Conservative Shadow Cabinet, then including myself, had decided, and publicly announced its decision, to oppose, on the ground that the Bill would do more harm than good. My speech was made in support and in defence of that decision from the point of view of a Member representing a constituency in one of the areas most affected; and it was so understood both by those to whom it was delivered and by the party officials who, in the normal course, were aware of its contents in advance.

In the seven months which have elapsed since I spoke I have been the target of endless abuse and vilification. No imputation or innuendo has been too vile or scurrilous for supposedly reputable journals to invent or repeat. On the other hand, I have been borne up by an astonishing manifestation, from among all classes of people and from all areas of the community, expressing relief and gratitude that the speech was made. . . .

The reaction to that speech revealed a deep and dangerous gulf in the nation, a gulf which is I fear no narrower today than it was then. I do not mean between the indigenous population and the immigrants. On the contrary, over the months and years the pressure upon me to oppose the growth in the number of immigrants has come as much from my immigrant constituents as from the rest, if not more so: in this matter I was convinced of speaking for and in the interest of all my constituents. Nor do I mean the gulf between those who do, and those who do not, know from personal experience the impact and reality of immigration. Knowledge of the facts and concern about them has been spreading rapidly in parts of the kingdom where a Commonwealth immigrant is never seen. I mean the gulf between the overwhelming majority of people throughout the country on the one side, and on the other side a tiny minority, with almost a monopoly hold upon the channels of communication, who seem determined not to know the facts and not to face the realities and who will resort to any device or extremity to blind both themselves and others. . . .

In the context of a Bill which the native inhabitants of this country were bound to see as directed against themselves, an important part of my argument at Birmingham was the fact of reverse discrimination—that it is not the true immigrant but the Briton who feels himself the 'toad beneath the harrow' in the areas where the immigrant population is spreading and taking root. This indeed was the background against which the opposition were justifiably claiming that the Race Relations Bill would do more harm than good. To illustrate it I described the typical situation of the last and usually elderly white inhabitants

of a street or area otherwise wholly occupied by immigrants, and I did so by citing an individual case from Wolverhampton in a correspondent's own words.

The outcry which followed illuminated like a lightning flash the gulf between those who do not know or want to know and the rest of the nation. Here were circumstances which those who know the facts now are being repeated over and over again, at this very moment, in the towns and the cities affected by immigration—often with aggravations more distressing than in the case I cited. It was ordinary, not extraordinary. Yet all at once the air was filled with denunciation: I was romancing; I had picked up a hoary, unverified legend; I had no evidence; nobody could find the old lady—no more than the class with the one white child! Where do these people live, who imagine that what I related was so remarkable and incredible that they had to conclude it was apocryphal? What do they suppose happens, or has been happening, or will be happening, as the growing immigrant numbers extend their areas of occupation? They must live either a long way off, or they must live with their eyes tight shut. . . .

The issue is not, as some people appear to imagine, one of being nice to the immigrants or strangers in our midst, however diverse their race or culture. The issue is an issue of numbers, now and especially in the future. And so I come to the question of numbers, and of the increase in numbers; for it is the very heart of the matter. As Lord Elton once put it: 'If it were known in my home village that the Archbishop of Canterbury were coming to live there, we should undoubtedly ring a peal on the church bells. If it were known that five archbishops were coming, I could still expect to see my neighbours exchanging excited congratulations at the street corners. But if it were known that fifty archbishops were coming, there would be a riot.'

First, let us get our sense of perspective. Let us look at present numbers. There are today in this country about 1-1/4 million Commonwealth immigrants, though the basis of the statistics is far from perfect and the number is likely to be more rather than less. Suppose that any Government fifteen years ago had declared: it is our intention that by 1968 1-1/4 million Afro-Asians shall have entered this country and settled in it. People would not have believed their ears. Of course, no government, no party would have dared to put forward such a proposal; if they had, they would have been hissed out of office. Yet the thing is no less absurd or monstrous now that it has become a reality than it would have seemed to everybody beforehand. It never was proposed or argued on grounds of supplying labour or skill. Indeed, it could not be; for that has nothing to do with immigration. The doctors, aliens as well as Commonwealth citizens, who have made it possible, by getting a few years of post-graduate experience in Britain, to expand the hospital service faster than would otherwise have been possible, have no more to do with immigration than have the *au pair* girls admitted for a year or two to give domestic help or the workers moving temporarily from one Common Market country to another. Those who still talk about needing immigrant doctors, dentists and teachers, are not really talking about immigration at all. As for unskilled labour, the mere attempt to justify mass importation of it would have been exploded by economists and trade unions alike: the remedy for shortage of labour in a developed economy is more capital and better organization. In short, it is only now that this has happened and the people of Britain are faced with a *fait accompli*, that all sorts of excuses are invented and we are told in terms of arrogant moral superiority that we have got a 'multi-racial society' and had better like it.

Yet if that were all, it could be endured. With their almost incredible tolerance the English—it is virtually only England which is affected—would settle down to live with what they neither asked for nor wanted nor were warned of nor understood. But the present, this 1-1/4 million reality—however inconceivable it would have been in prospect—this is not all. People look to the future, as, as they do so, they remember that they have been betrayed and misled in the past. It is our duty not to betray or mislead them again.

It is easy to understand how enormously strong is the temptation for all politicians to baulk at this vision of the future, and not least for my own party, the Conservative Party, which formed the Government of the country during the crucial years and would fain close its eyes and ears to the wholly unnecessary and avoidable havoc its own inaction wrought—a tragedy which need never have been enacted. If Britain had provided herself in 1956 instead of 1962 with what every other nation under the sun possesses—a law defining its own people—what a world of anguish past and future would never have been! Even those of us who inveighed against the British Nationality Act 1948 from the outset and who from inside and from outside Government urged legislation over the years, feel an oppressive sense of guilt and humiliation. The temptation to close our eyes to the future is correspondingly strong. But it is a temptation that has to be conquered.

Even more dangerous is the too common taunt: 'You did the wrong; you have no right to talk about it now.' Woe betide the nation that will not let its rulers admit their errors and try to remedy the consequences: there is no surer way to persist on a disastrous course until it is too late than to attach the penalty of mockery to those who say: 'We have done wrong.' . . .

On grounds—the prospective growth of numbers with its physical consequences, and the unacceptability of those consequences—rests the urgency of action. We can perhaps not reduce the eventual total of the immigrant and immigrant-descended population much, if at all, below its present size: with that, and with all that implies, we and our children and our children's children will have to cope until the slow mercy of the years absorbs even that unparalleled invasion of our body politic. What I believe we can do, and therefore must do, is to avert the impending disaster of its increase.

There are two, and, so far as I can see, only two measures available to this end. Both are obvious; one is far more important, and far more difficult, than the other. If further net immigration were virtually to cease at once, that would reduce the prospective total for 1985 by a further half million, and would have a somewhat more than proportionate effect on whatever is to be the rate of increase after 1985; for, as I have pointed out, the inflow, consisting as it does mostly of dependants, forms the basis for new family units in the future. I say 'virtually cease', because of course no one would wish an absolute veto on the settlement of individual Afro-Asians in this country in future, any more than of other aliens. But let there be no prevarication about what is meant. What is meant is that we would cease to admit not only new settlers and their dependants but the dependants or remaining dependants of immigrants already here. The first half of this presents no human difficulty: if we admit no new settlers, there is no problem about their dependants. The problem attaches to the reservoir of dependants who have not yet joined immigrants already here. In this case we have to decide between two evils, the denial of entry of an immigrant's dependants and the consequences of the prospective growth in numbers. But here the minor issue merges into the major one, that of repatriation.

I have argued that on any prudent view, quite apart from any subsequent immigration, the future prospect is unacceptable. Hence the key significance of repatriation or at any rate re-emigration. A policy of assisting repatriation by payment of fares and grants is part of the official policy of the Conservative Party. It is a just, rational and humane policy; it accepts that a wrong has unintentionally been done to the immigrant by placing him in a position where the future is as pregnant with trouble for him as for the rest of the population, and it accepts the duty of reinstating him as far as possible. As my colleage, Mr Boyd-Carpenter pointed out in a speech at Blackpool recently which has received too little attention, it would provide the fair answer for the immigrant here whose dependants were not permitted to join him. The question is what would be the practical scope and application of such a policy.

I believe that ignorance of the realities of Commonwealth immigration leads people seriously to underestimate the scope of the policy and thus to neglect and despise the chief key to the situation. Perhaps it is the historical associations of the world 'immigrant' which create in those remote from the facts the picture of individuals who have left their homes behind for ever to seek a new future in a far-off land, rather in the mood of those Victorian pictures of the immigrants' farewell.

Of course, there are many cases where individuals have uprooted themselves to come here; but in the mass it is much nearer the truth to think in terms of detachments from communities in the West Indies or India or Pakistan encamped in certain areas of England. They are still to a large extent a part, economically and socially, of the communities from which they have been detached and to which they regard themselves as belonging. As a recently published study of one of the West Indian islands put it thus:

> Migrant communities in Britain are linked to their home societies by an intricate network of ties and obligations. There are strong social pressures for members of a community to send back money to their families in the island, where most of them expect to return eventually . . . the ideology of migration and the social networks formed around it are so closely connected that it is rare for migrants to abandon one without leaving the other. Thus migrants who decide to stay permanently in Britain often cut themselves off from the others.

This description could apply, even more strongly, to the communities from India and Pakistan, whose total numbers now exceed the West Indian, and whose links with their homes are kept in being by a constant flow not only of remittances, amounting to many millions of pounds a year, but of personal visits and exchanges, the scale of which would astonish anyone not closely acquainted with the actual phenomenon of Commonwealth immigration in this country. The annual holiday 'back home' in the West Indies or in India or Pakistan is no rare feature of life in the immigrant communities.

Against this background a programme of large-scale voluntary but organized, financed and subsidized repatriation and re-emigration becomes indeed an administrative and political task of great magnitude, but something neither absurdly impracticable nor, still less, inhuman, but on the contrary as profoundly humane as it is far-sighted. Under a agreement between Ceylon and India for the repatriation of more than half a million Indians over fifteen years, 35,000 return to India each year with their assets. The Government of Guyana is anxious to promote the re-emigration to that country of West Indians and others who can help to build up its economy and develop its resources. A cursory survey carried out by a national newspaper six months ago indicated that over 20 per cent of immigrants interviewed would contemplate availing themselves of an opportunity to go home. It need not even follow that the income from work done here in Britain would be suddenly lost to the home communities if permanent settlement of population were replaced by what may countries in Europe and elsewhere are familiar with—the temporary, albeit often long-term, intake of labour.

The resettlement of a substantial proportion of the Commonwealth immigrants in Britain is not beyond the resources and abilities of this country, if it is undertaken as a national duty, in the successful discharge of which the interests both of the immigrants themselves and of the countries from which they came are engaged. It ought to be, and it could be, organized now on the scale which the urgency of the situation demands, preferably under a special Ministry of Repatriation or other authority charged with concentrating on this task.

At present large numbers of the offspring of immigrants, even those born here in Britain, remain integrated in the immigrant community which links them with their homeland overseas. With every passing year this will diminish. Sometimes people point to the increasing proportion of immigrant offspring born in this country as if the fact contained within itself the ultimate solution. The truth is the opposite. The West Indian or Asian does not, by being born in England, become an Englishman. In law he becomes a United Kingdom citizen by birth; in fact he is a West Indian or an Asian still. Unless he be one of a small minority—for number, I repeat again and again, is of the essence—he will by the very nature of things have lost one country without gaining another, lost one nationality without acquiring a new one. Time is running against us and them. With the lapse of a generation or so we shall at last have succeeded—to he benefit of nobody—in reproducing 'in England's green and pleasant land' the haunting tragedy of the United States.

The English as a nation have their own peculiar faults. One of them is that strange passivity in the face of danger or absurdity or provocation, which has more than once in our history lured observers into false conclusions—conclusions sometimes fatal to the observers themselves—about the underlying intentions and the true determination of our people. What so far no one could accuse us of is a propensity to abandon hope in the face of severe and even seemingly insurmountable obstacles. Dejection is not one of our national traits; but we must be told the truth and shown the danger, if we are to meet it. Rightly or wrongly, I for my part believe that the time for that has come.

SIGNIFICANCE

Although Powell's extreme proposals to cease all immigration to the United Kingdom and to offer assisted repatriation to New Commonwealth immigrants were never implemented, British immigration controls were progressively tightened during the following years. The 1971 Immigration Act eliminated the preferential status previously enjoyed by New Commonwealth immigrants and made them subject to the same controls as immigrants of other nationalities. Nevertheless, immigrants from the former colonies continued to enter the United Kingdom in substantial numbers during the 1970s, by an estimated 535,000 per year until 1978.

Race relations problems continued to threaten social stability during the 1970s, with the rise of the extreme right-wing National Front organization, who organized violent demonstrations throughout the decade, while Enoch Powell continued to enjoy a high level of public support for his views on immigration.

In the 1980s, however, immigration levels declined, particularly after 1988 when legislation came into force that eliminated the right for the dependants of pre–1973 immigrants to enter the country. Moreover, the 1983 Nationality Act clarified the law on entitlement to British citizenship and made it easier to enforce the immigration rules. As a result, immigration was no longer such a high profile political issue, and race relations improved.

FURTHER RESOURCES

Book

Paul, Kathleen. *Whitewashing Britain: Race and Citizenship in the Postwar Era*. Ithica, N.Y.: Cornell University Press, 1997.

Periodicals

Messina, Anthony M. "Immigration as a Political Dilemma in Britain: Implications for Western Europe." *Policy Studies Journal* (23) (4) (1995): 696–698.

Schnapper, Dominique. "The Debate on Immigration and the Crisis of National Identity." *West European Politics* (17) (2) (1994): 127–139.

The Most Memorable Times of Our Lives, 1968–1975

Essay

By: Rey Huerta

Date: 2003

Source: *Farmworkers Movement Documentation Project.* "Rey Huerta, 1968–1975: The Most Memorable Times of Our Lives." <http://www.farmworkermovement.org/> (accessed June 25, 2006).

About the Author: Rey Huerta, a Mexican-American, worked as an organizer for the United Farm Workers from 1968 to 1975. He was later employed as a math and science teacher, and currently tutors children and adults at his tutoring center in Coachella, California. Founded by César Chávez in 1962, the United Farm Workers was the premier organization for migrant workers in California.

INTRODUCTION

One of the poorest occupations in the United States is that of the landless, migrant farm worker. Migrant farm workers have long been a mainstay of the farms and ranches of California. Many of the workers, particularly the grape pickers, were organized by César Chávez and his United Farm Workers in the 1960s and 1970s to obtain better wages and working conditions. This labor struggle became one of the most publicized in American history, though it remained peaceful.

Prior to World War I, agriculture in the U.S. was largely family based and small scale. Independent family farmers, tenant farmers, and share cropping families lived on the land that they cultivated. For historical reasons, California was an exception. When California achieved statehood, former large Mexican estates were only partially broken up and a few thousand of California's wealthiest private proprietors soon owned most of the state's arable land. These landowners seldom resided on their land or directly worked the ground. To run the farms, they hired supervisors and small year-round crews that maintained machines and watched the crops. The growers authorized the hiring of large temporary workforces to harvest crops for a few weeks each year. The transient laborers were paid piecemeal for the number of pounds that they harvested each day. Workers lived in housing rented from the growers or in makeshift camps. Often pickers were not allowed to leave the ranches in the evening and were forced to buy groceries, toiletries, and other daily goods at exorbitant prices in company stores. As soon as a harvest was completed, a grower usually had no further need for the hundreds of field hands. They were quickly pushed and pulled to other farms.

Over time, little changed but the ethnic and racial composition of the huge migrating work force. At first, growers recruited down-on-their-luck miners, Native Americans, bankrupt former farmers, and newly arrived Europeans. At the start of the twentieth century, growers began using numbers of imported laborers from China, Japan, Mexico, and Hawaii. By the time that César Chávez organized the United Farm Workers (UFW) in 1962, the majority of the pickers were Mexicans. These Latinos occasionally engaged in local and spontaneous strikes (huelga, in Spanish) and slowdowns in hopes of securing better pay and working conditions. A few farm workers attempted to create permanent labor organizations. They did not succeed until Chávez and his fellow union organizers arrived.

▮ PRIMARY SOURCE

By 1970, I was ready to commit and join the union as a full-time volunteer. Of course, my family was not thrilled with my decision to join the union full time. The family vote came to four against one, not in my favor. It left me with no alternative but to claim five votes so the motion could carry! They could not stop crying. I had to persuade them that they would not starve to death, that they would have clothes and shoes to wear to school, and that the growers would not drive by and shoot at us. It took them quite a while to adjust to the discipline, but we all finally did.

At 3 A.M., it is so dark outside that a person cannot even see his hand in front of his face, but there we were, at the west end of Fresno with flags flying and headlights flashing. It was my first huelga. My wife and children were all jammed into our old car, except my youngest son, Ray, who was still sleeping in the trunk of the old Pontiac. When we arrived at the designated ranch, we immediately got out of our cars and started setting up picket lines around a peach grower's field. The huelga ladies knew their job and started to set up the huelga kitchen. We all needed our caffeine and tortillas con chile so that we could be energized for the long day ahead.

We were assigned to picket all day and then spend the night at this particular ranch. Our cars needed to be moved out of harm's way during the night, so we resorted to sleeping on the ground around the perimeter of the ranch to assure that the peach grower would not try to sneak scab workers by us in the middle of the night. This particular strike lasted six days and seven nights. The tactics were raw, but the outcome was a positive one: The grower agreed to negotiate a contract. The reason we selected to hit that peach grove was because we knew that the grower also had grape orchards that we could not locate. Striking his peach orchard forced him to disclose the location of the grapes! Si se puede! The strikers were jubilant. They did not expect such an easy victory. That was in the spring of 1970, and the other grape strikes and boycotts were still going strong. I was then assigned to the UFW Selma field office. I was to work directly under the supervision of Gil Padilla, the UFW treasurer and one of Cesar's

most trusted friends. Gil Padilla was also one of the UFW's top-notch organizers. Originally from Los Banos, California, Gil brought to the union years of experience in community organizing. He was very informed, diplomatic, and political; he could negotiate contacts and was a great leader. Gil reassigned me to Salinas right before the strike broke out. He felt it would be good training for me because I really did not have much strike experience.

Salinas was a rude awakening for me, as it was for most of the new volunteers arriving in the Salinas Valley for the lettuce strike. It was one of the first big gatherings of the UFW's finest recruits. Salinas was slated for a major strike. Fred Ross, Sr., along with Jerry Cohen, the UFW's legal point man and conciliari, were there to help Cesar schedule the various tasks needed as we grabbed the tiger by the tail. Marshall Ganz, Father Neri, Jim Drake and his charming wife, Susan, Eliseo Medina, LeRoy Chatfield, Chris Hartmire, and a whole collection of lawyers, organizers, various ministry folks, and office people were to take the thousands of calls and messages that would be generated from the strike. There were the huelga cooks and the security staff led by Richard Ybarra, Cesar's son-in-law. Also present were the many paralegals from all parts of the country. We were getting ready to do battle with California's agribusiness giants of the Salinas Valley, the West Coast lettuce industry. It looked to be a horrendous task, to say the least.

A chapter of the UFW's lettuce workers based in Calexico, California, was planning a general strike as they arrived to the Salinas Valley. The lettuce workers were on of our strongest groups, so Cesar decided to back the lettuce workers in their pursuit of a union contract that was to include seniority rights and a substantial pay increase for the arduous labor that the lettuce workers endured on a daily basis. The short-handled hoe would forever be outlawed in the lettuce fields of California because of the notoriety of its damage to a person's lower back. This was truly stoop labor in its cruelest form. Cesar put an end to it by having the notorious hoe banned from the fields in California.

Salinas is home to some of the largest lettuce, celery, cauliflower, artichoke, and strawberry growers in the country. Those growers have the money to support their whims. So who must have been running the city and county governments in the Salinas Valley? It was plain and simple: The multimillion-dollar giant agribusiness ran the show.

As soon as we set up the pickets, we began gaining immediate farmworker support as they started to leave the fields of the Salinas Valley. The growers and the courts got together soon enough and began handing down court injunctions like there was no tomorrow. They desperately tried to stop us from winning over their longtime farm laborers by trying to prevent such things as gathering in large numbers and limiting the area and space where we were striking or picketing.

The court injunctions were ludicrous. They soon arrested Cesar because he would not bow down and put an end to the strike! *Si se puede!* I recall our holding all-night candlelight vigils in front of the jail where Cesar was being held. There were thousands of supporters praying and chanting with us. We were out there for almost two weeks before they released Cesar from the Salinas County jail. Much to my dismay, I also spent a week in that same jail with 10 to 12 other strikers from one of the cauliflower companies for picketing a field that was covered by an injunction issued by the Salinas superior court. We were released after a three-day hunger strike; we were refusing to east the food that was given to us, which was primarily lettuce.

The cops chased us, the hired goons and thugs chased us, and the growers chased us. To add insult to injury, they even hired and brought in big dogs to chase us. We stood at the edge of the field next to the road waving our flags to attract the attention of the workers. The goons' supervisors would come at us with vicious dogs on leashes in an attempt to intimidate us enough to want to abandon our posts. Fat chance! Like a tree standing by the water, I remembered, we shall not be moved!

There were waves upon waves of red flags with the black eagle flying everywhere in and out of the city. One could drive along the highway from Salinas all the way south to Gonzales and beyond and see a continuous mass of flags waving in the coastal breezes. People waved at us in support of our struggle as they passed us in their autos. It was a beautiful sight: thousands of people, lined up for miles, waving their flags and shouting and singing with pride, "*Viva La Huelga*, Long Live the Strike," and as the chorus from the song of the time went:

Viva la revolucion,
Viva nuestra asociacion
Viva la huelga en el fil,
Viva la causa y la historia,
Viva raza llena de Gloria
La Victoria va cumplir.

We were enthusiastic and ready for all of the action. We took everything the growers and courts threw at us. My adrenaline was at a constant high and I was always ready to go and then some. We were operating on three or four hours of sleep each night. We got up before dawn in order to meet the workers as they tried to get into the fields on company buses. The *esquiroles* or scabs no longer drove into the fields in private autos. That year I also learned patience from Cesar. I learned to restrain the rage I felt

toward the establishment that was obviously purchased by the growers. As was expected, I had to learn to incorporate the nonviolence practiced by Cesar. I had to do some real practicing myself. Let me tell you, this was not easy for a barrio dude like me! To let the rednecks call us degrading names, to let them beat us, arrest us, then run over us— all these things were really stretching my commitment to the cause for justice. As one of the Brown Berets so aptly put it, "The courts don't mean justice; they mean just us."

SIGNIFICANCE

In 1965, Mexican American field hands spontaneously struck for better wages against a group of powerful vineyards. The strikers asked Chávez and the UFW to support the strike. To everyone's surprise, the strike lasted for five years. In the face of likely defeat, Chávez coined a novel strategy: consumer boycotts of the growers' products. UFW activists traveled throughout the U.S. and spoke to students and parishioners about the need to boycott grapes and wines. Supermarkets that stocked the growers' products were boycotted until they stopped doing so. In 1970, the growers agreed to accept union contracts, allowing the unionization of most of the industry. By then, the UFW claimed 50,000 dues-paying members, the most ever represented by a union in California. In the 1980s, a conservative political climate and disputes within UFW weakened the clout of the union considerably. By Chávez's death in 1993, the UFW had about 20,000 members.

The history of farm worker protests and movements in California highlights both the ongoing powerlessness of migrant workers and the power of the state's agribusiness. After a century of struggles, California farm hands remain among the poorest in America. The easy availably of replacement workers, often undocumented immigrants willing to work for little pay under poor conditions, has made it difficult for farm workers to exert pressure on the growers.

FURTHER RESOURCES
Books

Etulain, Richard W. *César Chávez: A Brief Biography with Documents*. Boston: Bedford/St. Martin's, 2002.

Hurt, R. Douglas. *American Agriculture: A Brief History*. Ames: Iowa State University Press, 2002.

Mooney, Patrick H., and Theo J. Majka. *Farmers' and Farm Workers' Movements: Social Protest in American Agriculture*. New York: Twayne, 1995.

Israel's Responsibility for and Policy Towards Diaspora Jewry

Book excerpt

By: Geula Cohen and Yitzhak Rabin

Date: November 26, 1975

Source: Cohen, Geula, and Yitzhak Rabin. *Major Knesset Debates*. Lanham, Md.: University Press of America, 1992.

About the Authors: Geula Cohen (b. 1925), an Israel politician, served in the Israeli Knesset from 1973 to 1992. In 2001 she was awarded the Israel Prize for Lifetime Achievement. Following twenty-seven years with the Israeli Defense Force, Yitzhak Rabin (1922–1995) joined the Likud party and served as Prime Minister from 1974 to 1977 and from 1992 to 1994. Rabin was awarded the Nobel Peace Prize in 1995, along with Yassar Arafat and Shimon Peres for their steps toward peace in the Middle East through the Oslo Accords. Rabin was assassinated in Tel Aviv after attending a rally in 1995.

INTRODUCTION

Anti-Semitism in the late nineteenth century throughout Europe became the catalyst for the movement to create of a Jewish homeland. This movement became referred to as Zionism. The most famous case of anti-Semitism occurred in France with the Dreyfus affair, in which a Jewish army captain was convicted of treason based on forged evidence, highlighting the institutionalized anti-Semitism in France. The Dreyfus affair influenced Jewish writers such as Leon Pinsker (1821–1891) and Theodore Herzl (1860–1904), who began to write about the Jewish experience of discrimination in Europe. In 1896, Herzl published *Der Judenstaat*, or the State of the Jews, which declared that the condition of the Diaspora, or Jews residing throughout the world, would continue to deteriorate. Under Herzl's leadership, the first Zionist Congress met in August of 1897 in Basle and established the goal of Zionism as the establishment of a Jewish homeland in Palestine, the ancient homeland of the Jewish people. The Zionist movement established itself as an international organization with a structure and institutions, including the Zionist General Council and the Zionist Executive. The Third Congress passed the first constitution for the organization in 1899.

Palestine at that time was part of the Ottoman Empire (Turkey) that ruled over much of the Middle East. The Ottomans were ethnically Turkish, while the people residing in Palestine were primarily Arabs, with some Jews as well. The Ottomans were opposed to the establishment of a Jewish homeland in Palestine. Western nations, at this time, viewed Palestine as a region that lacked a national identity. During World War I (1914–1918), the Ottoman Empire fought on the side of Germany and the Austro-Hungarian Empire (the Central Powers) against Great Britain, France, Russia and the other nations known as the Allied Powers. Britain negotiated with both Arabs and the Jews who resided in the Middle East in an effort to win their support against their Ottoman rulers. The British stated sympathy for Zionist goals in 1917 with the Balfour Declaration, which announced British intent to sponsor a national home for the Jews in Palestine after the war.

The Allied powers were victorious in World War I, and after the war British troops occupied Palestine and several other regions in the Middle East, becoming the dominant colonial power in the region. In an agreement reached at the San Remo Conference, which was drafted in 1920 and adopted by the League of Nations in 1922, the Principle Allied Powers divided the Middle East using self-interest to determine their individual country's mandates. As a provision under the Mandate for Palestine granted to Britain, an agency was created to represent the Jewish people and aid in the establishment of a Jewish homeland. The Zionist Organization established by Herzl was initially tasked as this agency. In 1929, the Jewish Agency for Palestine was created under the League of Nations Mandate for Palestine as an element of the World Zionist Organization in building a homeland for Jews.

While the Western powers carved up the region, Jews began to immigrate in larger numbers to Palestine. From 1919 to 1931 the Jewish population increased from 8 to 17 percent of the total population as their numbers increased from 60,000 to 175,000. Arabs became increasingly resistant to the increase in Jewish immigrants to Palestine during the period preceding World War II (1939–1945). After a series of violent conflicts, the British government published the White Paper of 1939 that established a new policy for Britain toward Zionism. The white paper announced British intention to seek an independent Palestinian state, governed by Jews and Arabs who shared authority. Zionists viewed the paper as a betrayal on the part of British policy makers and began to pursue support from the United States. where many Jews resided. As World War II came to an end and the details of the Holocaust became widely known, Zionists gained popular support for the creation of a Jewish homeland.

On the geopolitical stage, Britain and the U.S. recognized that the oil-rich Middle East would play an important role in the imminent Cold War with the Soviet Union. By 1948, the United Nations Resolution 181 terminated the Mandate for Palestine, under which the British had administered the region. The Jewish inhabitants of the region responded by declaring their independence and the statehood of Israel. Arab nations rejected the state of Israel while western powers acknowledged the new country.

▌ PRIMARY SOURCE

Introduction The relationship between Israel and Jews living abroad and, by the same token, the implications of Israel's character as a Jewish state have been fundamental issues echoed in many debates in the Knesset. They have, however, only seldom constituted the focus of a special debate. A motion for the agenda on the subject was presented by MK Geula Cohen on 26 November 1975, and was followed later on by a full-scale debate.

Sitting 231 of the Eighth Knesset
                    26 November 1975 (22 Kislev 5736)

G. Cohen (Likud): Distinguished Knesset, despite the Knesset's low labor morals . . . I hope things have not reached such a pass that I have to ask for House to forgive me for raising a purely Zionist issue . . . and asking whether we are still a Zionist state. . . .

In effect, what happened yesterday, when Jews who sought to settle in Judea and Samaria were removed, is sufficient indication . . . its ultimate implication being the establishment of a Palestinian state in the West Bank . . . and the condemnation of Zionism not only about our enemies. But today I will discuss Zionism from a different angle . . . that of the Jewish people, and ask to what extent the Government of Israel, as a Zionist government, is responsible for the fate of the entire Jewish people and is prepared to accept whatever derives from that and, accordingly, to appoint a Minister whose sole responsibility will be the Jewish people.

The only Jewish community . . . which cannot concern itself with the welfare of the Jewish people is the Jewish community in the State of Israel. In Israel's Knesset, which represents Israel's citizens, there is no possibility today of seriously discussing a topic connected with the Jews of the diaspora, whether it be immigration or Jewish education, assimilation or anti-Semitism, because there is no Minister in the Government who deals with the subject. . . .

That is no mere chance. The subject of the Jewish people does not appear on the agenda of the Knesset because it does not appear on the agenda of the State of Israel. The phenomenon I am referring to has its roots in a fundamental error . . . committed in the early years of the state's existence, when it decided not to take upon itself the responsibility for the Jewish people. . . . today, it cannot do so even if it wants to . . . although the state has accepted a situation of coexistence with the exile . . . (I am using the term deliberately), emptying of content all its statements about immigration and thereby relinquishing its role as a Zionist state. . . .

May I remind the House. . . . that the Zionist state was established in order to solve the problem of the Jewish people, and that its responsibility should extend beyond its territorial sovereignty to the place where the furthest-flung Jew resides. . . . Because if the Jews of the world may have a problem of dual loyalty, the Government of Zionist Israel can have only one loyalty, i.e., to every member of the Jewish people, wherever he or she may be.

The moral question as to what extent the Jewish people has empowered the Government of Israel to interfere in its affairs . . . was settled when Zionism—whose consequence is the state—came into being. . . . There may be no precedent in international law for one country's interference in the affairs of the citizens of another, but the Jewish people and its problems are so abnormal that they cannot be based on precedents. Such questions as in what ways to do it and whether we should intervene only when Jewish lives are threatened . . . can be asked only after the basic question of whether the Government of Israel regards itself as being responsible for the entire Jewish people has been answered. . . .

I expect to receive an answer to that question from the Prime Minister today, because if I had to answer it in the light of the behavior of all Israel's governments to date I would say that they hesitate to accept this responsibility, and that this has serious implications for the situation of the Jews of the exile as well as for the State of Israel. Officially, the Government has not divested itself of that responsibility . . . by transferring it to the Jewish Agency and the Zionist Organization, except in the spheres of financial and political aid for Israel's defense . . . this arrangement being anchored in an agreement signed in 1952, with coordinating committee between the Government and the Zionist Organization. . . . But that agreement is one which purportedly deals with the Jewish people and its problems, on the one hand, and the State of Israel and its problems, on the other . . . irrespective of the extent to which the Zionist organization is in fact Zionist and representative of diaspora Jewry. . . .

The inescapable fact is that the coordinating body cannot coordinate because it does not meet. Its chairman is the Prime Minister, and he is too busy with the problems of the State of Israel to convene it. Although it should meet at least once a month, it has not met more than twice or three times in the last two years . . . for the real question is not whether the Prime Minister has time for the problems of the Jewish people, but whether he is interested in them.... I assume he is interested...as was indicated by his admirable remarks in the debate arising from the U.N. resolutions on Zionism.... That was the first time I heard a Prime Minister speak in a truly Zionist spirit in this House...though the circumstances in which his warning to the Jews of the diaspora and his call to them to immigrate to Israel were issued were regrettable....

Be that as it may...why shouldn't a special Minister, someone who is genuinely concerned about and identifies with the Jewish people, take the Prime Minister's place as chairman of that committee...? The State of Israel, as a Zionist state, should not, from the very outset, have divested itself of responsibility for the fate of the Jewish people. This is even more so today, when the Jews of the exile will not make a move without Israel's approval and when Israel's fate determines the physical condition of the Jews of the diaspora.... Without a doubt, Israel does act on behalf of the Jews of the diaspora in various roundabout ways, but it must do so openly and officially....

There are also several contradictions in Israel's policy on this subject. On the one hand we hear the Foreign Minister declare, in Kissinger's wake, that the subject of Soviet Jewry is the internal concern of the Soviet authorities, while on the other the State of Israel sends Israeli citizenship documents to immigration activists in Russia.... Israel's responsibility for the diaspora is particularly necessary now...when assimilation and mixed marriage is rife, Jewish education is declining, anti-Semitism is increasing and immigration to Israel has become an infinitesimal trickle....

In the 1950s Ben-Gurion made a weak attempt to alter the situation and criticized the Zionist Organization...but his sole concern was immigration.... His approach was to turn his back and display pique, which is hardly a rational, useful or Zionist approach....

I am not unaware of the problems involved in our accepting this responsibility, particularly after having shrugged it off for twenty-seven years.... I live in this country and have also fought for it and know how much wars and struggles can distract a nation's attention from the more general problem of the Jewish people.... But we are all aware of the dreadful experience of the Holocaust and know now that it could be fatal to defer dealing with problems...for the enemies of the Jews are in a hurry to solve the problems of the Jewish people in their own way....

By neglecting to deal with the problem of the Jewish people we are also harming the State of Israel...cutting ourselves off from the historical process of redemption and the vision of the ingathering of the exiles and raising a barrier between Israelis and Jews.... All those things

have caused a diminution in every sphere of our life: withdrawal from parts of the land of Israel, negative immigration and retreats in the fields of culture, economics and morals.... A country which was created to be Zionist and does not act accordingly is not only non-Zionist, it is abnormal. The attempt to evade the Zionist mission and establish a normal country here is not succeeding. One might understand the desire to be normal, to be a country like any other, though when I look around at the normal countries I am not so very impressed. But even if we want to achieve that, we will not.

At any rate, in its declaration of intent, the state decided that it was Zionist. The only Zionist law which distinguishes this country is the Law of Return. This is the only country in the world most of whose potential inhabitants live outside it. Even in order to attain peace Israel will not abrogate the Law of Return.... But that law alone cannot bring immigrants to Israel...and what the country needs is a Zionist policy. I therefore propose that the Knesset hold an urgent debate on revising the state's responsibility for and policy towards the Jewish people, with all that that implies regarding the coordinating committee of the Zionist Organization, as well as on establishing a parallel Knesset committee to deal with the issue....

The Prime Minister, Y. Rabin: Mr. Speaker...the subject raised is without doubt an important one and concerns the basis of Israel's existence.... I will not repeat what is contained in the Government's guidelines regarding Israel and the diaspora. I am convinced that we are all united in realizing that the Jewish State is based on our firm and close link with our brethren abroad. Israel was established and exists for the entire Jewish nation, to ensure our national survival and continue Jewish history, not solely for its own inhabitants. That is no empty phrase, because it is reflected in our daily activities in every sphere.... I will not say that what we do is sufficient and that more could not be done to combat assimilation, heighten Jewish consciousness, encourage immigration and strengthen the bond between the State of Israel and the diaspora.

These obligations are of particular importance at this time, in view of the great and urgent challenges now on the agenda of the Jewish people...No one will dispute that the subject currently under discussion has to be given greater attention...but it cannot be said that nothing is being done.... I would like to remind the House of the law passed by the Knesset regarding the status of the Zionist Organization in 1952 and the agreement between the Government and the Zionist Executive in 1954.... Those documents embody both the basic ideology and the practical measures of and authority for its implementation...and considerable activity is being undertaken within those frameworks....

The Government, in conjunction with the Zionist Executive, is inviting Jewish leaders representing the major Jewish organizations of the free world to Jerusalem next week for the Jerusalem Conference for Jewish Solidarity, to express the solidarity of the Jewish people with Zionism and Israel and prepare a practical and detailed plan of action for 1976. There is a widespread awakening in Jewish communities all over the world.... The committee coordinating the work of the Government and the Zionist Organization met yesterday and the final details of the conference were worked out.... We hope that the conference will express the unity of the Jewish people in Israel and abroad, a unity which has grown stronger in the face of the attacks upon Zionism, the Jewish people and the State of Israel.... I support MK Cohen's proposal that the subject be discussed, which the Government will bring before the House.

(The proposal to place the subject on the agenda is adopted.)

SIGNIFICANCE

In 1952, the Knesset, the Israeli legislative body, adopted the World Zionist Organization-Jewish Agency Law. This legislation tasked the World Zionist Organization (WZO) with the development and settlement of the nascent state of Israel. Other aspects of the WZO mandate were the promotion of immigration to Israel and the absorption of immigrants from the Diaspora into the Israeli state. In 1954, the Israeli government and the Zionist executives met at the Jerusalem Conference for Jewish Solidarity. As a provision of the covenant that emerged from the conference, the WZO and the Jewish Agency were identified as the official representatives of Jews, whether residing in Israel or abroad. The WZO was given the task of focusing on the political and organization matters regarding Zionism, to include Jewish education in the Diaspora and the supervision of the Jewish National Fund. The Jewish Agency was tasked with the financial and economic activities regarding Zionism. As a result, the two organizations played a major role in the consolidation of the nascent Israeli state by absorbing and settling immigrants and gaining financial and moral support from the Diaspora.

Following the six-day war in 1967, the WZO and the Jewish Agency sought to strengthen ties between the Israeli state and the Diaspora. The WZO's primary concern was the development of the Diaspora through Jewish education, Zionist organizational work, and information and cultural programs. The Jewish Agency was tasked with fundraising to finance the resettlement issues of the immigrants, to include housing, social welfare, education and land settlement.

FURTHER RESOURCES

Books

Brenner, Michael. *Zionism: A Brief History*. Princeton, N.J.: Markus Weiner Publishers, 2003.

Sacher, Howard M. *A History of Israel*. New York: Alfred Knopf, 1979.

Periodicals

Bennis, Phyllis. "The United Nations and Palestine: Partition and its Aftermath." *Arab Studies Quarterly* 19 (June 22,1997).

Ovendale, Ritchie . "The Origins of the Arab-Israeli Conflict." *Historian*, January 1, 2002.

Web site

Library of Congress. "Israel Country Study." <http://countrystudies.us/israel/88.htm> (accessed June 15, 2006).

Plyler v. Doe

United States Supreme Court Strikes Down Texas Legislation That Denied the Use of Public Funds in the Education of the Children of Illegal Aliens

Legal decision

By: William J. Brennan, Jr.

Date: June 15, 1982

Source: *Plyler v. Doe*. 457 U.S. 202 (1982).

About the Author: The Supreme Court of the United States is comprised of eight justices and one chief justice. In 1982, the associate justices were John Paul Stevens, Thurgood Marshall, Lewis F. Powell, Jr., William H. Rehnquist, Sandra Day O'Connor, William J. Brennan, Jr., Byron R. White, and Harry A. Blackmun. Warren E. Burger was chief justice. William Brennan (1906–1997) authored the majority opinion of the court in its decision in *Plyler v. Doe*.

INTRODUCTION

The roots of the 1982 U.S. Supreme Court decision in *Plyler v. Doe* extend to a statutory scheme enacted in the state of Texas in 1975 known as the Alien Children Education Act. Texas passed legislation at that time that permitted local school boards to deny enrollment to the children of migrant Texas farm workers who were resident in the United States illegally. The majority of the children affected by this law were Mexican. In denying these children enrollment, the school boards, and ultimately the state, were not required to expend public monies on their education. The impetus for the 1975 legislation was a desire by Texas legislators to reduce the economic burdens placed on the state by its migrant worker population, specifically by the education and health care costs for these individuals.

The Plyler case was constituted as a class action, a legal proceeding where the plaintiff advances a claim on their own behalf and as representative of all other persons affected by the issue in dispute in the litigation. In Plyler, the affected class of persons was the school age children of Mexican migrant workers who wished to attend school in the Tyler, Texas, school district. While the class of plaintiffs was restricted to a single Texas school district, the U.S. Supreme Court ruling was binding on every school board in the United States.

The chief issue before the U.S. Supreme Court was the applicability of the Equal Protection Clause of the Fourteenth Amendment of the U.S. Constitution. The Court, in a five-to-four decision written by Associate Justice William Brennan, held that illegal aliens were persons who were entitled to constitutional protection. So long as the person is within the boundaries of the state and therefore subject to state laws, the protection applied.

The court also considered the issue of education as a fundamental right of every person in the United States. The court characterized education as a part of the fabric of society; to exclude the children of persons who were present in the United States illegally from taking a measure of shelter in that fabric was seen by the court as the perpetuation of needless hardship. The court also placed reliance on the fact that, in 1982, the nation did not possess a discernable national policy regarding the treatment of alien children that ought to move the court to place the Texas legislation within the bounds of such a policy.

The dissent in Plyler was authored by Chief Justice Warren Burger. The dissent draws a very clear demarcation between the powers of elected representatives to

Immigrant students hold a news conference demanding action on legislation to provide legal status for thousands of undocumented immigrant students. PHOTO BY SPENCER PLATT/GETTY IMAGES.

make social policy and the role of the court. The minority decision describes the majority approach as an unwarranted interference in the performance of the duties of the elected representatives of the state of Texas and their ultimate right to set social policy.

The minority decision strongly criticizes the majority viewpoint regarding the distinction to be drawn between children who have no direct control over their presence in the United States and their illegal resident parents. The minority were of the opinion that a state could treat the education of children differently if those were the offsprings of illegal aliens.

PRIMARY SOURCE

APPEAL FROM THE UNITED STATES COURT OF APPEALS FOR THE FIFTH CIRCUIT NO. 80–1538
Argued: December 1, 1981
Decided: June 15, 1982

Held: A Texas statute which withholds from local school districts any state funds for the education of children who were not "legally admitted" into the United States, and which authorizes local school districts to deny enrollment to such children, violates the Equal Protection Clause of the Fourteenth Amendment.Pp. 210–230.

(a) The illegal aliens who are plaintiffs in these cases challenging the statute may claim the benefit of the Equal Protection Clause, which provides that no State shall "deny to any person within its jurisdiction the equal protection of the laws." Whatever his status under the immigration laws, an alien is a "person" in any ordinary sense of that term. This Court's prior cases recognizing that illegal aliens are "persons" protected by the Due Process Clauses of the Fifth and Fourteenth Amendments, which Clauses do not include the phrase "within its jurisdiction," cannot be distinguished on the asserted ground that persons who have entered the country illegally are not "within the jurisdiction" of a State even if they are present within its boundaries and subject to its laws. Nor do the logic and history of the Fourteenth Amendment support such a construction. Instead, use of the phrase "within its jurisdiction" confirms the understanding that the Fourteenth Amendment's protection extends to anyone, citizen or stranger, who is subject to the laws of a State, and reaches into every corner of a State's territory. Pp. 210–216.

(b) The discrimination contained in the Texas statute cannot be considered rational unless it furthers some substantial goal of the State. Although undocumented resident aliens cannot be treated as a "suspect class," and although education is not a "fundamental right," so as to require the State to justify the statutory classification by showing that it serves a compelling governmental interest, nevertheless the Texas statute imposes a lifetime hardship on a discrete class of children not accountable for their disabling status. These children can neither affect their parents' conduct nor their own undocumented status. The deprivation of public education is not like the deprivation of some other governmental benefit. Public education has a pivotal role in maintaining the fabric of our society and in sustaining our political and cultural heritage; the deprivation of education takes an inestimable toll on the social, economic, intellectual, and psychological wellbeing of the individual, and poses an obstacle to individual achievement. In determining the rationality of the Texas statute, its costs to the Nation and to the innocent children may properly be considered. Pp. 216–224.

(c) The undocumented status of these children vel non does not establish a sufficient rational basis for denying them benefits that the State affords other residents. It is true that, when faced with an equal protection challenge respecting a State's differential treatment of aliens, the courts must be attentive to congressional policy concerning aliens. But in the area of special constitutional sensitivity presented by these cases, and in the absence of any contrary indication fairly discernible in the legislative record, no national policy is perceived that might justify the State in denying these children an elementary education. Pp. 224–226.

(d) Texas' statutory classification cannot be sustained as furthering its interest in the "preservation of the state's limited resources for the education of its lawful residents." While the State might have an interest in mitigating potentially harsh economic effects from an influx of illegal immigrants, the Texas statute does not offer an effective method of dealing with the problem. Even assuming that the net impact of illegal aliens on the economy is negative, charging tuition to undocumented children constitutes an ineffectual attempt to stem the tide of illegal immigration, at least when compared with the alternative of prohibiting employment of illegal aliens. Nor is there any merit to the suggestion that undocumented children are appropriately singled out for exclusion because of the special burdens they impose on the State's ability to provide high-quality public education. The record does not show that exclusion of undocumented children is likely to improve the overall quality of education in the State. Neither is there any merit to the claim that undocumented children are appropriately singled out because their unlawful presence within the United States renders them less likely than other children to remain within the State's boundaries and to put their education to productive social or political use within the State. Pp. 227–230.

No. 80–1638, 628 F.2d 448, and No. 80–1934, affirmed.

BRENNAN, J., delivered the opinion of the Court, in which MARSHALL, BLACKMUN, POWELL, and STEVENS, JJ., joined. MARSHALL, J.,post, p. 230, BLACKMUN, J., post, p. 231, and POWELL, J., post, p. 236, filed concurring opinions. BURGER, C.J., filed a dissenting opinion, in which WHITE, REHNQUIST, and O'CONNOR, JJ., joined, post, p. 242.

SIGNIFICANCE

From a civil procedure standpoint, the Plyler decision is of note since a number of diverse groups obtained standing as *amici curiae*, or friends of the court, to advance broad national arguments on what was conceived as a challenge to a Texas statute. Parties who obtained standing and who played a role in the outcome of the case included the federal government, a number of Texas school boards, and various groups engaged in the promotion of immigrant rights.

The majority decision in the Plyler case affirms a long line of American authorities that maintain that the Fourteenth Amendment will apply in the interpretation of any law where the applicant is physically located within the boundaries of the subject jurisdiction. This becomes a particularly important point in the Plyler decision, in light of the changes in American approaches to immigration that have occurred in the wake of the 9/11 attacks.

Although the case engaged a different set of issues, the ruling in Plyler may be regarded as a logical extension of the U.S. Supreme Court's decision in *Brown v. The Board of Education of Topeka*, where the court struck down the notion of separate but equal schools for black and white students, paving the way for the racial integration of the American public school system.

There are a number of aspects to the majority ruling in the Plyler case that have far reaching significance for national education. Education is asserted to be a concept that is distinct from other public benefits, yet education is not a fundamental right. The majority state clearly that children who have no control over their residency status should not be inflicted with the potential lifelong hardship of a limited education. It is implicit in the majority position that there exists an expectation that at some future time these children will be legal residents of the United States and that the cost of their current education will, therefore, not be wasted.

Plyler is regarded as one of three key appellate court decisions rendered in the United States prior to 1990 regarding the education of immigrant children. The other decisions are *Lau v. Nichols*, a 1973 decision concerning the right of immigrant children to English

as a second language instruction, and *Castenada v. Pickard*, a 1981 ruling concerning English as a second language programming.

In many respects, the minority decision presages many of the modern concerns expressed by conservative commentators in the United States regarding activist judges and interventionist courts. This element of American society often criticizes the legal system for not permitting elected bodies to function as they determine consistent with their constituency. The minority reasons in Plyler strongly advocate the proposition that the U.S. Constitution does not provide a cure for every social ill, nor does it provide judges with a mandate to attempt to resolve every social problem.

The significance of the Plyler decision was further underscored during the September 2005 Senate confirmation hearings concerning the nomination of John Roberts as chief justice of the U.S. Supreme Court. The prospective chief justice was questioned about his views concerning the Plyler decision; as a federal government lawyer in 1982, Roberts authored a memo criticizing the decision of the federal solicitor general not to file a legal memorandum in support of the Texas law.

The issues raised in the Plyler case are likely to remain current for years to come. In 2006, official estimates of the number of illegal residents in the United State varied from eleven million to thirteen million. The cost of education and other social services for these illegal residents to ensure compliance by government agencies with the provisions of the Fourteenth Amendment will remain an issue that attracts both political and broader public scrutiny.

FURTHER RESOURCES

Books

Louie, Vivian S. *Compelled to Excel: Immigration, Education and Opportunity and Chinese Americans*. Stanford, Calif.: Stanford University Press, 2004.

Suarez-Orozco, Carola, and Marcelo Suarez-Orozco. *Children of Immigration*. Cambridge, Mass.: Harvard University Press, 2001.

Periodicals

"Special Issue on Immigration and Education." *Harvard Educational Review* (Fall 2001).

Web sites

American Immigration Law Foundation. "Immigration Scare Tactics: Exaggerated Estimates of New Immigration Under S.2611." May 26, 2006. <http://www.ailf.org/ipc/policybrief/policybrief_2006_scaretactics.shtml> (accessed June 6, 2006).

Mexican Immigrants Crossing the Rio Grande

Photograph

By: Danny Lehman

Date: 1983

Source: © Danny Lehman/Corbis. Reproduced by permission.

About the Photographer: Corbis is a digital imaging/stock photography company, with headquarters in Seattle and offices worldwide.

INTRODUCTION

Illegal Mexican labor migration to the United States has a long history. Since the late nineteenth century, many Mexican citizens have crossed the border into the United States in search of employment. For many decades, it was relatively easy to cross the border, and migrants have been attracted by a ready supply of jobs, particularly in the agricultural sector, which has a continuous demand for a low-cost, flexible labor force.

Actual levels and patterns of labor migration from Mexico to the United States have changed over time, partly in response to economic and political conditions in Mexico, but also in response to various U.S. immigration policy initiatives.

Between the early 1940s and mid 1960s, migration from Mexico to the United States was generally short-term and circular in nature, and much of it occurred legally under the Bracero program, a scheme intended to provide labor for seasonal agriculture in the southern states. However, numbers of unauthorized migrants were also rising steadily at this time, putting

PRIMARY SOURCE

Mexican Emigrants Crossing the Rio Grande: Two Mexican women carrying three children cross the Rio Grande into the United States, near El Paso, Texas, 1983. © DANNY LEHMAN/CORBIS. REPRODUCED BY PERMISSION.

increasing pressure on the U.S. government to address the issue. In response, the Immigration and Nationality Act (1952) came into law, which introduced penalties for harboring undocumented migrants, but this legislation exempted agricultural employers in order to meet the needs for migrant labor, and did little to curb the flow of undocumented labor migrants.

With the end of the Bracero program in the mid 1960s, the number of undocumented workers from Mexico continued to rise steadily, but throughout the 1970s, most of the migration was still short term in nature, and the majority of migrants were males from rural areas in Mexico. By the 1980s, however, the patterns were changing. An economic crisis in Mexico in 1982 led to more Mexican citizens migrating in search of work, and it became increasingly common for women and family groups, and for urban as well as rural Mexicans, to enter the United States as undocumented workers. There was also a significant increase in the reported numbers of undocumented workers who stayed permanently in the United States, rather than returning to Mexico.

At the time this photograph of women and child emigrants crossing the Rio Grande River was taken in 1983, both politicians and the public in the United States were becoming increasingly concerned about the rapidly increasing levels of undocumented migration from Mexico. As a result, the United States increased measures to secure the borders. The Immigration Reform and Control Act of 1986 included a large increase in the number of border patrol agents, and the use of advanced technology to patrol and secure the border. These measures have made border crossings more difficult and hazardous than in the past, but they have failed to deter migrants from attempting to cross the border. As a result, there have been more accidental deaths among Mexicans attempting to enter the United States, an increased use by migrants of coyotes, people-smugglers, to facilitate their entry, and a consequent development of people smuggling as a major form of organized crime in Mexico.

PRIMARY SOURCE

MEXICAN EMIGRANTS CROSSING THE RIO GRANDE
See primary source image.

SIGNIFICANCE
Despite a policy emphasis in the United States on strengthening U.S.-Mexico border controls,

The Eagle Pass Border Patrol uses hover boats to patrol the Rio Grande river on the U.S.-Mexico border. © SHAUL SCHWARZ/CORBIS.

undocumented migration from Mexico has continued to increase. Furthermore, more Mexican migrants are believed to be settling permanently in the United States, although some research has indicated that the majority of migrants do eventually return to Mexico voluntarily. There has also been a reported increase since the 1980s in the proportion of Mexican labor migrants who are women, many of whom are following the traditional male migration pattern of working in the United States for temporary periods before returning home.

Mexican labor migration to the United States can be argued to have benefited both countries. For Mexico, it has eased unemployment and contributed to the economy in the form of remittances. The United States has in turn benefited from a low-cost, flexible labor force, which has met the needs in particular of seasonal agriculture and industry in the southern states.

However, there is a conflict between the needs of employers for a migrant labor force and the public pressure on the U.S. government to tackle undocumented migration and secure the borders in the interests of national security. There are also contradictions in U.S. policy between the need to protect the borders against undocumented migrants and infiltration by terrorists, on the one hand, and the need to open the borders to the legal passage of goods under the provisions of the NAFTA free trade agreement between the United States, Mexico and Canada.

FURTHER RESOURCES

Books

Monto, Alexander. *The Roots of Mexican Labor Migration.* Westport, Conn.: Praeger Publishers, 1994.

Periodicals

Canales, Alejandro I. "Mexican Labour Migration to the United States in the Age of Globalisation." *Journal of Ethnic and Migration Studies.* 29, 2003.

Cornelius, Wayne A. "Controlling 'unwanted' immigration: lessons from the United States, 1993–2004." *Journal of Ethnic and Migration Studies.* 31, 2005.

Espenshade, Thomas, J. "Unauthorized Immigration to the United States." *Annual Review of Sociology.* 21, 1995.

Griswold, Daniel T. "Confronting the Problem of Illegal Mexican Migration to the U.S." *USA Today (Society for the Advancement of Education).* 131, March 2003.

Amnesty: Who is Eligible

News article

By: Anonymous

Date: November 3, 1986

Source: "Amnesty: Who is Eligible." *The New York Times*, November 3, 1986.

About the Author: Founded in 1851, *The New York Times* is one of the largest national newspapers with a daily circulation of over one million copies.

INTRODUCTION

This news article reports on the eligibility criteria for legalization of unauthorized residence in the United States, which formed part of the 1986 Immigration and Control Act (IRCA). It highlights the anticipated difficulty that that undocumented immigrants might have had in providing evidence of their eligibility for legalization and the risky situation they could have put themselves in by declaring themselves illegally present. At the time, it was expected that

many illegal migrants would not apply for amnesty for these reasons.

The objective of the Immigration Reform and Control Act (IRCA) was to reduce the level of illegal migration and residence in the United States, and the Act was passed in response to rapidly increasing levels of undocumented migration, especially from Mexico. Research studies have estimated that by 1986 there may have been between three million and five million undocumented immigrants living in the United States.

IRCA aimed to tackle the problem of illegal migration and residence in several ways, including strengthening the operations of the U.S. Border Control. Its most radical measure, however, was the provision to legalize those undocumented migrants who had lived in the United States continuously since 1982. This was only finalized following a very lengthy process of debate and amendment to the original bill in Congress, during which there was considerable lobbying by various interest groups, including anti-immigrant organizations that were opposed to its proposals to legalize the status of existing undocumented residents, and civil rights groups and employer associations who supported the proposed amnesty, which would minimize disruption to the U.S. economy and take account of human rights issues in tackling undocumented residence.

The amnesty was introduced particularly to soften the immediate effects of the sanctions that the Act imposed on employers that knowingly recruited undocumented workers. The employment opportunities available in the United States were thought to be the driving force behind the increase in unauthorized migration and the new sanctions were intended to deter employers from recruiting undocumented migrants and new unauthorized migrants from entering the country.

In addition, the Act introduced temporary visas for seasonal agricultural workers, who were not required to meet the length of residence criteria applied to other unauthorized immigrants, but only had to have worked in seasonal agricultural jobs in the United States for at least ninety days in the preceding three years. This measure addressed the big demand in seasonal agricultural for temporary workers, which had traditionally been filled by migrants, many of them unauthorized.

Under the agreed amnesty provisions, eligible applicants were granted temporary resident alien status and were required to apply for permanent residence status within a year. Those receiving temporary employment visas under the Seasonal

Carlos Vaquerano, a Salvadoran immigrant and executive director of the Salvadoran American Leadership and Education Fund, stands in his office in Los Angeles. AP IMAGES.

Agricultural Workers Program would be allowed to apply for permanent residence after two years.

PRIMARY SOURCE

HOUSTON, Nov. 2— Under the new immigrant legislation, which President Reagan has said he will sign, legal status will be available for illegal aliens who have been "continuously physically present" in the United States since before Jan. 1, 1982, except for "brief, casual and innocent absences."

Those convicted of one felony or three or more misdemeanors are not eligible. Applications will be taken over a 12-month period beginning not later than 6 months after the law is enacted. Aliens must submit proof of continuous residence, preferably "employment-related," although the Attorney General may authorize other means. Documentation must be confirmed by "independent corroboration." Applicants must also demonstrate "minimal understanding of ordinary English" and knowledge of American government and history, or be studying these. Exceptions may be made for those over 65 years of age. Five years after becoming permanent legal residents, the immigrants may apply for citizenship.

It is uncertain just how many will apply for legal status, or how many will gain it. Some say, on the basis of foreign experience, that the number will be much smaller than expected. But Charles C. Foster, a leading Houston immigration lawyer, believes otherwise. "Once word gets out that the program is being administered in a reasonable manner and people are not being arrested," he said, "the problem will not be too few but too many."

Cheryl L. Schechter, a lawyer for Texas Center for Immigrant Legal Assistance, an arm of Catholic Charities in Houston, said she feared many legitimate applicants would have a terrible problem furnishing documentation, which they have carefully avoided all these years to thwart detection by the authorities. Much will depend, she said, on how the Immigration and Naturalization Service interprets the law.

It is a sign of the lingering fears that many illegal aliens around the country refused to have their names or pictures published when approached for interviews. In San Francisco, Henry Der, executive director of Chinese for Affirmative Action, advises applicants to be cautious for the moment.

Many of the aliens said they feared deportation before the amnesty program goes into effect. Under the legislation, any alien with a prima facie case for amnesty may not be deported by the immigration service and must be granted work authorization if he is apprehended before the application period commences.

Ironies abound in all this. For years, illegal aliens have done everything possible to avoid documenting their American existence and jobs; now, the Government says that, for them to remain here, they must prove they did everything they were not supposed to have. Moreover, to gain amnesty, one must prove "continuous unlawful residence"; those who maintained legal immigration status are ineligible to be legal permanent residents.

SIGNIFICANCE

In the event, more than 1.7 million people had applied for the main amnesty by December 1991 and ninety-five percent were granted temporary residence, of which the vast majority were subsequently approved for permanent residence. This indicates that the concerns about illegal immigrants being deterred by the eligibility criteria were unfounded. However, as there were no firm estimates of the number of undocumented immigrants in the United States before 1986, it is impossible to know how many remained clandestine. There were also around 1.3 million applicants for the Agricultural Workers amnesty, significantly more than had been expected, and again the vast majority were approved.

Subsequent research has indicated that the Immigration Reform and Control Act was not very successful in reducing illegal immigration to the United States. Although there was a short-term decline in the estimated stock of undocumented migrants following the passage of IRCA, this is likely to have been due mainly to the change in status of so many previously undocumented migrants. By 1989, however, the Immigration and Naturalization Service estimated that the number of undocumented residents in the United States remained at a level of around two to three million. This has been attributed partly to the ineffectiveness and lack of adequate enforcement of the employer sanctions, which has meant that there have been continuing job opportunities to attract unauthorized migrants to the United States. There was also evidence of fraud among applications for the Seasonal Agricultural Workers program, with false documents being submitted in many cases, and it has been argued that the existence of this program may even have increased illegal entry to the United States, by attracting new migrants who wished to apply fraudulently for residence under the scheme.

Some observers of the effects of the 1986 Act have argued that, rather than strengthening immigration control, it reflected the continuing liberalization of U.S. immigration policy.

FURTHER RESOURCES
Books

Briggs, Vernon, M. *Mass Immigration and the National Interest.* New York: Sharpe, M.E., 1992.

Delaet, Debra L. *U.S. Immigration Policy in an Age of Rights.* Westport, Conn.: Praeger Publishers, 2000.

LeMay, Michael C. *Anatomy of a Public Policy: The Reform of Contemporary American Immigration Law.* Westport, Conn.: Praeger Publishers, 1994.

Periodical

Espenshade, Thomas J. "Unauthorized Immigration to the United States." *Annual Review of Sociology* 21 (1995): 195–216.

Counting the Uncountable
Immigrant and Migrant, Documented and Undocumented Farm Workers in California

Book excerpt

By: Victor Garcia

Date: April 1992

Source: Garcia, Victor. *Counting the Uncountable, Immigrant and Migrant, Documented and Undocumented Farm Workers in California.* Washington, D.C.: GPO/Census Bureau, 1992.

About the Author: Victor Garcia is a Professor of Anthropology at the Indiana University of Pennsylvania. He has conducted many statistical projects for the United States Bureau of the Census.

INTRODUCTION

This report extract was taken from a special Census Bureau exercise to enumerate the Mexican and Mexican American resident households in California in 1990, using an ethnographic approach which collected detailed information on household characteristics in a sample area. Such exercises are often carried out in order to improve estimates of immigrant populations, which are often undercounted in the official Census. The Census requires respondents to complete a form with details of their household composition and basic characteristics, but some immigrants are unable or unwilling to provide this information, either because of language or literacy difficulties, or because they fear losing welfare benefits or being arrested for immigration offences if they provide the information requested. Accurate population estimates are needed by Federal and State governments in order to plan adequate public services and infrastructure and also to understand the nature of immigration and settlement in the United States.

Mexican resident households in California represent a section of the population for which it is difficult to obtain accurate information on numbers and characteristics. However, it is particularly important to obtain information about this group in order to plan social and economic policies and state budgets. As the ethnographic description shows, they are often economically disadvantaged, extremely poor and heavily dependent on public welfare. At the same time, their communities are connected in various ways with the problem of undocumented migration from Mexico, an issue which is of paramount concern to the government.

Permanent settlements of Mexican farm-worker communities first developed in California and other border states from the mid–1960s onwards, when the Bracero Program of 1944–1964 was terminated. Under this program, Mexicans had been brought into the United States to work for temporary periods in seasonal agricultural, but had generally returned to Mexico when their contracts ended. When the scheme was closed, local agricultural growers who feared shortages of low-cost labor helped many of the former Bracero workers to settle permanently in the United States, bringing their families with them. Over the following years, Mexicans continued to cross the border in large numbers to meet the continuing demand for cheap labor, many of them entering illegally as undocumented migrants, and the Mexican communities in California and other states continued to grow. The majority of the migrants who entered before 1986 acquired legal residence in the United States under The Special Agricultural Workers' Program (SAW) of the Immigration Reform and Control Act of 1986 (IRCA). This amnesty program was introduced by Congress in response to concerns that the new sanctions which were to be imposed on employers for hiring undocumented migrants would lead to severe shortages of labor, especially in agriculture. Overall, more than a million illegal immigrants were granted legal status under the program.

From the outset, the Mexican farm-worker communities have suffered greatly from exploitation by unscrupulous employers and middle-men, from a declining agricultural sector which cannot offer regular or full-time employment, and by a continuing influx of undocumented migrants from Mexico, who undercut the wages of the settled farm-workers. At the same time, some of these communities may be facilitating undocumented migration from Mexico, by providing a network of informants about job opportunities and providing their temporary accommodation to unauthorized migrants from Mexico.

Although most of the residents of the farm-worker communities have legal permanent residency in the United States, they are disadvantaged by being segregated in communities where the opportunities to acquire English language and employment-related skills are very poor. Some households have been able to improve their situation, usually by acquiring jobs in other sectors of the economy, but many remain heavily dependent on intermittent farm work and public benefits and are desperately poor.

Hispanic migrant workers harvesting lettuce. © JOSEPH SOHM; CHROMOSOHM INC./CORBIS. REPRODUCED BY PERMISSION.

PRIMARY SOURCE

The population in the ethnographic site is primarily made up of Mexican and Mexican American farm worker households who reside in a Californian farming community on a permanent basis. These proletariat households have no or few ties to the peasant economy in Mexico. In other words, the households are not comprised of peasant migrants who come to mind when we think of farm workers in California. Farm worker householders at the site do not pack up and leave when the harvest is poor or over, do not move to another harvest site nor do they return to a home base in Mexico. This California community is their home. However, some temporary household members, called *arrimados* in Spanish and who are related to the householder and spouse through kinship, reside locally during the lettuce harvest and return to Mexico after the season. . . .

The sample area is located in a new housing development in the western half of the farm worker town. The homes in this neighborhood are the newest in the community. The first dwellings were built in 1980; the most recent ones in 1986. Unlike residences in other neighborhoods, most of which were constructed immediately after World War II, the houses of the sample area are in excellent condition. Houses are structurally sound and well maintained. In addition, unlike other residences in the community, the properties are not altered to accommodate more people: they do not have illegal add-on rooms, secondary units in backyards, and garages converted into bedrooms. . . .

Recently, the community has suffered from chronic economic blight. The closure of nearly all of the agricultural enterprises in town coupled with changes in field production—which favor migrant workers over resident laborers—have resulted in a loss of city revenues and in greater unemployment and underemployment of the resident farm worker population.

According to preliminary 1990 Census data, the town has about 5,500 inhabitants, nearly eighty-five percent are of Mexican descent; a little under ten percent are of Asian extraction, mainly Japanese and Filipinos; the remainder are "white." Data from a 1988 survey reveal that the Mexican descent population is relatively young—the average age is twenty-six years (García, N.D.). The data also shows that a significant number of the Mexican descent population are ex-braceros [contracted workers] and their children. They and their children emigrated from the rural Central Plateau Region of Mexico where they had been campesinos [peasants] who practiced subsistence and cash-crop farming. Except for a common regional origin, this population has highly heterogeneous social characteristics, as it is comprised of both U.S. citizens and Mexican citizens who are permanent U.S. residents, Catholics and Protestants, lower and middle class, monolingual English and monolingual Spanish speakers, and bilingual speakers of both Spanish and English.

Resident farm workers work when they are able to find employment. The common vicissitudes of farm work—the weather and the commodity market—too often prevent local farm workers from obtaining gainful employment year-round. In addition, growers and other agricultural producers prefer to hire migratory labor which is highly exploitable and, as a result, resident workers have become a reserve labor force in the Valley. Resident workers, on the average, work anywhere from twelve weeks to thirty-six weeks out of the year. Those work weeks are not eight hour days, five days out of the week, but range from two to ten hours, three to six days out of the week.

Matters are further complicated by the incomes earned by the majority of the resident farm workers. Since local workers do not work directly for growers, but for labor contractors, their wages are at the minimum required by law, $4.50 an hour. Consequently, annual incomes are low. Income data from the 1988 survey, cited earlier, shows that annual incomes vary significantly, from $5,000 to $50,000 a year, with an average of $13,416. These annual incomes include Aid to Families with Dependent Children (AFDC), Social Security Supplement payments, unemployment compensation and disability benefits. Over half of the sample—ninety-three households—earn incomes at or below the official poverty level; and an additional forty-nine households—a little over a quarter of the sample—earn incomes that qualify them for social service programs.

The poverty that plagues farm workers manifests itself in many ways. In particular, it is obvious in their incomes, housing and home possessions, diet and nutrition, and social isolation. Their incomes are below or close to the poverty level. Their homes are often in need of repairs and are overcrowded. Their home possessions are used and inexpensive. Their diets consist of cheap foods which have very little nutritional content. They seldom can afford to attend community events. The economic plight of the farm workers is often attributed to their lack of a work ethic, but in reality their plight is the result of local labor practices adopted by growers and grower-shippers in the Valley.

The poverty and the low-income cycles that pull many of the farm worker households into their whirlwinds are broken in some cases. However, these instances are few; it seems that the only way out for them is to get out of farm work altogether. The households that are fortunate enough to escape the whirlwinds are those that have workers who are foremen, crew managers, machine operators. However, these positions are few and not available to everyone. Another way out for the households is to employ workers outside of agriculture, as laborers in assembly plants, cashiers and clerks at retail stores, clerks and typists in local government departments, and maintenance personal in many of the service establishments. However, these jobs are also limited in number, forcing many of the households to depend on farm work for their livelihood.

In spite of the poverty, the families do everything possible to keep their neighborhoods from looking run down. Homes are clean, yards are planted with roses and other flowers, and the streets are fee of litter. In addition, unlike other impoverished cities, it is not ridden with crime. In fact the local chief of police is quick to point this out, often boasting of the community's low crime rate, the lowest for a town of its size in the state. Most striking is a strong sense of community. Nearly all of the families know each other and in many cases they are related through fictive kin ties of compadrazgo, a relationship established between parents and godparents. This solidarity manifests itself on weekends, when locals get together for soccer matches and other recreational activities, and in September, when the local Mexican civic organization sponsors a parade and a three day festival to commemorate Mexican Independence Day....

The Alternative Enumeration was carried-out during a forty day period: from June 15th to June 30th, and the entire month of July 1990. After we received the match report in December 1991 from the Bureau of the Census, the follow-up research was completed from January 8th to January 16th, 1991.

The fieldwork and analysis of the Alternative Enumeration were conducted by the PI and RA. The two of us are both bilingual and bi-cultural. In fact, the RA is a native of Mexico: she was born and raised in that country. We found that our background was useful in establishing communication and building rapport with the Mexican and Mexican American households that we were not familiar with. In addition we discovered that our knowledge of the site and its residents, including their origins in Mexico, was useful in conducting the Alternative Enumeration. We knew when was the best time to make observations and to be seen strolling down the streets talking to local folks. During the week, the moments of opportunity were in the evenings after supper, and on the weekends, Saturday and Sunday afternoons....

SIGNIFICANCE

California's agricultural industry continues to decline, exacerbating the difficulties for Mexican farm-workers. The cultivation of high-value specialty crops has become the fastest growing area in Californian agriculture in recent years, but the labor-intensive nature of this work has meant that growers have tended to favor cheaper temporary migrant labor over the agricultural workers who are resident in the area. A 1997 U.S. Department of Labor report reported that the percentage of undocumented farm-workers in the United States increased from seven percent in 1989 to thirty-seven percent in 1995.

Although concerns are often raised about the adverse impact of undocumented migrants on the pay and conditions of low-skilled native workers, it can be seen that it is actually poor immigrant communities such as the Mexican farm-worker communities of California that are often most severely affected and that are less likely to be able to improve their situation. The high levels of unemployment and under-employment in these communities suggests that there is little need for increased numbers of agricultural workers and that it is primarily the recruitment practices of growers, favoring cheap migrant labor, that are

encouraging unauthorized migration. At the same time, the very existence of the Mexican settlements in the border region, and their family and kinship connections with communities within Mexico, may be a factor that is helping to facilitate continuing high levels of undocumented cross-border migration.

FURTHER RESOURCES
Books

Garcia, Victor. *Counting the Uncountable, Immigrant and Migrant, Documented and Undocumented Farm Workers in California.* Washington, D.C.: GPO/ Census Bureau, 1992.

Lowell, Lindsay B. ed. *Foreign Temporary Workers in America: Policies That Benefit the U.S. Economy.* Westport, Conn.: Quorum Books, 1999.

Periodicals

Rosenbaum, Rene Perez. "Toward a Criterion for Evaluating Migrant Farm Labor Policy Arguments." *Policy Studies Review.* 18, 2001.

Schlosser, Eric. "In the Strawberry Fields." *The Atlantic Monthly.* 276, 1995.

Language of Closet Racism: An Illustration

Online journal article

By: Paul Gorski

Date: 1995

Source: *EdChange Multicultural Pavilion.* "Language of Closet Racism: An Illustration." <http://www. edchange. org/ multicultural/papers/langofracism2.html> (accessed July 15, 2006).

About the Author: Paul Gorski is an assistant professor in the Graduate School of Education at Hamline University in St. Paul, Minnesota. He is an activist for equality and social justice, and he works as a consultant conducting training for schools and communities committed to equity and diversity issues. He serves on the board of directors of the National Association for Multicultural Education (NAME).

INTRODUCTION

In "Language of Racism," Paul Gorski argues that covert racism is endemic in American society today, though most people are unaware that they hold racist views. Gorski suggests that people don't recognize their own racism in part because the educational system both reflects and reinforces attitudes that legitimize the dominant position of white people in American society. Institutionalized racism is still believed to exist in many areas of life, despite the impact of civil rights legislation. It is argued that so-called "closet racists" are often oblivious of their own race issues, though they may recognize racism in the attitudes of others.

Overt racist policies and attitudes were prevalent in American society before the civil rights reforms of the 1960s and 1970s. As a result, black and white people were segregated in education, employment, public transportation, and other areas of life. Federal employment policies restricted black people to junior and low-skilled positions, and in the southern states black people did not even have the right to vote. Racial harassment and attacks on African Americans were common occurrences in many parts of the country.

Over time, the civil rights movement grew in strength, and in the early 1960s activists conducted many demonstrations, riots, and political lobbying campaigns for legislation to outlaw racial discrimination. They achieved major civil rights reforms during the 1960s and 1970s, starting with the landmark Civil Rights Act of 1964. This act outlawed discrimination on the basis of race, color, religion, sex, or national origin. In particular, it introduced employment legislation that prohibited discrimination by federal contractors in the recruitment, promotion, and training of employees. An Equal Employment Opportunity Commission was created to oversee the enforcement of the new legislation. However, the Civil Rights Act only required employers to provide equality of opportunity; it did not establish any requirement for affirmative action to promote the preferential treatment of black people in order to redress the existing inequalities in employment. Only in 1970 was a requirement introduced for federal contractors to implement affirmative actions in order to bring about proportional representation of different races in the workplace. Private employers and small companies were excluded from the requirements of the legislation, and though some larger private companies introduced their own voluntary programs, many African American workers remained without protection. For those that were covered, the 1991 Civil Rights Act strengthened the legislation by allowing all victims of employment discrimination the right to a jury trial and to compensation if successful.

Since the 1980s, however, there has been a decline in federal support for affirmative action programs designed to address these inequalities, with recent conservative governments quite strongly opposed to such programs. Among the majority white population, support has always been quite weak for affirmative action, with many holding the view that the equal opportunities legislation goes far enough and there should be no need for preferential treatment for black people.

Despite civil rights legislation, however, major inequalities remain between black and white people in terms of employment, earnings, education, and other socioeconomic indicators. Although black people are now represented in higher numbers at all levels in the workplace and have also made progress in other areas, the average incomes of African Americans remain well below those of white people, they are significantly less likely to own their own homes, and they have consistently higher unemployment levels.

PRIMARY SOURCE

Any person who has grown up in the American public school system has been educated to hold racial prejudices. To illustrate this point, ask any child to tell you about the first date in history he or she remembers learning: "In 1492 Columbus sailed the ocean blue." What happened in 1492? "Christopher Columbus discovered America." Did he? The history books I prefer to read have informed me that people were actually already here. Remember, the people who would eventually be driven from their sacred lands, forced to surrender their native tongue and customs, and "American-ize?"

The result of children learning such "facts" is a depreciation of an entire people—in this case, Native Americans.

So the American education system (with strong reinforcement from the media) has bred a nation of what I will call "closet racists." Closet racists are unaware of their prejudices. They have learned from text books presented to them by people who are supposedly knowledgeable enough to choose the best possible materials. They are trained, or more precisely, coerced into believing in "the system." If a child were to question a teacher's assertion that "Columbus discovered America," it is more likely that the child would be chastised for showing disrespect than the possibility of the teacher initiating a discussion on the discrepancy. A closet racist is defined, then, as simply a person with racial prejudices who is unaware of those prejudices as such, usually because he or she has never been afforded the opportunity to discuss racial prejudices as such.

The question arising from this assertion is clear: Where is the evidence of this nation of so-called "closet racists?" What links them? What are their characteristics?

The answer, emerging from years of experience facilitating conversations on race issues, interviewing specific cases, and participating in a variety of cultural diversity workshops, is equally clear: language. Closet racists share a distinct and surprisingly easily detectable language when observed in a discussion about race or racism. . . .

Who Are Closet Racists? Though everyone who has experienced the American education system is in some degree a closet racist, certain people, and indeed, certain groups, tend to portray the characteristics more than others. At the most basic level, people who have experienced consistent racial discrimination tend to be less assignable the label of closet racist. Such people have, through their personal experiences with discrimination, been afforded opportunities to discuss race issues. As Kim, an African-American student in a Multicultural Education class during Spring semester, 1995 explained,

> I live these issues every day. I can't escape them anywhere: stores, classes, the gym. Three, four, five things happen everyday to remind me that, no matter what white people believe, there is still a ton of prejudice out there. It reminds me to think about the things I do and say, and the prejudices I have.

In short, closet racism is a continuum. Those with the least exposure to racial issues fall toward the high end. Experience suggests that those falling on this end are usually "white," or "European-Americans," while "African-Americans" fall toward the low end. So-called "middle-man minorities" tend to be spread between the extremes.

Jen, a white woman, was chosen for the case study because her sheltered home-life and general unaware-ness of race issues have served as catalysts in her formation as a high-end closet racist. An admittedly extreme case, and for that reason purposively chosen, Jen illustrates clearly the language patterns of a closet racist.

The Three Strands of the Language of Closet Racism Three language indicators of closet racism are evident across the continuum. These are what I refer to as "strands" because, when woven together, they form the language web of closet racists. Again, strength of language and degree of racist attitudes change dramatically across the continuum, and as a result, these strands, or indicators, are more readily observable in certain individuals and groups than in others. They include fear, unaware-ness, and dis-ownership.

Consider the following excerpt taken from Jen's reaction paper from the first class meeting of Multicultural Education:

> The idea of political correctness with the black race astounds me. I found it extremely interesting that some blacks in our class prefer to be called African

> American. In all of my classes . . . I have felt like I was stepping on egg shells as to not offend the blacks in my class. I am honestly glad it is not that big of an issue to my fellow classmates—it promotes a more comfortable, genuine environment for me to be totally honest and carefree.

Jen reflected each strand of the language of closet racism within this short passage. These strands can be un-woven as follows:

1. Fear: "I have felt like I was stepping on egg shells as to not offend blacks in my classes."
2. Unaware-ness: "I found it extremely interesting that some blacks in our class prefer to be called African American."
3. Dis-ownership: "I am honestly glad it is not that big of an issue to my fellow classmates." . . .

Fear

We consider fear first, because it is, on the surface, the most surprising strand to find in the language. If closet racists do not consider themselves racists, then why would they show fear in discussing race issues? In the most simple terms, closet racists do not want other people to consider them racist, either. This is why white people developed "political correctness." The idea was to develop a system in which everyone knew what to say in order to allow everyone to avoid, as Jen mentioned," walking on egg shells."

Fear also becomes the catalyst for many closet racists' decisions on what information to offer (and likewise, what not to offer) during a discussion of race issues. As Jen explained in her second reaction paper:

> I was apprehensive to tell my group that my prejudice experience was within my family. I thought they would think that because my grandfather and father were racist, that I am as well—I thought they would dislike me.

She tended to elevate this apprehensive-ness during interviews, sometimes to the point of censoring herself. In one particular case, as she discussed the racial make-up of her hometown, her fear emerged quite blatantly:

> . . . and where I'm from there were two different types of black . . . there were . . . I don't want to say this. Is it all right if I say this? . . .

Her fear was clear, especially as she continued, deciding, in fact, to "say this." . . .

Jen feared being labeled a racist. Again, it is important to note that she did not consider herself a racist, which leads us to the second strand or indicator: unaware-ness.

Unaware-ness

Closet racists are unaware on several levels, illustrations for which can be found in language patterns. On the first level, as emphasized above, they are unaware of racial issues as racial issues. (How many white people insisted that race was never an "issue" in the O.J. Simpson trial?) Illustrating this point, Jen, in her first interview, suggested that at her high school, "there was not any sort of black/white issues or anything like that." She made this statement minutes before offering her story about the "two different types of black." In between the two statements she related stories of "some Ku Klux Klan there," "crosses burning, and stuff like that." But nonetheless, just as she did not label herself as a racist, she was unaware that the very issues she discussed were very racial in nature, and as such she did not label those issues in terms of race, either.

On another level, Jen failed to see the racial prejudice as such in the language of others. For example, she defended her grandmother: "my grandmother on my Mom's side is not prejudice." But as she continued, Jen, in her unawareness, all but labeled her grandmother a racist:

> ... but she refers to black people as "colored." Like when we have a Christmas party every year and Mark, a guy who lives around the corner from me, came to the party...and was the only black person there and she was like, "Who was that colored boy there?" She doesn't refer to him as "Mark," always "that colored boy."

On a third level, while Jen could sometimes point out racial prejudice in other places, she was quick to distance herself from that prejudice, as if she was somehow shielded from its permeation. In this sense, Jen was unaware of racism as it exists at the institutional level. Like many closet racists, Jen believed that racism could be found "here, there, and there," but that, in the correct circumstances, racism could be completely avoided. Again, this naivete could be recognized in her language, as in the following passage in which she compared her high school to the "other public high school" in her hometown:

> James Monroe was a predominantly black school, and the only white people that did go to school there were wealthy, and so there was like the wealthy and then there was African-Americans. There was a huge line between them, but there wasn't anything like that where I was.

This passage leads directly into the third strand of the language of closet racism.

Dis-ownership

Closet racists tend to avoid owning their views on race. They often point to other groups, using terms such as "they," or "those people," instead of refering to themselves. In the previous passage, Jen clearly utilized the language of dis-ownership, thus assessing blame to others. "There was a huge line between *them*." "I thought *they* would dislike me."

Closet racists, in avoiding using "I" and "me" statements in discussions of race issues, avoid accepting the responsibility for their perspectives, and in many cases, prejudices. Recent articles in the *Cavalier Daily* about so-called self-segregation at the University of Virginia have been drowned in this language. White columnists posed questions such as "Why do the African-American students sit together at lunch, congregate at the 'black bus stop,'" etc? "Why do they have organizations like the Black Student Alliance?" In shifting the responsibility to "the African-American students," the columnists dodged the intimidating possibility of accepting equal responsibility for the separation.

The Result of Closet Racism As is most clearly illustrated by the dis-ownership strand of the language of closet racism, closet racists will observe other groups segregating themselves, and suddenly race becomes an issue. But, for example, white students fail to notice that white students do not approach tables filled with African-American students during lunch. And white students clearly have congregation spots. . . .

The attractiveness—even if it exists at a subconscious level—of closet racism to those who retain it is that if one never labels himself or herself a racist, then (s)he is free from the obligation of doing something about it. For Jen and many others, closet racism becomes routine, easy, and comfortable. With blinders on their eyes, and the shield of manipulated language in their repertoire, closet racists can live a full life never confronting their own prejudices.

In fact, if the assertion holds up that white people tend to be toward the high end of the closet racist continuum, then the result of closet racism is clear. The phenomenon of closet racism is yet another catalyst in the cycle of discrimination experienced by racial minorities in America since the conception of this nation. . . .

So how, then, is the study of the language of closet racism useful? Sometimes people I've labeled as closet racists want to change themselves. Jen was one such person. The study of the language she used when discussing race (and other multicultural) issues, and how this language changed, helped me understand the stages she experienced on her trek toward race awareness and appreciation.

■

SIGNIFICANCE

There is little doubt that civil rights legislation has had only limited success in changing the patterns of racial inequality that developed over many decades of institutionalized discrimination and segregation. While a significant number of African Americans have achieved success, for the many black people who are disadvantaged by a lack of money, skills, and qualifications, and by a geographical concentration in areas of high unemployment and poverty, it has been difficult or impossible to take advantage of the formal equality of opportunity in education, employment, and housing.

What is unclear is the extent to which widespread "closet racism" or actual discrimination against black people is responsible for the continuing inequalities. The arguments put forward in this article offer one interpretation of how racism is perpetuated in society. The theory put forward by the author highlights the point that, regardless of the impact of formal legislation, people often hold deep-rooted beliefs and attitudes that may lead them, perhaps unknowingly, to act in ways that discriminate against African Americans and other racial minorities.

FURTHER RESOURCES

Books

Alexander, Neville, Antonio Ségrio Alfredo Guimaraes, Charles V. Hamilton, Lynn Huntley, and James Wilmot. *Beyond Racism: Race and Inequality in Brazil, South Africa, and the United States.* Boulder, Co.: Lynne Rienner, 2001.

Anderson, Terry H. *The Pursuit of Fairness: A History of Affirmative Action.* New York: Oxford University Press, 2004.

Batur, Pinar, Joe R. Feagin, and Hernán Vera. *White Racism: The Basics.* New York: Routledge, 2001.

Periodicals

Elliott, Euel and Andrew I. E. Ewoh. "The Evolution of an Issue: The Rise and Decline of Affirmative Action." *Policy Studies Review* (2000).

Web sites

EdChange Multicultural Pavilion. "Language of Closet Racism: An Illustration." <http://www.edchange.org/multicultural/papers/langofracism2.html> (accessed July 15, 2006).

Is Teaching 'La Causa' Grounds for Firing?

Online magazine article

By: Anonymous

Date: 1998

Source: "Is Teaching 'La Causa' Grounds for Firing?" *Rethinking Schools Online* 12 (3) (Spring 1998). <http://www.rethinkingschools.org/archive/12_03/cen-caus.shtml> (accessed July 21, 2006).

About the Author: Rethinking Schools is a nonprofit, independent publisher of educational materials, which was founded in 1986 by activist teachers. The organization advocates the reform of elementary and secondary education, with an emphasis on issues of equity and social justice.

INTRODUCTION

This article reports on a mid-1990s case in Vaughn, New Mexico, in which two sisters were dismissed from their teaching posts for teaching Chicano studies and racial tolerance studies to their middle and high school students, ninety percent of which were Latino, on the basis that the teaching materials used were racially divisive.

The Chicano movement developed among Mexican American students in the southwestern states in the 1960s and 1970s, when the broader civil rights movement was at its height. At this time, there had already been several generations of Mexican settlement in the United States, but the Mexican American descendants of the earlier settlers, many of whom were of mixed race, continued to face racism and discrimination in American society. In response to this, they formed a new ethnic identity, calling themselves Chicanos or Chicanas, and established activist groups to protest against unfair educational systems, which they felt discriminated against them, and to campaign on other issues affecting Chicano youth, such as alleged police brutality.

Chicano activist groups, which emerged in the late 1960s, included the Young Citizens for Community Action, subsequently the Brown Berets, who organized a series of large-scale strikes among high school students in 1968 to protest inequalities in the educational systems. In colleges, Mexican students formed the United Mexican American Students organization. In 1969, most of the separate Chicano groups merged to form the Movimiento Estudiantil Chicano de Aztlan, to fight the cause or "La Causa" of Chicanos. The main hero of the Chicano movement was César E. Chávez (1927–1993), the leader of the United Farm Workers, who fought for better pay and conditions for Mexican agricultural workers in the United States and organized a series of strikes among agricultural workers. Robert Kennedy (1925–1968) is also considered a hero in Chicano history because during the 1968 Presidential campaign he agreed to meet with a group of Chicano students, to help legitimize their case to the school board. The ideological basis for the movement varied between its sub-groups. However, some extremists supported a socialist revolution action against white Americans, while others were more nationalistic in their focus, campaigning for self-determination for Chicanos.

In the late 1970s, however, the Chicano movement lost strength, weakened by a lack of common or clear goals among its various sub-groups. Some elements, such as La Raza Unida Party in Texas, turned to mainstream politics and contested local elections to promote their cause. But the movement survived primarily as an academic discipline, with most southwestern universities establishing Chicano studies programs and departments. California State College, Los Angeles, was the first to establish a Chicano Studies department, in 1968, largely in response to demands from militant Mexican

American students. However, the Chicano studies programs have generally followed traditional mainstream accounts of Chicano history, rather than the more radical interpretations and the training for revolution which some students hoped they would cover.

When they were dismissed for teaching Chicano history, the Codova sisters turned to the American Civil Liberties Union (ACLU) for support and legal representation. This is a national non-profit association that defends individual rights and civil liberties in accordance with the constitution, through litigation, legislation, and training programs. Through the ACLU, the sisters sued the Vaughn District School Board for violating their rights under the First Amendment, part of the United States Bill of Rights, that prohibits Congress from passing laws that would restrict individual freedom of speech, religion and assembly, or the right to petition government for a redress of grievances.

César Chávez, the leader of the UFW (United Farm Workers) and a prominent Chicano spokespesman, takes part in a grape boycott in California, 1965. PHOTO BY MPI/GETTY IMAGES.

PRIMARY SOURCE

Patsy and Nadine Codova were considered outstanding teachers in the small town of Vaughn, NM. But in June 1996 they helped students at Vaughn Junior and Senior High School organize a MEChA club, a common student group in the Southwest which stands for Movimiento Estudiantil Chicano de Aztlan. And that, they believe, is when their troubles began.

That fall, Vaughn Superintendent Arthur Martinez told the Cordova sisters they could not teach anything "that reflects the MEChA philosophy." He accused Nadine of teaching "racial intolerance" and promoting "a militant attitude" in her students.

Under legal advice, the Cordova sisters asked that any further curriculum directives from Martinez be in writing. They believed that the superintendent's directives not only violated their rights under the First Amendment but were counter to the district's policies on handling complaints about curriculum. Nonetheless, they sought to comply until their lawyers could resolve matters.

By January of 1997, relations between the sisters and the superintendent were strained. Martinez told the sisters in writing that they could not use the supplementary text "500 Years of Chicano History," could not study Cesar Chavez and the United Farm Workers union, or hand out any materials that promote "la causa." Nadine argues that agricultural interests in the area were particularly concerned that students learning about Chavez and the UFW union.

But the prohibitions went beyond the UFW. The sisters were also told "to eliminate any reference to or discussion of Robert Kennedy, the U.S. Constitution, Dolores Huerta, justice, courage or non-violence," according to Nadine's attorney, Richard Rosenstock of the New Mexico Civil Liberties Union.

The controversy escalated when an Albuquerque newspaper ran a front-page story on Feb. 15 titled, "Chicano Studies Out in Vaughn." Rosenstock told **Rethinking Schools** that Martinez and his allies on the board were furious about the article. "As soon as this article comes out, he [Martinez] starts soliciting complaints from people from six or eight years ago and starts to put together a case against the Cordova sisters."

On Feb. 21, 1997, the sisters informed Martinez in writing that they hoped to use materials from the group Teaching Tolerance. They enclosed the table of contents from the group's curriculum package, "The Shadow of Hate: A History of Intolerance in America," copies of some articles, and the kit's statement of purpose. Martinez did not immediately respond.

At a board meeting Feb. 26 allegedly set up to resolve the problems, however, Martinez asked the sisters if they would stop using the Teaching Tolerance materials. The sisters said they would do so only if the request were in writing.

The Cordova sisters got an answer, of sorts, two days later. The town's chief of police walked into the school and handed them a letter telling them they were suspended on grounds of insubordination. That July, the board fired them. (For an excellent article on the case, see the August/September 1997 issue of *Teacher*.)

The Cordova sisters have filed suit in federal court to get their jobs back. They are confident they will win.

SIGNIFICANCE

In November 1998, the Cordova sisters won a half-million dollar settlement in their lawsuit against the Vaughn, New Mexico, School Board. Since then, they have received various awards for their action in standing up for the rights of ethnic minority students. These have included the Multi-Cultural Educators of the Year award from the National Association of Multi-Cultural Education, and the Guardian of Constitution Award from the New Mexico branch of the ACLU.

Although there is no firm evidence about the benefits of multi-cultural teaching for racial minority students, some researchers have identified positive effects, particularly in terms of confidence building among traditionally victimized groups, which is likely to improve educational performance. Those who are opposed to multi-cultural teaching, on the other hand, frequently argue that it can be racially divisive and can be a focus for the development of radical ethnic movements.

FURTHER RESOURCES

Books

Chávez, Ernesto. *Mi Raza Primero! (My People First!): Nationalism, Identity, and Insurgency in the Chicano Movement in Los Angeles, 1966–1978*. Berkeley: University of California Press, 2002.

Rosales, F. Arturo. *Chicano! The History of the Mexican American Civil Rights Movement*. Houston, Tex.: Arte Publico Press, 1996.

Taylor, Ronald B. *Chávez and the Farm Workers*. Boston: Beacon Press, 1975.

Periodical

Martinez, Elizabeth. "A View from New Mexico: Recollections of the Movimiento Left." *Monthly Review* 54 (July/August, 2002).

A Small Bengal, NW3

Book excerpt

By: Amit Chaudhuri

Date: February 1, 1999

Source: Chaudhuri, Amit. "A Small Bengal, NW3," *Granta*, (February 1, 1999).

About the Author: Amit Chaudhuri (b. 1962) is an Indian novelist, poet, and non-fiction writer who has been the recipient of many literary prizes. His first novel, *A Strange and Sublime Address*, won the Betty Trask Award and the Commonwealth Writers Prize. Other works include *Afternoon Raag* and *Freedom Song*.

INTRODUCTION

Immigrants from the Indian sub-continent and their descendents form one of the largest ethnic minority groups in Great Britain. Yet, up until the 1950s, there were very few Indians in the country and most of those who did come were transitory migrants, such as the students that are the subject of this book excerpt. Although many of them were only in Britain for a few years, they established their own ethnic or national communities in specific neighborhoods of London and other cities, setting a trend in which future mass immigration from the sub-continent and other former colonies would result in high geographical concentrations of specific ethnic groups.

Britain's links with its former colonies have influenced patterns of international migration of various kinds. Before the mass immigration of the late 1950s and the 1960s, the more wealthy nationals of the newly independent India and other former colonies started sending their children in significant numbers to study in Britain, a country with which they had a long historical association.

Indian migration increased rapidly during the 1950s and changed in nature, as successive post-war British governments encouraged low-skilled labor migrants to come to Britain to work in industries that were facing labor shortages. After 1962 in particular, the South Asian communities in the country increased rapidly in size, and the continuing policy of allowing dependants of migrant workers to immigrate with them encouraged more permanent settlement of Asians. These included substantial communities of Asian immigrants who were mainly employed in the textile industry in the Northwest of England, metal manufacturing in the Southeast and the Midlands, and in transport and catering throughout the country. Later waves of South Asian migrants brought more skilled and professional workers, especially health professionals, who were in demand in the National Health Service.

Around a third of all immigrants in the 1950s and 1960s settled in London, changing the character of many of the neighborhoods where they settled. This resulted in social tensions, as the working class white populations of these areas felt threatened by the large numbers of black and Asian immigrants, and many immigrants faced discrimination when applying for jobs or trying to rent accommodations in London. The hostility they often faced from landlords encouraged them to restrict themselves to particular neighborhoods where it was easier to find housing and contributed to the geographical concentration of particular ethnic groups. Race relations problems, such as the violence that broke out in Notting Hill in 1958 between West Indian immigrants and local white people, led to a tightening of immigration controls, and the implementation of Race Relations Acts intended to address the problems of racism and discrimination being faced by black and Asian immigrants.

Steps were also taken to tighten immigration controls and reduce the overall numbers of immigrants entering the country. It had been easy for people from the former British colonies to enter Britain in the 1950s and early 1960s, as they had been granted British citizenship under the 1948 British Nationality Act and there were no controls on their entry to the country. However, in response to concerns about rapidly rising levels of immigration, the 1962 Commonwealth Immigrants Act and the Immigration Act of 1971 were passed, with the eventual consequence that Commonwealth citizens came to be subject to the same immigration controls as other foreign nationals.

PRIMARY SOURCE

About five or six years after the war ended, and soon after India's independence and the beginning of the end of the British Empire, Belsize Park in the borough of Camden became home to a number of Indian, mainly Bengali, students. They lived in neighbouring houses, and were often neighbours in the same house; they talked with, and jostled, and cooked for, each other, and had small rivalries and sympathies between themselves; but they knew they were a transient lot, because they were here to pass exams, and very few intended to stay, to get swallowed by the London that had become their temporary home. Time went by quickly, although, in retrospect, the procession of years would sometimes seem long.

Strangely enough, while Kilburn came to be known as black and Irish area, and Golders Green a Jewish one, Belsize Park was never identified with its Bengali student population. Perhaps this was so because it was made up of itinerants rather than emigrants; most had left by the mid-Sixties—if not England, then at least Belsize Park. They were mainly young men and, now and again, women, in their late twenties or their thirties, diligent and intelligent on the whole, who had come to study for professional examinations whose names seemed to have been invented to enhance their job prospects: Chartered Accountancy, Cost Accountancy, MRCP, FRCP, FRCS. For these Bengalis, at least, there was a romance about degrees that had the words 'Chartered' or 'Royal' in them which will now probably seem absurd. The few who stayed on in England were often the ones who hadn't been able to get the degree they'd come here to acquire; they couldn't face their mothers and fathers without it; thus they drifted into the civic life of London, became railway clerks or council officials, or moved elsewhere, and eventually bought a house in Wimbledon or Sussex or Hampshire; at any rate, they left Belsize Park. Those who stayed on had their reasons—'staying on': those words had possibly as much resonance for them, though for entirely different reasons, as they did for the last Anglo-Indians—and none of those reasons, it is safe to suppose, had anything to do with an overwhelming attachment to England.

But most studied, and left; and, in Belsize Park, the emphasis was on exams and recreation. They'd brought Bengal with them though Bengal itself had become a state of mind, partitioned into two, half of it in India and half of it East Pakistan. They fell into a routine of buying 'wet fish', shopping at Finchley Road, going to work, listening to Tagore songs, in between bouts of memorizing the pulmonary functions of the heart of the intricacies of taxation law.

Some of the students had wives, and were newly married. The wife, like Draupadi in the *Mahabharata*, who married five brothers at once, not only played wife to her husband but often to all her husband's friends, making food for them, being indulgent to them when they were depressed, exhorting them to such hard, and generally lightening the air with her feminine presence. Later, the men would always remember these surrogate wives, the Mrs Mukherjis and Mrs Basus and Mrs Senguptas. In India, the new wife comes to her new home and is greeted by her husband's family and a way of life both pre-arranged and untested; every couple must, in the end, make what they will of their own lives. Here, in Belsize Park, the making of that life was both more naked and more secret; the new bride would be received not by her in-laws, but Cost Accountants to-be and would-be surgeons and physicians. She would come not to her husband's house but to a bedsit with wallpaper and cooking hobs which was now to be her own, and which cost three pounds and ten shillings a week.

Among the tenants was a young man who was supposed to be studying Chartered Accountancy but was actually doing everything but study. He was thinner than normal; his mother had died when he was seven years old. When he had left India in 1949, he had been twenty-seven years old; he had lost his homeland with Partition; and he had got engaged to his best friend's younger sister. In 1955, she travelled to London with her younger brother to marry the young man. They, my parents, were among the people who lived in Belsize Park in the Fifties....

Both, in the first yeas of their marriage, went out to work in the morning, and had their daily meeting-places outside work hours; during break-time, my mother would hurry to Jermyn Street, where my father worked for a few years in the Accounts Office of India House, and they would go for lunch or tea to the Lyons restaurant nearby. Once a week, they would have a Chinese dinner at the Cathay restaurant; watching, through a window, Piccadilly outside. Nearer the exams, my father would study at home while my mother went out to work as a clerk.

Without a harmonium or any other accompanying instrument, my mother would keep practicing the Tagore songs that she had learned as a child, in Sylhet, which had become part of East Pakistan. Her singing was full-throated; her voice would carry in the silent afternoons;

once, the spinster landlady, Miss Fox, came down to complain.

Then, in 1961, a year before I was born, my parents left for Bombay; my father had, after passing his exams, got a job that paid for his and my mother's fares back; the ship would take two weeks to reach India. As the ship sailed forth, my mother (so she tells me) stared at the cliffs of Dover to imprint them on her memory. In a year, she had conceived, and, at the age of thirty-seven, she gave birth to her first and only child in Calcutta.

This is what they left behind. Haverstock Hill leading on one side to Hampstead, and Belsize Avenue sloping downward to Swiss Cottage and Finchley Road on the other. Other lives begin; other stories; and the human capacity to create is at least as strong as the capacity to forget.

SIGNIFICANCE

The South Asian population of Britain increased significantly during the second half of the twentieth century. By 1991, there were 1.5 million South Asians in the country, accounting for 2.7 percent of the population. Within the South Asian population in Britain, around 840,000 were from India, 477,000 from Pakistan and 163,000 from Bangladesh. By the end of the century, South Asians owned more than fifty percent of the independent retail trade, accounted for nearly twenty percent of all hospital doctors and more than ten percent of pharmacists and were also successful in other areas of the economy. Their geographical distribution remains highly concentrated: In London, for example, most Indians live in ten boroughs to the west and east of the city.

As for the earlier immigrants who came to Britain to study or to work for short periods in the 1950s and 1960s, these mostly returned home as qualified professionals or businesspeople, and some will have entered politics and public life. Their association and familiarity with Britain, its legal and business systems, and way of life no doubt helped to shape the development of their own countries and to strengthen postcolonial links with Britain.

FURTHER RESOURCES
Books

Hansen, Randall. *Citizenship and Immigration in Postwar Britain*. Oxford: Oxford University Press, 2000.

Mcleod, John. *Postcolonial London: Rewriting the Metropolis*. London and New York: Routledge, 2004.

Paul, Kathleen. *Whitewashing Britain: Race and Citizenship in the Postwar Era*. Ithaca, N.Y.: Cornell University Press, 1997.

Spencer, Ian R.G. *British Immigration Policy since 1939: The Making of Multi-Racial Britain*. London and New York: Routledge, 1997.

Periodical

Parekh, Bhikhu. "South Asians in Britain." *History Today*, September 1, 1997.

Youth Employment in Agriculture

Report

By: Ruth Samardick

Date: June 2000

Source: U.S. Department of Labor

About the Author: Survey statistician Ruth Samardick works for the Office of the Assistant Secretary for Policy (OASP) within the U.S. Department of Labor. The Department of Labor is a cabinet department of the U.S. government. It is responsible for such duties as economic statistics, occupational safety, re-employment services, unemployment insurance benefits, and wage and hour standards.

A young migrant worker picks strawberries in a field in California's San Joaquin Valley. © PETER TURNLEY/CORBIS.

INTRODUCTION

During the 1990s, the U.S. Department of Labor (DOL) commissioned a national study on various aspects of paid workers including field packers and supervisors of crop agriculture. Crop agricultural work is defined by the DOL as any field work in such areas as cash grains, field crops, fruit and vegetable products, nursery products, and silage and fodder. The National Agricultural Workers' Survey (NAWS) summarized such data as basic demographics, education, legal status, family size, and working conditions based on interviews with 13,380 workers in the United States between the years 1993 and 1998.

The fifth chapter of the DOL's "Report on the Youth Labor Force" discusses youth employment in agriculture. Young workers in agriculture traditionally have different characteristics from those of their counterparts in other industries. Consequently, different problems occur to them and different government regulations apply to them. Between the years 1993 and 1998, 951 youths age fourteen to seventeen were

interviewed, and adult farm-working parents were interviewed about their children, who numbered 6,422 in all. NAWS asked questions concerning such subjects as age, gender, migration, place of birth, schooling, and work.

PRIMARY SOURCE

A demographic portrait of ten farmworkers can be drawn from the NAWS sample of 14- to 17-year-old respondents. Most teens who worked in agriculture were older—three-fourths of those between the ages of 14 and 17 who worked in the fields were aged 16 and 17. Like their adult counterparts, most (84 percent) teenage agricultural workers were young men.

Unlike the adult farmworker population, which was predominately (77 percent) foreign-born, most (52 percent) teen farmworkers were born in the United States. Most of the foreign-born minors working in agriculture did not come to this country as young children, but were recent arrivals. Of these foreign-born minor farmworkers, 3 in 4 (74 percent) came to the United States between the ages of 14 and 17, and 58 percent came at ages 16 or 17.

Many of the teens doing farmwork are *de facto* emancipated minors. More than one-half (54 percent) of the minor farmworkers do not live with a parent. Very few live without a parent but with some other member of their family. Overall, nearly half (48 percent) of the minor farmworker teenagers live in households without any member of their family.

The farmworker population is very poor—57 percent live in households below the Federal poverty threshold. . . .

Migrant farmworkers have an even harder time surviving than do settled farmworkers. NAWS defines a migrant as a person who travels 75 miles or more to do or seek farmwork. By this definition, teens were less likely to be migrants than were adults (36 percent versus 51 percent). However, those teens who are migrants live in very difficult conditions, usually without family supervision. According to NAWS, 4 in 5 migrant teens (80 percent) were *de facto* emancipated minors—not living with any other family member. The vast majority (91 percent) of minor migrant teens were foreign-born. . . .

Children with a migrant parent were more likely to work than were children whose parents are settled. Twenty-seven percent of all farmworkers' children live in a house with a migrant parent. However, 44 percent of children who work in the fields have a migrant parent, compared with just 27 percent of the children who do not work. (Again, because only 6 percent of the children are farmworkers, the average for all children tends toward the average of the 94 percent of children who do not work, despite significant differences between the two groups.) Children who work in the fields are more likely to migrate than are children who do not do farmwork. In almost all cases (99 percent), children who work in the fields accompany their migrant parent. . . .

Almost one-fourth of school-age children of farmworkers are behind in grade or have dropped out of school. Of the children of farmworkers, those who worked in the fields were more likely to be behind in school. Only 62 percent of children who did farmwork were learning at grade level compared with 78 percent of those who did not do farmwork. Twenty-two percent of the children doing farmwork were behind in grade and 16 percent had dropped out. While working in the fields may have affected their progress in school, children doing farmwork also had higher levels of other factors associated with being behind in school—they were more likely to be foreign-born and to be migrants. . . .

SIGNIFICANCE

Researchers with the DOL's Bureau of Labor Statistics (BLS) went to worksites of farmworkers to administer an employer-based survey and later administered a more detailed survey at locations convenient to the workers. With respect to NAWS, the researchers found that between the years 1993 and 1998 about seven percent of all farmworkers were between the ages of fourteen and seventeen years—or about 126,000 of 1.8 million U.S. farmworkers.

Other groups have documented youth employment in agricultural labor. For instance, the National Farm Workers Ministry estimates that, as of 2005, from 300,000 to 800,000 adolescent farmworkers work in the United States. Working hours for these children during the busy harvesting season can be over fourteen hours per day, seven days a week. According to Human Rights Watch, based on a 2000 survey, one-third of youth farmworkers receive less than the minimum wage.

The Fair Labor Standards Act makes it legal for any child age twelve years or older to perform agricultural work. Besides long working hours, conditions in agriculture have the potential to be dangerous for youths because of their lack of working experience. Consequently, even though youths make up only about seven percent of all farmworkers, their rate of fatalities is about forty percent, and about 100,000 youth workers report agricultural-based injuries each year.

Children who work in agricultural labor are also in increased danger of illness. According to the National Center for Farmworker Health, Inc., pesticide exposure is more toxic to children than to adults due to their small size. Children's smaller body mass tolerates smaller amounts of chemicals than do larger adult bodies. The U.S. federal government sets standards for pesticide residues in food that are acceptable for children to eat. However, similar standards are not established for children working to harvest foods. As one example, the Food Quality Protection Act of 1996 requires the U.S. Environmental Protection Agency (EPA) to consider children when limiting the amount of pesticides in food consumed by the public. However, the law excludes the EPA from considering occupational exposure to the same pesticides—that is, the law does not protect youth laborers who harvest these foods.

On the other hand, youth farmworkers are protected under various U.S. occupational health laws. For example, there are laws that require posting of notices about pesticide spraying. These postings state the minimum amount of time that workers must wait before they can safely return to the fields after spraying. However, both sides generally agree that youth farmworkers are exposed to higher dosages of pesticides through the foods they harvest than are the consumers of those foods.

Before 1997, the federal government had performed little research and enacted few laws on youth employment in agriculture. In fact, according to Associated Press science editor Matt Crenson, the National Institute of Occupational Safety and Health spent $2.5 million for research into child farmworker injuries in the same year the U.S. Department of Agriculture's Agricultural Research Service spent $700 million on livestock and crop studies. Beginning in 1997, however, the federal government began devoting more time and effort to occupational health and safety research on youth farmworkers. In addition, several organizations were formed around that same time to advocate better working conditions for youths employed in agriculture. For instance, the Children in the Fields Campaign was created by the Child Labor Coalition in 1997 to help protect working children.

In the past, most agricultural jobs were performed on small family farms. Youths worked on the farm as unpaid family workers. However, paid agricultural employment for youths has increased as the number of small family farms continues to decrease while large corporate farms increase. Adults working in agriculture within the United States are paid some of the lowest wages of any working group. Youths engaged in agriculture are paid even less. To make matters worse, youths working in agriculture face problems such as loss of educational opportunities, poor living and working conditions, separation from parents, and exposure to occupational hazards.

FURTHER RESOURCES
Books

Griffith, David Craig. *Working Poor: Farmworkers in the United States*. Philadelphia, PA: Temple University Press, 1995.

Human Rights Watch. *Fingers to the Bone: United States Failure to Protect Child Farmworkers*. New York: Human Rights Watch, 2000.

Levine, Marvin J. *Children for Hire: The Perils of Child Labor in the United States*. Westport, Conn.: Praeger, 2003.

Web sites

Association of Farmworker Opportunity Programs. "Child Labor—Children in the Fields: The Inequitable Treatment of Child Farmworkers." <http://www.afop.org/childlabor.htm> (accessed June 25, 2006).

Bureau of Labor Statistics, U.S. Department of Labor. "Report on the Youth Labor Force." <http://www.bls.gov/opub/rylf/rylfhome.htm> (accessed June 25, 2006).

Crenson, Matt. *Pangaea*. "Pesticides May Jeopardize Child Farmworkers' Health." December 9, 1997 <http://pangaea.org/street_children/americas/AP7.htm> (accessed June 25, 2006).

National Farm Worker Ministry. "Childhood and Child Labor." <http://www.nfwm.org/fw/childlabor.shtml> (accessed June 25, 2006).

Constitutional Amendment to Allow Foreign-Born Citizens to be President

Legislation

By: U.S. House of Representatives

Date: February 29, 2000

Source: U.S. Congress. House. *Constitutional Amendment to Allow Foreign-Born Citizens to be President*. HJR 88, 106th Congress, 2nd session. Available at: <http://commdocs.house.gov/committees/judiciary/hju 67306.000/hju67306_0f.htm> (accessed June 10, 2006).

About the Author: The U.S. House of Representatives and the U.S. Senate comprise the U.S. Congress, the legislative branch of the federal government. Members of the House may initiate the process of amending the U.S. Constitution.

INTRODUCTION

The decision of the Founding Fathers to break away from Great Britain and transform their colonies into a sovereign nation was motivated by a longing for self-determination. That desire led them to risk their personal fortunes and futures in a war against their former countrymen and their former king. Given their colonial experiences as subjects of an overseas monarch, they were understandably concerned that their new government not invest excessive power in a single person or family. Hence, they created an elaborate system of checks and balances within their new governmental system. The nation's founders were equally determined that their new government, particularly the chief executive, remain free of foreign influence. For this reason, they included a provision stating that the office of president cannot be held by a foreign-born person. That requirement remains in force today.

The Constitution's framers believed that while U.S. law should be amended, so that it can adjust to meet the changing needs of the country, the principles expounded in the Constitution itself should provide a timeless and relatively unchanging foundation for the remainder of U.S. law. For this reason, amending the Constitution requires significant effort.

While U.S. law is normally enacted with a simple majority vote of both houses of Congress and the signature of the president, an amendment to the Constitution requires a much larger mandate, beginning with a two-thirds majority vote in both houses of Congress. This requirement alone has made Congress the burial ground of virtually all proposed amendments. For example, an amendment proposed in 2006 would have defined marriage as a union between one man and one woman. It received less than half the votes cast in the Senate, and, thus, went no further.

If an amendment does receive the required supermajorities in both houses of Congress, it proceeds to a state-by-state vote. Each state determines when and if to hold its vote and a minimum of thirty-eight states are required to approve the amendment. Of the amendments reaching this stage, another twenty

California Governor Arnold Schwarzenegger speaks on the state's stalled budget negotiations at a fire station in Los Angeles, July 3, 2004. AP IMAGES.

percent fail to pass. The Equal Rights Amendment, guaranteeing equal rights for women, passed Congress in 1972, but was able to win approval in only thrity-five states, three short of the required minimum.

If a proposed amendment is able to gather enough state votes, it then becomes part of the U. S. Constitution. Of several thousand amendments proposed in Congress since the nation's founding, only thirty-three have been sent to the states; twenty-seven of those were ultimately added to the Constitution.

There is no limit to the number of times an amendment can be proposed in Congress, and some proposals are considered repeatedly. In 2000, Massachusetts Representative Barney Frank proposed a Constitutional amendment which would allow foreign-born American citizens to serve as President of the United States.

■ PRIMARY SOURCE

Proposing an amendment to the Constitution of the United States to make eligible for the Office of President a person who has been a United States citizen for twenty years.

IN THE HOUSE OF REPRESENTATIVES
FEBRUARY 29, 2000
Mr. FRANK of Massachusetts introduced the following joint resolution; which was referred to the Committee on the Judiciary

JOINT RESOLUTION

Proposing an amendment to the Constitution of the United States to make eligible for the Office of President a person who has been a United States citizen for twenty years.

Resolved by the Senate and House of Representatives of the United States of America in Congress assembled (two-thirds of each House concurring therein), That the following article is proposed as an amendment to the Constitution of the United States, which shall be valid to all intents and purposes as part of the Constitution when ratified by the legislatures of three-fourths of the several States within seven years after the date of its submission for ratification:

"Article—

"A person who is a citizen of the United States, who has been for twenty years a citizen of the United States, and who is otherwise eligible to the Office of President, is not ineligible to that Office by reason of not being a native born citizen of the United States."

SIGNIFICANCE

Although Congressman Frank's proposal made little progress in Congress, the idea of opening the presidency to all U.S. citizens appealed to Democrats and Republicans. Both major parties viewed the change as a potential winning issue with minority voters, particularly Hispanics. Republicans also had an interest in the future of California governor Arnold Schwarzenegger, an Austrian-born U.S. citizen since 1983. In 2003 and 2004, multiple versions of such an amendment were once again proposed by both parties. Though the details varied, each set a specific length of citizenship, ranging from fourteen to thirty-five years, after which an immigrant would become eligible to hold the presidency.

Supporters of such an amendment argue that as a nation of immigrants, the United States is the last place that separate classes of citizenship should exist. They note the distinguished service of such citizens as Secretaries of State Henry Kissinger and Madeline Albright, both of whom were foreign-born. They also point out that the birth requirement originated in an era when the United States was a small weak country, a situation which no longer exists.

Critics of the proposed change note that the United States is already unusually accepting of immigrant citizens, placing few other restrictions on them. These opponents also assert that the U.S. Constitution was intended to remain relatively unchanged, and that political motives and short-term objectives should not be permitted to change the provisions of this seminal document.

While there appear to be few outspoken critics of the proposal, the process of passing an amendment remains daunting. Successful amendment drives have often required a specific trigger event to galvanize public opinion and help propel the lengthy ratification process. A few supporters of the current proposal have suggested marrying it with another potentially popular change, such as removing term limits to allow a president to serve three terms.

FURTHER RESOURCES
Books

Amar, Akhil Reed. *America's Constitution: A Biography*. New York: Random House, 2005.

Cohen, Jeffrey, et al. *The Presidency*. New York: McGraw-Hill Humanities, 2003.

DeGregorio, William. *The Complete Book of U.S. Presidents*. Sixth edition. New York: Random House, 2001.

Periodicals

Govindarajan, Shweta. "Flag Amendment Proposal Passes First Test." *Congressional Quarterly Weekly* 64 (2006): 54.

Lawler, Peter A. "Toward a Consistent Ethic of Judicial Restraint." *Society* 43 (2006): 51–58.

Lloyd, Robert. "Rebuilding the American State." *Current History* 105 (2006): 229–233.

Web sites

Bill of Rights Institute. "The Bill of Rights." <http://www.billofrightsinstitute.org/Instructional/Resources/FoundingDocuments/Docs/TheBillofRights.htm> (accessed June 12, 2006).

Cornell Law School. "United States Constitution." <http://www.law.cornell.edu/constitution/constitution.table.html> (accessed June 12, 2006).

Puzzanghera, Jim. "Amendment Would Drop Requirement for President to be U.S.-Born." *Seattle Times*, September 16, 2004. <http://seattletimes.nwsource.com/html/nationworld/2002036961_amendment16.html> (accessed June 12, 2006).

The El Monte Experience

Book excerpt

By: Penda D. Hair

Date: March 2001

Source: Hair, Penda D. "The El Monte Experience." In *Louder than Words*. New York: Rockefeller Foundation, March 2001.

About the Author: Penda D. Hair is a researcher affiliated with the Rockefeller Foundation. Founded in 1913 by John D. Rockefeller, the foundation focuses on improving opportunities for poor people.

INTRODUCTION

Immigrants have long served as a major source of cheap labor for manufacturing. As the apparel industry globalized in the 1970s, it was expected that fewer immigrants would be needed to work in the United States since it was now possible to shift labor-intensive production activities out of high-wage countries into lower-wage nations. However, many manufacturers discovered that they could save money by importing workers to the United States and keeping them in a state of semi-slavery in modern sweatshops.

Most American sweatshops are located in U.S. territories where U.S. labor laws do not apply. Saipan, an island in the Northern Mariana Islands, maintains a number of U.S.-owned garment manufacturing companies that export $1 billion worth of clothing to the United States annually. Employees working on the factory line are paid about $2 below

Former sweatshop workers stand in front of the building where they were forced to labor as garment workers. AP IMAGES.

the U.S. federally required minimum wage. The vast majority of the workers, about ninety-eight percent, are immigrant women from China, the Philippines, Bangladesh, and Thailand.

These women are recruited by deception, through expensive recruiting fees. The workers are trapped in a state of indentured servitude until they pay off their travel fees. The workdays are seven days a week, twelve hours a day, with quota production requirements. The workers are required to live within the plant behind barbed-wire fences. Such working conditions received very little attention in the American media until the 1995 El Monte case revealed that similar sweatshops were being set up on the U.S. mainland and run by large Western transnational corporations.

PRIMARY SOURCE

Garment workers in Thailand making pennies per day dreamed of immigrating to the United States. One El

Monte worker remembered: "I had dreams about the United States since I was a little boy. [But] I thought, I have no education, I'm just a garment worker—how can I get to that place?" Another El Monte worker explained: "Everybody has a dream about America, a land of opportunity and freedom. You can make a fortune... if you come." When one of the enslaved workers first heard about a job in a factory in Los Angeles, he mused, "The name of the city—of angels—it must be good!"

The El Monte shop operators had a recruiter in Thailand, who claimed that immigrants would "just work regular 8 to 5, get a lot of pay and do what they did in Thailand." He even showed them a picture of a top-of-the-line factory. The rate of pay promised by the recruiter was so much that a garment worker would have to "work for the whole month in Thailand to make what she would make in a day or two of work in America." After hearing the recruiter's offer, one worker decided to "just get on the plane and go to the United States." Another worker stated: "I never imagined about any danger or that anything might happen . . . because I heard about the land of freedom and that law and police protect you."

Ready to pursue their drams, they quite their jobs, packed their bags and said goodbye to their families, promising to send money home as soon as they were settled. The recruiter gave each worker a bracelet and a thin necklace to wear for identification.

But the dream quickly turned sour. Once in America, the workers began to realize that the recruiter had lied to them. Rather than a fancy factory the recruiter had shown them in a photograph, they were taken to an apartment complex that had been converted into a garment factory in El Monte, a town a few miles east of Los Angeles. The workers met the head operator, the mastermind behind the entire operation, a sweet-talking Thai woman who asked everyone to call her Auntie. Auntie instructed the workers: "Don't talk to the people that lived here before you; they probably lie to you. Don't listen to all those things they put into your mind."

El Monte was grim. All calls were monitored; all mail was censored. High barbed-wire fences surrounded the complex, topped with metal spikes pointed inward. "We couldn't go anywhere, we couldn't get through the front gate because of the 24-hour armed guard." The operators constantly made violent threats to frighten workers into submission. They showed them pictures of an injured co-worker brutally beaten for trying to escape. They threatened to beat them, to kill their families and to burn down their homes in Thailand if they ever tried to escape. The operators also told the workers that if they contacted government officials, they would face prosecution for illegal entry into the country. They told the workers lies, such as, "If you got caught, the authorities . . . will shave your head."

"My hopes and dreams disappeared into thin air," said one worker. "I couldn't believe America had a place like this." Living quarters as well as working quarters were crowded, dirty and infested with rats and roaches. Often, just the act of breathing was difficult because fabric lint from the sewing clogged the air in inadequately ventilated rooms.

When one worker looked for the beds, she was told, 'don't even think about [a] bed." The workers had to sew their own mattresses. They slept on the floor, amongst the rats and roaches, sharing a room with up to eight other workers.

The workday was long and treacherous. Workers were at their machines by 7 A.M. and got only two breaks the entire day—15 minutes each for lunch and dinner. The shift ended only when the work order was complete, no matter how long it took. Exhausted workers often found themselves nodding off at the machines and drinking endless cups of coffee in the struggle to stay awake. Often, they didn't finish the job until 2 or 3 o'clock in the morning.

The El Monte operators ran a number of different "front shop" facilities in downtown Los Angeles that, at various times, employed up to 70 Latina workers. These workers were not enslaved, but labored in unsanitary conditions, making clothes for the same operators, manufacturers and retailers. One such sweatshop was an open warehouse with a wall partition in the middle, separating areas where finishing work was done from the area where shipment was made. The facility was crowded and extremely hot. Workers were told that they could not even bring their own fans because it would cost too much in electricity. The bathrooms were filthy, and air quality was poor. The workers were paid below minimum wage and denied overtime compensation.

At the Los Angeles facility, the finishing work—trimming, folding, packaging, buttonholes and buttons—was done after the garments had been sewn at the secret El Monte facility. The manufacturers and retailers inspected the front shops regularly, even as much as several times a day. The workers claimed in their litigation that the manufacturers and retailers know or should have known that all of the work was not being performed at the downtown shops.

Several Thai workers risked their lives to escape from the El Monte compound. In 1995, escaped workers took an additional risk to inform law-enforcement officials about the slave shop. Shortly after, a joint task force of federal and state law-enforcement agencies raided the El Monte operation.

The morning of the raid on El Monte, a male worker saw the police begin surrounding the compound. He immediately got scared and went to hide. Another worker, exhausted from work the night before, was sound asleep when a co-worker came to get him up. Everybody was screaming, "Pack!" For a time, some of the workers, in hushed tones, discussed whether to attempt a getaway. But all efforts to hide or escape were in vain. The workers were quickly rounded up and put on a bus bound for an Immigration and Naturalization Service (INS) detention facility.

For most, the bus trip was their first real glimpse of the outside world in the United States. As their relief at being free from El Monte settled in, they marveled at the sight of the passing city. "Oh, this is so beautiful, so light and shiny," thought one. "For once, everybody was happy."

But their happiness ended abruptly. The INS put them in the federal penitentiary at San Pedro Terminal Island, where they were forced to wear prison uniforms. During the daytime, they were taken to an INS holding cell in the basement of the federal building in Los Angeles, transported by bus in shackles. At night they were usually returned to the San Pedro prison, but they spent two nights in the INS holding tank, a concrete room with no beds.

SIGNIFICANCE

The El Monte case prompted the California state legislature in 1999 to enact AB 633, considered to be the country's toughest law targeting sweatshop operators who abuse apparel workers. The law has not been as successful as legislators expected. Garment workers' claims for wages and overtime quadrupled in the five years after the law's enactment from 565 in 1998 to 2,282 in 2004. Advocates for workers asserted that the claims reflect only a small fraction of the thousands of garment workers denied pay. The money owed to underpaid workers in Los Angeles County alone was estimated at $81 million annually. Clothing manufacturers in Los Angeles Country produced $13 billion in goods annually as of 2005. Additionally, workers who go through the state claims process end up recovering only about a third of the money that they are owed, with the contractors paying an average of $1,589 on claims that averaged $5,175. California has registered about 5,440 garment manufacturers with only forty-eight companies suffering an application denial or a registration revocation between 2000 and 2005. The meager number of firms that have been disciplined indicates to some worker advocates that the state is not effectively administering the law. California has been criticized for conducting superficial investigations of sweatshops and for overseeing a protracted claims process, which averages about two hundred days to complete.

There are hidden costs to cheap clothing. When manufacturers spend little on labor, these savings are not necessarily passed on to the consumer. A t-shirt purchased in Thailand or Indonesia is often made by an employee of a large U.S. transnational corporation who contracted out the labor for a few cents an hour per employee. While Americans are told that this will allow them to buy such clothing at cheaper prices, corporate moguls make more money from this arrangement instead of the workers or the consumers. Additionally, these dynamics lead workers in developing nations to believe that they might make more money if they move to the United States They immigrate only to discover that they are trapped in low-level minimum wage jobs or more dangerous or repetitive manufacturing jobs that American citizens refuse.

FURTHER RESOURCES
Books

Bonacich, Edna and Richard Appelbaum. *Behind the Label: Inequality in the Los Angeles Apparel Industry*. Berkeley, Calif.: University of California Press, 2000.

Rosen, Ellen. *Making Sweatshop: The Globalization of the U.S. Apparel Industry*. Berkeley, Calif.: University of California Press, 2002.

Ross, Robert J.S. *Slaves to Fashion: Poverty and Abuse in the New Sweatshops*. Ann Arbor, Mich.: University of Michigan Press, 2004.

International Adoptions

Transcript

By: James W. Ziglar

Date: May 22, 2002

Source: Ziglar, James W. "International Adoptions." *GPO /USCIS*, May 22, 2002 <http://www.uscis.gov/graphics/aboutus/congress/testimonies/2002 / 1ZIGHOUS. pdf> (accessed July 14, 2006).

About the Author: James W. Ziglar became Commissioner of the Immigration and Naturalization Service (INS) in the United States in 2001. In November 2002, Ziglar left the INS and was its last commissioner before INS services were folded into the Department of Homeland Security under a reorganization plan implemented by President George W. Bush's administration. Ziglar subsequently joined the Law School faculty at George Washington University.

INTRODUCTION

In the twentieth century, international adoptions increased after World War II, when tens of thousands of orphaned Jewish children were adopted throughout the United States and Europe. In addition, United States soldiers fighting in Germany and Japan produced a number of children who were half-American; immigration procedures changed to permit these children to enter the United States to live with their fathers or to be adopted by American families.

Many mainline Christian denominations, such as Lutherans, Seventh Day Adventists, and Catholics, encouraged international adoption and supported orphanages abroad; the plight of children suffering from poverty or neglect, in need of adoptive homes, was a subject addressed by religious volunteers and

Mark and Catherine Meister of Warner, New Hampshire, have three biological children and two adopted children, one from South Africa and another from Romania. © DAN HABIB/THE CONCORD MONITOR/CORBIS.

missionaries in coordinated activities in southeast Asian countries by the 1950s and 1960s. The Korean Conflict, in particular, brought home the issue of half-Korean, half-American children, who were shunned for their Amerasian status in Korea. Between 1953 and 1962, Americans adopted more than 15,000 children from abroad, many from South Korea. Religious and military families were some of the first to adopt internationally, a process that often fell outside of the supervision of child welfare agencies and was handled simply as a matter for the courts in the country of birth to approve.

Adoptions from Asian countries such as South Korean, China, Vietnam, and Cambodia have all increased since the 1960s. Many American soldiers who fought in the Vietnam War had children with Vietnamese women. As in South Korea, these half-American children were ostracized. In April 1975, more than 2,000 infants and children were evacuated from Saigon during "Operation Babylift," but thousands of other Amerasian children were left behind.

The 1987 Amerasian Homecoming Act, implemented in 1989, permitted more than 25,000 Amerasians from Vietnam to enter the United States. Though many of these new immigrants were teenagers, born in 1974 or 1975 as American involvement in Vietnam was ending, some were men and women in their twenties, fully grown adults seeking to escape difficulties in Vietnam.

Adoption from China increased in the 1990s as China's one-child policy led to the abandonment of female babies; in a culture that prized males, many couples sought to have a boy for their only child. At the same time, adoptions from Vietnam and Cambodia increased. In 2001 and 2003, Vietnam and Cambodia experienced corruption in the international adoption system as allegations of baby thefts, for purposes of selling abducted babies for international adoptions, came to light.

PRIMARY SOURCE

Mr. Chairman and Members of the Committee:

I welcome this opportunity to share with you my experience and objectives with respect to improving the Immigration and Naturalization Service's (INS) critical role in the international adoption arena. For those United States citizens who choose to open their hearts and homes to children from abroad, the INS shares with the Department of State responsibility for adjudicating orphan petitions and enabling a child's immigration to America.

The circumstances that arose in connection with the adoption of children from Cambodia and Vietnam in recent months thrust the INS into this issue early on in my tenure. The experience brings into sharp focus the many aspects of INS' global responsibilities: the interaction between our domestic and overseas offices and the Department of State, the interaction between U.S. immigration laws and the laws of the foreign sending countries, and the direct impact our work has on the hopes and dreams of United States citizens.

I am committed to working with you to improve INS' contribution to international adoptions. Along with the pressing security concerns of the day, I have made international adoptions a top priority for the INS. One of my first initiatives was to create a special Adoptions Task Force....The Task Force was created to undertake a special humanitarian initiative to review certain adoption cases in Cambodia. The Task Force has also undertaken a comprehensive review of the existing INS structure for dealing with international adoptions....

Largely Positive context For International Adoptions

The suspension of orphan visa processing in Cambodia was implemented for good reason: there are serious deficiencies in the Cambodian legal framework on adoptions, and there are very real human trafficking concerns. However, the controversies that have arisen recently in connection with Cambodia and Vietnam must not make us lose sight of the largely positive context in which we do our work. Although in need of improvement, the current procedures that are in place have worked for thousands of U.S. families each year. The majority of cases have happy endings.

INS' responsibilities

To the child

The INS' determination that a child is an orphan as defined under the Immigration and Nationality Act (INA), and is, therefore, eligible for immigration to the United States, is among the most sensitive adjudications we perform. In performing this task, the INS must bring to its work a core commitment to protect the interests of the child, which is at the heart of the process. Under the current statutory framework, we are obligated to make a determination as to whether or not this child is indeed an orphan—that is, a child without parents, as defined under the INA, and to uphold the laws that have been created to protect children in this process.

To the parents

We also have weighty responsibility to the American citizens—the prospective adoptive parents—who have invested their hearts, and often considerable resources, in this endeavor. The immigration process associated with adoption should not diminish the joys of providing a home to a child, but at the same time there are laws and procedures that must be honored. The INS must work to ensure that our efforts in upholding the law complement the commendable spirit that is at the core of the decision to open one's heart and home to a child.

International Context

Another factor that makes the international adoption process complex is that foreign countries in which parents seek to adopt are often characterized by extreme poverty and the accompanying societal uncertainties and pressures. These same countries may be struggling to establish the sound legal frameworks and well regulated adoption processes which would bring integrity to the intercountry adoption process and which make compliance with our immigration laws simpler. Also, even in relatively well-developed countries with strong legal systems, the legal adoption requirements can vary from country to country, even as they vary from state to state here, making the challenge of cooperation all the more complex and important....

Introducing "Hague-consistent" Safeguards for American Adoptive Parents: The "Adjudicate Orphan Status First" Initiative

Of all the changes the Task Force will address, the single most important operational improvement will be to introduce safeguards similar to the Hague Convention process for American adoptive parents as quickly as possible in certain more problematic countries. We are calling this the "adjudicate orphan status first" initiative.

The most serious problem with international adoptions is that in many countries, the process by which governments decide that birth parents are no longer providing care for their child and that the child is available for intercountry adoption is not always transparent.

As a consequence, some American prospective adoptive parents have experienced the heartbreaking situation in which they have traveled abroad and adopted a child, only to discover that the child does not meet the orphan definition and cannot immediately immigrate to the United States. For example, sometimes a foreign country allows Americans to adopt a child who is not an orphan because their laws are different than ours. Sometimes, particularly in poor and underdeveloped countries, unregulated and unscrupulous agents and facilitators take advantage of inadequate infrastructure and safeguards to lead American prospective adoptive parents to believe a particular child is an orphan when a professional review of the paperwork reveals serious problems and irregularities.

As I mentioned before, under the Hague Convention, signatory governments will be responsible for certifying that a child is eligible to immigrate under the laws of the prospective adoptive parents' country before they allow the adoption to take place. But prior to the Hague Convention being implemented and for non-signatory states, we are exploring ways to offer a voluntary service to prospective adoptive parents who are thinking about adopting in certain countries, in essence, to adjudicate orphan first. We are in the process of developing this process with the Department of State, and look forward to being in a position to share the details on this proposal shortly....

Communication

We will do our best to ensure that clear guidance is provided to prospective parents, adoption agencies, and other stakeholders on how the process works; what to expect at each stage in the adoption process; and the legal requirements that must be met for a child to immigrate to the United States in an international adoption. We continue to seek to explain to prospective parents that adoption and immigration are separate processes, and that, for example, fulfilling the adoption requirements of a foreign sending country does not necessarily mean that American immigration requirements have been met. We encourage other stakeholders, such as adoption agencies, to meet their own responsibilities in this regard. We will also continue to encourage domestic INS offices, and overseas posts, to communicate, openly and regularly with all the stakeholders in the adoptions process, including adoption agencies and prospective adoptive parents. As always, we seek to ensure that the latest information is available on the INS and State Department websites, so that everyone involved in the process has access to the best and most recent information available....

Conclusion: Caution That The Process Will Never Be Simple

Improving the immigration determinations for which INS is responsible has been a matter of the highest priority for the Service since I have become Commissioner. I believe that we have a plan that will take us in the right direction. Yet I must introduce a note of caution. We cannot lose sight of the fact that many international adoptions take place in the context of some of the poorest and most unstable and underdeveloped nations in the world. Even with the significant improvements to our process that will be introduced by the Adoptions Task Force, the introduction of the IAA, and some of our longer-term regulatory and structural improvements, we will still face a complex and difficult situation in many of the countries from which Americans seek to adopt. Unregulated and unscrupulous agents and facilitators, including those that operate on the internet, will continue, to try to insinuate themselves in the process, and to exploit the necessarily complex layers of interaction between agencies of different governments. We will need to continue to be vigilant that American citizens and the U.S. government do not unintentionally contribute to a situation where baby selling and buying can occur.

SIGNIFICANCE

International adoptions from China and Russia dominate the international adoption process, but other countries such as Ukraine, Cambodia, Kazakhstan, Guatemala, and Vietnam are the source of a substantial number of adoptions to such countries as the United States, Great Britain, Australia, and Italy. Between 1971 and 2001, more than 156,000 children from Asian countries were adopted in the United States.

The United States' immigration policies for determining eligibility for adoption are far more stringent than those procedures in many countries; as this testimony notes, in many instances children are placed for adoption in countries such as Cambodia or Vietnam, and the children are selected for adoption by U.S. citizens. During the document review process, however, the child's orphan status may come into question; in some countries, such as Ukraine, children are referred to as "social orphans" if one or both birth parents places the child in an orphanage. In some instances, the parents fail to relinquish parental rights yet for all intents and purposes abandon the child, leaving the child unadoptable. The U.S. vetting procedure unearths these cases, in part to prevent child bounty hunters from abducting children from parents who want them for the sake of selling the children on the black market for international adoption.

More than 265,000 children from countries other than the United States were adopted by U.S. citizens during the period 1971–2001; once the adoption is finalized in the United States, the children become U.S. citizens. In many instances, the children speak no English, the adoptive parents do not speak the child's native language, and the children face health and nutrition concerns. Ninety percent of all international adoptions to the United States involve children under the age of four; forty-six percent are under the age of one. As these children immigrate and assimilate into American culture, often with parents of a different ethnic background, they uniquely straddle two cultures within one family.

FURTHER RESOURCES

Books

McKelvey, Robert S. *The Dust of Life: America's Children Abandoned in Vietnam*. Seattle: University of Washington Press, 1999.

O'Halloran, Kerry. *The Politics of Adoption: International Perspectives on Law, Policy & Practice*. Dordrecht, The Netherlands: Springer, 2006.

Pertman, Adam. *Adoption Nation: How the Adoption Revolution is Transforming America*. New York: Basic Books, 2000.

Periodicals

Banghan, Huang, and Kay Johnson. "Infant Abandonment and Adoption in China." *Population and Development Review* 24 (3)(1998): 469–510.

Gunnar, Megan R. "International Adoption of Institutionally Reared Children: Research and Policy." *Development and Psychopathology* 12 (2002): 677–693.

Web site

United States Department of State. "International Adoption." <http://travel.state.gov/family/adoption/notices/notices_473.html> (accessed June 25, 2006).

U.S. Immigrant Educational Achievement

Chart

By: Luke J. Larsen, U.S. Census Bureau

Date: August 2003

Source: Adapted by Thomson Gale from data from: Larsen, Luke J. *The Foreign-Born Population in the U.S.: 2003*. U.S. Census Bureau, August 2003.

About the Author: Luke J. Larsen is a researcher in the U.S. Census Bureau, part of the United States Department of Commerce.

INTRODUCTION

Census charts show that in 2003 there were considerable differences between the overall levels of educational attainment of the native-born and foreign-born populations of the United States, and also between different groups within the foreign-born population. In particular, the lower levels of educational attainment among the foreign-born are accounted for almost entirely by lower levels of education among Latin American immigrants.

Overall, only sixty-seven percent of foreign born Americans, compared with 87.5 percent of the native born, had graduated from high-school. The percentage that had graduated from high school fell to forty-nine percent for those born in Latin American countries and, within this group, only thirty-eight percent of those born in Central America were high school graduates. In contrast, people who had been born in Asian countries or in other parts of the world had similar levels of educational attainment to the native-born population.

The data is taken from the Current Population Survey, a monthly sample survey of around fifty thousand U.S. households, conducted by the Bureau of the Census. Its main purpose is to collect employment-related data to feed into labor market policies, but the survey also generates information on the demographic characteristics of the U.S. population, including nativity and educational attainment levels.

The composition of the foreign-born population by levels of educational attainment largely reflects the immigration policies that have determined patterns of entry to the United States over the past few decades. In general, recent admissions policies have given priority to immigrants coming to the U.S. for the purpose of reunification with family members who are already U.S. citizens. To a slightly lesser extent, professionals and other high-skilled workers have been allowed to enter the U.S. to take up employment. As a result, a pattern has developed in which a high proportion of immigrants from Asian countries have come to the United States as highly skilled workers, while those from Mexico and other parts of Central and Latin America have come on family reunification visas and have generally had low levels of educational attainment.

Population by educational attainment and nativity: 2003

(As a percent of each population aged 25 and over)[1]

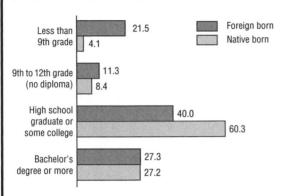

Less than 9th grade
Foreign born: 21.5
Native born: 4.1

9th to 12th grade (no diploma)
Foreign born: 11.3
Native born: 8.4

High school graduate or some college
Foreign born: 40.0
Native born: 60.3

Bachelor's degree or more
Foreign born: 27.3
Native born: 27.2

Legend: ■ Foreign born □ Native born

SOURCE: Luke J. Larsen, "Figure 7. Foreign-Born by World Region of Birth: 2003," in The Foreign-Born Population in the United States: 2003, Current Population Reports, P20-551, U.S. Census Bureau, August 2004, http://www.census.gov/prod/2004pubs/p20-551.pdf (accessed January 24, 2005).

Population with high school education or more, by nativity and world region of birth: 2003

(In percent)[1]

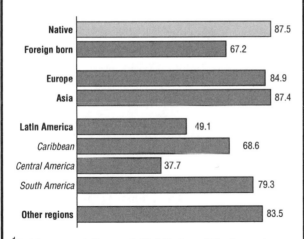

Native: 87.5
Foreign born: 67.2
Europe: 84.9
Asia: 87.4
Latin America: 49.1
Caribbean: 68.6
Central America: 37.7
South America: 79.3
Other regions: 83.5

[1]Each bar represents the percent of individuals aged 25 and over, who were born in the specified area, who have at least a high school education.

SOURCE: U.S. Census Bureau, August 2004,Current Population Survey, 2003 Annual Social and Economic Supplement.

■ PRIMARY SOURCE

U.S. Immigrant Educational Achievement: Latin American immigrants to the United States tend to be less well educated than native born Americans, but immigrants from other regions have a level of education roughly comparable to that of native born Americans. ADAPTED BY THOMSON GALE FROM DATA FROM THE U.S. BUREAU OF THE CENSUS.

However, these broad generalizations conceal the significant differences between immigrant groups from different regions of the world. For example, although many Asian immigrants are highly educated, the nationals of some Asian countries such as Cambodia and Laos have very low levels of education, on average. Similarly, Cubans and South American immigrants tend to be more highly educated than Mexican immigrants.

■ PRIMARY SOURCE

U.S. IMMIGRANT EDUCATIONAL ACHIEVEMENT
See primary source image.

SIGNIFICANCE

There have been particularly high levels of immigration to the United States over the last few decades, and the foreign-born now account for around twelve percent of the population. As a result, immigrant characteristics have an increasingly important impact on the overall educational distribution and labor market profile of the U.S. population. This is particularly true in states that have a disproportionately large immigrant population, such as California.

The majority of recent immigrants to the United States in recent years, both legal and undocumented, have been from Mexico, one of the countries whose immigrants have particularly low levels of educational attainment. Those with few qualifications are most likely to be employed in low-skilled jobs, receive lower wages and may claim more welfare benefits. This potentially has adverse consequences for the country in terms of overall skill levels, as well as other factors such as education and welfare costs.

Research has shown that family characteristics, including educational attainment, tend to be passed onto subsequent generations due to factors such as the language spoken at home and cultural views about the importance of education. This implies that there will be a general tendency for the American-born children of immigrants to attain similar levels of education to their parents and reinforce current labor market patterns, unless there are policy interventions such as special educational programs targeted at the children of immigrant families.

Concern about rising levels of legal and undocumented migration to the U.S. in the early twenty-first century has led to a growing demand for immigration reform. This provides an opportunity to take account of the labor market impacts of recent immigration patterns, and perhaps to incorporate a greater focus on educational attainment and skill levels within future admissions policies.

FURTHER RESOURCES
Books

Bosworth, Barry, Susan M. Collins, and Nora Claudia Lustig. *Coming Together? Mexico-United States Relations.* Washington, D.C.: Brookings Institution Press, 1997.

Krop, Richard A., Peter C. Rydell, and Georges Vernez. *Closing the Education Gap: Benefits and Costs.* Santa Monica, Calif.: Rand, 1999.

Periodicals

Hernandez, Donald J. "Demographic Change and the Life Circumstances of Immigrant Families." *The Future of Children* 14 (2004).

Kao, Grace and Jennifer S. Thompson. "Racial and Ethnic Stratification in Educational Achievement and Attainment." *Annual Review of Sociology* 29 (2003).

Immigrant Homes and Wealth and Poverty

Chart

By: Luke J. Larsen, U.S. Census Bureau

Date: August 2003

Source: Adapted by Thomson Gale from: Larsen, Luke J. *The Foreign-Born Population in the U.S.: 2003.* U.S. Census Bureau, August 2003.

About the Author: Luke J. Larsen is a researcher in the U.S. Census Bureau, a division of the United States Department of Commerce.

INTRODUCTION

The census chart below shows the distribution of household income for native-born and foreign-born members of the United States population and the distribution of income for individual foreign-born groups by region of birth. The data relates to 2002 and is from the Current Population Survey, a monthly sample survey of around fifty thousand U.S. households, conducted by the Bureau of the Census. The main purpose of the survey is to collect employment-related data, including data on individual and household incomes; it also collects information on the demographic characteristics of the population, including its composition by country of birth.

The distribution of the foreign-born population as a whole by household income in 2002 was not significantly different from that for the native-born population. Just a slightly higher percentage of the foreign born (24.6 percent) compared with the native-born (22.3 percent) were in households with a total annual income of less than $20,000, while 38.6 percent of the foreign-born compared with 44 percent of the native-born were in high-earning households with an income of $50,000 or more. Finally, 36.7 percent of the foreign-born were in households with an income of between $20,000 and $49,999, compared with 33.7 percent of the native-born.

However, these figures for the foreign-born concealed substantial differences in household income levels between the foreign-born groups from different parts of the world. Those born in Asian countries stood out as having the highest percentage of households earning $50,000 or more (53.8 percent) and the smallest percentage having low household incomes of less than $20,000 (18.5 percent). Asian immigrants therefore appeared to be performing much better economically than native-born Americans, as well as other foreign-born groups.

Conversely, foreign-born immigrants from the Caribbean and Central America were significantly more likely than the native-born to be living in households with a total income of less than $20,000 and were considerably less likely to be in households with incomes of $50,000 or more. Finally, those originating in South America, Europe, or other regions of the world had similar household income distributions to the native-born.

With the exception of the foreign-born from Asian countries, the majority of recent immigrants to the United States have been born in countries showing relatively low levels of household income compared with the native population. This may partly be due to their short length of time in the United States, since immigrants often face difficulties in securing well-paid work when they first arrive in a new country, perhaps because they do not speak the language, or do not have experience or qualifications that are recognized in the new country. Even highly qualified immigrants often have to take menial jobs when they first arrive. However, many research studies have shown that immigrants usually catch up with, or even exceed, the wage rates of the native population within a period of ten to twenty years.

Recent immigrants to the United States, particularly those from Mexico and other Central American countries, have tended to be those with low levels of educational attainment and skills, so it is not clear

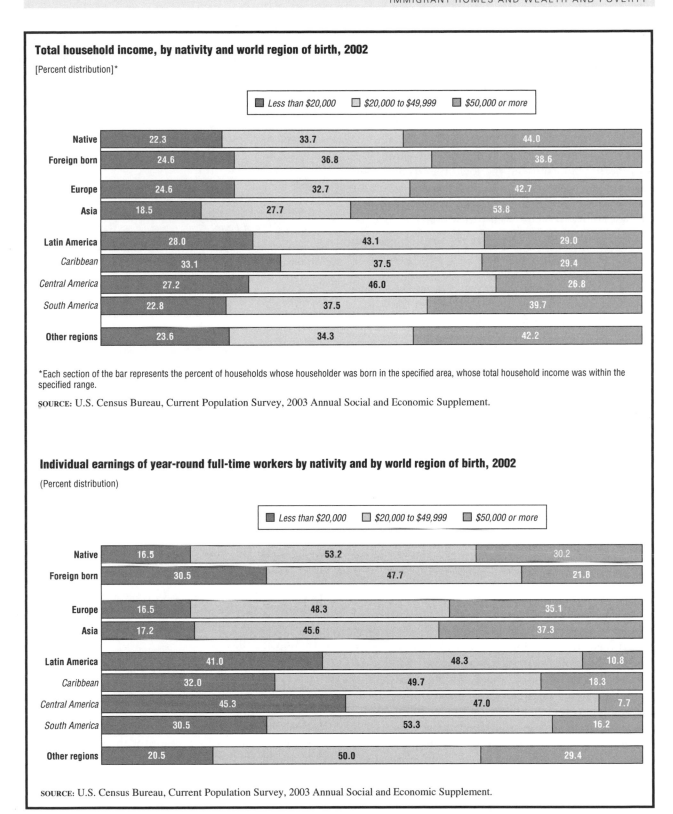

Total household income, by nativity and world region of birth, 2002

[Percent distribution]*

Legend: ■ Less than $20,000   □ $20,000 to $49,999   ■ $50,000 or more

Region	Less than $20,000	$20,000 to $49,999	$50,000 or more
Native	22.3	33.7	44.0
Foreign born	24.6	36.8	38.6
Europe	24.6	32.7	42.7
Asia	18.5	27.7	53.8
Latin America	28.0	43.1	29.0
Caribbean	33.1	37.5	29.4
Central America	27.2	46.0	26.8
South America	22.8	37.5	39.7
Other regions	23.6	34.3	42.2

*Each section of the bar represents the percent of households whose householder was born in the specified area, whose total household income was within the specified range.

SOURCE: U.S. Census Bureau, Current Population Survey, 2003 Annual Social and Economic Supplement.

Individual earnings of year-round full-time workers by nativity and by world region of birth, 2002

(Percent distribution)

Legend: ■ Less than $20,000   □ $20,000 to $49,999   ■ $50,000 or more

Region	Less than $20,000	$20,000 to $49,999	$50,000 or more
Native	16.5	53.2	30.2
Foreign born	30.5	47.7	21.8
Europe	16.5	48.3	35.1
Asia	17.2	45.6	37.3
Latin America	41.0	48.3	10.8
Caribbean	32.0	49.7	18.3
Central America	45.3	47.0	7.7
South America	30.5	53.3	16.2
Other regions	20.5	50.0	29.4

SOURCE: U.S. Census Bureau, Current Population Survey, 2003 Annual Social and Economic Supplement.

■ PRIMARY SOURCE

Immigrant Homes and Wealth and Poverty: As these charts show, Asian immigrants to the United States have tended to be very successful economically, while Central American and Caribbean immigrants have fared particularly poorly. ADAPTED BY THOMSON GALE FROM DATA FROM THE U.S. BUREAU OF THE CENSUS.

whether they will enjoy the same levels of economic success in the longer term as earlier immigrants, such as the Asians who entered the country in the 1970s and 1980s with very high levels of educational qualifications. In contrast to these Asian immigrants, nearly two-thirds of the foreign-born from Central America surveyed in 2003 had not completed high school.

In the case of the foreign-born from the Caribbean, who exhibited the lowest levels of household income overall, racial discrimination against black people in the labor force may also have an impact on their ability to secure well-paid work.

It is important to note that the data reflects the national distribution of household incomes by country of birth. The economic experiences of immigrants are likely to vary considerably between geographic areas as a result of factors such as local labor market conditions and whether there is a community network of their own nationals who can help them to secure jobs.

PRIMARY SOURCE

IMMIGRANT HOMES AND WEALTH AND POVERTY
See primary source image.

SIGNIFICANCE
Recent U.S. immigration policies have given priority to entry for family reunification rather than employment purposes. This has resulted in an influx of poorly educated, low-skilled immigrants who in general have performed less well economically than the native-born population.

It is becoming increasingly difficult for low-skilled workers to secure well-paid jobs in the U.S., regardless of national origin, since structural changes have reduced the availability of manufacturing and industrial work, and decreased wages in low-skilled service jobs. Continuing high levels of legal and undocumented migration among low-skilled immigrants along with an increase over time in the educational attainment levels of the native-born population are likely to increase the polarization between relatively highly paid natives and low-paid, low-skilled immigrants. This may result in social tensions and the need for policy interventions to address problems of poverty among immigrant communities.

The experience of earlier, more highly skilled immigrants has demonstrated that the foreign-born can contribute a great deal economically to the U.S. Greater emphasis on employment-based admissions in future immigration reform could potentially help to maximize the benefits of immigration to the country.

FURTHER RESOURCES
Books
Waldinger, Roger. *Strangers at the Gates: New Immigrants in Urban America*. Berkeley, Calif.: University of California Press, 2001.

Periodicals
Allen, James P. "How Successful are Recent Immigrants to the United States and Their Children?" *Yearbook of the Association of Pacific Coast Geographers* (January 2006).

Bernstein, Jared and Jeff Chapman. "Immigration and Poverty: How Are They Linked?" *Monthly Labor Review* 126 (2003).

Enchautegui, Maria E. "Low-Skilled Immigrants and the Changing American Labor Market." *Population and Development Review* 24 (1998).

Sehgal, Ellen. "Foreign Born in the U.S. Labor Market: The Results of a Special Survey." *Monthly Labor Review* (January 1985).

Vargas, Eugenio. "The Influence of Country of Birth and Other Variables on the Earnings of Immigrants: The Case of the United States in 1999 (Ethnicity and Immigration)." *The American Journal of Economics and Sociology* (January 2005).

U.S. Foreign Born by World Region of Birth

Chart

By: Luke J. Larsen

Date: August 2003

Source: Adapted by Thomson Gale from: Larsen, Luke J. *The Foreign-Born Population in the U.S.: 2003*. U.S. Census Bureau, August 2003.

About the Author: Luke J. Larsen is a researcher in the U.S. Census Bureau, a division of the United States Department of Commerce.

INTRODUCTION
In March 2003, according to official statistics based on the Continuous Population Survey (CPS), 11.7 percent of the population of the United States, or 33.5 million in total, were foreign-born. Of these, 53.3 percent had been born in Latin America, 25 percent had been born in Asia, 13.7 percent in Europe and

8 percent in other parts of the world. Among those born in Latin America, more than two-thirds were from Central America, including Mexico, and these accounted for more than a third of all the foreign born.

The Current Population Survey is a monthly sample survey of around fifty thousand U.S. households, conducted by the Bureau of the Census. Its main purpose is to collect employment-related data to feed into labor market policies, but the survey also generates information on the demographic characteristics of the U.S. population, including its composition by country of birth and ethnicity.

The distribution of the population by country of birth is a reflection of recent patterns of immigration to the United States. These are determined by a range of factors, including U.S. immigration policies, social and economic conditions in countries of origin, geographical proximity, and traditional linkages between these countries and the U.S. The main developments over the past few decades have been a significant decline in the numbers of European immigrants, a massive, ongoing increase in immigration from Mexico and other Latin American countries, and a significant increase in immigration from Asian countries. Overall, the developments can be attributed largely to the impact of changes in U.S. immigration policy, but they have also been influenced by conditions in the countries of origin and other factors.

Between 1929 and 1968, patterns of immigration to the United States had been shaped to a large extent by the National Origins Act, which imposed quotas on the number of immigrants from different countries. Within the quota system, relatively more immigrants were allowed from countries in the western hemisphere than from those in the eastern hemisphere. The 1965 Hart-Celler Act, which came into force in 1968, abolished the national origins quota system and sought to equalize the number of immigrants to the U.S. from the Western and Eastern hemispheres. Within the overall ceiling of immigrant visas allocated to each hemisphere, there were no longer any numerical limits for nationals of individual countries. The Act also introduced a preference system for use in prioritizing applications for entry, which emphasized the importance of family reunification over other reasons for applying. Moreover, the immediate relatives of U.S. citizens could be granted entry outside the quota system.

The 1965 Act had the effect of substantially increasing overall numbers of immigrants to the U.S. and changing the distribution of immigrants by national origin. By this time, immigration from Europe had declined significantly for reasons largely unrelated to immigration policies. Standards of living in European countries had increased in the post-war years and there was no longer much incentive for their nationals to emigrate. On the other hand, high levels of poverty and unemployment in Latin American countries, particularly Mexico, and their geographical proximity to the U.S. created a high level of demand for entry into the U.S. This was unleashed when the 1965 Act abolished national quotas, leading to a surge in levels of immigration from Mexico and other Latin American countries at this time. The lifting of quotas and the equalization of ceilings between the two hemispheres also led to a significant increase in immigration from Asian countries, especially China and the Philippines, although the overall numbers of immigrants from Asia were much lower than from Latin America. The Asian immigrant community was further increased by refugees from Vietnam, Laos, and Kampuchea at the time of the Vietnam War in the late 1970s, as well as by developments in U.S. refugee policies, which meant that refugees could become eligible for permanent residence after living in the United States for two years. Asians have also entered the U.S. in significant numbers as students—many have subsequently converted to permanent residence status, mainly under the occupational preference categories of the immigration acts, which allow entry to professionals and other highly qualified immigrants.

Other significant immigration policy developments have included the merging of the hemispherical quotas into one annual worldwide limit on immigration and the introduction of new quotas of twenty thousand visas to every country. Finally, in 1990, "diversity visas" were created that were intended to increase immigration from countries that were traditionally main sources of emigration to the U.S. but had been adversely affected by the 1965 Act, including some European countries. These developments have not had a major impact on the overall distribution of the foreign-born in the U.S. population, which had been established largely by the 1965 act. However, the continuing emphasis in immigration policy on family reunification has meant that existing communities have continued to expand as family members have joined the original immigrants. Moreover, the numbers of foreign born from Latin America, especially Mexico, was boosted in 1989 when the Legalization Program of the Immigration Reform and Control Act of 1986 created an amnesty for thousands of undocumented migrants already residing in the U.S., allowing them to become legal residents.

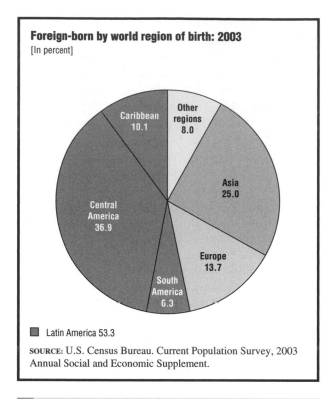

Foreign-born by world region of birth: 2003
[In percent]

Other regions 8.0
Caribbean 10.1
Asia 25.0
Central America 36.9
Europe 13.7
South America 6.3

■ Latin America 53.3

SOURCE: U.S. Census Bureau. Current Population Survey, 2003 Annual Social and Economic Supplement.

PRIMARY SOURCE

Reflecting the large flow of immigration from Mexico and Central America, in 2003 the majority of all foreign born people living in the United States were originally from Latin America. ADAPTED BY THOMSON GALE FROM DATA FROM THE U.S. BUREAU OF THE CENSUS.

PRIMARY SOURCE

U.S. FOREIGN BORN BY WORLD REGION OF BIRTH
See primary source image.

SIGNIFICANCE

Recent patterns of immigration to the U.S. have resulted in the creation of a large foreign-born population that is ethnically and culturally quite different from traditional immigrants to the United States. In the past, these were mainly European nationals who were relatively easily assimilated into American society.

In contrast, recent immigrants have tended to be more ethnically distinct from the native-born population and many have wanted to emphasize their own ethnic and cultural identities. Moreover, although some immigrants are highly skilled and well-educated, the majority of recent entrants have been low-skilled immigrants from poor countries, who have come on family reunification visas. This has had an impact on

the overall socio-economic distribution of the U.S. population and significant policy implications in a wide range of areas including education, employment, and welfare.

The ethnic diversity of the foreign-born enriches the cosmopolitan nature of U.S. society, but also means that the foreign-born are a more visible group, easily targeted by those opposed to increased immigration, and this creates potential for social and political unrest. In 2005–2006, there were heightened concerns about rapidly increasing levels of both legal and illegal immigration, particularly from Mexico and other Latin American countries. This resulted in clashes of pro-immigration and anti-immigration campaigners in demonstrations across the country.

FURTHER RESOURCES

Books

Segal, Uma A. *A Framework for Immigration: Asians in the United States.* New York: Columbia University Press, 2002.

Tichenor, Daniel, J. *Dividing Lines: The Politics of Immigration Control in America.* Princeton, N.J.: Princeton University Press, 2002.

Yang, Philip Q. *Post–1965 Immigration to the United States: Structural Determinants.* Westport, Conn.: Praeger, 1995.

Periodicals

Hochschild, Jennifer, L. "Looking Ahead: Racial Trends in the United States." *Daedalus* 134 (2005).

Civic Integration

Citizenship after 9/11

Speech

By: Eduardo Aguirre

Date: November 23, 2003

Source: Aguirre, Eduardo. "Civic Integration: Citizenship After 9/11." *United States Citizenship and Immigration Service.* November 13, 2003. <http://uscis. gov/graphics/aboutus/congress/testimonies/2003/ EA111303.pdf> (accessed June 7, 2006).

About the Author: Eduardo Aguirre is director of the United States Citizenship and Immigration Service, the federal agency overseeing the immigration and naturalization process.

INTRODUCTION

With the exception of a small number of Native Americans, the United States is populated entirely by immigrants and their descendents. Immigration to the United States has risen and fallen throughout the nation's history, propelled upward and downward by geopolitical and economic forces around the world. Immigration grew steadily throughout the 1800s, peaking with an influx of one million per year at the beginning of the twentieth century. The rate of immigration then fell sharply in the years leading up to World War I and remained relatively low throughout World War II. Immigration then began a steady climb that continued through the end of the twentieth century.

Dictated by public opinion and political whim, U.S. law has played a pivotal role in setting immigration patterns. Following World War I, Americans became less welcoming to immigrants from eastern and southern Europe. Congress responded by passing the Quota Act of 1921, and in 1924 President Calvin Coolidge signed an even more restrictive immigration bill into law. This act specified the maximum number of new citizens who would be accepted from each of a lengthy list of foreign countries. For each nation, the number of immigrants each year could not exceed two percent of the current number of immigrants from that nation already residing in the United States.

Under this policy, immigration was tightly capped at a specified level. Total immigration to the United States was initially set at only 165,000, less than one-fifth the pre-war level. Within that total, the quotas for individual countries varied widely. For example, in 1924, Great Britain was allowed 34,000 immigrants, while India was allowed only the minimum of 100. Italy, a country particularly impacted by the new law, found its prewar immigration levels of 200,000 slashed to just 4,000. Under the new policy, the ethnic makeup of the United States would remain largely unchanged.

A primary concern of U.S. immigration policy is the assurance of U.S. national security. Following the terrorist attacks of September 11, 2001, Americans began to reconsider the potential threat posed by immigrants. As the investigation of the attacks continued, several of the terrorists were found to have been living in the United States illegally, highlighting the relationship between immigration policy and national security. In the flurry of legislative activity following the attacks, the new Department of Homeland Security was created. As part of that action, the existing

U.S. Citizenship and Immigration Services employees and Servicemen watch a recorded message from President Bush. AP IMAGES.

Department of Immigration and Naturalization was transferred to the new department and renamed the Citizenship and Immigration Service.

In the wake of revelations that the 2001 terrorist attacks were financed, planned, and carried out by Islamic extremists of Middle Eastern descent, some of whom had been in the United States for many years, American policy-makers began wrestling with this newly recognized threat.

■ PRIMARY SOURCE

Good afternoon. Thank you, Bob, for that warm introduction. I am pleased to be here and speak to one of America's greatest privileges, Citizenship.

More specifically, I am here to talk about how Citizenship has changed since 9/11, and what USCIS is doing to refresh this American value.

An obvious place to start is by asking, what is Citizenship? Citizenship is, by definition, a condition of allegiance to, and participation in, a governmental jurisdiction. It means, for a collective order, a pledge of loyalty, commitment to actively participate in civics and community, and willingness to serve when and where called upon.

But, that is academic. The practical is—we each have a unique opinion of what it means to be a citizen in the greatest country in the world. And, where else but America could there be such freedom to differ on the one thing that we have in common.

America was built upon the principles of freedom, democracy and certain unalienable rights. The dreams and determination of immigrants, in whose footsteps I followed, enriched this land—socially, culturally and economically.

And, that record of contribution continues as we speak, immigrant soldiers are fighting for freedom to triumph over terror. Their willingness to give the ultimate sacrifice echoes the words, as engraved on the Statue of Liberty:

> "Give me your tired, your poor, your huddled masses yearning to breathe free, The wretched refuse of your teeming shore, Send these, the homeless, tempest-tossed, to me: I lift my lamp beside the golden door."

Make no mistake; we are today, as much a nation of immigrants as we have ever been. America's founding fathers knew this would be. George Washington, in his farewell address, noted "Citizens by birth or choice of a common country, that country has a right to concentrate your affections."

Washington's observations hold true. Citizenship begins within the individual but is nurtured by the country.

That is my task before you. The fateful day of September 11, 2001, emboldened our nation and united us through patriotism.

We each remember, with vivid clarity and overwhelming emotion, where we were and what we saw. We continue to try and make sense out of incomprehensible acts. And, we each, in our own way, say never again.

The Nation's resolve led to the creation of the new Department of Homeland Security, the dissolution of the Immigration and Naturalization Service, a fundamental transformation in the delivery of immigration services and an uncompromising commitment to the integrity of our immigration system. It also reinvigorated Citizenship, and its sinews have never been stronger.

The Administration and Congress called for, within the Homeland Security Act of 2002, the creation of an Office of Citizenship. This pioneering office is charged with promoting public awareness of the rights and responsibilities of this treasured value.

To put our ambitious agenda in context—by a show of hands, how many of you can trace your immigrant roots? In the private sector, I would call this redundant market research. Because, we all have an immigrant lineage of one form or another. That gives you insight into the size of our customer base everyone, citizen and non-citizen alike.

Now, some easier questions; not to show your hands, but ponder how many of you have a driver's license? How many of you got your license at the earliest possible age? Or, for the parents among us, how many of you recall the experience of your children earning a license?

In our country a license is a rite of passage, because to drive constitutes freedom to go, within reason, where you want, when you want. It also is an indisputable privilege, and one that is too often taken for granted.

Like a license, you have to earn Citizenship—a very different rite of passage—though the reward is beyond compare. And, like driver's education, the responsibilities that accompany the privilege of Citizenship do not culminate with a passing score and certificate. Rather, they multiply in number and scope.

The Office of Citizenship, within U.S. Citizenship and Immigration Services, is—loosely speaking—like a driving instruction program—coaching this rite of passage, for a nation-wide rediscovery of American Citizenship.

We are trying to take the concept of assimilation a step further, to what I call to Civic Integration. The difference between the two—is choice . . . more specifically, choice of allegiance.

America is as diverse as it is large. Today, a common denominator of our citizenry in a post-9/11 world is allegiance. Quite simply, we are one nation, indivisible, with liberty and justice for all.

Assimilation implies that government defines for the immigrant what it means to be American. We can, and should . . . do everything, but . . .

Defining what it means to be American is as much an individual right as our freedom to practice the faith, the politics and profession of one's choosing.

Government educates, facilitates and empowers potential new citizens to realize their respective American dreams. In the end, however, the decision to forge a personal and patriotic allegiance is up to the individual.

I want newly naturalized citizens to pick up the torch of American Citizenship and carry it for their children's generation. That is Civic Integration.

The Office of Citizenship will stress accountability and equip to that end. I am particularly pleased with our Immigrant Orientation Program, a pilot to provide legal immigrants with informational packets upon their initial arrival.

These packets will educate and inform on the expectations for Civic Integration as well as more clearly define the naturalization process.

At the grass-roots level, we will partner with groups like USA Freedom Corps to match new immigrants with community volunteers. And, we will soon have 30 Outreach Officers stationed in 17 strategic cities throughout the country, to carry out the President's charge that America continue to be "a nation that welcomes immigrants with open arms, not endless lines."

Any teacher will tell you that a proven barometer of knowledge is a test. So, we are looking at how we test potential new citizens.

We have convened a select and distinguished committee of university professors to identify the questions that best capture America and recommend as to how these questions should be framed. They began with English, and a corresponding study guide, and will turn next to Civics and History.

I cannot emphasize enough the significance of this undertaking. The current naturalization test is somewhat arbitrary. A candidate in San Francisco will, in all likelihood, not be asked the same questions as a candidate taking same exam on the same day in Boston. Inherently, this is now wrong; however, I think that we can do better!

In the current structure, an examiner will randomly select from a compilation of questions. This forces a candidate to memorize some 100 responses, instead of learning, grasping and retaining the answers to a strategic series of questions.

It comes down to meaning and substance. To compliment, we are making the naturalization ceremony more uniformly meaningful.

Because of the freedoms and economic opportunities that only America can provide, applications for naturalization have remained strong since 9/11. Last year, we welcomed more than 640,000 newly naturalized citizens to the American family.

Somewhere in America, right now, there is an administrative naturalization ceremony under way. Tomorrow, in Seattle, more than 100 service men and women, returning from Operation Iraqi Freedom, will take advantage of the President's Executive Order to expedite military naturalizations for those immigrant soldiers who bravely serve in the war against terror.

And, next week, I will join adoptive families in welcoming children in Miami to the table of America Citizenship.

Of course, the Oath of Allegiance is the most patriotic component to any naturalization ceremony.

And, having had the unique privilege of reciting the Oath as an immigrant, and now administering it as Director, I want to see it become even more so.

The Oath should not be altered in substance and solemnity, but it should be more crisp, fervent and meaningful—in keeping with the times. Renouncing and abjuring allegiances and fidelity to princes and potentates is confusing.

When a candidate raises his or her right hand to take this pledge, there is no guarantee that a new citizen will be a good citizen. However, we take an even bigger risk by using archaic language and convoluted grammar.

By choosing to become a Citizen, immigrants enter into a covenant with the Untied States. This covenant reserves the call to serve and bear arms, and demands loyalty to the Constitution and our laws.

One of the reasons the Department of Homeland Security was created is to prevent the wrong applicant from receiving an immigration benefit. Our comprehensive background checks, and effective risk management, sorts out the bad apples. Our initiatives for dramatically refreshing the citizenship process, including the Oath, will cultivate the good ones, and in so doing, we aim to sponsor new American patriots.

About a month ago, I was on CNN Moneyline with Lou Dobbs. The segment was billed by CNN as "The Great American Give Away." My message was that we give nothing away! In fact, we add value by making America more secure, preserving America's legacy of immigration, and celebrating America's ultimate privilege—Citizenship.

. . .

I remind you of what President Theodore Roosevelt, once noted, "The first requisite of a good citizen in this republic of ours is that he shall be able and willing to pull his weight."

My fellow citizens, one of the ways in which we are pulling our weight is by debating an issue as important as American Citizenship.

Thank you, and may God continue to bless America.

SIGNIFICANCE

While some Americans demanded an end to immigration from the Middle East, U.S. immigration policy has traditionally been resistant to such pressure. During the 1990s, a decade when the United States and Iraq were openly hostile and occasionally at war, 68,000 Iraqis were granted U.S. residency. As of 2006, even nations officially identified as sponsoring terrorism had not been barred from sending immigrants to the United States.

The question of how to deal with Muslim immigrants is not unique to the United States. European nations including France have wrestled with the proper response to growing Muslim populations within their borders. Unlike many previous immigrant groups, Muslims appear more likely to segregate themselves and less likely to assimilate into their new cultures. In many countries they have attempted to establish their own communities governed primarily by Islamic law and tradition, and as their birth rates far outstrip those of their host countries their influence is expected to grow. The fact that Islamic terrorists have in several cases been assisted by Muslim populations within their host countries raises further questions about appropriate policies toward them.

Present U.S. immigration policy limits the number of non-citizens who may become permanent U.S. residents and receive a document known as a Green Card. Applicants are considered based on their circumstances. Immediate family members of U.S. citizens, including spouses, minor children, and parents of adult citizens are admitted without quotas. Other family members, including married children of citizens and family members of Green Card holders are allowed to receive residency, but the total number is limited to 226,000 per year. As of 2006, no single country is allowed to send more than 25,620 immigrants, regardless of the country's population. Children born in the United States are automatically granted citizenship, a quirk of immigration law that has led to the practice of non-citizens entering the United States to deliver children, thus ensuring them

citizenship. In 2002, more than 600,000 foreign nationals became naturalized U.S. citizens.

FURTHER RESOURCES

Books

Freedman, Russell. *Immigrant Kids*. New York: Puffin, 1995.

Jacobson, Matthew Frye. *Whiteness of a Different Color: European Immigrants and the Alchemy of Race*. Cambridge, Mass.: Harvard University Press, 1999.

Portes, Alejandro, and Ruben G. Rumbaut. *Immigrant America: A Portrait*. Second Edition, Revised, Expanded, and Updated. Los Angeles: University of California Press, 1997.

Periodicals

Karaim, Reed. "Getting Real on the Border." *U.S. News & World Report* 140 (2006): 28.

Kelleher, C. C., et al. "The 'Americanisation' of Migrants: Evidence for the Contribution of Ethnicity, Social Deprivation, Lifestyle and Life-Course Processes to the mid–20th Century Coronary Heart Disease Epidemic in the U.S." *Social Science & Medicine* 63 (2006)485–500.

"Talking of Immigrants." *The Economist* 379 (2006): 50.

Web sites

The American Immigration Law Foundation. "Immigration Policy Center." <http://www.ailf.org/ipc/ipc_index.asp> (accessed June 7, 2006).

University of Missouri. Department of Sociology. "A Historical Look at U.S. Immigration Policy." <http://web. missouri. edu/~socbrent/immigr.htm> (accessed June 7, 2006).

The White House. "President Bush Proposes New Temporary Worker Program." January 2004. <http://www. whitehouse. gov / news / releases/2004/01/20040107-3.html> (accessed June 7, 2006).

Bishops' Conference Chairmen Support Farm Worker Proposal

Letter

By: Theodore Cardinal McCarrick and Thomas G. Wenski of the U.S. Conference of Catholic Bishops

Date: November 7, 2003

Source: *United States Conference of Catholic Bishops* "Bishops' Conference Chairmen Support Farm Worker Proposal." November 7, 2003. <http://216. 239.51.104/

search?q=cache:blvMSMjutmkJ:www.nccbuscc. org/ comm/archives/> (accessed July 15, 2006).

About the Author: The U.S. Conference of Catholic Bishops is an assembly of the Catholic Church hierarchy who work together to unify, coordinate, promote, and carry on Catholic activities in the United States; to organize and conduct religious, charitable, and social welfare work at home and abroad; to aid in education; and to care for immigrants. The bishops themselves constitute the membership of the Conference and are served by a staff of more than 350 lay people, priests, and deacons.

INTRODUCTION

The Agricultural Job Opportunities, Benefits, and Security Act (AgJobs) was an attempt to improve border security and provide workers for agricultural employers. While farmers need great numbers of temporary workers at harvest, there is a need for the Untied States to guarantee that terrorists are not arriving with the farm workers. In 2003, legislation was introduced to establish a guest worker program that would offer protections to farm workers while ensuring border security.

Policymakers have long recognized that many agricultural employers require temporary workers to help plant and harvest their crops in season. The Bracero program that began during World War II allowed the entry of between four and five million temporary foreign agricultural workers, principally from Mexico, to fill the farm labor shortage. Since the termination of the Bracero program in 1964, some farmers have relied on illegal aliens to harvest produce each season. It has been estimated that fifty to

Roman Catholic Archbishop Theodore E. McCarrick of Newark is appointed spiritual leader of the Washington Archdiocese by Pope John Paul II in Washington, November 21, 2000. © REUTERS/CORBIS.

seventy-five percent of farm workers are undocumented. As internal enforcement of immigration has increased, farms are struggling to find legal workers.

Because of the use of illegal workers to fill essential roles, lawmakers have been faced with the issue of how to balance the labor needs of the agriculture against the interest of the nation in controlling the border and upholding the law. The issue has been complicated by agribusinesses that have exploited the unskilled laborers, recognizing that their illegal status makes them vulnerable. Many undocumented workers cannot speak English and are unaware of even their most basic rights under U.S. labor laws. Because they are in the country illegally, they fear taking action against exploitative labor practices.

In the face of these problems, Congress has sought ways to control illegal immigration yet provide an agricultural workforce. The policy options fall into two categories: law enforcement and a tightly regulated influx of foreign farm labor. An enforcement-only policy will not work because the United States has 7,458 miles of land border and 88,600 miles of tidal shoreline. AgJobs proposes to let about 500,000 undocumented agricultural workers who have performed 100 hours of agricultural work in eighteen months to become legal residents. Most of the farm workers in the United States are Mexican nationals who are Catholic. The U.S. Conference of Catholic Bishops, an organization that has immigrant protection as part of its mandate, has taken a range of actions to support Catholic immigrants. In 2003, the Conference voiced support for AgJobs.

PRIMARY SOURCE

November 7, 2003

Dear Senator/Representative:

We write on behalf of the U.S. Conference of Catholic Bishops in general support of the Agricultural Job Opportunity, Benefits, and Security Act of 2003 (S. 1645, HR 3142). As introduced, the bipartisan measure would provide a path to permanent residency and citizenship for a number of undocumented farm workers. It also would make changes to the current H-2A nonimmigrant agricultural worker program. While we understand that there may be individual provisions within the bill that some may disagree with, we believe that it is a delicately balanced bill which deserves your support.

As you may know, the U.S. Catholic bishops have long advocated for the rights of farm workers, both workers residing in the United States and migrant workers from Mexico and other nations who toil in our agricultural fields.

Farm workers perform one of the most dangerous jobs in our nation, working long hours in difficult conditions. At the same time, by picking vegetables, fruits, and other crops all across our nation, their labor is among the most important to the welfare of the people of our nation.

Farm workers, especially those who are undocumented, are among the most vulnerable of workers in the United States. This is so, in part, because many of our nation's labor laws do not apply to their employment. Moreover, enforcement of their rights is often inadequate or non-existent. Undocumented migrant workers, who make up a significant percentage of the farm worker labor force, are even more susceptible to abuse and exploitation because of their irregular status.

For decades we have encouraged workable alternatives to the unjust status quo, which hurts both workers and employers and diminishes us as a nation. We are pleased that representatives of farm workers and agricultural employers have found common ground in this legislation.

As introduced, S. 1645 and HR 3142 represent, on balance, a positive improvement upon the current deplorable situation of migrant farm workers, many of whom are unable to organize or bargain with their employers. It is our view that the earned adjustment provisions, a central feature of the legislation, will enable many undocumented workers to "come out of the shadows" and assert their basic rights in the work place, creating an environment in the future which will benefit both foreign and U.S. farm workers.

Enactment of this legislation should not end Congress' obligation to take steps to improve the plight of farm workers in the United States. We note that S. 1645 and HR 3142 would freeze adverse effect wage levels for three years and relieve employers of the obligation to provide housing to workers, instead giving them the option, under certain circumstances, of providing a housing allowance to workers. It also would streamline the process for recruiting U.S. agricultural workers and for gaining government approval to hire foreign agricultural workers when shortages occur.

We urge Congress to examine these and other important areas more thoroughly in the near future to ensure that farm workers and their families are better able to support themselves in dignity. For example, we support increases in funding for low-income housing targeted at migrant workers so that decent and affordable housing is available in areas in which farm workers live and work. We also urge, consistent with provisions in the legislation, a reexamination of wage rate levels in the H-2A program so as to ensure that H-2A farm workers and their families receive a living wage and that U.S. workers are not adversely impacted by wage rates in the program.

In addition, we urge the appropriation of additional resources to enforce the U.S. worker recruitment requirements and worker protections in the program. Because of the many abuses which have occurred in past U.S. temporary worker programs, such as the Bracero program, the Catholic bishops' conference has been deeply skeptical of these programs. Appropriate enforcement of worker protections is essential to guarantee that future abuses in the H-2A program do not occur.

We welcome the efforts of those who negotiated this proposed legislation and we understand that many difficult choices had to be made in order to carefully construct this agreement between employers and workers. This legislation represents an important first step in ensuring that migrant farm workers fully enjoy the benefits of their labor in the future, eventually as legal permanent residents, and, if they so choose, U.S. citizens. We also believe enactment of this legislation would help in reexamining our nation's immigration laws and extending protection of the law to all undocumented workers in our midst.

We urge the swift enactment of this important measure as introduced. Substantial changes in the legislation that would adversely impact farm workers would require us to reevaluate our support.

As pastors, we are convinced that it is imperative to support this legislation as introduced. To take no action at this time could assign hundreds of thousands of farm workers in this nation to a permanent underclass, with no basic rights and no ability to live in dignity.

Sincerely,

His Eminence Theodore Cardinal McCarrick
Archbishop of Washington
Chairman, Domestic Policy Committee

Coadjutor Bishop of Orlando
Most Reverend Thomas G. Wenski
Chairman, Committee on Migration

SIGNIFICANCE

A number of immigration reform bills have been proposed to halt illegal immigration and the threat that such immigration poses to national security. Most of these bills do not include a guest worker program. AgJobs considers the unique needs of American agriculture while improving the quality of life for farm workers. It has gotten support from both the American Farm Bureau Federation and advocates for undocumented workers. It has not passed Congress as of mid–2006.

Despite bipartisan support in Congress, AgJobs appears unlikely to be approved by Congress. Some opponents of the bill argue that AgJobs would enable undocumented workers to jump ahead of the line of people who are seeking visas legally. Other opponents contend that it would provide a captive work force for agricultural interests. Granting amnesty to cater to a specific industry is also seen as making a mockery of efforts to halt illegal immigration.

FURTHER RESOURCES
Books

Acuna, Rodolfo. *Occupied America: A History of Chicanos*. New York: Pearson Longman, 2004.

Daniels, Roger. *Coming to America: A History of Immigration and Ethnicity in American Life*. New York: Harper Perennial, 2002.

Mitchell, Don. *The Lie of the Land: Migrant Workers and the California Landscape*. Minneapolis: University of Minnesota Press, 1996.

Ngai, Mae M. *Impossible Subjects: Illegal Aliens and the Making of Modern America*. Princeton, N.J.: Princeton University Press, 2005.

Top Ten Immigration Myths and Facts

Pamphlet

By: National Immigration Forum

Date: June 2003

Source: "Top Ten Immigration Myths and Facts." National Immigration Forum, 2003.

About the Author: The National Immigration Forum was established in 1982 with the mission of building public support in the United States for policies that welcome immigrants and refugees. It works closely with immigration support groups, advocacy organizations, and service providers across the United States and has been influential in helping to shape U.S. immigration policies.

INTRODUCTION

The National Immigration Forum (NIF) is an interest group that lobbies in support of pro-immigration policies. It regularly publishes pamphlets that provide information on the benefits of immigration to the United States, to encourage public support for its cause.

The National Immigration Forum was founded by Rick Swartz, a civil rights attorney and head of the Lawyers' Committee for Civil Rights Under Law. It was established in order to oppose proposed new immigration laws that included employer sanctions for hiring undocumented workers, and to lobby against the anti-immigration lobby led by the Federation for American Immigration Reform (FAIR). Funded from 1983 largely by the Ford Foundation, the National Immigration Forum created a powerful coalition of both right-wing and left-wing organizations who were against restrictive immigration reform. These included the business community, who were concerned about the impact on employers of restricting the availability of migrant labor, immigrant and ethnic community groups, the Catholic Church, and other church organizations that opposed the legislation on human rights grounds and in the interests of their own members.

The Forum lobbied successfully throughout the 1980s and 1990s in preventing the introduction of laws that would have reduced legal immigration to the United States. It played a key role in eliciting support for the provisions of the 1986 Immigration Reform and Control Act (IRCA), which provided amnesty for several million undocumented immigrants, and in watering down the employer sanctions so that they were difficult to enforce. As a result of its efforts, it has been reported, the Immigration Act of 1990, originally intended to control immigration, ultimately had the effect of increasing levels of legal immigration to the United States by around forty percent. The Forum has also been attributed with achieving the removal of all proposed controls on legal immigration from the 1996 Illegal Immigrant Reform and Immigrant Responsibility Act (IIRIRA).

Both the anti-immigration lobby and the pro-immigration lobby have increasingly drawn on the work of economists and researchers to provide data and information to support their respective policy perspectives. FAIR helped to establish the Center for Immigration Studies (CIS) in 1985, a think tank generating studies in support of restricting immigration, while the NIF has worked closely with the CATO institute, a research organization that shares its pro-immigration stance. The publications that have been produced in support of each perspective have been increasingly targeted at undermining the opposing evidence. For example, in 1995 the National Immigration Forum and the CATO Institute jointly produced a report entitled "Immigration: The Demographic and Economic Facts," which highlighted the positive economic benefits of immigration. The Federation for American Immigration Reform quickly responded with publications that opposed the NIF report's findings, and highlighted the costs to U.S. citizens of immigration, particularly undocumented (illegal) immigration.

PRIMARY SOURCE

Top 10 Immigration Myths and Facts
(See next page.)

Prepared by the National Immigration Forum, June 2003

SIGNIFICANCE

The National Immigration Forum's 2003 pamphlet provides useful information and data that can help to inform the immigration debate. However, it should be regarded as a partial rather than a comprehensive overview of the costs and benefits of immigration because the topics, wording, and statistics have been carefully chosen with the specific objective of advancing the pro-immigration argument. Similarly, publications produced by the anti-immigration lobby should be considered in the same light.

The "Myths and Benefits" pamphlet focuses on the general characteristics of immigrants and the contributions they make to the U.S. economy. However, much less is known about the costs and benefits of undocumented migration, and it is this aspect of immigration that has become of particular public concern and led to proposals for immigration reform in the mid 2000s. On the other hand, the publication list of the Federation for American Immigration Reform is heavily focused on the problems of illegal migration. Less attention has been given in the studies of the anti-immigration lobby to investigating the positive impacts that immigrants have had on the American economy and society.

American immigration reform has been heavily influenced over the past few decades by the lobbying of pressure groups, particularly the pro-immigration lobby, which includes many influential business leaders. However, as levels of undocumented migration to the United States continue to rise, and the issue receives a high level of media attention, the anti-immigration lobby is gaining public support. In this context, it may become increasingly difficult for the National Immigration Forum to influence the outcome of future legislation so that levels of immigration to the United States are not further restricted.

Myth	Fact	Source
1. Immigrants don't pay taxes	All immigrants pay taxes, whether income, property, sales, or other. As far as income tax payments go, sources vary in their accounts, but a range of studies find that immigrants pay between $90 and $140 billion a year in federal, state, and local taxes. Even undocumented immigrants pay income taxes, as evidenced by the Social Security Administration's "suspense file" (taxes that cannot be matched to worker's names and social security numbers), which grew $20 billion between 1990 and 1998.	National Academy of Sciences, Cato Institute, Urban Institute, Social Security Administration
2. Immigrants come here to take welfare	Immigrants come to work and reunite with family members. Immigrant labor force participation is consistently higher than native-born, and immigrant workers make up a larger share of the U.S. labor force (12.4%) than they do the U.S. population (11.5%). Moreover, the ratio between immigrant use of public benefits and the amount of taxes they pay is consistently favorable to the U.S., unless the "study" was undertaken by an anti-immigrant group. In one estimate, immigrants earn about $240 billion a year, pay about $90 billion a year in taxes, and use about $5 billion in public benefits. In another cut of the data, immigrant tax payments total $20 to $30 billion more than the amount of government services they use.	American Immigration Lawyers Association, Urban Institute
3. Immigrants send all their money back to their home countries	In addition to the consumer spending of immigrant households, immigrants and their businesses contribute $162 billion in tax revenue to U.S. federal, sate, and local governments. While it is true that immigrants remit billions of dollars a year to their home countries, this is one of the most targeted and effective forms of direct foreign investment.	Cato Institute, Inter-American Development Bank
4. Immigrants take jobs and opportunity away from Americans	The largest wave of immigration to the U.S. since the early 1900s coincided with our lowest national unemployment rate and fastest economic growth. Immigrant entrepreneurs create jobs for U.S. and foreign workers, and foreign-born students allow many U.S. graduate programs to keep their doors open. While there has been no comprehensive study done of immigrant-owned businesses, we have countless examples: in Silicon Valley, companies begun by Chinese and Indian immigrants generated more than $19.5 billion in sales and nearly 73,000 jobs in 2000.	Brookings Institution
5. Immigrants are a drain on the U.S. economy	During the 1990s half of all new workers were foreign-born, filling gaps left by native-born workers in both the high-and low-skill ends of the spectrum. Immigrants fill jobs in key sectors, start their own businesses, and contribute to a thriving economy. The net benefit of immigration to the U.S. is nearly $10 billion annually. As Alan Greenspan points out, 70% of immigrants arrive in prime working age. That means we haven't spent a penny on their education, yet they are transplanted into our workforce and will contribute $500 billion toward our social security system over the next 20 years.	National Academy of Sciences, Center for Labor Market Studies at Northeastern University, Federal Reserve

6. Immigrants don't want to learn English or become Americans	Within ten years of arrival, more than 75% of immigrants speak English well; moreover, demand for English classes at the adult level far exceeds supply. Greater than 33% of immigrants are naturalized citizens; given increased immigration in the 1990s, this figure will rise as more legal permanent residents become eligible for naturalization in the coming years. The number of immigrants naturalizing spiked sharply after two events: enactment of immigration and welfare reform laws in 1996, and the terrorist attacks in 2001.	U.S. Census Bureau, U.S. Department of Homeland Security (Bureau of Citizenship and Immigration Services)
7. Today's immigrants are different than those of 100 years ago	The percentage of the U.S. population that is foreign-born now stands at 11.5%; in the early 20th century it was approximately 15%. Similar to accusations about today's immigrants, those of 100 years ago initially often settled in mono-ethnic neighborhoods, spoke their native languages, and built up newspapers and businesses that catered to their fellow émigrés. They also experienced the same types of discrimination that today's immigrants face, and integrated within American culture at a similar rate. If we view history objectively, we remember that every new wave of immigrants has been met with suspicion and doubt and yet, ultimately, every past wave of immigrants has been vindicated and saluted.	U.S. Census Bureau
8. Most immigrants cross the border illegally	Around 75% have legal permanent (immigrant) visas; of the 25% that are undocumented, 40% overstayed temporary (non-immigrant) visas.	INS Statistical Yearbook
9. Weak U.S. border enforcement has lead to high undocumented immigration	From 1986 to 1998, the border Patrol's budget increased six-fold and the number of agents stationed on our southwest border doubled to 8,500. The border Patrol also toughened its enforcement strategy, heavily fortifying typical urban entry points and pushing migrants into dangerous desert areas, in hopes of deterring crossings. Instead, the undocumented immigrant population doubled in that timeframe, to 8 million—despite the legalization of nearly 3 million immigrants after the enactment of the Immigration Reform and Control Act in 1986. Insufficient legal avenues for immigrants to enter the U.S., compared with the number of jobs available to them, have created this current conundrum.	Cato Institute
10. The war on terrorism can be won through immigration restrictions	No security expert since September 11th, 2001 has said that restrictive immigration measures would have prevented the terrorist attacks—instead, the key is good use of good intelligence. Most of the 9/11 hijackers were here on legal visas. Since 9/11, the myriad of measures targeting immigrants in the name of national security have netted no terrorism prosecutions. In fact, several of these measures could have the opposite effect and actually make us less safe, as targeted communities of immigrants are afraid to come forward with information.	Newspaper articles, various security experts, and think tanks

FURTHER RESOURCES

Books

Graham, Hugh Davis. *Collision Course: The Strange Convergence of Affirmative Action and Immigration Policy in America*. New York: Oxford University Press, 2003.

Laham, Nicholas. *Ronald Reagan and the Politics of Immigration Reform*. Westport, CT: Praeger Publishers, 2000.

Lee, Kenneth K. *Huddled Masses, Muddled Laws: Why Contemporary Immigration Policy Fails to Reflect Public Opinion*. Westport, CT: Praeger Publishers, 1998.

Reimers, David M. *Unwelcome Strangers: American Identity and the Turn against Immigration.* New York: Columbia University Press, 1998.

Web sites

Federation for American Immigration Reform. "Federation for American Immigration Reform." <http://www. fairus. org/> (accessed June 16, 2006).

National Immigration Forum. "National Immigration Forum." <http://www.immigrationforum.org/> (accessed June 16, 2006).

What Immigrants and Refugees Need to Know about the New Tennessee Driver's License and "Certificate for Driving" Law

Document

By: Tennessee Immigrant and Refugee Rights Coalition

Date: June 28, 2004

Source: Tennessee Immigrant and Refugee Rights Coalition

About the Author: The Tennessee Immigrant and Refugee Rights Coalition is a statewide, immigrant and refugee-led collaboration whose mission is to empower immigrants and refugees to develop a unified voice, defend their rights, and create an atmosphere in which they are viewed as positive contributors to the state.

INTRODUCTION

The state of Tennessee began awarding full driver's license to illegal immigrants in early 2001 without requiring a social security number. More than 180,000 people obtained licenses before the September 11, 2001, terrorist attacks prompted national security fears about proof of identity. In July 2004, Tennessee Governor Phil Bredesen launched an initiative to grant driver's certificates to the state's immigrants rather than driver's licenses as both national security and road safety measures. The governor wanted to ensure that immigrants were familiar with traffic rules.

Tennessee became the first state to issue certificates, although Utah soon followed. Both undocumented and legal immigrants were eligible for the certificates. During the two year's of the programs existence, Tennessee issued 52,000 certificates. To

∧ sample State of Tennessee certificate for driving. AP IMAGES.

obtain certificates, applicants were required to provide two documents that showed they lived in Tennessee, such as a utility bill or a lease. They also had to provide a Social Security number or a sworn affidavit if they did not have a Social Security number. They were required to pass a vision test, a driving rules test, and a road test.

PRIMARY SOURCE

On May 29, 2004, Tennessee enacted a new law that changed the eligibility requirements for immigrant and refugee applicants for driver's licenses. On July 1, the Department of Safety will begin issuing the new "Certificate for Driving" to certain immigrants who will be ineligible for a regular driver's license under the new law. The purpose of this document is to clarify the new eligibility requirements and inform immigrants and refugees of their rights vis-à-vis the Department of Safety and law enforcement. The enclosed complaint form will help

TIRRC document instances of misapplication of the law and assist individuals who have been unfairly denied a driver's license or driving certificate, or who believe that their rights have been violated as a result of possessing a driving certificate. The contents of this document are as follows: . . .

1. What are the new requirements for immigrant and refugee applicants for driver's licenses/driving certificates?

Legal permanent residents (green card holders), refugees and asylees will continue to have access to a regular five-year driver's license. However, they will now be required to provide documentation of their status in addition to their social security card. In addition to proof of identity and proof of Tennessee residence, you will need to show one of the following documents:

INS I-55I Permanent Resident Alien Card

Foreign passport stamped by the U.S. Government indicating that the holder has been "Processed for I-55I"

Permanent resident Re-entry Permit (1-327)

Temporary I-55I stamp on Form 1-94, Arrival/Departure Record, with photograph of the applicant

U.S. Department of Receptions and Placement Program Assurance Form (Refugee) and I-94 stamped refugee

Form I-94 Record of Arrival and Departure stamped Asylee, Parolee or Parole, refugee, asylum, HP (humanitarian parolee) or PIP (public interest parolee)

Undocumented immigrants and nonimmigrants (temporary workers/students/visitors) will—as of July 1, 2004—no longer be able to obtain a regular driver's license. They can apply for a driving certificate—which will not be valid for identification—if they present two documents that prove their identity and two documents that prove they live in Tennessee. . . .

Please note that if an individual from one of these two categories (undocumented immigrant of visa holder) currently has a license, they can continue to use the license until it expires. Upon renewal, this individual will only have access to a driving certificate. For undocumented immigrants the driving certificate will be valid for one year. For nonimmigrants, the driving certificate will be valid until the expiration date of your visa, unless your visa is valid for less than one year, in which case the certificate will be valid for one year.

2. Will auto insurance companies accept the certificate for driving in lieu of a regular driver's license?

Although several insurance companies have indicated that they may insure drivers with driving certificates, none of them have made public statements to this effect. We expect this question will be answered after the first certificates are issued.

3. Will law enforcement accept the driving certificate as identification if I am stopped for a traffic violation?

According to the law, the driving certificate may be used for driving purposes only, and will not be valid for identification. It is still unclear whether or not the driving certificate will be accepted as ID by law enforcement for traffic violations. While some departments such as the Nashville Police Department and the Tennessee Highway Patrol have stated that they will accept the certificates as ID in these cases, other departments have not clarified their positions. In a situation where law enforcement does not accept the certificate as ID it could result in the arrest of those driving certificate holders who are stopped for a traffic violation if they do not have another valid form of ID. Until this issue with law enforcement is resolved, we recommend that certificate holders carry another form of ID, such as a passport if they possess one, while driving.

Important Note: We understand that many certificate holders may not have another form of ID, and we are actively working to address the problem of traffic violation procedures for these individuals. In the meantime, we recommend that immigrants who no longer qualify for a driver's license obtain and carry the driving certificate. Such individuals are more likely to be arrested for driving without a certificate than for driving with a certificate but no additional ID, and the former carries a more substantial penalty. If you learn of someone who has been arrested simply for driving with a certificate, please call the toll—free number below so that we can get him/her in contact with a legal advisor.

4. What is the position of the Tennessee Immigrant and Refugee Rights Coalition (TIRRC) regarding the new law?

The Tennessee Immigrant and Refugee Rights Coalition (TIRRC) believes that the best law for Tennessee is one that ensures access to driver's licensees for all Tennesseans. We are wary of the concept of a driving certificate, and are concerned that those who obtain the driving certificate will suffer discrimination simply for trying to obey the law.

TIRRC also believes that in order for the driving certificate to accomplish its purpose, immigrants must be able to use it without fear of being arrested. Therefore we urge the Bredesen administration to take action to ensure that law enforcement throughout the state will not arrest certificate holders solely because they have no other form of ID. The driving certificate is a statewide document that requires a consistent statewide response. We fear that leaving the decision of whether or not to accept the certificate as ID in the hands of local authorities will lead to abuses of the law and mistreatment of certificate holders. TIRRC will continue to pressure the administration to address this problem, while at the same time working with local law enforcement throughout Tennessee to encourage them to accept the certificate as ID on the road. Our success will depend on the help of individuals from across the state.

5. What should I do if I encounter problems or discrimination?

Since the law became effective at the end of May, TIRRC has already received several complaints from individuals who provided the proper documents but were denied a driver's license. This problem is likely to continue as staff at the driver's license station have not been thoroughly trained to recognize different kinds of immigration documents. We expect additional issues to arise, particularly regarding law enforcement procedures for driving certificate holders, after the Department of Safety begins issuing the certificates in July. In anticipation of these problems TIRRC has initiated a comprehensive outreach campaign to deal with confusion about the new requirements and identify unfair treatment/discrimination of immigrants associated with the driving certificate. As part of this effort we have established a toll-free hotline to register complaints and assist individuals in getting their driver's licenses and driving certificates. We have also developed and translated into various languages a complaint form to be used to document any type of problem or discrimination an individual believes they have encountered.

Potential complaints include the following:

An applicant provided proper documents for a driver's license or driving certificate and was rejected.
An applicant for a driving certificate was treated poorly by a driver's license testing station employee.
A certificate holder was treated unfairly by a law enforcement officer after showing his/her certificate.
A certificate holder was arrested by a law enforcement officer after showing his/her certificate. . . .

SIGNIFICANCE

The certificate program became a magnet for fraud when other states accepted the certificates as legal identification. Several of the September 11 hijackers used Virginia identification documents. This fact led to concerns that identification documents could be used by subsequent terrorists. While Tennessee attempted to address this concern, it did not devise an acceptable solution. The Tennessee Department of Safety suspended the certificate program on February 24, 2006, after a federal investigation found that rings were shuttling South and Central American immigrants with fake residency papers from as far away as New Jersey and Georgia to state licensing centers in Knoxville and Murfreesboro to take advantage of the program. Several state license examiners were convicted of accepting bribes for certificates and sentenced to prison terms. The state legislature stepped in to remedy the program's faults, with several legislators arguing that the program should be abolished as a national security threat.

The program was then reinstated in March. Legal immigrants were issued driving certificates valid for the period of their authorized stay, provided it is not less than one year or more than five years. Any immigrant who is not in the country legally is prohibited from being issued a certificate. The state legislature, as of mid–2006, is considering issuing driver's licenses to legal immigrants and abolishing the certificate program. The problem of how to provide identification to legal residents of the U.S. without providing a cloak to terrorists remains unresolved.

FURTHER RESOURCES

Books

Garfinkel, Simson. *Database Nation: The Death of Privacy in the Twenty-First Century*. Sebastopol, Calif.: O'reilly Media, 2001.

Harper, Jim. *Identity Crisis: How Identification is Overused and Misunderstood*. Washington, D.C.: Cato Institute, 2006.

O'Harrow, Robert. *No Place to Hide: Behind the Scenes of Our Emerging Surveillance Society*. New York: Free Press, 2005.

Web site

Tennessee Immigration and Refugee Rights Coalition. "Tennessee Immigration and Refugee Rights Coalition." <http://www.tnimmigrant.org/> (accessed June 21, 2006).

Your Rights and Responsibilities as a Permanent Resident

Pamphlet

By: United States Citizenship and Immigration Services

Date: 2004

Source: United States Citizenship and Immigration Services. *Welcome Guide to the United States: A Guide for New Immigrants;* "Your Rights and Responsibilities as a Permanent Resident." 2004. Available online at <http://www.uscis.gov/graphics/citizenship/rights.htm>(accessed July 14, 2006).

About the Author: The United States Citizenship and Immigration Services was created in 2002 as part of a reorganization within the United States government. The former agency responsible for immigration issues, Immigration and Naturalization Services, was dissolved, and many of its duties placed under the aegis of the Department of Homeland Security and the newly created USCIS to manage citizenship and immigration issues.

INTRODUCTION

The 1790 Naturalization Act was the first piece of legislation in the new United States to address immigration and naturalized citizenship. The Naturalization Act limited persons born outside of the United States from becoming citizens unless they were free white persons; free, former slaves of African ancestry could not, according to this law, ever achieve American citizenship.

The Fourteenth Amendment to the U.S. Constitution, ratified in 1868, changed this law: All persons born in the United States, regardless of race, sex, or nationality, were considered citizens. This "birthright citizenship" has become a cornerstone in immigration and citizenship policy; pregnant, undocumented immigrants often enter the United States illegally to give birth on U.S. soil. An estimated 200,000 to 400,000 "anchor babies" are born to these women each year; under current laws the mothers and fathers to these newly-born U.S. citizens cannot be deported. Once these babies reach the age of twenty-one, they can apply to bring relatives to the United States from their parents' home country. This "chain migration" allows extended families to migrate into the United States. Some European countries have eliminated birthright citizenship; in 2004, Ireland changed their constitution to require that at least one parent of a child born on Irish soil be an Irish citizen in order for the child to be deemed an Irish citizen.

Alfonso Aguilar, head of Homeland Security's Office of Citizenship, displays a new guide, written for recently arrived legal residents, during a news conference in Los Angeles. AP IMAGES.

In 1882, the Chinese Exclusion Act dramatically limited legal immigration for Asian persons; it was the first piece of legislation to target a specific ethnic group. The Immigration Act of 1917 limited Asian Indian immigration, and the 1924 Immigration Act changed the landscape of immigration for the next forty years, imposing stringent limits on all immigrants with the exception of those from most northern European countries. By 1965, an overhaul of the immigration process led to the U.S. borders opening for non-northern Europeans and eliminated the national origin quotas.

Legal immigrants to the United States fall into a wide range of documentation categories, from child care providers—au pairs—on a thirteen month J-1 visa, to workers in highly technical fields on H-1B visas, to permanent residents. Permanent residents—so called "green card" carriers, are legally permitted to work and live in the United States, though they are not citizens. As the following excerpt from the United States Citizenship and Immigration Services guidelines for permanent residents explains, permanent residents have rights and responsibilities within the United States.

▮ PRIMARY SOURCE

Your Rights and Responsibilities

What you do now as a permanent resident can affect your ability to become a U.S. citizen later. The process of becoming a U.S. citizen is called "naturalization."

As a permanent resident, you have the right to:

- Live and work permanently anywhere in the U.S.
- Apply to become a U.S. citizen once you are eligible.
- Request a visa for your husband or wife and unmarried children to live in the U.S.
- Get Social Security, Supplemental Security Income, and Medicare benefits, if you are eligible.
- Own property in the U.S.
- Apply for a driver's license in your state or territory.
- Leave and return to the U.S. under certain conditions.
- Attend public school and college.
- Join certain branches of the U.S. Armed Forces.
- Purchase or own a firearm, as long as there are no state or local restrictions saying you can't.

As a permanent resident, it is your responsibility to:

- Obey all federal, state, and local laws.
- Pay federal, state, and local income taxes.
- Register with the Selective Service (U.S. Armed Forces), if you are a male between ages 18 and 26. See page 11 for instructions.
- Maintain your immigration status.
- Carry proof of your permanent resident status at all times.
- Give your new address in writing to the Department of Homeland Security (DHS) within 10 days of each time you move. See page 12 for instructions.

Permanent residents are issued a valid Permanent Resident Card (Form I-551) as proof of their legal status in the United States. Some people call this a "Green Card." If you are a permanent resident who is 18 years or older, you must carry proof of your immigration status. You must show it to an immigration officer if asked for it. Your card is valid for 10 years and must be renewed before it expires. You should file Form I-90 to replace or renew your Permanent Resident Card. You can get this form at http://www.uscis.gov or by calling the USCIS Forms Line. There is a fee to file Form I-90. Your Permanent Resident Card shows that you are allowed to live and work in the United States. You also can use your Permanent Resident Card to re-enter the United States. If you are outside the U.S. for more than 12 months, you will need to show additional documentation to re-enter the U.S. as a permanent resident. See page 10 for more information on the documents required to re-enter the U.S. if you are out of the country for more than 12 months.

Maintaining Your Permanent Resident Status

There are some things you must do to maintain your permanent resident status. These are also important to remember if you plan to apply for U.S. citizenship in the future.

- Don't leave the United States for an extended period of time or move to another country to live there permanently.
- File federal and state income tax returns.
- Register with the Selective Service, if you are a male between the ages of 18 and 26.
- Give your new address to DHS.

Keep Your Immigration Status

Permanent residents who leave the United States for extended periods, or who cannot show their intent to live permanently in the U.S., may lose their permanent resident status. If you think you will be out of the U.S. for more than 12 months, you should apply for a re-entry permit before leaving the country. You should file Form I–131, Application for a Travel Document. A re-entry permit is valid for up to 2 years and shows that you are returning from a temporary visit abroad. You may show the re-entry permit at a port of entry.

You can get this form at http://www.uscis.gov or by calling the USCIS Forms Line. You must pay a fee to file Form I–131. If you are not able to return to the U.S. before your re-entry permit expires or you did not apply for a re-entry permit before leaving the U.S. and have been outside the U.S. for more than 12 months, you may be able to get a special immigrant Returning Resident (SB-1) visa overseas from the Department of State. There are special requirements for this visa. Visit http://www.state.gov or your nearest Department of State Consular Office overseas for more information.

File Tax Returns

As a permanent resident, you must file income tax returns and report your income to the Internal Revenue Service (IRS) and your state, city, or local tax department, if required. If you do not file income tax returns while living outside of the U.S. for any length of time, or if you say that you are a "non-immigrant" on your tax returns, the U.S. government may decide that you have given up your permanent resident status.

Register With the Selective Service

If you are a man and you are 18 to 26 years old, you must register with the Selective Service. When you register, you tell the government that you are available to serve in the U.S. Armed Forces. The United States does not have a military draft now. Permanent residents and citizens do not have to serve in the Armed Forces unless they want to. You can register at a United States post office or on the Internet. To register for Selective Service on the Internet, visit the Selective Service website: http://www.sss.gov. To speak with someone from the Selective Service, call 1-847-688-6888. This is not a free call. You can also find information on the USCIS website http://www.uscis.gov/graphics/howdoi/selsvc.htm.

Give Your New Address to DHS

Every time you move, you need to tell DHS your new address. You must file Form AR–11, Alien's Change of Address Card. You must file this form within 10 days of your move. There is no fee to file this form.

Send Form AR–11 to:
Department of Homeland Security
U.S. Citizenship and Immigration Services
Change of Address
P.O. Box 7134
London, KY 40742-7134

For more information, call USCIS at 1-800-375-5283 or visit http://www.uscis.gov/graphics/formsfee/forms/ar–11.htm.

If You Are a Conditional Resident

You may be in the U.S. as a conditional resident (CR). You are a CR if you were married for less than 2 years to your U.S. citizen or permanent resident spouse on the day your permanent resident status was granted. If you have children, they also may be CRs. Some immigrant investors are also conditional residents.

A CR has the same rights and responsibilities as a permanent resident. Conditional residents must file either Form I-751, Petition to Remove the Conditions on Residence, or Form I-829, Petition by Entrepreneur to Remove Conditions, within 2 years of the date they were granted conditional permanent resident status. This date is usually the expiration date of your Permanent Resident Card. You should file these forms within 90 days of the 2-year anniversary of when you got your conditional resident status. If you do not do this, you can lose your immigration status.

SIGNIFICANCE

Permanent resident status grants green card holders the ability to apply to bring relatives from their home countries to the United States legally. Approximately 400,000 people enter the United States legally each year, and in 2003, more than 700,000 people received permanent legal resident status. Legal immigration falls into three broad categories: family reunification, employment, and humanitarian/refugee status. Approximately seventy percent of all green card recipients meet the requirements for family reunification—this "chain migration," where a family member migrates to the United States and then sponsors family members in the country of origin for entry, represents the majority of all legal migration into the United States.

Sponsoring a relative to reunite a family is a complex process. In addition to providing the U.S. government with a wide range of information about the permanent resident and the immigration applicant, the green card holder must be capable, financially, of supporting the emigrating relative at 125 percent of the poverty line or higher. For many legal immigrants, who receive green card status but work low-paying jobs, that financial threshold is too high.

The immediate family members of U.S. citizens—children, spouses, and parents—do not need a visa number to enter the United States; they are placed on a fast track for approval. All other relatives of U.S. citizens or green card holders then receive entry visas based on a preference order dictated by the U.S. Citizenship and Immigration Services; reuniting families is a high priority for the process. Undocumented immigrants, however, cannot access any of these legal immigration processes for relatives in other countries, no matter how long the undocumented worker has resided in the United States, even if he or she has paid taxes into the federal and state government systems. Family members of undocumented workers wishing to enter the United States must do so by applying for legal entry or by entering illegally.

While the spouses of U.S. citizens receive fast track immigration approval, the spouses of legal permanent residents who are from countries other than the United States must wait to be assigned a visa number. This can separate families for years; ironically, immigrants on short-term visas, such as H-1B visas for employment, can bring their non-working spouses with them, but green card holders cannot readily do so. This separates families for long stretches of time; an estimated 1.5 million legal permanent residents wish to bring spouses and children from overseas but cannot. In 2006, the U.S. House of Representatives considered a bill to help with such family unity issues; as of this writing the bill was in commmittee.

FURTHER RESOURCES

Books

Borjas, George J. *Heaven's Door: Immigration Policy and the American Economy*. Princeton, N.J.: Princeton University Press, 1999.

Jacobson, David. *Rights across Borders: Immigration and the Decline of Citizenship*. Baltimore: Johns Hopkins University Press, 1996.

Steiner, Henry, and Philip Alston. *International Human Rights in Context: Law, Politics, Morals*. Oxford and New York: Oxford University Press, 2000.

Weissbrodt, David S., and Laura Danielson. *Immigration Law and Procedure in a Nutshell*. St. Paul, Minn: Thomson/West Group Publishing, 2005.

Web sites

United States Citizenship and Immigration Services. <http://www.uscis.gov/graphics/index.htm> (accessed June 30, 2006).

Discontent over Illegals in Arizona

News article

By: Wood, Daniel B.

Date: October 20, 2004

Source: Wood, Daniel B. "Discontent Over Illegals in Arizona." *The Christian Science Monitor* (October 20, 2004).

About the Author: Daniel B. Wood is a Staff Writer for the *Christian Science Monitor*, an international daily newspaper.

INTRODUCTION

The issue of illegal immigration into the United States reached a critical political point in 1994 in California with Proposition 187, a ballot initiative designed to prevent undocumented immigrants from accessing health care services, education, employment, or any form of social service assistance from government agencies. The law included specific actions for various social and health services, such as the following for education:

> For each child who cannot establish legal status in the United States, each school district shall continue to provide education for a period of ninety days from the date of the notice. Such ninety day period shall be utilized to accomplish an orderly transition to a school in the child's country of origin. Each school district shall fully cooperate in this transition effort to ensure that the educational needs of the child are best served for that period of time.

Other politicians and activists in border states such as Arizona, Texas, and New Mexico watched Proposition 187's journey with great interest.

Then-Governor Pete Wilson supported California's Proposition 187, and on November 8, 1994, the voters of California passed the ballot initiative with 59 percent of the vote. Wilson's approval ratings deteriorated quickly, largely as a result of his support for the legislation; many Hispanic voters quickly withdrew their allegiance to him and political analysts determined that approval of the Republican party among Hispanics suffered as a result of Proposition 187. Lawmakers and politicians in other border states viewed illegal immigration as a politically dangerous issue and retreated from cracking down on illegal immigration for some time.

In 1998, most of Proposition 187 was ruled unconstitutional, and newly-elected Democratic Governor Grey Davis let the law die out during mediation. The law's stringent withdrawal of social services from undocumented workers and immigrants, however, was appealing to many citizens and taxpayers in states that border Mexico, such as Arizona.

Proposition 200 in Arizona proposed limits on services that undocumented immigrants could access legally, with provisions that were similar to California's Proposition 187. In 2004, when the following article was written, the Minutemen Border Patrol, an all-volunteer border monitoring organization that stations armed volunteers along the border to call federal agents regarding illegal border crossings, was gaining momentum as part of the fight against illegal immigration. School systems struggled to incorporate children of undocumented immigrants,

A border guard on horseback escorts two illegal Mexican immigrants through Organ Pipe Cactus National Monument in Arizona, 1984.
© DANNY LEHMAN/CORBIS.

with a huge percentage of such students unable to speak English when enrolled in classes. Arizona spent more than $1 billion in social services for undocumented workers, placing a huge strain on state resources and provoking Proposition 200.

PRIMARY SOURCE

Prop. 200 on the state's ballot proposes limiting public benefits for the undocumented.

PHOENIX— At a suburban job center here where about 100 day laborers are lined up for work, Antonio Laguna speaks while his colleagues—illegal immigrants all—nod approval. "We help make this economy run smoothly, but now they want to crack down on us," says Mr. Laguna, husband and father of four who works for about $350 a week.

Outside a Wal-Mart downtown Judy Martinez, a third-generation Mexican-American, explains why legal American citizens like herself feel the time for a tougher approach has come. "They take jobs from legal citizens, and use up social services," notes Ms. Martinez, who says her own daughter Ciara has been passed over for several jobs given to illegals. "At the same time they drive up crime all over the city."

The two comments encapsulate an immigration controversy that is raising debate to decibel levels not heard since California's Prop. 187 tried to deny social services to illegals a decade ago.

Arizona's Proposition 200, on the Nov. 2 ballot wants state and local governments to verify the identity and immigration status of all applicants for certain public benefits, and to require government employees to report violations. It also asks proof of US citizenship for every person who registers to vote and for every voter to show ID at polls. Pollsters say citizens support it (by 42 percent to 29 percent, in a new poll), while public officials, Democratic and Republican leadership, and churches do not.

However the vote turns out, observers say the sheer intensity of concern here is symbolic of discontent that is growing in border and immigrant-rich Western states about the level of illegal immigration—and how little action is being taken by politicians nationally to stop it.

"There is a disconnect between politicians and the people," says Bruce Merrill, a pollster at Arizona State University, who has gotten more questions on this issue than any other over three decades of polling. He says many people want something done about the problem, but politicians are often afraid to act out of fear of alienating an increasingly powerful Hispanic voting bloc. Many people cite the steep drop in approval for California's former Gov. Pete Wilson and the California Republican Party after the passage there of the get-tough Prop. 187 in 1994 as evidence of what can happen. The GOP suffered a loss of Hispanic voters as a result.

"I think leaders here informally looked at California and saw what happened," he says. "Hispanics are 25 percent of the population now, but will be 40 percent in 10 to 12 years. So the strategy has been to not put things on the ballot that will motivate Hispanics."

Prop. 200 will provide the latest litmus test of how deep the public's discontent is over illegal immigration across the nation's southern border. Attitudes about the problem have hardened in recent years in some states, both out of concern about the economic impact, particularly in a time of slow job growth, and out of concern about the security threat posed since 9/11.

To be sure, the federal government has tried to stem the flow of illegal immigrants coming across the border with high-profile crackdowns in places like San Diego and southern Texas. Now the front-line battle is shifting to Arizona, where the border remains porous.

The concern over illegal immigration has intensified as the federal government has shifted more of the cost and control of welfare benefits to the states—further burdening state budgets. "Other states will be looking at whether this [Prop. 200] is a failure or a success so they can model theirs after what Arizona is doing," says Shirley Gunther, an analyst for ThinkAZ, an Arizona public policy group.

As in immigration policy battles of the past, propaganda wars are already afoot, delineating the costs and advantages that immigrants bring to the economy. Some anti-immigrant groups say they siphon more than $1 billion a year in social services from the Arizona treasury—$700 per family in the state. "Arizona has a serious problem on its hands in paying $1.3 billion a year in services to illegals," says Ira Mehlman of the Federation for American Immigration Reform, which helped gather signatures to qualify the initiative. "All [the state is] trying to do is provide a check to see if people are eligible to receive the benefits they are applying for."

But ASU's Merrill and other analysts question the $1.3 billion figure. "No research or statistics are available to make that claim," he says.

And there is the usual battle over what the proposition actually says and does, as well as the motives of supporters and detractors. Backers say passage will help the state by preventing illegal immigrants from receiving benefits they don't qualify for. They also say a separate provision of Prop. 200 will prevent voter fraud by keeping illegals from registering to vote.

Critics say Prop. 200 will do nothing to prevent illegals from crossing the border, but will only make it harder for citizens to vote. They also say it will be costly to implement, by requiring the processing of documentation (driver's license, passport, birth certificate) by registered voters.

Analysts at ThinkAZ say both sides are taking advantage of the measure's complexity to confuse voters. They also say the measure is written in such a way as to keep some key points vague. "Prop. 200 does not include a definition of the public benefits which it says are covered by the new law," says Ms. Gunther—an omission she says could require the intervention of either the state legislature or the courts if approved. She also says the measure does not remove federally mandated public benefits for illegals such as emergency healthcare, immunizations, and K–12 public education.

"They are trying to scare us into leaving the country," says Leonardo Flores, a 19-year-old in line at the labor center. "It's a cheap tactic to fool the very people who are doing the work of this state that others don't want to do."

SIGNIFICANCE

Proposition 200 requires proof of citizenship for voters and for access to state and local benefits. Unlike the California Proposition 187, the law does not restrict undocumented persons' access to education or healthcare. However, as the article notes, Proposition 200 is vague on key points, and would, like Proposition 187, spend a lengthy period of time being dissected by court judges seeking to determine the intent and scope of the law.

Federal and state politicians have found themselves at odds with each other regarding policy as well. President George W. Bush has supported a worker amnesty program and guest worker documents for Mexicans to come to the United States legally to work in agriculture and service industries. Arizona Republican Senator John McCain stated that unskilled laborers—many undocumented—do work that American citizens refuse to perform, at wages that help to sustain the U.S. economy. Opponents of such arguments, including state and local lawmakers and education administrators, point to the artificial suppression of wages caused by illegal immigration, job loss for citizens, and the strain that undocumented immigrants place on social service, education, and health care systems.

Voters passed Proposition 200 with fifty-six percent of the vote, and despite efforts to halt its implementation, the law went forward. Proposition 200 penalizes public officials and state workers who permit voting or access to state benefits from individuals without checking for immigration or citizenship documentation, with the state worker fined up to $700 for each offense.

President George W. Bush unveiled a new plan in May 2006 to send more than 6,000 National Guard troops to act as temporary border patrol agents and to train 3,000 new federal border patrol agents for service. Arizona lawmakers applauded the new program. In June 2006, the United States Congress considered legislation to change the standard "birthright citizenship" granted to those born in the United States. Undocumented immigrant women who enter the United States to give birth on U.S. soil have been accused by illegal immigration opponents of using these "anchor babies" to remain in the United States illegally. The Fourteenth Amendment to the U.S. Constitution, however, grants all persons born in the United States full citizenship rights; as of June 2006, the issue was still pending.

Competing economic analyses of undocumented immigrants' impact on Arizona's economy reveal part of the divide in the immigration debate: The Federation for American Immigration Reform claims that undocumented immigrants cost the state of Arizona more than $1.3 billion each year, while the Wells-Fargo Thunderbird School of Management's report details a $318 million surplus generated by undocumented workers' tax payments that helps the Arizona economy.

FURTHER RESOURCES
Books

Ellingwood, Ken. *Hard Line: Life and Death on the U.S.-Mexico Border*. New York: Pantheon Books, 2004.

Haines, David W., and Karen E. Rosenblum, eds. *Illegal Immigration in America: A Reference Handbook*. Westport, Conn.: Greenwood Press, 1999.

Yoshida, Chisato, and Alan Woodland. *The Economics of Illegal Immigration*. New York: Palgrave MacMillan, 2005.

Websites

Minuteman Project. <http://www.minutemanproject.com/default.asp?contentID=23> (accessed June 25, 2006).

Salon.com. "The Angry Patriot." <http://www.salon.com/news/feature/2005/05/11/minuteman> (accessed June 25, 2006).

United States Citizenship and Immigration Services. <http://www.uscis.gov/graphics/index.htm> (accessed June 25, 2006).

Immigrant Victims of Abuse are Illegally Denied Benefits, Suit Says

Newspaper article

By: Nina Bernstein

Date: December 13, 2005

Source: Bernstein, Nina. "Immigrant Victims of Abuse are Illegally Denied Benefits, Suit Says." *The New York Times* (December 13, 2005).

About the Author: A reporter for the *New York Times*, Nina Bernstein received the George Polk Award for distinguished metropolitan coverage in 1995. She is also the author of *The Lost Children of Winter* (2002), an investigative account of the consequences of New York City's child welfare system.

INTRODUCTION

The news article reports on a 2005 legal case being brought against government departments by immigrant women who were victims of domestic violence and were being denied welfare benefits by administrative systems that were failing to acknowledge their eligibility. Although immigrant victims of domestic violence often face particularly serious consequences of being denied benefits, this case also reflects the wider problems of poverty and hardship faced by immigrants who are deemed to be ineligible for welfare, or who fail to claim the benefits to which they are actually entitled.

Many immigrant women who experience violence fail to even report their problems to the authorities and to seek assistance to support themselves and their children without having to depend on an abusive husband.

This is sometimes because they are "undocumented" (illegal) immigrants or are uncertain of their immigration status and therefore fear repercussions from the immigration authorities. Others may avoid approaching the authorities because they cannot speak English well, or simply because they are unaware of the support and assistance that may be available to them.

Until the mid–1990s, most legal immigrants were eligible for welfare benefits in the United States on the same terms as U.S. citizens. With rising levels of legal and undocumented migration to the United States, however, the government decided to restrict eligibility to welfare in order to tackle immigrant abuse of the welfare system, deter potential migrants who were attracted by the welfare system, and reduce social security costs. Under the 1996 Welfare Reform Act, immigrants who arrived in the United States after August that year were banned from claiming benefits until they had lived in the United States for at least five years. The Act also transferred much of the responsibility for implementing welfare policies to local and state governments and introduced an element of discretion in terms of the criteria under which exceptions could be made for certain vulnerable groups, including victims of domestic violence. In practice this meant that states could deny welfare benefits to all non-citizens, with the exception of emergency Medicaid. Following widespread opposition to the 1996 Act, particularly by immigrant support groups, various amendments were introduced that did allow the granting of benefits to particular groups of non-citizens, but this resulted in considerable confusion about the rules, as well as administrative problems such as those reported in this news article, which led to many claims being erroneously rejected.

The overall impact of the legislation was a major decline among immigrants in the utilization of welfare programs such as Medicaid, Food Stamps and Temporary Assistance for Needy Families. Participation in such programs fell not only among those who were ineligible under the new rules, but among those who were entitled to the benefits, such as refugees and families with children that were U.S. citizens. Factors contributing to the decline in participation among these groups were likely to have included confusion about the eligibility rules, fear of reprisals from the immigration authorities if the household included illegal immigrants, insufficient information being made available to immigrant communities, and poor training of welfare office staff to recognize eligibility for assistance.

PRIMARY SOURCE

Hundreds of battered immigrant women and children are being illegally denied food stamps and other aid because of programming errors in New York welfare computers and faulty staff training, according to legal papers that poverty lawyers plan to file in federal court today.

The lawsuit is a last resort, the lawyers said, because city and state officials have failed to fix systemic problems that force many women to choose between staying safe and feeding their families, despite government policies aimed at supporting them until they can get on their feet.

At its most basic level, the problem lies in the pull-down computer menu that caseworkers use when they enter information about a noncitizen applying for aid. The list of eligible immigration categories mistakenly omits "battered qualified alien," the category in which these women and children fit. So workers systematically reject them, with faulty state training manuals compounding the problem, the lawyers said.

"We have clients who have chosen to return to the abuser rather than not have food for their children," said Elizabeth S. Saylor, a lawyer with the Domestic Violence Project of the Legal Aid Society, one of the groups bringing the lawsuit in federal court in Manhattan as a class action. "People try to escape, but what's worse for the children, to see their mom get abused, or to be in the shelter and go hungry?"

Bob McHugh, a spokesman for the city's Human Resources Administration, defended the agency. "We have worked every day, including with groups like Legal Aid, to make our delivery of service even better," he said. "They've chosen to litigate this matter, so let them have their day in court."

Officials at the state Office of Temporary and Disability Assistance and the state Department of Health, also named as defendants, said they could not comment before reviewing the papers.

The papers describe the dark side of a common immigration story. Many of the women had come with children to join a husband in New York after years of separation, when their visas came through. But the reunions turned ugly, often after the woman had become pregnant again.

The abuse, documented in orders of protection, police reports and letters from domestic violence shelters, is not in question.

More than a dozen plaintiffs, mostly identified only by initials, include a woman from Senegal helping to prosecute the man accused of torturing her and murdering her sister; a Mexican mother of three whose abusive husband tracked her from Texas to New York; and a Bangladeshi woman whose husband, since hospitalized for mental illness, repeatedly kicked her in the stomach while she was pregnant, then cut up her clothes and threatened to kill her when she tried to go to work after the birth of their second daughter.

Last year the Bangladeshi woman fled to a domestic violence shelter with her daughters, now 6 and 2. But when she applied for public benefits at a city Job Center, showing visas, work authorization cards, and proof of abuse, caseworkers wrongly told her that only the baby, a citizen, was eligible for aid, the papers say.

It took several efforts and a letter from a lawyer at the shelter to persuade officials that she and her 6-year-old were also eligible for help. Even then, supervisors could not figure out how to get around the computer system, the papers said, so it has repeatedly rejected the case for "errors."

Affidavits by lawyers who have handled scores of such cases depicted advocacy on behalf of individuals as a Kafkaesque cul de sac. Even though administrative "fair hearings" overrule denials, the decisions are worded too vaguely to overcome the conventional wisdom reinforced by the computer screen. A few times, workers managed to get around the system by filling in false information, but aid was soon cut off again, because the recipient's immigration documents did not match what had been entered in the computer.

In part, the situation reflects the complexities created when Congress restricted many federal benefits to newcomers in the 1996 welfare overhaul, then added a patchwork of exceptions. State programs filled other gaps.

"It's a nightmare," said a dressmaker from Jamaica who joined her husband legally with their two children last year, and fled with them to a homeless shelter when she was eight-and-a-half-months pregnant. Her abusive husband, she said, had threatened to feed rat poison to the children, who are 7 and 9.

A caseworker denied her and the older children food stamps, cash assistance and Medicaid because they had no Social Security numbers to satisfy one of the computer prompts. They are now subsisting on school lunches and her newborn's allotment of aid: $68.50 every two weeks, and $119 a month in food stamps.

In an affidavit, she wrote: "Although I am breastfeeding, I regularly do not eat enough because we do not have enough money. Because I am hungry, I oftentimes feel weak and suffer headaches. I have watched myself and my children lose weight and feel helpless to reverse it."

Friday evening, as the baby slept in the crowded lobby of the homeless shelter, the children reminisced about what they used to eat in Jamaica.

"Sometimes we had chicken and rice," the boy said.

"And we had dumplings," the girl remembered.

"Salt fish!" the boy added, eyeing the chips in the vending machines.

Asked if he wanted to go back to Jamaica, he fell silent. " I want to stay with my mommy," he whispered.

SIGNIFICANCE

A relatively high percentage of immigrant households live in poverty in the United States. It has been reported that twenty-one percent of all children with immigrant parents live below the official poverty line, compared with only fourteen percent of the children of U.S.-born parents. Policies that restrict the access of immigrants to welfare benefits or deter them from claiming benefits and delivery systems that erroneously reject their claims, may exacerbate the problems of poverty among immigrants in the United States. Children from poor households tend to experience lower levels of educational attainment, making it more difficult to escape their disadvantaged backgrounds later in life.

For victims of domestic abuse, receipt of welfare benefits has traditionally been a means of escaping an abusive domestic situation. Denying welfare benefits to battered immigrant women and their children may increase the overall incidence of domestic violence in the immigrant community, as many may be forced to stay in abusive relationships. At the same time, tight immigration laws may exacerbate the situation, if the women are forced to rely on their husband's citizenship or immigration status in order to secure their own legal residency.

In 2006, changes were introduced to the Medicaid system, requiring claimants to prove their U.S. citizenship. Although intended to tackle benefit fraud by undocumented immigrants, the experience of the 1996 welfare reform implementation suggests immigrants who are actually eligible may lose their benefits in practice unless steps are taken to improve delivery systems and increase awareness of entitlement among immigrants.

FURTHER RESOURCES
Book

Kretsedemas, Philip, and Ann Aparicio, eds. *Immigrants, Welfare Reform, and the Poverty of Policy.* New York: Praeger Publishers, 2004.

Periodicals

Chanley, Sharon A., and Nicholas O. Alozie. "Policy for the 'Deserving,' but Politically Weak: The 1996 Welfare

Reform Act and Battered Women." *Policy Studies Review* 18 (2) (Summer 2001): 1–26.

Shields, Margie K., and Richard E. Behrman. "Children of Immigrant Families: Analysis and Recommendations." *The Future of Children* 14 (2) (Summer 2004).

Thrupkaew, Noy. "No Huddled Masses Need Apply." *The American Prospect* 13 (13) (July 15, 2002).

15 Years on the Bottom Rung

Newspaper article

By: Anthony DePalma

Date: May 26, 2005

Source: DePalma, Anthony. "15 Years on the Bottom Rung." *New York Times* (May 26, 2005): A1.

About the Author: Anthony DePalma is an international business correspondent for the *New York Times*. He has written several books including *Here: A Biography of the New American Continent*.

INTRODUCTION

Horatio Alger (1832–1899), a contemporary of author Mark Twain, wrote more than 130 popular books. While the details varied, Alger's stories inevitably followed the same predictable formula: a young man is born into a poor family and finds himself facing a difficult life. But the hero of the story becomes convinced that his future can be brighter than his parents', and coupling a deep faith in his possibilities with extreme perseverance, the young man inevitably grows up to enjoy the rewards of his hard work. More than a century after his death, the term "Horatio Alger story" is still used to describe a person who climbs from rags to riches.

Alger's stories were appealing for their simplicity and their optimism. In Alger's world, no obstacle was too great to be overcome by persistence and ingenuity, suggesting that even in Alger's day his stories may have represented a somewhat idealized version of reality. Yet, the story of immigrants finding success in America continues to be told. Andy Grove, a co-founder and later President and CEO of Intel Corporation, was born in Hungary and immigrated in 1957. Ironically, the man responsible for perhaps the most American clothing item known, was an immigrant. Levi Strauss, after arriving from Germany, created the heavy-duty work pants known today as blue jeans.

In 1997, Thomas Stanley and William Danko published a book entitled *The Millionaire Next Door*. The book, summarizing their extensive research on millionaire households in America, was blunt in its assessment of the role immigrants play in fueling wealth in America. First and second generation immigrants are far more likely to amass large personal estates than their later generation descendents. The authors theorize that the values of thrift, hard work, and a willingness to take risks that immigrants often bring with them are the primary determinants of their success, and that these values tend to get lost as following generations become more Americanized.

Beyond the success of immigrant entrepreneurs, immigrants as a whole have also enjoyed economic success in recent years. The U.S. Bureau of the Census reports that from 1994 to 2000, immigrant poverty rates fell more than twice as fast as rates for other Americans. The same report notes that median family incomes among immigrant families climbed substantially faster than incomes of non-immigrant families. These changes, if sustained, suggest that immigrants will soon have poverty rates equal to the general U.S. population.

While immigrant success stories are inspiring, they do not provide the complete story, and some immigrants find far less success in America. Despite the substantial improvements in poverty rates, the Censure Bureau also reported that as of 2000 poverty rates for immigrants hovered near twenty percent, while those for U.S. natives were approximately half as high. This distinction may be partly due to the low educational level of many current immigrants. Immigrants with poor English skills and little formal education generally find it difficult to complete the education they need to improve their situation.

PRIMARY SOURCE

In the dark before dawn, when Madison Avenue was all but deserted and its pricey boutiques were still locked up tight, several Mexicans slipped quietly into 3 Guys, a restaurant that the Zagat guide once called "the most expensive coffee shop in New York."

For the next 10 hours they would fry eggs, grill burgers, pour coffee and wash dishes for a stream of customers from the Upper East Side of Manhattan. By 7:35 a.m., Eliot Spitzer, attorney general of New York, was holding a power breakfast back near the polished granite counter. In the same burgundy booth a few hours later, Michael A. Wiener, co-founder of the multibillion-dollar Infinity

A Greek family embarks on Ellis Island, to come to America. © BETTMANN/CORBIS.

Broadcasting, grabbed a bite with his wife, Zena. Just the day before, Uma Thurman slipped in for a quiet lunch with her children, but the paparazzi found her and she left.

More Mexicans filed in to begin their shifts throughout the morning, and by the time John Zannikos, one of the restaurant's three Greek owners, drove in from the North Jersey suburbs to work the lunch crowd, Madison Avenue was buzzing. So was 3 Guys.

"You got to wait a little bit," Mr. Zannikos said to a pride of elegant women who had spent the morning at the Whitney Museum of American Art, across Madison Avenue at 75th Street. For an illiterate immigrant who came to New York years ago with nothing but $100 in his pocket and a willingness to work etched on his heart, could any words have been sweeter to say?

With its wealthy clientele, middle-class owners and low-income work force, 3 Guys is a template of the class

divisions in America. But it is also the setting for two starkly different tales about breaching those divides.

The familiar story is Mr. Zannikos's. For him, the restaurant—don't dare call it a diner—with its $20 salads and elegant décor represents the American promise of upward mobility, one that has been fulfilled countless times for generations of hard-working immigrants.

But for Juan Manuel Peralta, a 34-year-old illegal immigrant who worked there for five years until he was fired last May, and for many of the other illegal Mexican immigrants in the back, restaurant work today is more like a dead end. They are finding the American dream of moving up far more elusive than it was for Mr. Zannikos. Despite his efforts to help them, they risk becoming stuck in a permanent underclass of the poor, the unskilled and the uneducated.

That is not to suggest that the nearly five million Mexicans who, like Mr. Peralta, are living in the United

States illegally will never emerge from the shadows. Many have, and undoubtedly many more will. But the sheer size of the influx—over 400,000 a year, with no end in sight—creates a problem all its own. It means there is an ever-growing pool of interchangeable workers, many of them shunting from one low-paying job to another. If one moves on, another one—or maybe two or three—is there to take his place.

Although Mr. Peralta arrived in New York almost 40 years after Mr. Zannikos, the two share a remarkably similar beginning. They came at the same age to the same section of New York City, without legal papers or more than a few words of English. Each dreamed of a better life. But monumental changes in the economy and in attitudes toward immigrants have made it far less likely that Mr. Peralta and his children will experience the same upward mobility as Mr. Zannikos and his family.

Of course, there is a chance that Mr. Peralta may yet take his place among the Mexican-Americans who have succeeded here. He realizes that he will probably not do as well as the few who have risen to high office or who were able to buy the vineyards where their grandfathers once picked grapes. But he still dreams that his children will someday join the millions who have lost their accents, gotten good educations and firmly achieved the American dream.

. . .

. . . Resentment and race subtly stand in their way, as does a lingering attachment to Mexico, which is so close that many immigrants do not put down deep roots here. They say they plan to stay only long enough to make some money and then go back home. Few ever do.

But the biggest obstacle is their illegal status. With few routes open to become legal, they remain, like Mr. Peralta, without rights, without security and without a clear path to a better future.

. . .

Little has changed for Mr. Peralta, a cook who has worked at menial jobs in the United States for the last 15 years. Though he makes more than he ever dreamed of in Mexico, his life is anything but middle class and setbacks are routine. Still, he has not given up hope. Querer es poder, he sometimes says: Want something badly enough and you will get it.

. . .

There is a break in the middle of the day at 3 Guys, after the lunchtime limousines leave and before the private schools let out. That was when Mr. Zannikos asked the Mexican cook who replaced Mr. Peralta to prepare some lunch for him. Then Mr. Zannikos carried the chicken breast on pita to the last table in the restaurant.

"My life story is a good story, a lot of success," he said, his accent still heavy. He was just a teenager when he left the Greek island of Chios, a few miles off the coast of Turkey. World War II had just ended, and Greece was in ruins. "There was only rich and poor, that's it," Mr. Zannikos said. "There was no middle class like you have here." He is 70 now, with short gray hair and soft eyes that can water at a mention of the past.

Because of the war, he said, he never got past the second grade, never learned to read or write. He signed on as a merchant seaman, and in 1953, when he was 19, his ship docked at Norfolk, Va. He went ashore one Saturday with no intention of ever returning to Greece. He left behind everything, including his travel documents. All he had in his pockets was $100 and the address of his mother's cousin in the Jackson Heights-Corona section of Queens.

Almost four decades later, Mr. Peralta underwent a similar rite of passage out of Mexico. He had finished the eighth grade in the poor southern state of Guerrero and saw nothing in his future there but fixing flat tires. His father, Inocencio, had once dreamed of going to the United States, but never had the money. In 1990, he borrowed enough to give his first-born son a chance.

Mr. Peralta was 19 when he boarded a smoky bus that carried him through the deserted hills of Guerrero and kept going until it reached the edge of Mexico. With eight other Mexicans he did not know, he crawled through a sewer tunnel that started in Tijuana and ended on the other side of the border, in what Mexicans call el Norte.

He had carried no documents, no photographs and no money, except what his father gave him to pay his shifty guide and to buy an airline ticket to New York. Deep in a pocket was the address of an uncle in the same section of Queens where Mr. Zannikos had gotten his start. By 1990, the area had gone from largely Greek to mostly Latino.

Starting over in the same working-class neighborhood, Mr. Peralta and Mr. Zannikos quickly learned that New York was full of opportunities and obstacles, often in equal measure.

On his first day there, Mr. Zannikos, scared and feeling lost, found the building he was looking for, but his mother's cousin had moved. He had no idea what to do until a Greek man passed by. Walk five blocks to the Deluxe Diner, the man said. He did.

The diner was full of Greek housepainters, including one who knew Mr. Zannikos's father. On the spot, they offered him a job painting closets, where his mistakes would be hidden. He painted until the weather turned cold. Another Greek hired him as a dishwasher at his coffee shop in the Bronx.

It was not easy, but Mr. Zannikos worked his way up to short-order cook, learning English as he went along. In 1956, immigration officials raided the coffee shop. He was deported, but after a short while he managed to sneak back into the country. Three years later he married a Puerto Rican from the Bronx. The marriage lasted only a year, but it put him on the road to becoming a citizen. Now he could buy his own restaurant, a greasy spoon in the South Bronx that catered to a late-night clientele of prostitutes and undercover police officers.

Since then, he has bought and sold more than a dozen New York diners, but none have been more successful than the original 3 Guys, which opened in 1978. He and his partners own two other restaurants with the same name farther up Madison Avenue, but they have never replicated the high-end appeal of the original.

"When employees come in I teach them, 'Hey, this is a different neighborhood,'" Mr. Zannikos said. What may be standard in some other diners is not tolerated here. There are no Greek flags or tourism posters. There is no television or twirling tower of cakes with cream pompadours. Waiters are forbidden to chew gum. No customer is ever called "Honey."

"They know their place and I know my place," Mr. Zannikos said of his customers. "It's as simple as that."

His place in society now is a far cry from his days in the Bronx. He and his second wife, June, live in Wyckoff, a New Jersey suburb where he pampers fig trees and dutifully looks after a bird feeder shaped like the Parthenon. They own a condominium in Florida. His three children all went far beyond his second-grade education, finishing high school or attending college.

They have all done well, as has Mr. Zannikos, who says he makes about $130,000 a year. He says he is not sensitive to class distinctions, but he admits he was bothered when some people mistook him for the caterer at fund-raising dinners for the local Greek church he helped build.

All in all, he thinks immigrants today have a better chance of moving up the class ladder than he did 50 years ago.

"At that time, no bank would give us any money, but today they give you credit cards in the mail," he said. "New York still gives you more opportunity that any other place. If you want to do things, you will."

He says he has done well, and he is content with his station in life. "I'm in the middle and I'm happy."

...

Mr. Peralta cannot guess what class Mr. Zannikos belongs to. But he is certain that it is much tougher for an immigrant to get ahead today than 50 years ago. And he has no doubt about his own class.

"La pobreza," he says. "Poverty."

It was not what he expected when he boarded the bus to the border, but it did not take long for him to realize that success in the United States required more than hard work. "A lot of it has to do with luck," he said during a lunch break on a stoop around the corner from the Queens diner where he went to work after 3 Guys.

"People come here, and in no more than a year or two they can buy their own house and have a car," Mr. Peralta said. "Me, I've been here 15 years, and if I die tomorrow, there wouldn't even be enough money to bury me."

In 1990, Mr. Peralta was in the vanguard of Mexican immigrants who bypassed the traditional barrios in border states to work in far-flung cities like Denver and New York. The 2000 census counted 186,872 Mexicans in New York, triple the 1990 figure, and there are undoubtedly many more today. The Mexican consulate, which serves the metropolitan region, has issued more than 500,000 ID cards just since 2001.

Fifty years ago, illegal immigration was a minor problem. Now it is a divisive national issue, pitting those who welcome cheap labor against those with concerns about border security and the cost of providing social services. Though newly arrived Mexicans often work in industries that rely on cheap labor, like restaurants and construction, they rarely organize. Most are desperate to stay out of sight.

Mr. Peralta hooked up with his uncle the morning he arrived in New York. He did not work for weeks until the bakery where the uncle worked had an opening, a part-time job making muffins. He took it, though he didn't know muffins from crumb cake. When he saw that he would not make enough to repay his father, he took a second job making night deliveries for a Manhattan diner. By the end of his first day he was so lost he had to spend all his tip money on a cab ride home.

He quit the diner, but working there even briefly opened his eyes to how easy it could be to make money in New York. Diners were everywhere, and so were jobs making deliveries, washing dishes or busing tables. In six months, Mr. Peralta had paid back the money his father gave him. He bounced from job to job and in 1995, eager to show off his newfound success, he went back to Mexico with his pockets full of money, and he married. He was 25 then, the same age at which Mr. Zannikos married. But the similarities end there.

When Mr. Zannikos jumped ship, he left Greece behind for good. Though he himself had no documents, the compatriots he encountered on his first days were here legally, like most other Greek immigrants, and could help him. Greeks had never come to the United States in large numbers—the 2000 census counted only 29,805 New Yorkers born in Greece—but they tended to settle in just a few areas, like the Astoria section of Queens, which became cohesive communities ready to help new arrivals.

Mr. Peralta, like many other Mexicans, is trying to make it on his own and has never severed his emotional or financial ties to home. After five years in New York's Latino community, he spoke little English and owned little more than the clothes on his back. He decided to return to Huamuxtitlán (pronounced wa-moosh-teet-LAHN), the dusty village beneath a flat-topped mountain where he was born.

"People thought that since I was coming back from el Norte, I would be so rich that I could spread money around," he said. Still, he felt privileged: his New York wages dwarfed the $1,000 a year he might have made in Mexico.

He met a shy, pretty girl named Matilde in Huamuxtitlán, married her and returned with her to New York, again illegally, all in a matter of weeks. Their first child was born in 1996. Mr. Peralta soon found that supporting a family made it harder to save money. Then, in 1999, he got the job at 3 Guys.

"Barba Yanni helped me learn how to prepare things the way customers like them," Mr. Peralta said, referring to Mr. Zannikos with a Greek title of respect that means Uncle John.

The restaurant became his school. He learned how to sauté a fish so that it looked like a work of art. The three partners lent him money and said they would help him get immigration documents. The pay was good.

But there were tensions with the other workers. Instead of hanging their orders on a rack, the waiters shouted them out, in Greek, Spanish and a kind of fractured English. Sometimes Mr. Peralta did not understand, and they argued. Soon he was known as a hothead.

Still, he worked hard, and every night he returned to his growing family. Matilde, now 27, cleaned houses until the second child, Heidi, was born three years ago. Now she tries to sell Mary Kay products to other mothers at Public School 12, which their son, Antony, 8, attends.

Most weeks, Mr. Peralta could make as much as $600. Over the course of a year that could come to over $30,000, enough to approach the lower middle class. But the life he leads is far from that and uncertainty hovers over everything about his life, starting with his paycheck.

To earn $600, he has to work at least 10 hours a day, six days a week, and that does not happen every week. Sometimes he is paid overtime for the extra hours, sometimes not. And, as he found out in May, he can be fired at

any time and bring in nothing, not even unemployment, until he lands another job. In 2004, he made about $24,000.

Because he is here illegally, Mr. Peralta can easily be exploited. He cannot file a complaint against his landlord for charging him $500 a month for a 9-foot-by-9-foot room in a Queens apartment that he shares with nine other Mexicans in three families who pay the remainder of the $2,000-a-month rent. All 13 share one bathroom, and the established pecking order means the Peraltas rarely get to use the kitchen. Eating out can be expensive.

Because they were born in New York, Mr. Peralta's children are United States citizens, and their health care is generally covered by Medicaid. But he has to pay out of his pocket whenever he or his wife sees a doctor. And forget about going to the dentist.

As many other Mexicans do, he wires money home, and it costs him $7 for every $100 he sends. When his uncle, his nephew and his sister asked him for money, he was expected to lend it. No one has paid him back. He has middle-class ornaments, like a cellphone and a DVD player, but no driver's license or Social Security card.

SIGNIFICANCE

In 2006, questions about U.S. immigration policy rose to the forefront of U.S. political debate. Facing increasing numbers of both legal and illegal immigrants from Mexico, Washington began to buzz with competing proposals to address the problem. The issues being debated ranged from securing the country's porous southern border to whether current illegal workers should be granted amnesty or expelled. Complicating the debate were questions about how each of the proposed changes might impact the U.S. economy.

Proponents of allowing illegal residents to remain recommended a guest worker program, which would allow illegal workers to register and remain in the United States with work permits. Such a program would help move illegal workers onto the tax rolls and allow them to continue working at jobs many Americans do not want. Further, such a program would, by definition, reduce the number of illegal aliens living in the United States.

Opponents of this plan argued that allowing illegal immigrants to obtain legal residency amounted to rewarding illegal behavior, potentially encouraging other Mexicans to enter the United States illegally. In response to lax border security, a group calling themselves the Minutemen carried out missions to apprehend illegal immigrants crossing into the United

States while simultaneously lobbying for the construction of a massive wall separating the United States and Mexico. Political analysts predicted that the issue would play an important role in the 2008 presidential election.

FURTHER RESOURCES

Books

Bernstein, Jared, et al. *Pulling Apart: A State-by-State Analysis of Income Trends.* Washington, D.C.: Economic Policy Institute and Center on Budget Policy Priorities, 2002.

Mills, Nicolaus. *Arguing Immigration: The Controversy and Crisis over the Future of Immigration.* New York: Touchstone, 1994.

Williams, Mary E., ed. *Immigration: Opposing Viewpoints.* Chicago: Greenhaven Press, 2003.

Periodicals

Ley, David. "Explaining Variations in Business Performance Among Immigrant Entrepreneurs in Canada." *Journal of Ethnic and Migration Studies* 32 (2006): 743–764.

"90's Boom Had Broad Impact; 2000 Census Cites Income Growth Among Poor, Upper Middle Class." *Washington Post* (June 5, 2000).

Scott, Janny. "Census Finds Immigrants Lower City's Income." *New York Times* (August 6, 2002).

Web sites

Carter, Jimmy. "Jimmy Carter Op-Ed: Employers in Quandary over Immigration Bill." *The Carter Center.* <http://www.cartercenter.org/> (accessed June 13, 2006).

Chapman, Jeff, and Jared Bernstein. "Immigration and Poverty: How Are They Linked?" *U.S. Bureau of Labor Statistics.* <http://www.bls.gov/opub/mlr/2003/04/art2full.pdf> (accessed June 13, 2006).

The White House. "Comprehensive Immigration Reform." <http://www.whitehouse.gov/infocus/immigration/> (accessed June 13, 2006).

Injured Soldier Naturalized at Walter Reed by USCIS Director

Press release

By: U.S. Department of Homeland Security

Date: March 8, 2005

Source: *U.S. Department of Homeland Security.* "Injured Soldier Naturalized at Walter Reed by USCIS

Director." <http://uscis.gov/graphics/publicaffairs/newsrels/WalterReedNatz03_08_05.pdf>(accessed June 13, 2006).

About the Author: The U.S. Department of Homeland Security was established in 2002. It is responsible for ensuring domestic safety, responding to natural disasters, and regulating the nation's borders.

INTRODUCTION

Armies have traditionally consisted of citizens from a warring country and mercenaries, professional soldiers hired for a specific conflict. The modern U.S. military is composed entirely of volunteers, though not all these volunteers are actually U.S. citizens. As of 2003, the U.S. Defense Department reported that approximately two percent of the U.S. military forces consisted of non-citizens. These 30,000 men and women were permanent residents of the United States who volunteered to serve in the military. Non-citizens are allowed to enlist in all branches of the military. About one-third of these soldiers are from Mexico, while the remainder are from other countries including Canada, India, China, and Vietnam.

Individuals may become U.S. citizens in several ways. A person born in the United States is automatically granted citizenship, regardless of his parents' country of citizenship. Similarly, a child born to U.S. citizens living abroad is automatically granted citizenship. Most American citizens today received citizenship as a result of being born in the United States.

Other men and women receive citizenship through a legal process known as naturalization. U.S. naturalization includes several requirements. Applicants must have been granted permanent resident status in the United States, and they must be at least eighteen years old at the time they apply. Applicants married to a U.S. citizen must be residents of the United States for three years before seeking citizenship, while applicants not married to a U.S. citizen must wait five years. Applicants are also required to demonstrate proficiency in English and are required to pass a test covering the basic principles of U.S. government and history. A record of criminal convictions may disqualify an applicant.

In 2002, in recognition of the sacrifices being made by non-citizens in the military, President Bush signed an executive order accelerating the naturalization process for non-citizen enlistees. Such orders are permitted during times of war, and past orders issued during both World Wars, Korea, Vietnam, and the 1991 Gulf War allowed accelerated eligibility for more than 100,000 non-citizens. Earning citizenship

U.S. Citizenship and Immigration Services Director Eduardo Aguirre administers the Oath of Allegiance to U.S. Army Spc. Victor Alfonso Rojas of Aurora, Illinois, during a ceremony at Walter Reed Army Medical Center in Washington, March 7, 2005. AP IMAGES.

also enabled the soldiers to remain in the armed forces beyond the normal time limits for non-citizens, benefiting both the individual and the service.

▮ PRIMARY SOURCE

Washington D.C.—U.S. Citizenship and Immigration Services Director Eduardo Aguirre swore in Army Specialist Victor Alfonso Rojas as a Untied States citizen in a private ceremony at Walter Reed Army Medical Center in Washington, D.C. With his father, senior Army officers, and many doctors, nurses, and other medical staff looking on, Rojas raised his right hand to take the Oath of Allegiance to fulfill his long held dream of becoming a U.S. citizen. He arrived at Walter Reed on Nov. 18, 2004, for treatment of the serious injuries he sustained during combat in Iraq.

"I feel really good about becoming a citizen. I was looking for this before going to Iraq." Rojas said after the ceremony, proudly pointing out that he was second member of his family to become a U.S. citizen.

On Nov. 16, 2004, Rojas was driving a vehicle as part of a convoy to collect fuel trucks at Camp Spiker in Iraq. While rendezvousing with a second convoy, he and the convoy suddenly found themselves under rocket-propelled grenade (RPG) attack. Although he received serious wounds to his right knee when a RPG round hit his vehicle, Rojas continued to drive, using his left leg to get the other soldiers with him in the vehicle out of the line of fire. As he was driving away, his vehicle took a second round, and he suffered additional injuries. Once clear of the attack and everyone was safe, Rojas sought treatment, and was evacuated due to his injuries.

Rojas immigrated to the U.S. from Zacatezas, Mexico, in 1997, settling with his family in Aurora, Ill. After graduating from East Aurora High School, where he participated in the Junior ROTC program, Rojas enlisted in the U.S. Army National Guard as a power generator repairman. In June 2003, Rojas was placed on active duty with the 33625 Maintenance Company and deployed to Iraq soon after

A selfless soldier, after the ceremony Rojas' immediate goal was to recover from his injuries and start running again so that he could rejoin his unit and fellow soldiers.

▮▮

SIGNIFICANCE

Though supporters and opponents of the proposed changes both recognize the contribution made by non-citizen soldiers and sailors, they differ on the appropriate response. Advocates of a liberalized citizenship policy argue that any person willing to risk his life fighting to defend the freedom of the United States has demonstrated his loyalty and should be granted citizenship quickly. Opponents of the change do not deny this line of reasoning; however, they worry that making military service an instant ticket to citizenship might prompt non-citizens to enlist solely to gain citizenship, potentially reducing the quality and effectiveness of the military.

Beginning in 2003, soldiers on active duty were legally allowed to complete the official naturalization ceremony outside the United States. As a result of this change, several hundred soldiers each year were able to become U.S. citizens without leaving their combat duty to return to the United States.

Under the terms of a 1990 law, non-citizens who died in combat with the U.S. military were eligible to be granted citizenship posthumously. This law recognized the sacrifice of men and women who had not yet received citizenship, but its provisions lasted only until 1992. In 2002, President Bush signed legislation re-establishing the citizenship opportunity for current members of the military. In addition to honoring the dead, this law allows dependents of deceased soldiers to count that soldier as a citizen for the purposes of their own citizenship applications. As of 2005, some military families began pressing to further expedite the posthumous citizenship process.

Several years into the Iraq war, some Hispanic advocacy groups charge that Hispanics are dying in disproportionately high numbers in combat. These critics accuse the U.S. military of targeting poorly educated Hispanics in order to meet recruiting quotas. In particular, critics claim that recruiters were promising educational benefits while knowing that only one in eight U.S. Hispanics ever qualify to attend college. U.S. Department of Defense data show that Hispanic enlistment reached record levels during the Iraq war.

FURTHER RESOURCES

Books

Barbour, Christine, et al. *Keeping the Republic: Power and Citizenship in American Politics*. Washington, D.C.: CQ Press, 2005.

Uschan, Michael V. *The Iraq War: Life of an American Soldier in Iraq*. New York: Lucent Books, 2004.

Zucchino, David, and Mark Bowden. *Thunder Run: The Armored Strike to Capture Baghdad*. New York: Atlantic Monthly Press, 2004.

Periodicals

"The Future Comes Apace." *National Review* 58 (2006): 56.

Kiely, Kathy. "For Legal Immigrants, Wait Can be Daunting." *USA Today* (May 16, 2006): 1a.

Martin, Kady, II. "Skating into Citizenship." *CQ Weekly* 64 (2006): 521.

Web sites

U.S. Army Judge Advocate General's Corps. "Naturalization Information for Military Personnel." <http://www.jagcnet.army.mil/JAGCNETInternet/Homepages/AC/Legal%20Assistance%20Home%20Page.nsf/0/6d81833c6d5d6df585256a05005d39c0/$FILE/MilitaryBrochurev77.pdf> (accessed June 13, 2006).

U.S. Office of Citizenship and Immigration Services. "Office of Citizenship." <http://www.uscis.gov/graphics/citizenship/index.htm> (accessed June 13, 2006).

White House. "President Attends Naturalization Ceremony." March 2006. <http://www.whitehouse.gov/news/releases/2006/03/20060327.html> (accessed June 13, 2006).

Riots and Rage

Magazine article

By: McNicoll, Tracy

Date: November 3, 2005

Source: McNicoll, Tracy. "Riots and Rage." *Newsweek* (November 3, 2005).

About the Author: Tracy McNicoll is a staff writer for *Newsweek*, one of the widest-circulating magazines in the United States. It focuses on current events around the world.

INTRODUCTION

France has a history of being a reluctant destination for immigrants. It never sent massive waves of emigrants to other countries and, until the late twentieth century, never accepted massive waves of immigrants. After 1945, France began relying on migrant labor to fill gaps in the labor force. Many of these migrants were Muslims who came from former French colonies in North Africa. They were not assimilated well into French life, and their children began to protest this exclusion with riots in 2005.

In France, the ideals of the French Revolution—liberty, equality, fraternity—still rule public policy. Race, religion, class, and color are not supposed to matter. Everyone who is a French citizen is automatically equal under French tradition and law. There is no affirmative action because ethnicity is not measured.

France established colonies in North Africa in the nineteenth century as part of its effort to maintain global strength. It lost these colonies, Morocco and Algeria, after World War II in 1945. At the same time, France needed workers and welcomed migrant laborers. According to ideals of the Revolution, these immigrants would blend seamlessly into French society. However, free movement of immigrants from Algeria gave way to attempts at migration control by the late 1960s. By the start of the twenty-first century, legal and illegal North African immigrants, mostly from Morocco, crossed into France almost daily. In France, many of the native French resented the

Muslim North African immigrants. As a result, the immigrants were marginalized and excluded.

In France, moving from one socio-economic level to another is becoming ever more difficult, as the economy crumbles. It is especially hard for those with North African names. These immigrants live in the poor suburbs surrounding Paris with little hope of escape to a better life. There is twenty-four percent unemployment in Clichy-sous-Bois, one of the 300 towns and cities struck by riots in autumn 2005. The French national average is ten percent. Some of the Muslims who rioted possess good degrees from good schools but they do not have the correct skin color or the correct address to secure employment. As the rioters emphasized, France has not fulfilled the Revolutionary hopes.

PRIMARY SOURCE

Wednesday is market day in this worn-down collection of housing projects northeast of Paris. Stalls are thrown up until midafternoon on a muddy stretch of parking lot. Their yellowed tarpaulins and worn umbrellas cut a swath of faded color through gray apartment blocks strung with laundry and pocked with satellite dishes. Veiled women, palms reddened with henna, move through November damp; hawkers offer everything from sportswear to the odd djellaba robes, pomegranates to shampoo, halal rabbit to teapots. It could be any immigrant neighborhood near the French capital, but this is Clichy-sous-Bois, flashpoint for this week's spreading violence between police and mostly-Muslim residents. It could also be the burial ground for the presidential aspirations of Interior Minister Nicolas Sarkozy.

On this day, the aromas of spices and North African pastries are perfuming the air. But beyond the tarpaulins there are also signs of the destruction wrought here since the last Wednesday market day. That was the day before angry youths took to the streets, burning cars and hurling projectiles at police and firefighters to protest the deaths of two neighborhood teenagers of African descent. The teens were electrocuted taking shelter in an enclosure surrounding a high-voltage electrical transformer. Residents say they were fleeing police; police insist this was not the case. The nightly violence has now spread through other similarly ghettoized suburbs that ring Paris. Dozens of police officers have been injured, hundreds of vehicles have been torched; rioters even set light to a kindergarten. President Jacques Chirac has appealed for calm and national newspapers offer five-alarm headlines like "The Republic is Catching Fire."

At the Clichy-sous-Bois market, the lot is spotted with burned-out cars. Splayed open and gray as the sky, their melted windshields collect in green lumps on sunken dashboards. This week's stalls have been built up around them. And then there's a new product being offered for sale. "I have tapes! Do you know where I can go with the tapes?" asks a man who bounds over like a long-lost friend when he realizes there's a journalist in the area. Identifying himself as Dany who lives "over there," he adds: "I have tapes of the riots. Every night. I have Oct. 28th, 29th, every night. Which do you think would be best, France 2 or France 3 or France 5?" Dany asks excitedly, rattling off the state television stations.

It is, however, going to take more than a few tapes to explain the precise dynamics behind the nightly battles of Clichy-sous-Bois. The electrocution deaths may have set the suburb ablaze, but it was a murky incident at a crowded mosque that seems to have aggravated the expanding cycle of violence. The two-story Bilal Mosque is behind the market, sharing a building with pastry and meat shops and the public bath known as a hammam. Four years after it opened, the mosque has no signs out front, but, for the faithful, it needs none. It was packed with some 700 people last Sunday night when the week's street violence drifted into its tiled prayer room on a cloud of tear gas. Worshipers fled tearful and barefoot into the night. Someone caught the pandemonium on a camera phone and put it up on the Internet.

Interior Minister Sarkozy has confirmed the type of canister lobbed at the mosque matched those issued to police in the area, but an investigation is underway to determine if it was actually fired by police. Whatever the outcome of the inquiry, the clashes clearly have damaged Sarkozy's prospects in his undeclared race for the presidency against another prospective right-wing candidate, Prime Minister Dominique de Villepin. De Villepin has taken the lead in the government's responses after Sarkozy was lambasted throughout the crisis for his controversial street talk, labeling the protesters as "racaille," which means rabble or scum.

To the hood-wearing kids loitering in front of the mosque on market day, domestic politics and official investigations don't much matter. "Another journalist!? You're all the same, all stupid. People talk to you and you take what you want and you throw the rest away," one disillusioned young teenager tells *Newsweek*. Asked what they saw during the clashes, they give knowing smiles: "Nothing. Didn't see anything, didn't hear anything, nothing." Still, they stick around, and new kids materialize to join the crowd, speaking up and shushing each other at turns. "They come around here and provoke us, the police. They go like this," says the first kid, holding up his middle finger. Another brings out what he says was one of the tear gas canisters fired Sunday night: "Here. See?"

Youngsters in this neighborhood of colorless tenements—and in others like it—know that their future prospects are bleak. "I'm thirty-five and I don't have work yet," says one man waiting outside the mosque. He gestures toward a plastic document folder he hugs while he waits; the folder, ostensibly holding the map to his job search, has a little French flag on it. Like many others, he declined to be identified.

Abderrahmane Bouhout, the Bilal Mosque's president, rattles off the problems. "People here are twenty, twenty-five, thirty, and they have no work. There are no jobs, there's no housing," he says. "[The kids' deaths] were a detonator." Bouhout has filed a complaint with the government about the tear gas incident and urges patience during the inquiry, careful not to provide another spark to the neighborhood pyre.

Reluctant to point fingers at politicians, Bouhout emphasizes intercommunal harmony, applauding local Christian clergy for their friendship. He hands over two small pieces of yellow paper, five by three inches. Their messages begin "Dear Muslim friends" in French and Arabic, and wish the Muslim faithful a happy Eid al-Fitr, the feast that ends the holy month of Ramadan, above a photocopied signature of the area's Roman Catholic bishop.

Bouhout has also helped an initiative to bring a precarious calm to his own neighborhood. While riots continued in neighboring communities, with protestors chasing a television crew from their car before setting it ablaze and briefly invading a police station on the country's seventh consecutive night of disturbances, Clichy-sous-Bois's angry youth are largely staying off the streets—at least for now. The reason? Appeals for calm by fifty "big brothers," neighborhood twentysomethings who have used their street cred to soothe the situation. The mentors have succeeded where police in riot gear have failed. But their very presence is yet another sign of the alienation of immigrants in the French Republic—and the need for a longer-term solution to their problems.

SIGNIFICANCE

In May 2006, the French National Assembly passed by 367 votes to 164, a new law that largely restricts immigration to educated and "desirable" workers. The legislation requires immigrants to learn French, respect the French way of life, and ends the old automatic right to French citizenship after ten years. It also sharply restricts the right of legal immigrants to bring family members to France to join them. Human rights groups have joined the opposition Socialist party and the Council of Christian Churches in fighting the new immigration law. They have pledged to

challenge the limits on family reunions in the European Court of Human Rights.

Meanwhile, the anti-immigration, extreme right candidate Jean-Marie Le Pen is expected to run again for the French presidency. He placed second in the 2002 elections. Unemployment remains high in the Muslim suburbs as does anger among the North Africans, complicating a possible solution to the French problem with immigration.

FURTHER RESOURCES
Books

Cornelius, Wayne A., ed., et al. *Controlling Immigration: A Global Perspective*. Stanford, CA: Stanford University Press, 2004.

Derderian, Richard C. *North Africans in Contemporary France: Becoming Visible*. New York: Palgrave Macmillan, 2004.

Australian Prime Minister Worries Over 'Extremist' Muslim Immigrants

News article

By: Phil Mercer

Date: February 20, 2006

Source: Mercer, Phil. "Australian Prime Minister Worries Over 'Extremist' Muslim Immigrants." *Voice of America News* (February 20, 2006).

About the Author: Phil Mercer is a contributor to Voice of America (VOA), part of an international news media organization sponsored by the government of the United States. The VOA was originally constituted as a radio network to provide current events information to both United States citizens living abroad and foreign nationals; the VOA today utilizes digital satellite and Internet communications as its broadcast media.

INTRODUCTION

The country of Australia, founded in 1901, is an aggregation of seven former British colonies that had been established on the Australian continent beginning in 1788. Through most of Australia's history, its immigrant population comprised a mixture of free Anglo-Saxon settlers and convicts transported from the British Isles to the colonies to serve their sentences. By 1901, these populations had blended to create a relatively homogeneous and predominately white society.

From the date of its independence, Australia was a bastion of patriotism and its policies conveyed a nationalist, Australian-first outlook. Although a nation with British roots, anti-English sentiment was a prominent feature of Australian nationalism. As the country grew from its birth through the 1960s, Australia was a nation that prized an identifiable Australian culture, where any visible minorities were expected to blend into the existing cultural fabric as opposed to maintaining a distinct cultural identity. The immigration practices of the Australian government as mandated through the 1960s have been described in academic literature as being in furtherance of a "White Australia" policy.

Australia legislated changes to its immigration policies in the 1970s that were intended to broaden the ability of non-white immigrants to migrate to Australia. Demographic studies confirm that since 1980, over 100,000 immigrants have arrived each

A young Muslim girl marches during a rally in Sydney on October 18, 2001, by students demanding the end to the bombing of Afghanistan. © REUTERS/CORBIS.

year in Australia, one of the highest per-capita rates of immigration in the world. The greatest percentage of these recent immigrants have arrived from Asia and Indonesia. There has been significant editorial commentary in the Australian media as to the rise in racially motivated incidents in the nation; a riot near Sydney that began with a confrontation between a white group and youths of Lebanese ancestry attracted national attention in January 2006.

When John Howard made the speech excerpted in the primary source below in February, 2006, he had been the Prime Minister of Australia for ten years. Howard, a politician who has exhibited a conservative approach to economic and social issues throughout his political career, had spoken out on how Australia should approach multiculturalism on numerous occasions. In 1988, while a member of the Australian parliament, Howard stated that it was his belief that Asian immigration to Australia was then at excessive levels, and that he feared that Australian cultural traditions would be overcome. In 2001, the Howard government provoked an international incident by boarding a Norwegian ship headed to Australia that contained Muslim asylum seekers from Indonesia. The combined effect of the 9/11 terrorist attacks on the United States and the 2002 bombing in neighboring Bali, Indonesia prompted a series of heightened internal security measures in Australia that directed attention to its Muslim minority (approximately 300,000 persons in a national population of twenty million).

PRIMARY SOURCE

Australian Prime Minister John Howard says he is concerned about "extremist" Muslim immigrants, insisting such people are antagonistic towards the wider community. Mr. Howard's remarks have sparked criticism from Islamic leaders in Australia. Prime Minister John Howard says there is a "small section of the Islamic population in Australia" that holds extremist views about relations with non-Muslims, the rights of women, and other contentious issues. He said such views pose a challenge to Australia's liberal immigration policy.

Australia's conservative leader was repeating comments for reporters that he had made in an earlier interview for a new book that details his forthcoming 10th anniversary as prime minister. Mr. Howard says radical elements within the country's Islamic community need to be confronted.

"It is not a problem we have ever faced with other immigrant communities, who become easily absorbed into the mainstream," he said. "We want people, when they come to Australia, to adopt Australian ways."

Mr. Howard's remarks have provoked criticism from Muslim leaders. They have insisted their community already feels under siege due to the U.S.-led war on terrorism, in which Australia is an eager participant, and recent race riots in Sydney, where white gangs targeted people of Arabic or Middle Eastern appearance.

The Australian Federation of Islamic Councils said the prime minister's comments were inflammatory at a time when tensions between Muslims and Western nations were already running high over controversial cartoons of the prophet Mohammed that originally ran in a Danish newspaper.

It is estimated that there are 300,000 Muslims in Australia. They have come from more than 70 countries, including Turkey and Lebanon. Islamic leaders have said that racism towards this minority group has been increasing in recent years, since the terrorist attacks in the United States in September 2001 and the bombings on the Indonesian island of Bali a year later. Islamic leaders have also expressed concern that new counter-terrorism laws in Australia will unfairly target Australia's Muslims.

Australia has never suffered a major terrorist attack on its own soil, but the 202 people killed on Bali in 2002 included 88 Australians, and the country is on a heightened state of alert. It has combat troops stationed in Iraq and Afghanistan.

SIGNIFICANCE

The comments of Australian Prime Minister John Howard in February 2006 reflect a growing concern on the part of many Australians about the future of Australian society in the face of the threats posed by terrorism beyond its borders, as well as a corresponding perception of the instability created by immigration posed within the country. Howard, a long time conservative presence in Australian national politics, echoed the sentiments of a significant segment of Australian society with his comments.

The Howard speech raises a number of issues in relation to Australian multicultural practices, the first of which is the distinction between the concepts of xenophobia and racism, two terms that are often used interchangeably. Xenophobia is a strong dislike, fear, or hostility towards foreign persons; racism is the subtle or active discrimination against persons who are of a different racial origin than

oneself. Racism does not depend upon a country of origin; similarly, xenophobia is not dependent upon race.

Neither xenophobia nor racism were perceived as particularly acute social problems in Australia when immigration to the country was made by predominately white persons. Australia through both the force of tradition and immigration practices encouraged the assimilation of all immigrant cultures into one definable Australian culture. In this respect Australia was similar to the traditional "melting pot" theory that was valued in the United States through the larger part of the history of immigration to America. Ethnic diversity as a stated societal goal as practiced in other nations that encouraged immigration, such as Canada, was not the rule in Australia.

The pressure to ensure tolerance toward all persons in Australia, particularly visible and ethnic minorities, had led to the passage in 1995 of the Racial Discrimination Act, which expressly prohibited a wide range of overt and indirect discrimination motivated by race. This Act was followed by the passage of the Racial Hatred Act, a statute that criminalized an equally broad range of conduct motivated by race. The existence of these statutes is significant in light of the statement made by Howard regarding the earlier assimilation of non-Muslim immigrants into Australian society and his stated desire that all immigrants "adopt Australian ways." Howard's reference to assimilation is in seeming contrast to the volume of immigration from backgrounds so clearly different from that of traditional white, Anglo-Saxon-rooted Australian society.

The corollary question raised by the prime minister's comments is how one precisely defines the "Australian ways" in that society. The more diverse the population a society becomes through immigration, the fewer common bonds will exist between its segments. As Australia has clearly pursued an immigration policy since the 1960s that has resulted in a society that includes both non-white and non-Christian persons, there would appear to be an implicit recognition that Australia is now designed to be a diverse, multicultural society.

It is of significance that the issues raised by Prime Minister Howard are those that have been advanced in a number of perspectives in American society in the wake of the 9/11 terrorist attacks. Australia has been a political ally of the United States and has provided military resources and troops to support the American initiatives in both Iraq and Afghanistan. The 2002 Bali terrorist attack that killed eighty-eight Australians and one hundred others occurred in Indonesia, a near northern neighbor to Australia and a country that is approximately ninety percent Muslim. After the 9/11 incursions, Bali served as a microcosmic example to Australians of the recent American experience with terrorism that was directly tied to a religious creed. It is not surprising that Howard would draw attention to Muslim extremism given this recent history.

FURTHER RESOURCES

Books

The Australian People, edited by James Jupp. Cambridge, U.K.: Cambridge University Press, 2001.

Horne, Donald. *10 Steps to a More Tolerant Australia*. Sydney: Penguin Australia, 2003.

Racism in Australia: Volume 180, Issues in Society, edited by Justin Healey. Thirroul, Australia: The Spinney Press, 2001.

Web sites

Government of Australia/Department of Foreign Affairs and Trade. "Human Rights." 200.5 <http://www.dfat.gov.au/hr/comm_hr/chr61_item6.html> (accessed June 28, 2006).

Refugees, Asylees, and Displaced Persons

Refugees, Asylees, and Displaced Persons

A refugee is a person who flees a nation or regime to escape persecution or violence. An asylee is an individual, unable or unwilling to return to her nation of origin, who seeks the protection of another nation. To seek asylum in the United States an individual must have a well-founded fear of persecution based on their race, ethnicity, religion, or political or social associations. Although the difference between these two groups rests on a technicality of immigration law, they share the experience of being uprooted from their homes by tragic or violent circumstance.

The refugee and asylee groups featured in this chapter have fled warfare, famine, political persecution, torture, and genocide. Throughout the chapter, images capture the drama of flight and the struggle for asylum: the Camarioca Boatlift from Cuba, a dangerous escape from the former communist bloc across the heavily guarded Berlin Wall, the Vietnamese boat people, and the controversial removal of the young Elian Gonzalez from the home of his relatives after he arrived from Cuba.

Several of the sources in this chapter highlight the plight of Jewish Holocaust victims after World War II. Allied-administered camps in Germany, Austria, Poland, and Italy housed over a quarter-million displaced persons (DPs). After its founding, the United Nations also administered aid and provided housing to DPs, but a long-term solution was slow in its evolution. Many victims did not have family or homes to which they could return; others feared further persecution or did not wish to return. Most Allied nations failed to intervene in the post-Holocaust immigration crisis for several years; many refused to alter their immigration laws to permit a mass immigration of DPs. The article "Displaced Persons Act of 1948" marks the dramatic change in U.S. policy that permitted large-scale immigration of DPs to the United States. Also included here are articles on the founding of the nation of Israel and influence of Zionism on post-Holocaust Jewish immigration.

In 2002, there were approximately sixteen million refugees across the globe who fled conflict and warfare. The editors of this volume on immigration have chosen to focus on refugees in a transnational context—those who have fled across international borders seeking refuge. The millions of internally displaced persons (IDPs) who have fled strife, but remained within their national borders, such as the recent victims of war and genocide in Sudan, are discussed in the volume on human rights.

Truman Statement on Displaced Persons

Newspaper article

By: Harry S. Truman

Date: December 22, 1945

Source: "Truman Statement on Displaced Persons." *The New York Times*, December 22, 1945.

About the Author: *The New York Times* is a daily newspaper, with a circulation of over one million copies, and was first published in New York City in 1851.

INTRODUCTION

At the end of the First World War, the 1919 Treaty of Versailles was the peace agreement negotiated between the victorious Allied nations of England, France, and the United States and defeated Germany. The refusal of the United States Senate to ratify the Treaty of Versailles meant that the United States would not join in a key product of the treaty, the League of Nations, when it was established in 1920. The United States pursued an isolationist foreign policy throughout the 1920s and 1930s; with a significant segment of the population opposed to the assistance provided by the Roosevelt administration to England after it declared war on Germany in September 1939.

It was against the backdrop of American inter-war history that President Harry Truman made his statement concerning American responsibility to Europe's displaced persons in December 1945. The prospect of a huge post-war population of displaced persons in Europe was one that was first anticipated by the Allied powers in 1944, when it became likely that Germany would ultimately be defeated by them in

People displaced by World War II gathered at a dispersal point in Ansalt, Germany, for repatriation to their home countries, 1945. © HULTON-DEUTSCH COLLECTION/CORBIS.

Europe. However, the issue was not immediately addressed at the time of the German surrender in May 1945 because American military attention immediately turned to the Pacific theater and the conclusion of the war with Japan.

In contrast to its view of foreign affairs in 1919, the United States in 1945 chose to take a leadership role with respect to achieving a solution regarding the displaced persons of Europe. Unlike its wartime ally, England, a country that had sustained widespread physical destruction as a result of the war, the United States possessed the resources to accommodate a significant influx of northern European immigration. The issue that confronted Truman in December 1945 was how the United States could provide leadership in the accommodation of the European refugees, while recognizing that there existed a significant portion of the American population who were opposed to the immigration of such persons to the United States.

By December 1945, it was clear that the boundaries of Eastern Europe would be redrawn, given the posture adopted by the Soviet Union concerning its military occupation of portions of the region. In addition to the displacement of millions of persons in Europe, there was the collateral question of whether the European Jewish peoples who were displaced could immigrate to a Jewish homeland in Palestine.

The participation of the United States in both the creation of the United Nations in 1945 and the conduct of the Nuremberg war trials are other contemporaneous examples of how the United States sought to pursue the assertive role in international matters reflected in the Truman statement on displaced persons.

PRIMARY SOURCE

Truman Statement on Displaced Persons

Washington, Dec. 22—The text of President Truman's statement on admission to this country of displaced persons and refugees in Europe, and his directive to Federal agencies on the matter were as follows:

Official Statement

The war has brought in its wake an appalling dislocation of populations in Europe. Many humanitarian organizations, including the Untied Nations Relief and the Rehabilitation Administration, are doing their utmost to solve the multitude of problems arising in connection with this dislocation of hundreds of thousands of persons. Every effort is being made to return the displaced persons and refugees in the various countries of Europe to their former homes. The great difficulty is that so many of these persons have no homes to which they may return. The immensity of the problem of displaced persons and refugees is almost beyond comprehension.

A number of countries in Europe, including Switzerland, Sweden, France and England, are working toward its solution. The United States shares the responsibility to relieve the suffering. To the extent that our present immigration laws permit, everything possible should be done at once to facilitate the entrance of some of these displaced persons and refugees into the United States.

In this way we may do something to relieve human misery and set an example to the other countries of the world which are able to receive some of these war sufferers. I feel that it is essential that we do this ourselves to show our good faith in requesting other nations to open their doors for this purpose. . . .

I hope that by early spring adequate consular facilities will be in operation in our zones in Europe, also that immigration can begin immediately upon the availability of ships.

I am informed that there are various measures now pending before the Congress which would either prohibit or severely reduce further immigration. I hope that such legislation will not be passed. This period of unspeakable human distress is not the time for us to close or to narrow our gates. I wish to emphasize however, that any effort to bring relief to these displaced persons and refugees must and will be strictly within the limits of the present quotas as imposed by law. . . .

The attached directive has been issued by me to the responsible Government agencies to carry out this policy. I wish to emphasize above all, that nothing in this directive will deprive a single American soldier or his wife or children of a berth on a vessel homeward bound, or delay their return.

This is the opportunity for America to set an example for the rest of the world in cooperation toward alleviating human misery.

The Directive

Memorandum to:

Secretary of State, Secretary of War, Attorney General, War Shipping Administrator, Surgeon General of the Public Health Service, Director General of UNRRA.

The grave dislocation of populations in Europe resulting from the war has produced human suffering that the people of the United States cannot and will not ignore. This Government should take every possible measure to facilitate full immigration to the United States under existing quota laws.

The war has most seriously disrupted our normal facilities for handling immigration matters in many parts of the world. At the same time the demands upon those facilities have increased manifold.

It is, therefore, necessary that immigration under the quotas be resumed initially in the areas of greatest need. I, therefore, direct the Secretary of State, the Secretary of War, the Attorney General, the Surgeon General of the Public Health Service, the War Shipping Administrator, and other appropriate officials to take the following action:

The Secretary of State is directed to establish with the utmost dispatch consular facilities at or near displaced person and refugee assembly center areas in the American zones of occupation. It shall be the responsibility of these consular officers, in conjunction with the immigrant inspectors, to determine as quickly as possible the eligibility of the applicants for visas and admission to the United States.

For this purpose the Secretary will, if necessary, divert the personnel and funds of his department from other functions in order to insure the most expeditious handling of this operation. In cooperation with the Attorney General he shall appoint as temporary vice consuls, authorized to issue visas, such offices of the Immigration and Naturalization Service as can be made available for this program.

Within the limits of administrative discretion, the officers of the Department of State assigned to this program shall make every effort to simplify and to hasten the process of issuing visas. If necessary, blocs of visa numbers may be assigned to each of the emergency consular establishments. Each such bloc may be used to meet the applications filed at the consular establishment to which the bloc is assigned. It is not intended, however, entirely to exclude the issuance of visas in other parts of the world.

Visas should be distributed fairly among persons of all faiths, creeds and nationalities. I desire that special attention be devoted to orphaned children to whom it is hoped the majority of visas will be issued. . . .

The Director General of the United Nations Relief and Rehabilitation Administration will be requested to provide all possible aid to the United States authorities in preparing these people for transportation to the United States and to assist in their care, particularly in the cases of children in transit and others needing special attention.

In order to insure the effective execution of this program, the Secretary of Sate, the Secretary of War, Attorney General, War Shipping Administrator and the Surgeon General of the Public Health Service shall appoint representatives to serve as members of an interdepartmental committee under the chairmanship of the Commissioner of Immigration and naturalization.

SIGNIFICANCE

The Truman statement of December 22, 1945, is part policy declaration and part executive order from President Truman. The official statement is significant for the strong language employed by Truman in the assertion of the leadership position to be taken by the United States in the assistance to be rendered to displaced persons in Europe. Commencing with the Potsdam Conference of July 1945, the Soviet Union had repeatedly indicated to the United States that the Soviet Union would resist any initiatives taken by the United States to control the movements of displaced persons resident in Soviet-controlled areas of Eastern Europe. It is for this reason that Truman emphasizes the assistance rendered to displaced persons would occur in reference to American zones of military occupation.

In December 1945, Truman faced significant political resistance regarding his domestic policies, many of which were an extension of the New Deal programs initiated by President Franklin Roosevelt in the mid–1930s. Truman's handling of foreign affairs issues such as the treatment of displaced persons assisted Truman in counteracting the resistance that he encountered on domestic policy issues, particularly those associated with curbing post war inflation.

The 1945 Truman statement had both an immediate as well as a long term impact upon American immigration policy and procedure. Truman's desire to facilitate the immigration of persons who had been displaced in Eastern Europe due to war was stated as operating within the framework of existing American immigration laws. The Truman statement foreshadowed significant changes to American immigration policy that were continued with the Displaced Persons Act of 1948 and the removal of many quotas and other immigration restrictions in 1952.

Truman advanced a policy that contrasted more than sixty years of prior American legislation that excluded most classes of nonwhite immigrants. Truman's reference to the acceptance of all nationalities, faiths, and creeds into the United States is an oblique reference to the restrictions imposed by federal legislation such as the Chinese Exclusion Act of 1882 and subsequent amendments that imposed specific quotas on identified persons and countries of origin.

The tone of the Truman statement also anticipated the wide ranging provisions of the 1947 Marshall Plan, a financial aid program that was conceived in the United States to assist in the economic reconstruction of Western Europe.

The language employed by Truman is consistent with the role of world leader that the United States had clearly pursued from the period commencing with its entry into World War II. In contrast to the isolationist sentiments that existed prior to 1941, Truman refers to a shared responsibility among nations regarding the solution to the plight of the displaced persons in Europe.

Truman strikes a balance between assistance being tendered as quickly as possible to displaced persons and any disruption of current American law and any perception that he was attempting to circumvent the power of Congress to legislate how immigration would legally occur in the United States. The Truman statement is at its strongest an indication that certain persons will be moved to the head of any line seeking consideration to enter the United States, without altering the rules as to whether such persons may ultimately be considered for admission into the United States.

The notion of establishing a mechanism in Europe to better assess claims made by displaced persons seeking to enter the United States was specifically set out in the subsequent 1948 Displaced Persons Act.

Although there is no specific mention of the ability of displaced Jewish persons to immigrate to America, the statement of policy made by President Truman occurred as the United States was attempting to facilitate the creation of a Jewish homeland in Palestine. It is clear from the position adopted by the Truman administration after December 1945 that it was the American hope that a significant European Jewish resettlement would occur in Palestine.

FURTHER RESOURCES

Books

Genizi, Haim. *America's Fair Share: The Administration and Resettlement of Displaced Persons, 1945–1952.* Detroit: Wayne State University Press, 1993.

Kochavi, Arieh J. *Post Holocaust Politics: Britain, the United States and Jewish Refugees, 1945–1948.* Chapel Hill: University of North Carolina Press, 2001.

London, Louise. *Whitehall and the Jews, 1933–1948.* Cambridge, U.K.; Cambridge University Press, 2001.

Web site

National Archives. "Truman and the Marx Brothers." 2001. <http://www.archives.gov/publication/prologue/2001/spring/truman-and-narx-brothers.html> (accessed June 7, 2006).

Message from the President of the United States Transmitting His Recommendation that Congress Enact Legislation to Enable Displaced Persons to Enter the United States as Immigrants

Statement

By: Harry S. Truman

Date: July 7, 1947

Source: "Message from the President of the United States Transmitting His Recommendation that Congress Enact Legislation to Enable Displaced Persons to Enter the United States as Immigrants," *Congressional Record.* 80th Congress, 1st sess., 1947, Vol. 19, pt. 74.

About the Author: Harry S. Truman (1884–1972) took office as the thirty-third President of the United States upon the death of President Franklin Roosevelt in 1945. Truman pursued a strong foreign policy and his terms in office were marked by conflict. He oversaw the end of World War II, most of the Korean War (1948–1952), and the beginning of the political conflict with the Soviet Union known as the Cold War. Truman was responsible for the decision to drop atomic bombs on Hiroshima and Nagasaki, Japan. On the domestic front, Truman worked to extend the New Deal reforms of his predecessor in the form of a "Fair Deal."

INTRODUCTION

The Second World War (1939–1945) displaced millions of people throughout Europe. At the end of the war the victorious Allies faced the problem of restoring them to their homes or finding them new places to live. Some of these refugees were ostarbeiter (eastern-workers) or laborers—often prisoners—forced to work in German factories and farms during the war. Other refugees were Jewish concentration camp survivors. Additional displaced persons were prisoners of war and civilians who had fled from the fighting.

Mass refugees in Europe were not a new phenomenon. Similar problems were caused by the First World War (1914–1918). At the end of World War I the League of Nations created the High Commission for Refugees to deal with the problem. This

Estonian refugees from the aftermath of World War II at port in Florida in 1946. They have arrived in the United States illegally after sailing across the Atlantic Ocean. © UPI/CORBIS-BETTMANN. REPRODUCED BY PERMISSION.

organization, led by Norwegian Fridtjof Nansen (1861–1930), relocated Russians, Armenians, Greeks, and Bulgarians displaced as a result of the war. In 1930, the League of Nations created the Nansen International Office for Refugees as a successor to the High Commission for Refugees. This office aided refugees from the Spanish Civil War (1936–1939) and aided Jews fleeing Nazi persecution as Hitler began his rise to power. However, as World War II began to spread across Europe, the League of Nations dissolved and so did the agencies created under it. In 1945, as World War II was coming to a close, the international community created a new international body to replace the League of Nations: the United Nations. Later in 1945, the United Nations Relief and Rehabilitation Administration (UNRRA) was created to assist war refugees.

In May 1945, approximately eight million foreign nationals were within German borders. The UNRRA established camps throughout the country to assist in dealing with these refugees. The situation was complicated because a significant number of refugees did not wish to return to their pre-war homes. Some of these were Jews who feared persecution upon return to their nation of origin. Others did not want to be sent to countries in Eastern Europe that had been occupied by the Soviet Union—led by the ruthless communist dictator Joseph Stalin—during the war. Roughly two million Russians were among the refugees in Germany. Some of them also feared persecution under Stalin, but under agreements reached by the Allies during the war they had no choice: all were repatriated to Russia. Even so, there were roughly one million other refugees in Germany that were unwilling to be repatriated to their countries of origin. As a result, the United States and its western European allies were forced to deal with relocating them. The International Refugee Organization was created to complete the mission of the UNRRA.

PRIMARY SOURCE

Legislation To Enable Displaced Persons To Enter The United States As Immigrants

Message

From

The President of the Untied Sates

Transmitting

His recommendation that Congress enable legislation to enable displaced persons to enter the United States as Immigrants

July 7,1947.—Referred to the committee on the Judiciary, and ordered to be printed

To the Congress of the United States:

On several occasions I have advocated legislation to enable a substantial number of displaced persons to enter the United States as immigrants. I stated this view in opening the second session of the General Assembly of the United Nations. In the message on the state of the Union on January 6, 1947, I said:

> The fact is that the executive agencies are now doing all that is reasonably possible under the limitation of existing law and established quotas. Congressional assistance in the form of new legislation is needed. I urge the Congress to turn its attention to this world problem, in an effort to find ways whereby we can fulfill our responsibilities to those thousands of homeless and suffering refugees of all faiths.

I express appreciation to the Congress for the attention already being given to this problem, and appreciation which appears to be generously shared by the public with increasing understanding of the facts and of our responsibilities.

Because of the urgency of this subject I should like again to call attention to some of its fundamental aspects. We are dealing here solely with an emergency problem growing out of the war—the disposition of a specific group of individuals, victims of war, who have come into the hands of our own and the other western Allied armies of occupation in Europe.

We should not forget how their destiny came into our hands. The Nazi armies, as they swept over Europe, uprooted many millions of men, women, and children from their homes and forced them to work for the German war economy. The Nazis annihilated millions by

hardship and persecution. Survivors were taken under the care of the western Allied armies, as these armies liberated them during the conquest of the enemy. Since the end of hostilities, the armies of occupation have been able to return to their homes some 7,000,000 of these people. But there still remain, in the western zones of Germany and Austria and in Italy, close to a million survivors who are unwilling by reason of political opinion and fear of persecution to return to the areas where they once had homes. The great majority come from the northern Baltic areas, Poland, the Russian Ukraine, and Yugoslavia.

The new International Refugee Organization, supported by the contributions of this and other countries, will aid in the care and resettlement of these displaced persons. But, as I have pointed out before, the International Refugee Organization is only a service organization. It cannot impose its will on member countries. Continuance of this Organization and our financial support of its work will be required as long as the problem of these homeless people remains unsolved.

It is unthinkable that they should be left indefinitely in camps in Europe. We cannot turn them out in Germany into the community of the very people who persecuted them. Moreover, the German economy, so devastated by war and so badly overcrowded with the return of people of German origin from neighboring countries, is approaching an economic suffocation which in itself is one of our major problems. Turning these displaced persons into such chaos would be disastrous for them and would seriously aggravate our problems there.

This Government has been firm in resisting any proposal to send these people back to their former homes by force, where it is evident that their unwillingness to return is based upon political considerations or fear of persecution. In this policy I am confident I have your support.

These victims of war and oppression look hopefully to the democratic countries to help them rebuild their lives and provide for the future of their children. We must not destroy their hope. The only civilized course is to enable these people to take new roots in friendly soil. Already certain countries of western Europe and Latin America have opened their doors to substantial numbers of these displaced persons. Plans for making homes for more of them in other countries are under consideration. But our plain duty requires that we join with other nations in solving this tragic problem.

We ourselves should admit a substantial number as immigrants. We have not yet been able to do this because our present statutory quotas applicable to the eastern European areas from which most of these people come are wholly inadequate for this purpose. Special legislation limited to this particular emergency will therefore be necessary if we are to share with other nations in this enterprise of offering an opportunity for a new life to these people.

I wish to emphasize that there is no proposal for a general revision of our immigration policy as now enunciated in our immigration statutes. There is no proposal to waive or lower our present prescribed standards for testing the fitness for admission of every immigrant, including these displaced persons. Those permitted to enter would still have to meet the admission requirements of our existing immigration laws. These laws provide adequate guaranties against the entry of those who are criminals or subversives, those likely to become public charges, and those who are otherwise undesirable.

These displaced persons are hardy and resourceful or they would not have survived. A survey of the occupational backgrounds of those in our assembly centers shows a wide variety of professions, crafts, and skills. These are people who oppose totalitarian rule, and who because of their burning faith in the principles of freedom and democracy have suffered untold privation and hardship. Because they are not Communists and are opposed to communism, they have staunchly resisted all efforts to induce them to return to Communist-controlled areas. In addition, they were our individual allies in the war.

In the light of the vast numbers of people of all countries that we have usefully assimilated into our national life, it is clear that we could readily absorb the relatively small number of these displaced persons who would be admitted. We should not forget that our Nation was founded by immigrants many of whom fled oppression and persecution. We have thrived on the energy and diversity of many peoples. It is a source of our strength that we number among our people all the major religions, races, and national origins.

Most of the individuals in the displaced persons centers already have strong roots in this country—by kinship, religion, or national origin. Their occupational background clearly indicates that they can quickly become useful members of our American communities. Their kinsmen, already in the United States, have been vital factors in farm and workshop for generations. They have made lasting contributions to our arts and sciences and political life. They have been numbered among our honored dead on every battlefield of war.

We are dealing with a human problem, a world tragedy. Let us remember that these are fellow human beings now living under conditions which frustrate hope; which make it impossible for them to take any steps, unaided, to build for themselves or their children the foundations of a new life. They live in corroding uncertainty of their future. Their fate is in our hands and must now be decided. Let us join in giving them a chance at decent and self-supporting lives.

I urge the Congress to press forward with its consideration of this subject and to pass suitable legislation as speedily as possible.

Harry S. Truman.

The White House, *July 7, 1947.*

SIGNIFICANCE

In the 1947 State of the Union Address, U.S. President Harry Truman called upon Congress to create legislation that would take action to assist those displaced persons located in Germany. In July 1947, after little action was taken, Truman sent another message to congress, once again urging legislation to be created on behalf of those displaced by the war. Finally, on the last day of session of the 80th Congress, the Displaced Persons Act of 1948 was passed. In his statement upon signing of the bill, Truman expressed his displeasure with the Act, but asserted that little action was better than none at all. The Displaced Persons Act of 1948 provided for the immigration of 400,000 people and 17,000 orphans into the United States. However, Truman suggested that that the bill was inherently discriminatory toward Jews and Catholics as it excluded those who had entered the American zones of Germany after a certain date. Truman asserted that those who fled into the American zones did so to escape persecution under the Soviet leadership. As such, Truman sought their inclusion in the act. In addition, Truman voiced his displeasure with the provision that displaced persons coming into the United States would count against future quotas. The issues raised by President Truman were revisited in 1952 with the Refugee Relief Act of 1953. This act allowed for an additional 200,000 displaced persons to migrate to the United States, coming from countries such as Poland, the Russian Ukraine, Yugoslavia and the Northern Baltic States.

By 1952, the United Nations High Commissioner for Refugees, which superseded the International Refugee Organization, had assisted approximately one million refugees immigrated to 113 countries.

FURTHER RESOURCES

Book

Wyman, Mark. *Europe's Displaced Persons 1945–1951.* New York: Associated University Presses, 1989.

Web sites

Truman Presidential Museum and Library. "Statement by the President upon Signing the Displaced Persons Act." June 25, 1948 <http://trumanlibrary.org/publicpapers/viewpapers.php?pid=1688> (accessed June 15, 2006).

National Commission on Terrorism. "Countering the Changing Threat of International Terrorism." January 1, 2004. <http://encyclopedia.laborlawtalk.com/Peter_Kropotkin> (accessed April 15, 2006).

Displaced Persons Act of 1948

Legislation

By: U.S. Congress

Date: June 25, 1948

Source: *Displaced Persons Act of 1948*, 62 Stat. 1009.

About the Author: The U.S. Congress is the legislative branch of American government. It is comprised of two branches, the Senate and the House of Representatives.

INTRODUCTION

The philosophy that provided the political foundation to the Displaced Persons Act of 1948 was first outlined by President Harry Truman in a policy statement published December 22, 1945. In the intervening two-year period, the Nuremberg war crimes trials of key Nazi leaders provided further evidence concerning the actions taken against Jews and other religious and ethnic groups during the German occupation of Europe between 1939 and 1945. The general approach of the United States towards the displaced persons of Europe was to help defined numbers of these individuals immigrate to America, while working with its former military allies to re-establish refugees in their homelands wherever possible.

Before World War II, immigration to the United States came from two primary sources. The first was Europe, most notably Great Britain, Germany, and Italy. While aspects of the integration of these groups into American society were controversial (the Irish and Italian communities of the eastern United States cities were notable examples), European immigration was relatively steady through the 1930s.

The second significant source of immigrants was Asia—first China beginning in 1849 and then Japan later in the nineteenth century. Asian immigration was such a contentious domestic issue that the United

States enacted a series of restrictive laws beginning in 1882 that significantly limited non-white immigration from any source; strict quotas were imposed for all Asian races after 1924. The limits placed upon Asian immigration were consistent with the generally isolationist stance adopted by the United States in its foreign relations after World War I, an attitude that was best reflected by the refusal of the U.S. Senate to ratify the 1919 Treaty of Versailles, the formal peace agreement ending World War I.

In May 1948, the United States supported the establishment of the Jewish state of Israel in the Palestine region of the Middle East. A significant motivation for the American support of Israel was the evidence of the horrors to which the European Jews had been subjected during World War II. Encouraging similarly displaced Europeans to immigrate to the United States was consistent with the philosophy that there existed an overwhelming humanitarian need to provide for displaced Europeans in a comprehensive fashion.

PRIMARY SOURCE

An ACT

To authorize for a limited period of time the admission into the United States of certain European displaced persons for permanent residence, and for other purposes.

Be it enacted by the Senate and House of Representatives of the United States of America in Congress assembled, That this Act may be cited as the Displaced Persons Act of 1948.

Sec. 2. When used in this Act the term—

(a) "Commission" means the Displaced Persons Commission created pursuant to this Act;

(b) "Displaced person" means any displaced person or refugee as defined in Annex I of the Constitution of the International Refugee Organization and who is the concern of the International Refugee Organization.

(c) "Eligible displaced person" means a displaced person as defined in subsection (b) above, (1) who on or after September 1, 1939, and on or before December 22, 1945, entered Germany, Austria, or Italy and who on January 1, 1948, was in Italy or the American sector, the British sector, or the French sector of either Berlin or Vienna or the American zone, the British zone, or the French zone of either Germany or Austria; or a person who, having resided in Germany or Austria, was a victim of persecution by the Nazi government and was detained in, or was obliged to flee from such persecution and was subsequently returned to, one of these countries as a result of enemy action, or of war circumstances, and on

Young refugees from Eastern Europe stand behind a chain link fence at a displaced persons camp in Paris, France, 1948. © JERRY COOKE/ CORBIS.

January 1, 1948, had not been firmly resettled therein, and (2) who is qualified under the immigration laws of the United States for admission into the United States for permanent residence, and (3) for whom assurances in accordance with the regulations of the Commission have been given that such person, if admitted into the United States, will be suitably employed without displacing some other person from employment and that such person, and the members of such person's family who shall accompany such person and who propose to live with such person, shall not become public charges and will have safe and sanitary housing without displacing some other person from such housing. The spouse and unmarried dependent child or children under twenty-one years of age of such an eligible displaced person shall, if otherwise qualified for admission into the United States for permanent residence, also be deemed eligible displaced persons.

(d) "Eligible displaced person" shall also mean a native of Czechoslovakia who has fled as a direct result of persecution or fear of persecution from that country since January 1, 1948, and (1) who is on the effective date of this Act in Italy or the American sector, the British sector, or the French sector of either Berlin or Vienna, or the American zone, the British zone, or the French zone of either Germany or Austria, and (2) who is qualified under the immigration laws of the United States for admission into the United States for permanent residence, and (3) for whom assurances in accordance with the regulations of the Commission have been given that such person, if admitted into the United States, will be suitably employed without displacing some other person from employment and that such person, and the members of such person's family who shall accompany such person and who propose to live with such person, shall not become public charges and will have safe and sanitary housing without displacing some other person from such housing. The spouse and unmarried dependent child or children under twenty-one years of age of such an eligible displaced person shall, if otherwise qualified for admission into the United States for permanent residence, also be deemed eligible displaced persons.

(e) "Eligible displaced orphan" means a displaced person (1) who is under the age of sixteen years, and (2) who is qualified under the immigration laws of the United States for admission into the United States for permanent residence, and (3) who is an orphan because of the death or disappearance of both parents, and (4) who, on or before the effective date of this Act, was in Italy or in the American sector, the British sector, or the French sector of either Berlin or Vienna or the American zone, the British zone or the French zone of either Germany or Austria, and (5) for whom satisfactory assurances in accordance with the regulations of the Commission have been given that such person, if admitted into the United States, will be cared for properly.

Sec. 3 (a) During the two fiscal years following the passage of this Act a number of immigration visas not to exceed two hundred and two thousand may be issued without regard to quota limitations for those years to eligible displaced persons as quota immigrants, as provided in subsection (b) of this section: Provided, That not less than 40 per centum of the visas issued pursuant to this Act shall be available exclusively to eligible displaced persons whose place of origin or country of nationality has been de facto annexed by a foreign power: Provided further, That not more than two thousand visas shall be issued to eligible displaced persons as defined in subsection (d) of section 2 of this Act.

(b) Upon the issuance of an immigration visa to any eligible displaced person as provided for in this Act, the consular officer shall use a quota number from the immigration quota of the country of the alien's nationality as defined in section 12 of the Act of May 26, 1924 (U.S.C., title 8, sec. 212), for the fiscal year then current at the time or, if no such quota number is available for said fiscal year, in that event for the first succeeding fiscal year in which a quota number is available: Provided, That not more than 50 per centum of any quota shall be so used in any fiscal year: Provided further, That eligible displaced orphans may be issued special nonquota immigration visas, except that the number of such special nonquota immigration visas shall not exceed three thousand.

Sec. 4. (a) Any alien who (1) entered the United States prior to April 1, 1948, and (2) is otherwise admissible under the immigration laws, and (3) is a displaced person residing in the United States as defined in this section may apply to the Attorney General for an adjustment of his immigration status. If the Attorney General shall, upon consideration of all the facts and circumstances of the case, determine that such alien is qualified under the provisions of this section, the Attorney General shall report to the Congress all of the pertinent facts in the case. If during the session of the Congress at which a case is reported, or prior to the end of the session of the Congress next following the session at which a case is reported, the Congress passes a concurrent resolution stating in substance that it favors the granting of the status of permanent residence to such alien the Attorney General is authorized, upon receipt of a fee of $18.00, which shall be deposited in the Treasury of the United States to the account of miscellaneous receipts, to record the admission of the alien for permanent residence as of the date of the alien's last entry into the United States. If prior to the end of the session of the Congress next following the session at which a case is reported, the Congress does not pass such resolution, the Attorney General shall thereupon deport such alien in the manner provided by law: Provided, That the number of displaced persons who shall be granted the status of permanent residence pursuant to this section shall not exceed 15,000. Upon the grant of status of permanent residence to such alien as provided for in this section, the Secretary of State shall, if the alien was a quota immigrant at the time of entry, reduce by one the immigration quota of the country of the alien's nationality as defined in Section 12 of the Immigration Act of May 26, 1924, for the fiscal year then current or the next succeeding fiscal year in which a quota number is available, but not more than 50 per centum of any quota shall be used for this purpose in any given fiscal year: Provided further, That quota deductions provided for in this section shall be made within the 50 per centum limitations contained in section 3(b) of this Act.

(b) When used in this section the term "Displaced Person residing in the United States" means a person who establishes that he lawfully entered the United States as a non-immigrant under section 3 or as a nonquota immigrant student under subdivision (e) of Section 4 of the Immigration Act of May 26, 1924, as amended, and that he is a person displaced from the country of his birth, or nationality, or of his last residence as a result of events subsequent to the out-break of World War II; and that he cannot return to any of such countries because of persecution or fear of persecution on account of race, religion or political opinions.

Sec. 5. Quota nationality for the purposes of this Act shall be determined in accordance with the provisions of Section 12 of the Immigration Act of 1924 (43 Stat. 160–161; 8 U.S.C. 212) and no eligible displaced person shall be issued an immigration visa if he is known or believed by the consular officer to be subject to exclusion from the United States under any provision of the immigration laws, with the exception of the contract labor clause of section 3 of the Immigration Act of February 5, 1917, as amended (39 Stat. 875-878; 8 U.S.C. 136), and that part of the said Act which excludes from the United States persons whose ticket or passage is paid by another or by any corporation, association, society, municipality, or foreign government, either directly or indirectly; and all eligible displaced persons and eligible displaced orphans shall be exempt from paying visa fees and head taxes.

Sec. 6. The preferences provided within the quotas by Section 6 of the Immigration Act of 1924 (43 Stat. 155–156; 47 Stat. 656; 45 Stat. 1009; 8 U.S.C. 206), shall not be applicable in the case of any eligible displaced person receiving an immigration visa under this Act, but in lieu of such preferences the following preferences, without priority in time of issuance of visas as between such preferences, shall be granted to eligible displaced persons and their family dependents who are the spouse or the unmarried dependent child or children under twenty-one years of age, in the consideration of visa applications:

(a) First. Eligible displaced persons who have been previously engaged in agricultural pursuits and who will be employed in the United States in agricultural pursuits: Provided, That not less than 30 per centum of the visas issued pursuant to this Act shall be made available exclusively to such persons; and Provided further, That the wife, and unmarried dependent child or children under twenty-one years of age, of such persons may, in accordance with the regulations of the Commission, be deemed to be of that class of persons who have been previously engaged in agricultural pursuits and who will be employed in the United States in agricultural pursuits.

(b) Second. Eligible displaced persons who are household, construction, clothing, and garment workers, and other workers needed in the locality in the United States in which such persons propose to reside; or eligible displaced

persons possessing special educational, scientific, technological or professional qualifications.

(c) Third. Eligible displaced persons who are the blood relatives of citizens or lawfully admitted alien residents of the United States, such relationship in either case being within the third degree of consanguinity computed according to the rules of the common law.

Sec. 7. Within the preferences provided in section 6, priority in the issuance of visas shall be given first to eligible displaced persons who during World War II bore arms against the enemies of the United States and are unable or unwilling to return to the countries of which they are nationals because of persecution or fear of persecution on account of race, religion or political opinions and second, to eligible displaced persons who, on January 1, 1948, were located in displaced persons camps and centers, but in exceptional cases visas may be issued to those eligible displaced persons located outside of displaced persons camps and centers upon a showing, in accordance with the regulations of the Commission, of special circumstances which would justify such issuance.

Sec. 8. There is hereby created a Commission to be known as the Displaced Persons Commission, consisting of three members to be appointed by the President, by and with the advice and consent of the Senate, for a term ending June 30, 1951, and one member of the Commission shall be designated by him as chairman. Each member of the Commission shall receive a salary at the rate of $10,000 per annum. There are hereby authorized to be appropriated such sums of money as may be necessary to enable the Commission to discharge its duties. Within the limits of such funds as may be appropriated to the Commission or as may be allocated to it by the President, the Commission may employ necessary personnel without regard to the Civil Service laws or the Classification Act of 1923, as amended, and make provisions for necessary supplies, facilities, and services to carry out the provisions and accomplish the purposes of this Act. It shall be the duty of the Commission to formulate and issue regulations, necessary under the provisions of this Act, and in compliance therewith, for the admission into the United States of eligible displaced orphans and eligible displaced persons. The Commission shall formulate and issue regulations for the purpose of obtaining the most general distribution and settlement of persons admitted under this Act throughout the United States and their Territories and possessions. It shall also be the duty of the Commission to report on February 1, 1949, and semiannually thereafter to the President and to the Congress on the situation regarding eligible displaced orphans, eligible displaced persons and displaced persons. Such report shall also include information respecting employment conditions and the housing situation in this country, the place and type of employment, and the residence of eligible displaced orphans and eligible displaced persons who have been admitted into the United States pursuant to the provisions of this Act. At the end of its term the Commission shall make a final report to the President and to the Congress.

Sec. 9. Every eligible displaced person, except an eligible displaced person who shall have derived his status because of being the spouse or an unmarried dependent child under twenty-one years of age of an eligible displaced person, who shall be admitted into the United States shall report, on the 1st day of January and on the 1st day of July of each year until he shall have made four reports to the Commission, respecting the employment, place of employment, and residence of such person and the members of such person's family and shall furnish such other information in connection with said employment and residence as the Commission shall by regulation prescribe: Provided, That if such person enters the United States within sixty days prior to either the 1st day of January or the 1st day of July, the first report need not be made until the next date on which a report is required to be made. Such report shall be made to the Commission during its term and thereafter to the Attorney General. Any person who willfully violates the provisions of this section shall, upon conviction thereof, be fined not to exceed $500, or be imprisoned not more than six months.

Sec., 10. No eligible displaced person shall be admitted into the United States unless there shall have first been a thorough investigation and written report made and prepared by such agency of the Government of the United States as the President shall designate, regarding such person's character, history, and eligibility under this Act. The burden of proof shall be upon the person who seeks to establish his eligibility under this Act. Any person who shall willfully make a misrepresentation for the purpose of gaining admission into the United States as an eligible displaced person shall thereafter not be admissible into the United States. No eligible displaced orphan or eligible displaced person shall be admitted into the United States under the provisions of this Act except in pursuance of the regulations of the Commission, but, except as otherwise expressly provided in this Act, the administration of this Act, under the provisions of this Act and the regulations of the Commission as herein provided, shall be by the officials who administer the other immigration laws of the United States. Except as otherwise authorized in this Act, all immigration laws, including deportation laws, shall be applicable to eligible displaced orphans and eligible displaced persons who apply to be or who are admitted into the United States pursuant to this Act.

Sec. 11. After June 30, 1948, no preference or priority shall be given to any person because of his status as a displaced person, or his status as an eligible displaced person, in the issuance of visas under the other immigration laws of the United States.

Sec. 12. The Secretary of State is hereby authorized and directed to immediately resume general consular activities in Germany and Austria to the end that the German and Austrian quotas shall be available for applicant's for immigration visas pursuant to the immigration laws. From and after June 30, 1948 and until July 1, 1950, notwithstanding the provisions of section 12 of the Immigration Act of May 26, 1924, as amended, 50 per centum of the German and Austrian quotas shall be available exclusively to persons of German ethnic origin who were born in Poland, Czechoslovakia, Hungary, Romania or Yugoslavia and who, on the effective date of this Act reside in Germany or Austria.

Sec. 13. No visas shall be issued under the provisions of this Act to any person who is or has been a member of, or participated in, any movement which is or has been hostile to the United States or the form of government of the United States.

Sec. 14. Any person or persons who knowingly violate or conspire to violate any provision of this Act, except section 9, shall be guilty of a felony, and upon conviction thereof shall be fined not less than $500 nor more than $10,000, or shall be imprisoned not less than two or more than ten years, or both.

Approved June 25, 1948.

SIGNIFICANCE

The Displaced Persons Act of 1948 represents the first legislative step taken in a seventeen-year process that would provide the framework for the most significant period of immigration in the history of the United States since the Civil War. The quotas that had been a fixture of immigration policies directed against non-white persons were modified in 1952, and the Immigration and Nationality Act abolished all quotas based upon the race of an applicant in 1965.

The generally vibrant post-war economy in the United States through the 1950s helped facilitate the entry of the European displaced persons into American society. The Act permitted over 400,000 displaced persons to enter the United States after 1948.

Consistent with the philosophy of the Displaced Persons Act, the United States supported an initiative at the United Nations to create the International Refugee Organization (IRO) in 1947. By 1951, the IRO had resettled approximately one million displaced persons throughout Europe. In 1951, the United Nations High Commission for Refugees (UNHCR) was created to further the work of resettlement in

Europe. Since 1951, a variety of world conflicts have broadened the mandate of the UNHCR and its successors in refugee resettlement.

The definition of persons who were legally permitted to seek immigration to the United States was carefully drafted in the Displaced Persons Act to ensure the widest possible acceptance of the program by the American public. Prospective immigrants were required to have both a resident sponsor in America as well as secure employment prior to their arrival. In addition, the employment could not be of a type that would displace an American citizen. This definition tended to alleviate concerns that America's compassion for European displaced persons would place a burden on American tax-payers.

In the period between President Truman's statement of December 1945, in which he proposed that the United States take a leadership role in rendering assistance to displaced persons, and the passage of the Displaced Persons Act in June 1948, there was a significant heightening of tension between the United States and the Soviet Union. These tensions would escalate into the Soviet blockade of German ports in July 1948. Anti-Communist feeling was beginning to emerge in the domestic politics of the United States. To provide a measure of control over the potential political influence that immigrant displaced persons might have in the United States, section 13 of the Act made any displaced person who had ever participated in activities "hostile" to the United States ineligible for immigration.

The definition of persons who were deemed to have participated in hostile activities was intended to exclude Communists, Socialists, and other perceived political agitators. There was no mechanism whereby the prospective immigrant could appeal such a finding by American immigration authorities. Conversely, the Act gave priority to those eligible displaced persons who fought against the enemies of the United States during the European conflict.

As the Cold War between the Soviet Union and the United States intensified during the 1950s, further American legislation was introduced to broaden the ability of European refugees to enter the United States. Most notable of these programs were the President's Escapee Program of 1952 and the Refugee Relief Act of 1953. The cumulative effect of these two statutes was to secure the admission into the United States of over 200,000 persons from regions controlled by the Soviet Union in Eastern Europe after 1945.

FURTHER RESOURCES

Books

Gruber, Ruth. *Exodus 1947: The Ship That Launched a Nation.* New York: Crown, 2000.

Loescher, Gil. *The UNHCR and World Politics: A Perilous Path.* Oxford, U.K.: Oxford University Press, 2001.

Web sites

Truman Presidential Museum and Library. "George L. Warren Papers." <http://www.trumanlibrary.org/hstpaper/warren.htm> (accessed June 7, 2006).

University of Dayton. "Asian Pacific Americans and Immigration Law." <http://academic.udayton.edu/race/02rights/immigr05.htm> (accessed June 8, 2006).

Camarioca Boat Lift

Photograph

By: Lee Lockwood

Date: October 1, 1965

Source: Lee Lockwood//Time Life Pictures/Getty Images.

About the Photographer: Lee Lockwood is an American photojournalist and author best known for his book *Castro's Cuba, Cuba's Fidel* (1967), which features a historic seven-day interview between Lockwood and the Cuban leader. The photograph is part of the collection at Getty Images, a worldwide provider of visual content materials to such communications groups as advertisers, broadcasters, designers, magazines, new media organizations, newspapers, and producers.

INTRODUCTION

On September 25, 1965, President Fidel Castro of Cuba made a surprise announcement that Cubans with relatives in the United States would be permitted to leave the island if their relatives asked for them. Men of military age—fourteen to twenty-seven—were not permitted to leave. Castro's announcement forced the United States to define its immigration policy toward Cuba and resulted in a doubling of the number of Cuban refugees in the United States from 211,000 to 411,000.

Castro came to power in January 1959. The Cuban Revolution that he led challenged long-standing American political and economic control of the island nation with a radical nationalist ideology. Castro sought to remedy the underdevelopment of Cuba by concentrating on a radical land reform policy, which took the large landed estates that belonged to the traditional elite who were also allies of American political and economic interests. In the environment of the Cold War, this policy appeared to be a step toward communism, a fear further heightened by the subsequent nationalization of the economy in 1960. Increasingly close ties between Cuba and the Soviet Union prompted the United States to end diplomatic relations with its neighbor in January 1961. Later that year, the United States attempted to remove Castro from power through the Bay of Pigs invasion. The failure of the operation moved Cuba closer to the Soviet Union, which then placed nuclear missiles on the island. This led to the Cuban missile crisis of 1962, when a full-scale invasion of the island was contemplated but rejected in favor of a U.S. Navy "quarantine" that isolated Cuba from the rest of the world. The crisis was resolved peacefully, but left U.S.-Cuban relations at a very hostile level.

Castro stated that he was allowing immigration because the United States used emigration from Cuba as a political weapon to make his government look bad. The United States had cut off normal avenues of exit following the 1962 Cuban missile crisis and would-be emigrants had resorted to using small, often-leaky boats to flee the communist dictatorship of Castro. U.S. commentators argued that Castro was permitting immigration to open talks with the United States to ultimately lead to normalized diplomatic relations, to ease internal problems by eliminating nonproductive Cubans, and to provide a safety valve by letting dissidents go to the United States. In October, hundreds of vessels of all sizes arrived at the Port of Camarioca in Cuba and, as promised, were allowed to pick up relatives and friends. Only normal delays and complications occurred.

■ PRIMARY SOURCE

Camarioca Boat Lift: Cuban exiles on board a small boat leaving Camarioca, Cuba, on its way to the United States. This was one of hundreds of small boats that carried Cubans to America druing the Camarioca Boat Lift of 1965. LEE LOCKWOOD//TIME LIFE PICTURES/GETTY IMAGES.

PRIMARY SOURCE

CAMARIOCA BOAT LIFT

See primary source image.

SIGNIFICANCE

The boat lift ended prematurely because of threatening weather. Only 5,000 of the estimated 200,000 emigrants had arrived in Florida. As the boat lift grew more dangerous, negotiations to end it and to establish a safer and more orderly passage intensified. On November 6, 1965, the United States and Cuba signed a "Memorandum of Understanding" that Cuba would permit immigration and the United States would accept emigrants, with relatives of those already living in the United States given first priority in processing and movement. The United States further agreed to provide air transportation to Miami for 3,000 to 4,000 Cuban emigrants per month.

The memorandum created a firestorm of protest in Florida. State officials publicly predicted economic chaos unless there was massive relocation of refugees outside of Florida and considerable federal help to the local areas. African-American leaders in Miami feared that Cubans would take jobs from their community. They also complained that African Americans, full-fledged American citizens, were not getting governmental assistance comparable to the quantity and quality of that given to the refugees. Tensions between African Americans and Cuban-Americans remained high in subsequent decades, partly contributing to race riots in the early 1980s.

The end of the Cold War and the collapse of the Soviet Union left Cuba increasingly isolated in the 1990s. In 1994, Castro, who had periodically created immigration problems for the United States by permitting floods of immigrants to leave Cuba, signed an immigration agreement that attempted to stop the rafters (emigrants who took anything that could float from Cuba in hopes of catching the Gulf Stream to Florida and who often drowned in the attempt). Castro allowed a legal immigration of 20,000 Cubans per year. Many of those who left were prompted to leave by the consumer goods and prosperity available to their relatives in Florida. As of 2006, an elderly Castro remains firmly in power and Cuba remains poverty-stricken. Observers expect that his death will trigger a flood of emigrants with the vast majority heading for American soil.

FURTHER RESOURCES

Books

Masud-Piloto, Felix Roberto. *From Welcomed Exiles to Illegal Immigrants: Cuban Migration to the U.S., 1959–1995.* Lanham, Md.: Rowman & Littlefield, 1996.

Pedraza-Bailey, Silvia. *Political and Economic Migrants in America: Cubans and Mexicans.* Austin, Tex.: University of Texas Press, 1985.

Perez, Louis A., Jr. *Cuba: Between Reform and Revolution.* New York: Oxford University Press, 1995.

Escapee in Lorry by Berlin Wall

Photograph

By: Anonymous

Date: September 20, 1965

Source: Photo by Express Newspapers/Getty Images.

About the Photographer: Getty Images provides photographs, film footage, and digital content, including current and historical photographs and political cartoons. The photographer is unknown.

INTRODUCTION

The year 1945 brought a welcome end to World War II, the bloodiest conflict in human history. The war cost fifty million lives and more than $2 trillion. As the armistice was signed, soldiers and civilians around the world made plans to return to their former lives. But even as the wartime powers began drawing down their armies, a new conflict was already brewing.

War produces unlikely, and at times unstable, alliances. As World War II wound to a close, it became increasingly obvious that the major Allied powers had very different expectations for post-war Europe and for Germany in particular. Under a 1945 agreement, post-war Germany was divided into four regions governed by the United States, France, Britain, and the Soviet Union. The capital city of Berlin, located within the Soviet sector, was partitioned along similar lines. But rising tensions between the East and West, coupled with deteriorating economic conditions in Germany, led to the Soviet withdrawal from the governing agreement. In 1948, the Soviets blockaded the western half of Berlin, cutting it off from outside supplies.

Facing the potential fall of West Berlin and unable to provide supplies by road or rail, the allies undertook an ambitious airlift to feed the city's citizens. Flying

The Berlin Wall under construction, August 18, 1961. © BETTMANN/CORBIS.

virtually non-stop for ten months, the effort brought a peaceful end to the blockade ten months later. In 1949, the three Allied sections of Germany united to form the Federal Republic of Germany and the Soviet sector became the German Democratic Republic. In 1952, the city of West Berlin was officially sealed off from the remainder of East Germany, though residents could still move between East and West Berlin. As living conditions deteriorated and Soviet rule became more oppressive, East Germans became increasingly likely to cross into West Germany through Berlin. More than two million are estimated to have fled the country between 1949 and 1961. Faced with a massive exodus to the West, the East German government made plans to close the border.

Early on Sunday, August 13, 1961, the East German government began constructing a barrier wall dividing Berlin. The initial barrier was temporary, created by stringing barbed-wire, blocking rail and subway lines, and stationing troops at strategic locations. The barricade ended travel between East and West Berlin, including daily commutes by

60,000 East Berlin residents who worked in the West. With the border secured, construction began on a more permanent partition.

The Berlin Wall stood as a symbol of Cold War hostilities and Soviet-bloc oppression, and was gradually upgraded through the years of its existence. Much more complex than its name implied, the wall was actually a complex series of obstacles designed to prevent East Germans from escaping. The actual concrete wall was twelve feet high, but before reaching it a fleeing East German would face two chain-link fences, barbed wire, guard towers manned with armed soldiers, patrol dogs, and a well-lit open expanse in which potential escapees were shot without warning. The wall stretched for ninety-six miles.

In the years following the wall's construction, conditions on the two sides of the border quickly diverged. The West German economy recovered, and the nation soon became a world economic power, while the East German economy languished under Soviet control. Seeking a better life in the

West, East Germans devised a series of ingenious escape methods. Tunnels were frequently dug beneath the border, often from inside buildings and at least once from a cemetery. Some refugees hid inside cars that were allowed to cross for official business. Two East German families collaborated to execute perhaps the most creative known escape. For months they purchased small pieces of light-weight cloth, painstakingly sewing them together in their basement to create a rudimentary hot air balloon. One night in 1979 they launched the balloon and drifted to freedom in West Germany.

Before the Berlin Wall evolved into the complex barrier it eventually became, it was far less secure. In a few places, East Germans simply cut the wires and walked through. The earliest days of the wall witnessed a spate of escapes using ropes and ladders, prompting East German authorities to outlaw the sale of rope and twine.

■ PRIMARY SOURCE

ESCAPEE IN LORRY BY BERLIN WALL
See primary source image.

SIGNIFICANCE

The Berlin Wall gradually became a focal point of Cold War rhetoric, a stark visual reminder of the ongoing conflict between East and West. As the Soviet economy began to weaken in the 1980s, its client states began to exercise more self-direction. In 1989, faced with growing domestic unrest, the East German Communist Party leader resigned. Hungary soon opened its border with Austria, and East Germans began following a circuitous route to West Germany, making the Berlin Wall less relevant. Following an announcement that travel restrictions between East and West would be loosened, massive crowds gathered at the wall and began chipping away small sections. By November, the wall's fall appeared inevitable, and over the course of several weeks East and West Germans demolished massive sections. In 1990, East and West Germany were formally reunited. Today, only memorial sections of the wall remain in Berlin.

FURTHER RESOURCES
Books
Cowley, Robert, ed. *The Cold War: A Military History*. New York: Random House, 2005.

Gaddis, John Lewis. *The Cold War: A New History*. New York: Penguin Press, 2005.

■ PRIMARY SOURCE

Escapee in Lorry by Berlin Wall: After using a ladder to escape over the Berlin Wall into West Berlin, East German Stanislaus Gefroerer hides in the back of a truck to avoid the attention of guards, September 20, 1965. PHOTO BY EXPRESS NEWSPAPERS/GETTY IMAGES.

Schmemann, Serge. *When the Wall Came Down: The Berlin Wall and the Fall of Soviet Communism*. New York: KingFisher, 1989.

Periodicals
Garvin, Glenn. "The New Berlin Wall." *New York Times Magazine* 155 (2005): 66–71.

Jeffrey, Terence P. "Border Fence Is Legitimate Self-Defense." *Human Events* 62 (2006): 5.

Mueller, Tom. "Beyond the Berlin Wall." *Smithsonian* 37 (2006): 94–102.

Web sites
George Washington University. "The Revolutions of 1989: New Documents from Soviet/East Europe Archives Reveal Why There Was No Crackdown." November 5, 1999. <http://www.gwu.edu/~nsarchiv/news/19991105/index.html> (accessed June 13, 2006).

PBS. "History's Great Escapes." <http://www.pbs.org/wgbh/nova/greatscape/history.html> (accessed June 13, 2006).

Ugandan Immigrants Arrive in London

Photograph

By: Anonymous

Date: September 18, 1972

Source: Photo by Keystone/Getty Images.

About the Author: This photograph is part of the collection at Getty Images, a worldwide provider of images, film, and digital materials to such communications groups as advertisers, broadcasters, designers, magazines, new media organizations, newspapers, and producers.

INTRODUCTION

One of the largest groups of refugees ever to be accepted into the United Kingdom was the Ugandan Asians who were expelled from their country in 1972. Uganda is a country in East Africa which was ruled as a British protectorate from 1894 to 1962, when it achieved independence. At that time, Uganda had a substantial minority population of ethnic Gujaratis from the Indian sub-continent, who had enjoyed great success in the country as traders and businessmen.

When African countries such as Uganda gained their independence, they faced great difficulties in building up their economies and establishing new nations, and their small Asian communities were used as convenient scapegoats for all their problems. They were blamed, for example, for taking money out of the country in the form of remittances to their home countries, and for monopolizing business and restricting opportunities for African entrepreneurs.

During the 1960s a steady flow of Ugandan Asians migrated to Britain, taking advantage of the British citizenship that was extended to all Britain's New Commonwealth nationals under the 1948 British Nationality Act. Their migration to Britain in the early-to mid-1960s was also facilitated by the provisions of the 1962 Commonwealth Immigrants Act that exempted all British citizens from immigration controls. However, in 1968, in response to concerns about rapidly rising immigration levels, the Labour government imposed new controls on British citizens from the New Commonwealth countries, which meant that they were not eligible to immigrate to Britain unless at least one of their parents or grandparents had been born or naturalized there. The Act was

General Idi Amin, in uniform, speaking in Cairo, Egypt. The so-called president of Uganda was a ruthless dictator blamed for tens of thousands of deaths in Uganda. AP/WIDE WORLD PHOTOS, INC. REPRODUCED BY PERMISSION.

criticized by the European Commission on Human Rights as being racist and directed particularly at East African Asians fleeing victimization.

It was perhaps the widespread condemnation of their actions in 1968 that influenced the British government to act more favorably towards the Ugandan Asians in 1972. Military dictator Idi Amin (1925–2003) had taken control of the country under a coup in 1971, following which he carried out a census of Asians in Uganda and publicly accused them of economic misconduct and for ethnic insularity. In 1972 Amin expelled all Asians from Uganda and seized their property. In response, Britain agreed to allow the entry of all of those refugees that it could not persuade other countries to accept. Around 23,000 were settled in other countries, such as Canada, while Britain took the remaining 27,000 or so, many of whom were destitute when they arrived in the country.

Because race relations were politically sensitive in Britain at this time, a Uganda Resettlement Board was set up with the purpose of dispersing the Ugandan Asian refugees away from existing centers of Asian settlement in Britain. However, this policy was unsuccessful, as most of the refugees gravitated towards areas in which they had a support network of relatives or friends. As a result, substantial East African Asian communities developed in areas of North London and the Midlands, especially Leicester. In total, around 103,588 East African

Ugandan Immigrants Arrive in London: Ugandan Asians arrive at Stansted Airport in Britain, shortly after Ugandan military dictator Idi Amin implemented a new regime expelling Asians from Uganda, 1972. PHOTO BY KEYSTONE/GETTY IMAGES.

Asians entered Britain, mainly from Uganda and Kenya, in the years up to 1973, but at this time immigration quotas were reinstated restricting the immigration of East African Asians to 5,000 per year.

UGANDAN IMMIGRANTS ARRIVE IN LONDON

See primary source image.

SIGNIFICANCE

While the Ugandan economy suffered badly as a result of the expulsion of the Gujarati community, this group transplanted their entrepreneurial talents to Great Britain and the other countries in which they settled, and become one of the most highly successful ethnic minorities. Ugandan Asians in Britain have dominated certain sectors of the retail trade, prospered in a range of business activities, and have been instrumental in helping to regenerate inner city areas.

The 1972 Ugandan Asian crisis had a major adverse impact on the effectiveness of the 1971 Immigration Act, which had been intended to reduce immigration into Britain from its former colonies. The surge in East African Asian immigration was also a major factor in the growth at this time of support for the extreme right-wing National Front, who organized violent demonstrations against immigration and ethnic minorities throughout the 1970s. This in turn helped to drive a policy emphasis on race relations legislation which over time helped to improve the situation for ethnic minorities in the United Kingdom.

FURTHER RESOURCES

Book

Spencer, Ian R. G. *British Immigration Policy since 1939: The Making of Multi-Racial Britain*. London and New York: Routledge, 1997.

Periodical

Mattausch, John. "From Subjects to Citizens: British 'East African Asians'." *Journal of Ethnic and Migration Studies* (24) (1) (1988): 121–142.

Yitzhak Rabin on the Centrality of Zionism to Israel's Existence

Speech

By: Yitzhak Rabin

Date: November 11, 1975

Source: Rabin, Yitzhak. *Major Knesset Debates: 1948–1981.* Lanham, Md: University Press of America, 1975.

About the Author: Yitzhak Rabin served in the Israeli Defense Force for twenty-seven years, reaching the position of IDF Chief of Staff. After his military service, Rabin served as the Israeli ambassador to the United States. In 1974, after joining the Labor Party, Rabin was elected Prime Minister and held the position until 1977. The Labor party regained the majority in 1992 and Rabin was once again elected Prime Minister. In 1994, Rabin, along with Yassar Arafat and Shimon Peres, was awarded the Nobel Peace Prize for the Oslo Declaration of Principles. In 1995, Rabin was assassinated after attending a rally in Tel Aviv.

INTRODUCTION

As the nineteenth century came to a close, anti-Semitism became apparent throughout Europe and fueled the movement for the creation of a Jewish homeland, which became referred to as Zionism. Following the assassination of the Tsar, Russian political problems were often blamed on Jews, making them targets of reprisal violence. In France, the Dreyfus affair, in which a Jewish army captain was convicted of treason based on forged evidence, highlighted the institutionalized anti-Semitism in France. Jewish writers such as Leon Pinsker and Theodore Herzl began to assert that Jews would continue to be the target of discrimination wherever they remained a minority. In

1896, Herzl published *Der Judenstaat*, or the *State of the Jews*, which declared that the condition of the Diaspora, or Jews residing throughout the world, would continue to deteriorate. Under Herzl's leadership, the first Zionist Congress met in August 1897 and the goal to gain a Jewish home was established. Chaim Weizmann led the Zionist movement after Herzl's death and met with British leaders in the hopes of gaining British support for a homeland. By 1907, Weizmann had visited Palestine and concluded that the region should be colonized by the Jews. As such, a trickle of immigrants began to move into the region.

During this time, Western nations viewed Palestine as a region that lacked national settlement. The approximately 200,000 Arabs that resided in the region lacked a formal government structure and were ethnically identified based on language rather than national identity. At the start of World War I, Britain negotiated policies with both Arabs and the Jews who resided in the Middle East. The 1917 Balfour Declaration stated the British sympathy for Zionist goals and British intent to sponsor a national home for the Jews. The British troops that occupied the Middle East allowed Britain to become the dominant power following the defeat of Germany and Turkey in World War I. At the San Remo Conference, which was drafted in 1920 and adopted by the League of Nations in 1922, the Principal Allied Powers divided the Middle East using self-interest to determine their individual country's mandates. While the Western powers carved up the region, Jews began to immigrate in larger numbers to Palestine. From 1919–1931, the total Jewish population increased from 60,000 to 175,000.

During the period preceding World War II, Arabs became increasingly resistant to the increase in Jewish immigrants to Palestine. After a series of violent conflicts resulted in the deaths of Britons, Jews, and Arabs, the British government published the White Paper of 1939, which established a new policy for Britain toward Zionism. The white paper asserted that Britain sought an independent Palestinian state, governed by Jews and Arabs who shared authority. Zionists perceived the paper as a betrayal on the part of British policy makers and began to pursue support from the United States where many of the Jewish Diaspora resided. As World War II came to an end, Zionists gained popular support for a Jewish state as the details of the Holocaust became publicized. In addition, Britain and the United States recognized that the oil-rich Middle East would play an important role in the looming Cold War with the Soviet Union. By 1948, the United Nations

At a news conference, Israeli prime minister Yitzhak Rabin states that Israel will insist on borders it can defend as part of any permanent peace settlement with Arabs. © BETTMANN/CORBIS.

Resolution 181 terminated the Mandate for Palestine, by which the British has administered the region. As a result, the Jewish inhabitants of the region declared their independence and the statehood of Israel. Arab nations rejected the state of Israel while western powers acknowledged the new country.

After the British left the nascent state, the surrounding Arab nations—including Egypt, Syria, Iraq, Lebanon, Jordan, and Saudi Arabia—declared war on Israel. Invasions by Egyptian, Syrian, and Jordanian forces began the Israeli War of Independence. The armistice for this war, signed in 1949, partitioned additional land to Israel than originally agreed to by the United Nations resolution. By 1967, the Cold War between the United States and the Soviet Union was in full force. Many Arab countries received military and financial support from the Soviet Union, while the United States, Britain, and France continued to support Israel. The six-day war occurred in June 1967 as a response to the actions of Egyptian President Gamal Abdel Nasser, who closed the straits of Tiran to Israeli shipping and expelled UN peacekeepers. In response, Israel launched attacks on the Egyptian air force and began an occupation of Sinai and Gaza, as well as the West Bank and Golan Heights. Peace was established through UN Resolution 242. However, many Arabs, including those within the Palestinian Liberation Organization, rejected the terms of the resolution. As a result, on October 6, 1973, Egyptian and Syrian forces launched an attack on Israel during the Jewish holy day of atonement, Yom Kippur. Both the United States and the Soviet Union aided in supplying their respective allies with arms. In an effort to respond to U.S. and western support of Israel during this war, the oil-producing nations under OPEC reduced their production of oil and halted their commerce with those nations—thus resulting in the Arab oil embargo of 1973.

PRIMARY SOURCE

Mr. Speaker, distinguished Knesset, yesterday the majority at the U.N. Assembly, serving Arab hostility, voted against the Jewish people, Zionism and the State of Israel. The majority at the Assembly approved resolutions which are factually and historically false, condemning Israel as a "racist state in occupied Palestine," and defining Zionism as "racism and racial discrimination." The prologue to the resolutions calls on all countries "to oppose that racist and imperialist ideology." Prior to that the Assembly approved two resolutions calling for the participation of the terrorist organization known as the PLO in the Geneva Conference and the establishment of a committee to supervise the implementation of those hostile resolutions.

By those three resolutions... the majority at the Assembly extended political support to the enemies of the Jewish people and the State of Israel who seek to undermine its moral, ideological and legal basis. By condemning Zionism as a supposedly racist theory, the people who initiated the resolution seek to deprive Israel of its right to exist, which is the result of the independent liberation movement of the Jewish people—Zionism.

We must not delude ourselves. This is not an abstract ideological debate, but a significant attack with clear political objectives, and as such it is unprecedented in the history of the struggle we have been engaged in for several decades. The aim of the Arab representatives and their supporters is to set Israel outside the pale and invalidate its very existence in order to prepare the political conditions for intensifying the struggle against Israel as an independent country and prepare the ground for the establishment of an Arafat-led state on Israel's ruins...

The resolutions... are barren in terms of *realpolitik*. Their content and timing stand in complete contradiction to the positive trend embodied in the Interim Agreement between Israel and Egypt. Progress towards peace and the solution of the conflict in our region, including the Palestinian problem, cannot be attained in the way indicated by the U.N. Assembly. Progress towards peace and the solution of the various problems is possible, but only while respecting the rights, existence, vocations and security of Israel. We will continue to follow that path despite bitter disappointments and the selfish appeasement of wealth and oil-producers.

What regimes rule in the Arab countries which imitated the resolution condemning Zionism and what moral right do they have to decide on matters of human and national rights? They are all countries which, since becoming independent, have been characterized by persecution, torture and even the destruction of minorities and ethnic groups within Assyrian minority. In recent times Iraq has tormented the Kurdish minority, causing massive bloodshed. In Sudan the black tribes to the south may have been slaughtered for years. In Egypt the Coptic minority has been accorded second-class status, and everyone remembers the treatment meted out to the inhabitants of the Gaza Strip when it was under Egyptian rule. Syria has always gloried in persecuting its minorities. Saudi Arabia still trades in slaves. In Lebanon the Maronite Christians are still fighting to survive. That is the true portrait and the moral mandate of the Arab countries which initiated those resolutions at the U.N. Assembly.

As for the PLO, which is invited to give its views on bringing peace to the Middle East, let it suffice to quote a few passages from its Manifesto:

"The liberation of Palestine is a national duty in order to repel the imperialist Zionist invasion from the great Arab homeland and purge Palestine of Zionist existence." "Claims as to the historical or spiritual bond between the Jews and Palestine are incompatible with historical truths." "Zionism is merely a virulently racist, aggressive movement which is expansionist-colonialist in its aims and fascist and Nazi in its means."

Who supported this base initiative? An examination of the list of countries which supported the resolution condemning Zionism reveals that it includes several countries whose regimes are dictatorial or totalitarian and whose histories are full of tyranny, repression and the disregard for human rights and dignity. It is hardly surprising, therefore, that the resolutions make no mention of human,

religious and social freedoms, knowing the initiators' own deficiencies in those areas.

We may draw encouragement from the countries which opposed the anti-Israel initiative... each one of which has a past which is distinguished by the ceaseless struggle for human freedom and national rights. They are enlightened democracies which have on more than one occasion fought against attempts to subordinate and subject man and society in the name of racist and reactionary theories... Once again it has been proved that the attitude of societies and people to the Jewish people is one of the touchstones of their enlightenment.

This is not the first time that November 10 has marked a significant event in the history of the Jewish people. Yesterday was the anniversary of *Kristallnacht* (the pogrom of 9 November 1938) in Nazi Germany... It is also the date on which the majority in the U.N. struck a mortal blow at the U.N. itself... By supporting this Arab scheme the U.N. has lost whatever moral and political validity it had, becoming the arena for clashes which have nothing to do with the principles and ideals for which it was established. Israel will not be the victim of these resolutions. It is the U.N. which has let itself beyond the pale... of universal principles....

There is not greater historical and moral distortion than what happened last night at the U.N. Assembly. The nation which throughout the generations has been the victim of racist persecution which is unparalleled in the history of mankind was once again the object of despicable attacks by benighted regimes. There is no greater and crueler irony than branding Zionism, which represents the struggle of an ancient nation for freedom in its land from the time our ancestors left ancient Egypt to this very day, and the nation which has contributed more than any other to the values of human freedom, as racist.

This requires the Jewish people in the diaspora and Israel to draw some basic conclusions. I call on the Jewish people in the diaspora to stand up to the plot against us, because Zionism, Judaism, the State of Israel and the Jewish people are all one and the same. At the basis of Jewish belief lies the link with the Land of Israel and the return to Zion... I call on the Jewish communities to make a greater effort to assure the welfare and future of the nation and State of Israel. I call on the entire Jewish nation to deepen Jewish consciousness, cultivate Jewish values and traditions and identify fully with the Jewish state. Today more than ever all Jews are responsible for one another. I call on Jewish youth throughout the world to immigrate to Israel and join us in fulfilling the Zionist vision.

I call on the nation in Zion to rise to the challenge before us. The attacks on Zionism and the Jewish state oblige us to reexamine our way of life and increase private and public efforts to fortify the State of Israel. Today more than ever we must rise above individual selfishness and comfort and devote ourselves completely to the objectives of Zionism. To those who rose up against us yesterday at the U.N., I say: we are no longer a helpless community. We are no longer a weak and frightened people. We are no longer despairing and hopeless. Something has happened since *Kristallnacht*. The Jewish nation now stands erect. The State of Israel has come into being. The State of Israel is firm, confident and strong. The State of Israel and its nation have decided once and for all to ensure that henceforth and forever "Israel shall dwell in safety in its land."

SIGNIFICANCE

In 1973 and 1974, the United Nations began to adopt a series of resolutions that highlighted the experience of Palestinian refugees, such as the first report of the Special Committee to Investigate Israeli Practices Affecting the Human Rights of the Population of the Occupied Territories. In addition, the international body called for a UN-sponsored conference on peace in the Middle East. In 1974, the Palestinian Liberation Organization was invited to participate in the plenary meetings and join in the UN assembly as a full observer. PLO leader Yassar Arafat delivered his "gun and olive branch" speech to the UN General Assembly and November 29, 1974 was designated as the International Day of Solidarity with the Palestinian People. On November 10, 1975, the UN adopted resolution 3379, passing with a vote of seventy-two in favor, thirty five against, and thirty-two abstentions. Within the text of this resolution, Zionism is equated to racism.

UN resolution 3379 was revoked on December 16, 1991 by UN resolution 4684, the complete text of which reads, "The general assembly decides to revoke the determination contained in its resolution 3379 (XXX) of 10 November 1975." Israel insisted on the revocation of the 1975 resolution before it would participate in the Madrid Peace Conference.

FURTHER RESOURCES

Books

Brenner, Michael. *Zionism: A Brief History*. Princeton, N.J.: Markus Weiner Publishers, 2003.

Sacher, H. M. *A History of Israel*. New York: Alfred Knopf, 1979.

Periodicals

Bennis, Phyllis. "The United Nations and Palestine: Partition and its Aftermath." *Arab Studies Quarterly* (June 22,1997).

Ovendale, Ritchie . "The Origins of the Arab-Israeli Conflict." *Historian* (January 1, 2002).

Vietnamese Boat People Arrive at Indonesia's Anambas Islands

Photograph

By: Jacques Pavlovsky

Date: August 5, 1979

Source: © Jacques Pavlovsky/Sygma/Corbis.

About the Photographer: Jacques Pavlovsky is a Paris-based photographer. This photograph is part of the collection of the Corbis Corporation, headquartered in Seattle, with a worldwide archive of over 70 million images.

INTRODUCTION

The fall of South Vietnam in April 1975 led to a mass migration of refugees fleeing communist rule. When communists leaders took control of South Vietnam, they ordered the systematic killings of former police officers, South Vietnamese soldiers, and others who had served in the South Vietnamese government. By 1976, some Southerners were being moved from cities to the country, while others were sent to reeducation camps for communist indoctrination or punishment.

Some early refugees were lucky enough to be taken out of the country by the United States, as its forces left the country. By early 1976, however, it was increasingly common for refugees to flee Vietnam by sea in the hopes of reaching Thailand, Malaysia, Indonesia, or Singapore. These refugees became known as boat people. The craft available to them were small, always packed with people, and often incapable of long journeys. The hazards of journeying on small, overcrowded watercraft combined with tales of inhuman treatment by pirates and, in some cases, governments, to draw international attention to the plight of the boat people.

PRIMARY SOURCE

Vietnamese Boat People Arrive at Indonesia's Anambas Islands: Vietnamese boat people refugees disembark at a refugee camp on Anambas Island in Indonesia. © JACQUES PAVLOVSKY/SYGMA/CORBIS.

The boat people were not greeted with open arms by their Southeast Asian neighbors. In Malaysia, Deputy Prime Minister Mahathir Mohamad issued statements that the boat people attempting to enter his country would be expelled, that they would be drowned if they tried to sink their boats in Malaysian waters in hope of rescue, and that he would seek legislation enabling Malaysia to shoot on sight any additional refugees trying to come ashore. However, Malaysia did accept 74,000 refugees by mid–1979.

Many of the refugees rejected by Malaysia went to Indonesia. Indonesia had several separate refugee areas, Galang Site 1A, and Galang Site 1B, and Galang Site 2. While life in these camps approached normality, a few temporary camps, such as Camp Kuku, became notorious for their inhumanity. Kuku housed about 500 boat people who were given little food and no medical assistance. Guards were notorious for beating the refugees and sexually assaulting the women, while officials took bribes before recommending resettlement. Most boat people who were housed in Galang first reached Indonesia at islands such as Natuna, Tarempa, and Anambas.

PRIMARY SOURCE

VIETNAMESE BOAT PEOPLE ARRIVE AT INDONESIA'S ANAMBAS ISLANDS

See primary source image.

SIGNIFICANCE

By July 1979, Vietnamese refugees were getting into boats at the rate of 65,000 persons per month. The Conference of Geneva, with fifty countries participating, was the first attempt at an international response to the mass exodus. The meeting led to pledges of resettlement for more than 260,000 refugees and financial pledges to the United Nations High Commissioner for Refugees (UNHCR) for the Indochina program amounting to $190 million. Perhaps more significantly, the gathering emphasized that the Vietnamese refugees were a worldwide concern not simply a regional issue.

In May 1979, the Vietnamese government reached an agreement with the UNHCR that eventually ended the crisis of the Vietnamese boat people. Under the terms of the agreement, Vietnam permitted the departure of Vietnamese citizens who wanted to leave the country to join relatives abroad or to work. More than two million refugees fled Vietnam in the years from 1975 to 1992, when the exodus largely ended. While some have flourished, many of the refugees have struggled to find countries willing to accept them for resettlement, and to become established in their new countries.

FURTHER RESOURCES
Books

Freeman, James M., and Nguyen Dinh Huu. *Voices from the Camps: Vietnamese Children Seeking Asylum.* Seattle: University of Washington Press, 2003.

Hitchcox, Linda. *Vietnamese Refugees in Southeast Asian Camps.* London: Macmillan, 1990.

Vietnamese boat people, refugees from Communist-dominated Vietnam, approach Indonesia's Anambas Island on August 5, 1979. © JACQUES PAVLOVSKY/SYGMA/CORBIS.

Stone, Scott C. S., and John E. McGowan. *Wrapped in the Wind's Shawl: Refugees of Southeast Asia and the Western World.* San Rafael, CA: Presidio, 1980.

Vo, Nghia M. *The Vietnamese Boat People, 1954 and 1975–1992.* Jefferson, NC: McFarland, 2006.

The Nguyen Family: From Vietnam to Chicago, 1975–1986

Book excerpt

By: Al Santoli

Date: 1993

Source: Dublin, Thomas, ed. *Immigrant Voices: New Lives in America, 1773–1986.* Urbana: University of Illinois Press, 1993.

About the Author: Al Santoli (b. 1949) is the senior vice-president of the American Foreign Policy Council and director of its Asia-Pacific Initiative. He is a specialist on security issues in the Asia-Pacific region and an author of works on military history, including *Everything We Had: An Oral History of the Vietnam War.*

INTRODUCTION

In the mid- to late–1970s, massive numbers of Vietnamese refugees settled in the United States. The first wave of refugees left South Vietnam in the aftermath of the Vietnam War in 1975, when their country was invaded by communist North Vietnam, following the withdrawal of United States support from the South. These were mainly well-educated, English-speaking upper or middle class Vietnamese, many of whom had been working for or associated with the U.S. government. They were airlifted out of the country by the United States to temporary refugee camps in other parts of Southeast Asia, and then resettled in the United States.

People pray on the eve of the 30th anniversary of the Fall of Saigon, April 29, 2005, at the Vietnam War Memorial in Westminster, California. Westminster's Little Sigon district is the nation's largest Vietnamese business district. PHOTO BY DAVID McNEW/GETTY IMAGES.

The emigration of refugees from South Vietnam continued throughout the 1970s, rising from approximately 1,500 per month in 1975 to more than 60,000 per month in 1979. However, the later waves of migrants were very different from those who had left immediately after the Communist invasion in 1975. The later refugees consisted mainly of poorer people with lower levels of education, who fled Vietnam in small boats. Many of these "boat people" perished at sea, while others were successful in reaching neighboring countries. However, the massive numbers involved and the concerns about the costs of accepting so many refugees led many countries to refuse them entry. In 1979, a United Nations Meeting on Refugees and Displaced Persons in South-East Asia in 1979 helped to resolve the situation by gaining formal agreement on the part of final resettlement countries such as the United States to take more Vietnamese refugees and to process their applications faster, in return for agreed temporary refuge in camps in Southeast Asian countries. By the end of 1979, nearly a quarter of a million Vietnamese refugees had been resettled in the United States.

Refugees from the first wave of migrants who left Vietnam for the United States, such as the family in this extract, were instrumental in establishing community organizations to help later arrivals, often with the support of federal and state agencies. The fact that they could mostly speak English and were well-educated helped their own assimilation into U.S. society and their ability to work with the government in this way. However, as the extract demonstrates, they initially encountered high levels of public hostility and discrimination on arrival in the United States. This was partly due to the high level of opposition among the general public to the Vietnam War, as well as concerns about refugees taking much-needed jobs in a time of economic recession and resentment about the assistance provided by the government to the refugees, which had not been available to other groups of immigrants.

As officially recognized refugees, the Vietnamese have been eligible to receive a wide range of social and welfare benefits in the United States to assist their resettlement. These have included cash and medical benefits on arrival, English-language and employment training, and assistance in finding homes and jobs. Those who meet certain criteria are also eligible for welfare assistance on the same means-tested basis as U.S. citizens, including Aid to Families with Dependent Children; Section 8 (subsidized) Housing, Supplemental Security Income (SSI), Medicaid and food stamps. However, the Vietnamese refugees were encouraged to find jobs and become financially independent as soon as possible, which meant that many had to take low-status and low-paying jobs for which they were over-qualified, bringing about a decline in their socio-economic status. They were also resettled throughout the country to spread the support costs, under the Refugee Dispersion Policy, but many subsequently drifted back to areas with large Vietnamese populations and informal support networks.

PRIMARY SOURCE

Trong: I have always believed that, if you just stay home and do nothing you are not a person whom others will respect. Since I came to Chicago in 1976, I've been involved in building the Vietnamese community. Of the twelve thousand Vietnamese who live in this city, more than half live in a fourteen-block area around the Argyle Street business strip, between Broadway and Sheridan roads.

Uptown is called the Ellis Island of Chicago. Some thirty languages are spoken in the area. Besides the Vietnamese, there are a thousand Cambodians, two hundred Laotians, and some Hmnong. But most of the people are American blacks, Appalachian whites who came from the coal mines of Kentucky and West Virginia, Mexicans, and some American Indians.

In 1975, when the refugees first began arriving, the area was a dumping ground for derelicts, mental patients, and everyone else the city didn't want. Drug addicts, gangs, and prostitutes hung out in abandoned buildings owned by absentee landlords. Some refugee families with children live in transient hotels alongside winos. Large multi-story housing projects like on the corner of Argyle and Sheridan were very dangerous. Refugees were constantly robbed and beaten.

The Argyle Street business strip had only a few struggling businesses, like small Chinese restaurants, a mom-and-pop bakery, and a tavern with naked dancers. Most storefronts were empty, with a lot of threatening people on the street.

When my wife and I came to Chicago, our major concern was to feed our five small children. We had Vietnamese pride and did not want to take public aid. We wanted the American community and authorities to respect us.

In Uptown, we felt like we were thrust from one war zone to another. Local community organizations strongly opposed the refugees. People talked about a "yellow Horde invasion." They started a lawsuit campaign against the city for bringing Indochinese into their area. They said, "Because the refugees are moving in, rents are going higher."

The absentee landlords in the neighborhood were horrible. The [community] organizations had started a boycott against them before the refugees arrived. This crated a lot of vacancies in some of the run-down buildings. The voluntary agencies who sponsored the refugees saw the cheap rents and placed refugee families in those apartments. That allowed slumlords to stay in business.

At the height of the tension, the city brought the community associations, some refugee leaders, and voluntary agency representatives into a room to talk. Commander Howard Patinkin of the police department moderated the session, because it was getting to the point of violence. At the meeting, the community groups realized that the refugees were good people, and an agreement was made for the voluntary agencies to coordinate with local residents.

Just trying to begin a new life here, we had so many difficulties. When I worked as a janitor at Water Tower Place, a co-worker told me, "Trong, do you know that America is overpopulated? We have more than two hundred million people. We don't need you. Go back where you belong." I was shocked to hear people trying to chase us out. I thought, "Who is going to feed the children?" In America, a single income can never feed the family. Even though our youngest was just a baby, my wife had to find work.

Hanh: When we first came to Chicago, I cried a lot. In the factory where I worked, there weren't many Americans. Most were Mexicans, some legal, but also many illegal aliens. They acted like, as Vietnamese say, "Old ghosts bully new ghosts." They cursed our people.

Some Mexicans said, "You come here and take our jobs. Go back wherever you came from." I was very upset and cried. They said so many things. Then one day some of them said, "You come here to make money, then go back home and live like kings." That was too much. I couldn't hold it in any more.

I told them in a very soft voice, "We are Vietnams people. You don't have enough education to know where our country is. Vietnam is a small country, but we did not come to America to look for jobs. We're political refugees. We can't go back home." I didn't call them bad names or anything, but I said, "You are the ones who come here to make money to bring back to your country. We spend our money here." After that, they didn't bother us very much.

Trong: In 1978, just before the boat-people crisis began, I found a job as a caseworker with Travelers and Immigrants Aid. My goal was to help those in need. After seven years in that job, when the Vietnamese community had become stabilized, I decided to open a restaurant. For my wife, working in a factory was such a heavy job. She tried so hard to stay with that type of work to help feed our family, but she was laid off on different occasions. When friends sometimes came to our home, they enjoyed my wife's cooking. They said, "Maybe one day open a restaurant, so we can eat your cooking more often."

They were joking, but it gave us the idea to open our own business. In June 1985, we opened this restaurant. We named it Song Huong, after the Perfume River in my home area of central Vietnam. . . .

Thanh: Our children were very young when we came here. So we have adjusted and let them have some freedom. We realize that we can't live the way we did in Vietnam. But we try to reach them to respect family life. I tell my children, "The U.S. is liberal. You have the right to drive a car. But when you see a 'One Way' sign, you can't ignore it and say, 'This is a free country, nobody can tell me what to do.' That will lead to a bad accident where you can get hurt. You must also think that way in terms of family rules."

Trong: Our oldest daughter is fifteen, I wouldn't be happy if a boy asked her to a dance at school or for a date, but it would be okay to go to a party at school, because it would be under supervision. Sometimes we compromise and allow her to go to a party at a friend's house if we know the parents.

Vietnamese tradition is not as strict with boys. I gave my son more freedom when he was in high school, but I had to know where he was going and who he was associating with. I told him, "I give you freedom, but you have to be home by 10:00 P.M., or midnight." If he didn't come home at the time limit—"Sorry," the next time he asks. But sometimes, when he was having a lot of fun and wanted to stay out a little longer, if he called me to ask permission, that was fine.

Last year, after Tran graduated from high school, he moved out on his own. That was a great shock for me. We didn't have enough money to send him to college, so he started working full-time to save for tuition. His high-school grades were average, but he is very artistic, a good drummer. In his free times, he practices a lot with his band. During days he works at a company downtown, and in the evenings he comes into our restaurant to help.

This first year of the restaurant business was miserable. Little by little, our customers have been building up. . . .

Thahn-Tram: When most American first meet me, they think that I'm seventeen or eighteen and was born here. When they find out that I'm only fourteen and was born in Vietnam, they are surprised.

I don't work at the restaurant on weekdays during the school year. But if I don't have any homework, I'll call the restaurant to see if my mom and dad need me. I come in all day on weekends and during the summer.

The best thing about working here is that I've gotten better at speaking Vietnamese. When I go to school in Des Plaines, there aren't Vietnamese to talk with. I only talk Vietnamese if I talk on the phone with friends in Uptown. But by working here, I've learned how to talk and write better.

I became a citizen with my parents two years ago. The whole family took the oath of citizenship together. Now most of my friends at school say that because I have my citizenship, I am American, no longer Vietnamese. I always tell them, "I'm still Vietnamese, no matter what I'm never going to be all American. I always have to stick to my country. . . ."

SIGNIFICANCE

The Vietnamese were one of the largest groups of refugees in recent decades, and their mass exodus from Vietnam resulted in the establishment of new national and international policies and legislation for dealing with political migrants. Their arrival in large numbers in the United States brought about a new distinction in the treatment of refugees and other immigrants in the provision of welfare, which resulted in considerable resentment from other immigrant groups who did not receive the same benefits as the Vietnamese.

The Vietnamese population of the United States continued to grow throughout the 1980s as new immigration policies allowed the entry of former military personnel and political prisoners, along with their family members. Around half of the Vietnamese American population in the United States now lives in California, but there are also substantial communities in Texas, Virginia, Washington, New York and a number of other states.

In general, the Vietnamese have been very successful economically in the United States, particularly the first wave immigrants who achieved average income levels comparable to the U.S. population as a whole by the mid–1980s. The success of the Vietnamese community is likely to be due to a combination of the government assistance that they have received, as well as their own educational ability or entrepreneurial skills. Additionally, the Vietnamese have drawn more heavily than other immigrant groups on their own family and community networks for support, which may have been a key factor in their success. Vietnamese can now be found in a wide range of occupations including professional jobs, retail, catering, and light manufacturing. In general, the community has experienced a high level of cultural assimilation, and their children have largely adopted American lifestyles and are achieving educational success. At the same time, fairly high levels of delinquency have been reported among Vietnamese youths, a phenomenon that may reflect continuing perceived or actual discrimination against them in American society.

FURTHER RESOURCES
Books

Hien Duc Do. *The Vietnamese Americans*. Westpost, Conn.: Greenwood Press, 1999.

Kibria, Nazli. *Family Tightrope: The Changing Lives of Vietnamese Americans*. Princeton, N.J.: Princeton University Press, 1993.

Periodicals

Menjivar, Cecilia. "Immigrant Kinship Networks: Vietnamese, Salvadoreans and Mexicans in Comparative Perspective." *Journal of Comparative Family Studies* 28 (1) (Spring 1997): 1–24.

Wood, Joseph. "Vietnamese American Place Making in Northern Virginia." *The Geographical Review* 87 (1) (1997): 58–72.

America's Haitian Influx

Book excerpt

By: Alistair Cooke

Date: June 25, 1993

Source: Cooke, Alistair. *Letters From America: 1946–2004*. New York: Allen Lane, 2004.

About the Author: Alistair Cooke was a British-born journalist and broadcaster, who lived and worked in the United States from the mid–1930s for the rest of his life. Between 1946 and 2004 he gave a fifteen-minute weekly talk about aspects of life in America, which was broadcast on BBC Radio. This became Britain's longest-running speech radio program. Alistair Cooke died in 2004, a few weeks after his retirement.

INTRODUCTION

In this book excerpt, a written record of one of the speeches of the broadcaster Alistair Cooke, the author reflects on the ways in which refugees and other migrants have been treated under United States immigration and reception policies, and how their treatment has often been inconsistent with the welcoming messages that are inscribed on the Statue of Liberty.

Although the United States has traditionally seen a current of immigration from many different countries of the world, Cooke illustrates that restrictive immigration measures and informal types of discrimination have reflected fears about the impact of large numbers of migrants from particular countries or ethnic groups. At the time this speech was written, the United States was experiencing an influx of asylum seekers from Haiti, who were regarded mainly as economic migrants rather than genuine refugees. These people were the target of restrictive admissions policies designed to deter further migration from Haiti to the United States.

Before the Immigration Act of 1924, immigration to the United States had been virtually unrestricted, and hundreds of thousands of immigrants arrived since the mid–nineteenth century, mostly from Western European countries. As Cooke notes, however, entry was never guaranteed, as migrants were subject to medical examinations on arrival and returned to their home countries if they showed signs of disease. Moreover, earlier legislative restrictions on the immigration of people from particular races, particularly the Chinese and Japanese were enacted, in response to outbreaks of xenophobic (foreign-fearing) attitudes and racial violence.

A boatload of Haitian refugees sailing into Biscayne Bay, near Miami, Florida, June 13, 1981. © NATHAN BENN/CORBIS.

During the early decades of the twentieth century, concerns about rapidly rising levels of immigration and its impact on American society led to a quota system that would control the numbers of immigrants to the United States from different countries. In order to maintain a stable racial distribution, quotas were based upon the number of immigrants from different countries already in the United States, and proportionately more immigrants from the western hemisphere were allowed entry than from the eastern hemisphere. In practice, the quotas allowed almost unrestricted immigration from western European countries, severely restricted immigration from southern and eastern Europe, and virtually banned immigration from Asia. The system remained in operation until 1968, when the quotas on immigrants from the western and eastern hemispheres were equalized, then later merged. New quotas of 20,000 visas were then applied to every country, leading to a surge in immigration from Latin America and Asia.

The United States has had less control over influxes of refugees fleeing persecution in their home countries, such as the Haitians in the early 1990s. Under the 1951 Geneva Convention relating to the Status of Refugees, people who flee their country because of a well-founded fear of persecution on the grounds of race, religion, nationality, membership of another social group, or political opinion, should not be returned to that country to face persecution or the threat of persecution. It is, however, up to immigration officers in the country in which they claim asylum to determine whether they show adequate proof of persecution or the threat of persecution.

The U.S. government chose to regard the majority of the Haitian boat people as economic migrants from a poverty-ridden country, rather than refugees fleeing a brutal regime. With the exception of small numbers of particularly vulnerable migrants, such as the HIV positive refugees mentioned by Cooke, the majority of the boat people were intercepted at sea and interviewed by immigration officers on board U.S. vessels. Until 1991, almost all were returned to Haiti as they could not demonstrate a well-founded fear of persecution. Later that year, when almost 10,000 Haitians fled their country, asylum interviews were held at the U.S. naval base at

Guantánamo Bay, Cuba, and at this time, about one-third were granted refugee status and allowed to enter the United States However, when the numbers of Haitian asylum seekers continued to increase over the following years, a new policy was adopted, in which the camps at Guantánamo Bay were used as a "safe haven" for those deemed to be genuine refugees, but none were granted entry to the United States.

PRIMARY SOURCE

There can hardly be an American born here who cannot recite the five thundering lines inscribed on the Statue of Liberty: the hectoring command—'Give me your tired, your poor, / Your huddled masses yearning to breath free/ The wretched refuse of your teeming shore.—/ Send these, the homeless tempest-tossed, to me:/ I lift my lamp beside the golden door.' Generous words, almost arrogant in their bravery. Whether they constitute fine poetry or doggerel, they touched the hearts and minds of millions of Europeans—always the poor, often the persecuted, very often the fugitives from military service. They were spurred to pack a few belongings, often no more than a blanket, a cooking pot, a prayer book, a corset, to climb aboard box cars deep inside Russia or Hungary or Lithuania or Germany and be carried to the great ports: Constantinople, Piraeus, Antwerp, Bremen, and then put aboard. There, in enclosures outside the embarkation city, they were bathed, de-loused, fed, their baggage and clothes fumigated. They were prepared for the land of the free.

We are talking about routine procedures employed with the fourteen and a half million immigrants who arrived here, mainly New York or Boston, in the first two decades of the twentieth century. Looking up in awe to the bosom of the colossal lady peering out towards Europe, they would very soon find out that the physical routine of getting into the United States was not quite what a poor foundling might expect of a new, compassionate mother.

Coming across the Atlantic, they were not so much allotted space as stowed aboard, as many as nine hundred in steerage. Sailing slowly up the lower bay of New York City, they would spot their first Americans climbing aboard from a Coast Guard cutter, two men and a woman: immigration inspectors, whose first job was to look over the ship's manifest, and see if the captain had recorded cases of contagious disease. Considering the frequency and unpredictability at the time of ravaging epidemics across the continent of Europe, they looked out first for signs of cholera, typhoid, tuberculosis. If you showed any sign of these fearsome diseases, you were at once taken off to quarantine on an island in the bay and got ready for early deportation.

Once the newcomers had been herded into a large reception hall, they would be tagged with numbers and grouped according to their native tongue, which for the vast majority of them was the only one they spoke. They moved, shadowed by interpreters, in lines past a doctor in a blue uniform, a man with a chalk in his hand—an instant diagnostician. He was certainly a fast one and had the confidence that comes from not knowing anything about CT scans, or MRIs, or PSAs. He saw an ageing man with purple lips and chalked on his back: H—possible heart disease. Separate this man! Children in arms stood down to see if they betrayed the limp of rickets. T on the back was the expulsion sign of tuberculosis. Two other doctors dipped into a bowl of disinfectant and folded a suspect eyelid back with a buttonhook. Trachoma—very prevalent in Southern and Eastern Europe and a sure harbinger of blindness. You, too, were on your way back home.

We won't follow the release of most of the healthy rest to railroad agents, con men, honest bosses, and sweatshop owners looking for, and getting in luscious numbers, an army of cheap laborers, for most of whom the prospect was better than life in the homeland.

The expectation, among the mass of the settled population, was that these strangers would settle in too. But with every wave of new immigrants there was always a booming counterwave of protest, from the people who'd been here a long time, two, three or more generations of what we now call the Anglos and their collateral Nordics—Swedes, Norwegians, Germans. They had run the country, its government, its institutions for a hundred years or more. So every breaking wave of new immigrants made a rude sound to the residents, and they protested, then they discriminated. Often Washington legislated, as it did in the 1920s and again in the 1950s against what were called "undesirable types", meaning Orientals, Southern and Eastern Europeans. Even as late as the time I first came here, in the early 1930s, there were still pasted on shop windows and employment agencies stickers left over from early in the century: "No Irish Need Apply." But now, equally new to me, just outside the entrance to an apartment building was a sign: a wooden post surmounted by a rectangle, a sort of mahogany plaque, very handsome, a meticulously printed sign of gold lettering on a black background. It said "Apartments To Let, Three To Six Rooms. Restricted." That last word was not put in as an afterthought. It was printed in the same fine style as the rest of the announcement. Restricted, I discovered, was shorthand for "No Jews Need Apply." This was standard practice here in New York, in Manhattan especially; the other four boroughs, getting most of their business and work from the legions of incoming Jews, could not afford to be so particular. That rather callous sign vanished. It came to be made illegal in the late 1940s, when a Republican Governor of New York, Thomas E. Dewey (who had two failing shots at the Presidency against

Franklin Roosevelt), pushed through the state legislature the first (in this country) fair employment and fair housing Act. (The practice of exclusion was not totally abandoned. It continued in parts of the Upper East Side, unofficially, without the dreaded word, discreetly, on tiptoe, in the English manner.) Today there are no signs, except scurrilous ones painted by hooligans. But in the teeming boroughs, in Queens, Staten Island, the Bronx, Brooklyn, blacks glare at the successful Korean fruiterers, the pious religious Jewish sects watch their step, people who once went to Chinatown for entertainment and exquisite cheap sandals now stay away, after hearing of boatloads of smuggled Chinese brought in here to swell the active army of gangsters. It is news to most of us that there have been for some time ruthless and very active Chinese gangs working profitably in—what else?—drugs.

But at the moment the victim, the scapegoat, everybody's feared interloper, is the Haitian. I mentioned lately the drastically changed ethnic composition of the fleet of New York's taxi drivers. Where once taxi drivers were first- or second-generation Irishmen, Italians, Germans, now, they are Puerto Ricans, Haitians, Russians, Israelis. Why should the arrivals from Haiti be so feared?

Well, since the Haitian military overthrew President Aristide almost two years ago, about forty thousand Haitians have fled from what is quite plainly a particularly brutal tyranny. They came floating in across the Caribbean and on to Florida, and hundreds, perhaps many thousands, of them never made it. Simply fell off their miserable little boats or sank with all hands. President Bush decided to apply the existing immigration laws which offer legal haven if you can prove that you are a political refugee escaping likely persecution. If you simply sought a better life, but could give no proof of past or pending persecution, you were returned to Haiti.

During the Presidential campaign, Mr. Clinton called this policy illegal and cruel and swore to reverse it and let in the Haitian masses huddled in their leaky boats. Tremendous joy throughout Haiti! At once, over a hundred thousand people helped to build more leaky boats. In the face of this totally unpredicted tidal wave, President Clinton reverted to the Bush policy. A national howl of pain from Haiti and cries of outrage from American liberals.

Last Monday the Supreme Court, nodding regretfully at the mention of the word cruelty, nevertheless ruled by eight to one that this policy, intercepting the unpersecuted ones, was constitutional. Just before this ruling was handed down, a hundred and twenty-five refugees from Haiti, who had been judged to be true political refugees, were released from the American naval base in Cuba and flown to Miami—some to New York—there to be allowed to be absorbed into the American way of life. They were designated a 'special group'. What was so special about

them—apart from an unconscionable long time they had been detained, is that they were all HIV positive, infected with the virus that causes AIDS.

So, in one action, freedom is available to diseased people who will at once be entitled to free medical care, to a home, to an interpreter, to daily maintenance. But in the more sweeping action, affecting all the boat people, the Supreme Court has added a phrase to Emma Lazarus's soaring invitation: 'Give me your tired, your poor, your huddled masses yearning to breathe free—but see they carry a return ticket.'

SIGNIFICANCE

In January 1995, after the fall of the dictatorship in Haiti, the United States began repatriating all Haitians from Guantánamo Bay. The safe haven policy had been successful in U.S. immigration policy terms in restricting the entry of vast numbers of Haitian nationals to the United States, while at the same time conforming to the requirements of international refugee law. The United Nations High Commissioner for Refugees (UNHCR) had approved the safe haven proposals as providing protection within the framework of the UN Refugee Convention. Many Haitians chose to return voluntarily to their country even before the change of government there, when it became clear they would not be granted asylum in the United States.

FURTHER RESOURCES
Books

Glazer, Nathan. *Clamor at the Gates: The New American Immigration.* New York: ICS Press, 1985.

Münz, Rainer. *Migrants, Refugees, and Foreign Policy: U.S. and German Policies toward Countries of Origin.* New York: Berghahn Books, 1997.

Zucker, Naomi Flink, and Norman L. Zucker. *Desperate Crossings: Seeking Refuge in America.* Armonk, New York: M.E. Sharpe, 1996.

Rwandan Refugees in Bukavu

Photograph

By: Jon Jones

Date: August 22, 1994

Source: © Jon Jones/Sygma/Corbis.

About the Photographer: Jon Jones is a photojournalist who has covered conflicts in places such as Rwanda, Bosnia,

Sri Lanka, and South Africa. He has been published in many major news magazines, including *Time*, *Newsweek*, *The New York Times*, and *Le Monde*. This image is part of the collection at Corbis, a Seattle-based organization with a repository of over seventy million images. Sygma is a division of Corbis.

INTRODUCTION

Shortly after the three-month Rwandan genocide of the Tutsi minority by the Hutu majority in 1994, approximately two million refugees fled Rwanda to the neighboring countries of Zaire (now the Democratic Republic of Congo), Tanzania, Uganda, and Burundi. The large exodus, called the Great Lakes Crisis, occurred over several days in July 1994. There were very few resources available to provide the food, medicine, shelter, and latrines the large number of refugees needed. The majority of the refugees were Hutus fleeing the Tutsi dominated Rwandan Patriotic Front (RPF), an army that had entered Rwanda to end the

genocide. The largest camps were found in eastern Zaire near the cities of Bukavu and Goma.

During the first few weeks of the refugee arrival in Zaire, Rwandans camped out on fields, at schools, on doorsteps, and in cemeteries. Many of the refugees arrived with only the possessions they could carry on their backs, and families were often separated amongst the dense crowds. Many refugees had injuries from the fighting in Rwanda, as well as injuries from the journey into Zaire. The camps were extremely dirty, and outbreaks of disease, particularly cholera, began killing refugees at the rate of 7,000 per week. The media coverage of the situation brought the issue to international attention, with United States President Bill Clinton calling the Rwandan situation the worst humanitarian crisis in a generation. Countries began sending large amounts of aid, enabling more than 200 relief organizations to rush in to start emergency relief operations. The United Nations High Commissioner for Refugees (UNHCR), the United Nations agency that works specifically for the needs of refugees, began

PRIMARY SOURCE

Rwandan Refugees in Bukavu: Refugees arrive in Bukavu, Zaire, fleeing genocide and violence in Rwanda, August 22, 1994. © JON JONES/SYGMA/CORBIS.

receiving more than one million dollars per month to expand its operations in Zaire. The United States military coordinated an international operation to move supplies and personnel relief into the Rwandan camps. The aid improved conditions in the camps, lowering the rates of disease and death.

Perpetrators and organizers of the Rwanda genocide were among the refugees, and they used the camps as a base to launch attacks against the RPF. As the camps became more organized, former Hutu leaders began to control the aid resources that were flowing in for the refugees. Many of the organizations working in the camps, including Doctors Without Borders, the International Rescue Committee, Oxfam, Save the Children, and CARE, began removing their aid workers, saying they could not ethically continue to provide aid that was being funneled to supporting the military objectives of the militant Hutus. The UNHCR maintained that the humanitarian efforts should continue, as the militants were a small minority compared to the thousands of men, women, and children relying on the aid. Smaller less experienced agencies began carrying out the humanitarian work left behind by the larger organizations. The UNHCR did report a

decrease in the ability to achieve the humanitarian objectives efficiently. Simultaneously, pressure was mounting on the new government of Rwanda by the World Bank, which was withholding development funds to Rwanda until the Government repatriated the refugees.

PRIMARY SOURCE

RWANDAN REFUGEES IN BUKAVU

See primary source image.

SIGNIFICANCE

The Hutu militants had an interest in maintaining the refugee camps near Bukavu and Goma, as the refugees served as protection for their activities. The international community attempted to negotiate a solution to the problem, but no agreement to repatriate the refugees was reached. In the following years, clashes occurred between the Hutu militias and Banyamulenge, ethnic Tutsis who had been living as a minority group in Eastern Zaire for several generations. The government of Zaire refused to remove the Hutu militants from

Rwandan refugees gather at Ruzizi Bridge waiting to cross into Bukavu, Zaire, July 1994. © HOWARD DAVIES/CORBIS.

Zaire, refusing the request of the Rwandan government. These growing tensions eventually led the Rwanda- and Uganda-backed Banyamulenge to take over Zaire. In 1997, the new government of Zaire worked to disband the Hutu militias near Bukavu. With the protection of the Rwandan government, many of the Rwandan refugees were then able to return to Rwanda where they would continue to receive further assistance. Later, a second revolution occurred in Zaire, as the Rwanda and Uganda coalitions fell apart. Although many of the refugees returned to Rwanda, a solution between the Tutsi government and the Hutu militants was only partially reached several years later.

Many aid organizations, including the UNHCR have used the Rwanda situation as a basis for discussing the role of international aid in the context of ethnic violence and military zones. The UNHCR redesigned its policy to ensure that commitments made to future humanitarian operations are kept by the aid organizations involved, regardless of the adversity that might arise.

FURTHER RESOURCES
Books

Khan, Shaharyan M., and Mary Robinson. *The Shallow Graves of Rwanda*. New York: St. Martin's Press, 2000.

The Office of the United Nations High Commissioner for Refugees. *The State of the World's Refugees: Human Displacement in the New Millennium*. New York: Oxford University Press, 2006.

Porter, Elisabeth J. *Researching Conflict in Africa: Insights and Experiences*. New York: United Nations University Press, 2005.

Umutesi, Marie B. *Surviving the Slaughter: The Ordeal of a Rwandan Refugee in Zaire*. Madison: University of Wisconsin Press, 2004.

Periodicals

Gibbs, Nance, and Bruce Crumley. "Cry the Forsaken Country." *Time* (August, 1 1994): 28–37.

Perlez, Jane. "The World; Aid Agencies Hope to Enlist Military Allies in the Future." *New York Times* (August 21 1994): Section 4, p.6.

Elian Gonzalez

Photograph

By: Alan Diaz

Date: April 22, 2000

Source: © Reuters/Corbis.

About the Photographer: Alan Diaz joined the Associated Press as a freelance photographer in 1994, and became a full time AP photographer in 2000. This photograph earned Diaz the Pulitzer Prize in 2002 for Breaking News Photography.

INTRODUCTION

In November 1999, Elizabet Brotons, her five year old son, Elian, and twelve other Cuban citizens attempted to cross the channel between Cuba and southern Florida by boat. Elian's mother and seven others died when their motorboat sank. Adrift on inner tubes, Elian and two adults survived; Elian was rescued by a fishermen named Donato Dalrymple in the seas off the coast of Florida.

Elian's parents were divorced, and Elizabet Brotons's boyfriend, who lived in Miami, smuggled Cuban refugees into the United States. Elizabet Brotons had taken the boy from Cuba without the permission of his father, Juan, who had remarried and had an infant son with his new wife. In the United States Elian was given over to the care of relatives who had fled Cuba when Fidel Castro had come to power in the 1960s; Elian's great-uncle, Lazaro, and his cousin, Marisleysis, were his primary caregivers, and would become embroiled in the custody battle that evolved over the next seven months.

Juan Gonzalez argued that Elian should be returned to Cuba to be with him; he had not granted his ex-wife permission to take Elian to the United States. Elian's Miami relatives, however, believed that Elizabet Brotons had embarked on the journey to give Elian a life in America; in their eyes returning the boy to Cuba would be an affront to his mother's sacrifice. Immigration authorities struggled with the issue. Elian was granted temporary permission to remain in the United States, and U.S. relatives began the process to apply for political and economic asylum for the little boy.

Fidel Castro issued a strongly worded demand for the boy's return; immigration officials ruled that he could stay, while Senator Jesse Helms called for special legislation to permit Elian to become a citizen of the United States. Nationwide polls showed that 56 percent of Americans believed Elian should be returned to his father, but among Cubans in south Florida that number shrank to 10 percent. U.S. policy toward Cuban refugees used the "wet feet/dry feet" approach: If a Cuban refugee can reach dry land—"dry feet"—he or she is eligible for asylum and citizenship under the 1966 Adjustment Act, which gives Cubans special status and citizenship eligibility after one year of residency. If, however, the refugee is captured by the Coast Guard in the water—"wet feet"—the refugee is returned to Cuba, possibly to face harsh penalties under Castro's Communist regime.

The Cuban community in south Florida took the firm position that Elian belonged in the United States. In January 2000 U.S. officials ruled that Elian should return, and asked that Juan Gonzalez come to take his son home. Fidel Castro refused to permit Gonzalez to leave, placing the burden on U.S. authorities, leading to speculation that Castro feared Gonzalez's defection. In the meantime Elian's relatives in the United States filed for custody of the child. By April 2000 Attorney General

Janet Reno determined that Elian's father, not his U.S. relatives, spoke for Elian's needs.

Marisleysis Gonzalez, Elian's second cousin, vocally asserted her family's refusal to give Elian over to U.S. authorities for deportation. When Castro permitted Elian's grandmothers to visit him in February 2000 Marisleysis Gonzalez claimed that Elian had rejected the grandmothers, while the grandmothers claimed that Elian seemed hardened and different. Cuban-American groups sided with Marisleysis and her father, Lazaro; Cuban activists threatened to encircle their home to prevent Elian's removal. A video was released by the U.S. relatives showing Elian saying he wished to remain in the United States; in a September 2005 interview,

PRIMARY SOURCE

Elian Gonzalez: Armed federal agents take custody of six-year-old Cuban refugee Elian Gonzalez on April 22, 2000. Gonzalez is being held by Donato Dalrymple, one of the fishermen who rescued Gonzalez at sea in 1999. © REUTERS/CORBIS.

however, Elian claimed to have been coached to make that statement.

Miami-Dade County Mayor Alex Penelas publicly stated that local authorities would not assist federal authorities with the boy's removal, leading to a showdown between federal and local authorities, and between the Cuban exile community and the U.S. Attorney General. In early April 2000 the Attorney General worked to negotiate with U.S. relatives for Elian's release, but the relatives insisted on retaining custody of Elian. An April 13, 2000, deadline for his release was defied by Lazaro and Marisleysis Gonzalez. On April 22, Janet Reno ordered U.S. officials to take Elian by force.

PRIMARY SOURCE

ELIAN GONZALEZ

See primary source image.

SIGNIFICANCE

In the early hours of April 22, 2000, Immigration and Naturalization Services agents stormed the Gonzalez house, bypassing volunteers who surrounded it. Using pepper spray and armed with rifles, the agents entered the home, where they found fisherman Donato Dalrymple holding Elian, crouched in a closet and hiding from the melee. Taken at gunpoint, Elian was handed over to a Spanish speaking social worker, Betty Mills, who assured Elian he was going home to see his father. More than 100 protestors were held at bay during the raid; after Elian's removal the crowd increased to more than 300, and Miami Mayor Joe Carollo issued a statement referring to the federal agents as "athiests" who "don't believe in God."

Elian was returned to his father within four hours of the raid; Juan Gonzalez traveled to Andrews Air Force Base for the reunion. For the next two months Elian and his father remained in the United States while Elian's Miami relatives exhausted all legal avenues for keeping him within the United States. The Cuban exiles argued that Elian had entered Florida under the "dry feet" rule, and that Elian should be granted political asylum. On June 1, 2000, the 11th Circuit Court of Appeals ruled that Juan Gonzalez was the only adult with legal authority to make decisions for Elian, and on June 28, 2000, the two returned to Cuba.

The Elian Gonzalez case tested issues of child custody, children's rights in immigration, political asylum, and Cuban-American policy and relations, and it caused huge political upheaval between the federal government and the Cuban exile community nationwide. The U.S. government determined that Elian's father—regardless of citizenship status in Cuba or elsewhere—had priority in custody and decision-making over all other interested adults, even in complex matters of immigration and asylum.

FURTHER RESOURCES

Periodical

Gibbs, Nancy, and Michael Duffy. "The Elian Grab." *Time Magazine*, May 1, 2000.

Web sites

BBCNews.com. "What Happened to Elian Gonzalez?" April 22, 2005 <http://news.bbc.co.uk/2/hi/americas/4471099.stm> (accessed June 28, 2006).

PBS Online Newshour. "The Elian Gonzalez Case." <http://www.pbs.org/newshour/bb/law/elian/> (accessed June 28, 2006).

U.S. Citizenship and Immigration Services. "Elian Gonzalez." <http://www.uscis.gov/graphics/publicaffairs/ElianG.htm> (accessed June 28, 2006).

Proposed Refugee Admission for Fiscal Year 2005

Government record

By: U.S. Department of Health and Human Services

Date: September 2004

Source: U.S. Department of Health and Human Services. *Proposed Refugee Admission for Fiscal Year 2005*. Report to the Congress. Department of State. Department of Homeland Security. Washington, D.C.: U.S. Department of Health and Human Services, 2004.

About the Author: The Proposed Refugee Admission is a report submitted to Congress by the Department of Health and Human Services in compliance with the Refugee Act of 1980. This report includes descriptions of the nature of the refugee situation, the number and allocation of refugees and resettlement analysis. The report includes plans and cost for resettlement, as well as, anticipated impact on the United States.

INTRODUCTION

In 1948, U.S. President Harry S. Truman signed the Displaced Persons Act. This legislation allowed approximately 400,000 people who had become refugees as a result of World War II to enter the United States. It was followed several years later by the Refugee Relief Act, which provided for the immigration of an additional 200,000 displaced persons. These were the first acts by the U.S. government to acknowledge the need of refugees to be resettled. In 1952, the standards for immigration to the United States were established in the Immigration and Nationality Act, which has been amended several times since its original implementation. In 1980, the U.S. Congress passed the Refugee Act, which directs the president to set annual ceilings on incoming refugees, including regional limits. As such, the president, in consultation with the congress, provides for the resettlement within the United States of refugees. Those seeking refugee status must display a founded fear of persecution based on political or religious ideology or race and ethnicity. Refugees can apply for permanent residency status after residing in the United States for one year. After five years of U.S. residence, the refugee becomes eligible for citizenship.

PRIMARY SOURCE

1. OVERVIEW OF U.S. REFUGEE POLICY

Resettlement to third countries, including the United States, is considered for refugees in urgent need of protection as well as for those for whom other durable solutions are not feasible. In seeking durable solutions for refugees, the United States generally gives priority to the safe voluntary return of refugees to their homelands. This policy, recognized in the Refugee Act of 1980, is also the preference of the international community, including the Office of the United Nations High Commissioner for Refugees (UNHCR). If safe voluntary repatriation is not feasible, other durable solutions are sought, including local integration in countries of asylum or resettlement in third countries. For many refugees, resettlement is the best, or perhaps only, alternative. Recognizing the importance of ensuring UNHCR's capacity to identify and to refer refugees in need of resettlement, the U.S. government has provided some 20 million dollars during the past seven years to expand the organization's resettlement infrastructure.

According to UNHCR, as of January 1, 2004 there were 9.9 million refugees in the world. An important foreign policy goal of the United States is to assist refugees worldwide. The United States therefore makes financial contributions to international organizations, as well as to non-governmental organizations. Under the authority in the Migration and Refugee Assistance Act of 1962, as amended, the United States contributes to the programs of UNHCR, the International Committee of the Red Cross (ICRC), the International Organization for Migration (IOM), and other international and non-governmental organizations that provide relief and assistance to refugees. Our assistance is targeted to address immediate protection needs of refugees as well as to ensure that basic needs for water, sanitation, food, health care, shelter, and education are met. The United States continues to press for the most effective use of international resources directed to the urgent needs of refugees and internally displaced persons. During FY 2004, the United States has supported major relief and repatriation programs throughout the world. Repatriation to countries including Afghanistan, Somalia, Angola, and Sierra Leone has proceeded on a large scale.

For many years, the United States was one of ten countries that worked with UNHCR on a regular basis to provide resettlement opportunities for persons in need of this form of international protection or durable solution. In 2003, UNHCR referred refugees to 24 countries for resettlement. The majority (86%) was referred to the United States, Canada, and Australia. In addition to New Zealand and the traditional Western European resettlement countries (Norway, Sweden, Denmark, Finland, the Netherlands, Great Britain), small numbers of referrals were accepted by Germany, Ireland, Italy, Belgium, Iceland, Austria, Switzerland, France, Spain, Chile, Brazil, Korea, and Mozambique. The European Union has recently endorsed a plan in support of refugee resettlement that may generate additional interest in participation of European countries.

While the overall number of refugees referred by UNHCR and the percentage resettled by various countries fluctuate from year to year, the United States is committed to providing an opportunity for U.S. resettlement to at least 50% of all UNHCR referrals. In calendar year 2003 the United States resettled 54% of all UNHCR-referred refugees resettled in third countries. . . .

The term 'refugee' means: (A) any person who is outside any country of such person's nationality or, in the case of a person having no nationality, is outside any country in which such person last habitually resided, and who is unable or unwilling to return to, and is unable or unwilling to avail himself or herself of the protection of that country because of persecution or a well-founded fear of persecution on account of race, religion, nationality, membership in a particular social group, or political opinion, or (B) in such circumstances as the President after appropriate consultation (as defined in section 207 (e) of this Act) may specify, any person who is within the country of such person's nationality or, in the case of a person having no nationality, within the country in which such person is habitually residing, and who is persecuted or who has a well-founded fear of persecution on account of race, religion, nationality, membership in a particular social group, or political opinion.

The term 'refugee' does not include any person who ordered, incited, assisted, or otherwise participated in the persecution of any person on account of race, religion, nationality, membership in a particular social group, or political opinion....

Refugees resettled in the United States contribute positively to the diversity and enrichment of our country. The U.S. program emphasizes the goal that refugees become economically self-sufficient as quickly as possible. Department of Health and Human Services-funded programs administered by individual states and the District of Columbia provide cash and medical assistance, training programs, employment, and other support services to arriving refugees. A variety of institutional providers perform these services, including the voluntary agencies that provide initial reception and placement services under cooperative agreements with the Department of State.

A. AFRICA

Resettlement in third countries outside the region is an essential durable solution for some African refugees. The possibility of third country resettlement can play an important protection role, given the political and economic volatility in many parts of Africa. With limited opportunities for complete, permanent integration in neighboring countries and often-protracted periods in refugee camps before voluntary repatriation becomes an option, the need for third country resettlement of African refugees will continue. All resettlement countries, in particular the United States, Canada, and Australia, accept resettlement referrals from Africa, but the U.S. program receives the majority of them. In recent years, UNHCR has increasingly viewed resettlement as an important tool of protection and durable solution for refugees in Africa.

5. FY 2004 U.S. Admissions

We anticipate exceeding the 25,000 refugee admissions ceiling for Africa in FY 2004. Four countries (Somalia, Liberia, Sudan, and Ethiopia) account for the majority of refugee arrivals, with two countries (Sierra Leone and Democratic Republic of Congo) accounting for fewer, yet significant numbers of refugee arrivals. Refugees also have been resettled from thirteen other African countries in smaller numbers.

We have taken steps to improve efficiency and to decrease vulnerability in the enhanced security procedures instituted in the aftermath of September 11, particularly the Security Advisory Opinion (SAO) component, which so impacted arrivals from Africa. Thanks to improved coordination with intelligence and law enforcement agencies and the addition of new staff at PRM dedicated to processing SAOs, delays caused by this enhanced security check were dramatically reduced in FY 2004. In addition, FY 2004 saw some improvement in the security conditions in some processing locations, such as Kakuma Camp in Kenya, where DHS officers were able to return in September 2003 and conduct interviews on a nearly continual basis throughout FY 2004. However, difficult security conditions persist in some locations, including many sites in Ethiopia. Sporadic violence in and around Kakuma threatened processing and required increased security for convoys of refugees and processing personnel into and out of the camp. Finally, USCIS has continued to verify claimed family relationships between U.S. anchor relatives and refugee applicants in the P-3 caseload in order to address the historically high levels of relationship fraud in the African P-3 program.

6. FY 2005 U.S. Resettlement Program

The proposed Africa ceiling of 20,000 is intended to respond to the resettlement needs of certain groups of African refugees, while realistically approaching the logistical and political realities of refugee processing in this complex working environment. PRM has actively engaged all appropriate offices within the Department of State, the voluntary agency community, UNHCR, and USCIS to help identify groups appropriate for resettlement that would likely qualify under U.S. law. As a result of these discussions, PRM has identified a number of groups for priority processing during FY 2004.

The estimate of 9,000 individuals in the pipeline of approved refugees who will likely arrive during FY 2005 includes P-1, P-2, and P-3 cases approved during FY 2004, including several thousand Somali Bantu in Kakuma.

PRM continues to work closely with UNHCR to strengthen its resettlement referral capacity in Africa. We are currently funding twelve resettlement positions in eight African countries: Ghana, Guinea, Ivory Coast, Senegal, Sierra Leone, Kenya, Ethiopia, and Tanzania. In return, PRM anticipates significant numbers of referrals from UNHCR in these countries during calendar year 2004 (many of whom will be processed in FY 2005).

In East Africa, we anticipate processing a group of approximately 1,750 Somali Benadir in Dadaab camp, Kenya, and approximately 1,000 minority clan Somalis in Nakivale Camp, Uganda. While we do not anticipate a large group referral from Mozambique, we do expect a continued increase in individual referrals of vulnerable cases from Marratane Camp. We also anticipate a referral of 2,000 or more Burundians in Tanzania—half of the total of 4,000 individuals that UNHCR intends to submit to all resettlement countries in the coming year.

In West Africa, we expect to process a group of 2,500 Liberian female-headed households who have experienced "double flight" to Ivory Coast and now Guinea, and a group of 1,500 Liberians in single-parent households in Ghana. We also anticipate smaller numbers of refugee referrals in Nigeria, Senegal, Gabon, and Sierra Leone, and will be examining the residual numbers of Sierra Leonean refugees throughout the region, given that the repatriation is coming to an end. In addition, UNHCR has indicated it may refer up to 500 Mauritanians in Senegal, pending negotiations between UNHCR and the governments of Mauritania, Senegal, and Mali.In Egypt, we expect fewer referrals of Sudanese than in previous years, given UNHCR Cairo's decision to suspend new registrations for refugee status determinations (RSDs) for Sudanese, following the May 26 signing of the framework for peace. However, cases in the RSD pipeline will be referred for possible resettlement and we have encouraged UNHCR to continue to refer vulnerable cases such as women at risk, and individuals from the Darfur region. At the same time, we expect referrals of Somalis in Egypt to increase. Small numbers of Sudanese and Somalis will continue to be processed in Syria and Lebanon.

7. Possible Future Groups

Other smaller groups of Somalis, Sudanese and Ethiopians are expected from both Dadaab and Kakuma. We continue to monitor the situation of the group of Eritrean Kunama in Ethiopia and have urged UNHCR to consider a group resettlement referral of those who do not choose to voluntarily repatriate to Eritrea by the end of 2004. In the Near East, we are working with UNHCR on possible referral of a group of Ethiopian former Navy personnel and their families in Yemen.

SIGNIFICANCE

According to the United Nations High Commissioner for Refugees (UNHCR), there were approximately 9.9 million refugees worldwide seeking to be resettled in 2004. The United States resettles more refugees than any other nation and between 2003 and 2004 provided $14 million in aid to the UNHCR. Those seeking to be resettled must demonstrate that they are the victims of persecution for religious, political, or other reasons. Refugees reside in holding camps around the world while they await settlement. In 2000, the United States resettled approximately 72,515 refugees.

Refugees awaiting entry into the United States fall under three categories, as determined by the Refugee Act of 1980: P-1, P-2, and P-3. The P-1 refugee have been identified and referred to the State Department for resettlement by the UNHCR, the U.S. embassy, or a non-governmental organization (NGO). Those groups of people identified as a special humanitarian concern represent the P-2 category. Finally, the P-3 category is for those family members of previously resettled refugees awaiting reunification.

However, on September 11, 2001, following the attacks on the World Trade Centers in New York, the resettlement of refugees slowed to a crawl in many countries. For the first months after the attacks, a moratorium was called on the entry of refugees into the United States. In Denmark, Germany and Britain, governments tightened refugee admissions. In 2002, the approximately 14,000 refugees were allowed to enter the United States and in 2003, that number rose to 28,000, somewhat shy of the 70,000 ceiling established by the president. In the months following the September 11 attacks, the U.S. Department of Justice officials advocated a slower pace of processing refugees to allow for better vetting and clearing the individuals of terrorist ties. Extra security checks, particularly in Arab or Muslim countries, resulted in a sharp decrease in refugees entering America. Additional security checks included a Federal Bureau of Investigation and Central Intelligence Agency review called the Security Advisory Opinion. The process to obtain was already overwhelmed by applicants desiring tourist, student and immigration visas. In addition, in developing nations, documentation needed for the report such as birth certificates can often be difficult to locate. As the U.S. State Department and newly formed Department of Homeland Security reviewed refugee immigration procedures, the discovery of fraud in the selection process resulted in additional delays for the resettlement of refugees from Africa. As a result of the increased security checks and the revelation of fraud, the admissions process slowed tremendously.

Refugees forced to remain in camps continued to experience frustrations. U.S.-based resettlement organizations were left without clients and began to be dismantled. In 2003, the situation at a refugee camp in Kenya led to violence. As a result, the U.S. caseworkers, who work to process and prepare the refugees as well as tend to their immediate needs, were forced to withdraw. Only after the U.S. State Department spent $500,000 to fortify the camps were the caseworkers returned to Kenya.

In June 2005, President Bush met with refugee advocates and two refugees who had been resettled in the United States. Following the meeting, the president authorized an additional $154.4 million for refugee admission and resettlement. The president also asked for an additional 20,000 refugees to be allowed entry into the United States.

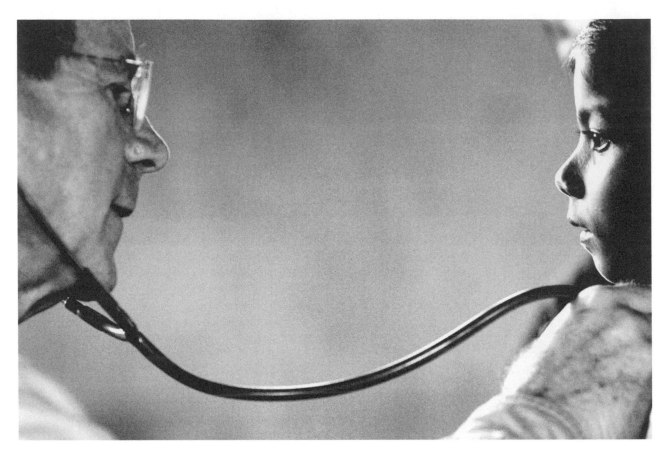

Northwest Medical Team's Dr. Bill Springer examines Niranji Kanesalingam for a cough in Palameen Madu, a fishing village on the east coast of Sri Lanka, January 3, 2005. © ROB FINCH/THE OREGONIAN/CORBIS.

FURTHER RESOURCES

Periodicals

Bixler, Mark. "Wavering Welcome: Foreign Policy Weighs Heavily on Refugees' Entry to US." *The Atlanta Journal and Constitution* (April 9, 2003): 30.

Hamburger, Tom, and Peter Wallsten. "Refugees' Tales Heard by Powerful Advocate of One." *Los Angeles Times*, February 14, 2005.

Hendrix, Anastasia. "Post 9/11 Delays Hurt US Bound Refugees." *San Francisco Chronicle* (November 30, 2003): A1.

Sheridan, Mary Beth. "Waiting for Ticket to Safety." *The Washington Post*, February 24, 2003.

Point of No Return

Magazine article

By: Mirta Ojito

Date: April 2005

Source: *Hispanic Magazine.com.* "Point of No Return: A Mariel Immigrant Remembers the Cuban Exodus That Shook Two Nations 25 Years Ago." April 2005. <http://www.hispaniconline.com/magazine/2005/april/Features/immigration.html> (accessed July 20, 2006).

About the Author: Mirta Ojito (b. 1964) is a professor of journalism and a Pulitzer Prize Winner. Institutions where she has taught include Columbia University, University of Miami, and New York University. She is the author of *Finding Manana: A Memoir of a Cuban Exodus* (2005).

INTRODUCTION

Mirta Ojito came to America during a time when immigration to the United States was welcome and President Carter was sympathetic to the plight of refugees. As an unoffending young teen, Ojito is keenly aware of the significance of the times. The times changed the future of not only her life, but also the lives of many compatriots and the demographic landscape of south Florida.

Cuban refugees fleeing to America aboard a shimp boat, at Key West, Florida, May 20, 1980. © BETTMANN/CORBIS. REPRODUCED BY PERMISSION.

The Mariel Boatlift that occurred some twenty-five years ago involved more than 125,000 Cubans immigrating to the Florida Coast of the United States. They traveled by way of the Mariel harbor on the west side of Cuba. The controversy surrounded the character of some of the immigrants who were released by Cuban President Fidel Castro (b. 1926). Castro used this opportunity to exile, along with professionals and families wishing to leave Cuba, many convicts and mentally disabled individuals to the United States. This behavior resulted after steps toward civil communications had supposedly been established between President Carter and Cuban government officials from Havana.

In 1977, President Carter desired open dialogue between the two countries and instituted formal lines of communication. There was a U.S. foreign sector established in Havana as well as in Washington, D.C. Though there were open communications, the relationship was far from conciliatory. Initially, Cuban government disallowed family visitations from former Cuban citizens, which contributed to the unstable relationship between the two countries. At this time however, Castro began to seek better relationships with the Cuban community living in America and permitted Cuban

Americans to visit friends and relatives in Cuba. These contacts caused Cubans to be more aware of the differences between Cuba and the United States.

PRIMARY SOURCE

Twenty-five years later you'd think it doesn't matter when people innocently ask me, "So, when did you come from Cuba?" and I tell them slowly and deliberately, "1980," which, of course, reveals a date but says nothing at all. I watch the faces of my inquisitors closely as they do their mental math and, invariably, the easy look of friendly curiosity turns into one of surprise, and, in some cases, horror. "Then," they say, "you must have come from Cuba in the boatlift." "Yes," I say calmly. "The Mariel boatlift." And then I have to explain myself because what follows is never pretty. Or polite. "But that's when all the criminals came from Cuba," they say and I sigh because it gets old to constantly have to justify myself as that which I'm not: not a criminal, not a mentally troubled refugee, and definitely not Tony Montana, Al Pacino's character in Scarface.

What I am, quite simply, is this: a Cuban woman who 25 years ago, at the age of 16, crossed the Florida Straits aboard a boat named MaÑana to escape a soul-crushing regime that, among other baffling indignities, had forced me to swear every day, for most of my life, that I would grow up to be like Che Guevara. And I was not alone.

From April to September 1980, more than 125,000 Cubans, mostly hard working, and many talented artists and intellectuals, left the island through the port of Mariel and reached the shores of Key West in what quickly came to be known as the Mariel boatlift—a chaotic event that managed to destabilize the Cuban government as no other event has in the 46 years Fidel Castro has been in power. The boatlift also contributed to Jimmy Carter's failure to regain the presidency for four more years and, eventually, changed U.S. immigration policy toward Cubans when, in 1994 and no doubt remembering the lessons learned in Mariel, President Bill Clinton announced that Cubans caught at sea would be returned to their country.

In the end, though, the story of the boatlift is a story like any other worth retelling: one in which regular people—not presidents or tyrants; diplomats or dissidents—take their lives in their own hands and, in the process, change history.

The boatlift started in 1977 with a thaw in the always-tense relations between Cuba and the U.S. Fresh in office and full of the optimism that only faith and good intentions can concede, President Carter announced that it was time for Washington and Havana to get along. The U.S. opened an Interests Section in Havana and Cuba did the same in Washington, which allowed the two countries to establish formal routes of communication despite their lack of formal relations. At the same time, the Cuban government reached out to the Cuban-American community as a way to gain favor with the White House, and a bridge was established, one that contributed to the release of thousands of political prisoners and that allowed Cubans to return to the island to visit relatives—a privilege that had long been denied to exiles.

The visits and the release of the prisoners put regular Cubans in touch with aspects of the Cuban Revolution and of the U.S. society that were unknown to us. First of all, many of us understood for the first time that we indeed lived in a country that regularly imprisoned, tortured and abused its opposition. That may seem commonplace now, but in 1980 it was a profound revelation for people like me: young people who had been told, from birth, that the revolution was good and just and right. The second thing we understood, suddenly and with great force, was that just about everything we had been told about the United States was a lie. Our returning relatives, loaded with gifts, told us stories of sacrifice and hardship, but they also told us about their vacations to Cancún and the Buicks parked in their garages and their bountiful Thanksgiving celebrations. They worked full time and, often, overtime, but their

skin was smooth and moisturized and the women had manicured long nails and white, shiny teeth.

Desperation and despair set in. Nothing was going to stand in the way of people whose mind was set on leaving the country, not even the gate of an embassy. On April 1, 1980, a man named Héctor Sanyustiz, accompanied by five others, drove a bus through the fence that surrounded the Peruvian Embassy in Havana and asked for political asylum. The Peruvian diplomat in charge of the embassy, a lawyer named Ernesto Pinto-Bazurco, offered it. Outraged that he couldn't get the gate-crashers back, Castro removed the Cuban guards from the embassy and proclaimed it open for anyone who wanted to leave the country. In less than 36 hours, there were more than 10,000 Cubans standing in what once were the grand and lovely gardens of the ambassador.

As the Peruvian Embassy crisis wore on, several countries offered help by taking a small number of refugees from the embassy. Among them, Spain, Costa Rica and Peru. But it was clear that Castro had another destination in mind. In April 1980, the Cuban government opened the port of Mariel and announced that all who wanted to leave the country could do so as long as a boat went to the port, west of Havana, to pick them up. Thousands of Cuban exiles, with little or no experience at sea, rushed to Key West and to the docks of the Miami River to hire boats to rescue their relatives.

Without doubt, Castro used the chaos of Mariel to unload on U.S. shores criminals and mentally unstable people, which gave the boatlift its unfortunate and still lingering reputation. But the most shocking element of Mariel has to be the sheer number of people who overwhelmed South Florida in only five months. In the first 20 days of the boatlift, the population of Miami had already increased by 10 percent. In one day alone, May 11, more than 5,000 people arrived in 18 hours, breaking all records of daily arrivals of immigrants in South Florida.

I was one of them. But when I think of May 11, I remember not so much how I arrived, though I remember that too, but how I left, the day before, at dusk.

I see myself surrounded by people and yet profoundly alone in this boat aptly named Mañana, and I remember trying to take it all in—the color of the water, the rough and yellowish shore, the white building atop a hill, the flag fluttering on the docks—and thinking that I was never going to see that island again. And I haven't, because even though I went back to Cuba in 1998, it was no longer the country I had left, and I didn't see it from the sea; I returned by airplane, which changes anyone's perspective.

Farewells from the sea are both definite and impossible to replicate in their romanticism. When the boat pulls away from shore, from the land you thought you'd never leave, you feel a detachment like no other, like the severing of a limb. Alone in that boat, though surrounded by people, you become your own small island, a chunk of land that floats away from the mainland. And though you may come back, as I did, the shore has reshaped in your absence, and the piece that was torn, the one that took you away, can never quite fit again.

SIGNIFICANCE

The tidal wave of new Cuban immigrants strained both the educational system and the provision of social services in South Florida, particularly in Miami. However, a study conducted several years later revealed that as a group, the Mariel refugees had made remarkable progress in assimilating into the South Florida economy and society. This success was due in large part to the willingness of the pre-existing Cuban community to assist the new arrivals, and the entrepreneurship and work ethic of most of the refugees themselves.

Despite their progress, many of the Mariel refugees continued to consider themselves victims of discrimination with the U.S. Cuban community, a unique minority-within-a-similar-minority situation. At the time of the study in 1985–1986, there remained a notable gap in employment and income between the refugees and the pre-existing community. Nevertheless, the majority of the refugees declared themselves satisfied with their current situation and said that if they had to make the choice again, they would make the same decision to come to the United States.

Ultimately, this episode led to the Clinton-Castro migration accord in the early 1990s, which established the "wet foot, dry foot" policy: Would-be immigrants intercepted at sea in boats ("wet foot") could be turned back, but anyone reaching the shores of the United States ("dry foot") would be accepted into the country. In 1999, this policy was used as an argument by the U.S.-based relatives of five-year-old Elian Gonzales, who was rescued by a fisherman off the coast of Flordia after the motorboat in which he was a passenger sank, killing his mother and seven other adults. They argued that under the "dry foot" policy, Elian was entitled to remain in the United States. The eventual decision, however, was that Elian's father's right to custody in Cuba took precedence over the "dry foot" rule.

FURTHER RESOURCES
Books

Ojito, Mirta A. *Finding Manana: A Memoir of a Cuban Exodus.* New York: Penguin Press, 2005.

Zucker, Norman L. *Desperate Crossings: Seeking Refuge in America.* Armonk, NY: M.E. Sharpe Inc., 1996.

Periodical

Portes, Alejandro, and Juan M. Clark. "Mariel Refugees: Six Years After." *Migration World* 15 (Fall 1987): 14–18.

Hmong Story Cloths

Photograph

By: Beth Schlanker

Date: November 10, 2005

Source: Schlanker, Beth. "Hmong Story Cloths." AP Images.

About the Author: Beth Schlanker is a contributing photographer to the Associated Press, a worldwide news agency based in New York.

INTRODUCTION

These Hmong story cloths are embroidered panels created by many Hmong refugee women who settled in the United States during the 1970s and 1980s. The panels illustrate the Hmong way of life and their experiences fleeing Laos in the aftermath of the Vietnam War. As a comparatively new folk art genre, story cloths were first made in the Thai refugee camps around 1975. The designs have changed over the years in response to American consumer tastes and exposure to new ideas.

The Hmong originated in China. In the early nineteenth century, in response to political and

A Hmong story cloth depicting the story of the Hmong helping the French fight the Japanese in Southeast Asia during World War II. The cloth is displayed at the home of Xao Yang Lee, a Hmong immigrant living in Sheboygan, Wisconsin. AP IMAGES.

cultural persecution by Chinese authorities, some Hmong moved south into Laos, where they formed one of about sixty ethnic groups. They had no written language until American missionaries created one for them in 1950. Anthropologists categorized the Hmong as a premodern people for their slash-and-burn agriculture and animistic religion.

In Laos, the Hmong were known as *meo*, or "savage" for their long tradition of fighting against authority in China, against the French colonizers in Laos, and against the local Laotian governments. With this history, the U.S. Central Intelligence Agency (CIA) recruited the Hmong to fight against the North Vietnamese, who were using Laos as a base for attacks against South Vietnamese and Americans in the Vietnam War. From 1960 to 1975, an estimated fifteen thousand Hmong died in the conflict. With the end of the war, many Hmong were forced to live in refugee camps, largely in neighboring Thailand. From these camps, about 150,000 have been resettled, with 100,000 immigrating to the United States and the rest heading to France, Australia, and Canada.

PRIMARY SOURCE

HMONG STORY CLOTHS
See primary source image.

SIGNIFICANCE

The Hmong have struggled to adjust to their new homelands. More so than other recent immigrants, they have been faced with dramatic lifestyle and cultural changes. An agricultural people with little experience with technology, they have been resettled in cities in highly developed countries. In the United States, they have chiefly been located in Minneapolis/

PRIMARY SOURCE

Hmong Story Cloths: A Hmong story cloth depicts lightning and a tornado, made in part by Xia Thao. It is used by a Minneapolis volunteer group to demonstrate safety tips for bad weather to Hmong immigrants unfamiliar with American weather. AP IMAGES.

St. Paul, with a far different cultural and geographical climate than Laos.

Some of the Hmong customs, such as polygamy, bride purchase, and bride kidnapping, are illegal in the West. This has forced them to abandon practices that date back centuries. The shift in the status accorded women has been a particularly noticeable change for the Hmong. In 1992, a Hmong woman, Choua Lee, was elected to the St. Paul school board, making her the first Hmong refugee to become an elected official.

The difficulties that most Hmong are experiencing in assimilating are evident in the low income levels of the Hmong. In the United States, the Hmong are the poorest ethnic group with about sixty percent of the people living below the poverty line in 1990. However, the Hmong have produced more offspring than the Cambodians and Laotians who also fled the Vietnam War at the time of the Hmong exodus. More than a third of the Hmong in the United States in 1990 were native-born. The children of the immigrants are successfully adjusting to American life, attending college, and becoming more prosperous than their parents.

FURTHER RESOURCES
Books

Chan, Sucheng. *Hmong Means Free: Life in Laos and America*. Philadelphia: Temple University Press, 1994.

Hamilton-Merritt, J. *Tragic Mountains: The Hmong, the Americans, and the Secret Wars for Laos, 1942–1992*. Bloomington, Ind.: Indiana University Press, 1993.

Hein, Jeremy. *From Vietnam, Laos, and Cambodia: A Refugee Experience in the United States*. New York: Twayne, 1995.

7 Immigration Reform: The Ongoing Debate

Immigration Reform: The Ongoing Debate

Immigration reform is the political term for proposed changes in U.S. immigration policy. Those who favor immigration reform claim that the current immigration system fails to function as it should. In 2005, U.S. lawmakers began a new campaign for immigration reform. Opinions on how to best change current immigration laws are diverse, from establishing a system of open immigration to curtailing most immigration altogether. Some assert that immigrant families are subjected to undue hardships and separations because of a stagnated visa system, or that undocumented immigrants who have lived and worked in the United States for several years should be given a path to citizenship. Others claim that illegal immigration poses a national security risk or that undocumented immigrant labor adversely affects the wages of all U.S. workers.

The debate is not limited to the halls of Congress or state legislatures. Public opinion is also divided on soultions to immigration issues. Strong feelings on immigration issues provoked stong actions. Scores of citizens have joined organizations that send volunteer-vigilantes to patrol the U.S.-Mexico border and search for undocumented immigrants. "The Minuteman Border Patrol" features images and discussion about one such controversial group. In the spring and summer of 2006, millions took to the streets to demonstrate on behalf of immigrant-friendly immigration reform. "500,000 Pack Streets to Protest Immigration Bills" describes one of the largest gatherings, presenting a look public opinion on immigrant reform in both immigrant and non-immigrant communities.

While immigration reform is often debated in the abstract, this chapter provides personal stories of those whose everyday lives are affected by immigration law and policy. "Amy's Story" is an account of one undocumented immigrant, raised and educated in the United States, who finds her undocumented status is a barrier to college education and lucrative employment. "Immigrants Lament: Have Degree, No Job" features similar accounts of the difficulties encountered even after college. Creating educational opportunities and a path to citizenship for undocumented children brought to the United States by their families has been a popular reform goal for several years. "An Irish Face on the Cause of Citizenship" dispels the myth that all undocumented immigrants are from the Americas.

At the heart of the debate over immigration reform are difficult questions about human rights, economic opportunities, national security, racism, xenophobia, poverty, exploitation, social policy, and employment. What are the responsibilities, if any, of more affluent nations to their less-affluent neighbors? How does international policy—from war to trade—affect immigration? What national concerns should, or can, be addressed through immigration policy?

California Proposition 187

Legislation

By: State of California

Date: 1994

Source: California Proposition 187. Available at: <http://www.usc.edu/isd/archives/ethnicstudies/historicdocs/prop187.txt> (accessed June 7, 2006).

About the Author: California is the most populous of the fifty states. It has a large Hispanic population and shares a lengthy border with Mexico.

INTRODUCTION

The state of California has a long history of voter activism. Californians pioneered the use of ballot initiatives as a tool to wrest control of state government away from their lawmakers; this technique reached its pinnacle when voters in the state voted to remove a sitting governor and replace him with famous actor Arnold Schwarzeneger. California has the largest economy among the fifty states and its prosperity attracts large numbers of legal and illegal immigrants from across the Mexican border.

As the state faced skyrocketing public expenditures during the 1990s, legislators and citizens began examining the cost of public assistance and education. Convinced that an inordinate share of California's funds was being spent to benefit illegal immigrants, legislators created Proposition 187, which came to a public vote in 1994. Proposition 187 required any person receiving public education or any other publicly funded benefit to prove U.S. citizenship. The measure was supported by Governor Pete Wilson and opposed by Hispanic advocacy groups who organized a mass march through the streets of Los Angeles. The measure passed with approximately fifty-nine percent of the vote and became California law.

A mother and her children wait to cross the border into California as illegal aliens. © DAVID TURNLEY/CORBIS.

PRIMARY SOURCE

This initiative measure is submitted to the people in accordance with the provisions of Article II, Section 8 of the Constitution.

This initiative measure adds sections to various codes; therefore, new provisions proposed to be added are printed in italic type to indicate that they are new.

PROPOSED LAW

SECTION 1. Findings and Declaration.

The People of California find and declare as follows:

That they have suffered and are suffering economic hardship caused by the presence of illegal aliens in this state.

That they have suffered and are suffering personal injury and damage caused by the criminal conduct of illegal aliens in this state.

That they have a right to the protection of their government from any person or persons entering this country unlawfully.

Therefore, the People of California declare their intention to provide for cooperation between their agencies of state and local government with the federal government, and to establish a system of required notification by and between such agencies to prevent illegal aliens in the United States from receiving benefits or public services in the State of California.

SECTION 2. Manufacture, Distribution or Sale of False Citizenship or Resident Alien Documents: Crime and Punishment.

Section 113 is added to the Penal Code, to read:

113. Any person who manufactures, distributes or sells false documents to conceal the true citizenship or resident alien status of another person is guilty of a felony, and shall be punished by imprisonment in the state prison for five years or by a fine of seventy-five thousand dollars ($75,000).

SECTION 3. Use of False Citizenship or Resident Alien Documents: Crime and Punishment.

Section 114 is added to the Penal Code, to read:

114. Any person who uses false documents to conceal his or her true citizenship or resident alien status is guilty of a felony, and shall be punished by imprisonment in the state prison for five years or by a fine of twenty-five thousand dollars ($25,000).

SECTION 4. Law Enforcement Cooperation with INS.

Section 834b is added to the Penal Code, to read:

834b. (a) Every law enforcement agency in California shall fully cooperate with the United States Immigration and Naturalization Service regarding any person who is arrested if he or she is suspected of being present in the United States in violation of federal immigration laws.

(b) With respect to any such person who is arrested, and suspected of being present in the United States in violation of federal immigration laws, every law enforcement agency shall do the following:

(1) Attempt to verify the legal status of such person as a citizen of the United States, an alien lawfully admitted as a permanent resident, an alien lawfully admitted for a temporary period of time or as an alien who is present in the United States in violation of immigration laws. The verification process may include, but shall not be limited to, questioning the person regarding his or her date and place of birth, and entry into the United States, and demanding documentation to indicate his or her legal status.

(2) Notify the person of his or her apparent status as an alien who is present in the United States in violation of federal immigration laws and inform him or her that, apart from any criminal justice proceedings, he or she must either obtain legal status or leave the United States.

(3) Notify the Attorney General of California and the United States Immigration and Naturalization Service of the apparent illegal status and provide any additional information that may be requested by any other public entity.

(c) Any legislative, administrative, or other action by a city, county, or other legally authorized local governmental entity with jurisdictional boundaries, or by a law enforcement agency, to prevent or limit the cooperation required by subdivision (a) is expressly prohibited.

SECTION 5. Exclusion of Illegal Aliens from Public Social Services.

Section 10001.5 is added to the Welfare and Institutions Code, to read:

10001.5. (a) In order to carry out the intention of the People of California that only citizens of the United States and aliens lawfully admitted to the United States may receive the benefits of public social services and to ensure that all persons employed in the providing of those services shall diligently protect public funds from misuse, the provisions of this section are adopted.

(b) A person shall not receive any public social services to which he or she may be otherwise entitled until the legal status of that person has been verified as one of the following:

(1) A citizen of the United States.

(2) An alien lawfully admitted as a permanent resident.

(3) An alien lawfully admitted for a temporary period of time.

(c) If any public entity in this state to whom a person has applied for public social services determines or reasonably suspects, based upon the information provided to it, that the person is an alien in the United States in violation of federal law, the following procedures shall be followed by the public entity:

(1) The entity shall not provide the person with benefits or services.

(2) The entity shall, in writing, notify the person of his or her apparent illegal immigration status, and that the person must either obtain legal status or leave the United States.

(3) The entity shall also notify the State Director of Social Services, the Attorney General of California, and the United States Immigration and Naturalization Service of the apparent illegal status, and shall provide any additional information that may be requested by any other public entity.

SECTION 6. Exclusion of Illegal Aliens from Publicly Funded Health Care.

Chapter 1.3 (commencing with Section 130) is added to Part 1 of Division 1 of the Health and Safety Code, to read:

Chapter 1.3. Publicly-Funded Health Care Services

130. (a) In order to carry out the intention of the People of California that, excepting emergency medical care as required by federal law, only citizens of the United States and aliens lawfully admitted to the United States may receive the benefits of publicly-funded health care, and to ensure that all persons employed in the providing of those services shall diligently protect public funds from misuse, the provisions of this section are adopted.

(b) A person shall not receive any health care services from a publicly-funded health care facility, to which he or she is otherwise entitled until the legal status of that person has been verified as one of the following:

(1) A citizen of the United States.

(2) An alien lawfully admitted as a permanent resident.

(3) An alien lawfully admitted for a temporary period of time.

(c) If any publicly-funded health care facility in this state from whom a person seeks health care services, other than emergency medical care as required by federal law, determines or reasonably suspects, based upon the information provided to it, that the person is an alien in the United States in violation of federal law, the following procedures shall be followed by the facility:

(1) The facility shall not provide the person with services.

(2) The facility shall, in writing, notify the person of his or her apparent illegal immigration status, and that the person must either obtain legal status or leave the United States.

(3) The facility shall also notify the State Director of Health Services, the Attorney General of California, and the United States Immigration and Naturalization Service of the apparent illegal status, and shall provide any additional information that may be requested by any other public entity.

(d) For purposes of this section "publicly-funded health care facility" shall be defined as specified in Sections 1200 and 1250 of this code as of January 1, 1993.

SECTION 7. Exclusion of Illegal Aliens from Public Elementary and Secondary Schools.

Section 48215 is added to the Education Code, to read:

48215. (a) No public elementary or secondary school shall admit, or permit the attendance of, any child who is not a citizen of the United States, an alien lawfully admitted as a permanent resident, or a person who is otherwise authorized under federal law to be present in the United States.

(b) Commencing January 1, 1995, each school district shall verify the legal status of each child enrolling in the school district for the first time in order to ensure the enrollment or attendance only of citizens, aliens lawfully admitted as permanent residents, or persons who are otherwise authorized to be present in the United States.

(c) By January 1, 1996, each school district shall have verified the legal status of each child already enrolled and in attendance in the school district in order to ensure the enrollment or attendance only of citizens, aliens lawfully admitted as permanent residents, or persons who are otherwise authorized under federal law to be present in the United States.

(d) By January 1, 1996, each school district shall also have verified the legal status of each parent or guardian of each child referred to in subdivisions (b) and (c), to determine whether such parent or guardian is one of the following:

(1) A citizen of the United States.

(2) An alien lawfully admitted as a permanent resident.

(3) An alien admitted lawfully for a temporary period of time.

(e) Each school district shall provide information to the State Superintendent of Public Instruction, the Attorney General of California, and the United States Immigration and Naturalization Service regarding any enrollee or pupil, or parent or guardian, attending a public elementary or secondary school in the school district determined or reasonably suspected to be in violation of federal immigration laws within forty-five days after becoming aware of an apparent violation. The notice shall also be provided to the parent or legal guardian of the enrollee or pupil, and shall state that an existing pupil may not continue to attend the school after ninety calendar days from the date of the notice, unless legal status is established.

(f) For each child who cannot establish legal status in the United States, each school district shall continue to provide education for a period of ninety days from the date of the notice. Such ninety day period shall be utilized to accomplish an orderly transition to a school in the child's country of origin. Each school district shall fully cooperate in this transition effort to ensure that the educational needs of the child are best served for that period of time.

SECTION 8. Exclusion of Illegal Aliens from Public Postsecondary Educational Institutions.

Section 66010.8 is added to the Education Code, to read:

66010.8. (a) No public institution of postsecondary education shall admit, enroll, or permit the attendance of any person who is not a citizen of the United States, an alien lawfully admitted as a permanent resident in the United States, or a person who is otherwise authorized under federal law to be present in the United States.

(b) Commencing with the first term or semester that begins after January 1, 1995, and at the commencement of each term or semester thereafter, each public postsecondary educational institution shall verify the status of each person enrolled or in attendance at that institution in order to ensure the enrollment or attendance only of United States citizens, aliens lawfully admitted as permanent residents in the United States, and persons who are otherwise authorized under federal law to be present in the United States.

(c) No later than 45 days after the admissions officer of a public postsecondary educational institution becomes aware of the application, enrollment, or attendance of a person determined to be, or who is under reasonable suspicion of being, in the United States in violation of federal immigration laws, that officer shall provide that information to the State Superintendent of Public Instruction, the Attorney General of California, and the United States Immigration and Naturalization Service. The information shall also be provided to the applicant, enrollee, or person admitted.

SECTION 9. Attorney General Cooperation with the INS.

Section 53069.65 is added to the Government Code, to read:

53069.65. Whenever the state or a city, or a county, or any other legally authorized local governmental entity with jurisdictional boundaries reports the presence of a person who is suspected of being present in the United States in violation of federal immigration laws to the Attorney General of California, that report shall be transmitted to the United States Immigration and Naturalization Service. The Attorney General shall be responsible for maintaining on-going and accurate records of such reports, and shall provide any additional information that may be requested by any other government entity.

SECTION 10. Amendment and Severability.

The statutory provisions contained in this measure may not be amended by the Legislature except to further its purposes by statute passed in each house by rollcall vote entered in the journal, two-thirds of the membership concurring, or by a statute that becomes effective only when approved by the voters.

In the event that any portion of this act or the application thereof to any person or circumstance is held invalid, that invalidity shall not affect any other provision or application of the act, which can be given effect without the invalid provision or application, and to that end the provisions of this act are severable.

SIGNIFICANCE

Immediately following its enactment, Proposition 187 was challenged in state court. Civil rights groups, including the Mexican-American Legal Defense/ Education Fund, the League of United Latin American Citizens, and the American Civil Liberties Union, quickly sought an injunction against the new measure, and on November 11 an injunction was issued pending a trial. The court based its action on a 1982 Texas ruling that required the state to provide public education for children of illegal immigrants residing in the state.

The Texas court set out two reasons for its ruling. First, it noted that the relative number of illegal immigrant children was small compared to the state's legal population, minimizing the economic impact on the state. Second, it observed that pending federal legislation was likely to grant amnesty to many of the children affected by the decision, meaning that these children were likely to be legally entitled to education in the near future. In the case of Proposition 187, the economic impact was also relatively small, but potential amnesty was not being considered.

Critics of Proposition 187 argued that the law violates the Constitution's guarantee of due process, since it directed state officials to withhold benefits without a court hearing. They also noted that California state law classifies education as a uniquely important service, demanding a more rigorous examination before it may be denied. Supporters of the law appealed to simple economics to make their case, arguing that the existing system unfairly forced tax-paying legal residents to subsidize health services and education for illegal aliens. They also argued that the law rewarded law-breakers by supporting individuals who entered the country illegally.

The legal battle over Proposition 187 dragged through the courts for years, as both sides filed briefs and sought friendlier venues. As the 1998 governor's election approached, candidate Gray Davis campaigned as an advocate of the law. Following his election, Davis submitted the law to arbitration, and the state's suit was eventually dropped, effectively killing the law. Hispanic groups applauded Davis's handling of the issue, while Proposition 187 fans claimed that he intentionally let the law die. Conservatives decried what they saw as the court system's hijacking of a legal election decision.

In the years since Proposition 187 was debated, immigration from Mexico has continued to be a point of contention. The U.S. border with Mexico is poorly policed and relatively porous, allowing easy entry for illegal immigrants. While immigration policy has been a politically thorny issue throughout the history of the nation, the extreme economic differences between the United States and Mexico provide tremendous incentive for poor Mexicans to move North. In 2006, President George W. Bush reopened the national debate about Mexican immigration and the millions of illegal immigrants already living in the United States.

FURTHER RESOURCES
Books

Daniels, Roger. *Coming to America: A History of Immigration and Ethnicity in American Life*. New York: Harper Perennial, 2002.

Mills, Nicholas. *Arguing Immigration: The Controversy and Crisis Over the Future of Immigration in America*. New York: Touchstone, 1994.

Oni, Kent A., and John M. Sloop. *Shifting Borders: Rhetoric, Immigration, and Californa's Proposition 187.* Philadelphia: Temple University Press, 2002.

Periodicals

"Another Rebellion." *The Economist* 373 (2004): 40.

Borjas, George J. "Welfare Reform and Immigrant Participation in Welfare Programs." *International Migration Review* 36 (2002): 1093–1123.

Valenty, Linda O., and Ronald D. Sylvia. "Thresholds for Tolerance: The Impact of Racial and Ethnic Population Composition on the Vote for California Propositions 187 and 209." *Social Science Journal* 41 (2004): 433–446.

Web sites

CNN. "Most of California's Prop. 187 Ruled Unconstitutional." <http://www.cnn.com/ALLPOLITICS/1998/03/19/prop.187/> (accessed June 7, 2006).

Skelton, George. "GOP's Prop. 187 Wounds Healing, But Dems Are Bleeding." *Los Angeles Times*, May 11, 2006. <http://www.latimes.com/news/local/la-me-cap11may11,1,6088958.column?coll=la-util-politics-cal> (accessed June 7, 2006).

York, Anthony. "R.I.P. Prop. 187." *Salon*, July 30, 1999. <http://www.salon.com/news/feature/1999/07/30/immigration/index.htm> (accessed June 7, 2006).

Blood on the Border

Magazine article

By: Southern Poverty Law Center

Date: 2001

Source: *Southern Poverty Law Center: Intelligence Report.* "Blood on the Border." 2001. http://www.splcenter.org/intel/intelreport/article.jsp?aid=230 (accessed July 25, 2006).

About the Author: The Southern Poverty Law Center Intelligence Project was established in 1981 to monitor hate groups and extremist activities throughout the United States. It also provides training to help law enforcement services and human rights groups combat organized racism. It publishes the quarterly *Intelligence Report* providing updates on the activities of more than 700 hate groups to law enforcement agencies, the media, and the public.

INTRODUCTION

The 2001 report "Blood on the Border" highlights the increasing threat to the United States of right-wing radicals and hate groups, who were growing in strength at that time in response to major increases in the immigration of nonwhite people to the country. In 2000, it was reported that there were 28.3 million immigrants in the United States; the majority were from Mexico, other Central or South American countries, the Caribbean, and East Asia. There were 7.9 million Mexican immigrants in the United States at that time. To some Americans, the new immigrants seemed very different ethnically and culturally.

Hate groups and other right-wing radical organizations who are opposed to nonwhite races have existed in the United States for a long time, but they have increased their activity and visibility in recent decades. This increase could be characterized as a backlash against the civil rights movement of the 1960s and 1970s, a movement that some radicals believe has threatened the national identity of the United States. The increase in hate-group activity may also be a response to changes in immigration laws that have favored nonwhite immigrants. Under these circumstances, right-wing groups have been able to increase their support among the general population, and some have moved into the mainstream, developing links with the anti-immigration movement, promoting their literature widely, and even contesting elections.

There are various types of right-wing radicals and hate groups, including the Ku Klux Klan, the skinhead movement, neo-Nazi groups, and some church organizations that use the scriptures to justify their white supremacist views. Although the specific ideologies, goals, and practices of these movements may vary, they share a virulent opposition to racial and ethnic minorities and often to other minority groups such as homosexuals and the disabled. Many advocate the use of violence or even murder in the name of preserving America's national white identity. They believe in the racial supremacy or superiority of white people, citing "scientific" evidence in proof of this, and they argue that nonwhite immigrants are taking jobs and living off welfare benefits in America, at a cost to the white population. Many of these organizations believe that there are conspiracies to undermine white dominance of the nation, either on the part of the government, which they believe to be run by Jews, or on the part of Mexico, which they believe is trying to lay claim to the southern U.S. states. There are close links between many of the groups in terms of information-sharing and the organization of rallies and other events, and their leaders and members are often associated with more than one organization.

In the mid-1990s, it was estimated that 25,000 Americans were actively involved in hate groups,

Members of the California Coalition for Immigration Reform argue with college students who oppose their views. AP IMAGES.

while a further 150,000 were likely to be "armchair racists" who do not actively participate but may receive literature and occasionally attend rallies. The Southern Poverty Law Center recorded an increase in the number of active hate groups in the United States from 240 in 1996 to 474 in 1998 and 676 in 2001. It is believed that the growth in the number of hate groups and in their membership was facilitated by the ease of communication via the internet and was influenced by particular forms of white power music among American youth. At the same time, there were increases in the amount and severity of violence being used by the groups against their victims, with many violent assaults and homicides being recorded. The members of such groups are often heavily armed in preparation for the race war that they believe is inevitable and by which they hope to achieve their goals either of banishing all nonwhites from the United States or of establishing separate territories for each racial group. However, the majority of racial hate crime is committed by individuals and small groups who are not connected with the organized hate movement.

■ **PRIMARY SOURCE**

In the frightening world of John Vinson's American Immigration Control Foundation (AICF), Americans are "fighting a war" with an "unseen enemy" who is rapidly ravishing the land.

A "raging flood" of Latins, Haitians and other Third Worlders "the greatest wave of immigration the world has ever witnessed" threatens America's "generally European" core with "foreign domination."

Already, Miami is a "Third World nightmare." "Illegal aliens" practice "voodoo" and leave stinking "human waste" in the streets. They bring crime, slums, urban sprawl and other troubles. "America is beautiful," says the narrator in one AICF videotape. "Why spoil it?"

John Vinson is not alone in his fears. The American radical right and even more so, the European is haunted by a specter: the day when white numerical dominance will end, sometime after 2050 in the United States.

The news last August that California had become the first large state to see its white population dip below 50 percent sent chills up the collective spine of the extreme right.

In the last year, radical groups around the country grew increasingly agitated over immigration. The pages of their publications filled with dire predictions of white racial extinction, a situation variously blamed on "corporate America" and a plot by Mexico.

Some held rallies in places where immigration is changing the local landscape, while others worked alongside more "mainstream" anti-immigrant groups to promote vigilantism.

Many wrote of the perils of foreign "takeovers" by non-whites. And David Duke, the former Klansman, started a group specifically to take advantage of nativist hatred. More and more, the radical right came to fear racial Armageddon at the hands of dark-skinned aliens.

"The brute fact," warned Sam Francis, editor of the white supremacist Council of Conservative Citizens' *Citizens Informer*, "is that unrestricted immigration has allowed the American Southwest to be invaded by aliens who may well in the near future... break the American nation apart."

Violence, too, is growing common both along the border and in places as far away as Long Island and Minnesota. In Pittsburgh last year, a lawyer allegedly went on a rampage against immigrants that left five non-whites dead.

Defeat and "Race War" in California   For the moment, anti-immigration activists face a dilemma. Since a major anti-immigrant proposition in California was overturned by the courts in 1998, opposition to immigration as a mainstream issue has faded.

As Francis complained angrily in a recent *Citizens Informer* editorial, "The Republicans in the last few years have almost entirely surrendered on immigration control."

Last fall, the only presidential candidate who ran on an anti-immigration platform—Pat Buchanan of the Reform Party—got just one percent of the vote, not the three-to-five percent many expected. A strong economy has meant few concerns about low-wage American jobs.

But that could change quickly. If, as many expect, the U.S. economy falls into a recession, all bets are off. In past downturns, Americans have passed harsh anti-immigration measures and violence has typically accelerated.

In Europe, recent hard times have seen outbursts of savage anti-immigrant attacks, including the fatal firebombings of several hotels full of foreign refugees.

Extremist nationalism is on the rise in the northern and central nations there and a similar phenomenon could easily hit the United States, given that immigration here already is at the highest levels since the massive wave of the early 1900s.

"I once interviewed a Spanish neo-fascist who talked about how capitalist society was like a diamond, very, very hard, almost impossible to break," says Martin Lee, an expert on the resurgence of fascism in Europe.

"But he said that if you found exactly the right pressure point, it could crack. For the European radical right, immigration has been that point for 30 years."

And what about America? "This is a precise situation which can start a race war," a hopeful "Tripp Henderson," a New Jersey member of the neo-Nazi National Alliance, wrote in a posting to an Alliance e-group.

"All it takes is for bodies to show up, and for the Mexicans in L.A. to start reprisals against Whites in California. Many wars have started over a single shot. I seriously urge any lone-wolf to leave a few bodies in the desert to get things warmed up."

Violence and Propaganda   Already, in an increasingly charged atmosphere along the U.S.-Mexican border, there has been violence. In the last year—the same period in which several Arizona ranchers made national news by "arresting" at gunpoint illegal aliens who crossed their lands—three would-be border-crossers have been killed in apparent vigilante violence.

One of them was shot from behind after asking a Texas rancher for water; he was left to bleed to death in the scrub brush. Seven others are confirmed wounded, and the toll will almost certainly go higher.

To the north, in Bloomington, Minn., a Hispanic man was clubbed and critically injured for speaking Spanish at a job site. In Farmingville, N.Y., a pair of tattooed racists were accused of posing as contractors to lure two undocumented Mexican workers to a warehouse where they were beaten severely.

This violence has been accompanied by renewed interest in immigration from two kinds of right-wing groups, some white supremacist and others less clearly so. Increasingly, these two sets of groups are finding common ground.

White supremacist groups almost by definition hate immigrants—at least dark-skinned ones. For groups from the National Alliance to the Klan to racist Skinhead crews, the Third World foreigner has always been an anathema.

But two of these racist groups are today particularly outspoken: the Council of Conservative Citizens (CCC) and its much smaller, more intellectual cousin, Jared Taylor's New Century Foundation, which publishes *American Renaissance* magazine.

The 15,000-plus-member CCC, led by Gordon Lee Baum, has taken up immigration issues ever more vigorously in the months since Sam Francis, a fired

Washington Times columnist who once chaired Vinson's AICF, took over as editor-in-chief of its *Citizens Informer*.

At the same time, *American Renaissance*, a journal dedicated to "proving" racial differences, has published Francis, California State University professor Roger McGrath and other anti-immigration ideologues. More and more, these two periodicals share both writers and politics.

Mexicans as "Cultural Cancer" Racist organizations like the CCC and the New Century Foundation have certainly helped beat the drum of anger at non-white immigrants, reaching thousands of people on the hard right with their messages.

But in many ways, it has been in a different milieu—in the circle of ostensibly more "mainstream" anti-immigration groups like AICF—that this movement has grown strong.

Vinson's videotape, "Immigration: Making America Less Beautiful?", is a lurid vision of barbarians at the gate and a classic example of the harsh anti-immigration propaganda now making the rounds.

To the strains of "America the Beautiful," it opens with Old Glory flapping, the U.S. Capitol, colonial houses and quiet streets. Suddenly, the music changes.

In Mexico, rough soldiers are saluting menacingly as they march by in red berets. Now, back to the Capitol, "America the Beautiful," blond-haired white kids tumbling down a slide. Then, to the border: a scary nightscope shot of Mexican illegals pouring across the line.

In a little while, a weeping woman will describe her son's murder by a "gang of illegals."

Glen Spencer's Voices of Citizens Together (VCT) almost makes AICF look tame by comparison. A Mexican invasion, Spencer warns in his own videotape, is racing across America "like wildfire." There are drugs in Iowa, gang takeovers in Nevada, and "traitors" in the Democratic Party, the Catholic Church and among the "corporate globalists."

Bringing crime, drugs, squalor and "immigration via the birth canal," Mexicans are a "cultural cancer" from which Western civilization "must be rescued." They are threatening the birthright left by the white colonists who "earned the right to stewardship of the land." And this invasion is no accident.

Working in league with communist Chicano activists and their allies in America, Spencer warns, Mexico is using a little-known but highly effective plan—a scheme already successful in "seizing power" in California—"to defeat America."

The name of the conspiracy is the "Plan de Aztlán." . . .

Leaving the Mainstream Much of [the] hard-line anti-immigrant movement today goes back to efforts in California to pass Proposition 187, which would have expelled illegal aliens from public schools and ended their access to benefits other than emergency medical treatment.

With the indispensable support of several key groups—in particular, Spencer's VCT and Barbara Coe's California Coalition for Immigration Reform (CCIR)—Prop 187 was approved in 1994 with 60 percent of the vote.

But in 1998, after years of court battles, the proposition was struck down, dealing a body blow to the mainstream anti-immigration movement.

It was later that year that VCT, CCIR and the more mainstream Federation for American Immigration Reform (FAIR) began working with the racist CCC. Coe, Spencer and Rick Oltman, FAIR's western regional representative, all came to Cullman, Ala., to speak at a 1998 anti-immigrant rally hosted by CCC.

The event, held to protest a swelling population of Mexican workers in the region, ended with the arrest of one of the rally's organizers. He was charged with violating a local ordinance regulating outdoor fires by burning a Mexican flag.

Vinson, for his part, began writing regular articles that year on the perils of immigration for the CCC's newspaper. Around the same time, Spencer began selling his videotape in full-page ads in the same paper.

(The CCC's racism, it should be noted, is not subtle. One recent commentary on the Florida CCC chapter's Web site, posted alongside a photo of an asylum-seeker, went like this: "THIS WORTHLESS, DIRT POOR, HAITIAN LEACH [sic] and her 3 BRATS have ABSOLUTELY NO RIGHT to be in this COUNTRY . . .!!!!!!!!!!!!!!!!")

In July 1999, the CCC organized an immigration panel at its semi-annual conference, held that summer in Washington, D.C. Speaking at the conference, where books with titles like *The Aryan Race* were offered for sale, were some key new luminaries of the anti-immigrant right: Vinson, Spencer and Lutton.

Also in 1999, Spencer sent copies of his remarkable video to every member of Congress. Hand-delivering the videos was Bettina McCann—the fiancée of the National Alliance's "military coordinator," neo-Nazi Steven Barry.

Picking the Scab In January 2000, David Duke, having recently abandoned attempts to appear nonracist, launched a new group he called the National Organization for European American Rights (NOFEAR). Explaining his new group's concerns at the National Press Club, Duke said, "If the present immigration rates continue . . . the European-American people will basically be lost as an entity."

Within a month, Duke was in Siler City, N.C., to tell about 100 people at an anti-immigration rally that they were losing their way of life to Hispanics who had come to work in local chicken-processing plants. The rally was organized by the National Alliance.

Last May, after national publicity surrounding Arizona rancher Roger Barnett's armed "arrests" of hundreds of illegals crossing his land, many anti-immigration groups came to Sierra Vista, Ariz., to back Barnett and others. Co-sponsoring the meeting were Spencer, Oltman and Coe (who referred to foreigners as "illegal alien savages").

Also attending, supposedly unbeknownst to the organizers, were two representatives of NOFEAR and unrobed members of an Arkansas Klan group. A Klan flier appeared on cars before the gathering.

In September, Spencer also traveled east to speak to a Long Island, N.Y., outfit called Sachem Quality of Life, a local anti-immigration group. His visit came just weeks after two Mexican day laborers were badly beaten in a warehouse, allegedly by white supremacists.

A few days after Spencer gave a fiery speech, a member of the Sachem group was arrested for threatening a local Hispanic family.

Spencer is active in other ways, as well. He hosts a syndicated radio show, "American Patrol Report," airing in 19 markets. He has interviewed Jared Taylor; former John Birch Society member Ezola Foster, Buchanan's running mate in the 2000 election; Kevin McDonald, a California State University professor who sees Jews behind U.S. immigration policies; and colleagues Coe and Oltman.

"Blood on the Border" In October, another anti-immigration delegation traveled to Arizona to lend its support to Roger Barnett, the controversial rancher who reportedly told a British newspaper that "tracking humans . . . is the biggest thrill."

This time it was a group known as Ranch Rescue, organized last summer by a Texan named Jack Foote. Foote, a conspiracy-oriented anti-immigration activist, had promised to "put a stop to . . . mass criminal trespass." When they arrived, Foote and a few followers spent time helping Barnett fix fences and "patrolling" his ranch.

Foote, who carried a large weapon and binoculars, has made a name for himself as a hard-liner. He reacted furiously, for instance, to an e-mail from a Mexican-American who accused him of racism.

"You and the vast majority of your fellow dog turds are ignorant, uneducated, and desperate for a life in a decent nation because the one you live in is nothing but a pile of dog shit made up of millions of worthless little dog turds like yourself," Foote wrote.

Finally, in December, the antigovernment separatist group known as the Republic of Texas (ROT) decided to "deploy" its "Texas Defense Forces" to part of the Mexican border to help "in controlling illegal border crossings."

ROT leader Daniel Miller said that any illegals who are intercepted in the operation planned for early this year "will be escorted back to the border and ordered to return."

That kind of talk bothers Miguel Escobar Valdéz.

Sitting in a drab, one-story building in Douglas, Ariz., not too far from Roger Barnett's ranch, the Mexican consul is leafing slowly through a lengthy report. Marked "CONFIDENTIAL," Escobar's report carries a title which leaves little to the imagination: "Incidents in Which Armed Private Citizens Threatened and Apprehended Individuals Presumed to be Undocumented Migrants."

One woman, the report says, was apparently fired on three times as she crossed a nearby ranch. Nine migrants say they were stopped by a local who fired half a dozen shots at them.

A group of 13 claims a rancher's wife set a German Shepherd on one of them while her husband held the rest at gunpoint. Armed ranchers forced two cars off a public road and held the 16 migrants in them until the Border Patrol showed up.

In incident after incident—28 in all, just in this small sector of the border over 17 months—angry white ranchers allegedly used weapons and threats, and sometimes violence, to "arrest" illegal aliens.

"I am very worried about the situation," Escobar said slowly as he spoke of the growing potential of an anti-immigration movement with an increasingly racist and vigilante edge. "We are all afraid of more blood on the border."

SIGNIFICANCE

When this report was written in 2001, immigration had faded as a mainstream political issue, due to a strong economy and few concerns about unemployment among the American-born population, and it was hoped that this would lead to a decline in support for hate groups. By 2005, however, immigration was firmly on the political agenda again, and white nationalist and other radical anti-immigration groups were increasing their influence in mainstream politics. Violent activity and vigilantism had also increased, particularly with the growth of so-called "Minutemen" vigilantes patrolling the U.S.-Mexico border region. In 2005 and 2006, there were demonstrations across the country in response to various immigration reform bills, demonstrations that resulted in violent clashes between anti-immigration and pro-immigration protesters, and at which hate groups were often strongly represented.

Within the political establishment, Republican Representative Tom Tancredo, who set up a congressional immigration-reform caucus to promote legislation to reduce both undocumented and legal immigration to the United States, has frequently attended the rallies and meetings of radical right-wing anti-immigration groups and has even praised the Minutemen initiative. However, there is still little support for extreme nationalist groups among the majority of the population, and the association of Tancredo and his anti-immigration colleagues with such groups may reduce rather than increase the level of popular support for tighter immigration policies.

FURTHER RESOURCES

Books

Perry, Barbara. *In the Name of Hate: Understanding Hate Crimes.* New York: Routledge, 2001.

Eatwell, Roger, and Cas Mudde. *Western Democracies and the New Extreme Right Challenge.* New York: Routledge, 2004.

Periodicals

Zeskind, Leonard. "The New Nativism: The Alarming Overlap between White Nationalists and Mainstream Anti-Immigrant Forces." *The American Prospect* 16 (2005).

Amy's Story

Essay

By: Anonymous

Date: 2002

Source: *Coalition of Student Advocates.* "Amy's Story." <http://www.cosaonline.org/stories.html> (accessed July 1, 2006).

About the Author: The Coalition of Student Advocates formed in October 2002 to lobby for legislation that would allow illegal immigrants who have graduated from American high schools to attend American universities.

INTRODUCTION

In the 1970s, widespread dissatisfaction with the nation's inability to control its borders prompted the American people to demand a change in immigration policy. Legislation passed over the next decades did not address the problems of naturalized immigrant children. The gap in the law led to calls for legislation that would allow immigrants students to be treated the same as native-born students.

The Refugee Act of 1980 indicated that Congress was ready, willing, and able to examine immigration reform. It was the first of several efforts to control the borders. The legislation set up a commission that issued recommendations that became the foundation for subsequent immigration laws in the 1980s and 1990s. The Immigration and Reform Control Act (IRCA) of 1986 provided a process by which immigrants who entered the country illegally could legalize their stay and eventually become naturalized U.S. citizens. Most of the immigrants who took advantage of IRCA came from Mexico, but more than 3,000 Taiwanese also became legal immigrants. The Immigration Act of 1990 included an authorization for the attorney general to grant temporary protected status to undocumented aliens subject to armed conflict. It also set a cap of 675,000 immigrants that has been regularly exceeded in subsequent years.

The various pieces of legislation did not resolve the crisis of border control or help all undocumented aliens who were long-term residents of the United States. Advocates for various groups of illegal immigrants proposed legislation that would address the needs of political and economic refugees. The Coalition of Student Advocates, one of the groups proposed immigration reform, focused on the concerns of naturalized students.

▮ PRIMARY SOURCE

Name: Amy

Location: New York

I am an American. I am also an undocumented immigrant.

Before I was born in 1978, my father was involved with the Tangwai. It was a movement in Taiwan whose main objective was to re-establish constitutional rights taken away by the Chinese Nationalists (Kuomingtang) after they had come into power in 1949. The grassroots-level work of the Tangwai eventually led to Taiwan's independence from China.

Involvement with the Tangwai was considered subversive at the time. As a means to silence my father, the Kuomingtang police power destroyed our home with sledgehammers. Our family stayed with one relative after another, running away in terror. We were afraid to be one of the other families involved with the Tangwai—the ones who seemed to disappear into thin air, or the individuals turning up with a bullet in their head. As I write this article, I am reluctant to say the scope of father's activity, as we still live with the fear of what can happen.

Roughly 100 students, some facing deportation, stage a mock graduation ceremony. Son Ah Yun leads the rally on Capitol Hill. AP IMAGES.

My father felt the best way to protect his wife and three daughters was to leave the island as soon as possible. After working with the U.S. Air Force in previous years, he believed America had much to offer. We left Taiwan on tourist visas in early 1982, with no intention to return.

I was three years old.

When we arrived in the United States, my parents did not contact lawyers. They did not know the language, and did not know anyone to turn to for help. Arriving in Los Angeles with only a few thousand U.S. dollars and three children to feed, one thing was clear: they needed money. Immediately, they began working. Despite having studied to become a civil engineer in Taiwan, my father became a cook in a restaurant, and my mother washed dishes.

The restaurant promised to file legalization papers on behalf of my parents, but in exchange my parents were to be paid very little. Everything seemed to cost more than expected in America. After working at three different restaurants simultaneously, my father decided the hours were lousy and the payoff was not enough to support a family. Instead of staying with this plan, my father became a motel manager in a bad neighborhood of San Bernardino. Here, he was to be paid a thousand dollars a month, and our family would receive living facilities—the manager's quarters—for free.

One year to the day we arrived in the United States, an armed gunman came into the manager's office and demanded the money from the cash register. He pointed the revolver just above the collarbone of my father's left shoulder, down into the torso region. My dad was naïve, and said the money was not his to give. So the gunman shot my father. He then took the money in the register, and ran to his motorcycle getaway where another person waited.

My father spent six months in the hospital, having repeated operations with complications resulting from adhesions. When I read the doctor's notes, my father's condition was reported as "stable, but the patient worries about how he will make money for his family."

When he finally recovered a year later, my father moved our family out of San Bernardino to a much safer neighborhood in the Los Angeles suburbs. He decided to leave previous plans behind and to go into business for himself. Utilizing his education in civil engineering, he started his own construction business.

Immigration laws have come and gone. The Immigration Reform and Control Act (IRCA) of 1986 gave a blanket amnesty for those who arrived before January 1, 1982. Our family arrived three and a half weeks after this deadline, and therefore did not qualify due to this technicality. We could not do anything about our status.

In second grade, in the multi-purpose room of my elementary school, I chimed along with others in music class,

This land is your land, This land is my land,

My sisters and I liked it here and wanted to belong. We got ourselves American names and worked hard to fit in. As I got older, I enjoyed participating in community service with my classmates. I usually spent afternoons finishing up on homework, nights watching Star Trek: The Next Generation or rehearsing with my high school marching band, playing the clarinet. I also hung out at the mall with my friends on the weekends.

From California , To the New York Islands,

But every year brought with it a sense of being unwelcome in a country we sought to call home. I was oblivious to immigration laws until I became older. When I was fifteen, I learned California Proposition 187 took away access to public services, including driver's licenses, from undocumented immigrants. It didn't matter that my parents paid income taxes every year since they had arrived in the U.S. It also made in-state college tuition for immigrants like me illegal, even though I had lived in California since I was three years old.

To the Redwood Forests, To the Gulf Stream Waters,

Further, lawyers were reluctant to take our case. Declaring amnesty was not going to work because Americans knew very little about the political upheaval in Taiwan. We therefore did not qualify as political asylum candidates, as Taiwan was not considered a "priority" country unlike China or Vietnam. Therefore, our best bet in becoming legal was to marry a U.S. citizen.

This land was made for you and me.

I finished high school with honors, and looked forward to college. "The FAFSA opens the door to the federal student aid process," the application said, "every step you take will get you closer to achieving your educational goals." One exception: I did not qualify because I couldn't check the little box saying I was a legal resident of the United States.

My father thought a college education was vital to success in America, so he and my mother worked like superheroes to put my sisters and myself through college, paying out-of-state tuition for each of us. My California state education cost $17,000 a year, more than three times the $4,500 tuition legal residents enjoyed.

As I entered college, I began to learn the boundaries which exist for an undocumented immigrant in America. One of the first things I did as a new college student was to visit the campus of a well-known academic university in San Diego. I was excited to see where I would be spending the next four years of my life. Our family rode southbound on the 5 freeway and watched as the landscape changed from evergreen trees to deep blue shores.

While driving through the San Onofre Mountains, a yellow highway sign caught my attention. It was posted in the middle of a highway, a yellow rectangular type with a silhouette of a three-member family holding hands and running, with the child flying up like a tail of a kite. The unmistakable word, CAUTION, was written across the top. It took only a moment for me to realize the sign was a warning to oncoming traffic about immigrants running across the eight-lane freeway, away from the border patrol.

As we drove further south, I became more mindful of my family's place in America. I looked across the freeway and observed that the northbound traffic had slowed down. Each car was individually stopped by border patrol agents.

"I don't want to come down here again," my mother said while looking out the window. "I don't feel safe."

In the years to follow, I tried not to fixate on my undocumented status. But in time I began hearing tales from my friends who studied abroad in Spain, England, and Australia. They would speak of their adventures backpacking through Europe, showing me pictures of these huge metal sculptures by Jean Tinguely in Paris. A friend said he realized he found the love of his life on one of the islands of Costa Rica.

I wanted more than anything to be a part of these adventures. I would feel this despair even when hearing my friends bragging about their latest exploits from Wednesday and Saturday nights spent down in nearby Tijuana. For example, when they returned home, they'd hold up a large chipped ceramic statue of a frog or an unauthorized replica of Homer Simpson and say, "Five, bucks! Can you believe it?"

Despite the fact that I would probably never have any use for these trinkets, I wanted more than anything to be in Mexico and other countries with my friends, creating new memories in my life. But I never ventured to go past the border. Despite my perfect English, I was afraid there would be something giving me away at the border check.

I believed if I traveled down to T.J. with my friends on a harmless night, the stories I would bring back would be much more tragic, assuming I could return at all.

To occupy myself, I thought perhaps I could get a job. I was hoping the advice attorneys had given us for years happened to be wrong—a misunderstanding. When I tried applying for employment at a retail clothing store, I was met with the same little box which stopped me from applying for the FAFSA: I needed some form of documentation to prove my legal status. According to something called the "I-9" form, I needed a U.S. passport or a green card, and a Social Security card to work. I didn't possess either of the first two documents, and the Social Security card I was issued as a child had some additional printing across the top which I never noticed before: "NOT VALID FOR EMPLOYMENT PURPOSES.'"

Without proper documentation, no one in my family was allowed to work in any setting requiring tax withholding—to file a 'W-2.' This meant no health insurance, no retirement benefits, or anything else to ensure our health and welfare.

I was afraid to fake documentation because I did not want to risk my own deportation. To do so would, in effect, also place my family in jeopardy. So instead, I worked odd cash-paying jobs. I helped people pack and move to new homes. I tutored high school kids. Neither paid much money. I even considered being an egg donor when I saw ads in the school newspaper.

Thanksgiving 1999. I would be graduating in six months. My father sat across from the black obsidian coffee table, with a large roasted bird placed on the reflective surface before us. It was prepared in my father's "traditional" Chinese style, with garlic, green onions, and soy sauce.

He cleared his throat. "So did you find a nice boy, someone to marry?"

I knew where this question was going. The immigration attorneys repeatedly told us it was the easiest way to become legal in this country. But the better years of college were spent in search of the perfect major, and not the perfect "husband."

My face became hot. I felt it was such an unfair question. I refused to accept marriage as a matter of convenience for my own immigration status. I wanted to tell him, "No, it goes against everything I was taught to believe—by you and everyone else."

But all I could do was to look down at my empty plate and say, "No, dad. I did not." Then my father sighed, and began carving the turkey.

I was at a loss for what I would do after graduation. On one hand, I could finish school and move back home with my parents. I hated the idea of moving back home, and would have done anything to avoid this fate. My other option was to stay in San Diego, learn the skills of a new profession, and, by my dad's words, "buy time" until I found a husband.

So I started law school. It seemed to be the right decision.

Spring 2001. Almost finished with my first year as a law student, I spoke to an attorney about the reinstatement of Section 245(i) . It was a law where undocumented immigrants were given the opportunity to apply for permanent residence without having to leave the U.S. The person filing for a green card either had to be related to a family member who was a legal resident, or had to be hired by a U.S. company.

This provided a loophole for the few who obtained employment with fake documentation. While not all immigrants use fake papers, the government in essence, was promising to look the other way for those who did when applying for green cards—just this one time.

I couldn't believe it. I never followed through with applying for a job because I believed it would have jeopardized my chances of gaining legal employment, legal residency, and ultimately U.S. citizenship. I was doing my best to play by the rules, but it wasn't paying off.

Attorneys were still unwilling to take my case: "Right now, you're just a scholar," one said to me, referring to my then-current status as a law student. "You don't have a job. You don't have an offer of employment. I'm sorry, I can't work with you."

Soon after, I learned for the first time that the American Bar Association does a background check on each person before taking the state bar. At this point, I no longer saw any reason to continue. I left law school and moved back home to the suburbs and got by, tutoring high school students in my neighborhood.

I look back at the twenty-two years I've spent in this country. I've been taught to love the United States and its values above all else. What I cherish most is the freedom to speak without concern of being persecuted by the government. My family did not have this freedom in Taiwan. And despite everything my family has experienced in this country, I would not choose to be anywhere else.

I hope the DREAM Act becomes a reality this year, as it will allow myself and others like me to become legal in a country we have come to love. If it is enacted, I have a to-do list. It is short because I am afraid to set my hopes too high. I will go out and find a secure job, finally utilizing my college degree. I will travel to other countries, including Taiwan, to put a physical setting to all the stories I heard as a child. Most importantly, I will stop living in fear.

But for now, it is still a dream.

SIGNIFICANCE

Until 1970, illegal immigrants to the United States were relatively rare. Subsequently, political turmoil and economic worries in their native countries as well as the increasing ease of transportation encouraged immigrants to enter the United States. By 2006, more than 35 million people living in the United States were born in other countries. This equals about 12 percent of the American population, the highest percentage of foreign-born since 1920. Of these people, an estimated 11 to 12 million are illegal immigrants. Approximately 60,000 undocumented immigrant children are estimated to graduate annually from U.S. high schools. These children, who often came to the United States at very young ages with their parents, are American in all but nationality. They speak English and possess American values. The problem of what to do with these Americanized illegal immigrants has entered the debate over illegal immigration.

Federal law does not permit financial aid to go to illegal immigrants and does not permit states to charge the lower in-state tuition to aliens. In 2003, Senators Orrin Hatch (R-UT) and Richard Durbin (D-IL) introduced the Development, Relief, and Education for Alien Minors Act (DREAM Act). The legislation permits states to determine residency for in-state tuition, protects students from the threat of deportation, and allows them to work legally. As of mid–2006, the legislation had yet to pass despite bipartisan support.

FURTHER RESOURCES

Books

Gimpel, James G., and James R. Edwards, Jr. *The Congressional Politics of Immigration Reform*. Needham Heights, Mass.: Allyn and Bacon, 1999.

Ngai, Mae M. *Impossible Subjects: Illegal Aliens and the Making of Modern America*. Princeton, N.J.: Princeton University Press, 2005.

Web site

Coalition of Student Advocates. "What is the DREAM Act?" <http://www.cosaonline.org/> (accessed July 1, 2006).

Huddled Masses, Please Stay Away

Magazine article

By: Anonymous

Date: June 22, 2002

Source: *The Economist*

About the Author: *The Economist* is an internationally focused political and economic publication based in Britain.

INTRODUCTION

The movement toward a united Europe began after World War II and culminated in the creation of the European Union. Following the destruction of Europe that occurred during World War II, six countries came together with the goal to create a common market in steel and coal. The member states—Belgium, Federated Republic of Germany, France, Italy, Luxembourg, and the Netherlands—sought to create economic cooperation between European neighbors in an effort to develop and sustain peace in the region. As a result, in 1951 the Treaty of Paris set up the European Coal and Steel Community. Shortly thereafter, the member states created a common market dealing with certain goods and services. In 1957, under the Treaties of Rome, the European Economic Community (EEC) was set up, and by 1968 customs duties between the member states were removed. Among the members, common policies on trade and agriculture were also developed in the 1960s. The success of this cooperation led to the first enlargement of the union to include Denmark, Ireland, and the United Kingdom. With the increased membership, leaders within the union sought to create a monetary union. By 1986, the membership had increased again with the addition of Greece, Spain, and Portugal. Following that expansion, additional programs were established to decrease the economic development gap between the member states. As the countries of Europe moved toward a unified economy, the EEC began to represent the member states as a unified front in the international community.

The Single European Act was signed in February 1986 and laid out the goal of completing a single European market by January 1, 1993. In December 1991, the members of the European Council, member states' presidents and prime ministers, adopted the Treaty on European Union. This treaty facilitated the name change of the EEC to become the European Union (EU) and set forth the goals of monetary union by 1999, European citizenship, and common policies regarding security. As the additional countries of Austria, Finland, and Sweden joined the EU, the organization moved toward its goals. In 2002, the member states replaced their individual currency with the euro (with some exceptions: the United Kingdom, Denmark, and Sweden are EU members who are not part of the monetary union and did not convert their currency to the euro). In 2004, the EU welcomed ten additional countries, many of which were former Soviet bloc countries. With the new states, EU membership rose to twenty-five nations. Among these states, the single currency and market has created a free flow of goods, services, capital, and people.

The free flow of people among EU member states, regardless of national origin, began in 1993 with the creation of the Schengen zone. In June 1985, seven EU states met in Schengen, Luxembourg, and signed a treaty to end the internal borders, checkpoints, and controls between signatories. As a result, the Schengen visa was created, allowing its holder to travel freely within much of the EU.

Since the creation of the Schengen visa, relatively large numbers of immigrants have entered the EU. Policies regarding the handling of refugees were addressed at the Dublin convention in 1997. The Dublin agreement affirmed cooperation with the United Nations High Commission on Refugees and sought to determine the status of refugees. The agreement was intended to clarify which Schengen member country was responsible for the refugee, to avoid passing the refugee between member states. Although the Dublin convention superseded previous bi-lateral agreements among individual EU states, it failed to be implemented within the EU. As a result, the refugee issue was revisited in 2003 with the Dublin II regulation.

▎ PRIMARY SOURCE

European leaders say they want harmonious EU action against illegal immigration. In reality, nearly all governments are still sticking to policies of their own.

"Give me your tired, your poor / Your huddled masses, yearning to breathe free", proclaims America's Statue of Liberty. If the European Union were to build a similar monument in Brussels, what message would it carry? Perhaps something like: "We have vacancies for a limited number of computer programmers and will reluctantly accept torture victims with convincing scars. Migrants looking for a better life can clear off."

As they prepare for a grand summit in Seville on June 21st-22nd, the EU's leaders have made it clear that controlling illegal immigration will be the top item on the agenda. This new-found urgency stems from the recent rise of populist anti-immigration parties across the Union,

including France's National Front, the Freedom Party in Austria, the Pim Fortuyn list in the Netherlands, the Northern League in Italy and the Danish People's Party. European leaders are worried that if they are not seen to act against illegal immigration, the far right will gain even more ground.

The EU's best guess is that the Union's domains absorb 500,000 illegals every year. Although the popular image of these people is formed by television pictures of Iraqis and Afghans trying to hop aboard trains that go through the Chunnel to Britain, or of Albanians struggling to cross the Adriatic to Italy in rickety boats, most illegal immigrants in the EU enter legally and simply stay on when their visas run out. Despite some politicians' steamy rhetoric, nobody really knows whether the flow of illegal immigrants is going up or down. It is known, however, that the number of refugees claiming political asylum in the Union has slowed sharply over the past decade. Last year 384,530 people claimed asylum, against 675,460 in 1992.

For several years EU leaders have been promising a common policy for both illegal immigration and asylum seekers. Now that the Union (bar Britain, Ireland and Denmark) has scrapped passport controls for travelling within it, logic suggests that a common approach to controlling the EU's external frontier should be forged. Having 15 different national regimes for asylum and naturalisation has also led to worries that illegal immigrants are "asylum shopping", and to recriminations between neighbouring countries like Britain and France, and Denmark and Sweden.

But while EU leaders love harmonisation in theory, in practice progress has been very sticky. A senior official at the European Commission, which has been trying to hammer out common policies, laments "a general unwillingness to change national systems whatever they may be." Britain, for instance, lets asylum seekers look for work six months after they have lodged their application; Germany makes them wait 12 months and France 18. Trying to find a common approach to family reunification has also proved fraught. Germany wants to prevent children older than 12 joining their parents; others see this as too tough. The Dutch want gays to be allowed to join their partners; the Spanish are dead against the idea. In theory, EU leaders also want a common time-frame for assessing asylum claims; in practice, many home ministers say they cannot give deadlines to judges.

It is unlikely that putting illegal immigration at the top of the agenda in Seville will lead to a breakthrough. The summiteers will look for progress in two specific areas. First, they will ponder the idea of an EU border-police to replace national frontier controls. That will be deemed a step too far for now, so instead there will be moves towards exchanging information on visas and an emphasis on greater co-operation between frontier police. Second, the leaders may try to pursue a British idea of trying to link foreign aid to countries' willingness to take back refugees whose asylum applications have been rejected. This may generate the headlines that EU leaders want about "tough action." But the reality will be messier. A link, maybe, as Italy plans; but no one will subordinate aid to the fight against illegal immigration.

So a genuine harmonisation of asylum policies will have to wait for another day. Commission officials hope that in about six months they may secure agreement on family reunification. Establishing common procedures for processing applications and appeals is likely to take much longer. In any case, some officials reckon that even if a fully harmonised set of EU rules is eventually achieved, it would be unlikely to ensure that all EU countries share a proportionately equal burden of asylum-seekers. That is because the laxness or otherwise of national regimes is only one factor determining where asylum seekers make their claims: family and cultural ties, work opportunities and language are just as important.

Liberals within the commission and elsewhere are hoping that the Seville summit will not strike too punitive a tone. "We might get something into the 13th paragraph of the summit statement, acknowledging that EU countries actually need immigrants," says one official wryly. But the argument that allowing more legal immigration is both the way to stem illegal immigration and to solve the problem of the EU's ageing population is widely viewed as too simple. As the same official points out, "We know from America's experience that allowing lots of legal immigration does not put a stop to illegal immigration." EU studies have also suggested that immigration alone will not be enough to make Europe's population younger.

So in calling for the harmonisation of EU policies on illegal immigration, European leaders are engaging in a great deal of double-talk. The number of asylum-seekers does not bear out talk of a worsening crisis. And the actions of political leaders do not suggest a great desire to surrender control of national immigration in favour of a common EU approach.

On the contrary. In the weeks before the Seville summit, several EU governments have taken unilateral measures to tighten up their own immigration regimes. Denmark has brought in a law cutting benefits to asylum seekers and making it harder to bring in spouses or elderly relatives. Italy will soon have one that would make non EU-citizens be fingerprinted if they want to live in the country. Britain's government has proposed

educating the children of asylum seekers outside the main school system. In Austria, immigrants will have to try harder to learn German. Other countries may well follow suit. EU governments can talk till they are blue in the face about a common approach. For now, unilateral action is still the order of the day.

SIGNIFICANCE

The summit in Seville, Spain, continued the dialogue between EU member states regarding the handling of immigrants. Those attending the conference called for stricter border controls and better coordination of visa policies and information on illegal immigrants. However, implementation of the policy became an area of contention. British prime minister Tony Blair proposed that development aid be used as a tool toward nations that do not work against human trafficking. French president Jacques Chirac, however, rejected this plan, saying that sanctions could create a deeper economic problem in the developing nations, thereby increasing migration.

The five major powers in the EU—France, Britain, Italy, Spain, and Germany—met in Evian, France, in June 2005 to continue the dialogue regarding the issues of immigration. This meeting focused on immigrants from Africa, the Middle East, and Asia. Members at the meeting sought consensus within the EU regarding greater security. One proposal included expanding the practice of fingerprinting visa applicants to make it easier to locate those who are carrying an expired visa. As the EU continues to seek a single policy, individual countries continue to create their own policies toward immigration control. In Spain, the Integrated External Vigilance System was unveiled in 2002. The $140 million surveillance system operates along the coastline closest to Morocco and is fitted with night-vision cameras and radar sensors.

FURTHER RESOURCES
Periodicals

Hannan, Daniel. "Bring Back Borders." *The Spectator* (June 29, 2002).

Wright, Tom. "Europeans Tackle Illegal Immigration." *International Herald Tribune* (July 6, 2005).

Web sites

CNN.com. "Immigration Tops EU Summit Agenda." June 20, 2002. <http://archives.cnn.com/2002/WORLD/europe/06/20/spain.summit/> (accessed June 15, 2006).

Human Rights Watch. "The Right to Asylum in the European Union." <http://www.hrw.org/worldreport/Helsinki-28.htm> (accessed June 15, 2006).

Immigrants Protest in Favor of Legalization Program in Spain

Photograph

By: Cesar Rangel

Date: June 11, 2004

Source: Caser Rangel/AFP/Getty Images.

About the Photographer: Cesar Rangel, a freelance photographer based in Barcelona, Spain, has contributed over 3,000 images to the Getty Images archives.

INTRODUCTION

This photograph portrays some of the estimated 1,700 immigrants that occupied two of Barcelona's main churches in June 2004 demanding the right to live and work in Spain legally. Following raids by the police, the immigrants left the churches peacefully, but continued to demonstrate on the streets, threatening to repeat the sit-ins if the government did not respond positively to their requests.

Similar demonstrations, as well as a hunger-strike, had been held by undocumented immigrants in Spain three years earlier, as a result the authorities agreed to review the papers of thousands of those who had not been approved for work and residency permits under a legalization scheme at that time.

In recent decades, Spain has experienced a steady increase in the numbers of both legal and undocumented labor migrants entering the country, mainly from nearby Morocco, but also from Pakistan, Latin American countries and other parts of the world. These people mainly work in unskilled or low-skilled jobs in the informal economy, especially in agricultural and construction work, catering, and the tourism industry. In 2003 and 2004, Spain received more legal immigrants than any other European Union (EU) nation, while at the same time, the numbers of undocumented migrants are also estimated to have increased rapidly.

Up until the mid–1980s, when Spain became a member of the EU and was put under pressure from other EU countries to control immigration, the country had no official immigration policy. When the first "foreigners' law" was passed in 1985, this created a new category of

Maria Garces, from Ambato, sleeps as she waits in line at the offices of the Foreign Ministry in Quito, Ecuador. AP IMAGES.

undocumented migrants who were already living and working in Spain. Policies over the next twenty years were mainly focused on attempting to control the number of immigrants entering and staying in the country, and little attention was given to integrating those already living there, whether legal or undocumented. However, Spain has enacted several regularization programs in recognition of the significant presence of undocumented immigrants and their contribution to the Spanish economy. Legalization programs, or amnesties, took place in 1986, 1991, and 1996. By the mid–1990s, under the socialist government of the time, steps were taken to recognize legal migrants as permanent rather than temporary members of society, by introducing six-year work permits, easing the family reunification rules and extending basic health and education rights to immigrants entering under family reunification visas.

When a conservative government was elected in 2000 under José María Aznar, immigration rules were tightened and the government refused to implement another regularization program. It made a clearer distinction than in the past between legal and undocumented migration, and enacted new laws that made living and working in Spain as an undocumented migrant a criminal act. Diplomatic relations suffered as Spain criticized Morocco for failing to tackle the problem of Moroccan illegal migration, and targeted Moroccans in its campaign to gain public support for its harsh policies against undocumented immigrants, linking the rise in Moroccan undocumented migration with increased crime rates in Spain.

In April 2004, a new socialist government under Prime Minister José Luis Rodríguez Zapatero came to power. Traditionally, the Socialists had been much more sympathetic to the plight of both legal and undocumented immigrants in Spain, and the new Government's announcement that it would improve the situation of undocumented immigrants raised the hopes of many, and gave rise to public statements of their demands, as in the Cathedral sit-in.

PRIMARY SOURCE

IMMIGRANTS PROTEST IN FAVOR OF LEGALIZATION PROGRAM IN SPAIN

See primary source image.

SIGNIFICANCE

Shortly after the immigrant demonstrations, in August 2004, the Spanish government announced a new policy under which immigrants holding

PRIMARY SOURCE

Immigrants Protest In Favor of Legalization Program in Spain: While locked in the Church of Pi of Barcelona, immigrants hold up their immigration papers as part of a protest to request the legalization of Spain's illegal immigrants, June 11, 2004. CASER RANGEL/AFP/GETTY IMAGES.

employment contracts would be provided legal status. However, only a small proportion of undocumented migrants have an employment contract, so the proposals fell far short of the demands of many thousands of immigrants for regularization of their status. More positively, President Zapatero promised to pursue a policy of extending undocumented migrants rights for health care, education and social services, and committed the government to reviewing a massive backlog of applications for regularized status.

Spain's economy will depend increasingly on labor migrants, as its working-age population is projected to start shrinking by 2010. However, it is under significant pressure from other European countries to control immigration, especially undocumented migration, as many migrants are currently passing through Spain and settling illegally in other parts of Europe. It will be necessary for Spain to implement policies which tackle the problem of illegal immigration more effectively than in the past, as well as dealing with the demands of a huge undocumented immigrant community already in the country, and facilitating the social integration of those it decides are entitled to stay.

FURTHER RESOURCES

Books

Balfour, Sebastian. *The Politics of Contemporary Spain.* Routledge, 2005.

Messina, Anthony M. *West European Immigration and Immigrant Policy in the New Century.* Praeger, 2002.

Periodicals

Sole, Carlota. "Immigration Policies in Southern Europe." *Journal of Ethnic and Migration Studies.* (November 30, 2004).

Levitin, Michael. "Labor pains: Spain's migrant-worker problem. (Of Several Minds)." *Commonweal.* September 24, 2004.

Illegal Immigrants Are Bolstering Social Security With Billions

Newspaper article

By: Eduardo Porter

Date: April 5, 2005

Source: Porter, Eduardo. "Illegal Immigrants Are Bolstering Social Security With Billions." *New York Times* (April 5, 2005).

About the Author: Eduardo Porter is an economics reporter for the *New York Times*, a daily newspaper with a circulation of over one million readers worldwide.

INTRODUCTION

The United States Social Security system is projected to be in crisis. It has been reported that unless social security contributions are increased or benefits reduced, the social security fund will be depleted before the middle of the twenty-first century (Board of Trustees, 2003). The contributions of undocumented workers are currently factored into social security projections, and plans in the mid-2000s to reform U.S. immigration laws and reduce levels of undocumented residence in the United States may therefore have a major impact on the future of social security system.

Official estimates in 2004 put the number of undocumented migrants living in the United States at 10.4 million; many believe that the true figure is much higher than this. A high proportion of these, particularly from Mexico and other Latin American countries, are labor migrants who use fake documents to secure employment in the United States It has been reported that the majority of undocumented migrants in the United States are paid at least the minimum wage, and that most of these workers and their employers regularly pay tax and social security contributions on their earnings. Some of these immigrants also hold fake social security cards and may therefore claim benefits. However, the welfare reform law of 1996 has made it very difficult even for legal immigrants who have been in the United States for less than five years, and especially for undocumented immigrants, to claim federally-funded benefits. Moreover, research has indicated that the majority of undocumented migrants stay for relatively short periods in the United States and eventually return to their home countries, with very few ever drawing a U.S. pension.

There is a substantial body of research into the fiscal costs and benefits of undocumented migrants to the U.S. economy, which takes into account their tax contributions, use of welfare services, benefits claims, and overall impact on U.S. wage levels. The findings are mixed and inconclusive, making it very difficult to interpret the real contribution of undocumented migrants to the U.S. social security system.

A research study of six thousand Mexican undocumented migrants reported that although around two thirds of them were paying income tax and social security contributions, only around ten percent had sent a child to a U.S. school and less than five percent had received any public benefits in the form of food stamps, welfare, or unemployment payments. In contrast, research by the Center for Immigration Studies reported that twenty-five percent of households headed by illegal Mexican immigrants had used a welfare program compared to only fifteen percent of households headed by U.S. nationals.

A 1984 study of unauthorized migrants in Texas found that the state gained fiscal benefits from its large undocumented migrant community due to their high tax payments and low use of public services, but similar research in Southern California around the same time found that undocumented migrants used more public services than their tax payments covered. In 1992, the Los Angeles County Internal Services Department

A man walks past a mural portraying various scenes from Irish life in Yonkers, New York, December 13, 2005. STAN HONDA/AFP/GETTY IMAGES.

estimated that undocumented migrants within the county represent a fiscal cost of around $440 per person. At the national level the picture is also mixed, with some research identifying an overall fiscal benefit from unauthorized migrants and other studies finding that they represent a cost to the U.S. economy.

■ PRIMARY SOURCE

STOCKTON, Calif.—Since illegally crossing the Mexican border into the United States six years ago, Ángel Martínez has done backbreaking work, harvesting asparagus, pruning grapevines and picking the ripe fruit. More recently, he has also washed trucks, often working as much as 70 hours a week, earning $8.50 to $12.75 an hour.

Not surprisingly, Mr. Martínez, 28, has not given much thought to Social Security's long-term financial problems. But Mr. Martínez—who comes from the state of Oaxaca in southern Mexico and hiked for two days through the desert to enter the United States near Tecate, some 20 miles east of Tijuana—contributes more than most Americans to the solvency of the nation's public retirement system.

Last year, Mr. Martínez paid about $2,000 toward Social Security and $450 for Medicare through payroll taxes withheld from his wages. Yet unlike most Americans, who will receive some form of a public pension in retirement and will be eligible for Medicare as soon as they turn 65, Mr. Martínez is not entitled to benefits.

He belongs to a big club. As the debate over Social Security heats up, the estimated seven million or so illegal immigrant workers in the United States are now providing the system with a subsidy of as much as $7 billion a year.

While it has been evident for years that illegal immigrants pay a variety of taxes, the extent of their contributions to Social Security is striking: the money added up to about 10 percent of last year's surplus—the difference between what the system currently receives in payroll taxes and what it doles out in pension benefits. Moreover, the money paid by illegal workers and their employers is factored into all the Social Security Administration's projections.

Illegal immigration, Marcelo Suárez-Orozco, co-director of immigration studies at New York University, noted sardonically, could provide "the fastest way to shore up the long-term finances of Social Security."

It is impossible to know exactly how many illegal immigrant workers pay taxes. But according to specialists, most of them do. Since 1986, when the Immigration Reform and Control Act set penalties for employers who knowingly hire illegal immigrants, most such workers have been forced to buy fake IDs to get a job.

Currently available for about $150 on street corners in just about any immigrant neighborhood in California, a typical fake ID package includes a green card and a Social Security card. It provides cover for employers, who, if asked, can plausibly assert that they believe all their workers are legal. It also means that workers must be paid by the book—with payroll tax deductions.

IRCA, as the immigration act is known, did little to deter employers from hiring illegal immigrants or to discourage them from working. But for Social Security's finances, it was a great piece of legislation.

Starting in the late 1980s, the Social Security Administration received a flood of W-2 earnings reports with incorrect—sometimes simply fictitious—Social Security numbers. It stashed them in what it calls the "earnings suspense file" in the hope that someday it would figure out whom they belonged to.

The file has been mushrooming ever since: $189 billion worth of wages ended up recorded in the suspense file over the 1990s, two and a half times the amount of the 1980s.

In the current decade, the file is growing, on average, by more than $50 billion a year, generating $6 billion to $7 billion in Social Security tax revenue and about $1.5 billion in Medicare taxes.

In 2002 alone, the last year with figures released by the Social Security Administration, nine million W-2s with incorrect Social Security numbers landed in the suspense file, accounting for $56 billion in earnings, or about 1.5 percent of total reported wages.

Social Security officials do not know what fraction of the suspense file corresponds to the earnings of illegal immigrants. But they suspect that the portion is significant.

"Our assumption is that about three-quarters of other-than-legal immigrants pay payroll taxes," said Stephen C. Goss, Social Security's chief actuary, using the agency's term for illegal immigration.

Other researchers say illegal immigrants are the main contributors to the suspense file. "Illegal immigrants account for the vast majority of the suspense file," said Nick Theodore, the director of the Center for Urban Economic Development at the University of Illinois at Chicago. "Especially its growth over the 1990s, as more and more undocumented immigrants entered the work force."

Using data from the Census Bureau's current population survey, Steven Camarota, director of research at the Center for Immigration Studies, an advocacy group in Washington that favors more limits on immigration, estimated that 3.8 million households headed by illegal immigrants generated $6.4 billion in Social Security taxes in 2002.

A comparative handful of former illegal immigrant workers who have obtained legal residence have been able to accredit their previous earnings to their new legal Social Security numbers. Mr. Camarota is among those opposed to granting a broad amnesty to illegal immigrants, arguing that, among other things, they might claim Social Security benefits and put further financial stress on the system.

The mismatched W-2s fit like a glove on illegal immigrants' known geographic distribution and the patchwork of jobs they typically hold. An audit found that more than half of the 100 employers filing the most earnings reports with false Social Security numbers from 1997 through 2001 came from just three states: California, Texas and Illinois. According to an analysis by the Government Accountability Office, about 17 percent of the businesses with inaccurate W-2s were restaurants, 10 percent were construction companies and 7 percent were farm operations.

Most immigration helps Social Security's finances, because new immigrants tend to be of working age and contribute more than they take from the system. A simulation by Social Security's actuaries found that if net immigration ran at 1.3 million a year instead of the 900,000 in their central assumption, the system's 75-year funding gap would narrow to 1.67 percent of total payroll, from 1.92 percent—savings that come out to half a trillion dollars, valued in today's money.

Illegal immigrants help even more because they will never collect benefits. According to Mr. Goss, without the flow of payroll taxes from wages in the suspense file, the system's long-term funding hole over 75 years would be 10 percent deeper.

Yet to immigrants, the lack of retirement benefits is just part of the package of hardship they took on when they decided to make the trek north. Tying vines in a vineyard some 30 miles north of Stockton, Florencio Tapia, 20, from Guerrero, along Mexico's Pacific coast, has no idea what the money being withheld from his paycheck is for. "I haven't asked," Mr. Tapia said.

For illegal immigrants, Social Security numbers are simply a tool needed to work on this side of the border. Retirement does not enter the picture.

"There will be a moment when I won't be able to continue working," Mr. Martínez acknowledges. "But that's many years off."

Mario Avalos, a naturalized Nicaraguan immigrant who prepares income tax returns for many workers in the area, including immigrants without legal papers, observes that many older workers return home to Mexico. "Among my clients," he said, "I can't recall anybody over 60 without papers."

No doubt most illegal immigrants would prefer to avoid Social Security altogether. As part of its efforts to properly assign the growing pile of unassigned wages, Social Security sends about 130,000 letters a year to employers with large numbers of mismatched pay statements.

Though not an intended consequence of these so-called no-match letters, in many cases employers who get them dismiss the workers affected. Or the workers—fearing that immigration authorities might be on their trail—just leave.

Last February, for instance, discrepancies in Social Security numbers put an end to the job of Minerva Ortega, 25, from Zacatecas, in northern Mexico, who worked in the cheese department at a warehouse for Mike Campbell & Associates, a distributor for Trader Joe's, a popular discount food retailer with a large operation in California.

The company asked dozens of workers to prove that they had cleared up or were in the process of clearing up the "discrepancy between the information on our payroll related to your employment and the S.S.A.'s records." Most could not.

Ms. Ortega said about 150 workers lost their jobs. In a statement, Mike Campbell said that it did not fire any of the workers, but Robert Camarena, a company official, acknowledged that many left.

Ms. Ortega is now looking for work again. She does not want to go back to the fields, so she is holding out for a better-paid factory job. Whatever work she finds, though, she intends to go on the payroll with the same Social Security number she has now, a number that will not jibe with federal records.

With this number, she will continue paying taxes. Last year she paid about $1,200 in Social Security taxes, matched by her employer, on an income of $19,000.

She will never see the money again, she realizes, but at least she will have a job in the United States.

"I don't pay much attention," Ms. Ortega said. "I know I don't get any benefit."

SIGNIFICANCE

Concerns about high levels of undocumented migration to the United States, particularly from Mexico, have led to the introduction of two competing immigration reform bills, both of which could impact significantly on the U.S. social security system.

Republican proposals to make illegal immigration and the employment of undocumented workers a federal crime, if effectively enforced, would be likely to reduce the numbers of undocumented workers contributing to the tax and social security system, leading to the need to raise contributions or reduce benefits to make up the difference. These proposals were passed in the House of Representatives in December 2005, but are strongly opposed by pro-immigrant groups and many Democrat politicians.

An alternative bill that has received cross-party support in the Senate proposes the introduction of a guest worker program, which would be likely to legalize the status of many of the existing migrants. Although this would mean they would continue making tax and social security payments, it would also put pressure on the social security system by extending the eligibility to benefits to a larger number of immigrants.

The article is controversial in that it highlights the extent to which the United States social security system depends on the contributions of unauthorized migrants, and raises the possibility that the United States would benefit from more, rather than less, undocumented immigration. Although there is no firm research evidence to support this, the question of how much undocumented immigrants contribute to the U.S. economy and social security system is likely to come under increasing scrutiny in the immigration reform debate of 2006.

FURTHER RESOURCES
Periodicals

Espenshade, Thomas J. "Unauthorized Immigration to the United States." *Annual Review of Sociology* 21 (1995).

Howling, Stephanie, A. "Generational Equity, Generational Interdependence, and the Framing of the Debate Over Social Security Reform." *Journal of Sociology and Social Welfare* (September 1, 2003).

"Do Borders Matter to President Bush? Critics of His Proposed "Guest-Worker" Program Claims It Will

Open the Floodgates to More Illegal Immigration and Endanger the Ideal of a Stable Middle Class in America." *Insight on the News* (March 1, 2004).

Bill on Illegal-Immigrant Aid Draws Fire

Newspaper article

By: Rachel B. Swarns

Date: December 30, 2005

Source: Swarns, Rachel B. "Bill on Illegal-Immigrant Aid Draws Fire." *New York Times* (December 30, 2005).

About the Author: Rachel B. Swarns is a reporter for the *New York Times*, a quality daily U.S. newspaper that was founded in 1851. The *New York Times* is published in New York City and is distributed to many other countries.

INTRODUCTION

In December 2005, the U.S. House of Representatives passed a border security bill aimed at strengthening enforcement of immigration control and reducing undocumented migration to the United States. Mass rallies were held nationwide to protest against the bill, particularly the provision that made it a felony for anyone to assist an undocumented immigrant to enter the United States or to remain in the United States illegally. This provision of the bill was primarily intended to punish smugglers who assist undocumented migrants to enter the United States and employers who deliberately hire people known to be illegal residents or those without proper documentation.

It has been estimated that up to forty percent of undocumented migrants, particularly those from Mexico, use the services of agents, or people smugglers, to arrange their entry to the United States. The use of smugglers is believed to have increased since policies aimed at strengthening the border control have made land crossings into the United States increasingly difficult. As a result, large criminal groups specializing in people smuggling have developed in Mexico, with many smaller agents also involved. Research has found that the typical fees paid to a smuggler by a Mexican migrant increased more than threefold since the launch of "Operation Gatekeeper" in 1994, and by 2004 were often in excess of $2,000.

The border security bill aims to deter such activity by imposing hefty penalties and jail sentences on those found guilty of this crime.

Employers of undocumented migrants are also targeted by the bill. Although many employers may unknowingly employ illegal migrants, particularly if they hold faked documents, the proposed legislation is aimed at those with a deliberate strategy of hiring undocumented migrants, perhaps in order to reduce wage costs. Under the 1986 Immigration Reform and Control Act (IRCA), employers found to have knowingly employed undocumented migrants are liable to fines. However, this legislation has been ineffective in reducing levels of employment of undocumented migrants, in part due to a loophole in the law that does not require employers to verify the documents presented by potential employees. More significant, however, has been the lack of funding for enforcement of those provisions of the legislation dealing with employers, and a focus on strengthening border controls as the primary measure in combating illegal immigration. As a result, the number of workplace inspections conducted between 1992 and 2002 fell by more than seventy percent and, in 2003, only four employers were prosecuted for employing undocumented migrants.

The intention of the December 2005 bill was to make federal crimes of activities such as people smuggling and the employment of unauthorized migrants. However, a wide range of religious institutions, advocacy organizations, and immigrant support organizations also come into contact with undocumented migrants and may actively seek to provide them with various forms of humanitarian and welfare support and other assistance. These groups were concerned that they also would be liable to prosecution if the bill were to become law. They embarked on a campaign of opposition to the proposed legislation, spearheaded by the Catholic Church.

The Catholic Church in the United States has traditionally supported immigrant groups in both a political and practical sense. Church officials at the highest levels have openly criticized immigration policies that are felt to be harmful to the interests of immigrants, such as the Illegal Immigration Reform and Immigrant Responsibility Act and the Welfare Reform Act of 1996. In 2000, the United States Conference of Catholic Bishops called publicly for the respect of immigrants' rights. The Catholic Church, along with other religious organizations, also provides many practical services to assist immigrants in submitting applications for immigration or political asylum. A wide range of

Rosa Elia Navejas looks up the statue called "The Undocumented Christ" at Our Lady of Refuge Catholic Church in Eagle Pass, Texas, December 6, 2005. AP IMAGES.

other immigrant support groups, some organized along ethnic or religious lines, provide similar assistance to immigrants, and some go even further in helping them to learn English and find jobs in the United States. For ethical reasons, these organizations often do not discriminate on the basis of immigration status when providing services.

PRIMARY SOURCE

WASHINGTON, Dec. 29— Churches, social service agencies and immigration groups across the country are rallying against a provision in the recently passed House border-security bill that would make it a federal crime to offer services or assistance to illegal immigrants.

The measure would broaden the nation's immigrant-smuggling law so that people who assist or shield illegal immigrants would be subject to prosecution. Offenders, who might include priests, nurses or social workers, could face up to five years in prison.

The proposal would also allow the authorities to seize some assets of those convicted of such a crime.

Proponents of the legislation have argued that such provisions would make it harder for illegal immigrants to thrive in the United States by discouraging people from helping them. The legislation, which cleared the House this month, could also subject the spouses and colleagues of illegal workers to prosecution.

Several Republicans and Democrats in Congress say the measure appears unlikely to become law. But the legislation has touched off an outcry among groups that teach English and offer job training, medical assistance and other services to immigrants.

The United States Conference of Catholic Bishops has written to members of Congress and called on President Bush to oppose the measure publicly. In Manhattan, scores of immigrants demonstrated against the bill last week. Here in the Washington area, a coalition of immigrant-services groups is planning rallies, visits to members of Congress and a letter-writing campaign to try to prevent the immigration bill from becoming law.

"We are going to fight this legislation," said Gustavo Torres, executive director of Casa of Maryland, one of the advocacy groups rallying against the measure. "The immigrant community is very upset about this."

Mr. Torres's group offers job placement services and English classes to thousands of immigrants each year. On Wednesday, as he greeted day laborers looking for work at his center in Silver Spring, Md., Mr. Torres said he could not imagine being forced to turn away the needy because they lacked legal papers.

"We never ask for documentation," he said. "Our mission is to help anyone in need of service, regardless of their immigration status. We are proud of that." Speaking for the Conference of Catholic Bishops, Bishop Gerald R. Barnes of San Bernardino, Calif., said the measure threatened church workers and doctors as well as ordinary citizens who provided urgent or life-saving assistance to illegal immigrants.

"Current legislation does not require humanitarian groups to ascertain the legal status of an individual prior to providing assistance," Bishop Barnes wrote this month in a letter to Congress. "The legislation would place parish, diocesan and social service program staff at risk of criminal prosecution simply for performing their jobs."

Supporters of the border-security bill say they are trying to crack down on a culture of indifference to the nation's immigration laws that has allowed 11 million illegal immigrants to live in this country.

The legislation would make it a federal crime to live in the United States illegally, which would turn millions of illegal immigrants into felons, ineligible to win any legal status. It would also stiffen the penalties for employers who hire illegal immigrants.

"This legislation aims to prevent illegal immigration and re-establish respect for our immigration laws," said Representative F. James Sensenbrenner Jr., Republican of Wisconsin, who introduced the legislation in the House.

"Those breaking the law will be held accountable," Mr. Sensenbrenner said, "whether they are smugglers cruelly trafficking in human beings, employers hiring illegal workers or alien gang members terrorizing communities."

President Bush has also praised the legislation.

"America is a nation built on the rule of law, and this bill will help us protect our borders and crack down on illegal entry into the United States," Mr. Bush said after the House passed the measure. "Securing our borders is essential to securing the homeland."

In his statement, Mr. Bush did not comment on the provision that is causing such a furor among churches and nonprofit groups. A White House spokesman referred questions about Mr. Bush's position on the matter to the Justice Department.

John Nowacki, a spokesman for the department, declined to answer questions about whether the Bush administration supported the provision.

White House officials have emphasized in recent weeks, however, that Mr. Bush still believes that any immigration legislation should include a guest worker program that would grant millions of undocumented workers the right to work temporarily in this country.

The House bill does not include a guest worker program, but the Senate is expected to consider such a plan early next year. A guest worker plan would give legal status to millions of illegal immigrants. If that were to happen, the measure outlawing assistance to illegal immigrants might be removed or end up having little effect.

But advocates for immigration said they were still deeply disheartened that Mr. Bush and members of Congress had not spoken out against the House measure.

"It's mind-boggling," said Julie Dinnerstein, deputy director for immigration policy at the New York Immigration Coalition, which sponsored last week's rally in New York.

"I think our courts should be focused on people who are doing terrible things," Ms. Dinnerstein said. "Do we need to send a bunch of priests or ministers or nurses to jail?"

SIGNIFICANCE

Major public demonstrations against the border security bill were held across the country during early 2006. In May 2006, the Senate passed an alternative bill that did not propose any change to the law on assisting undocumented migrants, although it did support further strengthening of immigration enforcement. The Senate bill addressed the interests of undocumented migrants already in the United States and the needs of U.S. employers by proposing a guest worker program. Under this program, undocumented immigrants already residing in the United States would be eligible to apply for guest worker status.

Both houses of Congress must agree on an immigration bill before it can become law. As of mid–2006, it was unclear whether such an agreement would be reached on the proposal to make providing assistance to undocumented migrants a federal crime. The outcry from the church and immigrant support organizations has highlighted the complexity of defining such a crime, given the wide range of organizations and service providers that undocumented migrants may contact and the ethical issues often involved in these interactions.

FURTHER RESOURCES

Books

DeLaet, Debra L. *U.S. Immigration Policy in an Age of Rights.* Westport, Conn.: Praeger, 2000.

Periodicals

Cornelius, Wayne A. "Controlling 'Unwanted' Immigration: Lessons from the United States, 1993–2004." *Journal of Ethnic and Migration Studies* (July 2005).

Menjivar, Cecilia. "Religion and Immigration in Comparative Perspective: Catholic and Evangelical Salvadorans in San Francisco." *Sociology of Religion* (Spring 2003).

The Minutemen Border Patrol

Photograph

By: David McNew

Date: July 19, 2005

Source: Photo by David McNew/Getty Images.

About the Photographer: Photographer David McNew is a member of the National Press Photographers Association and has won regional as well as national awards for his work. This image is part of the collection maintained by Getty Images.

INTRODUCTION

In 2002, Chris Simcox, an Arizona newspaper publisher, created the Civil Homeland Defense Corps, the precursor to the Minuteman Civil Defense Corps, known informally as the Minutemen or the Minutemen Border Patrol. Simcox has stated that the terrorist attacks on September 11, 2001—at the World Trade Center and the Pentagon, and in southwestern Pennsylvania—triggered in him a sense of outrage and a desire to help defend the United States from outside aggressors.

The Minutemen Border Patrol's slogans, "Americans doing the jobs Congress won't do" and "Operating within the law to support enforcement of the law," reflect a dissatisfaction with Congress and law enforcement in the United States regarding illegal immigration and border patrol. According to the Minutemen and Simcox, their group's effort to patrol the U.S. borders with Canada and Mexico is a coordinated, all-volunteer venture to protect the United States from terrorists, and to prevent immigrants from entering the country illegally to take jobs, use government assistance, enroll in schools, and use U.S. healthcare illegally. Simcox and other group members claim not to be anti-immigrant but to be against illegal immigration; the group views President George W. Bush (1946–) and the Republican-controlled Congress as ineffective agents in securing the borders.

In 2003 Simcox was arrested during a patrol of the Arizona-Mexico border; he was found on national park land, carrying a loaded pistol and a police scanner. Simcox has stated his belief that federal border patrol agents are too lax in their work. He has claimed to witness immigrants crossing the border with armed guards while border agents do nothing to prevent the crossing. In 2004 Jim Gilchrist founded the Minuteman Project, an organization similar to Chris Simcox's Minuteman Civil Defense Corps, with an anti-violence, anti-separatist message, promoting monitoring as a method for assisting federal border patrol agents. The two men combined their groups in 2005.

By 2005 the Minutemen Border Patrol was active in border states such as Arizona, Texas, Vermont, New York, and Idaho. On April 1, 2005, the group organized a 900-person effort along a twenty-three-mile stretch of the Arizona-Mexico border; by the end of April, the Minutemen claimed that illegal crossings dropped from more than 800 per day to approximately 13 per day, a 98 percent decrease. Simcox considered the effort a success, proof that his organization was necessary and effective in managing border crossings.

PRIMARY SOURCE

THE MINUTEMEN BORDER PATROL
See primary source image.

SIGNIFICANCE

California governor Arnold Schwarzenegger hailed the Minutemen Border Patrol as a positive force in controlling illegal crossings, stating that "They've done a terrific job. And they have cut down the crossing of illegal immigrants by a huge percentage." President Bush labeled the Minutemen Border Patrol volunteers "vigilantes," a comment that fed a growing divide in the Republican party and among

PRIMARY SOURCE

The Minutemen Border Patrol: Thomas McMullen prepares his gear, including camouflage, spotting scope, and a pistol, for a covert approach in the controversial nightly patrol by citizen volunteers searching for people crossing into the U.S. illegally from Mexico, on July 19, 2005. PHOTO BY DAVID MCNEW/GETTY IMAGES.

conservatives in the United States. The Minutemen and their followers disagree sharply with President Bush's worker amnesty proposals and guest worker programs.

Unlike other volunteer border patrol groups, such as Ranch Rescue, the Minutemen do not advocate the use of violence in preventing border crossings. Chris Simcox suggests that volunteers use video cameras to document crossings and carry cell phones or two-way radios to communicate with authorities. He advises volunteers to approach persons crossing the border to ask about their citizenship status. This last measure has led to accusations by Minutemen opponents that racism and racial profiling fuel the group's actions. Critics allege that Minutemen have approached persons of color on or near borders, asking them whether they speak English, where they live, and where they work, while not asking such questions of caucasian people in the same areas.

The Minutemen Border Patrol assert that illegal immigration is responsible for a loss of high-paying American jobs, health care crises in emergency rooms, overcrowded schools in border areas, and other social and economic problems in border states. As of late 2005, the Minutemen Border Patrol claimed to have more than 15,000 volunteers. In April 2006, massive immigration protests involving more than four million protestors across the United States were organized to oppose a Republican plan to crack down on illegal immigration. In May 2006, during the Memorial Day weekend, Minutemen volunteers began to construct a fence along the Arizona-Mexico border on private land, with encouragement from the land's owner. While a December 2005 bill, passed by the U.S. Congress, provided more money for federal border patrol agents and fences, the private effort gained significant attention and criticism from Mexican

Wes Bramhall, from Tucson, Arizona, stands in front of a United States Border Patrol Station, rallying for more support from the U.S. government in preventing illegal immigrants from crossing the U.S.-Mexico border, in Naco, Arizona. © SAUL LOEB/EPA/EPA/CORBIS.

authorities such as Bishop Renato Ascencio Leon, who called the group's actions "xenophobic."

In May 2006 President Bush ordered 6,000 National Guard troops to work as border patrol substitutes, and he created 3,000 federal border patrol agent jobs. This action reversed his 2004 signing of a budget that eliminated nearly 10,000 border patrol positions. Simcox hailed the addition of border patrol troops and agents but stated that 30,000—not 6,000—troops were needed to adequately patrol the borders with Mexico and Canada and to prevent illegal immigrants from coming into the United States.

FURTHER RESOURCES
Books
Ellingwood, Ken. *Hard Line: Life and Death on the U.S.-Mexican Border*. New York: Pantheon, 2004.

Haines, David W., and Karen E. Rosenblum, eds. *Illegal Immigration in America: A Reference Handbook*. Westport, Conn.: Greenwood Press, 1999.

Yoshida, Chisa To, and Alan Woodland. *The Economics of Illegal Immigration*. New York: Palgrave MacMillan, 2005.

Websites
Minuteman Civil Defense Corps. <http://www.minutemanhq.com/hq/> (accessed June 25, 2006).

Minuteman Project. <http://www.minutemanproject.com/default.asp?contentID=23> (accessed June 25, 2006).

Salon.com. "The Angry Patriot." <http://www.salon.com/news/feature/2005/05/11/minuteman> (accessed June 25, 2006).

United States Citizenship and Immigration Services. <http://www.uscis.gov/graphics/index.htm> (accessed June 25, 2006).

Tom Tancredo's Wall

The Colorado Congressman Tries to Make America the World's Biggest Gated Community

Newspaper editorial

By: Tom Tancredo

Date: December 29, 2005

Source: *WSJ.com Opinion Journal.* "Tom Tancredo's Wall: The Colorado Congressman Tries to Make America the World's Biggest Gated Community." December 29, 2005. <http://www.opinionjournal.com/editorial/feature.html?id=110007740> (accessed July 26, 2006).

About the Author: Thomas Gerard "Tom" Tancredo is a Republican politician who has been a member of the U.S. House of Representatives since 1999 and represents the 6th Congressional District of Colorado. He is a leading figure in the Republican campaign for tighter immigration controls and is chairman of the House Immigration Reform Caucus.

INTRODUCTION

The proposals for a barrier along the southern border of the United States, referred to in Republican Congressman Tom Tancredo's speech of December 2005, were those contained in the Republican Bill on immigration reform that was passed by the House of Representatives that month. The Bill proposed tough measures to strengthen the border and to tackle the problem of illegal migration to the United States, particularly from Mexico. It has been estimated that more than four-fifths of recent Mexican immigrants to the United States are undocumented migrants and that more than half of all undocumented immigrants in the United States are from Mexico.

U.S. governments have progressively been tightening the border controls since the passing of the Immigration Reform and Control Act (IRCA) in 1986. Under the provisions of IRCA, the number of

Rep. Tom Tancredo, R-Colo., holds a shirt after signing up as a volunteer with the Minuteman Project in Tombstone, Arizona, April 1, 2005. AP IMAGES.

border control agents were increased, advanced surveillance technology was introduced in the border region, and high security fences were erected in some areas known to be commonly used to gain entry to the United States. Over the following years, there were a number of major initiatives that stepped up border control patrols in specific high-risk areas and were intended to deter potential illegal migrants. These included "Operation Hold the Line" in the El Paso, Texas, area in 1993 and Operation Gatekeeper in the San Diego region the following year. Although these specific initiatives were reported to have had immediate effects in reducing numbers of apprehensions, overall levels of undocumented entry from Mexico have continued to increase. The impact of building security fences in specific areas has apparently been to redistribute entries to other parts of the border and to increase the use of agents to facilitate entry. There is little evidence that the measures have had much of a deterrent effect on potential migrants.

It is often argued that the tightening of the U.S. border with Mexico has been ineffective in reducing illegal immigration to the United States because the border control measures have not been accompanied by effective application of the laws against the employment of undocumented immigrants. IRCA had introduced legal sanctions against employers who knowingly hired unauthorized migrants, but these had not been effectively enforced by the Immigration and Naturalization Service (INS), partly due to limited staffing and budgets in their workplace enforcement wing. As long as employers continue to offer jobs to low-cost illegal migrants, they will continue to find ways of entering the country. One reported effect of tightening the border without reducing employment opportunities was that undocumented migrants started to settle for longer periods in the United States, rather than traveling between the United States and Mexico to meet the demands for seasonal labor.

The Republican Bill of December 2005 proposed hard-line measures that were intended to tackle undocumented migration more effectively. These measures included building a 700-mile long two-layer security fence along the border, increasing the number of border control agents, and making it a felony to enter or settle in the United States illegally or to assist anyone else to do so, for example, by employing them. The Bill made no provision for a guest worker scheme or for any legal route to settlement for the estimated 11.5 million undocumented migrants already living and working in the country, who could be subject to deportation.

PRIMARY SOURCE

"We have a supply and a demand problem. The supply problem is coming across the border. We are in this bill doing something very specific about that with the inclusion of the amendment, with the passage of the amendment, to build some barrier along at least 700 miles of our southern border. I hope we continue with that, by the way, along the entire border, to the extent it is feasible, and the northern border we could start next."

—*Rep. Tom Tancredo (R., Colo.)*

So there you have it. Tom Tancredo has done everyone a favor by stating plainly the immigration rejectionists' endgame—turn the United States into the world's largest gated community. The House took a step in that direction this month by passing another immigration "reform" bill heavy with border control and business harassment and light on anything that will work in the real world.

For the past two decades, border enforcement has been the main focus of immigration policy; by any measure, the results are pitiful. According to the Migration Policy Institute, "The number of unauthorized migrants in the United States has risen to almost 11 million from about four million over the past 20 years, despite a 519% increase in funding and a 221% increase in staffing for border patrol programs."

Given that record, it's hard to see the House Republican bill as much more than preening about illegal immigration. The legislation is aimed at placating a small but vocal constituency that wants the borders somehow sealed, come what may to the economy, American traditions of liberty or the Republican Party's relationship with the increasingly important Latino vote.

Besides mandating the construction of walls and fences along the 2,000-mile Mexican border, the bill radically expands the definition of terms like "alien smuggler," "harboring," "shielding" and "transporting." Hence all manner of people would become criminally liable and subject to fines, property forfeiture and imprisonment—the landscaper who gives a co-worker a ride to a job; the legal resident who takes in an undocumented relative; a Catholic Charities shelter providing beds and meals to anyone who walks through the door.

Sponsors of the legislation, led by House Judiciary Chairman James Sensenbrenner and Homeland Security Chairman Peter King, don't stop at targeting good Samaritans. They're also forcing the business community to simultaneously create jobs and kill jobs. The bill would make it incumbent on employers to establish the immigration status of all hires and empower local police to enforce federal immigration laws. This means small-business owners soon could find themselves not only inconvenienced by a mandated hiring database system but also threatened with the prospect of bankruptcy due to repeated raids and high fines. Some will throw in the towel on the GOP.

Perhaps the bill's most revealing feature is the one that makes it a criminal offense, rather than a civil violation, to be in the country illegally. This would effectively turn the country's 11 million or so illegal aliens into felons and automatically disqualify them from gaining legal status— ever. The provision gives lie to the claim we keep hearing from Mr. Tancredo and GOP Congressional leaders that they're open to a guest-worker program for illegal aliens so long as we first beef up the border.

This also smears the law-abiding aliens with the law-breakers. If a bill with this anti-guest-worker provision ever became law, millions of otherwise well-behaved people who have become integral parts of thousands of U.S. communities would have every incentive to stay in the shadows lest they be deported. As a matter of law enforcement priorities if nothing else, this is crazy. In truth, this bill in its current form has no chance of becoming law. The Senate will take up immigration reform soon and is expected to produce something more feasible.

President Bush has said repeatedly that he'll only sign a comprehensive immigration reform bill; that means creating *legal* pathways for foreign labor to enter the country and fill jobs Americans simply won't do anymore. Regrettably, the White House, in a sop to the throw-'em-all-out faction, praised the House vote. By voicing no disapproval of these over-the-top provisions, Mr. Bush legitimizes the forces that will make it hard to pass useful reform. And so a highly divisive problem may fester without solution into the next elections. At some point, the president of the United States will have to get behind the Statue of Liberty or Tom Tancredo's wall.

SIGNIFICANCE

The Republican Bill met with much protest from Democrats, some Republicans, the business community, and pro-immigrant groups. It was argued that the proposed measures for dealing with undocumented migration were too harsh, that it did not take into account the economy's need for migrant labor, and that it was impractical in making no allowance for a legal route to settlement for the millions of unauthorized migrants already in the country. Demonstrations against the Bill were held across the nation during the following months.

In May 2005, the Senate passed an alternative Democrat-led Immigration Reform Bill with cross-party support. While this proposed legislation also provided for building a high security fence along the border and increasing the number of border control agents, it did not propose to criminalize unauthorized migrants. It included provisions for a guest worker visa scheme and an agricultural worker temporary visa scheme, while also proposing giving illegal migrants who had been in the country for a minimum length of time the option to apply for legal settlement. By mid–2006, neither bill had yet been passed by both houses, a necessary prerequisite for becoming law. The issue of immigration reform looked likely to be a major factor influencing the outcome of the 2006 mid-term elections in November.

FURTHER RESOURCES

Periodicals

Cornelius, Wayne A. "Controlling 'unwanted' Immigration: Lessons from the United States, 1993–2004." *Journal of Ethnic and Migration Studies* 31 (4) (July 2005): 775–794.

Espenshade, Thomas J. "Unauthorized Immigration to the United States." *Annual Review of Sociology* 21 (1995): 195–216.

Web site

BBC News. "US Immigration Debate: Key Players." <http://news.bbc.co.uk/2/hi/americas/4955768.stm> (accessed July 7, 2006).

House Votes for 698 Miles of Fences on Mexico Border

Newspaper article

By: Rachel B. Swarns

Date: December 16, 2005

Source: Swarns, Rachel B. "House Votes for 698 Miles of Fences on Mexico Border." *New York Times*. December 16, 2005.

About the Author: Rachel B. Swarns is a reporter for the *New York Times*, a New York newspaper with a daily circulation of over one million copies.

INTRODUCTION

Since the early 1990s, a major focus in United States immigration policy has been on securing the land border with Mexico and reducing levels of undocumented migration to the United States, as well as tackling other cross-border crimes such as drug smuggling. In December 2005, the House of Representatives passed a bill intended to further

Two men on the Mexican side of the U.S.-Mexico border fence above Smuggler's Gulch in Imperial Beach, California. AP IMAGES.

strengthen the border with measures including the construction of high security fences for some 700 miles along the United States border with Mexico.

Mexicans account for a high percentage of all undocumented immigrants to the United States. Of the estimated 10.4 million undocumented immigrants living in the United States in 2004, fifty-seven percent were from Mexico. Up to eighty-five percent of recent Mexican immigrants to the United States have entered as undocumented migrants, many using the services of people traffickers (coyotes) to facilitate their entry.

Drug smuggling from Mexico is also an increasing problem. The U.S. State Department estimates that by the mid–1990s, around ten percent of the cocaine, twenty to thirty percent of the heroin, and up to eighty percent of the marijuana being brought into the United States arrives via Mexico. The Drug Enforcement Administration has also calculated that Mexico earns more than $7 billion annually from illegal drug trading.

Although a security fence already exists along some sections of the border known to be used by undocumented migrants, it is easily penetrable and has been ineffective in deterring migrants. Long stretches of the border have no fence and are unmarked. However, there has been a significant strengthening of border control since the early 1990s, with a major increase in border control agents and the use of advanced technology to detect unauthorized migrants. These have often been introduced under specific initiatives such as Operation Gatekeeper, launched in the San Diego border region in 1994.

The proposal to construct a high security fence along a lengthy stretch of the 1,951-mile U.S. border with Mexico is controversial, especially in Mexico. It is seen as being in conflict with the provisions of the North American Free Trade Agreement (NAFTA), intended to facilitate free trade and the legal movement of goods between the United States and Mexico. There is already a high degree of integration between the Mexican and U.S. economies. With an estimated 230 million people and 82 million vehicles entering the United States from Mexico every year, it remains difficult to secure the border against illegal activity, while leaving it open to legitimate crossings and trade.

■ PRIMARY SOURCE

WASHINGTON, Dec. 15—House Republicans voted on Thursday night to toughen a border security bill by requiring the Department of Homeland Security to build five fences along 698 miles of the United States border with Mexico to block the flow of illegal immigrants and drugs into this country.

The amendment to the bill would require the construction of the fences along stretches of land in California, New Mexico, Texas and Arizona that have been deemed among the most porous corridors of the border.

The vote on the amendment was a victory for conservatives who had long sought to build such a fences along the Mexican border. But the vote was sharply assailed by Democrats, who compared the fences to the Berlin Wall in Germany. Twelve Republicans also voted against the amendment.

Representative David Dreier, Republican of California, hailed the fences as a necessary tool to ensure border security. Construction of the barriers is to include two layers of reinforced fencing, cameras, lighting and sensors near Tecate and Calexico on the California border; Columbus, N.M.; and El Paso, Del Rio, Eagle Pass, Laredo and Brownsville in Texas.

The border security bill, which cracks down on illegal immigration and now mandates the construction of the fences, is expected to pass the House on Friday.

"Border fences are a security tool with proven results," Mr. Dreier said. "This amendment allows us to target our federal resources where they are needed most: five specific border crossings with the highest number of immigrant deaths, instances of drug smuggling and illegal crossings."

The vote on the amendment came on a day when the tough border security bill survived an unexpected tactical challenge from several Republicans. The bill was criticized by some moderates because it does not grant millions of undocumented workers the right to work temporarily in the United States and by some conservatives who argued that the measure was not tough enough.

The unusual revolt highlighted the schism within the Republican Party over the volatile issue of immigration. Business leaders, traditional allies of the party, have lobbied fiercely against the bill, which contains strict employment verification requirements that many executives view as a burden.

Republican leaders stamped out the rebellion after an emergency meeting. But one Republican, Jim Kolbe of Arizona, said he and his allies would continue to try to stop the bill, which has been endorsed by the Republican leadership and some conservatives but attacked by business executives, church leaders and advocates for immigrants.

The bill would require mandatory detention of many immigrants, stiffen the penalties for employers who hire them and broaden the immigrant-smuggling statute to include employees of social service agencies and church groups who offer services to undocumented workers.

It would not create the temporary guest worker program that President Bush has urged to legalize the status of the 11 million illegal immigrants believed to be living in this country.

Seeking to sink the legislation, several Republicans took the tactical step on Thursday of voting against a rule that had to pass to allow the measure to go up for a vote. Some conservatives, who felt the bill was not tough enough, also voted against the rule.

"Unfortunately, the bill before us today does nothing to solve the real problems of immigration," Mr. Kolbe told lawmakers. "But we are going to go down this path, continue this charade, continue lying to the American people, continue pretending we are doing something to prevent illegal immigration."

In addition to Mr. Kolbe, six other Republicans voted against the rule: Representatives Fred Upton of Michigan, Christopher Shays of Connecticut, Jim Leach of Iowa, Heather A. Wilson of New Mexico, J.D. Hayworth of Arizona, and John Hostettler of Indiana.

Mr. Kolbe spoke as faxed letters from the United States Chamber of Commerce warned lawmakers that in its annual ratings of members of Congress, it would penalize any legislator who voted for the rule that would allow the measure to go to the floor for a vote.

By midafternoon, the party's leaders had beaten back the challenge, at least for the day. Representative F. James Sensenbrenner Jr., Republican of Wisconsin, sharply criticized those expressing support for what many conservatives describe as an amnesty for illegal immigrants.

"This bill doesn't give amnesty to illegal aliens and it shouldn't because that would reward someone for breaking our laws," said Mr. Sensenbrenner, who had introduced the border security bill.

SIGNIFICANCE

The House of Representatives passed the border security bill in December 2005, with strong Republican support. However, the issue of immigration reform opened up major rifts within the party and between the Republicans and their traditional allies in the business community, who were opposed to the strong emphasis on enforcement of the immigration rules without any provision for a guest worker program to meet the needs of U.S. employers for migrant workers.

In May 2005, the Senate passed an alternative bill with cross-party support that did include a proposal for a temporary worker program. The Senate bill also supported the building of a high security fence along the border. By mid–2006 neither bill had been passed by both houses, a necessary prerequisite for becoming law, but since both proposed the building of a border fence, it is likely that this will be included in the agreed package of immigration reform.

Such a policy may have an adverse impact on diplomatic relations with Mexico, which has generally co-operated with the United States in recent years on tackling undocumented migration and cross-border crime, but is likely to be opposed to the construction of a border fence. Within the United States, supporters of a border fence see it as a powerful, visible symbol of its efforts to prevent unauthorized migration, as well as a weapon in the fight against international terrorism.

FURTHER RESOURCES
Books

Delaet, Debra L. *U.S. Immigration Policy in an Age of Rights*. Westport, Conn.: Praeger Publishers, 2000.

Monto, Alexander. *The Roots of Mexican Labor Migration*. Westport, Conn.: Praeger Publishers, 1994.

Periodicals

Andreas, Peter. "The Making of Amerexico: (Mis)handling Illegal Immigration." *World Policy Journal* (June 22, 1994).

Andreas, Peter. "U.S.-Mexico: Open Markets, Closed Border." *Foreign Policy* (June 22, 1996).

Burnor, Emily. "Under the Fence: US-Mexican Immigration Issues.(AMERICAS)." *Harvard International Review* (June 22, 2005).

Cornelius, Wayne A. "Controlling 'Unwanted' Immigration: Lessons from the United States, 1993–2004." *Journal of Ethnic and Migration Studies* (July 7, 2005).

Griswold, Daniel T. "Confronting the Problem of Illegal Mexican Migration to the U.S." *USA Today (Society for the Advancement of Education)* 131 (March 2003).

Kruys, Brig Gen George. "Controlling Land Borders: a Comparison of the United States of America, Germany and South Africa." *Strategic Review for Southern Africa* (November 1, 2002).

Immigrants' Lament: Have Degree, No Job

News article

By: Miriam Jordan

Date: April 28, 2005

Source: Jordan, Miriam. "Immigrants' Lament: Have Degree, No Job." *College Journal*, from the *Wall Street Journal* (April 28, 2005).

About the Author: Miriam Jordan is a staff reporter for the *Wall Street Journal*. The *Wall Street Journal* is an international daily newspaper based in New York.

INTRODUCTION

The state of Kansas has a law that allows students to pay in-state tuition if they have graduated from high schools in that state, regardless of immigration status. In 2004, the state was sued by a group of university students and their parents—they argued that the state law contradicted federal immigration laws and essentially that it was unfair for illegal residents to receive the benefit of in-state tuition. These students were out-of-state residents and thus were not beneficiaries of in-state tuition. The court dismissed the case on July 5, 2005, citing the plaintiff's lack of evidence of injury on which to base their claim. (Kansas state law K.S.A. 76–731a granted tuition rates, but did not deny anyone benefits).

If passed by the Congress, the Development, Relief, and Education for Alien Minors (DREAM) Act would give states the ability to provide higher education benefits to the children of illegal immigrants. In addition, the DREAM Act would give these students the opportunity to obtain legal status.

In March 2006, the DREAM Act passed the Senate Judiciary Committee as an amendment to a larger immigration bill. Critics doubted this bill would be passed in 2006. Advocates of the DREAM Act contend that the bill is more about the future of young people rather than immigration policy. The children of illegal immigrants who have grown up in America are caught in the middle of the immigration dispute.

PRIMARY SOURCE

Suffering from a severe shortage of nurses, U.S. hospitals have recruited thousands of workers from countries such as the Philippines, Jamaica and Mexico.

Meanwhile, Julieta Garibay's nursing degree from a prestigious Texas university isn't helping her land a job with any hospital. The most she can do is volunteer.

Ms. Garibay, 24 years old, who came to the U.S. as a child, is an illegal immigrant. She is part of an emerging class of young immigrants facing a new quandary: They are educated, but unable to get work because of their immigration status.

Their dilemma promises to be an increasing problem as more illegal immigrants attend U.S. colleges. The U.S. Supreme Court ruled in 1982 that all children, regardless of immigration status, are entitled to attend elementary and secondary school for free. But higher education is largely a state matter.

In 2001, Texas became the first state to pass a law allowing undocumented immigrant students who graduated from a state high school to pay resident tuition at public universities. Since then, eight more states have passed similar laws, and bills are before legislators in several other states. In a few states, financial aid is available. For Ms. Garibay, whose single mother is a cleaning lady, the in-state tuition legislation opened up an otherwise unaffordable opportunity.

However, as the first crop of students—about several hundred—who benefited from the Texas bill prepare to graduate in coming months, they find themselves unemployable. Their legal limbo is turning Texas into the test case for what happens to the new class of educated but illegal graduates.

"We have this irony—young adults who are trained and ready to join the work force but are unable to do so legally," says Josh Bernstein, director of federal policy at the National Immigration Law Center in Washington, D.C.

Lawmakers say they anticipated that this problem could arise but hoped Congress would pass a bill to legalize these students. Such a bill is expected to be introduced in the Senate in coming months.

Distressed students are knocking on the door of Tito Guerrero, president of Stephen F. Austin State University in Nacogdoches, Texas. "We have been living blissfully for four years," he says. "Now these kids are graduating, and I don't know what to tell them."

Supporters of the in-state tuition policy argue that it enables immigrant students to make a bigger contribution to the U.S. economy and society than if they are deprived of a higher education. Critics say the policy amounts to a tax giveaway for people who shouldn't be here in the first place. Kansas, which passed an in-state tuition bill last year, is facing a lawsuit in federal court from opponents who charge that such a measure violates the U.S. Constitution and immigration law. The first hearing is scheduled for May 10.

Come May 20, Carlos Hernandez, 22, will have a degree in petroleum engineering from the University of Texas at Austin. One reason Mr. Hernandez, the son of a waitress and a construction worker, chose the major is that the university proclaims a high rate of job-placement for graduates of its program. But during a recent job interview with oil giant ChevronTexaco Corp., Mr. Hernandez says an upbeat recruiter turned sour on hearing about his immigration status.

Companies sometimes sponsor foreign workers with specialized skills, making a case for permanent residency, or a green card. But laws that apply to undocumented immigrants make it impossible for businesses to sponsor these youngsters because they have been living in the country illegally.

"There is very high demand for petroleum engineers in the energy sector," says Don Campbell, a Chevron spokesman. But there is no way around the legal requirements for working in the U.S. "We follow immigration law," he says.

Mr. Hernandez hasn't even been able to get a paid internship. "I have enjoyed every minute of my studies," he says during a break from his senior design project. But, "I am really bummed out."

Immigrant advocates say the only solution for students like Mr. Hernandez and Ms. Garibay is passage of the so-called Dream Act, which would allow those who came to the U.S. as children at least five years ago to get temporary legal residency upon completion of high school. Those who attended college or joined the military would become eligible for permanent residency.

Congress recessed last year without taking action on the Development, Relief and Education for Alien Minors Act. The bill, which has bipartisan support, is expected to be re-introduced by Sen. Orrin Hatch (R., Utah). "The federal government needs to pass the Dream Act so these students can get on with their lives," says Mr. Bernstein of the immigration advocacy center.

Amid the national furor over illegal immigration, the fate of the bill remains unclear. "Current politics are making this radioactive right now," says Travis Reindl, director of state policy analysis at the American Association of State Colleges and Universities, a nonpartisan group.

Opponents say they are determined to stall it and still are angry about giving illegal immigrants in-state tuition. "We can't hold taxpayers accountable to providing discounted education to people in this country illegally," says Congressman Steve King (R., Iowa). Mr. King acknowledges that the students are likely to pay more taxes as professionals than as blue-collar workers if they remain in the U.S. But, he says, "we can't make economic arguments" in favor of illegal immigration.

About 1.7 million illegal minors reside in the U.S., according to the Pew Hispanic Center, a Washington think tank. Although there are no official statistics, it is estimated that a very small number of students are taking advantage of the in-state tuition program in most states.

In California, undocumented immigrants benefiting from in-state tuition account for less than 1% of the two million students at community colleges and state universities. In Kansas, only 30 undocumented students availed themselves of the program at state institutions last fall; the state had predicted 370.

"Opponents' fear that our colleges would be flooded with illegal immigrants should be assuaged," says Kip Peterson, spokesman for the Kansas Board of Regents, which oversees higher education in the state.

Most of the illegal-immigrant students are from Latin America, but Asian, African and European students are also benefiting.

Many immigrant students are ill-prepared academically for college or can't afford it, even with in-state tuition. (Most states, including California, don't offer financial aid to illegal immigrants; Texas, Oklahoma and New Mexico are the exceptions.) In addition, education officials say many school administrators aren't spreading the word—because they are unaware of the law or don't understand it.

Mr. Hernandez, the petroleum-engineering student, didn't hear about the program from his college counselor at the Galveston, Texas, high school he attended. His mother learned about it on Spanish-language television.

Steve Murdock, chief demographer of Texas, says helping any Hispanic student get ahead should be a no-brainer: "It's not about the individual," he says. As the Latino population swells, "how well our Hispanic population does is how well Texas and other states will do." The Texas labor force, for one, will be less well-qualified in 2040 than in 2000, according to his projections.

Some undocumented students are using the tools of American democracy to lobby their cause. In February, Ms. Garibay was among a group from Texas who traveled to Washington to lobby Congress in support of the Dream Act. They have formed a coalition called Jovenes Imigrantes Por Un Futuro Mejor, or Young Immigrants for a Better Future, with chapters at several colleges.

"So many kids without papers just stop studying and have babies," says Ms. Garibay, who is scheduled to graduate this summer from the University of Texas at Austin. "We have studied and want to be productive, but we have no prospects."

SIGNIFICANCE

The American Dream Act (the DREAM Act was introduced to the U.S. House of Representatives under this new name) proposes a number of provisions for undocumented residents, including:

- Restoring state's rights to provide in-state tuition to undocumented residents;
- Allowing children of illegal immigrants to attain citizenship;
- Allowing these students to be considered for legal resident status on a conditional basis if they: entered the United States before age sixteen, lived in the United States for five years by the date the law is passed, demonstrate good moral character and no criminal record, have attained a high school diploma or GED in the United States;
- Allowing for this conditional status to be lifted after six years if the student has completed college or finished two years in good standing, or has served in the military for at least two years.

Opponents charge that this form of legislation violates the civil rights of students who are not given these benefits (in-state tuition rates, for instance). Several complaints were filed with the Department of Homeland Security against Texas and New York. However, advocates of the American Dream Act say that this legislation will provide many benefits to America in the long run. They assert that young people need a head start in life. They state the Dream Act will benefit society as a whole in several ways:

- By reducing high school drop-out rates—which cost taxpayers billions of dollars each year—by eliminating barriers and incentivizing students to achieve;
- With more high school and college graduates, the economy will be stimulated to the tune of hundreds of billions of dollars;

- In addition to increased earnings and tax revenues, providing a way for young people to get jobs will help fill workplace vacancies;
- The act rewards character by granting provisions to individuals that choose to work hard and contribute to the community in which they have grown up.

FURTHER RESOURCES

Books

Daniels, Roger. *Guarding the Golden Door: American Immigration Policy and Immigrants since 1882*. New York: Hill and Wang, 2004.

Hing, Bill O., and Anthony D. Romero. *Defining America Through Immigration Policy*. Philadelphia: Temple University Press, 2004 .

Periodicals

Del Conte, Natali T. "Out of the Shadows." *Hispanic Magazine* (March 2006).

Yoo, Lana. "Students Work to Pass DREAM Act." *Daily Bruin* (September 30, 2005).

Web sites

National Immigration Law Center. "DREAM Act: Basic Information." April 2006. <http://nilc.org/immlawpolicy/DREAM/index.htm> (accessed June 28, 2006).

We Want to Stop People from Crossing into America Illegally

Speech

By: President George W. Bush

Date: October 22, 2005

Source: *White House Office of the Press Secretary*. "President's Weekly Radio Address." October 22, 2005. <http://www.whitehouse.gov/news/releases/2005/10/print/20051022.html> (accessed June 15, 2005).

About the Author: George W. Bush is the forty-third president of the United States. He is currently in his second term as president, having originally been sworn into office on January 20, 2001, and again on January 20, 2005, after re-election on November 2, 2004.

INTRODUCTION

This radio address by President George W. Bush announced his signing of the Homeland Security

Mexicans illegally crossing the U.S. Border. © DAVID TURNLEY/CORBIS.

Appropriations Act of 2005 into law in October 2005. The Act contained a package of measures designed to strengthen the enforcement of the immigration laws and to reduce levels of undocumented migration into the United States, particularly across the land border between the United States and Mexico.

The problem of undocumented migration across America's land borders has been regarded as a potential threat to national security, particularly since the terrorist attack on the World Trade Center on September 11, 2001. Immigration control at airports and seaports has been tightened in order to prevent further terrorist attacks, but the government has been concerned that terrorists and criminals could slip over the Mexican border, along with the many undocumented migrant workers who enter the United States by land.

In order to address the issue of national security, the Department of Homeland Security (DHS) was established in 2003, and this department took over responsibility for immigration services and the enforcement of immigration control. Although the department handles a wide range of immigration functions, including the processing of visa and citizenship applications, the policy focus on national security and increases in funding in this area have led to a major emphasis on enforcement functions and on the development of measures to reduce levels of undocumented migration. DHS has responsibility for the apprehension of undocumented immigrants, management of the detention process and the mechanisms for keeping in contact with non-detained undocumented migrants, and the enforcement of orders to remove from the United States those not legally entitled to remain there.

The Department of Homeland Security has reported success in increasing numbers of apprehensions and in removing undocumented migrants from the country. However, many of the removed migrants subsequently return to the United States, and so far, there is little evidence that the increased enforcement effort has had any deterrent effect, with an overall increase in the numbers of undocumented migrants occurring during the early 2000s. However, migration patterns do appear to have changed, especially in response to the strengthened border control, with the use of different, more hazardous entry routes, the increased use of smugglers, and a tendency for undocumented migrants to stay longer once they are in the United States, rather than take the risk of repeated re-entries.

The continued high level of undocumented migration and increasing numbers of apprehensions has put great pressure on detention facilities in the United States, and has led to the use of other, less reliable, mechanisms for maintaining contact with undocumented migrants pending their removal from the United States. The Homeland Security Appropriations Act of 2005 addresses the need to strengthen all areas of immigration control and enforcement, including detention capacity and the speed of removals processes, so that improvements made in one area do not create excessive pressures in other areas.

PRIMARY SOURCE

THE PRESIDENT: Good morning. This week I signed into law a bill that supports our ongoing efforts to defend our homeland.

To defend this country, we have to enforce our borders. When our borders are not secure, terrorists, drug dealers, and criminals find it easier to sneak into America. My administration has a clear strategy for dealing with this problem: We want to stop people from crossing into America illegally, and to quickly return the illegal immigrants we catch back to their home countries.

For the past four years, we've been implementing this strategy. To stop illegal immigrants from coming across our borders, we've added manpower, upgraded our technology, and taken the final steps necessary to complete a fourteen-mile barrier running along the San Diego border with Mexico. To enforce our immigration laws within our borders, we've hired more immigration agents, gone after criminal gangs, and targeted smugglers and coyotes who traffic in human beings. We are getting results: Since 2001, we have removed more than 4.8 million illegal immigrants from the United States, including more than 300,000 with criminal records.

Our border patrol and immigration agents are doing a fine job, but we still have a problem. Too many illegal immigrants are coming in, and we're capturing many more non-Mexican illegal immigrants than we can send home. And one of the biggest reasons we cannot send them back is that we lack space in our detention facilities to hold them until they are removed. When there's no bed available, non-Mexicans who are caught entering our country illegally are given a slip that tells them to come back for a court appearance. Most never show up. And then they disappear back into the shadows of our communities. This is called "catch-and-release," and it is unacceptable.

The bill I signed includes $7.5 billion that will help us address the problem of illegal immigration in two important ways. First, it provides more than $2.3 billion for the Border Patrol so we can keep more illegal immigrants from getting into the country in the first place. These funds will help us hire a thousand new border patrol agents, improve our technology and intelligence, expand and improve Border Patrol stations, and install and improve fencing, lighting, vehicle barriers, and roads along our border areas. I appreciate the help Congress has given us for our common goal of creating more secure borders.

Second, this bill also provides $3.7 billion for Immigration and Customs Enforcement so we can find and return the illegal immigrants who are entering our country. With these funds, we can expand the holding capacity of our detention facilities by ten percent. This will allow us to hold more non-Mexican illegal immigrants while we process them through a program we call "expedited removal." This will make the process faster and more efficient. Putting more non-Mexican illegal immigrants through expedited removal is crucial to sending back people who have come here illegally. As Secretary Chertoff told the Senate this week, our goal is to return every single illegal entrant, with no exceptions. And this bill puts us on the path to do that.

For Mexicans who cross into America illegally, we have a different plan, but the same goal. Now, most of the 900,000 illegal immigrants from Mexico who are caught each year are immediately escorted back across the border. The problem is that these illegal immigrants are able to connect with another smuggler or coyote and come right back in. So one part of the solution is a program called "interior repatriation" where we fly or bus these illegal immigrants all the way back to their hometowns in the interior of Mexico. By returning illegal Mexican immigrants to their homes, far away from desert crossings, we're saving lives and making it more difficult for them to turn right around and cross back into America.

As we improve and expand our efforts to secure our borders, we must also recognize that enforcement cannot work unless it's part of a comprehensive immigration reform that includes a temporary worker program. If an employer has a job that no American is willing to take, we need to find a way to fill that demand by matching willing employers with willing workers from foreign countries on a temporary and legal basis. I'll work with members of Congress to create a program that will provide for our economy's labor needs without harming American workers, and without granting amnesty, and that will relieve pressure on our borders.

A critical part of any temporary worker program is ensuring that our immigration laws are enforced at work sites. America is a country of laws; we must not allow dishonest employers to flout those laws. So we've doubled the resources for work site enforcement since 2004.

We have much more work ahead of us. But the Homeland Security bill I signed this week provides vital support for our efforts to deal with the problem of illegal immigration, and make all Americans safer and more secure.

Thank you for listening.

SIGNIFICANCE

The president's address attempts to make a clear link between undocumented migration and the risk of terrorist attack on the United States. Major increases in levels of undocumented migration in recent years have highlighted the weaknesses in American border control that could allow potential terrorists to enter the country. Generally, public concerns about the impact of rising numbers of undocumented migrants in the United States have put pressure on government officials to address the problem. The increasing focus on undocumented migration in the context of terrorism and other types of crime is controversial, but may help to gain public support for tough immigration policies.

Undocumented migration remained high on the political agenda following the passing of the Homeland Security Bill. In December 2005, the Immigration Rights Bill was passed by the House of Representatives, which proposed introducing stiff penalties for undocumented migrants and anyone assisting them to enter the United States, and making undocumented migration a felony, and also proposed the fencing of some 700 miles of the U.S.-Mexican border to try to reduce the number of illegal border crossings. In May 2006, the Senate passed the Comprehensive Immigration Reform Act. This bill acknowledged the labor market need for migrant workers, and proposed a guest worker program under which migrant applicants would be matched with U.S. employers that had unfilled vacancies, while also proposing measures to strengthen border control and enforcement.

By mid–2006, little progress had been made towards further reform of the immigration laws, as neither of these bills had been agreed on by both the House and the Senate. However, it is likely that the main focus of U.S. immigration policy in the foreseeable future will continue to be on stronger enforcement of the immigration controls.

FURTHER RESOURCES

Periodicals

Cornelius, Wayne A. "Controlling 'Unwanted' Immigration: Lessons from the United States, 1993–2004." *Annual Review of Sociology* 21 (1995).

Espenshade, Thomas J. "Unauthorized Immigration to the United States." *Annual Review of Sociology* 21 (1995).

Jonas, S. and Tactaquin, C. "Latino Immigrants Rights in the Shadow of the National Security State: Responses to Domestic Preemptive Strikes." *Social Justice* 31 (2004).

Web sites

White House Office of the Press Secretary. "President's Weekly Radio Address." October 22, 2005. <http://www.whitehouse.gov/news/releases/2005/10/print/20051022.html> (accessed June 15, 2005).

UK Immigration and the 2005 General Election

Magazine article

By: Anonymous

Date: April 7, 2005

Source: "UK Immigration and the 2005 General Election." *The Economist* (April 7, 2005).

About the Author: *The Economist* is a news magazine that has been published weekly since 1843. Produced in London but with a worldwide readership, it covers international affairs, politics, business and finance issues, and has an editorial stance in support of free trade and fiscal conservatism. The article is taken from the online version of the magazine, *The Economist.com*.

INTRODUCTION

In 2005 immigration was high on the political agenda in Britain, and was expected to be one of the key factors influencing the outcome of the general election in May that year.

The two main political parties in the United Kingdom, the Labour Party and the Conservatives, or Tories, have traditionally had different policy perspectives on immigration, ever since Britain first experienced large-scale immigration to the country in the 1950s. Although both parties have been keen to control the overall numbers of immigrants entering Britain, the Conservatives have generally been much more strongly opposed to uncontrolled immigration into Britain, whilst Labour Party has focused more on the benefits that migrants can offer to the country, and has taken the lead in introducing Race Relations legislation to help immigrants integrate successfully into British society.

Immigration first became a central issue in British politics during the 1950s and 1960s, when both main parties became concerned about very large and rapid increases in immigration from the New Commonwealth countries such as India, Pakistan, and the West Indies. The nationals of these countries had been granted British citizenship under the British Nationality Act of 1948 and had the right of free entry into the United Kingdom. The 1971 Immigration Act, implemented by the Conservative Government, made Commonwealth citizens subject to the same immigration controls as other foreign nationals and significantly reduced the numbers of immigrants. To a large extent, the political focus shifted onto race relations issues rather than immigration during the 1970s and early 1980s, when a series of violent race riots broke out within the largely immigrant communities of Britain's inner cities.

Recent concerns about immigration have focused not on legal immigration through normal channels, but on the surge in asylum applicants and undocumented immigrants since the late 1990s, which Britain has experienced along with other European countries. The problems were exacerbated by the failure of processing systems within the Immigration and Nationality Directorate of the U.K. Home Office, which led to very long delays in processing asylum applications and problems in keeping in contact with asylum applicants while their claims were being considered. As a result, it has been claimed that large numbers of applicants simply settled in the country as undocumented immigrants, along with the increasing numbers who are believed to have entered the country clandestinely, smuggled in within trucks for example.

The task of dealing with these immigration issues fell to the Labour government which has been in power since 1994, under Prime Minister Tony Blair. This government introduced an Immigration Act in 1999 that focused on improving the efficiency of immigration control systems, and clearing the backlog in asylum applications. It also introduced new measures for dispersing asylum applicants to accommodation around the country, to address public concerns about concentrations of large numbers in particular areas, and brought in a controversial system under which they were given vouchers rather than money to buy food and other necessities. The 1999 Act also introduced policies to encourage more skilled migration to Britain, a

theme that was taken up in the 2002 White Paper and which continued to be important in the 2005 election campaign.

Despite approaching the issue from different perspectives, the Election Manifestos of both parties in 2005 proposed a points system to help identify who should be allowed to enter Britain, on the basis of qualifications and experience. The difference was that the Tories wanted to introduce such as system as a means of deciding how to allocate visas under new annual quotas for both immigrant groups, whereas the Labour Party wanted to increase migration of those migrants who could contribute positively to the economy.

The election Manifestos of both parties also included measures to tighten the border controls. For the Conservatives, under party leader Michael Howard, this formed one of the key issues of their election campaign, and focused on increasing the numbers of immigration officers and establishing a new border police force. The Labour Party, on the other hand, planned to introduce new technology to improve the efficiency of immigration control, such as fingerprinting, biometric passports and ID cards, and a new information technology system to monitor both entry to and departure from the United Kingdom.

PRIMARY SOURCE

If the Conservatives could choose a single issue on which to fight the 2005 general election, it would be immigration. Over the past eight years, Labour has muscled in on traditional Tory terrain such as economic policy and law and order. When it comes to keeping out foreigners, though, the Conservatives (and only they) are as confident and sure-footed as a champion boxer. "People will face a clear choice at the next election," declared Michael Howard in January: "unlimited immigration under Mr. Blair or limited, controlled immigration with the Conservatives."

It is not unusual for politicians to make a fuss about immigration in the months before a general election. The Conservatives have done so on three out of the last four occasions in which they have contested an election from a position of opposition, in 1970, 1979 and 2001. But immigration is more central to this year's campaign than to any before. That is partly because the public seems to be more concerned about the issue, partly because the Tories have distinct proposals, and partly because the charge that Labour has radically altered immigration policy during the past eight years is, for once, true.

Although it looms large as a political issue, immigration into Britain is relatively paltry. In 2003, the nation accepted 140,000 settlers from outside the European Union. That is 0.3% of the adult population of Britain. By contrast, Canada reckons to let in 1% of its total population in new settlers every year. The British remain overwhelmingly home-grown, with about 5% of the population born abroad, compared with 9% of Germans, 12% of Americans and 23% of Australians.

Yet the accusation that the nation's borders have become more porous under Labour is fair. Immigration into Britain may not be high, compared with some other industrialised countries, but it is a lot higher than it was under the last Conservative government. From the early 1980s to the mid–1990s, the number of new settlers held steady at 50,000–60,000 per year. Since 2000, settlement has topped 100,000. Britain has gone from being a nation of low immigration to a nation of medium immigration—by European standards, perhaps even high immigration.

The main reason for that is rising numbers of foreign workers. They have come to Britain partly because there are jobs to be had and partly because the government has set about dismantling many of the barriers to movement erected before 1997. Obtaining a work permit is easier, thanks to a relaxation of rules requiring proof that no British or European citizen can be found to perform a job. Highly skilled workers are actively courted, as they are by Canada and Australia. The effect has been striking. Between 1997 and 2003, the number of work-permit holders and their dependants admitted to Britain each year rose from 63,000 to 119,000.

Had all the new arrivals been white American businessmen, the rising tide would probably have gone unnoticed. Had they come from Commonwealth countries such as Jamaica and India, they might have been tolerated, since the natives are already accustomed to the presence of such migrants. Instead of which, the new arrivals are diverse, ranging from Somalis to Slovaks. They are likely to be Muslim, male, young and travelling alone—four characteristics that Britons find unnerving. Worst of all, migrant workers have been joined by newcomers clutching not job offers or wedding rings, but false documents and purported evidence of abuse at home.

It has been Labour's misfortune to hold power in an era of persecution. Since 1997, enormities in Yugoslavia, Afghanistan, Somalia, Iraq and Zimbabwe have displaced millions, of whom a small but noticeable fraction found their way to Britain. The number of people claiming asylum rose from 32,500 in 1997 to 84,000 in 2002. Other European countries were similarly burdened, but Britain took more than most. One reason is that, Yugoslavia excepted, all these countries have historical links to Britain (and Kosovans fleeing ex-Yugoslavia will have noted that some of their liberators were British). A report for the Home Office in 2002 found that many refugees had chosen Britain because it was rich and free. As a Yemeni man put it, "Europe is democratic. You can go to Hyde Park and you can shout."

The British regard themselves as kind-hearted folk, and in some senses they are (Britons gave more in private donations to victims of the Asian tsunami than anyone except Americans or Germans). But they are hostile to migrants' tales of woe. A 2000 Eurobarometer poll found that only 12% of Britons would unreservedly accept refugees even if they proved genuine—fewer than any other country in Europe. And the fact that many self-styled refugees are plainly not afflicted makes for harder hearts. Britons can tolerate competition, but they cannot abide queue-jumpers. Public anger over the past eight years has focused more on asylum-seekers than on any other kind of immigrant.

The government has responded in two ways. First, it tried to accelerate the processing of asylum claims so people are not condemned to idleness for months or even years. That reform began catastrophically, with technological failure and lost paperwork on a vast scale. By 1999, the backlog of cases reached 125,000, which meant that the immigration service was utterly unable to cope with unprecedented numbers of asylum claimants in the following three years. Since then, the situation has gradually improved. Amnesties and bureaucratic reform have helped cut the backlog to less than 10,000.

The second strategy has been to make life difficult for asylum-seekers. Egged on by conservative newspapers, and believing that tough policies would restore confidence, the government has done what it can within the law. Cash handouts to asylum-seekers were set at indigent levels—£31.15 per week for a young single person; £39.34 for a lone parent. Support to failed claimants was cut off. Borders were tightened, partly by investing in scanning systems (to spot people hidden in trucks) but mostly by demanding visas of migrants from hotspots such as Zimbabwe.

When the law has obstructed change, the government has tried to undermine the law. In 2004, the then-home secretary, David Blunkett, tried to curtail judges' powers to review asylum decisions. Such reviews had exposed shabbiness in the immigration service and laid down more liberal precedents for judging claims. Mr Blunkett's move was stymied following an extraordinary outburst from the Lord Chief Justice. But efforts to curtail legal aid for asylum cases were successful, as were new laws that allowed the police to raid the offices of immigration solicitors.

The tough stuff worked, in the sense that fewer people applied for asylum in 2004 than in any year since 1998 (whether the system had got any better at sifting genuine claims from false ones is less certain). Reduced numbers, in turn, meant a calmer electorate. Polls by MORI, a pollster, show that the proportion of Britons citing immigration and race as one of the two most important issues facing the nation declined gradually from a pre-campaign peak of 39% in May 2002 to 26% in January 2005. It then shot up again when Labour and the Tories unveiled their policies.

The question facing the parties now is whether Britons are hostile to asylum-seekers or to immigrants in general. If they are worried only about asylum-seekers (and, perhaps, illegal immigrants) it is good news for Labour. Numbers are convincingly down, so the issue is likely to shift few votes. If, on the other hand, voters dislike the lot of them, Labour may be in trouble. When it comes to economic migrants, the charge that Labour has allowed more people in is irrefutable. Not surprisingly, the Tories have therefore made a determined effort to fudge the distinction between asylum-seekers and the rest.

Michael Howard's pitch is simple: immigration is out of control. He insists, first, that there are a lot more foreigners coming into Britain; and, second, that the processing of refugees has been incompetent. Both claims are true, but the implicit charge—that immigration has risen because of government incompetence—is off target. Immigration has risen because of foreign wars and work permits. The former are, by their nature, beyond control, while the number of work permits has increased as a result of deliberate policy.

The Tories want to set a quota for the total number of migrant workers—a quota which, they hint, will be much lower than the numbers allowed in under Labour. Would-be immigrants will be judged according to a points system, with permits given only to those who possess skills that the government deems to be in short supply. As for asylum-seekers, they will no longer be allowed to travel to Britain. If they make it past toughened border controls, they will be packed off to overseas processing centres while their claims are heard. They, too, will be subject to quotas.

Labour's response to these proposals has been less critical than defensive. Rather than attack the Tories' plans as illiberal, it questioned the cost. In February, it published a "five-year plan" that featured similar proposals for a points system for economic migrants, along with more tough language about asylum-seekers. In some ways, Labour's proposals consolidated its liberal immigration policy. Highly skilled migrants will now be known as Tier 1 applicants, but will be assessed in much the same way as before; skilled migrants will now be known as Tier 2 applicants and will be able to apply for settlement after five years. And so on. But Labour also hinted that unskilled

workers would no longer be able to work their way towards citizenship. The Liberal Democrats stayed out of the fray, loftily declaring that politicians should not engage in a "bidding war" over immigration. Yet they, like the Conservatives, want an annual immigration quota.

For those who support immigration, there are just two points of light. The first is that the immigration debate is taking place in Parliament and the media rather than on the streets. With the exception of one incident in Glasgow, there have been no large-scale marches or organised attacks against immigrants to match those of the 1970s. The second reason for optimism is that the political discussion has been dominated by the three main parties. In many areas, voters in next month's election will be able to cast their ballot for the UK Independence Party (which opposes immigration and European integration) or the British National Party (which opposes immigration and everything non-white). Neither party is expected to do well.

SIGNIFICANCE

Despite the strong emphasis of the Conservative Party during the election campaign on the need for tighter immigration controls, it failed to win the election and the successful Labour Party entered its third term in office. The Labour Government proceeded to implement its own proposed policies on immigration, announcing in March 2006 the introduction of a new five-tier points system for those applying to come to the United Kingdom to take up employment.

Although the numbers of applicants claiming asylum in Britain declined from 2001 onwards, the public and politicians alike remained concerned about the problem of undocumented migration and the numbers of unauthorized immigrants already living in the country. By mid–2006 the Labour Party was considering the possibility of an amnesty for these people, while taking forward its plans to tighten border controls and introduce national security measures such as ID cards to prevent further increases in illegal entry.

FURTHER RESOURCES
Periodicals

Duvell, Franck, and Jordan, Bill. "Immigration Control and the Management of Economic Migration in the United Kingdom: Organisational Culture, Implementation, Enforcement and Identity Processes in Public Services." *Journal of Ethnic and Migration Studies* 29 (2003).

Luedtke, Adam. "The Politics of European Union Immigration Policy: Institutions, Salience, and Harmonization." *Policy Studies Journal* (February 1, 2004).

Rowthorn, Robert. "The Economic Effects of Immigration into the United Kingdom." *Population and Development Review* (December 1, 2004).

Zimmermann, Klaus, F. "Immigrant Performance and Selective Immigration Policy: A European Perspective." *National Institute Economic Review* (October 1, 2005).

Web site

Home Office Immigration and Nationality Directorate. "Legislation." <http://www.ind.homeoffice.gov.uk/lawandpolicy/legislation/> (accessed June 29, 2006).

Come Hither

Illegal Immigration to the United States

Magazine article

By: Anonymous

Date: December 1, 2005

Source: *The Economist.* "Come Hither." December 1, 2005. <http://www.economist.com/world/na/displaystory.cfm?story_id=5249522> (accessed June 12, 2006).

About the Author: *The Economist* is a weekly news magazine based in London, England. *The Economist* was founded in 1843.

U.S. President George W. Bush poses with new American citizens after a swearing in ceremony on Ellis Island, July 10, 2001. © REUTERS/CORBIS.

INTRODUCTION

The U.S.-Mexico border is lengthy and difficult to police. In the late twentieth and early twenty-first century the availability of relatively well-paying jobs in the United States encouraged tens of millions of people—mostly Mexicans but many other nationalities as well—to attempt to cross the border and illegaly immigrate to the United States. On November 28, 2005, President Bush proposed a major reform in how the United States deals with illegal immigrants in a speech at Davis-Mothan Air Force Base in Arizona. At the time of the speech, U.S. government estimates suggested that between eleven million and thirteen million undocumented immigrants were resident in the United States.

The massive flow of illegal immigrants into the United States inspires mixed feelings among U.S. citizens. Few in the United States believe that breaking immigration law is appropriate. Furthermore, some argue that illegal immigrants are a drain on social services. For instance, in 1982 the Supreme Court struck down a Texas law that prohibited the expenditure of public funds on the school aged children of migrant Mexican farm workers. Some believe that illegal immigrants depress wages or steal jobs from native-born Americans. On the other hand, many in the United States appreciate access to a ready and available supply of inexpensive Mexican labor. And they question if many American citizens truly desire the menial jobs that illegal immigrants typically hold.

The massive flow of illegal immigrants across the border also raises questions about the security of the United States. President Bush's speech carries an implicit reference to the consequences of the 9/11 terrorist attacks upon the United States, and the concurrent belief that American borders generally have been insecure against foreign incursion. By better controlling the borders, President Bush hopes to not only reduce illegal immigration but also protect the United States from terrorists, drug smugglers, and other criminals.

President Bush emphasizes the ability of the United States to be a welcoming society and a lawful society at the same time. At the end of the Civil War in

1865, there were no limitations upon who could enter and take up residency in the United States. It was the establishment of a distinct American society in the latter part of the nineteenth century that the nation built by immigration enacted entry and residence restrictions.

■ PRIMARY SOURCE

George Bush has promoted a sensible immigration plan, to the horror of many of his supporters. But the devil is in the details. THERE is a state of emergency on the border between Arizona and Mexico, with all the confusion that entails. The radio hisses: "We've got a 'failure to yield'." A Border Patrol agent has ordered a vehicle to pull over and seen it speed off instead. He needs back-up. Patrolman Jim Hawkins races towards the scene. Passing a suspicious-looking pick-up truck en route, he sighs that he doesn't have time to stop. A few minutes later, however, the patrolman who called for help manages to catch his prey unassisted, though the driver assaults him, so Mr. Hawkins goes looking for the suspicious pick-up truck. There was someone in it using what looked like a Border Patrol radio, he explains, which could mean that it was a people-smuggler.

Mr. Hawkins's instincts are shrewd, but wrong. The pick-up's driver is using a Border Patrol radio because he is, in fact, a Border Patrol agent, who had impounded the vehicle after finding two dozen illegal aliens squeezed in the back. Their disguise was averagely cunning. They came in a convoy: two pick-ups, each with a sheet of plywood over the bed, painted the same color as the truck itself to make it look like the bed was empty, when in fact it was packed with Mexicans. Some forty of them—men, women and children—sit glumly beneath a mesquite tree, waiting to be processed. The one smuggler who failed to escape into the roadside bushes stands even more glumly to one side, in handcuffs.

A few miles away and eleven days later, on November 28th, George Bush gave a speech about illegal immigration. "America has always been a compassionate nation that values the newcomer and takes great pride in our immigrant heritage," the president told patrolmen at an air base in Tucson, Arizona. "Yet we're also a nation built on the rule of law, and those who enter the country illegally violate the law. The American people should not have to choose between a welcoming society and a lawful society. We can have both."

He then outlined a plan to curb illegal immigration without starving the fruit-picking and construction industries of labor, and without offering "amnesty" to illegals currently on American soil. Given how upset people get about this issue, how hard it is to tackle and how deeply it divides Mr. Bush's own party, political strategists might doubt Mr. Bush's wisdom in making it the last big domestic battle of a wretched year. For Americans outside the Beltway, however, the questions are: "Is it a good plan?" and "Will it work?"

The problem is familiar. Unlike other rich countries, the United States shares a long border with a poor and populous neighbor. According to the Pew Hispanic Centre, nearly 500,000 unskilled migrants arrive every year to do the kind of strenuous, low-paid jobs that Americans shun. Yet the United States issues only 5,000 visas a year for unskilled foreigners seeking year-round work. As Tamar Jacoby of the conservative Manhattan Institute explained to the Senate in July: "A Mexican without family in the US who wants to do something other than farm work has virtually no legal way to enter the country. And even a man with family here must wait from six to twenty-two years for a visa."

So they come illegally, as the stampede of sandy footprints at popular crossing-points attests. Many are caught, but most aren't. Since the penalty for capture is repatriation, the only deterrent to trying again is the $1,500 a head the "coyotes" or smugglers charge. Coyote gangs do not hesitate to beat, rob or kill migrants who enter "their" territory without paying.

Meanwhile, many other foreigners enter America legally but then either stay on after their visas have expired or work when they are not supposed to. All told, there are an estimated eleven million "illegal aliens."

Many Americans do not mind. The illegals undoubtedly boost the economy. They wash dishes more cheaply than locals would, benefiting anybody who ever goes to a restaurant. Without Mexicans, vegetables would go unpicked and nursing homes would be filthy. But others object strongly to illegal immigration. Three reasons are usually cited.

The first is economic. The middle classes may love illegal gardeners, but many unskilled Americans fear being displaced by them, or forced to accept lower wages. "Keep them fools out," says Alvin Pablo, an unemployed landscaper in Tucson, who says that Mexicans took his job. A recent study by the Congressional Budget Office found that the negative effect of migrants on the wages of unskilled Americans was less clear, and probably lower, than people imagine: it reduced them by something between zero and ten percent. But this will hardly comfort Mr. Pablo, who favors erecting a huge fence along the border.

The second gripe about America's porous borders is that they might let terrorists in. A Texan lawmaker claimed this month that al-Qaeda operatives have moved to Mexico, learned Spanish and been caught slipping into the United States disguised as economic migrants. Mr. Bush mentioned terrorism twice in his speech in Tucson.

The third complaint about illegal aliens is that they are illegal. The failure to enforce immigration laws undermines the rule of law itself. Or, as many employers would put it, the fact that America does not issue enough visas to unskilled workers forces them to break the law.

Mr. Bush is trying to please as many grumblers as he can. His plan is two-pronged: he wants to tighten controls at the border, while simultaneously relieving pressure on it by "creating a legal channel for those who enter America to do an honest day's labor," through a new temporary worker program.

More guards, more permits. For the first prong, Mr. Bush is relying on cash and technology. He boasted this week of having increased funding for border security by sixty percent since taking office. True enough, but, as Ms. Jacoby told the Senate, the number of Border Patrol agents has tripled since 1986, and their budget risen tenfold, without noticeably staunching the flow of illegals.

Mr. Bush argued that "cutting-edge equipment like overhead surveillance drones" can give agents a "broader reach." The border patrollers agree. An unmanned spy plane can hover over the border for ten–twelve hours, beams Michael Nicely, the Border Patrol chief for the Tucson sector. His men have all manner of gizmos, from "stop sticks" that slowly deflate the tires of fleeing cars to "pepperball launching systems"—glorified paintball guns that immobilize rowdy smugglers.

Captured migrants sometimes have no idea how they were spotted. Carmen Vasquez, interviewed in a holding pen in Nogales, says she was tip-toeing through the mountains with her family after dark when she was suddenly surrounded by Border Patrol agents on roaring quad bikes. Agent Hawkins explains (though not to Ms. Vasquez) that she was seen through an infra-red camera on a distant hilltop. "Don't let anyone tell you we can't control our borders," says Mr. Nicely, "We just need more resources." He mentions lights, fences, infra-red cameras and helicopters (of which he already has fifty-three—four times more than are available to help feed Sudan's stricken Darfur region).

As well as catching more illegals, Mr. Bush wants to deal more rationally with those who are caught. He wants to end "catch and release," the policy whereby four-fifths of non-Mexican illegals, when caught, are released pending an appearance before a judge, to which seventy-five percent of them fail to show up. He also touted the success of a pilot scheme in west Arizona where illegal Mexicans, instead of being repatriated to border towns, were flown and then bused back to their hometowns. With further to

walk, only 8% of the 35,000 deportees so dealt with were caught again.

But can more gadgets and tougher rules beat market forces? As she waited to be "voluntarily repatriated," Ms. Vasquez said she would like to come back soon. Her sister, she said, makes $1,000 a month cleaning hotel rooms in Florida—ten times what she could earn back home.

Which brings us to the more controversial, and promising, part of Mr. Bush's plan. To "match willing foreign workers with willing American employers to fill jobs that Americans will not do," he proposes letting illegal aliens currently in America register for legal status. After paying fines and back taxes, they would then be allowed to work for a fixed period, after which they would have to return home. He insisted that this would not constitute an "amnesty." Right-wingers said it did. "Now we've finally caught the president in a lie," fumed Neal Boortz, a talk-radio host.

Whether a temporary worker scheme gets off the ground depends on Congress. The Senate is soon to consider two bills. One, sponsored by John McCain (an Arizona Republican) and Ted Kennedy (a Democrat from Massachusetts), calls for a guest-worker program much like Mr. Bush's. The other, sponsored by John Cornyn of Texas and Jon Kyl of Arizona, both Republicans, lays more emphasis on enforcement. This week, Mr. Bush praised both Mr. McCain and Mr. Kyl.

However the bills are blended together, a guest-worker program will work only if it meets two criteria. First, it must allow a realistic number of temporary work permits—enough to match the demand for migrant labor. Second, employers who hire illegals must be punished, as they rarely have been in the past. Mr. Bush touted a program called "Basic Pilot," which allows firms to check with a federal database to see whether a prospective worker is legal. And he boasted that swoops on worksites under "Operation Rollback," which was "completed" this year, resulted in the arrest of hundreds of illegal aliens and convictions against a dozen employers.

Hundreds of arrests when the total number of illegals is around eleven million? That is the kind of number that enrages Chris Simcox, the head of the Minutemen, a group that patrols the border and organizes protests much further inside the country (such as outside a day centre for illegal aliens in Virginia, where they can hook up with employers). He fumes at the "hypocrisy" of "a federal government that will not enforce the rule of law." He adds: "That's going to lead to anarchy, [and] out-of-control cultural change in this country."

The mainstream media paint the Minutemen as spiteful and clueless vigilantes. One of them dressed an illegal alien in a T-shirt with the slogan: "Bryan Barton caught me crossing the border and all I got was this lousy T-shirt." Against this, Mr. Barton was expelled, and in parts of conservative America Minutemen are heroes. A recent CBS poll found that seventy-five percent of Americans— and eighty-seven percent of Republicans—think more should be done to keep illegal aliens out. That is why Mr. Bush has to sound tough.

But not only tough. For a start, the Republicans are keen to woo Latino voters, who are quick to punish politicians who bash their immigrant cousins. Moreover, conservative whites are not as xenophobic as their bumper stickers. They may wax indignant about the need for higher fences, but when asked detailed questions about what should happen to the illegals already in the United States, they quickly turn pragmatic. A recent poll of likely Republican voters by the Manhattan Institute found that only a third favored mass deportations, and only thirteen percent thought it was possible to deport all eleven million illegals.

Most encouragingly for Mr. Bush, when asked if they would favor a comprehensive bill that included both tougher enforcement (at the border, and in workplaces) and a way for illegals to get temporary work permits that might, with good behavior, lead to citizenship, seventy-two percent of these Republicans said yes. The tired, poor, huddled masses are still welcome.

SIGNIFICANCE

The approach to resolving illegal Mexican immigration as advocated by President George Bush in November 2005 is a significant departure from the traditional methods taken previously by the United States. Bush recommended what was characterized by many political commentators as an amnesty for undocumented immigrants.

The undocumented Mexican population in the United States, centered in the border states of California, Arizona, and Texas, has posed a long term problem for American authorities. The length of the border, measuring 2,000 miles (3,200 km) and the rugged and lightly populated lands along much of its extent presents a law enforcement challenge of its own. As the example described in the *Economist* article illustrates, the ability of American authorities to effectively police this border is blunted by both the sheer numbers and the determination of economically disadvantaged Mexicans to risk capture.

The magnitude of the effort to resolve the illegal entry of Mexicans into the United States is reflected by the United States Border Patrol capture of over 1.2 million persons attempting such entries in 2005.

The attempts by Mexican citizens to breach the American border are an example of how illegal immigration is now a multi-faceted issue. For virtually the entire period in which the United States has regulated immigration, the relevant legislation defined the illegal classes of persons in terms of being 'alien'. Aliens could be either persons seeking better economic opportunities or political refugees. The modern problem of illegal Mexican entries into the United States is restricted to that of an economic migration into the United States; there are no particular political ideologies motivating immigration.

It is equally clear that the huge undocumented immigrant presence in the United States now represents over three percent of the current American population. A number of economic studies have established that the undocumented immigrant population, a large percentage of which is employed in either service industries or unskilled laboring work such as construction, has no worse than a neutral impact upon the function of the American economy. The economic effect of illegal Mexican immigration may be a beneficial one for these sectors, given that such workers often are employed at lesser wage rates than American citizens.

The economic significance of undocumented immigrants in the United States is countered by a widely held negative American perception that is rooted in three separate areas—fear of future—economic displacement on the part of established American workers; fear of terrorism, through poorly secured borders; the notion of fair play, as an amnesty for present undocumented immigrants is perceived as taking such persons ahead of other persons in other countries who wish to enter the United States legally and who have adhered to all application procedures.

The Bush policy statements invoked very strong feelings from a number of disparate elements of American society. Those who advocate a traditionalist approach that advances the rule of law have lobbied the federal government to deport all undocumented immigrants. A prominent group, the Minutemen, established a physical presence along various parts of the Mexican border to prevent illegal entries from Mexico. Bush confirmed his November 2005 position with a similar articulation of the border plan and the desired implementation in a further speech delivered in May 2006. An important aspect of the Bush initiative is a screening process for the illegal residents and their passage of an American criminal background check.

Of significance is whether the Bush initiative is an amnesty; President Bush stated that it was not an amnesty, in the sense of a general pardon for the offences of illegal immigration. A better characterization of the Bush approach is it constituting an amelioration of the illegal status of selected persons, as the proposed plan does not guarantee naturalization or ultimate American citizenship for the persons affected.

The Bush initiatives were also accompanied by the deployment of 6,000 National Guard forces along the Arizona/Mexico border in May 2006, to assist in border enforcement. The Mexican government protested the action as a further step by the United States to militarize the border between the two countries.

The Bush initiatives were also significant in that the focus on the security of the border has a predominately economic aspect, through the control of the entry of undocumented persons; in the 1980s, while undocumented immigration was an important factor, United States-Mexico border security was also directed towards the stoppage of the entry of illegal drugs into the United States, primarily cocaine and methamphetamines.

FURTHER RESOURCES

Books

Nevins, Joseph. *Operation Gatekeeper: The Rise of the Illegal Alien and the Making of the U.S.-Mexico Boundary*. New York: Routledge, 2002.

Pitti, Stephen J. *The Devil in Silicon Valley: Northern California, Race and Mexican Americans*. Princeton, New Jersey: Princeton University Press, 2003.

Truett, Samuel, and Elliot Young, eds. *Continental Crossroads: Remapping U.S.-Mexico Borderlands History*. Raleigh, North Carolina: Duke University Press, 2004.

Web sites

Business Week. "The Economic Progress of Immigrants." December 2, 2005. <http://www.businessweek.com/the_thread/economicsunbound/archives/2005/12/the_economic_pr.html> (accessed June 12, 2006).

Points System Will Favor Skilled Immigrant Workers, Says Clarke

News article

By: Richard Ford

Date: March 8, 2006

Source: *www.timesonline.co.uk*. Ford, Richard. "Points System Will Favor Skilled Immigrant Workers, Says Clarke." March 8, 2006. <http://www.timesonline.co.uk/article/0,,2–2075110,00.html> (accessed June 28, 2006).

About the Author: *Timesonline.co.uk* is the online version of *The Times* and *The Sunday Times* newspapers. Richard Ford is a reporter for *The Times*, a daily newspaper published in the United Kingdom since 1785.

INTRODUCTION

In March 2006, the British Labor government announced plans for a new points-based system for evaluating applications for immigration into the country for employment purposes, to be introduced the following year. The proposed new scheme was similar in nature to those already being operated in other countries, such as Australia and Canada, where points are awarded for such factors as qualifications, work experience, and language skills.

The scheme was intended to facilitate the entry to and settlement in the United Kingdom of highly-skilled and qualified people who could make significant contributions to the country and its economy, as well as addressing periodic labor shortages in specifically defined areas by allowing the short-term temporary migration of lower-skilled people with relevant training or work experience.

The new five-tier scheme will replace a complex system of work permits and other employment visas, which had evolved over time to include around eighty different categories of application, depending on the applicant's occupational group and nationality. The new system was intended to reduce confusion on the part of applicants and employers alike, while being more responsive to the needs of the economy.

The two top tiers of the new scheme will apply to highly skilled professionals and experts, and other qualified workers whose skills are needed in the United Kingdom, with the applications of people in these categories being evaluated in terms of qualifications, experience and existing salaries. Since Britain wants to attract skilled migrants who contribute to the country in the long term, the successful applicants will have the right to apply for permanent settlement after specified time periods, and will be allowed to bring their family members to Britain. No other migrant workers will be allowed to apply to settle permanently in the United Kingdom.

Under the new scheme, low-skilled workers from outside the European Union will only be allowed to enter Britain on a temporary basis, without their dependants, if they are need to fill specific temporary labor shortages. This is largely a response to the expansion of the European Union, which means that Britain is now likely to be able to fill most of its unskilled and low-skilled labor requirements with EU migrants, who are in general allowed to live and work in Britain without restriction. Many unskilled workers from the Eastern European countries that joined the EU in May 2004 have already migrated to Britain and boosted the unskilled and low-skilled labor force. By establishing a specific body to provide advice to the government on areas of labor shortage, the government is attempting to ensure that the immigration system is specifically tailored to the needs of the economy. It is also moving more closely towards the sort of 'guest worker' schemes operated by other Western European countries such as Germany.

Underpinning the development of this new system by the government was a policy perspective which sees immigration as essential to the future well being of the country. It has been predicted that, without net migration, the population of the United Kingdom of working age will fall by around 2 million by the end of the first quarter of the twenty-first century, while the number of people of retirement age will increase by up to three million. This situation would be likely to create severe skills and labor shortages as well as difficulties for the provision and funding of health, social services, and pension systems.

■ PRIMARY SOURCE

Britain is to close the door on low-skilled migrants from outside Western Europe seeking work in the country under plans for a points-based immigration system.

Charles Clarke, the Home Secretary, outlined plans yesterday for a scheme aimed at attracting the brightest and best workers.

A new five-tier system will allow only skilled workers to settle permanently, with the low and unskilled allowed entry for periods of up to a year before leaving. Companies and colleges will help the Government to police the system by sponsoring skilled workers and students. They will be expected to report to the Home Office when people fail to turn up and take jobs or college places or go absent for lengthy periods.

Low-skilled workers will enter the country only if a skills shortage in particular sectors is found. They will not be allowed to bring spouses or children with them. The low skilled may be made to hand over a financial bond, possess a return ticket or have money docked from their pay and put in a bank in their home country to ensure that they leave Britain.

They will only be allowed to come if a new body identifies labor shortages in particular areas of the economy, such as the building or catering industries. Mr. Clarke told a press conference that the five-tier scheme will replace the existing eighty work and study routes into the country.

He said that the plans would benefit the economy and protect British borders. Mr. Clarke added: "Crucially, it will allow us to ensure that only those people with the skills the UK needs come to this country, while preventing those without these skills applying."

Home Office documents outlining the proposals admitted that migration to Britain could leave the existing population "concerned about the impact on jobs, public services and their way of life."

It outlined a scheme in which most low-skilled workers will be expected in future to come from the EU and applicant states. Under the system migrants will be awarded points based on factors such as their age, qualifications, previous earnings and whether they have a job offer.

Tony McNulty, the Immigration Minister, said that the strategy would reduce immigration by the "wrong" sort of people.

Damian Green, the Shadow Immigration Minister, said: "We welcome a points-based system in principle—it is something we have been suggesting for a long time."

The CBI and TUC gave their support to the scheme, which ministers hope to begin implementing by 2008.

Julia Onslow-Cole, head of global immigration at CMS Cameron McKenna, an employment law firm, said: "I think that good employers have nothing to fear from this scheme. The scheme rewards good employers by giving a light touch to their immigration needs."

The Five Tiers

1. Highly skilled (such as a doctor) seventy-five points required. Bachelor degree thirty, Masters thirty-five, PhD fifty. Points for previous wages, weighted to take account of home country: five for £18,000 salary to forty-five for £45,000-plus. Points for age: Under twenty-seven years, twenty points; thirty to thirty-one, five points. Allowed to apply to settle in Britain permanently after two years. Allowed to bring dependants.

2. Skilled workers (such as nurses) fifty points required. Bachelor degree ten points, Masters ten, PhD fifteen, NVQ level three, five. Points for likely UK earnings: £15,000 to £18,000, five points, rising to twenty for

£21,000-plus. Allowed to apply for settlement in UK after five years. Allowed to bring dependants.

3. Low-skilled in areas such as agriculture. No points system. Migrants only enter when there is a shortage of workers in a sector. Applicants may need open return ticket. Not allowed to apply for settlement.

4. Students. Must provide evidence they are studying with an accredited college. Allowed to remain in Britain for duration of study. Not allowed to apply for settlement. Allowed to bring dependants if over sixteen.

5. Temporary workers, au pairs, sports people in competitions, musicians on tour. Allowed in Britain for up to two years. Not allowed to apply for settlement. Temporary workers allowed to bring dependants; gap-year students no dependants.

SIGNIFICANCE

Already, studies have shown that U.K. businesses are facing difficulties in recruiting local staff, and increasingly rely on migrant workers to fill their vacancies. Moreover, although the evidence is not conclusive, several research studies have demonstrated that migrants offer net economic benefits, since they are more likely to be of working age and in employment than the native population, and over the course of their lifetime they pay more in taxes than they receive in public services and benefits. Studies have also found, however, that immigrants tend to be concentrated among both the highest paid and lowest paid members of the workforce, so it is important to ensure that immigration systems facilitate the entry of those who are most likely to be succeed economically.

Additionally, the new scheme is intended to play an important role in tightening the control of immigration to Britain and reducing the numbers of undocumented migrants. Many of these undocumented migrants are overstayers, who originally entered Britain on employment or student visas and failed to leave the country when their visas expired, or never even took up their jobs or college places. Various aspects of the new scheme are designed to address this problem, including the requirement for some low-skilled migrants to put down a financial bond, refundable only when they leave the country, and for employers and colleges to be involved in policing the scheme.

The proposals have received support from the main opposition party in Britain, the Conservatives, as well as the main employers' organization, the Confederation of British Industry, and the main association of worker unions, the Trades Unions Congress. Supporters of a points-based immigration system argue that it is more transparent and fair to applicants, as well as being more effective in contributing to the needs of the economy. Opponents of the scheme contend, however, that it is likely to lead to increased levels of unauthorized immigration, since many sectors of the economy, such as cleaning and catering, rely heavily on low-cost non-European Union labor and will continue to attract such workers.

FURTHER RESOURCES

Books

Glover, S., C. Gott, A. Loizillon, J. Portes, R. Price, S. Spencer, V. Srinivasan, and C. Willis, *Migration: an Economic and Social Analysis, RDS Occasional Paper No. 67.* The Home Office Research, Development and Statistics Directorate, 2001.

Web sites

TimesOnLine. "Points System Will Favor Skilled Immigrant Workers, says Clarke." March 8, 2006. <http://www.timesonline.co.uk/article/0,,2–2075110,00.html> (accessed June 28, 2006).

Holland Launches the Immigrant Quiz

Newspaper article

By: Nicola Smith

Date: March 12, 2006

Source: Smith, Nicola. "Holland Launches the Immigrant Quiz." *The Times* (March 12, 2006).

About the Author: Nicola Smith is a reporter for *The Times*, a daily newspaper published in the United Kingdom since 1785.

INTRODUCTION

The article reports on the introduction in March 2006 of a compulsory civic integration examination as part of the application procedure for immigration to the Netherlands. The test, which would take place in the Dutch embassy in the applicant's country of origin, would involve watching a controversial video about the more liberal aspects of life in the permissive society of the Netherlands, such as nudity and homosexuality, and being tested on Dutch culture and history.

Prospective immigrants would also be required to pass a Dutch language examination. The proposed tests reflected new hard-line immigration policies being adopted in the Netherlands by the center-right coalition government elected to power in 2003.

Until this time, the Netherlands had a fairly liberal immigration policy. Traditionally, most of the country's immigrants were migrants from its former colonies such as Surinam and the Antilles or guest workers from Turkey and Morocco who were brought in to solve labor shortages after the second word war. From the 1990s onwards, the majority of immigrants were European Union (EU) nationals, who could enter and live in the Netherlands without restriction, and large numbers of asylum seekers and refugees, mainly from the Middle East and Eastern Europe. By 2002, eighteen percent of the Netherlands population of sixteen million had been born outside the country.

Although the Netherlands' immigration policies were not very restrictive in the past, making it relatively easy for migrant workers and their families to settle in the country, immigrants have never integrated well into Dutch society, and the government had made little effort to assimilate them. On the contrary, immigrants had been encouraged to preserve their own cultural identities, in much the same way as the Dutch Protestant and Catholic communities had traditionally formed different "pillars" in society, with their own schools, churches and other social and economic institutions. This non-assimilation approach resulted in the development of immigrant enclaves and in the exclusion of many immigrants from opportunities to gain the education and skills needed to succeed economically. On average, immigrants attain much lower educational levels than the native Dutch population and are three times more likely to be unemployed. This situation has been reinforced by the existence in the Netherlands of a very generous welfare system, which has enabled immigrants to live comfortably there without any need to learn the language or enter the labor market. In the 1990s, targeted integration policies were introduced that were intended to help immigrants learn the Dutch language, correct educational shortcomings, and help immigrants to acquire job-related skills, but have had very limited success.

Rising levels of unemployment and economic stagnation in the 1990s led many native Dutch people to become resentful about the large and visible immigrant populations, who they blamed for their country's difficulties. The consequence of this resentment was an increasing number of racially-motivated hate crimes, with Muslims especially targeted after the September 11, 2001, terrorist attacks on the World Trade Center in New York. There were also increasing numbers of attacks by young Muslims on the homosexual community, on the Netherlands' Jewish community, and on those perceived to be critical of Islam. In 2004, a radical Dutch film-maker, Theo van Gogh, was murdered by a Muslim radical after the release of his film "Submission," which criticized the treatment of women in Islamic cultures. The Somali-born ex-Muslim woman Ayaan Hirsi Ali, who had written the film script, and was at the time a member of Parliament in the Netherlands, also received death threats and was forced into hiding.

The center-right coalition government that took power in 2003 under Jan Peter Bakenenede shifted the immigration policy focus from integration to tough immigration control, in response to increasing concerns about racial and religious-related violence and the increasing size of the immigrant population. Soon after taking up power, the government announced plans to evict failed asylum seekers from temporary housing and deport them to their home countries, to introduce the mandatory citizenship tests and integration programs, and other hard-line policy measures to curb levels of immigration to the Netherlands.

PRIMARY SOURCE

TWO MEN kissing in a park and a topless woman bather are featured in a film that will be shown to would-be immigrants to the Netherlands.

The reactions of applicants—including Muslims—will be examined to see whether they are able to accept the country's liberal attitudes.

From this Wednesday, the DVD—which also shows the often crime-ridden ghettos where poorer immigrants might end up living—will form part of an entrance test, in Dutch, covering the language and culture of Holland.

Those sitting the test will be expected to identify William of Orange and to know which country Crown Princess Maxima comes from (Argentina) and whether hitting women and female circumcision are permitted.

Muslim leaders in Holland say the film is offensive. "It really is a provocation aimed to limit immigration. It has nothing to do with the rights of homosexuals. Even Dutch people don't want to see that," said Abdou Menebhi, the Moroccan-born director of Emcemo, an organisation that helps immigrants to settle.

He added: "They are trying to find every pretext to show that people should not come to the Netherlands because they are fundamentalist or not emancipated. They confront people with these things and then judge them afterwards."

Famile Arslan, 34, an immigration lawyer of Turkish origin, agreed. "I have lived here for 30 years and have never been witness to two men kissing in the park. So why are they confronting people with that?" she said.

She accused the government of preaching tolerance about civil rights while targeting non-westerners with harsh and discriminatory immigration curbs.

The new test—the first of its kind in the world—marks another step in the transformation of Holland from one of Europe's most liberal countries to the one cracking down hardest on immigration.

Rita Verdonk, the immigration minister known as Iron Rita, has introduced compulsory integration classes, higher age limits for marriage to people from abroad and the removal of residency permits if immigrants commit petty crimes. She has also talked of banning the burqa.

The measures were prompted in part by outrage over the 2004 murder of Theo Van Gogh, who had made a film about the oppression of women in Muslim communities.

Applicants will sit the exam at one of 138 embassies around the world. They will answer 15 minutes of questions and those who pass the first stage will have to complete two "citizenship" tests over five years and swear a pledge of allegiance to Holland and its constitution.

The centre-right government of Jan Peter Balkenende, the prime minister, believes the tests will provide an objective way of assessing the suitability of applicants by gauging how well prepared they are to make the transition to Dutch life and their willingness to integrate.

Critics complain that people living in the mountains of Morocco or rural villages in Pakistan will not be able to make the long journey to cities for Dutch language lessons. According to Instituut Oranje, a Dutch language school, someone with a low level of education would require 250 hours of tuition, costing £1,200, to pass the tests.

The total bill of £1,495—including £55 for a preparatory test pack and DVD and £240 for the exam—makes the process unaffordable for many.

Dirk Nieuwboer, a Dutch journalist based in Istanbul, said the multiple-choice cultural test included a question about how to behave in a cafe if two men at the next table started kissing. "There was another question about which former Dutch colony a particular spice came from," said Nieuwboer. "Most Dutch people don't know these things."

However, Jeroen Dijsselbloem, a socialist from the parliament's immigration committee, said the film had been created to help prepare people for "open-minded" attitudes on issues such as homosexuality. "We have lots of homo-discrimination, especially by Muslim youngsters who harass gay men and women on the streets. It is an issue here."

A spokeswoman for Verdonk said an edited version of the DVD would be available for showing in Middle Eastern countries such as Iran where it would be illegal to possess images of homosexuality.

SIGNIFICANCE

Controversy over the proposed citizenship tests and other hard-line immigration policies was a leading factor in the collapse of Bakenenede's government in June 2006. Many officials in the city governments had refused to co-operate with the arrangements for deporting asylum seekers, and there had been international outcry over the citizenship tests. The government finally collapsed when the smallest party in the coalition, D-66, refused to work with Immigration Minister Rita Verdonk, in protest at her hard-line immigration policies and her decision to revoke the citizenship of Ayaan Hirsi Ali. A temporary government was established at the request of Queen Beatrix under former Christian Democrat Prime Minister Ruud Lubbers, and a general election is scheduled for November 2006.

FURTHER RESOURCES

Book

Alicea, Marixsa, and Maura I. Toro-Morn. *Migration and Immigration: A Global View*. Westport, Conn.: Greenwood Press, 2004.

Periodicals

Schilling, Timothy P. "Innundated: Immigration & the Dutch." *Commonweal* 131 (February 27, 2004).

"Tolerance on Trial." *The Wilson Quarterly* 29 (March 22, 2005).

An Irish Face on the Cause of Citizenship

Newspaper article

By: Nina Bernstein and Matthew Sweeney

Date: March 16, 2006

Supporters of the Irish Lobby for Immigration Reform rally in front of the U.S. Capitol on March 8, 2006, to show support for the McCain-Kennedy Immigration Bill that would provide legal status to undocumented immigrants already in the United States. AP IMAGES.

Source: Bernstein, Nina, and Matthew Sweeney. "An Irish Face on the Cause of Citizenship." *New York Times* (March 16, 2006).

About the Author: Nina Bernstein and Matthew Sweeney are reporters for the *New York Times*, a daily newspaper with a circulation of over one million readers worldwide.

INTRODUCTION

Irish nationals account for only a very small proportion of the total number of unauthorized immigrants in the United States. A 2004 estimate of the total number of undocumented migrants in the United States put the figure at 10.4 million, of which more than half were from Mexico, and a further quarter were from other Latin American countries. There is no official estimate of the number of undocumented Irish immigrants in the United States, but one research study in the early 1990s roughly gauged the total to be only around fifty thousand nationwide.

Although the United States has a substantial existing Irish-American community, most of the Irish undocumented immigrants as of 2006 are recent migrants who entered the United States during the 1980s to escape poor economic conditions and high levels of unemployment in Ireland at that time. Most entered legally as tourists and overstayed their visas, taking work mainly in low-skilled jobs in the construction and catering industries, or as au pairs. Being white, English-speaking immigrants, they have been able to integrate easily into U.S. society, and have received relatively little attention from the immigration authorities.

When the Immigration Reform and Control Act (IRCA) of 1986 introduced sanctions for employers who hired undocumented workers, this made it increasingly difficult for the Irish, along with other unauthorized immigrants, to secure work. As a result, the Irish undocumented migrant community mobilized themselves politically to fight for immigration reform, through organizations such as the Irish

Immigration Reform Movement, Project Irish Outreach, and the ethnic newspaper the *Irish Voice*. They have done so very successfully, capitalizing on their Irish ethnicity and drawing support from the established Irish-American community, including many prominent politicians and business leaders. Their main success to date is often regarded as the establishment of a special visa program in 1986, which aimed to redress the balance of the Hart-Celler Act of 1965 in favor of the Irish and other European immigrants.

The Hart-Celler Act had sought to equalize the number of immigrants to the United States from the Western and Eastern hemispheres, severely restricting legal immigration from Europe. Lobbying by the Irish was a main factor in the implementation of the NP5 Visa Program in 1986, which aimed to increase emigration from some of the countries who had traditionally been main sources of immigration to the United States but had been adversely affected by the Hart-Celler Act. Although the Irish political lobby campaigned on behalf of many countries affected by the Act, in the end around sixteen thousand of all the visas allocated, forty-one percent of the total, were obtained by Irish applicants. Around a third of these applicants were reportedly already living illegally in the United States.

The political successes of the Irish undocumented immigrant community have roused mixed views from other immigrant groups, some of whom resent the preferential treatment that the Irish are perceived to have received in immigration law, and others who welcome the Irish efforts to champion the cause of undocumented migrants.

The Irish Lobby for Immigration Reform is a group that was newly established to lobby on behalf of Irish undocumented immigrants in the debate on immigration reform taking place in the mid 2000s. Along with other undocumented immigrant groups, the Irish were concerned about the impact of the border security bill passed by the House of Representatives in December 2005. The bill proposed making it a felony to enter or live in the United States without documentation, or to assist anyone else to do so. Members of the community are being urged to support an alternative bill passed by the Senate in May 2006, which included provision for a guest worker program that existing undocumented immigrants would be eligible to apply for.

▰ PRIMARY SOURCE

Rory Dolan's, a restaurant in Yonkers, was packed with hundreds of illegal Irish immigrants on that rainy Friday night in January when the Irish Lobby for Immigration Reform called its first meeting. Niall O'Dowd, the chairman, soon had them cheering.

"You're not just some guy or some woman in the Bronx, you're part of a movement," Mr. O'Dowd told the crowd of construction workers, students and nannies. He was urging them to support a piece of Senate legislation that would let them work legally toward citizenship, rather than punishing them with prison time, as competing bills would.

For months, coalitions of Latino, Asian and African immigrants from 50 countries have been championing the same measure with scant attention, even from New York's Democratic senators. But the Irish struck out on their own six weeks ago, and as so often before in the history of American immigration policy, they have landed center stage.

Last week, when Senators Hillary Rodham Clinton and Charles E. Schumer declared their support for a new path to citizenship, and denounced criminal penalties recently passed by the House of Representatives, they did so not at the large, predominantly Hispanic immigrant march on Washington, but at the much smaller Irish rally held there the following day.

Some in the immigrant coalitions resent being passed over, and worry that the Irish are angling for a separate deal. Others welcome the clout and razzmatazz the Irish bring to a beleaguered cause. And both groups can point to an extraordinary Irish track record of lobbying triumphs, like the creation of thousands of special visas in the 1980's and 90's that one historian of immigration, Roger Daniels, calls "affirmative action for white Europeans."

Mainly, though, they marvel at the bipartisan muscle and positive spin the illegal Irish can still muster, even as their numbers dwindle to perhaps 25,000 to 50,000 across the country—those left behind by a tide of return migration to a now-prosperous Ireland.

This week, as the Senate Judiciary Committee wrestles with a comprehensive immigration bill, towns across the country are preparing to celebrate their Irish roots. On Friday, St. Patrick's Day, President Bush is to meet with Ireland's prime minister, Bertie Ahern, who has vowed to put the legalization of the Irish at the top of his agenda. And Irish Lobby volunteers are ready to leverage the attention, with "Legalize the Irish" T-shirts and pressure on senators like Rick Santorum, Republican of Pennsylvania, who is in a tight race against Bob Casey Jr., a Democrat of Irish ancestry.

The new Irish dynamic is all the more striking because the Republican Party is fiercely split over immigration, and many Democrats have hung back from the fray, judging the issue too hot to handle in an election year.

"They're still good at the game," said Linda Dowling Almeida, who teaches the history of Irish immigration at New York University. She and other historians noted that in the mid–19th century, Irish immigrants used the clout of urban political machines and leadership by the Roman Catholic Church to beat back a nativist movement that saw them as a threat to national security and American culture.

More recently, Mr. O'Dowd, the publisher of The Irish Voice, was himself part of a lobby that leaned on legislators with Irish heritage to engineer more than 48,000 visas for the Irish, legalizing many who had re-greened old Celtic neighborhoods in New York, Boston and Philadelphia.

But much has changed. After 9/11, a groundswell of anger over illegal immigration converged with national security concerns, propelling a populist revolt across party lines. Immigration is now seen as a no-win issue in electoral politics. And both opponents and supporters of legalization take a more jaundiced view of the Irish role in the debate.

"They're essentially saying, 'Look, we're good European illegal immigrants,'" said Mark Krikorian, director of the Center for Immigration Studies, which supports the House and Senate measures that would turn "unlawful presence," now a civil violation, into a crime. "The reason they've been more successful is the same reason it appeals to editors—immigration nostalgia from 150 years ago."

He added: "Can they be bought off by a special program for a handful of remaining illegals? I'm not saying it's a good idea, but you just start talking about the old sod and singing 'danny Boy,' and of course it's possible."

A special measure for the Irish would be hard to pass today, countered Muzaffar Chishti, the director of the New York office of Migration Policy Institute, a nonpartisan research organization that has generally supported immigrant amnesties. In earlier campaigns, he recalled, an Irish lobby worked with other immigrant groups, and all won pieces of their agenda.

"It was extremely important for the optics on Capitol Hill," Mr. Chishti said. "The Irish were also very savvy about it at that time. They knew that they would get some special Irish treatment, but they also wanted to make it look like they were part of the immigrant coalition."

Today, the lobby's most crucial role, he said, may be changing the political calculus of Democrats who have shunned the immigration issue as a no-win choice between responding to Latinos and looking tough on immigration. Many Irish-Americans are swing voters, he said, and "it becomes sort of a tipping point for the Democratic Party."

For now, Mr. O'Dowd said, the Irish Lobby's focus is entirely on supporting the McCain-Kennedy bill, which would allow illegal immigrants who qualify to pay a $2,000 fine and work toward citizenship. But if no such measure emerges from Congress, he added, the Irish Lobby will push for any special arrangement it can get—"as will every other ethnic group in the country."

Special visas for the Irish "would be brilliant," said Valery O'Donnell, a house cleaner and single mother of 7-year-old twins who was at the Rory Dolan's meeting, and said she had lived in New York illegally for 13 years. "There's no harm in us. We're all out here to work hard."

But several immigrant advocates in New York said that even the hint of special treatment for the Irish would inflame the hurt feelings that began in February when Senator Schumer first spoke out on immigration at an Irish Lobby event in Woodside, Queens, after declining invitations by veteran immigrant organizations more representative of an estimated 700,000 illegal immigrants in the state. The Pew Hispanic Center estimates that 78 percent of the nation's nearly 12 million illegal immigrants are from Mexico or elsewhere in Latin America.

Spokesmen for the two senators said that their appearances had been determined only by what fit their schedules, and that their support for immigrants was not meant for a specific group.

Some immigrant leaders were not convinced. Juan Carlos Ruiz, the coordinator of the predominantly Hispanic rally of 40,000 held March 7 on Capitol Hill, said that only one senator had shown up there, without speaking: Richard J. Durbin, an Illinois Democrat. The next day, Mr. Ruiz said, when he and his 14-year-old son stopped by the Irish gathering of about 2,400 and realized that the speakers included Senators Edward M. Kennedy, John McCain, as well as Senators Clinton and Schumer, his son asked, "Why didn't the senators come to our rally?"

"I was heartbroken," Mr. Ruiz said. "I needed to explain to him: 'the immigrants of color, for these senators we are not important enough for them to make a space in their calendar.' "

He added: "The Irish are not at fault. They are suffering the same troubles that we are. But it is discrimination."

Monami Maulik, a leader in another coalition, Immigrant Communities in Action, echoed his sentiment. "For a lot of us, this is a current civil rights struggle," she said.

But when the phrase was repeated to Mr. O'Dowd, he countered: "It's not about that at all. It's about how you change the law." For years, he added, he has lobbied to win nearly lost causes, including helping to broker a ceasefire in Northern Ireland. "It's not about being fair, it's about being good," he said. "It's about getting it done."

SIGNIFICANCE

Proposals to reform immigration law in the mid–2000s have been focused primarily on addressing the problem of unauthorized migration from Mexico and other parts of Latin America. However, this news article highlights the fact that undocumented migrants from Ireland and a range of other countries would also be affected by any new legislation. This has implications for the viability of proposed enforcement measures such as the prosecution of employers under federal law, since white European migrants are less visible than other ethnic groups, and it is arguably more difficult to identify them as unauthorized immigrants if they hold convincing fake documents.

The article also serves as a reminder that many undocumented migrants were originally legal immigrants who have overstayed their visas, and that immigration enforcement policies therefore need to address this problem in addition to strengthening control of the land borders.

The Irish have traditionally been able to influence U.S. immigration reform, due to their ability to capitalize on their ethnic links with the established Irish-American community, and it is possible that their interests and political lobbying will affect the outcomes of the 2006 immigration reform debate in their favor. However, this is likely to be difficult to achieve in the current climate, when public concern about levels of undocumented migration is at an all time high, and enforcement of the immigration laws is also being presented as a weapon in the war against terrorism.

FURTHER RESOURCES

Books

Corcoran, Mary P. *Irish Illegals: Transients between Two Societies*. Westport, Conn.: Greenwood Press, 1993.

Delaet, Debra. *U.S. Immigration Policy in an Age of Rights*. Westport, Conn.: Praeger, 2000.

Tichenor, Daniel J. *Dividing Lines: The Politics of Immigration Control in America*. Princeton, N.J.: Princeton University Press, 2002.

Web sites

Irishabroad.com. <http://www.irishabroad.com> (accessed June 26, 2006).

500,000 Pack Streets to Protest Immigration Bills

News article

By: Teresa Watanabe and Hector Becerra

Date: March 26, 2006

Source: *Los Angeles Times. latimes.com*. March 26, 2006. <http://pqasb.pqarchiver.com/latimes/access/> (accessed June 15, 2006).

About the Author: Teresa Watanabe and Hector Becerra are reporters for the *Los Angeles Times*, a daily newspaper published in Los Angeles, California. The article is taken from the online version of the newspaper.

INTRODUCTION

In the early months of 2006, mass demonstrations were held across the United States in protest of the immigration bill that had been passed by the House of Representatives in December 2005. The rally held in Los Angeles in March was one of the largest, reflecting the sizeable immigrant community and numerous immigrant advocacy groups located in this area.

The House bill was passed in response to concern about increasing levels of immigration, especially undocumented immigration, to the United States. Its main provisions included the proposal that illegal entry or illegal presence in the United States should be made a felony, and that any attempt to assist a person to enter or remain in the United States illegally should also be made a felony. It proposed steep increases in the penalties for undocumented entry, and for the assistance or employment of undocumented migrants, and recommended that a fence should be constructed along 700 miles of the U.S.-Mexico border. Under the House bill, there would be no route to legal residence or to U.S. citizenship for any undocumented immigrants.

Protest against the House bill came not only from immigrants and immigrant support groups but from the church, charities and other organizations that provide humanitarian aid to undocumented migrants. Although the proposal to make assistance to undocumented migrants a felony was primarily directed at people smugglers and those who deliberately employ or provide a safe harbor for undocumented migrants within the United States, these groups were concerned that they would also be liable for penalties and imprisonment for providing assistance to immigrants. Immigrants

A crowd of 500,000 Hispanic workers and immigrants march in downtown Los Angeles to protest against the anti-immigrant H.R. 4437 federal bill. © GENE BLEVINS/LA DAILY NEWS/CORBIS.

and their supporters also stressed the important role that immigrants play in the U.S. economy.

The mass mobilization of opposition to the House bill across ethnic groups, as well as the involvement of the Catholic church in the protests, raised the political sensitivity of immigration reform. In recent years, immigrant votes, particularly from the Latin-American community, have become increasingly influential in U.S. politics and helped to shape immigration policy. For example, the Democrats capitalized heavily on promoting their party to the Hispanic community in the 1996, 1998 and 2000 elections, and on campaigning against the tough immigration reforms being proposed by the Republicans. In addition, the business community is generally opposed to tougher immigration laws, which would make it more difficult for employers to recruit immigrants to unfilled vacancies. By the mid–2000s, conflicts had emerged both within and between the main political parties regarding the future of immigration reform. The most pressing issue had become the problem of undocumented migration, and how to deal with

this while retaining the political support of the business community and major immigrant groups.

■ PRIMARY SOURCE

A crowd estimated by police at more than 500,000 boisterously marched in Los Angeles on Saturday to protest federal legislation that would crack down on undocumented immigrants, penalize those who help them and build a security wall along the U.S. southern border.

Spirited but peaceful marchers—ordinary immigrants alongside labor, religious and civil rights groups—stretched more than twenty blocks along Spring Street, Broadway and Main Street to City Hall, tooting kazoos, waving American flags and chanting, *"Sí se puede!"* (Yes we can!).

Attendance at the demonstration far surpassed the number of people who protested against the Vietnam War and Proposition 187, a 1994 state initiative that sought to deny public benefits to undocumented migrants but was struck down by the courts. Police said there were no arrests or injuries except for a few cases of exhaustion.

At a time when Congress prepares to crack down further on illegal immigration and self-appointed militias patrol the U.S. border to stem the flow, Saturday's rally represented a massive response, part of what immigration advocates are calling an unprecedented effort to mobilize immigrants and their supporters nationwide.

It coincides with an initiative on the part of the Roman Catholic Church, spearheaded by Cardinal Roger M. Mahony, archbishop of Los Angeles, to defy a House bill that would make aiding undocumented immigrants a felony. And it signals the burgeoning political clout of Latinos, especially in California.

"There has never been this kind of mobilization in the immigrant community ever," said Joshua Hoyt, executive director of the Illinois Coalition for Immigrant and Refugee Rights. "They have kicked the sleeping giant. It's the beginning of a massive immigrant civil rights struggle."

The demonstrators, many wearing white shirts to symbolize peace, included both longtime residents and the newly arrived, bound by a desire for a better life.

Arbelica Lazo, forty, illegally emigrated from El Salvador two decades ago but said she now owns two businesses and pays $7,000 in income taxes each year.

Jose Alberto Salvador, thirty-three, came here illegally four months ago to find work to support the wife and five children he left behind. In his native Guatemala, he said, what little work he could find paid $10 a day.

"As much as we need this country, we love this country," Salvador said, waving both the American and Guatemalan flags. "This country gives us opportunities we don't get at home."

On Monday, the U.S. Senate Judiciary Committee is scheduled to resume work on a comprehensive immigration reform proposal. The Senate committee's version includes elements of various bills, including a guest worker program and a path to legalization for the nation's 10 million to 12 million undocumented immigrants proposed by Sens. John McCain (Republican-Arizona) and Edward M. Kennedy (Democrat-Massachusetts.)

In addition, Senate Majority Leader Bill Frist (Republican-Tennessee.) has introduced a bill that would strengthen border security, crack down on employers of illegal immigrants and increase the number of visas for workers. Frist has said he would take his bill to the floor Tuesday if the committee does not finish its work Monday.

Ultimately, the House and Senate bills must be reconciled before a law can be passed.

President Bush has advocated a guest worker program and attracted significant Latino support for his views.

In his Saturday radio address, Bush urged all sides of the emotional debate to tone down their rhetoric, calling for a balanced approach between more secure borders and more temporary foreign workers.

Largely in response to the debate in Washington, hundreds of thousands of people in recent weeks have staged marches in more than a dozen cities calling for immigration reform.

In Denver, police said Saturday that more than 50,000 people gathered downtown at Civic Center Park next to the Capitol to urge the state Senate to reject a resolution supporting a ballot issue that would deny many government services to illegal immigrants in Colorado.

Hundreds rallied in Reno, the Associated Press reported.

On Friday, tens of thousands of people were estimated to have staged school walkouts, marches and work stoppages in Los Angeles, Phoenix, Atlanta and other cities.

In addition, several cities, including Los Angeles, have passed resolutions opposing the House legislation. At least one city, Maywood, declared itself a "sanctuary" for undocumented immigrants.

Despite the significant opposition to the crackdown on illegal immigrants shown by the turnout in recent rallies, a recent Zogby poll found sixty-two percent of Americans surveyed wanted more restrictive immigration policies, and a Field Poll last month found that the majority of California voters surveyed believed illegal immigration was hurting the state.

"Polling has consistently shown that Americans don't want guest workers or amnesty," said Caroline Espinosa, spokeswoman for NumbersUSA, a Washington-based immigration control group that says its e-mail list of one million and 140,000-member roster of activists have more than doubled in the last year.

Espinosa said current levels of both legal and illegal immigration would push the U.S. population to 420 million by 2050, "leading to a tremendously negative impact on the quality of life in the United States."

According to a U.S. Census Bureau survey a year ago, the nation's 35.2 million immigrants—legal and illegal—represent a record number. California led the country with nearly 10 million, constituting twenty-eight percent of the state's population overall and one-third of its work force.

The swelling number of immigrants has clearly influenced the political calculus of those involved in the issue, including political and religious groups. The Republican Party, for instance, is split among those who want tougher restrictions, those who fear alienating the Latino vote and business owners who are pressing for more laborers—mostly Latin Americans—to fill blue-collar jobs in construction, cleaning, gardening and other industries.

Some Republicans fear that pushing too hard against illegal immigrants could backfire nationally, as with Proposition 187. Strong Republican support of that measure helped spur record numbers of California Latinos to become U.S. citizens and register to vote. Those voters subsequently helped the Democrats regain political control in the state.

"There is no doubt Proposition 187 had a devastating impact on the [California] Republican Party," said Allan Hoffenblum, a Republican political consultant. "Now the Republicans in Congress better beware: If they come across as too shrill, with a racist tone, all of a sudden you're going to see Republicans in cities with a high Latino population start losing their seats."

The effects of the nation's growing Latino presence also are evident in religious communities. This week, for instance, the president of the 30-million-member National Assn. of Evangelicals is scheduled to issue a statement supporting immigration reform, including a guest worker program. It will be in concert with the National Hispanic Christian Leadership Conference, said the Rev. Samuel Rodriguez, conference president.

Rodriguez, whose Sacramento-based group serves the nation's 18 million evangelical Christian Latinos, said it took "a lot of persuasion" to broker the joint statement with Ted Haggard, president of the evangelicals group. Rodriguez said he warned the group that failure to support comprehensive immigration reform would have long-term political repercussions.

Latino evangelical Christians voted for Bush at a forty percent higher rate than Latinos overall, he said, but they would probably turn away from conservative candidates and causes without support on immigration.

"I had to do a lot of asking: Will Hispanics ever vote for conservative candidates again, or partner with white evangelicals if they were silent while our brothers and sisters and cousins were being sent out of the county on buses?" Rodriguez said.

Churches were just one force behind Saturday's rally.

Several immigrant advocates said that the ethnic media were a significant factor in drawing crowds. News outlets repeatedly publicized it and even exhorted marchers to wear white shirts. Churches announced the rally too. Although a police spokeswoman estimated the crowd at 500,000 based on helicopter surveillance, rally organizers said it was closer to one million.

Los Angeles Mayor Antonio Villaraigosa briefly addressed the rally.

"We cannot criminalize people who are working, people who are contributing to our economy and contributing to the nation," Villaraigosa said.

In contrast to demonstrations twelve years ago against Proposition 187, Saturday's rally featured more American flags than those from any other country. Flag vendors were soon overwhelmed by demonstrators holding out dollar bills.

Father Michael Kennedy, a longtime immigrant advocate and pastor of Dolores Mission Church in Boyle Heights, said that past demonstrations were more heavily Mexican or Mexican American, but the House bill had rallied protesters across religious, national and ethnic lines.

One was Korean immigrant Dae Joong Yoon, executive director of the Korean Resource Center in Los Angeles. Yoon said the Korean community was more inflamed over the House bill than Proposition 187 because it would penalize not only undocumented immigrants but also businesses that hired them and anyone who helped them.

He said the Korean-language media has intensified coverage of the House bill in recent weeks.

"The Korean community is shocked and outraged over this inhumane legislation," Yoon said. "Everybody would be affected by it."

SIGNIFICANCE

In May 2006, the U.S. Senate passed an alternative immigration bill, which was also designed to address the problem of undocumented immigration, while acknowledging the key role that immigrant workers play in the U.S. economy, and the need for a plan to deal with the millions of undocumented migrant workers already in the country. The bill was intended to address the concerns of pro-immigrant groups as well as those in favor of tougher policies on undocumented migration.

This bill proposed a guest worker program, under which immigrants already in the United States and those from overseas would be able to apply for unfilled vacancies. If successful, they would be granted a three-year temporary residence permit, renewable once, and would subsequently be allowed to apply for permanent residence through normal immigration channels. Those undocumented migrants who had been in the United States for more than five years would be allowed to stay and to gain legal status, after payment of fines and unpaid taxes, while those who had been in the United States for more than two years would be required to return to the border and submit an application to return. All undocumented migrants who had been in the United States for less than two years would be required to leave the country. In order to help prevent further undocumented migration, particularly from Mexico, the Senate bill supported the building of a fence along the Mexico-United States border, and proposed increased funding for more Border Control agents and for increased detention facilities for those undocumented migrants who were apprehended within the country.

Although the Senate bill received support across party lines, many Republicans and some Democrats remained fiercely opposed to any legislation that would reward the illegal act of undocumented migration with legalization of status. Since any bill has to be passed by both houses before it can become law, it will be necessary to achieve a compromise, which has majority support in both Houses. In the meantime, both parties face the risk of alienating key segments of the electorate on the immigration issue in an important mid-term election year.

FURTHER RESOURCES

Books

Delaet, Debra L. *U.S. Immigration Policy in an Age of Rights.* Praeger, 2000.

Periodicals

Cornelius, Wayne A. "Controlling 'unwanted' immigration: lessons from the United States, 1993–2004." *Annual Review of Sociology.* 21, 1995.

Espenshade, Thomas J. "Unauthorized Immigration to the United States." *Annual Review of Sociology.* 21, 1995.

Jonas, S., and C. Tactaquin. "Latino Immigrants Rights in the Shadow of the National Security State: Responses to Domestic Preemptive Strikes." *Social Justice.* 31, 2004.

Web sites

Los Angeles Times. "latimes.com." March 26, 2006 <http://pqasb.pqarchiver.com/latimes/access/> (accessed June 15, 2006).

Real Injustice

Newspaper editorial

By: The *Washington Post*

Date: March 18, 2006

Source: "Real Injustice." *Washington Post*, (March 18, 2006), A20.

About the Author: Founded in 1877, The *Washington Post* is located in the nation's capital and is famed for its reporting on U.S. political issues.

INTRODUCTION

In an effort to boost national security, Congress passed the Real ID Act. Designed to stop terrorists from moving easily around the United States, the legislation is projected to have the unintended consequence of keeping law-abiding would-be immigrants out of the country as well.

The Real ID Act came about in response to the September 11, 2001, terrorist acts. The 9/11 Commission noted that all but one of hijackers had obtained some form of U.S. identification document, some fraudulently. The documents made it easier for the hijackers to board airplanes, rent cars, and carry out other activities as part of their plot. As a result, the commission recommended that the federal government should set standards for birth certificates, driver's licenses, and other identification materials.

The Intelligence Reform and Terrorist Prevention Act, signed into law in December 2004, addressed the issue of identification security. It created a collaborative process between federal officials, governors, state legislators, and motor vehicle administrators for developing minimum standards for drivers' licenses and avoided the creation of a national ID. In March 2005, Real ID supporters attached their measure to an emergency spending bill to fund tsunami relief efforts and military operations in Iraq and Afghanistan. As a result, the bill passed through without much discussion and the ID committee was disbanded. The new law placed full responsibility upon the states to develop drivers' licenses that contain machine-readable technology and are valid for eight years. The new licenses must be in place by May 2008, with minimal federal financial assistance provided for development and implementation. The Real ID law has since come under attack from a range of groups, including advocates for immigrants.

PRIMARY SOURCE

WHEN CONGRESS passed the Real ID Act last year, it presumably did not intend to prevent human rights victims all over the world from entering the United States. Its goal was to keep terrorists and those who support them from resettling in the United States as refugees. The legislative language, however, was irresponsibly broad; its effects have been cruel to people already oppressed by vile regimes and terrorist groups. The law needs to be changed.

Terrorists were excluded from the United States even before the Real ID Act, but the law made substantial changes to keep out donors to terrorist groups or others who provide them "material support." The trouble is that, because of the new law and its interaction with existing

Aracely Lara, left, of El Salvador, and Guillermina Castellanos of Mexico, right, march during an immigration protest outside the home of Sen. Dianne Feinstein D-Calif., in San Francisco. AP IMAGES.

provisions, the legal definitions of terrorism, terrorist organizations and material support are so broad that they include countless people who deserve the United States' protection, not exclusion.

The law bars associates of any group that contains "two or more individuals, whether organized or not, [which] engages in, or has a subgroup which engages in" activities as general as using an "explosive, firearm or other weapon or dangerous device." The law contains no exceptions for people who are forced to support a group, or for children, or for tiny contributions, or for contributions that took place decades ago. It does not make any distinction between an al-Qaeda member and an armed combatant against a murderous regime. While the government has waiver authority in some cases, it has not yet used this power.

The results are terrible. According to the office of the U.N. High Commissioner for Refugees and to officials and academics who have looked at the issue, here are some people who may be barred from entry to the United States: Colombians who were forced to help the leftist insurgency

of the Revolutionary Armed Forces of Colombia; thousands of Karen and Chin nationals who suffered brutal repression at the hands of the Burmese military junta; Liberian, Somali and Vietnamese Montagnard victims of terrorism and repression; and some dissident Cubans who aided anti-Castro forces in the 1960s. The administration recently acknowledged in one asylum proceeding that those who fought with or aided the Northern Alliance against the Taliban or who supported the African National Congress against South Africa's apartheid government would be excluded, too.

A spokesman for House Judiciary Committee Chairman F. James Sensenbrenner Jr. (R-Wis.), who championed the Real ID Act, says the law's waiver authority gives the government the flexibility it needs to deal with such cases. And the problem could be alleviated if the administration would use that authority aggressively. But that would address only some of the cases, and only by having the government forgiving "terrorism" on the part of refugees whom it should not be labeling terrorists in the first place. This problem can be solved only by Congress. If this mess is not what Mr. Sensenbrenner had in mind, he ought to do something to clean it up.

SIGNIFICANCE

Critics of the Real ID Act argue that it is both unnecessary and impossible to provide more than 200 million Americans with new, standardized, electronically readable ID materials within only a few years. In 2006, the National Governor Association, National Conference of State Legislators, and the American Association of Motor Vehicle Administrators declared the act requirements to be unworkable. Instead, the groups suggested, the federal government should decide which states have the best systems for document verification and license requirements and help other states adopt those practices.

Several states are considering ways to opt out of Real ID. Federal officials have responded to this threat by warning that identification issued in states that do not comply with the law will not be accepted to board airplanes or enter federal buildings. No state and no federal officials are discussing ways to modify the legislation to help victims of human rights abuses.

FURTHER RESOURCES
Books

Garfinkel, Simson. *Database Nation: The Death of Privacy in the Twenty-First Century*. Sebastopol, CA: O'reilly Media, 2001.

Harper, Jim. *Identity Crisis: How Identification is Overused and Misunderstood*. Washington, D.C.: Cato Institute, 2006.

O'Harrow, Robert. *No Place to Hide: Behind the Scenes of Our Emerging Surveillance Society*. New York: Free Press, 2005.

8 Multiculturalism

Multiculturalism

Immigration involves not only the movement of peoples, but also the movement of cultures. Immigrants carry with them the foundations of their cultural identity: language, food, religion, traditions, social patterns, leisure activities, and family structures. The cultural patterns of an immigrant's indigenous community or country of origin can sometimes conflict with social customs and laws of their new county. In turn, social attitudes and cultural tolerance of the destination country influence the immigrant's dilemma of how and to what degree they desire to assimilate.

Multiculturalism is the acceptance of a number of cultures within a multiethnic society. Multiculturalism as officially adopted public policy is controversial. Those who favor a policy of multiculturalism assert that it promotes respect for individual differences, fosters diversity, and promotes beneficial cultural evolution. Many supporters claim it promotes tolerance and equality by not requiring individuals to fully assimilate or integrate into the dominant or traditional culture of their surroundings. Opponents charge that multicultural policy undermines social cohesiveness and encourages individual interests over common interests. Some critics claim it exacerbates social tensions over individual differences; some claim it destroys a society's traditional majority culture.

This chapter includes sources on both sides of the political debate over multiculturalism as a viable public policy. Featured are the Canadian Multicultural Act and the Australian national policy on multiculturalism. In contrast, "Berlusconi Warns Against Multiculturalism" presents opposing opinions to the adoption of national multicultural policy.

In the United States, the social theory of the "melting-pot" remains in tension with the more recent "salad-bowl" theory. Whereas the melting pot required amalgamation of diverse elements into an evolving but cohesive whole, the salad bowl permits individuals to retain their cultural identity within the whole—like the ingredients in a salad.

Without a comprehensive national policy, many multicultural programs in the United States are left to individual states. National multicultural initiatives have included the adoption of Black History and Asian-American history months. Within this chapter, the lingering debate over bilingual education best represents the overarching debate over multicultural policy in the United States. Several sources discuss the promotion and effectiveness of bilingual education, as well as attempts by states to ban the practice.

Finally, multiculturalism can refer to a cultural phenomenon divorced from politics. Caribbean-influenced rhythms and Spanish-language pop songs have achieved mainstream radio popularity. Fusion food adopts cooking styles and ingredients of diverse ethnic traditions. The fruits of multiculturalism and immigration are seen in everyday life. From ethnic enclaves in urban areas to ethnic foods in grocery stores, people experience the fusion of different cultures.

1933 World's Fair in Chicago

Poster

By: Glen C. Sheffer

Date: 1932

Source: © Swim Ink 2, LLC/Corbis.

About the Artist: Glen C. Sheffer was an illustrator known for painting landscapes, figures, and humans in action. Sheffer's impressionist works have been on exhibit in Chicago. This image is part of the collection at Corbis Corporation, headquartered in Seattle, with a worldwide archive of over seventy million images.

INTRODUCTION

The official title of the 1933 World's Fair in Chicago was A Century of Progress International Exposition. The Fair was organized to mark Chicago's one hundred year anniversary. The mission of the Fair was to demonstrate the significance of scientific and technological discoveries to industry and modern society and how those discoveries were being made. The Fair also showcased modern advancements in art, literature, and architecture from across the globe. Exhibits from all over the world included new automobile designs, houses of the future, and babies living in incubators. There was also an abundance of international carnival entertainment at the Fair, including the Skyride, a cable-suspended people mover higher than any building in Chicago. The midway provided games, a roller coaster, shows, and food. A Century of Progress was the second World's Fair in Chicago, the first being a tribute to the 400 years since the arrival of Christopher Columbus in 1893.

To represent modernity and the future, the buildings of the 1933 Fair were painted in many different colors, and were tall and angular in shape. This style contrasted the earlier 1893 Fair, whose buildings were all white and had curving shapes. To keep the focus on the technological exhibits inside the buildings, organizers did not build lasting monuments as seen in some of the previous World Fairs, such as the Eiffel Tower built for the Paris World Fair in 1889. In another attempt to represent the future, thousands of lights were used to light up the buildings and midway area at night. The actual site of the Fair was 427 acres, located just south of Chicago's downtown. The majority of the site was built by filling in the coast of Lake Michigan with landfill. The site later became Meigs Field airstrip, and a large convention center called McCormick Place.

A Century of Progress received sanctioning from the Bureau of International Exhibitions (BIE). The Convention on International Exhibitions established BIE in Paris in 1928 to give oversight and guidance to international exhibitions. The international community recognized the need for BIE to regulate the frequency and quality of exhibitions that had begun to occur quite frequently. The 1933 Fair was categorized by the BIE as a universal exhibition, as it covered a theme pertinent to citizens throughout the world. Smaller events sanctioned by the BIE are typically more specialized than universal exhibitions, concentrating on issues important to the host country, and other countries in the region. The BIE is not involved with trade fairs and other commercial exhibitions.

PRIMARY SOURCE

1933 World's Fair in Chicago: A poster advertising the 1933 World's Fair in Chicago. © SWIM INK 2, LLC/CORBIS.

PRIMARY SOURCE

1933 WORLD'S FAIR IN CHICAGO

See primary source image.

SIGNIFICANCE

One of the main objectives of the Chicago World's Fair was not only to highlight finished products, but also to illustrate how products were made and how science worked. The General Motors exhibit, for example, contained a functioning Chevrolet production line. Such exhibits showed the contributions factories were making to modern society. Organizers considered this an important aspect of the Fair, as many of the visitors were themselves factory workers, and such events would enable them to see the importance of their daily work. Although the Fair was designed to show that Chicago had entered an era of sophistication, some historians say this goal was not met, as many visitors were most captivated by the lights and popular entertainment the Fair provided. The Fair also brought foreign cultures to the masses. Though its main emphasis was on technology, popular exhibits and entertainers showcased cultures from across the globe. One of the most popular events was Sally Rand, an exotic fan dancer whose show made her famous at the Fair. While all World's Fairs punctuated events with multicultural entertainments, they all promoted a vision of uniting cultures through technology. The exhibits of 1930s World's Fairs promoted a common vision of modernity that crossed—and even blurred—cultural bounds.

The Fair was unique in that it was not paid for with government money. A Century of Progress was created as a non-profit corporation to organize the Fair, with members paying a fee to cover startup costs. Later, citizens of Chicago formed the World's Fair Legion, which generated further funds to organize the Fair. Over 100,000 people paid five dollars to be a member of the Legion. Corporate sponsors and private citizens financed the rest of the costs. The Fair opened on May 27, 1933 and closed for the first time on November 12, 1933. Because of its popularity, the Fair reopened on May 26, 1934 and had its final closing on October 31, 1934. The extension of the Fair resulted in over thirty-nine million admissions to the Fair, providing enough revenue to pay off its accrued debts. In contrast, many other World's Fairs have relied heavily on government subsidies.

FURTHER RESOURCES
Books

Armour, Nelson H. *The Conquest of Chicago: Visiting the 1933 World's Fair*. Manhattan, Kansas: Sunflower University Press, February 2004.

Cutler, Dawes Rufus. *A Century of Progress: Chicago World's Fair Centennial Celebration*. Chicago, Ill.: Century of Progress, 1933.

Periodicals

Chase, Al. "Opening of Exposition Great Occasion of Week." *Chicago Daily Tribune*. Part 8 May 21 (1933): e1.

Eve, Cousin. "A Century of Progress Has Greatest Home Exhibit of Modern Times." *Chicago Daily Tribune*. Part 1 June 4 (1933):24.

New York Times. "1934 World's Fair Largely Revamped." *New York Times*. Section 1 April 1 (1934):29.

Web sites

Bureau International des Expositions. "Bureau International des Expositions." <http://www.bie-paris.org/main/index.php?lang=1> (accessed June 26, 2006).

The Immigrant Strain

Book excerpt

By: Alastair Cooke

Date: May 6, 1946

Source: Cooke, Alastair. *Letters From America, 1946–2004*. London: Penguin, 2005.

About the Author: Alastair Cooke (1908–2004) was a British journalist who worked as the Washington correspondent for the *Guardian* newspaper during World War II. Cooke was resident in the United States from 1946 until his death in 2004. His weekly radio commentary, *Letters from America*, was nationally broadcast in the United States from 1946 to 2004.

INTRODUCTION

"The Immigrant Strain" was written in the wake of the successful alliance made between the United States and Great Britain during World War II. Cooke writes from the immediacy of that wartime alliance, an alliance that was an extension of hundreds of years of shared history that had created a similar cultural, linguistic, and political outlook between these two countries.

In 1946, the relative geopolitical position of each nation had profoundly changed due to the war. For the first time in their collective history, the United States was a demonstrably superior world power to Great Britain, in terms of both military might and international political influence. Cooke's *Letters from America* did not provide his audience in either Britain or America with supposed insights concerning an old colonial holding. Instead, Cooke connected his observations concerning American life into broader themes so as to better explain the function of the world's now most powerful country.

Cooke himself was representative of this sense of allied cultures and experiences. He lived in the United States for almost sixty years; he was educated at Cambridge in England, as well as at both Harvard and Yale. Cooke's avuncular but never pandering style was a constant in both the forty-eight years of his *Letters from America* series, as well as in his work as a host of many British television productions shown on the American national public broadcaster PBS. When Cooke referred to the English generally as being more foreign and more familiar to Americans than any other nationality, he neatly encapsulated his own experience as a commentator on American affairs.

Cooke's title is a clever introduction to the themes that he amplifies in the article itself. His use of 'strain' is both a reference to the different nationalities that are bound together to form the American population, as well as an allusion to the tensions that existed in 1946 in the broader American population as a result of immigration.

The affectionate tone adopted by Cooke towards American life in 1946 was a recurring element in his *Letters from America* series for the fifty-eight years of its existence. Cooke's manner and his insightful but rarely judgmental approach made him one of the most recognizable voices in the American media.

◼ PRIMARY SOURCE

An item came over the news-tape the other day about somebody who wanted to organize a National Hobby Club. There is nothing earthshaking in this, but it opens up a field of speculation about Britons and Americans that I should like to graze around in.

. . .

Active Americans do many things. And in different parts of the country they do routinely things that other parts of the country have never heard about. But by and large they do what other people, what their neighbours, do. There is a good reason for this, and you will be glad to hear we don't have to go back to the Indians for it.

Hobbies, I suggest, are essentially a tribal habit and appear most in a homogeneous nation. English boys in school sit beside other boys who are called Adams and Smith and Rendall and Barnes and Gibbs. They do not have to use up much of their competitive energy showing who is more English than another. A nation which says, "it isn't done", is much more settled as a community than one which says, "It's un-American." Only thirty years ago Theodore Roosevelt made a campaign of urging immigrant Americans to forget their roots, to cease being 'hyphenated Americans'. But there are still in America two generations, the sons and grandsons of immigrants, who are trying to outlive the oddity of their family's ways. For it is a stigma for an American to talk with a foreign accent rather than with an American accent. This is snobbery, of course, but the people who instantly recognize it as such are enviably free from the problem. If it is snobbery, even in this land, it is a real humiliation: it is not the urge of insecure people to be different from others; it is the more pressing urge to be the same, and it is acutely felt among people who are insecure just because they *are* different. In very many American cities where there are large populations of immigrants, this is what happens. The son is, let us say, an Italian. As a boy he is brought up with a mixture of American and Italian habits. He plays baseball, but the big meal of the week is ravioli, and he is allowed little gulps of red wine. (If he is a Pole, he is dolled up once a year and marched in the parade on Pulaski Day.) Then he goes to school. There he mixes with boys called Taylor and Smith and also with other boys called Schenck and Costello and O'Dwyer and Koshunski. He begins to find in time that ravioli is a mild joke at school.

Of course, there are millions of Americans who eat ravioli who are not Italian-Americans, but they are untouched by the kind of problem I am discussing. Ravioli is an American dish by now. And that is another thing. The boy notices that just so much as his own habits and speech were instilled by his parents, by so much does he tend not to fit in. By so much he runs the risk of being a joke; which is no joke to a child. And then, at about the age of 12, an awful thing happens. It is happening all over America all the time, and produces recrimination and heartbreak to the folks still left who came originally from the old country—from Poland or Italy or Czechoslovakia or Russia or Germany or wherever—and who will never master the American language. The boy notices that they speak with an accent. He never knew this before. But now it crowds in on him. Now he starts his own rebellion. And that is serious enough to many fine parents so that in scores, perhaps hundreds, of American cities that schools run night classes for parents, in the English language, to help them keep the affection and respect of their sons and daughters, or grandsons and granddaughters. It is a great theme in American life, and it cannot be dismissed by superficial horror or irritated appeals to decent feeling. In time, of course, masses of such sons and daughters outlive the threat of seeming different. And then, but only then, can they begin to cherish some of their oddity, especially in the way of food and festivals. Their strangeness becomes a grace note to the solid tune of their Americanism. But by that time they are sure of themselves and so able to look on their parents again—God help them—with affection.

So you see how sure of your standing with your companions you have to be to start, in boyhood, cooking up interests that will set you apart from your fellows. It will be no surprise now, I think, to hear from my Englishman that nearly all the members of his natural history club in New York were older men with Anglo-Saxon names—families that have been here for a hundred years or more, that have never felt anything but American. They start with the great advantage of being already something that the Poles and the Germans and the Czechs and the Italians have to get to be the hard way.

You may wonder how an Englishman, and an English accent, fit into all this. Well, Englishmen who live here, no matter how long—first-generation Englishmen—are a special case. They may hope to be mistaken for Bostonians (but not by Bostonians). Yet if they affect any more Americanism than that which has grown into their characters, they do themselves much hurt, and both the country they came from and the country they adopted. There are Irish-American and Czech-Americans and Polish-Americans and German-Americans and Swedish-Americans and Italian-Americans and Greek-Americans. But there are only 'Englishmen in America'. They are always apart and always at once more foreign and more familiar.

And an English accent is by now just another foreign sound. There was a time when an English accent would take an Englishman into homes on the East Coast socially more elevated than the home he left behind him. Such Englishmen were secretly delighted to discover this while believing they were only being taken at their true worth. But the hosts knew better. This social observation was a favourite theme of American writers, New Englanders especially, in the early nineteenth century. Washington Irving once boiled over about a certain kind of British traveller: "While Englishmen of philosophical spirit and cultivated minds have been sent from England to penetrate the deserts and to study the manners and customs of barbarous nations, it has been left to the broken-down tradesman, the scheming adventurer, the wandering mechanic, the Manchester and Birmingham agent, to be her oracles respecting America." You can still run into the type. Or you could say more accurately that this attitude is one part of most Englishmen's character that is aroused by a visit to America. But the day is long past when Americans imitated English habits in order to be fashionable. There is, however,

one peculiar hangover from that period. It is the convention of speaking English on the American stage. Unlike the British and the Germans, the Americans seem never to have worked out a type of stage speech true to the reality of the life around them. Except in comedies. In most historical American plays, and plays of polite life, the characters talk a form of British English. If you chide Americans about this and say, correctly, that these people in real life would not talk at all like that, they say: "Well, of course not; they're actors, aren't they?" I always feel in London that no matter how trivial the play, the characters being played would talk more or less that way in life. In this country it is understood as a convention, having nothing to do with social honesty, that actors should adopt an unreal mid-Atlantic lingo known, with a straight face, as Stage Standard. You may have noticed that even in American movies most American historical characters and members of congress talk a form of British, while what are called 'character parts' talk American.

Englishmen can hardly be blamed if they assume that Americans share their sneaking belief that no American can be distinguished and yet sound American at the same time. It has given some otherwise shrewd English dramatic critics the idea that really educated Americans talk like Englishmen. The fact is that educated Southerners, New Yorkers, Chicagoans or New Englanders could never be mistaken for Britons. And there is something wrong if they could be mistaken for each other. It is a fairly safe rule that if in life you meet an American who sounds English, he is either a transplanted Englishman, or one of those homeless Americans forlornly bearing up under the 'advantages' of an education in Europe. Or he is a phoney. The American dramatic critic, Mr. George Jean Nathan, was not intending to be facetious, but merely expressing a perennial American puzzle, when he wrote: "After thirty years of theatergoing, I still can't make up my mind whether actors talk and behave like Englishmen or whether Englishmen talk and behave like actors."

. . .

SIGNIFICANCE

Cooke's observations of America through the dual lenses of local residency and his British nationality are clear in a number of respects. The most trenchant of these is his analysis of how immigrants to the United States in 1946 became American over time in both their manners and their outlook. Cooke's analysis remained an accurate depiction of the American approach to its treatment of European newcomers and the manner in which these persons were absorbed into the fabric of American society, particularly as the Displaced Persons Act of 1948 created an influx of European immigration in the years that followed.

Without specifically employing the expression, Cooke describes the classic melting pot theory of American immigration practices, long held as the most desirable manner in which to assimilate newcomers into American society. Cooke's depiction of the Italian immigrant child seeking to conform with his new surroundings would have been applicable to any immigrant arriving in the United States in this period.

Many American citizens at this time espoused the melting pot theory of immigration, since it was thought to reduce the risk of subversive political elements undermining the existing American community. In the years following World War II, a particular concern was the potential entry of Communism or other similar left-leaning ideologies. By encouraging immigrants to conform to the existing America culture, the national government believed the risk of subversion was reduced. Cooke's use of the expression 'un-American' is reflective of the growing fear in 1946 that Communism, in particular, posed a significant threat to American society.

Cooke also observes that being English in America is different than being a member of any other immigrant class in the country. It is a rule of human nature that people tend to feel most comfortable in the company of those persons who are most similar to them. Today, according to the United States Census Bureau, approximately sixty-six percent of the American population is of non-Hispanic Caucasian ancestry, a demographic that possesses a similar genetic background to that of the majority of the population of modern England. The English language spoken in both countries, while subject to various regional inflections and expressions, is very similar. Since Cooke's letter in 1946, the United States and Great Britain have been significant trade partners, as well as allies in foreign military actions such as the conflict in Iraq. Two notable pairs of American president and English Prime Minister (Ronald Reagan and Margaret Thatcher, George W. Bush and Tony Blair) have enjoyed very close personal and political relations in the period since 1980. With the possible exception of the relationship of the United States with Canada, it is clear that the American/British connection has remained remarkably vibrant as the world's political structure has become more fractured.

Cooke observed in 1946 that there was a sentiment held by many Americans that it was impossible to be distinguished and to sound American at the same time. Implicit in this sentiment is the perception that Americans then felt the need for a form of endorsement from a settled nation such as England before

American opinions could be taken at face value. With the speed that information can be disseminated today, and the resultant availability of learned commentaries from every corner of the world and from persons of diverse backgrounds, it is likely that this sentiment as expressed by Cooke has less resonance today.

Sixty years later immigration and immigrants have taken on an entirely different character in America, yet Cooke's observations about the relationship between the existing population and its newcomers remain apt. In 2006, official estimates regarding the number of illegal immigrants to the United States ranged form 11 million to 13 million persons. Unlike the post-World War II Italian family, these immigrants are often persons of color who identify not with the mainstream of American society, but their identifiable segment of that society. These issues are compounded by the specter of home-grown terrorism raised since the September 11, 2001 attacks.

Since the 1950s, the American population has grown from 151 million to over 300 million people living in the United States as of 2006. Growth in the Asian (currently four percent of the population) and Hispanic communities (fourteen percent of the population) between 2006 and 2050 is expected to represent the bulk of the expansion of the American population. Cooke's implicit melting pot analysis could not have foreseen the growth of both groups, each with a non-English language heritage.

FURTHER RESOURCES
Books

Brownstone, David, and Irene M. Franck. *Facts about American Immigration*. New York: H. W. Wilson, 2002.

Ueda, Reed, ed. *A Companion to American Immigration*. Boston: Blackwell Publishing, 2006.

Web sites

Glendon, Mary Ann. "Principled Immigration." *Harvard Law School*, May 25, 2006. <http://www.law.harvard.edu/news/2006/05/25_glendon.php> (accessed June 6, 2006).

New February Activities Focus on Black History Importance

Newspaper article

By: Rollie Atkinson

Date: February 14, 1976

Source: Atkinson, Rollie. "New February Activities Focus on Black History Importance." *The News* (February 14, 1976).

About the Author: Rollie Atkinson was a staff writer for the *News*, a newspaper for Frederick County, Maryland, that is now known as the *Frederick News-Post*.

INTRODUCTION

The year 2006 marks the eightieth anniversary of black history celebrations. In February 1926, Harvard-trained historian Carter G. Woodson (1875–1950) introduced the annual Negro History Week. Woodson hoped to promote pride within the black community and to foster more awareness and appreciation of African Americans and their contributions to society. Racism was widespread and blatant from the late 1800s to the mid-1900s. From 1890 to 1925, one black American was lynched every 2.5 days. (Lynching is an act in which a mob of citizens execute someone, usually by hanging, without due process of law.) Against the backdrop of extreme prejudice and pervasive stereotyping of black Americans as inferior citizens, Woodson sought to portray black Americans in a more complex and humane manner.

Negro History Week was an opportunity for people to learn about and reflect on the achievements of black men and women. It was also a time for the affirmation of goals and dreams. For mainstream America, it was an opportunity to look beyond the common caricatures of poverty and hopelessness to more realistic representations of family and faith.

This celebration became more popular in the 1940s. With the aid of "negro history kits," photos and posters, social and civic groups held lectures, rallies, and other events. In the 1960s, Negro History Week became Black History Month. Black History Month continues today as an annual celebration held

Teenagers in Birmingham, Alabama begin a segregation protest march that ended in them being sprayed by high-pressure hoses and attacked by snapping police dogs on national television, May 4, 1963. © BETTMANN/CORBIS.

in February. In turn, this observance has generated other explorations of American history such as Asian American Month (April), National Hispanic Heritage Month (mid-September to mid-October), Native American Heritage Month (November), and Women's History Month (March).

It was a common misconception eighty years ago that black people had no history worth studying. Today, during Black History Month, books, documentaries, television programs, and other media on the subject abound. Furthermore, African American history is now regarded as a respectable academic undertaking for historians and scholars alike. Scholars continue to debate, however, whether the social, psychological, and economic advances Woodson hoped for have been achieved. At the beginning of the twenty-first century, academics and historians wonder whether Black History Month is still relevant today.

PRIMARY SOURCE

For all of this week and the remainder of February special focus will be given to black history.

Why black history?

Black history, the study of events and people which together comprise the heritage and culture of Afro-Americans, for one-and-a-half centuries was largely ignored, maligned and forgotten. "To know where we are going we must know from where we came," is how one local black explains the importance of black history.

The Association for the Study of Negro Life and History first celebrated Negro History Week in February 1926. Now Black History Week, the occasion is held annually during the week of February containing both Abraham Lincoln's and black abolitionist Frederick Douglass's birthdates.

In past years, Frederick's NAACP organization has always led in coordinating Black History Week projects. This year, however, NAACP president Lord Nickens saw that other local groups were interested enough in black history to organize their own activities.

Several programs have been scheduled at Fort Detrick and Fort Ritchie and in addition to planned classroom topics throughout county schools, local high schools sponsored black history programs and displays this week.

This Sunday in the Ft. Detrick Chapel (building No. 924) a Fellowship program will feature the "Echoneers" of Baltimores First Apostolic Faith Institutional Church.

Later this month on the 28th a soul disco dance will be held in further observance of Black History Month in Ft. Detrick's NCO Club. Ft. Detrick also sponsored a youth talent show, soul food dinner and presentation by Mary Carter Smith, well-known African folklorist.

The February issue of *Frederick Foundations,* The *News-Post*'s monthly Bicentennial supplement, will feature the history of blacks and other minorities.

For a long time, prior to the 20th century, there was little interest in preserving black history. Only recently has much significant black history been uncovered.

Old records mostly ignored and left out mention of blacks. They were not considered citizens as Frederick's own Roger Brooke Taney decreed in his famous Dred Scott Decision as Chief Justice of the U.S. Supreme Court. A black was mentioned in official documents only as a piece of property along with cattle and furnishings for tax purposes or when they were given or able to buy their freedom.

A Frederick County document of the 1860s lists nearly 100 pages of names of freed slaves after the Civil War and passage of the 14th Amendment. The Book of Freed Negroes is now in the hands of the Maryland Hall of Records in Annapolis.

William O. Lee a local black who has collected Frederick black history claims that the first record of a Mack in Frederick was made in 1743 when Lord Baltimore made a land grant to a John Dorsey for a land parcel west of the Linganore Creek.

Official history, collected by whites, does not list the race of Dorsey but Lee claims, "The Mack people of New Market remember that he was black." Near the beginning of the Civil War, recorded history tells the story, of a former slave Greensburg Barton who bought land three miles east of Frederick on the eastern bank of the Monocacy River.

As other blacks moved to this area the community of Bartonsville grew up. In Frederick, it was not until shortly before 1920 that blacks were given the right to vote. While several local civic organizations for blacks were begun at about this time blacks still found it difficult to get their names in public accounts and records.

Reports of an active Ku Klux Klan in the vicinity and several actual raids and threatened lynchings served to deter blacks from speaking out too loudly. Progress and equality came begrudgingly to local blacks who in recent years following the Civil Rights crusade of Dr. Martin Luther King and others now share with whites in many more equal opportunities.

SIGNIFICANCE

When Dr. Carter G. Woodson set out to share and publicize the rich history of African Americans, he unwittingly played a role in a revolution in American history. Around the same time black Americans were being persecuted and lynched, Native Americans were being relocated and driven off their land by the U.S. government. While black Americans were enduring segregation and Jim Crow, American women were fighting for equal rights as well as the right to vote. Black history is one thread of American history that was buried. Historians acknowledge that uncovering black history has enriched the tradition of American history and sparked others to research their history as well. Black history month sparked historical recovery on a number of fronts and has contributed to a more accurate and complex depiction of America.

Integrating black history into the framework of formal education is the next big step, according to Roger Wilkins, professor of history at George Mason University in Virginia:

> I'm old enough to remember how history was taught…. And in Grand Rapids, Michigan, I was taught white history. When I graduated from high school, if you believed everything that our teachers told us, you would have thought that no black person had done anything useful in the history of the world. And then, although I love the University of Michigan, I went there for seven years, and I was never assigned a book, a play, a poem or an essay written by a black person. I never had a black professor; never had a female professor, either, for that matter.

Historians agree that a more concerted effort is needed to move black history away from a segregated celebration into a more inclusive celebration of American history. In fact, historians are attempting to add other missing and uncovered histories to the discourse and celebration of American history, including Native American history, Asian American history, women's history, and others. The next step is the scholarly integration of each of these disciplines into the study of American history as a whole.

FURTHER RESOURCES

Books

Willis, Deborah. *Reflections in Black: A History of Black Photographers, 1840 to the Present.* New York: W. W. Norton, 2000.

Periodicals

Considine, Austin. "Black History Month Events: A Slice of American History." *New York Times* (February 3, 2006).

Crowder, Ralph L. "Historical Significance of Black History Month." *Black History Bulletin* (January 1, 2002).

Wells, Barry S. "Why We Celebrate Black History Month." *The Post-Standard* (February 17, 2002).

Reagan Signs into Law National Holiday

Newspaper article

By: Anonymous

Date: November 3, 1983

Source: "Reagan Signs into Law National Holiday." *The Post-Standard* (November 3, 1983).

About the Author: This article was contributed by a staff writer for the *Post-Standard*, a newspaper serving the city of Syracuse, New York, and its surrounding localities. The author is unknown.

INTRODUCTION

American clergyman and civil rights leader Martin Luther King, Jr. (1929–1968) held that all citizens of the United States—and all peoples of the world—should have equal rights. He stated that all Americans should have the right to work, pursue an education, and use all the facilities available in the United States. King held the ideal that only peaceful (nonviolent) means should be used to settle disagreements.

King became a minister like his father and grandfather. He married Coretta Scott after both had attended college in Boston, Massachusetts. The couple then moved to Montgomery, Alabama. King hoped to help peacefully settle the racial problems the community was having between African Americans and whites. In 1955, King led a lengthy protest against busing laws in Montgomery after African-American civil rights activist Rosa Parks (1913–2005) was arrested for refusing to give up her seat to a white man while riding a city bus. Over the next few years, King led peaceful protests to change existing laws that barred African Americans from using public facilities and services reserved for white Americans, such as drinking fountains, eating establishments, and restrooms. In 1963, King led a March on Washington, D.C. in which he gave his famous *I Have a Dream* speech. In 1964, King was awarded the Nobel Peace Prize.

On April 4, 1968, King was assassinated in Memphis, Tennessee, after leading a rally for African American sanitation workers who were protesting inequitable wages with comparable white workers.

After King's death, support grew to establish a day to honor his activism with regard to civil rights. Coretta Scott King staged the first observance of King's birthday. Representative John Conyers (D–Michigan) first introduced a Congressional bill to establish a national

President Ronald Reagan signs a bill making Martin Luther King Jr.'s birthday a national holiday, November 2, 1983. King's widow, Coretta Scott King, looks on (second from left). © CORBIS.

holiday in honor of Martin Luther King, Jr. When the bill failed, six million signatures were submitted to the U.S. Congress in support of the holiday. Conyers and Representative Shirley Chisholm (D–New York) resubmitted the Congressional bill several times. The 1982 and 1983 civil rights marches in Washington, D.C. added urgency and additional pressures on members of Congress to pass the bill.

In November 1983, President Ronald Reagan signed a bill declaring that the third Monday of every January, beginning in 1986, would be celebrated as a national holiday, named Martin Luther King, Jr. Day. The day occurs each year around the time of King's birth on January 15. The first observance of Martin Luther King, Jr. Day was January 20, 1986. Beginning in 2000, the day became an official national holiday in all fifty states.

■ PRIMARY SOURCE

REAGAN SIGNS INTO LAW NATIONAL HOLIDAY

With Martin Luther King's widow at his side, President Reagan signed legislation Wednesday he once opposed that honors the slain civil rights leader with a national holiday each year. Reagan said King had "stirred our nation to the very depths of its soul" in battling racial discrimination.

Congressional leaders and veterans of the civil rights movement, including Jesse Jackson, the Rev. Ralph Abernathy and Atlanta Mayor Andrew Young, filled the Rose Garden for the signing ceremony.

The proceedings climaxed as the crowd softly sang "We Shall Overcome"—the anthem of King's nonviolent crusade against segregation.

His widow, Coretta Scott King, told the crowd, "America is a more democratic nation, a more just nation, a more peaceful nation because Martin Luther King became her pre-eminent non-violent commander."

While saying the nation had made huge strides in civil rights, Reagan declared, "traces of bigotry still mar America."

He said King's holiday should serve as reminder to follow the principles that King espoused: "Thou shalt love thy god with all they heart, and thou shalt love thy neighbor as thyself."

Recalling Kings' historic address to 250,000 people at the Lincoln Memorial in 1963, at the height of civil rights battles, Reagan said:

"If American history grows from two centuries to 29, his words that day will never be forgotten: 'I have a dream that one day on the red hills of Georgia, the sons of former slaves and the sons of former slave owners will be able to sit down together at the table of brotherhood."

The legislation makes the third Monday in January a legal public holiday, beginning in 1986.

For the day of the signing ceremony, at least, civil rights leaders put aside their policy differences with the administration and their anger over Reagan's earlier opposition to honoring him with a national holiday.

"Well, we've all had high and low moments, and this is one of his high moments," said Jackson, an outspoken Reagan critic and newly announced candidate for the Democratic presidential nomination.

Jackson said the only thing that mattered was Reagan's signature on the bill.

"The effect is that the civil rights movement and its place in American history is institutionalized, and that's very significant." Jackson said.

Reagan originally had expressed concern over the cost of honoring King with a national holiday, and said he would have preferred a day of recognition.

At a news conference October. 19, Reagan said he decided to sign the legislation "since they (congress) seem bent on making it a national holiday." At that same session, Reagan publicly speculated on whether secret FBI files would show that King was a Communist sympathizer. For that remark, the resident later apologized to Mrs. King.

Reagan also wrote former New Hampshire Gov. Meldrin Thomson that the public's perception of King was "based on an image, not reality."

Mrs. King told reporters she had accepted Reagan's apology for his news conference remark. As for his letter to Thomson, she said, "I am not questioning motives at this point. I think we have to accept what people say, and then we watch what they do."

White House deputy press secretary Larry Speakes noted Reagan's apology to Mrs. King and said, "I don't think a day like today calls for discussion from us on that kind of controversy."

SIGNIFICANCE

The actions of Martin Luther King, Jr. in leading nonviolent protests against racial discrimination and segregation in the United States during the 1950s and 1960s played an important role in persuading many Americans of all races and backgrounds to support the cause of civil rights. After his death, the struggle for racial justice continued. King became a symbol to people who were discriminated against because of their race. His life symbolized the courage and perseverance that one person can maintain when believing wrongs had been committed by one race onto another race of people. His death symbolized the extremes that one person must sometimes go to in order to stand up for deep-rooted moral and ethical principles.

The Martin Luther King, Jr. Memorial Center (or sometimes simply called The King Center) is a research institute located in Atlanta, Georgia, within the Martin Luther King, Jr. National Historic Site. King's birthplace, the Ebenezer Baptist Church, and King's final resting place are also located within the grounds. The King Center was established to memorialize King, to promote his teachings, and to preserve his papers and historical documents.

The lectures, speeches, and dialogues that King used in thirteen years of civil rights activities united a generation of Americans to make significant improvements in U.S. society. He inspired many people with his charismatic leadership skills, courage, and devotion to a cause that eventually ended his life. King's actions, words, and commitment gave hope and direction to African Americans and the poor in the United States and to disadvantaged people throughout the world.

Martin Luther King, Jr. Day is observed each year as a day to emphasize the principles that King believed are important in the United States and throughout the world. Among those principles are nonviolent direct action, peace, rational and nondestructive social change, volunteerism, social justice, and class and racial equity. The holiday is an observance of the life and legacy of Martin Luther King, Jr. The day honors the man who is known as one of the greatest American leaders of racial equality and justice. As Coretta Scott King stated in a biography of her husband, "This is not a black holiday; it is a peoples' holiday. And it is the young people of all races and religions who hold the keys to the fulfillment of this dream."

FURTHER RESOURCES
Books

I Have a Dream: Martin Luther King, Jr. and the Future of Multicultural America, edited by James Echols. Minneapolis, Minn.: Fortress Press, 2004.

King, Jr., Martin Luther. Strength to Love. New York: Harper and Row, 1963.

———. Stride Toward Freedom. New York: Harper and Row, 1958.

———. *Why We Can't Wait*. New York: Harper and Row, 1963.

Kotz, Nick. *The Judgment Days: Lyndon Baines Johnson, Martin Luther King, Jr., and the Laws That Changed America*. Boston: Houghton Mifflin, 2005.

Ling, Peter J. *Martin Luther King, Jr.* New York: Routledge, 2002.

Web sites

Coretta Scott King, The King Center. "The Meaning of the Martin Luther King, Jr. Holiday." <http://www.thekingcenter.org/holiday/index.asp> (accessed June 28, 2006).

The King Center. <http://www.thekingcenter.org/index.asp> (accessed June 28, 2006).

Canadian Multiculturalism Act

Legislation

By: Government of Canada

Date: July 21, 1988

Source: "Canadian Multiculturalism Act." R.S., 1985 c. 24 (4th Supplement), as amended through 2002. Government of Canada, 2002.

About the Author: The legislative power of the Canadian government is vested in its Parliament, an entity composed of an elected House of Commons and an appointed Senate. When proposed legislation has been passed by both parliamentary bodies, the enactment becomes law upon receiving Royal Assent, a largely symbolic process of confirmation carried out by the Governor General or their designate.

INTRODUCTION

The passage of the Canadian Multiculturalism Act in 1988 represented a confirmation of the approach taken to cultural diversity in Canada since the country had begun to encourage wholesale immigration from nontraditional sources in the 1960s.

Unlike the neighboring United States, where its initial racial diversity occurred through the emancipation of its African American slave class before and after the Civil War (1861–1865), Canada was established as a multicultural society from the time of the capture of the French colony of Quebec by the British in 1759. British North America, as the English colony in Canada became known, was governed as a single political unit with distinct English and French communities.

British colonial authorities did not seek to assimilate the French population of British North America, nor did Britain engage in a involuntary resettlement of the French as it had done with the Acadians of the eastern Canadian coast that Britain relocated to Louisiana between 1775 and 1778. The British North American administrators permitted the French language, culture, and the practice of the Roman Catholic faith in what is now the Canadian province of Quebec through the entire British colonial period. While the colonial relationship between the English and the French was often fractious, there was never any serious effort to assimilate French culture into that of the English majority. When Canada was granted independence from Britain in 1867, the French and English peoples of Canada were explicitly recognized as the two founding peoples of the country. It is this cultural duality that is the foundation to all subsequent Canadian immigration policies.

The French and English communities have remained the dominant cultural forces in Canada. The relationship between the province of Quebec and English Canada was often referred to as "the two solitudes," where there was an absence of outright conflict but little integration of the two cultures, notwithstanding government policies such as bilingualism in the federal government service.

The dual-nation cultural structure of Canada after 1867 did not encourage liberal immigration practices in relation to peoples of other racial or ethnic backgrounds. Canada acted vigorously to exclude Chinese workers after the trans-continental railway was completed through the use of a significant proportion of Chinese labor in 1885. Canada explicitly encouraged northern Europeans to take up farming on the Canadian prairies after 1900 in preference to other races and nationalities. Canada also interned over 22,000 males of Japanese ancestry during the Second World War: Canada did not intern persons of German or Italian origin during the course of the conflict.

In the post Second World War period, Canada accepted a large number of persons who had been displaced from their European homelands. Canada also encouraged the immigration of northern Europeans, particularly British and Dutch persons during this period.

The federal government moved to a more liberal immigration policy in the 1960s, and Canada's racial and ethnic diversity expanded to embrace a multitude of cultures. The 1982 enshrinement of the primary document of the Canadian constitution, the Charter of Rights and Freedoms, elevated the concept of

French general and president Charles De Gaulle arrives in Quebec, Canada, on July 23, 1964, to a crowd of people carrying signs calling for a Free Quebec. In a speech the next day De Gallue would famously declare "Long live free Quebec." © ALAIN NOGUES/CORBIS SYGMA.

Canadian multiculturalism to an entrenched constitutional principle.

In 1988, Canada enjoyed an international reputation as a nation with one of the most liberal immigration policies in the world. The Multiculturalism Act confirmed Canada's ongoing commitment to the promotion of ethnic and cultural diversity.

PRIMARY SOURCE

CANADIAN MULTICULTURALISM ACT
MULTICULTURALISM POLICY OF CANADA

3. (1) It is hereby declared to be the policy of the Government of Canada to

   (a) recognize and promote the understanding that multiculturalism reflects the cultural and racial diversity of Canadian society and acknowledge the freedom of all members of Canadian society to preserve, enhance and share their cultural heritage;

   (b) recognize and promote the understanding that multiculturalism is a fundamental characteristic of the Canadian heritage and identity and that it provides an invaluable resource in the shaping of Canada's future;

   (c) promote the full and equitable participation of individuals and communities of all origins in the continuing evolution and shaping of all aspects of Canadian society and assist them in the elimination of any barrier to that participation;

   (d) recognize the existence of communities whose members share a common origin and their historic contribution to Canadian society, and enhance their development;

   (e) ensure that all individuals receive equal treatment and equal protection under the law, while respecting and valuing their diversity;

   (f) encourage and assist the social, cultural, economic and political institutions of Canada to be both respectful and inclusive of Canada's multicultural character;

   (g) promote the understanding and creativity that arise from the interaction between individuals and communities of different origins;

(h) foster the recognition and appreciation of the diverse cultures of Canadian society and promote the reflection and the evolving expressions of those cultures;

(i) preserve and enhance the use of languages other than English and French, while strengthening the status and use of the official languages of Canada; and

(j) advance multiculturalism throughout Canada in harmony with the national commitment to the official languages of Canada.

(2) It is further declared to be the policy of the Government of Canada that all federal institutions shall

(a) ensure that Canadians of all origins have an equal opportunity to obtain employment and advancement in those institutions;

(b) promote policies, programs and practices that enhance the ability of individuals and communities of all origins to contribute to the continuing evolution of Canada;

(c) promote policies, programs and practices that enhance the understanding of and respect for the diversity of the members of Canadian society;

(d) collect statistical data in order to enable the development of policies, programs and practices that are sensitive and responsive to the multicultural reality of Canada;

(e) make use, as appropriate, of the language skills and cultural understanding of individuals of all origins; and

(f) generally, carry on their activities in a manner that is sensitive and responsive to the multicultural reality of Canada.

IMPLEMENTATION OF THE MULTICULTURALISM POLICY OF CANADA

4. The Minister, in consultation with other ministers of the Crown, shall encourage and promote a coordinated approach to the implementation of the multiculturalism policy of Canada and may provide advice and assistance in the development and implementation of programs and practices in support of the policy.

5. (1) The Minister shall take such measures as the Minister considers appropriate to implement the multiculturalism policy of Canada and, without limiting the generality of the foregoing, may

(a) encourage and assist individuals, organizations and institutions to project the multicultural reality of Canada in their activities in Canada and abroad;

(b) undertake and assist research relating to Canadian multiculturalism and foster scholarship in the field;

(c) encourage and promote exchanges and cooperation among the diverse communities of Canada;

(d) encourage and assist the business community, labour organizations, voluntary and other private organizations, as well as public institutions, in ensuring full participation in Canadian society, including the social and economic aspects, of individuals of all origins and their communities, and in promoting respect and appreciation for the multicultural reality of Canada;

(e) encourage the preservation, enhancement, sharing and evolving expression of the multicultural heritage of Canada;

(f) facilitate the acquisition, retention and use of all languages that contribute to the multicultural heritage of Canada;

(g) assist ethno-cultural minority communities to conduct activities with a view to overcoming any discriminatory barrier and, in particular, discrimination based on race or national or ethnic origin;

(h) provide support to individuals, groups or organizations for the purpose of preserving, enhancing and promoting multiculturalism in Canada; and

(i) undertake such other projects or programs in respect of multiculturalism, not by law assigned to any other federal institution, as are designed to promote the multiculturalism policy of Canada.

(2) The Minister may enter into an agreement or arrangement with any province respecting the implementation of the multiculturalism policy of Canada.

(3) The Minister may, with the approval of the Governor in Council, enter into an agreement or arrangement with the government of any foreign state in order to foster the multicultural character of Canada.

6. (1) The ministers of the Crown, other than the Minister, shall, in the execution of their respective mandates, take such measures as they consider appropriate to implement the multiculturalism policy of Canada.

(2) A minister of the Crown, other than the Minister, may enter into an agreement or arrangement with any province respecting the implementation of the multiculturalism policy of Canada.

7. (1) The Minister may establish an advisory committee to advise and assist the Minister on the implementation of this Act and any other matter relating to multiculturalism and, in consultation with such organizations representing multicultural interests as the Minister deems appropriate, may appoint the members and designate the chairman and other officers of the committee.

(2) Each member of the advisory committee shall be paid such remuneration for the member's services as may be fixed by the Minister and is entitled to be paid the reasonable travel and living expenses incurred by the member while absent from the member's ordinary place of residence in connection with the work of the committee.

(3) The chairman of the advisory committee shall, within four months after the end of each fiscal year, submit to the Minister a report on the activities of the committee for that year and on any other matter relating to the implementation of the multiculturalism policy of Canada that the chairman considers appropriate.

GENERAL

8. The Minister shall cause to be laid before each House of Parliament, not later than the fifth sitting day of that House after January 31 next following the end of each fiscal year, a report on the operation of this Act for that fiscal year.

9. The operation of this Act and any report made pursuant to section 8 shall be reviewed on a permanent basis by such committee of the House, of the Senate or of both Houses of Parliament as may be designated or established for the purpose.

SIGNIFICANCE

The sweeping language of the Multiculturalism Act of 1988 confirms why this legislation has been referred to as the high water mark of Canadian multiculturalism. The legislative intent evident from the words of the enactment must be assessed in light of the sequence of political and social events since its passage. Canada's cultural fabric has sustained significant pressure in the years since 1988 in a manner that has challenged the Canadian multicultural identity.

As with the United States and Australia, two other nations built through immigration, various political forces in Canada have opposed the promotion of cultural diversity at various periods. In the early 1960s, prime minister John Diefenbaker (1895–1979) attacked such diversity as representing "hyphenated Canadianism," where immigrant persons were encouraged to be something other than citizens of one Canada. The province of Quebec also resisted non-white immigration as a means of protecting its French culture from incursion; ironically, immigration from Haiti to Montreal created a large French-speaking, non-white community in that city.

The face of Canada changed quickly. In the period between 1967 and 2006, approximately ninety percent of all immigrants settled in urban centers, most of these in Toronto, Montreal, and Vancouver. The Greater Toronto Area, with its population of over 4.5 million people, is one of the most racially and ethnically diverse regions in the world. As an example, over 350,000 Muslims live in Toronto, a population that did not exist to any significant degree in 1967. There are an estimated 400,000 persons of Chinese heritage in the Toronto area, and federal projections suggest that one half of the Toronto population will be composed of visible minority persons by 2017.

With the rapid growth of immigrant communities, Toronto has been the focal point of numerous debates concerning racial and ethnic tolerance and diversity. A rising violent crime rate in Toronto during the 1990s revealed a disproportionate number of persons of color in conflict with the law. In addition, large segments of the population expressed concerns over the public costs associated with immigration, particularly health and social assistance benefits. This demographic debate sparked controversy over whether Canada was truly as welcoming to diversity as the Multiculturalism Act proclaimed.

The terrorist attacks of September 11, 2001 in the neighboring United States brought renewed attention to Canada's multiculturalism. American officials expressed particular concern that Canada's immigration policies created an environment where terrorists could take up residency in Canada for the purpose of organizing further attacks upon American targets. The highest levels of the United States government criticized Canadian immigration and border security as an indirect threat to American homeland security, urging Canada to tighten its immigration procedures.

The issue as to whether Canada is a de facto refuge for anti-American terrorists prompted strong domestic sentiments to be expressed concerning modern Canadian multiculturalism. Many Canadians, particularly members of the different immigrant groups who had come to Canada within the previous thirty years, urged the Canadian government to continue to promote racial and cultural diversity; Canada's population growth from twenty million people in 1967 to the 2006 census estimate of over thirty million people is attributable largely to immigration. In June, 2006, the arrest of seventeen alleged Muslim terrorists in the Toronto area, most of whom were persons born in Canada to immigrant parents of Middle Eastern origins, re-kindled this issue.

The Multiculturalism Act expressly provides that racial and cultural diversity is a fundamental characteristic of the Canadian heritage; equal protection and treatment under the law are implicit to such protections. A debate in the province of Ontario arose in 2005 regarding the Muslim religious law known as *sharia* and whether these laws could be enforced in Muslim communities in Ontario in substitution for the civil law. Proponents of *sharia* pointed to the principles of multiculturalism and equality enshrined in the Act and in the Charter of Rights.

In a unique aspect of Canadian criminal law, aboriginal persons convicted of a crime may take be entitled to be judged according to the decision of a sentencing circle, where representatives of the aboriginal community—not an appointed judge—determine the appropriate sentence to be imposed. The sentencing circle is recognition on the part of the Canadian justice system that the issues faced by aboriginal offenders require a different approach, one consistent with the philosophy of both the Multiculturalism Act and the Charter of Rights and Freedoms.

FURTHER RESOURCES

Books

Barry, Brian. *Culture and Equality: An Egalitarian View of Multiculturalism*. Cambridge, Mass.: Harvard University Press, 2002.

Bissoonath, Neil. *Selling Illusions: The Cult of Multiculturalism in Canada*. Toronto: Penguin Canada, 2002.

Periodicals

Kealey, Linda. "Letters in Canada / Who Killed Canadian History?" *University of Toronto Quarterly* 69 (1999/2000).

Bilingual Education: A Critique

Essay excerpt

By: Peter Duignan

Date: 1992

Source: *The Hoover Institution*. "Bilingual Education: A Critique." <http://www.hoover.org/publications/he/2896386.html?show=essay> (accessed July 9, 2006).

About the Author: Peter J. Duignan is a senior fellow at the Hoover Institution on War, Revolution and Peace at Stanford University. The Hoover Institution is a public policy research center devoted to the study of politics, economics, and political economy. Peter J. Duignan has extensive experience researching and writing in a wide range of domestic and international policy areas. His areas of expertise include immigration to the United States and Hispanics in the United States.

INTRODUCTION

The essay "Bilingual Education: A Critique" highlights the impact that recent waves of non-English-speaking immigrants have had on the educational system in the United States and how approaches to the education of non-English-speaking children have changed over time. Although this excerpt focuses on the period from 1986 onwards, there has been a fierce debate in the United States about bilingual education ever since it was introduced in the 1960s. The Bilingual Education Act of 1968 first required states to provide education in the first languages of Limited English Proficient (LEP) children for one year, at which stage it was considered they should be sufficiently proficient in English to transfer into mainstream English-language education. The legislation was underpinned by research evidence from a 1953 UNESCO study that indicated that immigrant children who were initially educated in their native language did better at school than those who were taught in the language of their new country from their arrival in the educational system.

During the 1970s, however, the nature of bilingual education in the United States changed, partly in response to the landmark *Lau v. Nichols* case of 1974, in which it was ruled that non-English-speaking Chinese students in San Francisco were being denied access to and participation in educational programs since all the teaching and teaching materials were in English. Following this case, the Supreme Court ruled that school districts should be required to take "affirmative steps" to address the language issues that prevented non-English-speaking children from having equal access to educational programs. From this point onwards, bilingual education was no longer employed primarily as a transitional measure to ease LEP students into mainstream education; it became a parallel scheme offering ongoing education in native languages. It was also increasingly seen as a tool to promote multiculturalism in American society. The growing importance of and federal funding for bilingual education programs was largely the result of political lobbying by influential immigrant groups such as Hispanic Americans, who argued that the reasons for the low educational attainment and high drop-out rate of their children included their difficulties in English and various ways in which they were discriminated against in the mainstream education system.

In 1986, the Legalization Program of the Immigration Reform and Control Act provided amnesty for many thousands of undocumented residents, mostly from Mexico and other Latin American countries, and swelled the school population with non-English-speaking children. Federal

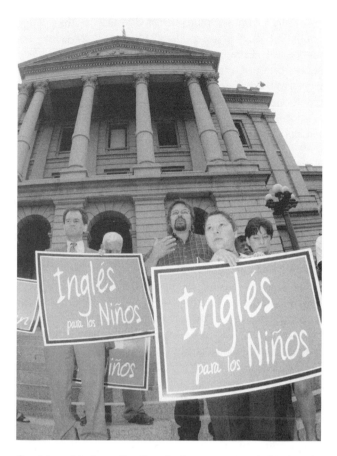

Guadalupe Martinez (front) and other protestors hold signs in front of the state capitol in Denver. They are opposed to mandatory bilingual education for Spanish speaking students, preferring that children have the option to be placed in English immersion classes, 2001. AP IMAGES.

funding was provided for numerous bilingual education programs across the country, especially in states and cities with large numbers of immigrant families. Between 1985 and 1990, the number of LEP students in U.S. schools reportedly increased by fifty-one percent, with around three-quarters believed to be Spanish-speaking. By the late 1990s, at least five percent of all public school children in grades K–12 were LEP students.

Since its inception, there has never been any consensus about the value of bilingual education for non-English-speaking students. Those in favor of bilingual education argue that it enables immigrant children to keep up with their English-speaking peers, particularly in subjects such as mathematics and science. Critics of the system believe that it delays the development of proficiency in English and can have an adverse impact on

successful assimilation into American society. The findings of research into the benefits of bilingual education have been inconclusive but have provided some evidence of higher educational achievement among those LEP students who did receive some bilingual education.

Bilingual education has also become controversial for other reasons, closely tied in with the wider immigration debate. While multiculturalists have supported it as a way of helping immigrant groups to retain their language and cultural identity, the anti-immigration movement has argued that immigrants already in the United States should be required to learn English and assimilate into American culture. Many resent the use of federal funding for immigrant education programs, while even within the immigrant population there have been arguments about the relative allocation of funding among ethnic groups.

PRIMARY SOURCE

Bilingual education since 1986 The legalization of illegal immigrants in 1986 brought millions of Asians and Spanish speakers to the United States. Schools became more crowded in big cities that had large Spanish-speaking populations. The flood of illegals continued as well, further inundating the schools and public services.

In the previous peak years of immigration (1900–1910), the old immigrants, however diverse, all derived from the Judeo-Christian tradition. The new immigrants include not only Hispanics, but also Muslims, Confucians, Buddhists, adherents of Shinto, and votaries of Voodoo. Given such cultural multiplicity, and bilingualism and cultural maintenance programs—anti-immigrationists argue—the United States may split linguistically and spiritually in future.

Immigration has had numerous unintended consequences. The old-style immigrant was usually a European. Since 1965, the new-style immigrant mostly comes from Asian, Latin American, or Caribbean countries whose political and social traditions greatly differ from those of the United States. The new immigrants (much like previous immigrants), moreover, have higher birth-rates than the natives. Hence immigrants have a disproportionately powerful impact on the United States' demographic composition and school population. The post-1970 population growth, according to demographer Leon F. Bouvier, is nearly all due to immigration. (Immigrants now account for 37.1 percent of all new population growth, compared with 27 percent at the peak years of immigration.)

Does this matter? Did not the United States, in the olden days, successfully absorb Irish, Germans, Poles, and many other nationalities? True enough, argue the anti-immigrationists. But the position has changed. In the late nineteenth and early twentieth centuries, the United States had a confident core culture. The United States insisted that newcomers should assimilate and learn English—and so they did; there was little or no bilingual education. By contrast, the new immigrants come at a time when the cultural self-reliance of the United States has eroded. Mexican and Asian activists have learned from the civil rights struggles conducted by black Americans and thus demand bilingual education and seek group rights, "brown pride," and restoration of "brown dignity," while rejecting assimilation and Western culture. The new immigrants, or rather their self-appointed spokespeople, now desire official recognition as groups and proportional representation—requirements incompatible with the operation of a free market. Group rights are demanded in the makeup of electoral districts, in employment, in the awarding of official contracts, in education, in every sphere of public life. Opposition to such programs, it is falsely claimed, is yet one more proof of white America's inherent racism.

Multiculturists want to preserve immigrant cultures and languages, not absorb or assimilate the American culture. (The melting-pot metaphor is rejected by multiculturists.) The United States, the anti-immigration argument continues, therefore must restrict immigration and at the same time promote cultural assimilation. Otherwise multiculturalism will lead to political fragmentation and disaster. Imagine the United States as a Bosnia of continental proportions—without a sense of common nationhood, a common language and culture, a common political heritage, with dozens of contending ethnic groups and a population of half a billion! These problems will become even harder to face because immigration has exacerbated income inequalities within the United States, worsened the economic prospects of poorly educated black Americans and recent Hispanic immigrants, disrupted local communities, and—through sheer force of numbers—further injured the environment. The United States, argue critics such as Peter Brimelow, will in the long run cease to be a mainly white nation; its ethnic character will be transformed—this without proper policy discussion and against the declared will of America's overwhelming majority. Nativists are accused of hysteria when they talk about a threatened Mexican *reconquista* of California. Nativists incur equal censure when they charge foreign-born activists with scorning the *anglo-sajones* and their values. But nativist fears merely reflect the ethnic propaganda common in campus rallies held by ethnic militants.

Critics of immigration such as Brimelow (*Alien Nation*) doubt that assimilation can work today as it once did. The number of Hispanic immigrants is growing; affirmative action, bilingual education, and multiculturalism are roadblocks to assimilation and Americanization. The new immigrants are less well educated than previous immigrants, are not forced to learn English, and enter a labor market ill equipped for well-paying jobs. Wages for the unskilled have actually declined in the 1980s and 1990s, and new illegal immigrants will work for lower wages, thus replacing earlier immigrants.

In the field of public education the Americanizing of immigrant children has fallen into disrepute. The method of teaching English by the immersion method has been widely replaced by bilingual education (now required by nine states in all school districts with a designated number of limited-English-proficient [LEP] students). In Massachusetts, twenty LEP students in one language group in a district will trigger native-language instruction, even if there are only two students in each grade in a separate classroom taught by a certified bilingual teacher. As a result, forty thousand students in fifty-one Massachusetts school districts received bilingual education in 1993–94. Spanish-speaking students, who represent more than half of the LEP population in Massachusetts, are taught to read and write Spanish and also are instructed in Spanish in other academic subjects. But thousands of Cape Verdeans are instructed in a pidgin Portuguese-Crioulo—though the majority do not know the language; indeed in Cape Verde only Portuguese is taught since Crioulo is a spoken language, not a written one. Teachers in Massachusetts had to invent and print up Crioulo materials. Such examples have intensified the debate on bilingual education.

A recent study by the National Research Council, however, found that the arguments in favor of bilingual education were based on a number of myths. There was no evidence of long-term advantages in teaching LEP children in their native language. Further, teaching these children to read in English first, not in their native language, did them no harm. In contrast, emphasizing cultural and ethnic differences in the classroom was counterproductive. It caused stereotyping, did not improve the self-esteem of minority children, and reinforced the differences of these children from the others. Nor was there any research support for the idea that teachers who were themselves members of minority groups were more effective than others who worked with children from those same groups. The study concluded that the U.S. Department of Education's management of bilingual education research had been a total failure, wasting hundreds of millions of dollars, using the research agenda for political purposes to justify a program that had not proven its worth, and keeping its research from educators who could use it to improve their school programs.

I agree with Charles L. Glenn, a bilingual specialist, who insists that there is no reason to spend more years searching for a "model" teaching program, while another generation of language-minority students is damaged by inferior schooling. And there is certainly no reason to put any future research in the hands of the Office of Bilingual Education and Minority Languages Affairs (OBEMLA).

I would leave considerable latitude to local authorities to determine their own needs in public education. But I reject "cultural maintenance" as a legitimate object of public education. U.S. citizens and residents alike have an indefeasible right to speak whatever language, and practice whatever customs they please in their own homes. But the aim of public education should be to assimilate the immigrants—not to preserve their status as cultural aliens. (Assimilation means to learn English, become part of American society, follow American laws, values, and institutions, and know American history—in short, become Americanized.) Bilingualism not only divides Americans but also limits Latinos' job and education opportunities because of their poor English and low graduation rates.

SIGNIFICANCE

By the late 1990s, there was increasing evidence that bilingual education was not achieving its objectives of improving the educational and economic performance of non-English-speaking immigrants such as Latinos. Some argued that the programs actually exacerbated the problems of such groups.

In 1998, the state of California abolished most of its bilingual education programs under Proposition 227 and replaced these with one-year English-immersion programs. Arizona followed suit in 2000 and Massachusetts in 2002. Under English-immersion programs, teaching is mainly in English, with the students' native language used only for the purpose of clarifying and explaining points. Although immigrant student test scores in California improved following Proposition 227, it has been argued that the improvements were due to factors unrelated to the abolition of bilingual education. A number of longitudinal studies have indicated that there is little difference in educational attainment between students who receive bilingual education and those who receive English-immersion education.

One of the main problems with bilingual education is that there has been a lack of adequately trained teachers and high-quality teaching materials, making it difficult to assess the impact of this type of education. Evaluations of bilingual programs are also complicated by a range of factors such as immigrant segregation into disadvantaged areas and schools.

FURTHER RESOURCES
Books
Brisk, Maria Estela. *Bilingual Education: From Compensatory to Quality Schooling*. Mahwah, N.J.: Lawrence Erlbaum Associates, 1998.

Periodicals
Gersten, Russell and John Woodward. "The Language-Minority Student and Special Education: Issues, Trends, and Paradoxes." *Exceptional Children* 60 (2000).

Mora, Marie T. "English-Language Assistance Programs, English-Skill Acquisition and the Academic Progress of High School Language Minority Students." *Policy Studies Journal* 28 (2000).

Web sites
The Hoover Institution. "Bilingual Education: A Critique." <http://www.hoover.org/publications/he/2896386.html?show=essay> (accessed July 9, 2006).

History of Bilingual Education

Photograph

By: Jeffry W. Myers

Date: 1994

Source: Corbis Corporation

About the Photographer: Jeffry M. Myers is a photographer and an author based in Seattle, Washington. This photograph is a part of the collection maintained by Corbis Corporation, a worldwide provider of visual content materials to such communications groups as advertisers, broadcasters, designers, magazines, and newspapers.

INTRODUCTION

In the United States, bilingual education includes any form of instruction in the nation's school systems where the English language is partnered with another language for classroom use. Bilingual education has a long history in the United

States, often mirroring the predominate immigration patterns of a particular era.

At the time of the foundation of the American nation prior to 1800, bilingual education was a highly localized matter. In 1839, the state of Ohio became the first jurisdiction to formally endorse a form of bilingual instruction, when the teaching of its large population of German immigrant schoolchildren in both the English and German languages was established in the state public education system.

Louisiana enacted similar legislation for the instruction of the children of its French-speaking population in 1847; the Cajuns, as the descendants of the Acadian immigrants to Louisiana were known, had been a part of the Louisiana population since the 1740s. The New Mexico Territory also passed a law permitting bilingual instruction in English and Spanish in 1850.

By 1900, twelve American states had a form of legislated bilingual public school education. There were also informal and localized bilingual educational programs, often organized by specific immigrant or religious groups, in many American cities at this time.

The move of the United States to a more isolationist stance in foreign relations was reflected in the national educational policies after 1918. Persons who did not speak English as a first language were often perceived as potentially disloyal and un-American. By 1925, most American states had allowed their bilingual education programs to fade away.

The changes in the composition of American society after World War II brought pressures upon the public education system to accommodate increasing numbers of students who did not speak English as their first language. Various studies of the performance of such students in English-only instructional environments tended to confirm that the American education system was not permitting these students to advance at the same rate as their classmates.

In 1968, the U.S. Congress enacted the first Bilingual Education Act. In 1973, the U.S. Supreme Court ruled in the *Lau v. Nichols* decision that schools are obligated to take sufficient steps to assist non-English-speaking students to overcome linguistic barriers in the classroom. The federal statute passed by the U.S. Congress in 1974, the Equal Educational Opportunities Act, provided a framework within which bilingual instruction could occur as an aspect of state-supported education.

At the time that this photograph was taken in Seattle in 1994, bilingual education was once again well established in many American school districts.

███ **PRIMARY SOURCE**

HISTORY OF BILINGUAL EDUCATION
See primary source image.

███ ████

SIGNIFICANCE

A crucial consequence of both the Equal Educational Opportunities Act and its application in various American states was the development of an accepted national standard as to what bilingual education actually means in practice. Although the standard can be articulated in different ways, most educational programs aimed at students whose first language is not English utilize a three-part approach.

The first part of the standard involves the use of a properly researched and tested program that ensures that students who have English as a second language have equal opportunities to succeed within the educational system. The second aspect of bilingual education is proper implementation of this instructional program. Adequate resources, including properly qualified teachers and appropriate instructional materials and supplies, must be provided to ensure the true implementation of the course of study. The third component of the standard is the existence of an ongoing monitoring system to assess the effectiveness of the bilingual program in preparing students for either further education or the workplace.

In a number of school districts, resolutions have been proposed that seek to remove various forms of bilingual educational programming from the school system. The best known of these resolutions was the 1998 Unz resolution in the state of California. The proponents of this resolution sought to replace bilingual education with a system known as English immersion, where students are required to take all classroom instruction in the English language regardless of their native language. Supporters of the Unz initiative pointed to studies suggesting that California students taught solely in English performed at least as well on standardized tests as did bilingual education students. These opponents of bilingual education also noted the additional costs required to provide bilingual instruction in public schools.

The passage of the Unz initiative in California, a state with a growing Spanish-speaking population, triggered similar voter initiatives in other states. The most significant political success for the English instruction advocates came in Arizona, despite the established practice of instructing the students living on Arizona's native reserves in their native language.

PRIMARY SOURCE

History of Bilingual Education: Children in a bilingual classroom in Seattle, Washington, 1994. © JEFFRY W. MYERS/CORBIS.

Whether the Unz initiative or similarly constructed legislative measures would successfully pass a legal challenge based on the precedent set in *Lau v. Nichols* and the cases that followed remains an open question. The ultimate sanction for school boards that choose to eliminate bilingual language instruction where the demographics suggest it should be provided is loss of federal education funding.

In other parts of the United States, bilingual education has prospered. For example, in Maine, a state adjacent to the Canadian province of Quebec and its French-speaking population, French language instruction is provided in school districts where the population warrants this programming.

In 2001, the U.S. Congress passed the No Child Left Behind Act. An omnibus educational act with a number of different educational objectives, the act also provides a three-year window during which students who do not speak English as their first language may take mandated assessment tests in their native languages. After three years, the act requires that all assessments be conducted in English.

FURTHER RESOURCES

Books

Blanc, Michel H. A., and Josiane Hammers, editors. *Bilinguality and Bilingualism*. Cambridge, U.K: Cambridge University Press, 2000.

Cran, William, and Robert MacNeil. *Do You Speak American?*. New York: Doubleday, 2005.

Slotsky, Susan. *Losing Our Language*. New York: The Free Press, 1999.

Web sites

Rethinking Schools Online. "History of Bilingual Education." <http://www.rethinkingschools.org/special_reports/bilingual/langhst.shtml> (accessed June 7, 2006).

Attacks on Foreigners and Immigrants in Post-Reunification Germany

Book excerpt

By: Maryellen Fullerton

Date: April 1995

Source: Fullerton, Maryellen. *Germany for Germans: Xenophobia and Racist Violence in Germany*. New York: Human Rights Watch, 1995.

About the Author: A professor of law at Brooklyn Law School, Maryellen Fullerton is an expert on procedural law, focusing on federal jurisdiction in the United States as well as on refugee and asylum systems in many countries worldwide. She has written books concerning Germany's refugee policies for Human Rights Watch, and has co-edited three volumes concerning migration in Hungary. Human Rights Watch is a non-governmental organization established in 1978 to monitor and promote the observance of internationally recognized human rights in Africa, the Americas, Asia, and the Middle East, as well as the signatories of the Helsinki accords.

INTRODUCTION

This report highlighted concerns about the increasing number of violent racial and anti-Semitic attacks that had been taking place in Germany in the early 1990s since reunification of the country in 1989. The incorporation of the large but economically weak German Democratic Republic into the Federal Republic of Germany, following the collapse of socialism, had resulted in major economic and social pressures on the whole country, and some blamed Germany's large and increasing immigrant community for their problems. Extreme-right wing groups, such as the Neo-Nazi movement, were able to exploit these conditions to gain support, particularly in the former German Democratic Republic, where conditions were particularly severe and unemployment levels very high. These movements blamed foreigners for the country's problems, encouraged the growth of xenophobic (anti-foreigner) attitudes, and encouraged their members to carry out violent racist attacks on immigrants.

Ever since the 1950s Germany's immigration levels have been among the highest in the world. Immigrants in Germany fall into three broad categories. The largest group consists of those who entered under the 'guest worker' programs of the 1960s and early 1970s, mainly from Turkey and Morocco. Many of these guest workers later settled permanently in Germany, bringing family members to join them. Second, there are a substantial number of ethnic Germans from former Eastern European Communist countries such as Russia and Poland. Hundreds of thousands of these people, who held German citizenship, entered Germany every year from the late 1980s until 1993 when the citizenship rules were changed. Finally, like other European countries Germany experienced a major influx of asylum seekers in the 1980s and 1990s, from Eastern Europe and other parts of the world.

Despite the high levels of immigration that Germany has experienced, successive German governments until recently did not regard immigration as a significant policy issue in Germany, and have tended to treat its immigrant population as temporary settlers. As a result, there was traditionally little attempt to integrate or assimilate them, and immigrants developed their own communities outside mainstream German society. This was the case in the German Democratic Republic as well as in the West. In 1989 East Germany had a non-Russian foreign-born population of around 190,000, including many from Vietnam and Mozambique, who had entered the country as labor migrants under government agreements, and were accommodated in special housing away from the native population. Typically, Germany's immigrants in both the east and the west are economically disadvantaged compared with native Germans, and their living conditions are often poor. This separation of Germany's native and immigrant communities has led to a situation in which there is widespread distrust and fear of foreigners on the part of some sections of the population, particularly the working class youths most affected by the economic upheavals of reunification.

The violent attacks on foreigners that began in eastern Germany soon after reunification had disturbing connotations with the Jewish Holocaust, when millions of Jews were rounded up and killed under the Nazi regime in the 1930s and 1940s. Soon after unification, slogans such as "Germany for the Germans" and "foreigners out" were commonly used by the radical right wing groups that beat up foreigners on the streets of eastern Germany, and carried out arson attacks on their homes. Initially, asylum seekers and refugees were the main targets, but soon the violence spread to include attacks on ethnic Germans and the large community of Turkish immigrants. Violent anti-Semitic acts were also carried out, but because there were very few Jewish people living in Germany by this time, these were mainly directed at symbolic targets such as Jewish cemeteries and museums rather than individuals.

Before long, xenophobic attitudes and radical right-wing movements including neo-Nazism spread across the country, with increasing numbers of attacks on foreigners taking place in the former Federal Republic. Although many of the attacks were perpetrated by small, unorganized individuals and groups, extremist right-wing parties also gained support in mainstream politics in the early 1990s, garnering a significant proportion of votes in some municipal elections.

Concerned at the growth of racist movements, the Government banned about twenty neo-Nazi and other extreme right-wing groups in the early 1990s, and increased the powers of the police and the judiciary to deal with racial violence. Among the general population there was widespread disgust at the violent attacks on foreigners, and public demonstrations were held in protest against right-wing radicalism, including candlelit processions known as "human chains of light," intended to show solidarity with immigrants.

The German Government also tackled the problems by changing the laws on asylum and citizenship, which made it more difficult for foreigners to enter the country and almost immediately reduced levels of immigration significantly. The Asylum Law of 1993 gave Germany the power to turn away any asylum seekers from countries where there was deemed to be no threat to their safety, or those who had passed through another safe country on their way to Germany. Laws were also passed limiting the entry of ethnic Germans from countries such as Poland and Russia, who had automatically been granted citizenship before this time.

PRIMARY SOURCE

GERMANY FOR GERMANS

Attacks on Foreigners and Immigrants in post-Reunification Germany

The Federal Republic of Germany has undergone an entire epoch of history in the past five years since trainloads of East Germans crossed into Hungary and Czechoslovakia searching for a route to the West in the spring and summer of 1989. In November 1989, people rushed over the Berlin Wall, border crossings opened, and crowds danced on top of the grim edifice that had scarred the city once known as the "capital of Europe." The euphoria culminated one year later in December 1990 in the Treaty of Unification. Two states became one: the former German Democratic Republic (GDR) was transformed into five federal states (Bundeslander) that joined with the existing eleven federal states to constitute the Federal Republic of Germany.

This transformation has been accompanied by heady euphoria at freedom of movement, freedom of assembly, freedom of speech, and freedom to buy a fabulous array of consumer goods provided by a free market economy. It has also been accompanied by a dramatic increase in unemployment in the East and heavy tax burdens on the more prosperous citizens of the West. Resentment of these two economic consequences of unification has led to bitterness with the present and nostalgia for the past. Many former citizens of the GDR feel a loss of a sense of community, as well as a loss of jobs and social support. Many also feel a loss of their bearings and values. In the former West Germany many citizens resent the economic cost of unification and are angry that the social process of unification is not already complete.

This darker side of the transformation has had a violent, sometimes murderous, aspect. The racism endemic in many societies has exploded in a public way in Germany in the past five years. Hostility against foreigners, a phenomenon seen in many countries, has linked up with right-wing and neo-Nazi movements in Germany to yield incidents of violence and brutality. Television audiences around the world watched with horror as the local population in certain German cities crowded around and supported neo-Nazi assaults and arson attacks on defenseless asylum seekers. People whose only offense was that they did not look German have been killed. Other "foreigners" have been driven from their houses. Widespread beatings of "foreigners" seem to have become a regular feature of major holidays in some places in Germany.

It is clear that racist attacks and killings are not unique to Germany. Genocide has been committed in Rwanda and the former Yugoslavia. Many violent attacks against foreigners have occurred in France, England, Sweden, and other West European democracies in the early 1990s. However, the German government was slow to respond to attacks on foreigners and to initiate specific measures to combat right-wing violence. In fact, the federal government must shoulder much of the blame for the increase in right-wing violence that took place during the first years following unification. What is more, history has left a special legacy for Germany. The massive persecution and execution of "non-Aryans" during the Nazi era set a backdrop for violence against foreigners that is too vivid to forget.

Taken as a whole, Germany has been confronted with a disturbing escalation in violent crimes against those who are different, and especially those who are perceived as not ethnic German during the period since unification. For example, between 1990 and 1992, there was over an 800 percent increase in the number of attacks on foreigners.

Due, in part, to more forceful government measures to combat xenophobic violence, there has been a significant decrease in the number of violent crimes against foreigners in Germany in the last two years. Government statistics indicate that, from 1992 to 1994, there was a 46 percent decline in the number of violent attacks against non-Germans. The government has expanded the number of police and prosecutors trained to investigate and prosecute cases of xenophobic violence. It has also restricted the right to asylum, a step long urged by the extreme right, thereby expropriating a major aspect of the far right's political platform, at least temporarily.

Despite the significant drop in the number of violent attacks, however, the figures were still significantly higher in 1994 than prior to 1991. Figures for 1994 were still more than 400 percent higher than comparable figures for 1990. According to the Office to Protect the Constitution, 1,233 violent attacks motivated by xenophobia were reported to the German authorities in the first eleven months of 1994. According to foreigners' rights groups, a large number of attacks also went unreported.

There were also troubling failures by local and federal authorities in responding to specific cases of violence. Although the police response to attacks on foreigners does appear to have improved significantly over the past two years, many foreigners are still under the impression that they cannot rely on the German police to protect them. This impression is based, in part, on foreigners' experiences with the police during the 1990-92 period. What is more, foreigners' rights groups and our own research indicate that there is a growing problem of police brutality against foreigners, which makes it very difficult to assess whether foreigners are reporting xenophobic crimes as frequently as they may have done in previous years. This is especially so for foreigners whose residency status has not been determined or for illegal aliens who fear deportation. These groups are particularly vulnerable to violence, and the least likely to report such violence to German authorities.

Moreover, other forms of xenophobic violence appear to be on the increase in Germany. Anti-Semitic crimes soared during 1994. Government statistics indicate that an estimated 1,040 anti-Semitic crimes occurred during 1994, representing a 60 percent increase over 1993. Of these, fifty-six were violent offenses. Although this category of crimes includes criminal harassment and intimidation, it also includes expressive conduct that Human Rights Watch/Helsinki believes should not be criminalized. Such statistics may, however, be a measure of the depth of anti-Semitic sentiment in the society, and as such are troublesome. A growing number of right-wing crimes against other minorities, such as the handicapped and homosexuals, was also reported....

Throughout 1991 and 1992, the German government coupled its condemnation of violent attacks on foreigners with a call for restricting the number of asylum seekers in Germany. "By linking these two issues, the government fail[ed] to acknowledge the severity of the crimes being committed against foreigners by German citizens. Instead it subtly shift[ed] the focus and the blame to the foreigners themselves." On May 26, 1993, the Bundestag (parliament) voted 521 to 132 to amend the country's constitutionally-guaranteed right to asylum. Since July 1, 1993, when the new asylum law took effect, the right of asylum does not exist for refugees who pass through safe countries before they reach Germany or who come from homelands deemed safe. Legislation defines safe transit countries and safe home countries. Since July 1993, there has been a significant reduction in the number of foreigners legally entering Germany. Government statistics indicate that the number of foreigners seeking asylum in Germany decreased by 60 percent from 1993 to 1994.

The asylum debate has left a legacy that continues to have a negative impact burden of right-wing violence on the victims—the asylum seekers—rather than on the perpetrators. Schmalz-Jacobsen, the federal commissioner for foreigners' affairs, put it succinctly: "The asylum debate was irresponsible at times. It is easy to destroy a climate, and hard to create one." Numerous others agree that the asylum debate encouraged hostility and violence against foreigners in Germany, Ernst Uhrlau, the director of the Office to Protect the Constitution in Hamburg, noted that the impact of the asylum debate was great on the youths who participated in spontaneous violence against foreigners.

The government had pushed for restrictions on the right to asylum, arguing that it was necessary to prevent a further escalation of xenophobic violence. However, on May 29, 1993, only three days after the Bundestag voted to restrict the right of asylum, five long-time Turkish residents died when four youths allegedly set fire to their house in the town of Solingen. This was the worst single attack on foreigners since unification and set off yet another wave of attacks on foreigners....

SIGNIFICANCE

Despite the measures taken by the Germany government in the mid–1990s to address the problem of right-wing violence against immigrants, the attacks increased in frequency during the second half of the decade. In 2000 a record high of 10,000 attacks were reported.

Integration programs and language training schemes have been introduced to help immigrants assimilate better into German society, but these appear to be having little impact on the problems, with anti-immigrant movements growing in strength. The extreme right-wing National Democratic Party has been gaining support in mainstream politics, particularly in the former East Germany, where it won parliamentary seats in 2004.

This presents a major challenge to the German government, which needs to address the problems of racism and anti-immigrant feeling, while at the same time acknowledging that Germany will need increased numbers of immigrants in the future due to its changing demographic profile and the need for more working-age people in the labor force.

FURTHER RESOURCES

Books

Bergmann, Werner, Erb Rainer, and Hermann Kurthen, eds. *Antisemitism and Xenophobia in Germany after Unification*. New York: Oxford University Press, 1997.

Kitschelt, Herbert, and Wolfgang Street. *Germany: Beyond the Stable State*. Portland, Ore., and London: Frank Cass, 2004.

Niven, Bill. *Facing the Nazi Past: United Germany and the Legacy of the Third Reich*. London and New York: Routledge, 2002.

Periodicals

Anderson, Lieselotte. "Immigration and Social Peace in United Germany." *Daedalus* 123 (Winter 1994): 85–106.

Bering-Jensen, Henrik. "A Flood of Strangers in Estranged Lands." *Insight on the News*, January 4, 1993.

Klusmeyer, Douglas B. "Aliens, Immigrants, and Citizens: The Politics of Inclusion in the Federal Republic of Germany." *Daedalus* 122 (3) (1993): 81–114.

Rosenthal, John. "Anti-Semitism and Ethnicity in Europe." *Policy Review* 121 (2003): 37–58.

Resolution of the Board of Education Adopting the Report and Recommendations of the African-American Task Force

A Policy Statement and Directing the Superintendent of Schools to Devise a Program to Improve the English Language Acquisition and Application Skills of African-American Students

Policy Statement

By: Oakland Unified School District Board

Date: December 18, 1996

Source: *Linguist List*. "Original Oakland Resolution on Ebonics." December 18, 1996 <http://linguistlist.org/ topics/ebonics/ebonics-res1.html> (accessed July 16, 2006).

About the Author: The Governing Board is the elected policy-making body for the Oakland, California, Unified School District, which serves over 50,000 students. The *Linguist List* is a major online source of information and resources on languages and language analysis. It is maintained by linguistics professors and graduate students and jointly edited by Eastern Michigan University and Wayne State University.

INTRODUCTION

In December 1996 the Oakland Unified School District Board in California passed a resolution that formally recognized Ebonics as the official language of the 28,000 African American students in the District, and proposed special educational programs directed at this language group.

The term "Ebonics" was first used in a 1975 book by Robert Williams to describe the language used by American descendents of slaves from West Africa and the Niger-Congo region. The language is also commonly known as "Black English" or "African American Vernacular English" (AAVE). The Linguistic Society of America has confirmed that African American communications have a unique linguistic style, and the Oakland Resolution was based on the principle that Ebonics is a legitimate, distinct language and not just an English dialect.

Oakland was one of the few school districts in America at that time which had a majority of African-American students, and the district was facing severe problems of educational under-achievement within this ethnic group, whose typical grade point average was a D+. African-Americans accounted for 71 percent of all special needs students in the district at that time. Underpinning the Resolution was the belief that the low educational achievement and other problems of African-American students were related to their difficulties in Standard English, which was not the language they normally spoke at home. It proposed the implementation of a training program for the district's teachers that would help them to identify how Ebonics could be used in education to improve African-American student performance, in the same way as other bilingual language programs that qualified for federal funding under Title VII. Under this legislation, schools can apply for funding for bilingual education programs for their Limited English Proficiency (LEP) or No English Proficiency (NEP) students. The majority of bilingual educational programs are directed at Latino and Asian students.

There was a national outcry in response to the Oakland Resolution, with critics arguing that Ebonics was not a distinct language at all, and that Ebonics programs should not be eligible for federal or state funding. Some accused the Oakland school board of trying to appropriate federal funding intended for non-English speaking immigrants. Almost immediately, Secretary Richard Riley announced that Ebonics was nothing other than an English dialect and stated that Title VII funding was only for programs directed at non-English speaking students. As a result, the original Resolution was retracted and it was replaced in January 1997 with a much revised, toned-down version.

Much of the controversy over the Oakland Resolution was apparently due to its misrepresentation in the media, where it was portrayed as a proposal to replace the teaching of Standard English with Ebonics in Oakwood, rather than a proposal to develop programs using Ebonics as a tool in the teaching of Standard English. In fact, this was not new: The educational method known as 'contrastive analysis,' which involved comparing Ebonics and Standard English, had been in use in a number of states, including California, since the 1960s, and was believed to be helping to improve the educational performance of Ebonics speakers.

A bill was introduced in the Senate in March 1997 that proposed eliminating specific sources of federal funding for nonstandard English educational programs, particularly "Ebonics, Black English, Black language or African American Vernacular English." However, the Ebonics debate continued, with those in favor of recognizing Ebonics as a formal language arguing that it would improve the educational prospects of African American students, while others asserted that it is not a separate language, and that Ebonics programs should not therefore be eligible for special funding.

▮ PRIMARY SOURCE

RESOLUTION OF THE BOARD OF EDUCATION ADOPTING THE REPORT AND RECOMMENDATIONS OF THE AFRICAN-AMERICAN TASK FORCE; A POLICY STATEMENT AND DIRECTING THE SUPERINTENDENT OF SCHOOLS TO DEVISE A PROGRAM TO IMPROVE THE ENGLISH LANGUAGE ACQUISITION AND APPLICATION SKILLS OF AFRICAN-AMERICAN STUDENTS.

No. $597-0063

Whereas, numerous validated scholarly studies demonstrate that African American students as part of their culture and history as African people possess and utilize a language described in various scholarly approaches as "Ebonics"- (literally Black sounds) or Pan African Communication Behaviors or African Language Systems; and

Whereas, these studies have also demonstrated that African Language Systems are genetically-based and not a dialect of English; and

Whereas, these studies demonstrate that such West and Niger-Congo African languages have been officially recognized and addressed in the mainstream public educational community as worthy of study, understanding or application of its principles, laws and structures for the benefit of African American students both in terms of positive appreciation of the language and these students' acquisition and mastery of English language skills; and

Whereas, such recognition by scholars has given rise over the past 15 years to legislation passed by the State of California recognizing the unique language stature of descendants of slaves, with such legislation being prejudicially and unconstitutionally vetoed repeatedly by various California state governors; and

Whereas, judicial cases in states other than California have recognized the unique language stature of African American pupils, and such recognition by courts has resulted in court-mandated educational programs which have substantially benefitted African American children in the interest of vindicating their equal protection of the law rights under the 14th Amendment to the United States Constitution; and

Whereas, the Federal Bilingual Education Act (20 USC 1402 et seq.) mandates that local educational agencies "build their capacities to establish, implement and sustain programs of instruction for children and youth of limited English proficiency,"and

Whereas, the interests of the Oakland Unified School District in providing equal opportunities for all of its students dictate limited English proficient educational programs recognizing the English language acquisition and improvement skills of African American students are as fundamental as is application of bilingual education principles for others whose primary languages are other than English; and

Whereas, the standardized tests and grade scores of African American students in reading and language art skills measuring their application of English skills are substantially below state and national norms and that such deficiencies will be remedied by application of a program featuring African Language Systems principles in instructing African American children both in their primary language and in English, and

Whereas, standardized tests and grade scores will be remedied by application of a program with teachers and aides who are certified in the methodology of featuring African Language Systems principles in instructing African American children both in their primary language and in English. The certified teachers of these students will be provided incentives including, but not limited to salary differentials,

Now, therefore, be it resolved that the Board of Education officially recognizes the existence and the cultural and historic bases of West and Niger-Congo African Language Systems, and each language as the predominantly primary language of African American students; and

Be it further resolved that the Board of Education hereby adopts the report recommendations and attached Policy Statement of the District's African American Task Force on language stature of African American speech; and

Be it further resolved that the Superintendent in conjunction with her staff shall immediately devise and implement the best possible academic program for imparting instruction to African American students in their primary language for the combined purposes of maintaining the legitimacy and richness of such language whether it is known as "Ebonics," "African Language Systems," "Pan African Communication Behaviors" or other description, and to facilitate their acquisition and mastery of English language skills; and

Be it further resolved that the Board of Education hereby commits to earmark District general and special funding as is reasonably necessary and appropriate to enable the Superintendent and her staff to accomplish the foregoing; and

Be it further resolved that the Superintendent and her staff shall utilize the input of the entire Oakland educational community as well as state and federal scholarly and educational input in devising such a program; and

Be it further resolved, that periodic reports on the progress of the creation and implementation of such an educational program shall be made to Board of Education at least once per month commencing at the Board meeting of December 18, 1996.

POLICY STATEMENT

There is persuasive empirical evidence that, predicated on analysis of the phonology, morphology and syntax that currently exists as systematic, rule governed and predictable patterns exist in the grammar of African-American speech. The validated and persuasive linguistic evidence is that African-Americans (1) have retained a West and Niger-Congo African linguistic structure in the substratum of their speech and (2) by this criteria are not native speakers of black dialect or any other dialect of English.

Moreover, there is persuasive empirical evidence that, owing to their history as United States slave descendants of West and Niger-Congo African origin, to the extent that African-Americans have been born into, reared in, and continue to live in linguistic environments that are different from the Euro-American English speaking population, African-American people and their children, are from home environments in which a language other than English language is dominant within the meaning of "environment where a Language other than English is dominant" as defined in Public Law 1–13-382 (20 U.S.C. 7402, et seq.).

The policy of the Oakland Unified School District (OUSD) is that all pupils are equal and are to be treated equally. Hence, all pupils who have difficulty speaking, reading, writing or understanding the English language and whose difficulties may deny to them the opportunity to learn successfully in classrooms where the language of instruction is English or to participate fully in classrooms where the language of instruction is English or to participate fully in our society are to be treated equally regardless of their race or national origin.

As in the case of Asian-American, Latino-American, Native American and all other pupils in this District who come from backgrounds or environments where a language other than English is dominant, African-American pupils shall not, because of their race, be subtly dehumanized, stigmatized, discriminated against or denied. Asian-American, Latino-American, Native American and all other language different children are provided general funds for bilingual education, English as Second Language (ESL) and State and Federal (Title VIII) Bilingual education programs to address their limited and non-English proficient (LEP/NEP) needs. African-American pupils are equally entitled to be tested and, where appropriate, shall be provided general funds and State and Federal (Title VIII) bilingual education and ESL programs to specifically address their LEP/NEP needs.

All classroom teachers and aids who are bilingual in Nigritian Ebonics (African-American Language) and English shall be given the same salary differentials and merit increases that are provided to teachers of the non-African American LEP pupils in the OUSD.

With a view toward assuring that parents of African-American pupils are given the knowledge base necessary to make informed choices, it shall be the policy of the Oakland Unified School District that all parents of LEP (Limited English Proficient) pupils are to be provided the opportunity to partake of any and all language and culture specific teacher education and training classes designed to address their child's LEP needs.

On all home language surveys given to parents of pupils requesting home language identification or designations, a description of the District's programmatic consequences of their choices will be contained.

Nothing in this Policy shall preclude or prevent African-American parents who view their child's limited English proficiency as being non-standard English, as opposed to being West and Niger-Congo African Language based, from exercising their right to choose and to have their child's speech disorders and English Language deficits addressed by special education and/or other District programs.

SIGNIFICANCE

The Ebonics debate has never been fully resolved, and surfaces from time to time, particularly in the context of the continued low performance of African American students compared with other groups. In 2001, for example, it was reported that African Americans were three times more likely to have special educational needs than white students.

Many factors may be contributing to the low educational performance of African Americans, including language-related issues. In the case of non-English speaking students, such as Hispanics for example, research has shown that educational performance can be improved by the provision of bilingual education. Because Ebonics is not recognized as a distinct language that is eligible for bilingual education program funding, it is difficult to investigate whether special language programs could raise the educational levels of African American students. The Ebonics debate of the late 1990s did, however, serve to highlight the problem of low educational achievement within this group, bringing to public attention the need for measures to address the issue.

FURTHER RESOURCES

Books

Baugh, John. *Beyond Ebonics: Linguistic Pride and Racial Prejudice*. Oxford: Oxford University Press, 2000.

Delpit, Lisa, and Theresa Perry. *The Real Ebonics Debate: Power, Language, and the Education of African-American Children*. Boston: Beacon Press, 1998.

Wheeler, Rebecca. *The Workings of Language: From Prescriptions to Perspectives*. Westport, Conn., and London: Praeger Publishers, 1999.

Periodical

Crozier, Karen, and Smith, Ernie. "Ebonics Is Not Black English." *Western Journal of Black Studies* 2 (22) (1998): 109–116.

Jewish Alumnus Sues University of Pennsylvania over 'Water Buffalo' Incident

Magazine article

By: Robert Leiter

Date: April 19, 1996

Source: *J.—The Jewish News Weekly of Northern California*

About the Author: Robert Leiter is the Literary Editor of the *Jewish Exponent*, a weekly newspaper based in Philadelphia, Pennsylvania. He is widely published on topics related to Jewish life in the United States.

INTRODUCTION

The right to free speech is among the most cherished individual liberties. The freedom to speak without fear of punishment is a fundamental privilege protected under international law. The opening paragraph of the U.S. Bill of Rights explicitly prohibits any federal law restricting individual freedom of speech, and most other nations offer similar protections.

While U.S. law guarantees freedom of speech, it also provides for a balance between the rights of individuals, so that one citizen's rights do not extend so far as to encroach on the rights of another. In practical terms, this means that one's free speech rights may be limited if exercising those rights would infringe on the rights of another. One well-known example of such a scenario involves a movie-goer who falsely yells "Fire" in a crowded theater, knowing that this will create panic and potential injury to others. In such a case, the man's right to speech is limited by the other patrons' right to safety.

Individual free speech is sometimes legally limited by a higher need. National security concerns frequently dictate limits on how classified information may be used. Threats against the life or safety of the U.S. president are prohibited by law and punishable by up to five years in prison. False speech, such as offering untrue testimony in a legal proceeding or providing false financial data for a publicly traded corporation, is also prohibited and punishable by law.

Other specific types of speech are outlawed in various regions of the world. Ten countries in Europe prohibit Holocaust denial, the assertion that the German extermination of Jews during World War II never occurred. Canadians can be jailed for up to fourteen years for promoting genocide or hatred against any specifically identifiable group, while Icelanders can be jailed for two years simply for insulting or publicly ridiculing a person because of his nationality, religion, or sexual orientation. The prohibition of such hate speech is based on the belief that when used repeatedly, such words can intimidate or threaten the safety of others. Racial and gender slurs are two examples of typical hate speech.

PHILADELPHIA (JTA)—Eden Jacobowitz, whose late night cry of "water buffalo" turned the second half of his freshman year at the University of Pennsylvania into a "politically correct" nightmare, is suing his alma mater for damages, both mental and physical.

According to his attorney, Edward Rubenstone, the complaint was filed in the civil court division of Philadelphia's Common Pleas Court on Feb. 13. Jacobowitz is seeking damages "in excess of $50,000, plus interest and costs of suit, plus punitive damages."

The charges against Penn include gross negligence, breach of contract, reckless or intentional infliction of emotional distress, invasion of privacy and defamation.

The lawsuit stems from an incident that began just before midnight on Jan. 13, 1993, when Jacobowitz was in his dorm room working on an English paper.

Several black sorority women were making noise in front of the dorm. Jacobowitz remembers yelling, "Shut up, you water buffalo."

When the women hollered back that they were looking for a party, he added, "If you're looking for a party, there's a zoo a mile from here."

The sorority members, incensed by the yelling, called the campus police.

When the police asked Jacobowitz if he knew the race of the women, he said yes, but that it had no relevance to what he had shouted.

Some of the sorority women said that Jacobowitz had yelled "black water buffalo," but he insisted he had never mentioned race or color.

An Israeli-born Orthodox Jew from Long Island, N.Y., Jacobowitz explained at the time of the original case that his use of the term "water buffalo" came from the Hebrew word "behema," which can mean "water buffalo" but has often been used by Hebrew speakers as a mild rebuff when someone commits a thoughtless act.

Robin Read, who was then with the university's Judicial Inquiry Office, decided, however, that the water buffalo reference was racist.

In March 1993, she told Jacobowitz that no further action would be taken if he would apologize to the women and admit that he harassed them racially; if he would lead a sensitivity seminar on race in his dormitory; and if he would agree to have the incident recorded in his permanent transcript.

When Jacobowitz refused, Read told him he would have to attend a judicial inquiry.

The hearing took place on May 14, 1993. Three days later, the university published the tribunal's findings denying Jacobowitz's request for a dismissal of charges, and postponed a trial until the fall.

Almost immediately, the sorority women called a news conference and withdrew all charges, saying that undue publicity had deprived them of a fair hearing.

As far as the university was concerned, the case was officially closed.

But, after Jacobowitz graduated, he decided to see if he had a case and contacted Rubenstone.

"We charge breach of contract," Jacobowitz said in an interview last week, "because when you decide to go to a school, you basically sign an agreement that you'll abide by the rules and the school will treat you fairly and justly according to their standards.

"But the school violated their own policies by continuing the case on and on when it was clear that the charges had no merit."

Jacobowitz, the complaint says, is seeking damages because the prosecution of the case "impaired his academic career." He had to take incompletes in two of his second-semester freshman courses, and the ongoing case caused him to feel "fear, alienation and depression" while on campus.

He also suffered from a respiratory condition that began in the spring of his freshman year and persisted for at least six months.

"I definitely want damages," Jacobowitz said. "I think they owe it to me. Because when you enter an Ivy League school and are paying Ivy League prices and you get the door slammed in your face, then you're owed something."

Earlier this month Penn's attorney filed written objections to the complaint in court, according to Barbara Beck, director of news and public affairs at the university.

"The objection makes it clear that the university believes that the complaint has no merit and should be promptly dismissed," Beck said.

"The university plans to defend itself vigorously," she added.

Rubenstone dismissed Penn's objection as "pretty standard stuff," but acknowledged that the case would take some time.

Jacobowitz, whose degree from Penn is in communications, is doing temporary work for a medical company in the Philadelphia area while he waits for responses from the numerous law schools to which he has applied.

SIGNIFICANCE

The Pennsylvania case focused renewed national attention on free speech and individual rights. In particular, the case raised difficult questions about how hate speech is defined and at what point free speech becomes unacceptable. Supporters of the women involved claim that their right to safety and security was infringed by the comment, which they perceived as racist. Eden Jacobowitz's supporters take the position that free speech includes the right to insult others.

The issue of offensive speech continues to attract attention. In 2005, the NCAA, which oversees most college athletics, announced a ban on the use of Native American imagery or mascots in post-season play, finding that their use constitutes hostile and offensive speech. Eighteen schools, including the Florida State University Seminoles, were affected by the ban. Following a vigorous appeal by Florida State and the Florida Seminole tribe, the school was granted an exemption to the rule. Carthage College elected to change its mascot from the Redmen to the Red Men and eliminate Indian imagery, while the Southeastern Oklahoma State University Savages became the Savage Storm. As of 2006, several schools were still appealing the NCAA ruling. Critics of the policy characterize it as an unreasonable application of hate speech restrictions and an example of political correctness run amok.

The conflict between free speech and hate speech is not a recent development. Speaking in 1919, U.S. Supreme Court Justice Oliver Wendell Holmes addressed this conflict by pointing out that the U.S. Constitution defends individual speech of all kinds, including speech that others may find repugnant or distasteful. Holmes argued that even ideas that may be seen as dangerous should be allowed to compete freely in the marketplace of common discussion. He contended that such ideas, once fully examined, would be unable to withstand public scrutiny and be discarded.

After graduating from the University of Pennsylvania, Eden Jacobowitz enrolled in law school. His 1996 lawsuit, claiming emotional distress and violation of contract, sought $50,000 in damages. In 1997, Jacobowitz settled his lawsuit for an undisclosed amount under $10,000.

FURTHER RESOURCES

Books

Brown, Michael K., et al. *Whitewashing Race: The Myth of a Color-Blind Society*. Los Angeles: University of California Press, 2003.

Kors, Alan Charles, and Harvey A. Silvergate. *The Shadow University: The Betrayal of Liberty on America's Campuses*. New York: The Free Press, 1998.

Satel, Sally. *P.C., M.D.: How Political Correctness is Corrupting Medicine*. New York: Basic Books, 2000.

Periodicals

Buckley, William F. "Church/State at Dartmouth." *National Review* 57 (2005): 70–71.

Chong, Dennis. "Free Speech and Multiculturalism In and Out of the Academy." *Political Psychology* 27 (2006): 29–54.

"Remember Detroit." *Economist* 378 (2006): 11.

Web sites

The Free Press. "Shadow University: The Betrayal of Liberty on America's Campuses." <http://www.shadowuniv.com/> (accessed June 8, 2006).

Ganzhorn, Derek. "'Politically Correctness' Hides Depth of Racism in America." *University of Minnesota Register*, November 3, 2005. <http://www.morris.umn.edu/register/> (accessed June 7, 2006).

Knott, Tom. "A Need to Pass the Peace Pipe." *Washington Times*, August 19, 2005. <http://washingtontimes.com/sports/20050819–125544-4353r.htm> (accessed June 8, 2006).

Proposition 227

Initiative

By: Ron Unz

Date: June 2, 1998

Source: *California Secretary of State*. "Proposition 227." <http://primary98.ss.ca.gov/VoterGuide/Propositions/227.htm> (accessed June 10, 2006).

About the Author: Ron Unz, a physicist and chairman of a software company in California, drafted Proposition 227 and led the campaign to pass the initiative.

INTRODUCTION

On June 2, 1998, Californians approved a mandate for English-only instruction in the public schools by a margin of sixty-one percent to thirty-nine percent. Proposition 227 came in response to fears that national unity would be damaged by encouraging the use of Spanish in schools and in other arenas. The legislation was part of a wave of anti-immigrant sentiment that swept the United States at that time.

In the United States, bilingual education was not uncommon in the eighteenth and nineteenth centuries. Linguistic diversity was acknowledged and tolerated, if not always encouraged. In California, both English and Spanish schools existed. In the Midwest,

German-language schools served the large number of German immigrants. French-language public schools served the French-speaking communities in Louisiana and northern New England. Other languages such as Norwegian, Lithuanian, and Czech were part of the curriculum in areas with large numbers of immigrants from these areas.

In the late nineteenth century, the movement for the Common School, or public school, and compulsory education gained momentum as large numbers of poorly educated immigrants arrived on American shores. The influx of these immigrants, who were predominantly Catholics from southern and eastern Europe, prompted a strong xenophobic (anti-foreigner) reaction among the native-born, who were chiefly Protestants of northern and western European stock. Local leaders became increasingly worried about changes in their communities resulting from a swelling among the ranks of the children of the foreign-born. Mandatory education served as a means to ensure that the children of immigrants were assimilated into American (in other words, Anglo-Saxon/northern European Protestant) culture. Public schools came to be seen as the primary institution for this duty.

This task of assimilating foreign children raised the issue of a common language of instruction that would represent American society. The loss of the national-origin language represented the abandonment of the foreign culture of origin. State legislatures began to pass laws regulating the language of public school instruction. California, among others, passed an English-only instruction law. In 1923, in *Meyer v. Nebraska*, the Supreme Court stopped the English-only trend by ruling that a Nebraska state law prohibiting the teaching of a foreign language to elementary students was unconstitutional. Following this decision, the strict English-only instruction laws were generally either repealed or ignored. However, the Supreme Court had also declared in *Meyer v. Nebraska* that the United States is an English-speaking country and schools could require the use of English. At the millennium, English-only legislation made a comeback.

A student in the first and second grade class stands in a bilingual classroom in Manzanita Elementary School in Oakland, California.
© DAVID BUTOW/CORBIS SABA.

Ron Unz, a multimillionaire software developer and former Republican candidate for governor, conceived and financed the campaign for Proposition 227. He entitled the bill English for the Children. Unlike previous English-only advocates, Unz made special efforts to separate opposition to bilingual education from anti-immigrant and anti-Latino views.

■ PRIMARY SOURCE

Chapter 3. English Language Education for Immigrant Children
Article 1. Findings and Declarations

300. The People of California find and declare as follows:

(a) Whereas, The English language is the national public language of the United States of America and of the State of California, is spoken by the vast majority of California residents, and is also the leading world language for science, technology, and international business, thereby being the language of economic opportunity; and

(b) Whereas, Immigrant parents are eager to have their children acquire a good knowledge of English, thereby allowing them to fully participate in the American Dream of economic and social advancement; and

(c) Whereas, The government and the public schools of California have a moral obligation and a constitutional duty to provide all of California's children, regardless of their ethnicity or national origins, with the skills necessary to become productive members of our society, and of these skills, literacy in the English language is among the most important; and

(d) Whereas, The public schools of California currently do a poor job of educating immigrant children, wasting financial resources on costly experimental language programs whose failure over the past two decades is demonstrated by the current high drop-out rates and low English literacy levels of many immigrant children; and

(e) Whereas, Young immigrant children can easily acquire full fluency in a new language, such as English, if they are heavily exposed to that language in the classroom at an early age.

(f) Therefore, It is resolved that: all children in California public schools shall be taught English as rapidly and effectively as possible.

Article 2. English Language Education

305. Subject to the exceptions provided in Article 3 (commencing with Section 310), all children in California public schools shall be taught English by being taught in English. In particular, this shall require that all children be placed in English language classrooms. Children who are English learners shall be educated through sheltered English immersion during a temporary transition period not normally intended to exceed one year. Local schools shall be permitted to place in the same classroom English learners of different ages but whose degree of English proficiency is similar. Local schools shall be encouraged to mix together in the same classroom English learners from different native-language groups but with the same degree of English fluency. Once English learners have acquired a good working knowledge of English, they shall be transferred to English language mainstream classrooms. As much as possible, current supplemental funding for English learners shall be maintained, subject to possible modification under Article 8 (commencing with Section 335) below.

306. The definitions of the terms used in this article and in Article 3 (commencing with Section 310) are as follows:

(a) "English learner" means a child who does not speak English or whose native language is not English and who is not currently able to perform ordinary classroom work in English, also known as a Limited English Proficiency or LEP child.

(b) "English language classroom" means a classroom in which the language of instruction used by the teaching personnel is overwhelmingly the English language, and in which such teaching personnel possess a good knowledge of the English language.

(c) "English language mainstream classroom" means a classroom in which the pupils either are native English language speakers or already have acquired reasonable fluency in English.

(d) "Sheltered English immersion" or "structured English immersion" means an English language acquisition process for young children in which nearly all classroom instruction is in English but with the curriculum and presentation designed for children who are learning the language.

(e) "Bilingual education/native language instruction" means a language acquisition process for pupils in which much or all instruction, textbooks, and teaching materials are in the child's native language.

Article 3. Parental Exceptions

310. The requirements of Section 305 may be waived with the prior written informed consent, to be provided annually, of the child's parents or legal guardian under the circumstances specified below and in Section 311. Such

informed consent shall require that said parents or legal guardian personally visit the school to apply for the waiver and that they there be provided a full description of the educational materials to be used in the different educational program choices and all the educational opportunities available to the child. Under such parental waiver conditions, children may be transferred to classes where they are taught English and other subjects through bilingual education techniques or other generally recognized educational methodologies permitted by law. Individual schools in which 20 pupils or more of a given grade level receive a waiver shall be required to offer such a class; otherwise, they must allow the pupils to transfer to a public school in which such a class is offered.

311. The circumstances in which a parental exception waiver may be granted under Section 310 are as follows:

(a) Children who already know English: the child already possesses good English language skills, as measured by standardized tests of English vocabulary comprehension, reading, and writing, in which the child scores at or above the state average for his or her grade level or at or above the 5th grade average, whichever is lower; or

(b) Older children: the child is age 10 years or older, and it is the informed belief of the school principal and educational staff that an alternate course of educational study would be better suited to the child's rapid acquisition of basic English language skills; or

(c) Children with special needs: the child already has been placed for a period of not less than thirty days during that school year in an English language classroom and it is subsequently the informed belief of the school principal and educational staff that the child has such special physical, emotional, psychological, or educational needs that an alternate course of educational study would be better suited to the child's overall educational development. A written description of these special needs must be provided and any such decision is to be made subject to the examination and approval of the local school superintendent, under guidelines established by and subject to the review of the local Board of Education and ultimately the State Board of Education. The existence of such special needs shall not compel issuance of a waiver, and the parents shall be fully informed of their right to refuse to agree to a waiver.

Article 4. Community-Based English Tutoring

315. In furtherance of its constitutional and legal requirement to offer special language assistance to children coming from backgrounds of limited English proficiency, the state shall encourage family members and others to provide personal English language tutoring to such children, and support these efforts by raising the general level of English language knowledge in the community. Commencing with the fiscal year in which this initiative is enacted and for each of the nine fiscal years following thereafter, a sum of fifty million dollars ($50,000,000) per year is hereby appropriated from the General Fund for the purpose of providing additional funding for free or subsidized programs of adult English language instruction to parents or other members of the community who pledge to provide personal English language tutoring to California school children with limited English proficiency.

316. Programs funded pursuant to this section shall be provided through schools or community organizations. Funding for these programs shall be administered by the Office of the Superintendent of Public Instruction, and shall be disbursed at the discretion of the local school boards, under reasonable guidelines established by, and subject to the review of, the State Board of Education.

Article 5. Legal Standing and Parental Enforcement

320. As detailed in Article 2 (commencing with Section 305) and Article 3 (commencing with Section 310), all California school children have the right to be provided with an English language public education. If a California school child has been denied the option of an English language instructional curriculum in public school, the child's parent or legal guardian shall have legal standing to sue for enforcement of the provisions of this statute, and if successful shall be awarded normal and customary attorney's fees and actual damages, but not punitive or consequential damages. Any school board member or other elected official or public school teacher or administrator who willfully and repeatedly refuses to implement the terms of this statute by providing such an English language educational option at an available public school to a California school child may be held personally liable for fees and actual damages by the child's parents or legal guardian.

Article 6. Severability

325. If any part or parts of this statute are found to be in conflict with federal law or the United States or the California State Constitution, the statute shall be implemented to the maximum extent that federal law, and the United States and the California State Constitution permit. Any provision held invalid shall be severed from the remaining portions of this statute.

Article 7. Operative Date

330. This initiative shall become operative for all school terms which begin more than sixty days following the date on which it becomes effective.

Article 8. Amendment

335. The provisions of this act may be amended by a statute that becomes effective upon approval by the electorate or by a statute to further the act's purpose passed by a two-thirds vote of each house of the Legislature and signed by the Governor.

Article 9. Interpretation

340. Under circumstances in which portions of this statute are subject to conflicting interpretations, Section 300 shall be assumed to contain the governing intent of the statute.

SIGNIFICANCE

California, in the year that Proposition 227 passed, legally admitted 62,113 people from Mexico. In numbers of immigrants admitted annually and number of Mexican immigrants admitted, it ranked first among all states.

In the 1990s, issues of demographic change polarized Californians. Immigration, race, ethnicity, and language became the topics of heated debates. Public schools became a particular area of concern. The enrollment of limited-English-proficient (LEP) children more than doubled between 1988 and 1998 to 1.4 million children. In 1998, English learners represented about twenty-five percent of California K–12 students and about thirty-three percent of those entering first grade. This remarkable growth stems not only from rising immigration but also from higher birthrates in language-minority communities. Between 1990 and 1996, as the state's population increased by 2.6 million, nine out of ten of the new Californians were Latinos or Asian Americans. These groups expanded to twenty-nine percent and eleven percent, respectively, of state residents, while African Americans held steady at seven percent and non-Latino whites slipped to fifty-three percent. Approaching minority status for the first time since the Gold Rush days of the 1840s, many white Californians began to feel threatened by the impending shift in political power and resentful about paying taxes to benefit other people's children, particularly Spanish-speaking children.

Ron Unz has exported his anti-bilingual campaign to other states, including Arizona and Massachusetts. His timing is especially good, as a debate over poorly controlled immigration from Mexico is fueling the fire for English-only legislation. Meanwhile, only a few bilingual educators have entered the political arena. They argue that the key issue is not finding a program that works for all children and all localities, but rather finding a set of program components that works for the children in a particular community, given that community's goals, demographics, and resources. The efforts of the educators to depoliticize bilingual education have not had a strong impact as of 2006.

Also in 2006, a report commissioned by the California legislature showed some educational gains brought about after implementation of Proposition 227, along with some continuing barriers to improved public education for those students for whom English is a second language. Students across all language classifications in all grades have experienced performance gains on state achievement tests, for example. The likelihood of an English learner to achieve successful completion of the academic criteria needed to reclassify them as fluent English proficient status after ten years in California schools, however, is less than forty percent.

FURTHER RESOURCES

Books

Adams, Karen L. and Daniel T. Brink, eds. *Perspectives on Official English: The Campaign for English as the Official Language of the USA.* Berlin: Mouton de Gruyter, 1990.

Crawford, James. *At War with Diversity: U.S. Language Policy in an Age of Anxiety.* Clevedon, England: Multilingual Matters, 2000.

Del Valle, Sandra. *Language Rights and the Law in the United States: Finding Our Voices.* Clevedon, England: Multilingual Matters, 2003.

Padilla, Amado M., Halford H. Fairchild, and Concepcion M. Valdez. *Bilingual Education: Issues and Strategies.* Newbury Park, Calif.: Sage, 1990.

Checking the Immigrant Friendliness of Your Schools

Chart

By: Northwest Regional Education Laboratory

Date: September 6, 2001

Source: *Northwest Regional Education Laboratory.* "Improving Education for Immigrant Students." September 6, 2001 <http://www.nwrel.org/cnorse/booklets/immigration/5.html> (accessed July 1, 2006).

About the Author: The Northwest Regional Education Laboratory provides research and development assistance to educational, governmental, and community agencies as well as businesses and labor organizations. It chiefly serves the states of Alaska, Idaho, Montana, Oregon, and Washington.

INTRODUCTION

Children pose a unique immigration problem. While they are under the control of parents, they are also subject to the demands of educational officials. In the past, parents and educators often clashed over cultural values. In the late twentieth century, educational leaders became more supportive of multiculturalism. As an alternative to forcing Americanization upon children, they looked for ways to welcome immigrant students and celebrate other ethnicities.

When the period of mass immigration began in the mid-nineteenth century, many Americans began to think of the expanding public school system as a place in which devotion to America could be taught along with reading, writing, and arithmetic. In most public schools, American meant Protestant American and the curriculum included Bible-reading and school prayer. As a result, Roman Catholics formed private schools that used Catholic Bibles instead of the King James version. Protestant ethnic denominations then began to create schools that taught in non-English languages, typically German. Some of these schools offered English as foreign language. By 1890, a rising chorus of complaints led to legislation banning instruction in foreign languages in some states and localities. This legislation reached its peak during the anti-German hysteria of World War I when many states banned the teaching of the German language.

The vast majority of immigrant children have always received instruction in English and have become Americanized. In the latter half of the twentieth century, under the impact of large numbers of Spanish-speaking children, many public schools developed a system of bilingual education under which students who did not have a good command of English could attend classes taught in Spanish in schools that were otherwise instructing in English. These classes were enormously controversial. Opponents argued that they allowed children to avoid becoming Americanized and, by doing so, posed a threat to the survival of the American way of life; supporters claimed the classes enabled children to excel and become more confident by being relieved of the burden of learning basic facts and skills through a second language. Despite the continuing controversy, educators have continued to offer programs that promote multiculturalism. The program by the Northwest Regional Education Laboratory was made public a few days before the September 11, 2001 terrorist attacks reshaped the debate over immigration by increasing fears of immigrants.

■ PRIMARY SOURCE

CHECKING THE IMMIGRANT FRIENDLINESS OF YOUR SCHOOLS

See primary source image.

SIGNIFICANCE

The debate over immigration and multiculturalism expanded at the turn of the millennium to include birthright citizenship for the children of illegal immigrants. The issue has the potential to reshape public education by prompting children to avoid schools for fear of deportation or arrest.

The Fourteenth Amendment provides citizenship to anyone born in the United States. Originally constructed to give citizenship rights to African Americans, it has since given citizenship to the children of illegal immigrants. Legal status allows these children to attend public schools without fear of being deported. However, only about half of developed countries grant birthright citizenship. Most require that one parent be a citizen. Policymakers in the United States have considered reforming the law to make the citizenship of children born in the Unites States follow the citizenship of their parents. They argue that undocumented aliens have demonstrated by their illegal entry into the United States that they do not respect American laws and that their children should not benefit by their lawbreaking. The issue is likely to continue to be raised as long as the subject of illegal immigration is a matter of serious national concern.

Self-Report Card—Teacher

Like good student assessments, this self-report card for classroom teachers is designed to help measure your own progress while identifying ideas for improving your classroom.

Always	Usually	Rarely	Never	Checklist for measuring the immigrant-friendliness of your classroom
☐	☐	☐	☐	Am I familiar with the values, traditions, and customs of students in my classroom?
☐	☐	☐	☐	Am I knowledgeable about the immigration experience of my students' families?
☐	☐	☐	☐	Do I visit at home with the families of immigrant students in my classroom to gain insight into the students' lives and support systems?
☐	☐	☐	☐	Do I learn some vocabulary in the native language of my students to better communicate with them?
☐	☐	☐	☐	Do I encourage immigrant parents to help their children maintain their native language at home while learning English at school?
☐	☐	☐	☐	Do I base my academic expectations on the individual ability of each student rather than on broad or stereotypical assumptions?
☐	☐	☐	☐	Do I understand the English and native-language skills of each student so I can develop individually appropriate classroom and homework assignments?
☐	☐	☐	☐	Do I seek additional, culture-specific assistance to provide appropriate instruction before referring an immigrant student to remedial classes?
☐	☐	☐	☐	Do I use peer teaching, where limited-English-proficient students can participate and practice English-language skills in small groups?
☐	☐	☐	☐	Do I allow students to develop their English-language skills in class without feeling embarrassed or intimidated?
☐	☐	☐	☐	Are all students actively involved in classroom instruction and other classroom activities?
☐	☐	☐	☐	Are classroom seating arrangements balanced by ethnicity as well as by gender?
☐	☐	☐	☐	Are reading materials provided in the native languages represented in my classroom?

Self-Report Card—Administrator

Administrators can take several steps to make their districts and schools more supportive and welcoming to immigrant students.

Always	Usually	Rarely	Never	Checklist for measuring the immigrant-friendliness of your school
☐	☐	☐	☐	Do I participate and encourage participation in formal, multicultural courses available within my community?
☐	☐	☐	☐	Do I provide inservice training to staff on equity, multicultural, and immigrant education issues?
☐	☐	☐	☐	Do I hire trained professionals available to provide long-term consultation and analysis for school district planners and classroom teachers?
☐	☐	☐	☐	Do I provide resources for planners and teachers to develop multicultural programs?
☐	☐	☐	☐	Do I develop relationships with surrounding ethnic communities to assist the school with translation, cultural interpretation, and other needs?
☐	☐	☐	☐	Are printed materials (bulletin boards, school publications, etc.) available in the home languages of all children in the school?
☐	☐	☐	☐	Do school clubs and activities reflect the ethnic makeup of the student populations?
☐	☐	☐	☐	Are signs of intolerance dealt with immediately and according to the school's antiharassment policies?
☐	☐	☐	☐	Are immigrant families participating in teacher conferences?

PRIMARY SOURCE

Checking the Immigrant Friendliness of Your Schools: These self-assessment tools are designed to help school teachers and administrators evaluate and improve the immigrant-friendliness of their schools. ADAPTED BY THOMSON GALE FROM "IMPROVING EDUCATION FOR IMMIGRANT STUDENTS." *NORTHWEST REGIONAL EDUCATION LABORATORY.* SEPTEMBER 6, 2001.

FURTHER RESOURCES
Books
Crawford, James. *At War with Diversity: U.S. Language Policy in an Age of Anxiety.* Clevedon, U.K.: Multilingual Matters, 2000.

Dinnerstein, Leonard, Roger L. Nichols, and David M. Reimers. *Natives and Strangers: A Multicultural History of Americans.* New York: Oxford University Press, 1996.

Padilla, Amado M., Halford H. Fairchild, and Concepcion M. Valdez. *Bilingual Education: Issues and Strategies.* Newbury Park, CA: Sage, 1990.

Weiss, Bernard J., ed. *American Education and the European Immigrant, 1840–1940.* Urbana: University of Illinois Press, 1982.

President George W. Bush and Secretary Elaine L. Chao Celebrating Asian Pacific American Heritage Month

Speech

By: Elaine L. Chao and George W. Bush

Date: May 17, 2002

Source: *Office of the Secretary, U.S. Department of Labor.* "President George W. Bush and Secretary of Labor Elaine L. Chao Celebrating Asian Pacific American Heritage Month, East Room, The White House, Washington, D.C., May 17, 2002." <http://

www.dol.gov/_sec/media/speeches/ 20020517_POTUS_APA. htm> (accessed June 28, 2006).

About the Author: Elaine L. Chao (1953–) is the twenty-fourth U.S. secretary of labor (2001–) of the United States. Secretary Chao is the first Asian-American woman and the first Chinese-American appointed to the federal cabinet. George W. Bush (1946–) is the forty-third president of the United States (2001–). Before becoming U.S. president, Bush served as governor of the state of Texas for two consecutive terms beginning in 1994.

INTRODUCTION

Asian Pacific American Heritage Month (APAHM), held annually each May in the United

Secretary of Labor Elaine Chao introduces President Bush as he prepares to deliver remarks at the Asian Pacific American Heritage Month ceremonies in the White House, Washington, May 17, 2002. AP IMAGES.

States, is a celebration of U.S. citizens that are descended from natives of Asia and the Pacific Islands (which includes Hawaii and other Pacific islands). Local, state, and national activities, festivals, and educational activities are held throughout May in celebration and in acknowledgment of the contributions made by Asian/Pacific-Island Americans to U.S. society.

Beginning in the 1970s, Chinese-American speaker and consultant Jeanie F. Jew—who was also president of the Organization of Chinese-American Women—identified the need to celebrate the accomplishments of Asian/Pacific-Island Americans— similar to the way, for example, that African Americans and others celebrate Black History Month. In 1976, Jew sought the help of Representative Frank Horton (D–New York). Horton and Norman Y. Mineta (D–California), in June 1977, introduced House Resolution 540 into the agenda of the House of Representatives for the express purpose of the president to proclaim the first ten days of May as Asian/Pacific Heritage Week. Senators Daniel K. Inouye (D–Hawaii) and Spark Matsunaga (D–Hawaii) introduced a similar Senate bill in July 1977. The U.S. Congress subsequently passed each bill. In October 1978, President Jimmy Carter signed a Joint Resolution that declared Asian American Heritage Week be held annually during the first week of May. The decision was made to celebrate it in May in order to coincide with the immigration of the first Japanese to the United States on May 7, 1843 and the efforts of Chinese workers in building the transcontinental railroad that was completed on May 10, 1869. The first Asian Pacific American Heritage Week was celebrated in May 1979.

Congress later expanded the celebration to one month in length and, in May 1992, President George H. W. Bush officially renamed the celebration Asian Pacific American Heritage Month. APAHM was enacted by Public Law 102-450 on October 28, 1992, to honor the achievements of Asian/Pacific-Island Americans and to recognize their contributions to the United States.

PRIMARY SOURCE

Secretary Chao: Good afternoon. Thank you all for being here. Not long ago, our President spoke of the nation's need for "citizens who hear the call of duty ... who care for their families ... and who treat their neighbors with respect and compassion." While he was calling every American to service, he was also describing the values that define the Asian Pacific American community.

Duty ... family ... respect ... and compassion. These are the values that have sustained us—and our ancestors before us—in coming to America. How grateful we are to have a President who personally lives out the values that have led us—and calls each of us to pursue them with renewed vigor.

Let me add one more ideal to the list that has inspired our community: the American Dream ... the desire to be free ... to work hard and succeed ... so that we may pass on a better life to the generations that follow.

Most of us carried the American Dream in our hearts long before we ever reached these shores. Though we left behind family, friends and all that was familiar, we knew that the dream that burned in our hearts was well worth the sacrifice.

We also have a President who came to Washington from a distant and exotic land: Texas. Like all of us, he came here for a purpose: to preserve and expand the American Dream. Our President believes that politics is not about who you know—it's about what you accomplish.

Power doesn't come from a position, it comes from what you believe in—and whether you have the courage to stand up for it in the face of opposition. Our President believes in—and stands up for—giving all Americans access to a good education, the dignity of work, including those currently on welfare. He believes in cutting taxes, so families have more to save and invest. And he believes deeply in reaching out and opening doors.

That's why, in just the first year of his Administration, he appointed more Asian Pacific Americans to senior positions than ever in American history—including two Asian Pacific Americans to his cabinet.

A politician will tell you what you want to hear; but a leader does what he says. We have such a leader—one who shares our values and stands up for our dreams—our President, George W. Bush.

President Bush: Elaine, thank you very much. Welcome to your house—the White House. I want you to know, [Secretary of Transportation] Norm [Mineta], I welcome Republicans, Democrats—people who don't care—all Americans. You're welcome here. I am honored to welcome you. I didn't realize you sponsored the legislation that my Dad—we call him Number 41—signed, which permanently made the celebration of Asian and Pacific American culture a month-long event. And that's what we're honoring today.

I'm so proud to be the President of a diverse nation, a nation with 13 million Americans of Asian or Pacific Island heritage. What a great country, to welcome such diversity. Whether you're here by birth, or whether you're in America by choice, you contribute to the vitality of our life. And for that, we are grateful.

I also appreciate service to our government, and our country. I picked two fabulous members of my Cabinet from Asian-Pacific backgrounds. You've seen them both. One lady who wasn't born in America, yet because of the dreams of her mother and father, and because our country can be a welcoming country, was able to get a good education, and here she sits in the Cabinet of the President of the United States.

Another man, a man not of the same political party as I am, but a man who loves his country just as much as I do; a person who, as a young boy, was interned in a camp for Japanese Americans on our own soil—a moment that is not a good chapter in our history—and yet had the courage to fight for change and for the dignity of every American, and now sits in the Cabinet of the President of the United States. I am fortunate to have them in my Cabinet. I appreciate their advice, and I appreciate the great job they're doing on behalf of all Americans. All Americans.

I want to thank Senator Inouye for being here. He's one of the fine distinguished members of the United States Senate. He's an ally when it comes to defending our nation. He understands what it means to serve your country and be prepared for the defense of America. Senator, you're doing a great job. Thank you for coming. I also want to thank Congressman David Wu from Oregon for being here, as well.

I want to thank Delegate Faleomavaega. Did I even come close? Well, at least I gave it my best shot, Eni. How about just Eni? Thank you for coming from the American Samoa. We've got friends of ours from Guam, the Guam Senate—Senate Leader Edward Calvo and the House Speaker, Tony Unpingco. Thank you all for coming. I'm honored you both are here. You are welcome.

I want to thank Susan Allen, the President of the U.S. Pan Asian American Chamber of Commerce. Thank you, Susan, it's great to see you again.

Richard, I want to thank you for filling this room and the whole house with incredible music. Man, what a talent. And I appreciate you sharing it with us. You help make a special day more special. And Lisa, thank you for bringing your beauty here.

I'm looking around for Dat Nguyen. Is he here? He's supposed to be here. Yes, he's a Texan. He's a mighty Texas A&M Aggie, middle linebacker for the Dallas Cowboys, came from a Vietnamese family. He's a great story. And I just wish they'd win a couple more games.

I want to thank John Tsu, the Chairman of the White House Initiative on Asian Americans and Pacific Islanders. John, thank you very much. And Russell Wong, a great actor, for being here as well. And welcome to you all.

The history of Asian Pacific Americans is really a history of great patriotism, people who were willing to sacrifice. Incredibly enough, Asian Pacific Americans fought in the Civil War, and, of course, World War II and the war on terror.

It's a story of hard work. Many of you have had relatives who came here early, early on in our country, that worked the railroad, helped build the infrastructure necessary for America to grow. It's a story of great achievement and great success—I mean, look at our Olympic teams; Asian Americans on our Olympic teams, helping a unified country achieve in sports. It's a story of great business success, great cultural success.

It's a story of influence on our society—scientific influence, architectural influence, music, art, significant contribution to our country. And for that, all of us are grateful.

SIGNIFICANCE

Asian/Pacific-Island Americans contribute significantly to U.S. society. For instance, the U.S. Census Bureau states that Asian/Pacific Island Americans are the fastest-growing racial group in the United States. According to the 2005 census, approximately 13.5 percent (about 39 million) of the U.S. population state that their bloodlines derive from people of Asian and Pacific Island descent. As of July 2004, about five percent of the population—about 14 million people in the United States—are considered primarily of Asian or Pacific Island descent. With 4.8 million citizens, the state of California has the largest population of Asian/Pacific Island-Americans. The state of Hawaii has the largest percentage (about fifty-eight percent) of Asian/Pacific Island-Americans within its population. The Census Bureau lists about thirty Asian and Pacific Islander groups in the United States, including Burmese, Cambodian, Chinese, Filipinos, Indian, Japanese, Korean, Laotian, Indonesian, Malaysian, and Vietnamese.

In addition, from the U.S. Census Bureau, forty-nine percent of all Asian-Americans aged twenty-five years or older have at least a bachelor's degree. This percentage is the highest proportion of college graduates of any ethnic or racial group in the United States. Eighty-seven percent of Asian-Americans (within this same age bracket) are high school graduates, and twenty percent possess an advanced educational degree. About fifteen percent of Native Hawaiians and other Pacific Islanders have at least a bachelor's degree, with eighty-four percent of them having high school diplomas and four percent with graduate degrees. Asian-Americans also hold the highest median household income for any racial group in the United States—at $57,518. Pacific-Island-Americans have a median household income of $51,687. Forty-six percent of Asian-Americans and twenty-three percent of Pacific-Island Americans—sixteen years of age or older—work in management or professional and related occupations.

Many organizations have formed as a result of Asian Pacific American Heritage Month (APAHM). For example, in 1992 the Asian/Pacific American Heritage Association (APAHA) was formed to "promote the Asian/Pacific American culture, heritage, and awareness through celebration events and educational outreach—leading to the month of May, Asian/Pacific American Heritage Month." Members of APAHA coordinate their efforts with community, cultural, and educational groups in order to provide continuing educational, cultural, and scholarship programs to the Asian/Pacific Island community in the United States.

Asian/Pacific-Island Americans have played an important role in the development of the United States. The importance of Asian/Pacific-Island Americans to the United States was first officially recognized in the 1970s. Asian Pacific American Heritage Month has come to signify a time to celebrate the contributions, heritage, and traditions of Asian/Pacific-Island Americans to America's history, culture, and society.

FURTHER RESOURCES

Books

Asian Americans: Contemporary Trends and Issues, edited by Pyong Gap Min. Thousand Oaks, Calif.: Pine Forge Press, 2006.

The Asian Pacific American Heritage: A Companion to Literature and Arts, edited by George J. Leonard. New York: Garland Publishing, 1999.

Barringer, Herbert R. *Asians and Pacific Islanders in the United States*. New York: Russell Sage Foundation, 1993.

The New Face of Asian Pacific America, edited by Eric Lai and Dennis Arguelles. San Francisco, Calif.: AsianWeek, with UCLA's Asian American Studies Center Press, 2003.

Remapping Asian American History, edited by Sucheng Chan. Walnut Creek, Calif.: AltaMira Press, 2003.

Web sites

Asian/Pacific American Heritage Association (APAHA). <http://www.apaha.org> (accessed June 28, 2006).

Australian Multiculturalism—The Policy

Government record

By: Australian Government

Date: May 2003

Source: *Department of Immigration and Multicultural Affairs, Australian Government.* "Multicultural Australia: United in Diversity." May 2003. <http://www.immi.gov.au/living-in-australia/a-diverse-australia/government-policy/index.htm> (accessed July 1, 2006).

About the Author: The Australian Government has a long history of supporting only British immigration to Australia. Multiculturalism has been a concern only since the 1960s.

INTRODUCTION

Australia is largely a nation of immigrants. It ranks as the fourth largest country of immigrant settlement in the past century, after the U.S., Canada, and Brazil. Despite this history, Australian governments promoted policies that discriminated against Aborigines and blocked immigration by non-Europeans. The Australian embrace of multiculturalism is recent and occasionally reluctant.

Europeans began to settle Australia in 1788. They have always been the favored group. From the 1880s onward, there has been discussion in Australian society about Australia being one nation, one people, and a homogenous group of citizens. The concern led to the White Australia policy in 1901 that banned all Asian and African immigration. It was part of an equation that linked civilization to the Anglo-Saxon race. After World War II, the Australian government reluctantly began to support immigration from southern and eastern Europe. It did so because not enough British, Dutch, and German immigrants could be induced to migrate even with subsidized passage costs. The White Australia policy was dismantled in the 1960s at a time when there was a general consensus that a more ethnically diverse intake of immigrants was more appropriate for Australia.

Beginning in 1975, waves of Indo-Chinese refugees from the Vietnam War fled to Australia. This immigration coupled with growing family reunion migration and the movement of skilled workers to bring cultural diversity to Australia. These changes generated some opposition with the One Nation political party forming in 1997 to oppose immigration. Soon after its creation, One Nation garnered 9% in public opinion polls and obtained 25% of the primary vote in the state of Queensland. It reflected resistance to diversity, particularly among lower income Australians who feared being marginalized.

The Australian government officially supports a multicultural Australia. In 2003, it updated the 1999 *New Agenda for Multicultural Australia* by issuing *Multicultural Australia: United in Diversity*. The new plan set the strategic direction for Australia until 2006.

Tribes from around Australia particpate in the Yeperenye Festival, celebrating 100 years of Australian Federation. © JOHN VAN HASSELT/ CORBIS.

PRIMARY SOURCE

The Government is committed to ensuring that all Australians have the opportunity to be active and equal participants in Australian society, free to live their lives and maintain their cultural traditions.

Australian multiculturalism recognizes, accepts, respects, and celebrates cultural diversity. It embraces the heritage of indigenous Australians, early European settlement, our Australia-grown customs and those of the diverse range of immigrants now coming to this country.

The Government's aim is to build on our success as a culturally diverse, accepting and open society, united through a shared future, and a commitment to our nation, its democratic institutions and values, and the rule of law. This vision is reflected in the four principles that underpin multicultural policy.

Responsibilities of all—all Australians have a civic duty to support those basic structures and principles of Australian society which guarantee us our freedom and equality and enable diversity in our society to flourish;

Respect for each person—subject to the law, all Australians have the right to express their own culture and beliefs and have a reciprocal obligation to respect the right of others to do the same;

Fairness for each person—all Australians are entitled to equality of treatment and opportunity. Social equity allows us all to contribute to the social, political, and economic life of Australia, free from discrimination, including on the grounds of race, culture, religion, language, location, gender, or place of birth; and

Benefits for all—all Australians benefit from productive diversity, that is, the significant cultural, social, and economic dividends arising from the diversity of our population. Diversity works for all Australians.

SIGNIFICANCE

With a stable political system and strong economy, Australia is one of the most culturally diverse countries in the world. About six million migrants have settled in Australia since the end of World War

II in 1945. Increasingly, these immigrants are from Asia, reflecting Australia's position as a key nation in the Asia-Pacific region. Australia's population is projected to become even more diverse over the next few decades.

The Islamist terrorist attacks of September 11, 2001 in the U.S. and October 12, 2002 in Bali changed the global environment. Many Australians called for immigration restrictions as a way to guard national security. Multiculturalism came under attack for allowing radical Islamists to preach a message of intolerance. In this climate, the Australian government of John Howard reiterated its support of multiculturalism.

FURTHER RESOURCES

Books

Burnley, Ian H. *The Impact of Immigration on Australia: A Demographic Approach.* South Melbourne, Australia: Oxford University Press, 2001.

Clarke, Frank G. *The History of Australia.* Westport, CT: Greenwood Press, 2002.

Moore, Andrew. *The Right Road: A History of Right-Wing Politics in Australia.* Melbourne, Australia: Oxford University Press, 1995.

McClatchy Adds "Diversity Day"as an Annual Holiday

News article

By: Anonymous

Date: October 7, 2003

Source: PR Newswire, The McClatchy Company

About the Author: PR Newswire, a subsidiary of United Business Media based in London, England, is a leading global media company in news and information distribution. It is a part of PR Newswire Association LLC, which provides electronic distribution, measurement, translation, and broadcast services to associations, corporations, governments, labor organizations, non-profits, and other customers worldwide.

INTRODUCTION

Founded by James McClatchy in 1857, The McClatchy Company is a leading newspaper and Internet publisher based in Sacramento, California. It owns twelve daily newspapers and sixteen community

newspapers—with a total circulation of about 1.4 million daily subscribers and, on average, 1.9 million subscribers for its Sunday papers. Its largest newspaper is the *Star Tribune*, based in Minneapolis-St. Paul, Minnesota, while its oldest paper (which was founded in 1857) and its second largest, is *The Sacramento Bee*, based in Sacramento, California. The company employs about 9,300 people. The newspaper was awarded thirteen Pulitzer Prizes throughout its history, with five gold medals for public service.

Chairman of the board, president, and chief executive officer Gary B. Pruitt has been chairman of the board since 2001 (he became a board director in 1995), president since 1995, and CEO since 1996. Before that time, Pruitt was chief operating officer from 1995 to 1996 and vice-president of operations and technology from 1994 to 1995. From 1991 to 1994, he was the publisher of *The Fresno Bee*. Earlier, Pruitt was its corporate secretary and general counsel from 1991 to 1987, and its counsel from 1987 to 1984.

According to the agreement between Northern California Media Workers, Guild/Typographical Union-CWA, Local 39521 and McClatchy Newspapers, Inc., who is the publisher of *The Sacramento Bee*, the Diversity Day agreement states: "Diversity Day will be celebrated to coincide with Martin Luther King Day. If an employee wishes to select an alternate day, they must do so in writing during open enrollment. Selection of an alternate day is subject to supervisor approval." and "Diversity Day is not a floating holiday and it may not be used as an extension of vacation, sick leave, another holiday or any other form of paid time off. The Company reserves the right to deny a paid day off for a requested Diversity Day if business needs necessitate or if the selected day does not coincide with a religious, ethnic or diversity event."

■ PRIMARY SOURCE

Sacramento, California., Oct. 7 /PRNewswire-FirstCall/—Gary Pruitt, chairman and chief executive officer of The McClatchy Company (NYSE: MNI), today announced the recognition of a new holiday called Diversity Day, which will be added to the company's holiday calendar beginning in 2004.

"Giving our employees paid time off to honor the various cultures, heritages and faiths represented by our work force is an important addition to McClatchy's benefits package," Pruitt said. "It also strengthens our continuing

Keanu Rhum and Emily Phosy study the globe. They are both first grade students at Van Allen Elementary School, Mount Pleasant Iowa, February 27, 2004. The activity is part of the school's Diversity Day activities. AP IMAGES.

efforts to diversify our work force so that it better reflects the communities we serve."

The additional holiday will allow employees to designate a specific date to use as their Diversity Day. The day must be taken off for diversity-related events such as Cesar Chavez Day, Chinese New Year or Yom Kippur, and cannot be used simply as a floating holiday.

Employees who don't select a specific date will automatically receive the Martin Luther King Jr. holiday, which is the third Monday of January.

"We believe Diversity Day is an important addition to our benefits package and a powerful reminder to our employees of the company's commitment to diversity," Peter CaJacob, vice president, human resources, said.

"We've made this commitment not just because it is good business, but because it is the right thing to do," Pruitt added.

SIGNIFICANCE

Diversity is defined within a society such as the United States, as the presence of a wide variety of demographic and philosophical differences within its citizens. Such differences include abilities/disabilities, ethnicities and nationalities, experiences, interests and aspirations, languages, levels of education, opinions and philosophies, physical features, politics, religious beliefs and faith, sexuality and gender identity, socio-economic backgrounds, and skills and professions. In cultures outside the United States, diversity is sometimes called multiculturalism, or tolerance.

Diversity Day is sometimes celebrated by companies in the United States, such as The McClatchy Company, to recognize the value of the company's widely varied work force. Many companies contend that they can prosper and grow better when a wide diversity of people is employed within their organizations. Schools often celebrate diversity day in order to educate students on the subject of diversity in society and within their own classrooms.

People are sometimes treated differently based upon such characteristics as color, ethnic origins, gender, marital status, nationality, or race. U.S. law is designed to encourage diversity and prevent discrimination in the workplace. For example, companies must hire employees without regard to such factors as age, gender, and race. The government, by enacting such laws, hopes to eliminate discrimination within the workplace and promote equal opportunities. Such laws, for example, assure that disabled people—whose particular disability does not affect the performance of their job—receive equal treatment at work over colleagues who are not disabled. Equal opportunity laws also assure that employees are paid the same rate of pay for performing the same job without regard to age or gender.

Practices that promote diversity places value on individuals and groups. For Diversity Day celebrations, the promotion of open communication between people of different lifestyles and backgrounds helps increase knowledge and understanding about others. Such individuals are then likely to be less prejudicial of others. Consequently, work environments where equality and mutual respect are important more likely result in successful, supportive, and caring individuals and groups.

After September 11, 2001, 185 nations adopted the United Nation's Educational, Scientific, and Cultural Organization (UNESCO's) Universal Declaration on Cultural Diversity, which states that cultural differences should not divide people but rather bring them together. The Declaration maintains that mutual communications and understanding between societies can produce a more peaceful world. Leaders of UNESCO also proclaimed May 21 as Diversity Day (officially called World Day for Cultural Diversity for Dialogue and Development.). On October 2005, the General Counsel of UNESCO adopted the Convention on the Protection and Promotion of the Diversity of Cultural Expressions. The Adoption, which was created to safeguard cultural diversity around the world, states the legal rights and obligations of countries and their citizens with respect to international cooperation.

FURTHER RESOURCES
Books

Bucher, Richard D. and Patricia L. Bucher. *Diversity Consciousness: Opening Our Minds to People, Cultures, and Opportunities.* Upper Saddle River, NJ: Merrill, 2004.

Cox, Taylor. *Creating the Multicultural Organization: A Strategy for Capturing the Power of Diversity.* San Francisco, CA: Jossey-Bass, 2001.

Web sites

The Better World Project. "Diversity Day." <http://www.diversityday.net/> (accessed June 26, 2006).

Northern California Media Workers Guild/Typographical Union. "Agreement 2004–2006, Northern California Media Workers Guild/Typographical Union-CWA, Local 39521 and McClatchy Newspapers, Inc., Publisher of the Sacramento Bee." <http://www.mediaworkers.org/sacbee/sacbeecontract.html> (accessed June 26, 2006).

United Nations. "World Day for Cultural Diversity for Dialogue and Development: May 21." <http://www.un.org/depts/dhl/cultural_diversity/> (accessed June 26, 2006).

United Nation's Educational, Scientific, and Cultural Organization (UNESCO). "UNESCO Universal Declaration on Cultural Diversity—2001." <http://portal.unesco.org/culture/en/> (accessed June 26, 2006).

Gratz et al v. Bollinger

U.S. Supreme Court Rules on University Affirmative Action Policies

Judicial decision

By: William H. Rehnquist

Date: June 23, 2003

Source: *Gratz et al v. Bollinger,* 539 U.S. 244 (2003).

About the Author: William H. Rehnquist (1924–2005) was appointed to the U.S. Supreme Court as an associate justice in 1972. Rehnquist was subsequently appointed Chief Justice of the Court in 1986, serving in that capacity until his death in 2005. The Supreme Court of the United States is the nation's highest court, a body composed of eight associate justices and one chief justice.

INTRODUCTION

The decision of the U.S. Supreme Court in *Gratz* represents an aspect of the evolving debate about racial issues in American education. Beginning with the landmark decision of *Brown v. Board of Education* in 1954, in which the Supreme Court ruled that "separate but equal" educational systems for black and white students was a violation of the equality provisions of the U.S. Constitution, race has been a recurring theme in American education.

In the wake of the *Brown* decision, where the issue determined by the Supreme Court was the integration

Barbara Grutter (l) and Jennifer Gratz (right) speak with reporters outside the U.S. Supreme Court on April 1, 2003. They are two of the plaintiffs in the case against the University of Michigan's affirmative action program heard at the Court that day. AP/WIDE WORLD PHOTOS. REPRODUCED BY PERMISSION.

of a public high school, universities contended with racial integration throughout the late 1950s and early 1960s, particularly in institutions located in the southern states. A prominent example was the University of Mississippi, where riots were precipitated by efforts to integrate its undergraduate programs in 1962.

Once the principle of the integration of black and white students was relatively settled in American universities, many institutions moved to implement programs that encouraged a greater population of black students. These measures, generally categorized as affirmative action, sought to increase the enrollment of black and other visible minority students by creating admission procedures that tended to create a favorable environment for the black applicants. The most common of these affirmative action measures was to specify

that black applicants would be rated differently in the admissions process than white applicants.

Affirmative action programs were intended to address the underrepresentation of the black population at large in university programs. Critics of affirmative action initiatives pointed to the fact that such measures tended to discriminate against otherwise qualified applicants who were white.

The first significant legal test of affirmative action in university admissions took place in 1978, when the Supreme Court, in the case of *Regents of the University of California v. Bakke*, endorsed affirmative action in university admissions in certain circumstances; the Court ruled that the race of an applicant could be a valid admissions consideration, so long as the race of a particular candidate was part of a wide variety of admission criteria, including grades, personal background, and other factors.

The *Gratz* case arose as a challenge to the undergraduate admissions procedures at the University of Michigan in the 1990s. The white applicants, Jennifer Gratz and Patrick Hamacher, were qualified students applying to the College of Literature, Science, and the Arts (LSA) in 1995 and 1997, respectively. At that time, the university had a points system whereby a black, Hispanic, or Native American applicant automatically received additional points, improving their chances for admission. Gratz and Hamacher were denied admission, while, they contended, less academically qualified persons of color were admitted to the university.

■ PRIMARY SOURCE

Petitioners filed this class action alleging that the University's use of racial preferences in undergraduate admissions violated the Equal Protection Clause of the Fourteenth Amendment, Title VI of the Civil Rights Act of 1964, and 42 U.S.C. §1981. They sought compensatory and punitive damages for past violations, declaratory relief finding that respondents violated their rights to nondiscriminatory treatment, an injunction prohibiting respondents from continuing to discriminate on the basis of race, and an order requiring the LSA to offer Hamacher admission as a transfer student. The District Court granted petitioners' motion to certify a class consisting of individuals who applied for and were denied admission to the LSA for academic year 1995 and forward and who are members of racial or ethnic groups that respondents treated less favorably on the basis of race. Hamacher, whose claim was found to challenge racial discrimination on a classwide basis, was designated as the class representative. On cross-motions for summary judgment, respondents relied on Justice Powell's principal opinion in *Regents of Univ. of Cal. v. Bakke,* 438 U.S. 265, 317, which expressed the view that the consideration of race as a factor in admissions might in some cases serve a compelling government interest. Respondents contended that the LSA has just such an interest in the educational benefits that result from having a racially and ethnically diverse student body and that its program is narrowly tailored to serve that interest. The Court agreed with respondents as to the LSA's current admissions guidelines and granted them summary judgment in that respect. However, the Court also found that the LSA's admissions guidelines for 1995 through 1998 operated as the functional equivalent of a quota running afoul of Justice Powell's *Bakke* opinion, and thus granted petitioners summary

judgment with respect to respondents' admissions programs for those years. While interlocutory appeals were pending in the Sixth Circuit, that court issued an opinion in *Grutter v. Bollinger,* post, p. ___, upholding the admissions program used by the University's Law School. This Court granted certiorari in both cases, even though the Sixth Circuit had not yet rendered judgment in this one.

Held:

1. Petitioners have standing to seek declaratory and injunctive relief. The Court rejects *Justice Stevens'* contention that, because Hamacher did not actually apply for admission as a transfer student, his future injury claim is at best conjectural or hypothetical rather than real and immediate. The "injury in fact" necessary to establish standing in this type of case is the denial of equal treatment resulting from the imposition of the barrier, not the ultimate inability to obtain the benefit. *Northeastern Fla. Chapter, Associated Gen. Contractors of America v. Jacksonville,* 508 U.S. 656, 666. In the face of such a barrier, to establish standing, a party need only demonstrate that it is able and ready to perform and that a discriminatory policy prevents it from doing so on an equal basis. *Ibid.* In bringing his equal protection challenge against the University's use of race in undergraduate admissions, Hamacher alleged that the University had denied him the opportunity to compete for admission on an equal basis. Hamacher was denied admission to the University as a freshman applicant even though an underrepresented minority applicant with his qualifications would have been admitted. After being denied admission, Hamacher demonstrated that he was "able and ready" to apply as a transfer student should the University cease to use race in undergraduate admissions. He therefore has standing to seek prospective relief with respect to the University's continued use of race. Also rejected is *Justice Stevens'* contention that such use in undergraduate transfer admissions differs from the University's use of race in undergraduate freshman admissions, so that Hamacher lacks standing to represent absent class members challenging the latter. Each year the OUA produces a document setting forth guidelines for those seeking admission to the LSA, including freshman and transfer applicants. The transfer applicant guidelines specifically cross-reference factors and qualifications considered in assessing freshman applicants. In fact, the criteria used to determine whether a transfer applicant will contribute to diversity are *identical* to those used to evaluate freshman applicants. The *only* difference is that all underrepresented minority freshman applicants receive 20 points and "virtually" all who are

minimally qualified are admitted, while "generally" all minimally qualified minority transfer applicants are admitted outright. While this difference might be relevant to a narrow tailoring analysis, it clearly has no effect on petitioners' standing to challenge the University's use of race in undergraduate admissions and its assertion that diversity is a compelling state interest justifying its consideration of the race of its undergraduate applicants. See *General Telephone Co. of Southwest v. Falcon*, 457 U.S. 147, 159; *Blum v. Yaretsky*, 457 U.S. 991, distinguished. The District Court's carefully considered decision to certify this class action is correct. Cf. *Coopers & Lybrand v. Livesay*, 437 U. S. 463, 469. Hamacher's personal stake, in view of both his past injury and the potential injury he faced at the time of certification, demonstrates that he may maintain the action. Pp. 11–20.

2. Because the University's use of race in its current freshman admissions policy is not narrowly tailored to achieve respondents' asserted interest in diversity, the policy violates the Equal Protection Clause. For the reasons set forth in *Grutter v. Bollinger, post*, at 15-21, the Court has today rejected petitioners' argument that diversity cannot constitute a compelling state interest. However, the Court finds that the University's current policy, which automatically distributes 20 points, or one-fifth of the points needed to guarantee admission, to every single "underrepresented minority" applicant solely because of race, is not narrowly tailored to achieve educational diversity. In *Bakke*, Justice Powell explained his view that it would be permissible for a university to employ an admissions program in which "race or ethnic background may be deemed a 'plus' in a particular applicant's file." 438 U.S., at 317. He emphasized, however, the importance of considering each particular applicant as an individual, assessing all of the qualities that individual possesses, and in turn, evaluating that individual's ability to contribute to the unique setting of higher education. The admissions program Justice Powell described did not contemplate that any single characteristic automatically ensured a specific and identifiable contribution to a university's diversity. See *id.*, at 315. The current LSA policy does not provide the individualized consideration Justice Powell contemplated. The only consideration that accompanies the 20-point automatic distribution to all applicants from underrepresented minorities is a factual review to determine whether an individual is a member of one of these minority groups. Moreover, unlike Justice Powell's example, where the race of a "particular black applicant" could be considered without being decisive, see *id.*, at 317, the LSA's 20-point distribution has the effect of making "the factor of race . . . decisive" for virtually every minimally qualified underrepresented minority applicant, *ibid*. The fact that the LSA has created the possibility of an applicant's file being flagged for individualized consideration only emphasizes the flaws of the University's system as a whole when compared to that described by Justice Powell. The record does not reveal precisely how many applications are flagged, but it is undisputed that such consideration is the exception and not the rule in the LSA's program. Also, this individualized review is only provided *after* admissions counselors automatically distribute the University's version of a "plus" that makes race a decisive factor for virtually every minimally qualified underrepresented minority applicant. The Court rejects respondents' contention that the volume of applications and the presentation of applicant information make it impractical for the LSA to use the admissions system upheld today in *Grutter*. The fact that the implementation of a program capable of providing individualized consideration might present administrative challenges does not render constitutional an otherwise problematic system. . . .

SIGNIFICANCE

The *Gratz* decision represents only one-half of the university admissions equation decided by the Supreme Court in 2003; the other component was determined in the case of *Grutter et al v. Bollinger*, a 2003 case that challenged the admissions procedures in place at the University of Michigan's Law School. In *Gratz*, the majority of the Court clearly finds the use of a racial "points" structure in the university's undergraduate admissions system to be akin to a rigid quota and therefore inconsistent with the holistic approach that the Court had endorsed in *Bakke* concerning admissions standards.

The Michigan undergraduate admissions system also scored other attributes of applicants that were unrelated to race. These qualities included athletic participation, the socioeconomic circumstances of the applicant, Michigan residency, and demonstrated leadership skills.

The *Grutter* case, like *Bakke*, arose in a professional school setting where the overall competition to win acceptance into the faculty was significantly higher than at the undergraduate admissions level. The Court was clearly prepared to accept that there are different factors at play between the *Gratz* undergraduate scenario and the *Grutter* professional school application. In *Grutter*, the affirmative action applications system was upheld because the court found that the University of Michigan Law School admissions procedures sufficiently considered each applicant as an individual and that race was not a predominate factor in acceptance into the law school, unlike the points system employed for Michigan undergraduates.

In both cases, as in *Bakke*, the Supreme Court was careful to emphasize that the concept of racial diversity was a meaningful and a legitimate objective of an American university. Implicit in the reasoning in both *Gratz* and *Grutter* is the proposition that while the university application process may be perceived as one based upon the principles of a pure meritocracy, the creation of an ideal university learning environment can properly go beyond scholastically qualified applicants to specifically include minority candidates without breaching the equality rights of a person who is denied admission.

The dissenting opinions in *Gratz* echoed some of the broader-based societal reasons as to why the university could justify its points system for blacks and other identified minorities. Justice Ruth Bader Ginsburg, the author of the minority judgment, saw the university admissions process in classic affirmative action terms: so long as racism exists in society at large, coupled with inequities of opportunity and income, points systems and quota systems of all kinds will be necessary to achieve equality over time.

A further significant facet of the *Gratz* decision was the organization whose counsel advanced the arguments against the affirmative action programs at the University of Michigan. *Gratz* was a class action suit brought by the Center for Individual Rights, a conservative legal advocacy group based in Washington, D.C., that also acted for the applicant in the *Grutter* decision. The Center for Individual Rights advocates numerous conservative causes; the organization is styled as a counterbalance to the perceived liberal influence in the American justice system cast by organizations such as the American Civil Liberties Union.

Of interest is the time frame within which the *Gratz* proceeding (and its companion, *Grutter*) unfolded between the denial of admission at the University of Michigan and the decisions of the Supreme Court. When the ruling came eight years after the 1995 application, Gratz had moved ahead with her life and career aspirations, and admission into the university's freshman class was no longer a realistic remedy. *Gratz* represents a relatively rare instance of the advancement of a pure legal principle versus the seeking of personal benefit.

FURTHER RESOURCES

Books

Ibarra, Robert A. *Beyond Affirmative Action: Reframing the Context of Higher Education*. Madison: University of Wisconsin Press, 2001.

Schunck, Peter H. *Diversity in America: Keeping Government at a Safe Distance*. Cambridge, Mass.: Harvard University Press, 2003.

Web sites

National Public Radio. "Split Ruling on Affirmative Action." June 23, 2003 <http://www.npr.org/news/special/michigan> (accessed June 14, 2006).

University of Pittsburgh Law School. "Learning from Living: The University of Michigan Affirmative Action Cases." September 5, 2003 <http://www.jurist.law.pitt.edu/forum/symposium-aa/bell.php> (accessed June13,2006).

University of Pittsburgh Law School. "Some Observations on Grutter." September 5, 2003 <http://www.jurist.law.pitt.edu/forum/symposium-aa/shields.php> (accessed June 13, 2006).

Civic Leaders call for Calm as Rumours Fly

News article

By: Hugh Muir and Riazat Butt

Date: October 25, 2005

Source: Muir, Hugh, and Riazat Butt. "Civic Leaders call for Calm as Rumours Fly." Guardian Unlimited, October 25, 2005.

About the Author: Hugh Muir and Riazat Butt are writers for Guardian Unlimited, a news website owned by the British Guardian Media Group. The website contains most of the content of The Guardian and The Observer newspapers, as well as additional content and a rolling news service.

INTRODUCTION

The article reports on a race riot that broke out in Birmingham, England in October 2005, between the city's Pakistani and African-Caribbean communities.

The riot was sparked by an incident in which a teenage African-Caribbean girl was allegedly gang raped by several young Pakistanis. The situation spiraled out of control when the African-Caribbean community press urged black locals not to patronize Asian retail establishments. There were demonstrations against Asians over the course of the following week, which resulted in violent clashes between the two ethnic groups, during which an innocent young passer-by was stabbed to death. Although many local people took part in the demonstrations, it was claimed

Andy Warhol's *Birmingham Race Riot.* © ANDY WARHOL FOUNDATION/CORBIS.

that race activists from other parts of the country were the main perpetrators. There were rumors, for example, that there may have been involvement by the "Yardies", or Jamaican-born gangsters, and by "The Nation of Islam," an association of Muslims who hold extreme anti-white views. The riots were soon quelled by the police, and did not reach the scale of those that had occurred in Handsworth, another area of Birmingham, twenty years earlier.

Race riots have sporadically broken out in some inner cities of the United Kingdom ever since the late 1950s, peaking in their frequency and intensity during the 1970s and early 1980s. They have usually been sparked by specific incidents, but more generally are believed to be related to dissatisfaction among ethnic minority youths about their relative economic dis-

advantage, racial discrimination against them in the labor market and other areas of life, and their harassment or perceived harassment by others in society, including the police and extreme right-wing activists.

Britain's inner cities have high proportions of ethnic minority people in their populations, and many of these experience economic disadvantage. Research has shown that young African-Caribbean men in the United Kingdom are twice as likely to be unemployed as young white men and that those in employment are generally paid less than their white counterparts. Pakistani and Bangladeshi young men are even more likely to be unemployed than African-Caribbean men. In Birmingham, where 18.5 percent of the 2001 population was from the Indian sub-continent, and 10.6 percent was from other ethnic minority groups, including African-Caribbeans, ethnic minorities were significantly over-represented in the low-income segment of the city's population.

Some of the worst race-related riots in Britain occurred in 1981 in Toxteth, Liverpool, and Brixton, South London. In these cases, violence was directed at the police by black youths, following recent police campaigns in which young black people had been stopped and searched by the police on the streets of these areas. In the same year, violence broke out in Southall, West London, when right-wing supporters of the National Front, which opposes all immigrants and non-whites in British society, attacked some young Asians, provoking angry retaliations from the Asian community. The Asians also attacked the police who were attempting to restore order, protesting that they were not doing enough to protect their community. The racial violence soon spread to other parts of the country, including Moss Side in Manchester and Handsworth in Birmingham, where violence again flared in 1985.

◼ PRIMARY SOURCE

Police and civic leaders in Birmingham yesterday issued fresh appeals for calm during another day of rumours and speculation that threatened to spark fresh trouble between the city's Pakistani and African-Caribbean communities.

There were unsubstantiated claims that large numbers of young Pakistani men were ready to enter the fray and have only been held back by the orders of their religious leaders.

Last night the MP for the area, Khalid Mahmood, demanded that those who claim that a young black woman was raped by Asian men either provide evidence that a crime took place or help to calm the situation.

"The Home Office have made concessions on the immigration issues [concerning the alleged rape victim,] police have given assurances as well and would give the alleged victim total anonymity. Nobody has come forward," he said. "This can't be allowed to continue on rumour. They have to produce the evidence or back down and say it was a mistake."

Within the African-Caribbean community, activists also sought to calm tensions. But efforts to impose normality were hampered by a succession of rumours and incidents, all of which heightened fears that the violence may intensify. Reports of violence around the city were seized upon by residents, and one Asian taxi driver was mugged while television cameras filmed the assault....

One activist said: "I am hearing reports that there are busloads of Pakistanis on their way from Leicester. I have

had calls from Yardies in London asking if we need help, and have heard that the Nation of Islam are ready to come up. No one knows how much of this is true, but we are in a dangerous situation."...

But the angry mood in the black community was further inflamed by the black newspaper the Voice, which reported on its front page the alleged rape of a black girl by Pakistani men and published an editorial urging black shoppers to avoid Asian-run stores. Mahmood Hussain, a councillor who represents Lozells, the district where the main rioting took place, said a series of urgent cross-community meetings were now taking place. "We need to bring some calm to the area. We are in a situation where a minority are taking advantage of this tension. I don't know if there will be any more trouble, but I hope not."

Those who experienced the Handsworth riots that scarred the city two decades ago are particularly keen to avoid a schism.

One shopkeeper, Nazir Ahmed, saw his father's shop burnt down then. "We rebuilt things and Lozells has come a long way since those dark days," he said. "Now is a time for us as a community to show solidarity."

◼▰

SIGNIFICANCE

From the end of the 1980s race riots have been less frequent in Britain's inner cities, but continue to occur from time to time.

Britain's Race Relations Act of 1976, and Race Relations (Amendment) Act of 2000, make it unlawful to discriminate against anyone on grounds of race, color, nationality (including citizenship), or ethnic or national origin, and require public authorities to promote racial equality, particularly in the areas of jobs, education and housing. However, despite legislative efforts to increase equality among Britain's races, ethnic minorities are still concentrated in the poorest areas of the country and their members do less well at school and in the job market, overall, than the native white population. This creates underlying tensions that still sometimes emerge in violent demonstrations, particularly in response to attacks by other social groups.

Some observers have noted that race riots, particularly those of the early 1980s, have brought to public attention the situation faced by African-Caribbean and Asian communities in the poor inner cities, including poor housing and high levels of unemployment, and thus helped to promote the development of policies and legislation to improve their circumstances. The overall decline in racial violence over the past twenty years may reflect these positive developments, but the comparative peace is a fragile one, as shown by the ease with which violence broke out in Birmingham in 2005.

FURTHER RESOURCES

Books

Berthoud, Richard. *Young Caribbean Men and the Labour Market: A Comparison with Other Ethnic Groups.* York, U.K.: York Publishing Services, 1999.

Blackstone, Tessa, Bhikhur Parekh, and Peter Sanders. *Race Relations in Britain: A Developing Agenda.* London: Routledge, 1998.

Centre for Contemporary Cultural Studies. *The Empire Strikes Back: Race and Racism in 70s Britain.* London: Routledge, 1992.

John, Gus. *Taking a Stand.* Manchester, U.K.: Gus John Partnership, 2006.

Music: The Shakira Dialectic

Newspaper article

By: Jon Pareles

Date: November 13, 2005

Source: Pareles, Jon. "The Shakira Dialectic." *New York Times* (November 13, 2005).

About the Author: Jon Pareles is the chief pop music critic for the *New York Times*, a daily newspaper with a circulation of over one million readers worldwide.

INTRODUCTION

Shakira exploded onto the international music scene in 1996 with the album *Pies Descalzos (Bare Feet)*. The release fist caught fire in Latin America and eventually hit number one in sales in eight countries.

In 1998, Shakira teamed up with record producer Emilio Estefan (husband of Latina singer Gloria Estefan) and released *Donde Estan Los Ladrones? (Where are the Thieves?)*. This album, a hybrid of Arab influences, Colombian rhythms, and Western pop, was lauded by critics as a breakthrough. The title track, "Ojos Asi" (These Eyes), garnered a Latin Grammy Award in 2000. The same year, she won a second Latin Grammy for "Octavo Dia" and an MTV Video Music Award.

As of 2006, Shakira's new single "Hips Don't Lie," featuring Wyclef Jean, vaulted her to Number One on the Billboard charts.

■ PRIMARY SOURCE

LONDON—On the cover of her new album, "Oral Fixation, Vol. 2," the Colombian pop singer and songwriter Shakira plays Eve, clothed only in strategic leaves. Perched next to her in a tree is a baby girl, reaching for the apple Shakira holds in her hand.

For obvious reasons, it's eye-catching, as was the cover of the Spanish-language companion album Shakira released in June, "Fijación Oral, Vol. 1," which showed her fully dressed and holding the same baby to her breast. Although it had been four years since her previous album, "Fijación Oral, Vol. 1" zoomed to No. 4 on the Billboard pop charts.

As an attention-getter, a pop star showing skin needs no further justification. Yet Shakira, 28, has other ideas about her latest chosen image. "I want to attribute to Eve one more reason to bite the forbidden fruit, and that would be her oral fixation," she said in an interview. "I've always felt that I've been a very oral person. It's my biggest source of pleasure."

"From a psychoanalytical point of view, we start discovering the world through our mouths in the very first stage of our lives, when we're just born," she continued. "The first album cover is more Freudian, and the second one more resembles Jung, because Eve is a universal archetype. I tried to keep a unity between the two album covers, and I chose to use some Renaissance iconography. Mother and child and original sin are recurrent concepts of the Renaissance period, and I wanted the historical character."

Psychoanalysis, biblical revisionism, Renaissance paintings. Not to mention DNA-level multiculturalism, torrid dance moves and an ear for rhythms and hooks from all over. Fulfilling the basic needs of current pop—a catchy song, a pretty face—doesn't begin to match Shakira's gleeful ambitions. She is pop's 21st-century Latina bombshell, a sweetly upbeat face of globalization, and then some.

"I'm not the one who's causing this to happen," she said. "I'm just a consequence of the great musical momentum and the great changes we are going through in the world."

And she just might seduce the world. Gabriel García Márquez, the Nobel Prize-winning novelist from Colombia, wrote, "She has invented her own brand of innocent sensuality." Chatting over Indian samosas and chicken tikka, she seems candid, confident, light-hearted and completely disarming.

In her new single, "Don't Bother," Shakira sings about being rejected in favor of a woman who's tall and "fat-free," but insists she'll get over it. The video clip, after a flashback of lovemaking in the shower, shows her taking vengeance: she has the man's car crushed.

"Did it hurt?" she said, laughing, curious about a male viewer's reaction. "A man's car is like an extension of their ego and their manhood. I thought this would be a video that would make women say, 'Yeah, yeah!' and it would make men feel"—she gave a pained sound: "'Ohh...'" She giggled.

Songs and videos "exorcise the bad things that could happen to your relationship," she said. "Inside me there's a real jealous beast I'm trying to tame."

Still, she said: "My videos represent the artist in me very well, but not the kind of woman I am. When they watch my videos, people might think that I'm very sexually aggressive person, but I am completely the opposite. I'm very shy of my body. The most I can show is my belly. I admire people who can do nudes for the love of art. I can't. And I wear enough to cover what my mother wishes I cover."

"I think art, music should be sensual," she added. "Not necessarily sexual. I think that's a huge difference between that N and that X. It's more than the 11 letters of difference. Sensual is everything that refers to the delight of the senses. And that's what artists do, is stimulate the senses in any possible way. I don't think I have to hang myself a little sign that says 'Hey, I'm sexy,' and then take it off and now say, 'Hey, now I'm serious.' I can just fluctuate and oscillate from one side to the other whenever my instincts tell me to."

If her songs hadn't become international pop hits, Shakira would have been lauded as an innovator in Latin alternative rock. Her lyrics, almost always about romance, mix generalized pop sentiments with unlikely confessional nuggets. In the ballad "Your Embrace" on her new album, Shakira wonders, "What's the use of a 24-inch waist if you don't touch me/Tell me what's the use again of being on TV every day if you don't watch me?"

And her music has a savvy but nearly unhinged eclecticism. Another new song, "Animal City," starts with an Arabic-flamenco vocal flourish, switches to synth-pop, tosses in some surf guitar and tops it with mariachi horns: "Never mind the rules we break," she sings. Even in her more conventional rock or pop songs, her voice is untamed, or rather, her voices: a tearful, sultry alto; a cutting, breaking rock attack; a girlish lilt; a whispery insinuation. It's deliberate yet willful, sure of its impulses.

No boardroom plan for crossover success could have devised a figure like Shakira. Her mother is Colombian, her father Lebanese; in Arabic, Shakira means "woman full of grace." "I look for the most primal elements of both cultures, and I bring them into my music," she said. "I think that that's why I am probably a romantic and a passionate person. But I also have a very disciplined side, very disciplined and very demanding. Sometimes my sense of responsibility is my worst torturer."

Shakira speaks Spanish, Portuguese and English, and wants to learn more languages. She calls herself a nomad; she has houses in the Bahamas, where she now lives, and in Miami, while she still regularly visits her hometown, Barranquilla, on Colombia's Caribbean coast. Her Middle Eastern side comes out in vocal arabesques and belly-dance moves, but she's also steeped in rock, pop and disco; the first album she owned, on a cassette, was Donna Summer's "Bad Girls."

"I feel comfortable in my pop shoes," Shakira said. "They let me walk in any direction. I like to go from one extreme to the other. One day I feel that I want to do a song with reggaetón influence, I do it. The next day I feel I need to do a song with rock elements to it, I do it. And sometimes I try to see if an Argentine bandoneón"—the accordion used in tango—"can survive in a song with fluegelhorns."

Shakira was taking a break from rehearsing her band in a South London warehouse, getting ready for television and radio appearances that would, in the next week, take her to Denmark, Germany, Italy and Portugal. A petite figure in a black T-shirt and jeans, she was multi-tasking; the night would include not only an interview and rehearsal but also a costume fitting, a quick takeout dinner and, sometime after midnight, a flight to Copenhagen. Her arm had a bright red burn mark from the curling iron that had styled her blonde Botticelli ringlets: "A good excuse for getting a tattoo," she said with a laugh.

Singing as she faced her band, her big, tremulous alto rose unamplified across the room. As a song ended, the band members looked to her and she asked, in a gentle uptalk: "Do you think we could have a little more dynamically? So it can grow? So it can move higher?"

Shakira has been in charge of her own music for a decade. She began writing songs at 8 and was signed to a recording contract at 13. In Bogotá, she made two albums of Latin pop that, she said, "don't represent me at all." She had a brief stint acting in a Colombian soap opera; she doesn't think she was very good at it. Then, with "Pies Descalzos" ("Bare Feet"), released in 1996, Shakira started producing herself with collaborators she chose.

"I was always very sure of what I wanted to hear," she said. "I had to fight to be heard: 'don't play that melody in this part, play the other one.' Guys don't like women telling them what to do. It reminds them of their mothers, or something like that."

She added: "I don't want to sound like a feminist saying this. But it's true, it's a man's world."

Shakira was already a star across Latin America by the end of the 1990's. So she set out to learn English well enough to write lyrics, and she conquered the rest of the world with "Laundry Service," which sold three million copies in the United States and an estimated 10 million more worldwide.

Between albums, Shakira wrote 60 songs, some in Spanish and some in English, and winnowed them down to 20 before deciding to make two albums, one in each language. As usual, she says, she agonized over details. "I'm a perfectionist in recovery," she said, laughing. "I'm trying to deal with that monster inside of me that wants to do everything right. Or better than right."

She took a full month, she said, tweaking "La Tortura," the first single from "Fijación Oral, Vol. 1," which mixed Colombian cumbia, Puerto Rican reggaetón, Jamaican dancehall, rock guitars, electronic blips and guest vocals by a major pop star from Spain (Alejandro Sanz). "If there's a problem, then I need to fix it," she said, "and it's painful because you don't know what to fix, you know? The bass sounds, the drum sounds—I changed them many times. That's a song that needed clearly the right, the accurate production. If I went a little bit left or little bit far right, the song would suffer and get affected. And I struggled with the song until I finally got it." And she was still working on "Oral Fixation, Vol. 2" after its single, "Don't Bother," had been released. She was under deadline pressure by that point but, she says, "You can't ripen a fruit by hitting it with rocks."

"Fijación Oral, Vol. 1" reconnected Shakira with her longtime Spanish-speaking fans. "Oral Fixation, Vol. 2" includes English versions (though not direct translations) of two songs from "Vol. 1"; the other nine are new. Perhaps because the songs are in English rather than Spanish, the music moves closer to Anglo rock and pop, dipping into folk-rock, power ballads and the Cure. "Sometimes a melody suggests in what language that song should be written," she said. "I just learned to listen to what the song wants to tell me."

Although "Vol. 1" holds more unconventional songs, the rock songs on "Vol. 2" still have Shakira's own quirks. Along with her love songs, this time Shakira also looks beyond the domestic. The opening song, "How Do You Do," begins with prayers for forgiveness—recurring in Arabic, Hebrew, Latin and English—then fires off a series of tough questions at a deity.

And she ends the album with "East Timor," which is not an earnest anthem about one more troubled place in the world, but an ironically perky, synthesizer-pumped dance tune with lyrics about the ways happy-talk media and pop culture distract us from sufferings far away: "It's all right, at least there's half the truth/Hearing what we want's the secret of eternal youth," she sings, adding, "I'll keep selling records and you've got your MTV." She almost dropped "East Timor" from the album. "For a second I thought, people are not going to understand this," she said. "They are going to think I'm trying to talk about world peace, and to find ways to fix problems that are so complex, not even critics or politicians can find the solutions. And then a 28-year-old girl from Barranquilla is going to find solutions? I just wrote this song because it was an impulse."

Rehearsal beckoned; in a few days, Shakira would be singing the songs in public for the first time. "Just today," she said, "I'm starting to get in touch with the songs from the performer point of view. O.K., how am I going to interpret this with my body? How am I going to start to have now a physical relationship with my songs?"

The band kicked into "Hey You," a flirtatious song with a 1960's Merseybeat bounce. In it, Shakira offers herself to a man as everything from queen to cook to slave: "I'd like to be the owner of the zipper on your jeans, and that thing that makes you happy." As she sang, she stood still at first, then let the music carry her. Her shoulders start to roll, her feet picked up the rhythm, and soon her hips started to swivel.

"My hips tell me where and when I should move," she had said before returning to work with the band. "And my hips don't lie—my hips tell me the truth."

SIGNIFICANCE

Shakira Isabel Mebarak Ripoll was born in Barranquilla, Colombia on February 9, 1977. Her father's Lebanese background (her mother is Colombian) was an important influence—her music is crafted with Arabic ambiance. In addition, the name, Shakira, means "woman full of grace" in Arabic.

Undoubtedly, her Caribbean roots—Barranquilla is on the Caribbean coast—have also influenced her music. Music critics regard Shakira as a Latin hybrid and cross-over success for infusing her albums with pan-Caribbean rhythms, rock, and pop. She is often compared to a chameleon because her repertoire ranges from rocker to ballads to Puerto Rican reggaeton (a blend of hip-hop and Jamaican dancehall) and Columbian cumbia.

One in eight Americans is Hispanic, and Latin Alternative music is gaining momentum. Music industry experts acknowledge that as demographic changes continue to favor young bilingual audiences, innovative music that fuses cultures, much like Shakira's, will continue to gain in popularity.

FURTHER RESOURCES

Periodicals

Fred Bronson. "Chart Beat: 'Hips' Hops to No. 1." *Billboard* (June 8, 2006).

Jon Pareles. "At the Jingle Ball, It was Nerds vs. Braggarts." *New York Times* (December 19, 2005).

Web sites

New York Times. "Alternative View: Latinos Say Rock is More Than Just Reggaeton." August 8, 2005. <http://www.nytimes.com/2005/08/08/arts/music/> (accessed June 22, 2006).

Shakira. <http://www.shakira.com> (accessed June 22, 2006).

Confederate Will Remain in Name of Vanderbilt Dorm

Newspaper article

By: Michael Cass

Date: July 12, 2005

Source: Cass, Michael. "Confederate Will Remain in Name of Vanderbilt Dorm." *The Tennessean. (July 12, 2005).*

About the Author: Michael Cass is a staff writer for *The Tennessean,* the major daily newspaper for middle Tennessee.

INTRODUCTION

In 2002, Vanderbilt University proposed to sandblast the word "Confederate" from the frieze of the campus building known as Confederate Memorial Hall. The building was built in 1935 with a $50,000 donation by the United Daughters of the Confederacy (UDC). Vanderbilt's proposal set off a firestorm of protest over the best way to commemorate its Southern past.

Vanderbilt University, along with other Southern colleges and universities, seeks to recruit African American students, faculty, and staff. Such recruitment efforts have sometimes been hampered by Confederate symbols. While the descendents of

Dr. Eddie Hamilton, a Vanderbilt University Medical School graduate, stands in front of Confederate Memorial Hall on the Vanderbilt University campus in Nashville, Tennessee, May 17, 2005. Hamiliton has offered $50,000 to a Southern heritage group to buy the naming rights to the building. AP IMAGES.

Confederates view their ancestors as heroic, African Americans regard the Civil War as an effort by the South to continue the slave system, and symbols of the Confederacy are seen as part of a hostile climate for blacks instead of an effort to remember the past.

In 2002, Vanderbilt Chancellor Gordon Gee cited the need to create a welcoming environment as part of diversity efforts when he decided to remove the word "Confederate" from Memorial Hall. The issue had been a topic of debate at the private university since the residence hall was renovated in 1988. The UDC wanted the name to remain to honor the men from Tennessee who died in the Civil War, and successfully pursued the matter in court. While frustrated in its efforts to make the physical change, "Confederate" has been dropped from all maps and literature that refer to the building. The university has also established an annual lecture series to address diversity topics.

PRIMARY SOURCE

The words Confederate Memorial Hall—words that evoke images of slavery for some people and fallen heroes for others—will remain inscribed in stone on a Vanderbilt University building after a three-year legal battle.

Vanderbilt decided not to appeal a state court ruling ordering that the Nashville school either keep the inscription on the building or pay damages that could have topped $1 million to the United Daughters of the Confederacy, university spokes-man Michael Schoenfeld said yesterday.

The UDC's Tennessee division raised $50,000 during the Great Depression to help pay for the building, which was part of the former George Peabody College for Teachers at the time, and vigorously challenged Vanderbilt's plans to remove the name in 2002. Peabody merged with Vanderbilt in 1979.

Schoenfeld said the university, which had hoped to create what it considered a more welcoming environment by taking down a word some find offensive, is dropping the matter and leaving the full name on the seventy-year-old residence hall.

"We believed the best option for Vanderbilt at this time was to move on," he said. "Taking on this issue was something important for the university to do, and taking it any further was reaching a point of diminishing returns."

UDC representatives said they were thrilled by the decision, which followed a May 3 ruling by the Tennessee Court of Appeals.

"Slavery was terrible, and the Civil War was terrible in terms of the blood shed," said Doug Jones, a Nashville-based attorney for the organization. "But we don't need to forget it."

Vanderbilt said that simply bringing attention to the issue was a victory, and that the building's new name in all other official references, Memorial Hall, was taking hold on campus.

The legal fight concerned only the Confederate Memorial Hall inscription on the building's stone pediment. The Court of Appeals ruled that the inscription must stay up as long as the building does.

The university plans to create an annual lecture series or other educational events to keep issues of race, history, memory and the Civil War on students' minds, Schoenfeld said.

Dr. Eddie Hamilton, a Nashville physician and Vanderbilt School of Medicine graduate who had offered to give $50,000 to help Vanderbilt remove the name by paying damages to the UDC, said he was disappointed but not surprised by the decision. He said the university never contacted him about his offer, which he had hoped would inspire other donations.

Hamilton, an African-American, compared Confederate symbols with Nazi swastikas, which he said would not be allowed to stay on a building in Tennessee.

"Slavery was evil, and the Confederacy supported slavery," he said. "For us to be even having a discussion of whether it should come down is inappropriate. But life goes on. We, as a race of people, this is not going to affect us in terms of slowing down our progress."

But Jones and Deanna Bryant, president of the UDC's Tennessee division, said most of the soldiers honored by Confederate Memorial Hall were not slave owners. They were simply men "trying to defend their homes," said Jones, who is a former president of the Battle of Nashville Preservation Society.

"It's a victory for the entire South," Bryant, who lives in Franklin, said of the decision to keep the inscription on the building. "Regardless, the War Between the States happened. Just because somebody doesn't like something, you can't erase it from the history books."

SIGNIFICANCE

The Civil War remains the bloodiest conflict in American history, killing more people than all other American wars combined. During the Civil War, 112,000 Union soldiers and 94,000 Confederates were killed in combat. Another 197,000 Union men and 140,000 Confederates died of disease. Prison claimed 64,000 Union soldiers and 26,000 Confederates. The 633,000 total deaths do not reflect the men who were physically or psychologically wounded.

In this light, it is not surprising that the war is also the most commemorated in American history. Even before the war ended in 1865, Americans struggled over how to memorialize the experience. Since then, remembrance of the war has produced a vast set of monuments, speeches, poems, reenactments, films, and other works. In this commemoration, Americans have created a kind of public art that addresses issues of nationhood, race relations, gender roles, and multiculturalism. The response to this art has changed over time. The birth and flowering of the civil rights movement led to challenges of commemoration that celebrated the Southern side of the war. In clashes over the display of the Confederate battle flag and other Confederate memorabilia, African Americans have argued that the portrayal of the war should not celebrate a South that sought to enslave blacks. As the continuing debate indicates, issues surrounding the war continue to play a role in American society.

FURTHER RESOURCES

Books

Blight, David W. *Beyond the Battlefield: Race, Memory, and the American Civil War*. Amherst: University of Massachusetts Press, 2002.

Fahs, Alice and Joan Waugh, eds. *The Memory of the Civil War in American Culture*. Chapel Hill: University of North Carolina Press, 2004.

Neff, John R. *Honoring the Civil War Dead: Commemoration and the Problem of Reconciliation*. Lawrence: University Press of Kansas, 2005.

A Southern Star Rises in the Low Country

Newspaper article

By: R.W. Apple, Jr.

Date: March 15, 2006

Source: Apple, R.W., Jr. "A Southern Star Rises in the Low Country." *New York Times* (March 15, 2006).

About the Author: R. W. Apple, Jr. is an Associate Editor for the *New York Times*. Apple began working at the *Times* in 1963 and has served as Washington Bureau Chief, Chief Washington Correspondent, and Chief Correspondent of the Newspaper. He has covered the Vietnam War, the Iranian revolution, and the 1991 Persian Gulf War. Apple also wrote the book, *Apple's Europe*. He serves as the Director of the American Institute of Wine and Food.

INTRODUCTION

The city of Charleston, South Carolina, has a long history covering its 300 years of existence. The Spanish were the first to arrive in South Carolina in 1514, followed by the French Huguenots who settled in 1562. The Spanish struggled with Native Americans and later, the English and abandoned their settlements, along with the French. The first permanent settlement in South Carolina occurred in 1670 when the English settled at Albemarle Point on the Ashley River. King Charles II granted the Carolina territories to eight English noblemen called the Lords Proprietors. The English successfully created a plantation economy similar to those in the West Indies and brought in Barbadians to work the plantations. African slaves were soon needed as a result of the plantation boom, and by 1708, the majority of the plantation population was African slaves. In 1719, the colonists revolted against proprietary rule and South Carolina became a royal province.

Charleston then began to fulfill its destiny to become a major port town for the new world and in the 1750s, the proliferation of rice and indigo led to wealth for farmers and merchants. As merchants from the city traded with Bermuda and the Caribbean Islands, the population during this period began to change as well. Immigrants from Germany, Scotland, Ireland, and Wales permeated the city. In addition, increased trade led to a further expansion of plantations, thereby increasing the African slave population as well. Often the African slaves that were brought together in America were from different tribal groups and could not understand each other's language. As a result, the Gullah language and culture emerged as a combination of West African religion, culture, and language. Additionally, Sephardic Jews—those of Spanish and Portuguese descent—began to migrate to Charleston, leading it to become one of the largest Sephardic Jewish communities in North America.

As the cultural diversity of the city's immigrants grew, ethnic societies formed throughout Charleston. In 1737, the French Huguenots created the South Carolina Society. Germans were brought together in the German Friendly Society in 1766. In addition, the Irish were represented by the Hibernian Society beginning in 1801.

By the mid-eighteenth century, Charleston was the cultural and economic center of the South. However, the city and state of South Carolina were devastated during the American Civil War. On April 12, 1861, the first shots of the war were fired in Charleston Harbor. Although Charleston was spared the destruction that many cities in the south endured, the plantation-based economy was displaced by the end of slavery. Over the next decades, Charleston would struggle to reestablish its prewar status. In an attempt to rejuvenate the city's pre-war status, Charleston hosted the 1901 South Carolina Interstate and West Indian Exposition. The city hoped to become the primary port facilitating trade between the United States and Latin America and the Caribbean. The exposition was not a success. The port, however, would eventually develop into a gateway for modern-day trade with the U.S.

PRIMARY SOURCE

Eating well, very well, is nothing new in the marshy, island-rimmed Lowcountry of South Carolina. The complex and amply documented culinary traditions of this elegant peninsular city and its hinterland stretch back into Colonial times.

In 1742, Eliza Lucas Pinckney, born in Antigua, educated in London, wrote from her family's plantation on Wappoo Creek: "The country abounds with wild fowl, venison, and fish. The pork exceeds any I ever tasted anywhere. The turkeys are extremely fine, especially the wild, and indeed all the poultry is exceeding good. Peaches, nectarines, and melons of all sorts are extremely fine and in profusion." Decades before the Revolution, she cultivated rice and figs, baked macaroons with West Indies coconut, and macerated peach kernels in wine, brandy, orange flower water, and sugar to produce the cordial ratafia.

Notable early cookbooks were compiled by her daughter, Harriott Pinckney Horry (1770), and another relative, Sarah Rutledge ("The Carolina Housewife," 1847). Miss Rutledge included recipes for shrimp, crabs, oysters and shad—all Charleston mainstays a century and a half later—as well as daubes and ragouts introduced to South Carolina by the French Protestants known as Huguenots. Nor did she omit savory dishes based on ingredients brought by slaves from West Africa, such as okra, sesame seeds (known here as benne, exactly as in Senegal), peanuts, and black-eyed field peas—the key ingredient, along with rice, in that quintessential Lowcountry treat Hoppin' John.

But the Civil War and its aftermath took a heavy toll, devastating the aristocratic families like the Pinckneys and the Rutledges (from both of which my wife, Betsey, descends) and fastening a straitjacket of poverty on the Lowcountry that stayed in place for almost a hundred years.

These days Charleston is again a boom town, with soaring real estate prices and growing suburbs like Mount Pleasant, which is linked to the city by a spectacular $650 million suspension bridge, opened in 2005. Packed with restaurants old and new, the area has become one of the South's important culinary capitals—a worthy rival, if on a smaller scale, for New Orleans, at a time when many of that city's eating places are struggling to regain their footing after the hurricanes of 2005.

To mark its arrival in the gastronomic big time, Charleston staged its first Food and Wine Festival early in March, drawing more than 5,000 people over three days. Chefs and other food experts came from across the South to size up the situation, and many of them were impressed.

"The seeds have been here for a long time," said John T. Edge, director of the Southern Foodways Alliance at the University of Mississippi, "and now they're sprouting, at the most opportune moment." Frank Stitt, the chef and owner of the heralded Highlands Bar and Grill in Birmingham, Ala., agreed that "Charleston is poised to take its place alongside New Orleans, and the process won't take long."

Unlike New Orleans, Charleston was slow to develop a restaurant culture, and the best cooking was long confined to private kitchens. As late as 1958, when I first visited the city, in search of architectural rather than epicurean thrills, it had only one significant restaurant, Perdita's, which specialized in she-crab soup, made with the orange roe of the female of the species. Not incidentally, the definitive sherry-laced version of that soup is said to have been perfected early in the twentieth century by William Deas, butler to a local grande dame named Blanche Rhett, who produced a cookbook in the 30's.

Betsey can remember street vendors calling out "Swimpee! Swimpee!" when she was a young girl. They have disappeared, along with most of the sweet, tiny creek shrimp that they sold and the habit in many households of eating shrimp and grits for breakfast, lunch, and dinner, sometimes in the same day. Still, that dish, usually made with larger if still succulent bay and ocean shrimp, has become the emblem of Charleston restaurant cooking in recent times, as ubiquitous as pizza in Naples.

Today, though, a new sophistication is sweeping across the city and its suburbs as chefs with fresh ideas arrive from places like Boston, New York, Chicago, and Houston, eager to use local ingredients in new ways shaped by their own experience.

As the newcomers have poured in, some of the old masters have decamped—first Louis Osteen took his rich duck and quail specialties, his oyster stews and cobblers, to Pawleys Island, almost two hours up the coast, while more recently Michael Kramer, the Californian who put McCrady's on the culinary map, headed north to Chicago, and Rose Durden abdicated her seemingly permanent post in the kitchen of Carolina's.

Many of the town's classicists continue to turn out their classics, of course. The food-mad pilgrim can still revel in Robert Carter's moist, towering seven-layer coconut cake at the Peninsula Grill and Bob Waggoner's authentic, brightly spiced Frogmore Stew (a Lowcountry witch's brew that includes shrimp, crab, corn and sausage) at the Charleston Grill. And night after night at the cozy little Hominy Grill, Robert Stehling sends out carefully handmade versions of a myriad of regional delicacies, like okra and shrimp beignets, shad roe (perfectly sautéed and prettily poised on a heap of stone-ground grits) and buttermilk pie, which beats a buttermilk sky any old day.

There is much to like about Fig, Mike Lata's pared-down dining room on Meeting Street, Charleston's main stem. Things like the mustardy deviled eggs served while you read the menu, for example, and a warm salad of shrimp, pancetta, radicchio, and cherry tomatoes, and a wine list filled with fairly priced, seldom-encountered gems such as Brick House Oregon pinot noir, made by my friend Doug Tunnell, and the matchless Armagnacs of Francis Darroze.

Mr. Lata, a thirty-three-year-old New Englander who came to Charleston by way of New Orleans and Atlanta, turns out a superb hanger steak with caramelized shallots and an old-fashioned bordelaise sauce, and a paprika-infused Portuguese seafood stew. His luscious pudding made with Carolina Gold Rice puts other local versions to shame.

But Fig's strongest suit is vegetables—appropriate enough in a city and a region where the three- or four-vegetable plate lunch remains a treasured tradition.

An adherent of the Slow Food movement, Mr. Lata knows when to gild and when not to. He dresses a billowing bowlful of tender pale green Bibb lettuce, grown on nearby Wadmalaw Island by Dan Kennerty, with freckles of dark green herbs and a sherry vinaigrette, nothing more. His roasted beets are sweet simplicity, too. But he transforms the seasonal produce of Celeste Albers, turning hardy winter chard into a voluptuous gratin and pairing pan-roasted cauliflower with mustard butter. Only the turmeric-flavored cauliflower dishes in India excited me quite as much.

"The food Celeste brings me is so perfect that you're frustrated the rest of the year when you have to make do with the ordinary stuff," Mr. Lata said, and he frets that the proliferation of golf courses, gated residential communities, and shopping centers here is squeezing farmers out, narrowing the range of products available to chefs. . . .

A bit farther out of town, on Daniel Island, which once belonged to the Guggenheim family, Ken Vedrinski has given the area perhaps its most cosmopolitan restaurant, Sienna, a stylish, polished wood and stainless steel room with an open kitchen. Born in Ohio into a Polish-American family, he was largely raised by an Italian-American grandmother who proved to be his primary culinary influence.

Mr. Vedrinski likes bold flavors that "pop off the plate," he told me, and that showed in the array of Italian-style raw fish—crudo—that he served to a group of us, including Mickey Bakst, a veteran of the Michigan restaurant wars, who as maître d'hôtel has breathed animation into the Charleston Grill at Charleston Place, a rather sterile space that once epitomized the forbidding feel of hotel dining rooms.

The crudo at Sienna was every bit the equal of its celebrated counterpart, David Pasternak's at Esca in Manhattan, utilizing fish from near and far: local flounder, grouper, and oysters, tuna from the Northeast, ivory king salmon from the Northwest. Each got its own topping: olive oil for some, citrus juices for others, balsamic vinegar, even highly perfumed moscato vinaigrette.

Adapting a technique from Siggi Hall, Iceland's leading chef, Mr. Vedrinski bonds a ciabatta crust to a salmon scallop, a substitute for the crisp skin that he said "most Americans just won't eat," and serves it with a bracing cold salad of tomatoes, capers, garlic, and onions. He serves the classic Lowcountry combination of pork and shellfish in the form of intensely piggy guanciale, made from hog jowls, and lightly cooked shrimp over noodles hand-cut with a chitarra, a guitar-shaped tool.

We sampled all that, and two more irresistible plates—tiny veal meatballs, made to Grandma Volpe's recipe with impossibly ethereal gnocchi, and an unctuous rice pudding gelato made by Shun Li, the youthful Chinese-American pastry chef—before waddling out to our car, happily sated. Sienna's remarkably fastidious, decidedly modern Italian cooking could stand muster in New York, or in Milan for that matter.

Some people argue that Charleston lacks the lovable holes-in-the-wall that underpin the more ambitious restaurants in great food towns, places like the bouchons of Lyon, say, or the street-food stalls of Singapore. To a degree that's true, especially downtown. As much of the local food gossip these days centers on who serves the best beef—the Oak Steakhouse, Grill 225 or Mo Sussman's, the three main combatants in the city's red-hot steak skirmishes—as on who turns out the best shrimp and grits.

But move away from the center, to outlying areas where commercial pressures are not so intense, and you find plenty of joints where the old verities are served.

Take oysters. Charleston loves 'em, especially the uncultivated beauties, "meaty, juicy, salty," that John Martin Taylor, the Lowcountry food maven, gushes about, "continually washed by the incredible flow of our eight-foot tide," then plucked from the mud of the salt marshes and "garnished only by the glint of the January sun."

All through the colder months, oysters in vast quantities are cooked over raging fires and consumed at outdoors open-them-yourself oyster roasts, accompanied by heroic quantities of beer. Much the same experience can be had all year, in less raucous surroundings, at Bowens Island Restaurant, a humble cinder-block place on James Island, south of Charleston, where clusters of oysters from the Ashley River are steamed under wet burlap on a sizzling metal plate, then shoveled unceremoniously onto your table. Add saltines, hot sauce, maybe a squirt of lemon to replace that "glint of the January sun," and the requisite beer.

A ramshackle roadside place called See Wee, on Highway 17 leading north toward Myrtle Beach, is blessed with virtuoso practitioners of another old Lowcountry art, frying. Frying oysters, frying pickles, and delicately frying green tomatoes—the best of my seventy-one years, cut thin, dusted with corn flour and plunged into the hot fat for just a few moments, served up crisp and golden with a mild horseradish sauce. But most of all, frying shrimp, as well as any Tokyo tempura master, without a scintilla of heaviness or a smidgen of grease to mar the love affair 'twixt crustacean and palate.

As is always the case, freshness is the key here. Shrimp start deteriorating the minute they leave the water, so you eat them best close to the sea. The See Wee sign promises that—"Local Shrimp," it says, "God Bless the USA"—and at the same time suggests an unhappy reality. Carolina shrimpers, like Maryland crabbers, are menaced by low-cost foreign competition.

The restaurant's unusual name? It commemorates a small, ill-starred Indian tribe who took to their canoes in the seventeenth century, hoping to cross the Atlantic to trade deerskins with the king of England. Most quickly drowned; the rest were captured and sold into slavery and death in the Caribbean.

Closer to town, on the same stretch of Highway 17, stands an unpretentious little monument to the Gullah people, as the African-Americans who inhabited the coastal islands are known, and their culinary culture. Gullah Cuisine, it is called, and it is the place to get over your allergy to that mucilaginous vegetable the okra pod. Charlotte Jenkins, sixty-three, the kindly, soft-spoken proprietor, cured me in ten minutes flat with her smoky, robust shrimp-and-andouille gumbo, thickened with okra (and not, like most Louisiana gumbos, with roux or filé); her deep-fried okra; and her distinctive yellow rice with crisp, vividly green okra. Mrs. Jenkins's sweet braised cabbage, her extra-cheesy macaroni and her state-of-the-art fried chicken were all richly worth the trip out from town as well.

The happy, appreciative crowd at Saturday lunch was as heterogeneous as you could imagine: black, white and Hispanic, working class and middle class, local and Yankee, young and old. Parked outside were a Lexus, a Mercedes, a Harley, several pickups and a lot of battered third-hand jalopies. This, I said to my wife, was the South we fantasized about but almost never found in the days when I traipsed around the region in the 1960's, covering Martin Luther King.

SIGNIFICANCE

In a 2005 census of Charleston, the city population was found to be approximately 116,000 people. Of that, sixty-three percent of the population is white, and thirty-four percent of the population is black or African-American. One percent of the population is either Asian-American or of Hispanic ancestry. The remaining population is Native American or Pacific Islander.

Charleston's cultural makeup is based on the intermingling of ethnicities available in the city and has emerged as a fusion of the elite and the working class. The first settlers to Charleston began the cultural phenomenon by bringing with them transplants from the Caribbean and from Africa. While these slaves worked their plantations, their children were schooled in the aristocratic traditions in Europe. The American Civil War ended the plantation economy but did not end the high versus low country reality of Charleston's landscape.

FURTHER RESOURCES

Books

McInnis, Maurie D. *The Politics of Taste in Antebellum Charleston*. Chapel Hill: University of North Carolina Press, 2005.

Web sites

National Park Service's Park Register. "Charleston—community history." <http://www.cr.nps.gov/nr/travel/Charleston/intro.htm> (accessed June 15, 2006).

South Caroline State Government. "A Brief History of South Carolina." <http://www.state.sc.us/scdah/history.htm> (accessed June 15, 2006).

Dancehall with a Different Accent

Newspaper article

By: Kelefa Sanneh

Date: March 8, 2006

Source: Sanneh, Kelefa. "Dancehall with a Different Accent." *The New York Times*. (March 8, 2006).

About the Author: Kelefa Sanneh writes about pop music for *The New York Times*, and also serves as deputy editor for *Transition Magazine*. His main focus is the transition of hip-hop into the mainstream, and how this compares to the development of rap music.

INTRODUCTION

American popular music has evolved over the past century and a half, changing and morphing based on various influences, both cultural and political. The increased rate of immigration to the United States starting in the mid-nineteenth century resulted in a wealth of new ethnic types of music, primarily European, getting absorbed into the American culture, and when those ethnic groups mingled, their music affected that of other groups. In addition, following the Civil War and the freeing of the slaves in the late 1860s, African Americans migrated in large numbers, seeking out employment opportunities in major cities. Their musical styles and preferences went with them and began to influence the rhythms and sounds of the music in the areas where they settled. In the decades that followed, American music continued to develop with input from different cultures, altering with each change in the patterns of immigration to the United States, and based on which cultures dominated society.

■ PRIMARY SOURCE

On Monday night, America's most popular reggae singer took the stage wearing a black hat and a long black coat, but it wasn't a costume. The singer is Matisyahu, a former hippie from White Plains. Once he followed Phish. Now he follows the teachings of Hasidic Judaism. And tons of fans follow him.

Monday's concert was the first of two sold-out shows at the Hammerstein Ballroom. And yesterday he released his major-label debut album, "Youth" (JDub/Or/Epic), which is all but certain to enter the pop charts near the top. The record is dull, and the concert was often worse.

Still, once you hear Matisyahu's music, you may wonder why someone didn't think of this sooner. The plaintive, minor-key melodies of reggae aren't so far removed from the melodies Matisyahu would have heard, and sung, when he attended the Carlebach Shul, on the Upper West Side. And the imagery of Rastafarianism borrows heavily from Jewish tradition: Matisyahu is by no means the first reggae star to sing of Mount Zion, although he might be the first one who has had a chance to go there.

Matisyahu's black hat also helps obscure something that might otherwise be more obvious: his race. He is a student of the Chabad-Lubavitch philosophy, but he is also a white reggae singer with an all-white band, playing (on Monday night, anyway) to an almost all-white crowd. Yet he has mainly avoided thorny questions about cultural appropriation. He looks like an anomaly, but if you think of him as a white pop star drawing from a black musical tradition, then he may seem like a more familiar figure.

His sound owes a lot to early dancehall reggae stars like Barrington Levy and Eek-a-Mouse, who delivered half-sung lyrics over bass-heavy grooves. On "Youth," which was mainly produced by Bill Laswell, he is sometimes accompanied by electronics and backup vocals. The Hammerstein concert was sparser: a three-man band played the music while Matisyahu sang and twisted and hopped.

His heavy-handed lyrics (like "Fan the fire for the flame of the youth"), delivered in a slightly Jamaican-inflected accent, don't benefit from the stripped-down arrangements. And while he worked hard to entertain—rapping in double-time, beat-boxing, showing off some exuberant, high-stepping dance moves—he rarely sounded like the musical conqueror he wants to be.

Perhaps Matisyahu's fans aren't familiar with a little-known group of performers who still make great reggae records: Jamaicans. Maybe they are waiting for a shopping list of the best recent reggae CD's from Jamaica. So here's a start: Richie Spice, "Spice in Your Life" (Fifth Element); Luciano, "Lessons of Life" (Shanachie); Sizzla, "Da Real Thing" (VP).

Matisyahu has built a following by bypassing reggae fanatics (many of his fans come from the jam-band world). That explains why he outsells and outdraws his Jamaican counterparts. And it may also explain why some listeners find his music so exciting. Certainly no one seemed disappointed after Monday's concert. And as the crowd filed out, a wry young black woman working the door could be overheard singing to herself. It was a line from an older reggae song: "Could You Be Loved," by Bob Marley. "Don't let them fool you," she sang.

■

SIGNIFICANCE

The earliest musical influences in America were religious hymns or spirituals, folk music, and work songs sung primarily by slaves as they labored on plantations. The songs were strong in their narrative aspects and passed along stories of the development of the nation and the suffering of the people living there. Folk music traveled westward with the pioneers, and with the building of the railroads. Once slavery ended, African Americans congregated in cities such as New Orleans, Memphis, Chicago, and New York, working their way north in search of job opportunities. The rhythms of their music began to spread as they traveled and settled in different parts of the country, developing into ragtime, formalized blues music, and eventually jazz. For

Hasidic reggae singer Matisyahu performs in Aspen, Colorado, at the Belly Up, on February 5, 2006. © LYNN GOLDSMITH/CORBIS.

individuals without a great deal of money for things such as instruments, the steady beats and low tones of blues and jazz could be produced by homemade string instruments and drums, and augmented by vocals. Ragtime in particular spread throughout dance halls, adding an additional level of entertainment. Immigrants from Europe brought the sounds of their individual countries—Irish jigs, Polish polkas, Russian mazurkas—which began to blend as they populated both the cities and the frontier.

In the mid-twentieth century, rock and roll sprouted from the rhythms of African American music, and its birth is often attributed to singer Chuck Berry, whose steady beats and catchy tunes were first heard in the mid–1950s. Although Berry was black, his music had wide appeal, and white teenagers were as anxious to dance to his songs as black teens were. Segregation was still in full force in the United States, but the music industry ignored

social prejudices in favor of making money, and record labels began to actively search out other performers who could provide more music in a similar vein. White musicians began to emulate the rock-and-roll style, with performers such as Elvis Presley shooting to popularity. Country and folk music blended with the work of the softer rock singers, resulting in a quieter sound and harmonizing. By the 1960s, music was being imported from Great Britain in the so-called "British Invasion," as groups such as The Beatles grew in notoriety, further developing the sound.

By the close of the twentieth century, rock and roll music had subdivided into a variety of sounds, each the result of its own external influence. A shift in the immigrant population resulted in yet another series of musical influences. Urban music morphed into rap, which combined politics, poetry, and steady rhythms that resembled chanting. Caribbean music, with its lyrical rhythms and reggae sounds began to affect the sounds of modern American music. Hip-hop also developed from urban, African American and Latin rhythms, and was heavily influenced by the dance scene. But even as these musical influences changed the sounds of different popular music genres, the question of authenticity began to arise. Many of these musical types are based in the experiences and history of the culture from which they stem, and in some cases those individuals resent other cultures appropriating their music. While rap began as a predominantly African American form of expression, white and Hispanic musicians have adopted the format, as well as the lifestyle that many perceive to accompany that music. Is this simply a case of others enjoying and appreciating an art form, or is the life experience that generated that music truly necessary in order to justify participation? As music continues to evolve, and society struggles to determine whether cultures should blend or remain separate and distinct, the question as to whether Americans should maintain their original heritage over a unified identity will affect not only the numerous subgenres of popular music, but all aspects of culture in the United States.

FURTHER RESOURCES
Books

Landeck, Beatrice. *Echoes of Africa in Folk Songs of the Americas*. David MacKay Co., 1969.

Rose, Tricia. *Black Noise: Rap Music and Black Culture in Contemporary America*. Wesleyan University Press, 1994.

Szatmary, David. *Rockin'in Time: A Social History of Rock and Roll*. Prentice Hall Press, 2006.

Web sites

Roots World. "World Music." 2006 <http://www.rootsworld.com/rw/> (accessed June 25, 2006).

University of Virginia. "Jazz Roots, 1890–1935 <http://xroads.virginia.edu/~ASI/musi212/brandi/bmain.html> (accessed June 25, 2006).

Berlusconi Warns Against Multiculturalism

News article

By: Alessandra Rizzo

Date: March 28, 2006

Source: Rizzo, Alessandra. "Berlusconi Warns Against Multiculturalism." Associated Press, March 28, 2006.

About the Author: Alessandra Rizzo is a regular contributor to the Associated Press, a worldwide news agency based in New York.

INTRODUCTION

In 2000, there were more than one million legal immigrants living in Italy. Immigrant communities were diverse, consisting of Africans from Morocco, Senegal, and Tunisia (a total of 310,748); Asians from China, India, and the Philippines (a total of 192,864); and Europeans from Albania, former Yugoslavia, Poland, and Romania (a total of 382,924). The legal immigrant population also included people of the Americas, including Brazil, Peru, Colombia, and the Dominican Republic. In contrast, there were nearly 600,000 illegal immigrants residing in Italy. Cities with the highest concentration of immigrants are Rome and Milan.

Italy has the unique distinction of serving as a bridge to other countries in Europe. Shiploads of immigrants regularly arrive with people seeking refuge from war and armed conflicts. At the same time, Italy is experiencing a labor shortage in Northern regions. Although most immigrants live and work in central and northern Italy (thirty-four and fifty-four percent,

respectively), public opinion correlates immigration with poverty and crime.

In 2002, Prime Minister Berlusconi passed new legislation to regulate immigration for legal and illegal immigrants. Some fear the new Law No. 189 (the Bossi-Fini law), which is stricter than previous measures, will hurt the economy. Others argue that the law is beneficial because it requires employers to sign contracts for decent housing and return travel expenses, fixed wages, and set lengths of employment.

Those in favor of the law assert it benefits the country by improving living standards of immigrants and providing a more selective process for immigrant laborers.

PRIMARY SOURCE

ROME (AP)—Prime Minister Silvio Berlusconi said he does not want Italy to become a multiethnic, multicultural country, drawing plaudits from a right-wing ally and criticism from center-left opponents.

Berlusconi, a conservative, faces a stiff challenge in next month's national election, with opinion polls putting him behind his opponent, former premier Romano Prodi.

The poor economy, a main worry for voters in this election, has fed concerns about immigration by right-wing parties in Berlusconi's coalition, although the kind of work usually done by immigrants is shunned by many Italians. Surveys show that some Italians also perceive immigrants as being linked to crime.

"We don't want Italy to become a multiethnic, multicultural country. We are proud of our traditions," Berlusconi said Monday on state-run radio.

Berlusconi's government has put in place a tough immigration policy, including legislation cracking down on illegal immigration. The 2002 law allows only immigrants with job contracts to obtain residency permits.

"We want to open (our borders) to foreigners who flee countries where their lives or liberties are at risk," said Berlusconi, adding those who come to Italy to work also are welcome. "We don't want to welcome all those who come here to bring about damage and danger to Italian citizens."

Thousands of illegal immigrants come to Italy every year, mostly crossing the Mediterranean from North Africa on rickety boats. The latest group of more than 200 landed Monday on Lampedusa, a tiny island off Sicily.

Most immigrants, if they elude police, move on to other European countries.

The Northern League, a right-wing anti-immigrant party, welcomed Berlusconi's remarks.

"Here's the Berlusconi we want," said Roberto Calderoli, a Northern League leader who was forced to quit as reforms minister last month after he wore a T-shirt on state TV decorated with caricatures of the Prophet Muhammad. "Our values, our identity, our history, our traditions" must be defended against immigration, the Italian news agency ANSA quoted him as saying.

Paolo Cento of the opposition Greens party criticized Berlusconi, saying "the multiethnic society is a reality and an asset that must be handled," ANSA said.

SIGNIFICANCE

Italy is in a state of political and social adjustment. Social scientists have been trying to understand the world's racial and ethnic interactions since World War II. Nearly sixty years later, race and ethnicity remains a difficult social topic to predict. Historically, Italy was a country of emigrants—with an exodus in the late 1800's and early 1900's of immigrants to the United States. In the twenty-first century, Italy must grapple with the reverse—an exodus from other countries to its shores. In addition, with one of the world's lowest fertility rates, fewer Italian workers and more immigrants on the way mean that migration management will be an issue for years to come.

Due to its position as a bridge to Western Europe, Italy has been criticized by the European Union for its immigration policies, especially with regard to implementation and enforcement. Critics doubt Italy's ability to regulate its vulnerable shoreline (4,720 miles, or 7,600 kilometers). Some tout the new Bossi-Fini law as the answer to Italy's immigration problem, while others assert that improved border management and economic support in developing countries is the answer.

FURTHER RESOURCES

Books

Grills, R. D. and J. C. Pratt. *The Politics of Recognizing Difference: Multiculturalism Italian-Style*. Aldershot, U.K.: Ashgate, 2002.

Periodicals

Kowalczyk, Jaime and Thomas S. Popkewitz. "Multiculturalism, Recognition and Abjection: (Re)mapping Italian Identity." *Policy Futures in Education* 3 (2005): 423–435.

Rex, John. "Empire, Race, and Ethnicity." *International Journal of Comparative Sociology* 45 (2004): 161–177.

Web sites

Migration Information Source. "Italy." <http://www.migrationinformation.org/Resources/italy.cfm> (accessed June 26, 2006).

Why Aren't Black Business Tycoons Celebrated During Black History Month?

News article

By: Jeffrey J. Matthews

Date: February 27, 2006

Source: *History News Network*. "Why Aren't Black Business Tycoons Celebrated during Black History Month?" February 27, 2006 <http://hnn.us/articles/22169.html> (accessed July 17, 2006).

About the Author: Jeffrey J. Matthews is the Director of the Business Leadership Program at the University of Puget Sound in Tacoma, Washington, where he teaches courses in leadership, international business, and history. He is also the author of *Alanson B. Houghton: Ambassador of the New Era* (2004).

INTRODUCTION

This article questions why the history of black people in the United States pays insufficient attention to the achievements of black entrepreneurs and executives such as the renowned John Harold Johnson, who owned *Ebony Magazine* and numerous other business enterprises.

An annual period to commemorate Black History has been observed in the United States since 1926, when it was first organized by a Harvard scholar Dr. Carter G. Woodson (1875–1950). Woodson was keen to bring the story of African Americans into mainstream historical study and designated a week in February as Negro History week, in which black contributions to American society were celebrated. Over time, it has evolved into the annual Black History Month.

However, as the author of this article notes, the main focus of African America history has always been on slavery and on the experiences of black people as workers and subordinates. Although there is evidence of entrepreneurship among black people even before the Civil War, these accomplishments are generally given little or no discussion in history books.

Jason Hines, (third from left), a tenor with the Kuumba Singers of Harvard University, and a student at Harvard Law School, sings a solo during a choral performance at a service honoring Black History Month held at The Memorial Church in Cambridge, Massachusetts, February 17, 2002. AP IMAGES.

In the eighteenth century, the vast majority of African Americans in the United States were slaves, working as agricultural field-hands on the cotton, rice, and sugar plantations. After the abolition of slavery in 1864, many blacks continued working in agriculture, mainly as poor sharecroppers and tenant farmers. With industrialization and urbanization, a high percentage of blacks moved to the towns, and into unskilled and low-skilled service occupations and manual labor. Over the course of the twentieth century they have consistently had higher unemployment and under-employment rates than white people and other ethnic minorities such as the Latinos.

The relatively high rates of poverty and disadvantage among blacks have led to a focus in history and social science on these characteristics and on investigating the factors that contribute to them. However, studies have tended to ignore or sideline the phenomenon of black entrepreneurship, which also has a long history. Even during the time of

slavery, there are reports that many blacks in the southern states were planters, shareholders, or other businessmen, and many amassed hundreds of thousands of dollars.

Although some of these black entrepreneurs lost their fortunes during the Civil War, others continued their business activities and many black enterprises survived into the twentieth century. A new group of black businesspeople also emerged among the former slaves, some of whom had worked as artisans and were able to transfer their skills easily to new business enterprises, serving white as well as black communities. Indeed, the difficulties faced by African Americans in overcoming racial discrimination in the labor market and securing well-paying jobs has encouraged many of them to turn to self-employment, some simply making a living as individual traders and service providers, and others becoming highly successful businesspeople with very profitable enterprises.

In the late twentieth century, particularly after the Civil Rights Act of 1964 made illegal any discrimination on the basis of color, race, or gender, the number of African American owned businesses grew tremendously, particularly as black people had greater access to sources of funding than in the past. Despite the impressive growth, however, blacks remained under-represented in business compared to their percentage of the population. In the 1990s, it was reported that just over three percent of all United States businesses were owned by black people and these companies accounted for only one percent of total annual business receipts, even though African Americans comprised around thirteen percent of the population at this time. Moreover, although African Americans were achieving success in some niche areas such as the funeral business, black companies in more competitive sectors, such as retailing, were experiencing high rates of failure.

Some scholars have argued that the reasons for African Americans' low level involvement in business include the lack of an entrepreneurial tradition among black people, and the inability to develop the sort of business networks and ethnic credit facilities that have been important in other minority communities. However, others argue that it has been the impact of discrimination and racism against black people that has stifled their greater participation in entrepreneurial activity.

■ PRIMARY SOURCE

It's February and that means it's Black History Month, a designated time to commemorate and celebrate black contributions to American society. Unfortunately, the historic achievement of African American businesspeople is too often neglected this month, and every month.

For more than two decades, a number of historians, led largely by the pathbreaking scholarship of Professor Juliet E.K. Walker of the University of Texas, have been working to expand our knowledge of the rich tradition of black entrepreneurs, managers, and corporate executives. Too few people, including U.S. historians, have taken notice.

This historical neglect might have changed after last year, which witnessed the passing of one of the greatest entrepreneurs in American history. John Harold Johnson, the grandson of slaves, rose from Depression-era Arkansas roots to reach to the pinnacle of commercial success. By 1982 he had earned a place on the Forbes 400 list of richest Americans—the first African American so recognized. By the time of his death, at the age of eighty-seven, his fortune was thought to exceed half a billion dollars.

Johnson's business career began in 1936 when he accepted a part-time position with the black-owned Supreme Life Insurance Company of Chicago. In 1942, using his mother's furniture as collateral for a loan and advance proceeds from charter subscribers, he began his storied entrepreneurial career by creating the monthly news magazine *Negro Digest*. Three years later, he launched the legendary *Ebony* magazine, and in 1951 he began publishing the pocket-sized newsweekly *Jet*. By 1955, Johnson was an established millionaire and his publishing company reported a combined circulation of 2.6 million.

Of course what makes Johnson's success story even more remarkable is that he, like other black entrepreneurs and businesspeople, was forced to overcome severe racism. Early on, for example, when he approached First National Bank of Chicago for a business loan, he was told "Boy, we don't make any loans to colored people." Years later, a white property owner refused to sell his office building to Johnson because he was black. Undeterred, Johnson hired a white attorney to act surreptitiously on his behalf and he proceeded to buy the property at fair market value.

Another obstacle was convincing white advertising agencies and corporate executives to advertise in Johnson's magazines. He found some limited success with the companies Chesterfield and Kotex, but the significant financial breakthrough came in 1947 when this consummate salesman attracted the loyalty of Eugene F. McDonald, Zenith Radio's president, who not only bought major blocks of advertising but also encouraged other major corporations to do the same. As a result, business historian Robert Weems argues that Johnson "emerged as the major intermediary between corporate America and black consumers." Many years later, Johnson joined Zenith's board of directors.

Clearly Johnson was an ambitious capitalist, but he also was committed to both black economic empowerment and to enhancing the image of African Americans in the media. Over decades, Johnson employed and trained thousands of black Americans and he supported the activities of many black entrepreneurs, especially those in the advertising industry. On a broader scale, the eminent psychologist and Civil Rights leader Kenneth B. Clark concluded that "It is almost impossible to measure the morale-building value of [Ebony]. The mere fact of its existence and success has been an inspiration to the Negro masses."

John Johnson's business activities extended beyond magazine publishing and real estate investments. He owned multiple radio stations, sponsored several television shows, and manufactured hair care products. In 1973, he founded Fashion Fair Cosmetics, which after losing $5 million during its first five years of operation, grew to become America's largest black-owned cosmetics company with international sales in North and Latin America, in Europe, and in Africa. Other Johnson business lines included travel services, a mail order operation, fashion shows, clothing, and book publishing.

Beyond commerce, Johnson left a legacy of philanthropy that was most often committed to education. He was especially dedicated to the United Negro College Fund, and it is estimated that his companies helped to raise more than $51 million in scholarships throughout the country. Several years before his death, he donated $4 million to Howard University's School of Communications, which now bears his name. He also actively supported the Urban League, the National Association for the Advancement of Colored People, and the National Conference of Christians and Jews.

Not withstanding the above, John Johnson was a controversial figure. Employees complained about his autocratic leadership style, with some even referring to Johnson Publishing as the "plantation." In 1985, Fortune magazine labeled him as "one of the toughest bosses to work for." Johnson's publications were also criticized for offering too much "fluff" at the expense of critical reporting on the continuing inequities of American society. In response, Johnson often pointed to specific stories he had published related to the civil rights struggle, but he also reminded his critics that he was "a businessman, not a social worker."

For most of his life Johnson preached that a strong work ethic and sheer perseverance could overcome racial prejudice. But the accomplished millionaire came to question this precept, writing in his autobiography, *Succeeding Against the Odds*: "the closer I get to the top the more I realize that I'm never going to be fully accepted on merit and money alone. And that a different generation of Blacks—and a different generation of Whites—will know the final victory."

It is difficult to exaggerate John Johnson's influence on American society. And while the extent of his commercial success is truly exceptional, he is but one of countless examples of the inspirational black business tradition in American history. That tradition deserves more attention not only during Black History Month but also in the pages of our classroom history books.

SIGNIFICANCE

By focusing on the study of black people primarily as slaves and workers, mainstream history and social science may serve to perpetuate inequalities between blacks and whites in American society. In consistently portraying black people as subordinates, rather than equal participants in the modern American economy and society, these studies may create or strengthen beliefs and attitudes that legitimize racism at both personal and institutional levels and in turn prevent the greater involvement of black people in business.

A body of research into black business has been developing among white academics in recent years, with an emphasis so far on the study of black financial institutions such as insurance companies. This may help to highlight the achievements of black business people and contribute to a better understanding of the factors which have promoted as well as restricted entrepreneurship among African Americans.

FURTHER RESOURCES

Books

Walker, Juliet E. K. *Encyclopedia of African American Business History*. Westport, Conn.: Greenwood Press, 1999.

Walker, Juliet E. K. *The History of Black Business in America: Capitalism, Race, Entrepreneurship*. New York: Macmillan Press, 1998.

Periodicals

Dagbovie, Pero Gaglo. "Making Black History Practical and Popular: Carter G. Woodson, the Proto Black Studies Movement, and the Struggle for Black Liberation." *The Western Journal of Black Studies*. 28 (June 22, 2004): 372–383.

House, Bessie. "Does Economic Culture and Social Capital Matter?: An Analysis of African-American Entrepreneurs in Cleveland, Ohio." *The Western Journal of Black Studies* 24 (September 22, 2000): 183–192.

Sources Consulted

BOOKS AND WEBSITES

A Century of Lawmaking. "Library of Congress." <http://rs6.loc.gov/ammem/amlaw/lawhome.html> (accessed on June 24, 2006).

Abbott, Carl, Stephen J. Leonard, and Thomas J. Noel. *Colorado: A History of the Centennial State.* Boulder: University Press of Colorado, 2001.

Acuna, Rodolfo. *Occupied America: A History of Chicanos.* New York: Pearson Longman, 2004.

Adams, Karen L. and Daniel T. Brink, eds. *Perspectives on Official English: The Campaign for English as the Official Language of the USA.* Berlin: Mouton de Gruyter, 1990.

Agency for Healthcare Research and Quality. "Agency for Healthcare Research and Quality." <http://www.ahrq.gov> (accessed on June 24, 2006).

Aguirre, Eduardo. *"Civic Integration: Citizenship After 9/11." United States Citizenship and Immigration Service. November 13, 2003. <http://uscis.gov/graphics/aboutus/congress/testimonies/2003/EA111303.pdf> (accessed June 7, 2006).*

AIDS Research Institute (ARI). "AIDS Research Institute (ARI)." <http://ari.ucsf.edu> (accessed on June 24, 2006).

Alexander, Neville, Antonio Ségrio Alfredo Guimaraes, Charles V. Hamilton, Lynn Huntley, and James Wilmot. *Beyond Racism: Race and Inequality in Brazil, South Africa, and the United States.* Boulder, Co.: Lynne Rienner, 2001.

Alicea, Marixsa, and Toro-Morn, Maura I. *Migration and Immigration: A Global View.* Westport, Conn.: Greenwood Press, 2004.

Amar, Akhil Reed. *America's Constitution: A Biography.* New York: Random House, 2005.

American Immigration Law Foundation. "America's Heritage: A History of U.S. Immigration." March 29, 2006. <http://www.ailf.org/exhibit> (accessed June 26, 2006).

American Immigration Law Foundation. "Immigration Policy Center." <http://www.ailf.org/ipc/ipc_index.asp> (accessed June 7, 2006).

American Memory. "Library of Congress." <http://memory.loc.gov/ammem/index.html> (accessed on June 24, 2006).

American Rhetoric. "American Rhetoric." <http://www.americanrhetoric.com/> (accessed on June 24, 2006).

Amnesty International. "Amnesty International." <http://www.amnesty.org/> (accessed on June 24, 2006).

Anbinder, Tyler. *Nativism and Slavery: The Northern Know Nothings and the Politics of the 1850s.* New York: Oxford University Press, 1994.

Andersen, Arlow W. *The Norwegian-Americans.* Boston: Twayne, 1975.

Anderson, Terry H. *The Pursuit of Fairness: A History of Affirmative Action.* New York: Oxford University Press, 2004.

Angel Island Association. "Angel Island State Park." <http://www.angelisland.org> (accessed June 29, 2006).

Angel Island Immigration Station Foundation (AIISF). <http://www.aiisf.org> (accessed June 29, 2006).

Asian/Pacific American Heritage Association (APAHA). <http://www.apaha.org> (accessed June 28, 2006).

Association of Farmworker Opportunity Programs. "Child Labor—Children in the Fields: The Inequitable Treatment of Child Farmworkers." <http://www.afop.org/childlabor.htm> (accessed June 25, 2006).

Australian Government Culture and Recreation Portal. "European Discovery and the Colonisation of

Australia." <http://www.cultureandrecreation.gov.au/articles/australianhistory> (accessed June 28, 2006).

Avalon Project at Yale Law School. "An Act Respecting Alien Enemies." <http://www.yale.edu/lawweb/avalon/statutes/alien.htm> (accessed June 26, 2006).

Balfour, Sebastian. *The Politics of Contemporary Spain.* Routledge, 2005.

Barbour, Christine, et al. *Keeping the Republic: Power and Citizenship in American Politics.* Washington, D.C.: CQ Press, 2005.

Barringer, Herbert R. *Asians and Pacific Islanders in the United States.* New York: Russell Sage Foundation, 1993.

Barry, John M. *The Great Influenza: The Epic Story of the Deadliest Plague in History.* New York: Penguin Books, 2004.

Baugh, John. *Beyond Ebonics: Linguistic Pride and Racial Prejudice.* Oxford: Oxford University Press, 2000.

Bergmann, Werner, Erb Rainer, and Hermann Kurthen, eds. *Antisemitism and Xenophobia in Germany after Unification.* New York: Oxford University Press, 1997.

Bernstein, Jared, et al. *Pulling Apart: A State-by-State Analysis of Income Trends.* Washington, D.C.: Economic Policy Institute and Center on Budget Policy Priorities, 2002.

Berthoud, Richard. *Young Caribbean Men and the Labour Market: A Comparison with Other Ethnic Groups.* York, U.K.: York Publishing Services, 1999.

Better World Project. "Diversity Day." <http://www.diversityday.net/> (accessed June 26, 2006).

Bill of Rights Institute. "The Bill of Rights." <http://www.billofrightsinstitute.org/Instructional/Resources/FoundingDocuments/Docs/TheBillofRights.htm> (accessed June 12, 2006).

Bissoonath, Neil. *Selling Illusions: The Cult of Multiculturalism in Canada.* Toronto: Penguin Canada, 2002.

Blackstone, Tessa, Bhikhur Parekh, and Peter Sanders. *Race Relations in Britain: A Developing Agenda.* London: Routledge, 1998.

Blanc, Michel H. A., and Josiane Hammers, editors. *Bilinguality and Bilingualism.* Cambridge, U.K: Cambridge University Press, 2000.

Blegen, Theodore C. *Norwegian Migration to America, 1825–1860.* Northfield, MN: The Norwegian-American Historical Association, 1931.

Blight, David W. *Beyond the Battlefield: Race, Memory, and the American Civil War.* Amherst: University of Massachusetts Press, 2002.

Blum, John Morton. *V Was for Victory. Politics and American Culture during World War II.* New York: Harcourt Brace Jovanovich, 1976.

Bogen, Elizabeth. *Immigration in New York.* New York: Praeger Publishers, 1987.

Bok, Edward. *The Americanization of Edward Bok*, chapter 39. New York: Charles Scribner's Sons, 1921.

Bonacich, Edna and Richard Appelbaum. *Behind the Label: Inequality in the Los Angeles Apparel Industry.* Berkeley, Calif.: University of California Press, 2000.

Borjas, George J. *Heaven's Door: Immigration Policy and the American Economy.* Princeton, N.J.: Princeton University Press, 1999.

Bosworth, Barry, Susan M. Collins, and Nora Claudia Lustig. *Coming Together? Mexico-United States Relations.* Washington, D.C.: Brookings Institution Press, 1997.

Brechin, Gray. "The Wasp: Stinging Editorials and Political Cartoons." *Bancroftiana*, Fall 2002, <http://bancroft.berkeley.edu/events/bancroftiana/121/wasp.html> (accessed June 5, 2006).

Breitman, Richard, and Alan M. Kraut. *American Refugee Policy and European Jewry, 1933–1945.* Bloomington: Indiana University Press, 1987.

Brenner, Michael. *Zionism: A Brief History.* Princeton, N.J.: Markus Weiner Publishers, 2003.

Briggs, Vernon, M. *Mass Immigration and the National Interest.* New York: Sharpe, M.E., 1992.

Brigham Young University. "The World War I Document Archive." <http://www.lib.byu.edu/~rdh/wwi/> (accessed June 8, 2006).

Brisk, Maria Estela. *Bilingual Education: From Compensatory to Quality Schooling.* Mahwah, N.J.: Lawrence Erlbaum Associates, 1998.

British Library. "British Library Images Online." <http://www.imagesonline.bl.uk/britishlibrary/> (accessed on June 24, 2006).

Brock, William Ranulf, *Scotus Americanus: A Survey of the Sources for Links between Scotland and America in the Eighteenth Century.* Edinburgh: Edinburgh University Press, 1982.

Brown, Michael K., et al. *Whitewashing Race: The Myth of a Color-Blind Society.* Los Angeles: University of California Press, 2003.

Brownstone, David M., Irene M. Franck, and Douglass Brownstone. *Island of Hope, Island of Tears.* New York: Metro Books, 2003.

Brownstone, David, and Irene M. Franck. *Facts about American Immigration.* New York: H. W. Wilson, 2002.

Bucher, Richard D. and Patricia L. Bucher. *Diversity Consciousness: Opening Our Minds to People, Cultures, and Opportunities.* Upper Saddle River, NJ: Merrill, 2004.

Bureau International des Expositions. "Bureau International des Expositions." <http://www.bie-paris.org/main/index.php?lang=1> (accessed June 26, 2006).

Bureau of Labor Statistics, U.S. Department of Labor. "Report on the Youth Labor Force." <http://www.bls.gov/opub/rylf/rylfhome.htm> (accessed June 25, 2006).

Burnley, Ian H. *The Impact of Immigration on Australia: A Demographic Approach*. South Melbourne, Australia: Oxford University Press, 2001.

California Proposition 187. Available at: <http://www.usc.edu/isd/archives/ethnicstudies/historicdocs/prop187.txt> *(accessed June 7, 2006).*

California Secretary of State. "Proposition 227." <http://primary98.ss.ca.gov/VoterGuide/Propositions/227.htm> (accessed June 10, 2006).

Calonius, Erik. *The Wanderer: The Last American Slave Ship and the Conspiracy That Set Its Sails*. New York: St. Martin's Press, 2006.

Cambridge University. "Cambridge University, Institute of Public Health." <http://www.iph.cam.ac.uk> (accessed on June 24, 2006).

Cameron Riley, Hawkesbury Historical Society. "The 1804 Australian Rebellion and Battle of Vinegar Hill." November 2003. <http://www.hawkesburyhistory.org.au/articles/Battle_of_Vinegar.html> (accessed June 28, 2006).

Canot, Theodore. *Adventures of an African Slaver; Being a True Account of the Life of Captain Theodore Canot, Trader in Gold, Ivory & Slaves on the coast of Guinea*. Garden City, N.Y.: Garden City Pub. Co, 1928.

Carter Center. "There's Hope in Liberia's History: An Op-Ed by Jimmy Carter." July 13, 2003 <http://www.cartercenter.org/doc1366.htm> (accessed June 7, 2006).

Carter, Jimmy. *"Jimmy Carter Op-Ed: Employers in Quandary over Immigration Bill."* The Carter Center. <http://www.cartercenter.org/> (accessed June 13, 2006).

Casper, Scott E., and Lucinda M. Long. *Moving Stories: Migration and the American West, 1850–2000*. Reno: University of Nevada Press, 2001.

CDC (Centers for Disease Control and Prevention). "CDCSite Index A-Z." <http://www.cdc.gov/az.do> (accessed on June 24, 2006).

Census Bureau. "United States Census Bureau." <http://www.census.gov/> (accessed on June 24, 2006).

Central Pacific Railroad Photographic History Museum. "Chinese-American Contribution to Transcontinental Railroad." <http://cprr.org/Museum/Chinese.html> (accessed June 25, 2006).

Central Pacific Railroad Photographic History Museum. "Report of the Joint Special Committee to Investigate Chinese Immigration." <http://cprr.org/Museum/Chinese_Immigration.html> (accessed June 11, 2006).

Centre for Contemporary Cultural Studies. *The Empire Strikes Back: Race and Racism in 70s Britain*. London: Routledge, 1992.

Chávez, Ernesto. *Mi Raza Primero! (My People First!): Nationalism, Identity, and Insurgency in the Chicano Movement in Los Angeles, 1966–1978*. Berkeley: University of California Press, 2002.

Chambers, John Whiteclay. *The Tyranny of Change: America in the Progressive Era, 1890–1920*. New York: St. Martin's Press, 2000.

Chan, Sucheng. *Hmong Means Free: Life in Laos and America*. Philadelphia: Temple University Press, 1994.

Chapman, Jeff, and Jared Bernstein. "Immigration and Poverty: How Are They Linked?" U.S. Bureau of Labor Statistics. <http://www.bls.gov/opub/mlr/2003/04/art2full.pdf> (accessed June 13, 2006).

City of Botany Bay. "The History of Botany Bay." <http://www.botanybay.nsw.gov.au/city/history.htm> (accessed June 28, 2006).

Clarke, Frank G. *The History of Australia*. Westport, CT: Greenwood Press, 2002.

Clegg, Claude A., III. *The Price of Liberty: African Americans and the Making of Liberia*. Charlotte, N.C.: University of North Carolina Press, 2003.

CNN.com. "Immigration Tops EU Summit Agenda." June 20, 2002 <http://archives.cnn.com/2002/WORLD/europe/06/20/spain.summit/> (accessed June 15, 2006).

CNN. "Most of California's Prop. 187 Ruled Unconstitutional." <http://www.cnn.com/ALLPOLITICS/1998/03/19/prop.187/> (accessed June 7, 2006).

Coalition of Student Advocates. "Amy's Story." <http://www.cosaonline.org/stories.html> (accessed July 1, 2006).

Coalition of Student Advocates. "What is the DREAM Act?" <http://www.cosaonline.org/> (accessed July 1, 2006).

Cohen, Geula, and Yitzhak Rabin. *Major Knesset Debates*. Lanham, Md.: University Press of America, 1992.

Cohen, Jeffrey, et al. *The Presidency*. New York: McGraw-Hill Humanities, 2003.

Cohen, Rose. *Out of the Shadow: A Russian Jewish Girlhood on the Lower East Side*. Ithaca, N.Y.: Cornell University Press, 1993.

Columbia University Digital Knowledge Ventures. "The Architecture and Development of New York City: Living Together." <http://nycarchitecture.columbia.edu> (accessed June 28, 2006).

Cooke, Alastair. *Letters From America, 1946–2004*. London: Penguin, 2005.

Corcoran, Mary P. *Irish Illegals: Transients between Two Societies*. Westport, Conn.: Greenwood Press, 1993.

Coretta Scott King, The King Center. "The Meaning of the Martin Luther King, Jr. Holiday." <http://www.thekingcenter.org/holiday/index.asp> (accessed June 28, 2006).

Cornelius, Wayne A., ed., et al. *Controlling Immigration: A Global Perspective*. Stanford, CA: Stanford University Press, 2004.

Cornell Law School. "United States Constitution." <http://www.law.cornell.edu/constitution/constitution.table.html> (accessed June 12, 2006).

Cornell University: Making of America archives. "The American Missionary." <http://cdl.library.cornell.edu/moa/browse.journals/amis.html> (accessed June 11, 2006).

Cowley, Robert, ed. *The Cold War: A Military History.* New York: Random House, 2005.

Cox, Taylor. *Creating the Multicultural Organization: A Strategy for Capturing the Power of Diversity.* San Francisco, CA: Jossey-Bass, 2001.

Cran, William and Robert MacNeil. *Do You Speak American?* New York: Doubleday, 2005.

Crawford, James. *At War with Diversity: U.S. Language Policy in an Age of Anxiety.* Clevedon, England: Multilingual Matters, 2000.

Crenson, Matt. Pangaea. "Pesticides May Jeopardize Child Farmworkers' Health." December 9, 1997 <http://pangaea.org/street_children/americas/AP7.htm> (accessed June 25, 2006).

Cronin, Mike. *A History of Ireland.* New York: Palgrave, 2001.

Cutler, Dawes Rufus. *A Century of Progress: Chicago World's Fair Centennial Celebration.* Chicago, Ill.: Century of Progress, 1933.

Daniels, Roger. *Coming to America: A History of Immigration and Ethnicity in American Life.* New York: Harper Perennial, 2002.

Daniels, Roger. *Guarding the Golden Door: American Immigration Policy and Immigrants since 1882.* New York: Oxford University Press, 1996.

Daniels, Roger. *Politics of Prejudice: The Anti-Japanese Movement in California.* Berkeley, Calif.: University of California Press, 1999.

Dawidowicz, Lucy. *The War Against the Jews, 1933–1945.* London: Weidenfeld and Nicolson, 1975.

DeGregorio, William. *The Complete Book of U.S. Presidents.* Sixth edition. New York: Random House, 2001.

Del Valle, Sandra. *Language Rights and the Law in the United States: Finding Our Voices.* Clevedon, England: Multilingual Matters, 2003.

Delaet, Debra L. *U.S. Immigration Policy in an Age of Rights.* Praeger, 2000.

Delaet, Debra L. *U.S. Immigration Policy in an Age of Rights.* Westport, Conn.: Praeger Publishers, 2000.

Delaet, Debra. *U.S. Immigration Policy in an Age of Rights.* Westport, Conn.: Praeger, 2000.

Delpit, Lisa, and Theresa Perry. *The Real Ebonics Debate: Power, Language, and the Education of African-American Children.* Boston: Beacon Press, 1998.

Department of Immigration and Multicultural Affairs, Australian Government. "Multicultural Australia: United in Diversity." May 2003. <http://www.immi.gov.au/living-in-australia/a-diverse-australia/government-policy/index.htm> (accessed July 1, 2006).

Department of Translation Studies, University of Tampere. "Italian Immigration to the United States." January 2000 <http://www.uta.fi/FAST/US2/PAPS/db-italy.html> (accessed July 22, 2006).

Derderian, Richard C. *North Africans in Contemporary France: Becoming Visible.* New York: Palgrave Macmillan, 2004.

Diner, Hasia. *Jews in America.* New York: Oxford University Press, 1999.

Dinnerstein, Leonard, Roger L. Nichols, and David M. Reimers. *Natives and Strangers: A Multicultural History of Americans.* New York: Oxford University Press, 1996.

Doctors Without Borders. "Doctors Without Borders." <http://www.doctorswithoutborders.org/> (accessed on June 24, 2006).

Donnelly, Jack. *Universal Human Rights in Theory and Practice.* Ithaca, New York: Cornell University Press, 2002.

Dow, George F. *Slave Ships and Slaving.* Salem, Mass.: Marine Research Society, 1927.

Dower, John W. *War without Mercy: Race and Power in the Pacific War.* New York: Pantheon, 1987.

Dublin, Thomas, ed. *Immigrant Voices: New Lives in America, 1773–1986.* University of Illinois Press, 1993.

Dudley-Edwards, R. and Desmond T. Williams. *The Great Famine: Studies in Irish History, 1845–52.* New York: New York University Press, 1957.

Duncan, Cynthia M., ed. *Rural Poverty in America.* New York: Auburn House, 1992.

Eatwell, Roger and Cas Mudde. *Western Democracies and the New Extreme Right Challenge.* New York: Routledge, 2004.

EdChange Multicultural Pavilion. "Language of Closet Racism: An Illustration." <http://www.edchange.org/multicultural/papers/langofracism2.html> (accessed July 15, 2006).

Eldershaw, M. Barnard. *Phillip of Australia.* Sydney, Australia: Augus & Robertson, 1972.

Ellingwood, Ken. *Hard Line: Life and Death on the U.S. Mexican Border.* New York: Pantheon, 2004.

Erickson, Charlotte. *Leaving England: Essays on British Emigration in the Nineteenth Century.* Ithaca, NY: Cornell University Press, 1994.

Ets, Marie Hall. *Rosa: The Life of an Italian Immigrant.* Madison: University of Wisconsin Press, 1999.

Etulain, Richard W. *César Chávez: A Brief Biography with Documents.* Boston: Bedford/St. Martin's, 2002.

Fahs, Alice and Joan Waugh, eds. *The Memory of the Civil War in American Culture.* Chapel Hill: University of North Carolina Press, 2004.

Farmworkers Movement Documentation Project. "Rey Huerta, 1968–1975: The Most Memorable Times of Our Lives."<http://www.farmworkermovement.org/> (accessed June 25, 2006).

Federal Government Agencies Directory. "Louisiana State University." <http://www.lib.lsu.edu/gov/fedgov.html> (accessed on June 24, 2006).

Federation for American Immigration Reform. "Federation for American Immigration Reform." <http://www.fairus.org/> (accessed June 16, 2006).

Federation of American Scientists. "Federation of American Scientists, ProMED Initiative." <http://www.fas.org/promed> (accessed on June 24, 2006).

FedStats. "FedStats." <http://www.fedstats.gov> (accessed on June 24, 2006).

Ferrie, Joseph P. *Yankeys Now: Immigrants in the Antebellum United States, 1840–1860.* New York: Oxford University Press, 1999.

Findlaw. "Findlaw/West." <http://public.findlaw.com/library/> (accessed on June 24, 2006).

Foster, R. F. *The Oxford History of Ireland.* New York: Oxford University Press, 2001.

Freedman, Russell. *Immigrant Kids.* New York: Puffin, 1995.

Freeman, James M. and Nguyen Dinh Huu. *Voices from the Camps: Vietnamese Children Seeking Asylum.* Seattle: University of Washington Press, 2003.

Friedland, Klaus, ed. *Maritime Aspects of Migration.* Cologne, Germany: Bohlau, 1989.

Friedman-Kasaba, Kathie. *Memories of Migration: Gender, Ethnicity, and Work in the Lives of Jewish and Italian Women in New York, 1870–1924.* Albany, NY: State University of New York Press, 1996.

Fullerton, Maryellen. *Germany for Germans: Xenophobia and Racist Violence in Germany.* New York: Human Rights Watch, 1995.

Gabaccia, Donna R. *From Sicily to Elizabeth Street: Housing and Social Change among Italian Immigrants, 1880–1930.* Albany, N.Y.: State University Press of New York, 1984.

Gabaccia, Donna. *From the Other Side: Women, Gender, and Immigrant Life in the U.S., 1820–1990.* Bloomington: Indiana University Press, 1994.

Gaddis, John Lewis. *The Cold War: A New History.* New York: Penguin Press, 2005.

Gallman, Matthew J. *Receiving Erin's Children: Philadelphia, Liverpool, and the Irish Famine Migration, 1845–1855.* Chapel Hill, N.C.: University of North Carolina Press, 2000.

Ganzhorn, Derek. "'Politically Correctness' Hides Depth of Racism in America." *University of Minnesota Register,* November 3, 2005. <http://www.morris.umn.edu/register/> (accessed June 7, 2006).

GAO (Government Account Office). "Site Map." <http://www.gao.gov/sitemap.html> (accessed on June 24, 2006).

Garcia, Victor. *Counting the Uncountable, Immigrant and Migrant, Documented and Undocumented Farm Workers in California.* Washington, D.C.: GPO/ Census Bureau, 1992.

Gardner, Martha. *The Qualities of a Citizen: Women, Immigration, and Citizenship, 1870–1965.* Princeton, N.J.: Princeton University Press, 2005.

Garfinkel, Simson. *Database Nation: The Death of Privacy in the Twenty-First Century.* Sebastopol, Calif.: O'reilly Media, 2001.

Genizi, Haim. *America's Fair Share: The Administration and Resettlement of Displaced Persons, 1945–1952.* Detroit: Wayne State University Press, 1993.

George Washington University. "The Revolutions of 1989: New Documents from Soviet/East Europe Archives Reveal Why There Was No Crackdown." November 5, 1999. <http://www.gwu.edu/~nsarchiv/news/19991105/index.html> (accessed June 13, 2006).

Gillen, Mollie. *The Search for John Small: First Fleet.* North Sydney, Australia: Library of Australia History, 1985.

Gimpel, James G. *Separate Destinations: Migration, Immigration, and the Politics of Places.* Ann Arbor: University of Michigan Press, 1999.

Gimpel, James G., and James R. Edwards, Jr. *The Congressional Politics of Immigration Reform.* Needham Heights, Mass.: Allyn and Bacon, 1999.

Glazer, Nathan, and Moynihan, Daniel P. *Beyond the Melting Pot, Second Edition: The Negroes, Puerto Ricans, Jews, Italians, and Irish of New York City.* Cambridge, Mass.: The MIT Press, 1970.

Glazer, Nathan. *Clamor at the Gates: The New American Immigration.* New York: ICS Press, 1985.

Glazier, Jack. *Dispersing the Ghetto: The Relocation of Jewish Immigrants across America.* Ithaca, N.Y.: Cornell University Press , 1998.

Glendon, Mary Ann. "Principled Immigration." *Harvard Law School,* May 25, 2006. <http://www.law.harvard.edu/news/2006/05/25_glendon.php> (accessed June 6, 2006).

Glenn, Evelyn N. *Unequal Freedom: How Race and Gender Shaped American Citizenship and Labor.* Cambridge, MA: Harvard University Press, 2002.

Glover, S., Gott, C., Loizillon, A., Portes J., Price, R., Spencer, S., Srinivasan, V. and Willis, C. *Migration: an Economic and Social Analysis, RDS Occasional Paper No. 67.* The Home Office Research, Development and Statistics Directorate, 2001.

Godley, Andrew. *Jewish Immigrant Entrepreneurship in New York and London, 1880–1914: Enterprise and Culture.* New York: Palgrave, 2001.

Gordon, Milton M. *Assimilation in American Life: The Role of Race, Religion, and National Origin*. New York: Oxford University Press, 1964.

Government of Australia/Department of Foreign Affairs and Trade. "Human Rights." 200.5 <http://www.dfat.gov.au/hr/comm_hr/chr61_item6.html> (accessed June 28, 2006).

Gowdey, David. *Before the Wind: True Stories about Sailing*. Camden, Maine: International Marine, 1994.

Graham, Hugh Davis. *Collision Course: The Strange Convergence of Affirmative Action and Immigration Policy in America*. New York: Oxford University Press, 2003.

Great Buildings.com. "The Statue of Liberty." 2006 <http://www.greatbuildings.com/buildings/Statue_of_Liberty.html> (accessed June 24, 2006).

Griffith, David Craig. *Working Poor: Farmworkers in the United States*. Philadelphia, PA: Temple University Press, 1995.

Grills, R. D. and J. C. Pratt. *The Politics of Recognizing Difference: Multiculturalism Italian-Style*. Aldershot, U.K.: Ashgate, 2002.

Gruber, Ruth. *Exodus 1947: The Ship That Launched a Nation*. New York: Crown, 2000.

Gyory, Andrew. *Closing the Gate: Race, Politics, and the Chinese Exclusion Act*. Chapel Hill, N.C.: University of North Carolina Press, 1998.

Hackemer, Kurt. *The U.S. Navy and the Origins of the Military Industrial Complex, 1847–1883*. Washington, D.C.: Naval Institute Press, 2001.

Haines, David W., and Karen E. Rosenblum, eds. *Illegal Immigration in America: A Reference Handbook*. Westport, Conn.: Greenwood Press, 1999.

Hamilton-Merritt, J. *Tragic Mountains: The Hmong, the Americans, and the Secret Wars for Laos, 1942–1992*. Bloomington, Ind.: Indiana University Press, 1993.

Hansen, Randall. *Citizenship and Immigration in Postwar Britain*. Oxford: Oxford University Press, 2000.

Harper, Jim. *Identity Crisis: How Identification is Overused and Misunderstood*. Washington, D.C.: Cato Institute, 2006.

Health Resources and Services Administration (HRSA). "Health Resources and Services Administration (HRSA)." <http://www.hrsa.gov> (accessed on June 24, 2006).

Hein, Jeremy. *From Vietnam, Laos, and Cambodia: A Refugee Experience in the United States*. New York: Twayne, 1995.

Henriksen, Louise Levitas. *Anzia Yezierska: A Writer's Life*. New Brunswick, N.J.: Rutgers University Press, 1988.

Hien Duc Do. *The Vietnamese Americans*. Westpost, Conn.: Greenwood Press, 1999.

Hindus, Milton. *The Jewish East Side, 1881–1924*. New Brunswick, N.J.: Transaction Publishers, 1996.

Hing, Bill O. and Anthony D. Romero. *Defining America Through Immigration Policy*. Philadelphia: Temple University Press, 2004 .

Hirobe, Izumi. *Japanese Pride, American Prejudice*. Stanford, Calif.: Stanford University Press, 2001.

Historical Society of Pennsylvania. "Irish Immigrant Ballads." <http://www.hsp.org/default.aspx?id=580> (accessed June 29, 2006).

History News Network. "Why Aren't Black Business Tycoons Celebrated during Black History Month?" February 27, 2006 <http://hnn.us/articles/22169.html> (accessed July 17, 2006).

Hitchcox, Linda. *Vietnamese Refugees in Southeast Asian Camps*. London: Macmillan, 1990.

Home Office Immigration and Nationality Directorate. "Legislation." <http://www.ind.homeoffice.gov.uk/lawandpolicy/legislation/> (accessed June 29, 2006).

Hopkinson, Deborah. *Shutting Out the Sky: Life in the Tenements of New York, 1880–1924*. New York: Orchard, 2003.

Horne, Donald. *10 Steps to a More Tolerant Australia*. Sydney: Penguin Australia, 2003.

Hostetler, John. *Amish Society*. Baltimore: Johns Hopkins University Press, 1993.

Human Rights Watch. *Fingers to the Bone: United States Failure to Protect Child Farmworkers*. New York: Human Rights Watch, 2000.

Human Rights Watch. "Human Rights Watch." <http://www.hrw.org/> (accessed on June 24, 2006).

Human Rights Watch. "The Right to Asylum in the European Union." <http://www.hrw.org/worldreport/Helsinki-28.htm> (accessed June 15, 2006).

Hurt, R. Douglas. *American Agriculture: A Brief History*. Ames: Iowa State University Press, 2002.

Hutchinson, E.P. *Legislative History of American Immigration Policy, 1798–1965*. Philadelphia: University of Pennsylvania Press, 1981.

Ibarra, Robert A. *Beyond Affirmative Action: Reframing the Context of Higher Education*. Madison: University of Wisconsin Press, 2001.

Ignatiev, Noel. *How the Irish Became White*. New York: Routledge, 1996.

Illinois Institute of Technology. "World's Columbian Exposition of 1893." <http://columbus.gl.iit.edu/> (accessed June 12, 2006).

Irish Culture and Customs. "Padraic Pearse." <http://www.irishcultureandcustoms.com/Poetry/PadraicPearse.html> (accessed July 15, 2006).

Irish History Online. "Welcome to Irish History Online." <http://www.irishhistoryonline.ie/> (accessed June 23, 2006).

Irishabroad.com. <http://www.irishabroad.com> (accessed June 26, 2006).

Ishay, Micheline. *The History of Human Rights: From Ancient Times to the Globalization Era.* Berkeley: University of California Press, 2004.

Jacobson, David. *Rights across Borders: Immigration and the Decline of Citizenship.* Baltimore: Johns Hopkins University Press, 1996.

Jacobson, Matthew Frye. *Whiteness of a Different Color: European Immigrants and the Alchemy of Race.* Cambridge, Mass.: Harvard University Press, 1999.

Jayasuriya, Laksiri, and Kee Pookong. *The Asianisation of Australia?: Some Facts about the Myths.* Carlton South, Australia: Melbourne University Press, 1999.

Jeffrey, Julie Roy. *Great Silent Army of Abolitionism: Ordinary Women in the Antislavery Movement.* Chapel Hill: University of North Carolina Press, 1998.

Jewish Women's Archive. "Exhibit: Women of Valour: Emma Lazarus." 2006. <http://www.jwa.org/exhibits/wov/lazarus/el12.html> (accessed June 20, 2006).

John, Gus. *Taking a Stand.* Manchester, U.K.: Gus John Partnership, 2006.

Jones, Maldwyn Allen. *American Immigration.* Chicago: University of Chicago Press, 1960.

Joseph, Samuel. *Jewish Immigration to the United States from 1881 to 1910.* New York: Columbia University Press, 1914.

Kazal, Russell M. *Becoming Old Stock: The Paradox of German-American Identity.* Princeton, N.J.: Princeton University Press, 2004.

Keene, Jennifer D. *The U.S. and the First War.* New York: Longman, 2000.

Keller, Morton. *The Art and Politics of Thomas Nast.* New York: Oxford University Press, 1968.

Kerber, Linda K. *No Constitutional Right to be Ladies: Women and the Obligations of Citizenship.* New York: Hill and Wang, 1998.

Ketchum, Alton. *Uncle Sam: The Man and the Legend.* New York: Hill and Wang, 1959.

Kettner, James H. *The Development of American Citizenship, 1608–1870.* Chapel Hill: University of North Carolina Press, 1978.

Khan, Shaharyan M., and Mary Robinson. *The Shallow Graves of Rwanda.* New York: St. Martin's Press, 2000.

Kibria, Nazli. *Family Tightrope: The Changing Lives of Vietnamese Americans.* Princeton, N.J.: Princeton University Press, 1993.

King Center. <http://www.thekingcenter.org/index.asp> (accessed June 28, 2006).

King, Jr., Martin Luther. *Strength to Love.* New York: Harper and Row, 1963.

Kitschelt, Herbert, and Wolfgang Street. *Germany: Beyond the Stable State.* Portland, Ore., and London: Frank Cass, 2004.

Klein, Herbert S. *The Atlantic Slave Trade.* Cambridge, U.K.: Cambridge University Press, 1999.

Knott, Tom. "*A Need to Pass the Peace Pipe.*" *Washington Times*, August 19, 2005. <http://washingtontimes.com/sports/20050819–125544-4353r.htm> (accessed June 8, 2006).

Kochavi, Arieh J. *Post Holocaust Politics: Britain, the United States and Jewish Refugees, 1945–1948.* Chapel Hill: University of North Carolina Press, 2001.

Kors, Alan Charles, and Harvey A. Silvergate. *The Shadow University: The Betrayal of Liberty on America's Campuses.* New York: The Free Press, 1998.

Kotz, Nick. *The Judgment Days: Lyndon Baines Johnson, Martin Luther King, Jr., and the Laws That Changed America.* Boston: Houghton Mifflin, 2005.

Krabbendam, Hans. *The Model Man: A Life of Edward William Bok, 1863–1930.* Amsterdam: Rodep, 2001.

Kretsedemas, Philip, and Ann Aparicio, eds. *Immigrants, Welfare Reform, and the Poverty of Policy.* New York: Praeger Publishers, 2004.

Krop, Richard A., Peter C. Rydell, and Georges Vernez. *Closing the Education Gap: Benefits and Costs.* Santa Monica, Calif.: Rand, 1999.

Kwong, Peter. *Forbidden Workers: Chinese Immigrants and American Labor.* New York: New Press, 1998.

Labor and Labor Movements. "American Sociological Association." <http://www.bgsu.edu/departments/soc/prof/mason/ASA/> (accessed on June 24, 2006).

LaGumina, Salvatore J. *From Steerage to Suburb: Long Island Italians.* New York: Center for Migration Studies, 1988.

LaGumina, Salvatore J. *From Steerage to Suburb: Long Island Italians.* New York: Center for Migration Studies, 1988.

Laham, Nicholas. *Ronald Reagan and the Politics of Immigration Reform.* Westport, CT: Praeger Publishers, 2000.

Lai, Him Mark, Genny Lim, and Judy Yung. *Poetry and History of Chinese Immigrants on Angel Island, 1910–1940.* Seattle, Wash.: University of Washington Press, 1999.

Landeck, Beatrice. *Echoes of Africa in Folk Songs of the Americas.* David MacKay Co., 1969.

Leavitt, Thomas W. *Hollingworth Letters: Technical Change in the Textile Industry 1826–1937.* Cambridge, MA: MIT Press/ Society for the History of Technology, 1969.

Lee, Erika. *At America's Gates: Chinese Immigration During the Exclusion Era, 1882–1943.* Chapel Hill, N.C.: University of North Carolina Press, 2003.

Lee, Kenneth K. *Huddled Masses, Muddled Laws: Why Contemporary Immigration Policy Fails to Reflect Public Opinion.* Westport, CT: Praeger Publishers, 1998.

Legal Information Institute, Cornell University. "Code of Federal Regulations." <http://www4.law.cornell.edu/cfr/> (accessed on June 24, 2006).

LeMay, Michael C. *Anatomy of a Public Policy: The Reform of Contemporary American Immigration Law.* Westport, Conn.: Praeger Publishers, 1994.

LeMay, Michael, and Elliott R. Barkan, eds. *U.S. Immigration and Naturalization Laws and Issues: A Documentary History.* Westport, CT: Greenwood Press, 1999.

Levine, Marvin J. *Children for Hire: The Perils of Child Labor in the United States.* Westport, Conn.: Praeger, 2003.

Levitt, Jeremy. *The Evolution of Deadly Conflict in Liberia: From 'Paternaltarianism' to State Collapse.* Durham, N.C.: Carolina Academic Press, 2005.

Library of Congress. "Library of Congress Online Catalog." <http://catalog.loc.gov/cgi-bin/Pwebrecon.cgi?DB=local&PAGE=First> (accessed on June 24, 2006).

Library of Congress/American Memory. "The Chinese in California 1850–1925." <http://memory.loc.gov/ammem/award99/cubhtml/cichome.html> (accessed June 5, 2006).

Library of Congress. "A Century of Immigration: 1820–1934." September 7, 2005 <http://www.loc.gov/exhibits/haventohome/haven-century.html> (accessed June 24, 2006).

Library of Congress. "Israel Country Study." <http://countrystudies.us/israel/88.htm> (accessed June 15, 2006).

Library of Congress. "Norwegian-American Immigration and Local History." June 28, 2005 <http://www.loc.gov/rr/genealogy/bib_guid/norway.html> (accessed June 13, 2006).

Ling, Peter J. *Martin Luther King, Jr.* New York: Routledge, 2002.

Linguist List. "Original Oakland Resolution on Ebonics." December 18, 1996 <http://linguistlist.org/topics/ebonics/ebonics-res1.html> (accessed July 16, 2006).

Loescher, Gil. *The UNHCR and World Politics: A Perilous Path.* Oxford, U.K.: Oxford University Press, 2001.

Loewen, Harry and Steven Nolt. *Through Fire and Water: An Overview of Mennonite History.* Scottsdale, PA: Herald Press, 1996.

Loewen, Royden. *Hidden Worlds: Revisiting the Mennonite Migrants of the 1870s.* Winnipeg, Manitoba: University of Manitoba Press, 2001.

London, Louise. *Whitehall and the Jews, 1933–1948.* Cambridge, U.K.; Cambridge University Press, 2001.

Louie, Vivian S. *Compelled to Excel: Immigration, Education and Opportunity and Chinese Americans.* Stanford, Calif.: Stanford University Press, 2004.

Lowell, Lindsay B. ed. *Foreign Temporary Workers in America: Policies That Benefit the U.S. Economy.* Westport, Conn.: Quorum Books, 1999.

Lum, Lydia. *Angel Island: Immigrant Journeys of Chinese-Americans.* <http://www.angel-island.com> (accessed June 29, 2006).

Münz; Rainer. *Migrants, Refugees, and Foreign Policy: U.S. and German Policies toward Countries of Origin.* New York: Berghahn Books, 1997.

Mackay, David. *A Place of Exile: European Settlement of New South Wales.* Melbourne, Australia: Oxford University Press, 1985.

Making of America. "Cornell University." <http://cdl.library.cornell.edu/moa/> (accessed on June 24, 2006).

Mangione, Jerre and Ben Morreale. *La Storia: Five Centuries of the Italian American Experience.* New York: Harper Collins, 1992.

Masud-Piloto, Felix Roberto. *From Welcomed Exiles to Illegal Immigrants: Cuban Migration to the U.S., 1959–1995.* Lanham, Md.: Rowman & Littlefield, 1996.

Maxwell-Stewart, Hamish and Cassandra Pybus. *American Citizens, British Slaves: Yankee Political Prisoners in an Australian Penal Colony 1839–1850.* Melbourne, Australia: Melbourne University Press, 2002.

Mayer, Henry. *All on Fire: William Lloyd Garrison and the Abolition of Slavery.* New York: St. Martin's Press, 2000.

McCullough, David G. *John Adams.* New York: Simon and Schuster, 2001.

McInnis, Maurie D. *The Politics of Taste in Antebellum Charleston.* Chapel Hill: University of North Carolina Press, 2005.

McKelvey, Robert S. *The Dust of Life: America's Children Abandoned in Vietnam.* Seattle: University of Washington Press, 1999.

Mcleod, John. *Postcolonial London: Rewriting the Metropolis.* London and New York: Routledge, 2004.

McPherson, J. H. T. *History of Liberia.* Kieler, Mont.: Kessinger Publishing, 2004.

McPherson, J. H. T. *The Cholera Years: The United States in 1832, 1849, and 1866.* Chicago: University of Chicago Press, 1987.

Merriman, Eve. *Emma Lazarus Rediscovered.* New York: Biblio Press, 1999.

Messina, Anthony M. *West European Immigration and Immigrant Policy in the New Century.* Praeger, 2002.

Migration Information Source. "Italy." <http://www.migrationinformation.org/Resources/italy.cfm> (accessed June 26, 2006).

Mills, Nicholas. *Arguing Immigration: The Controversy and Crisis Over the Future of Immigration in America.* New York: Touchstone, 1994.

Mitchell, Don. *The Lie of the Land: Migrant Workers and the California Landscape.* Minneapolis: University of Minnesota Press, 1996.

Modern American Poetry. "Angel Island: Guardian of the Western Gate." <http://www.english.uiuc.edu/maps/poets/a_f/angel/natale.htm> (accessed June 29, 2006).

Molony, John. *The Penguin Bicentennial History of Australia: The Story of 200 Years.* Ringwood, Victoria, Australia: Penguin Books, 1988.

Monto, Alexander. *The Roots of Mexican Labor Migration.* Westport, Conn.: Praeger Publishers, 1994.

Mooney, Patrick H., and Theo J. Majka. *Farmers' and Farm Workers' Movements: Social Protest in American Agriculture.* New York: Twayne, 1995.

Moore, Andrew. *The Right Road: A History of Right-Wing Politics in Australia.* Melbourne, Australia: Oxford University Press, 1995.

Moreno, Barry. *Ellis Island.* Charleston, S.C.: Arcadia Publishing, 2003.

Morgan, Sharon. *Land Settlement in Early Tasmania: Creating an Antipodean England.* Cambridge, UK: Cambridge University Press, 1992.

Morgan, Ted. *Reds: McCarthyism in Twentieth-Century America.* New York: Random House, 2004.

Mulrooney, Margaret M. *Fleeing the Famine: North America and Irish Refugees, 1845–1851.* Westport, Conn.: Praeger, 2003.

Nast, Thomas. *Thomas Nast's Christmas Drawings.* New York: Dover Publications, 1978.

National Archives and Records Administration "Chinese Immigration and the Chinese in the United States." <http://www.archives.gov/locations/finding-aids/chinese-immigration.html> (accessed June 25, 2006).

National Archives of Ireland. "Transportation of Irish Convicts to Australia (1791–1853)." <http://www.nationalarchives.ie/topics/transportation/transp1.htm> (accessed June 19, 2006).

National Archives. "Constitution of the United States: Amendments 11–27." <http://www.archives.gov/national-archives-experience/charters/constitution_amendments_11-27.html> (accessed June 28, 2006).

National Archives. "Truman and the Marx Brothers." 2001 <http://www.archives.gov/publication/prologue/2001/spring/truman-and-narx-brothers.html> (accessed June 7, 2006).

National Commission on Terrorism. "Countering the Changing Threat of International Terrorism." January 1, 2004. <http://encyclopedia.laborlawtalk.com/Peter_Kropotkin> (accessed April 15, 2006).

National Farm Worker Ministry. "Childhood and Child Labor." <http://www.nfwm.org/fw/childlabor.shtml> (accessed June 25, 2006).

National Immigration Forum. "National Immigration Forum." <http://www.immigrationforum.org/> (accessed June 16, 2006).

National Immigration Law Center. "DREAM Act: Basic Information." April 2006. <http://nilc.org/immlawpolicy/DREAM/index.htm> (accessed June 28, 2006).

National Park Service's Park Register. "Charleston—community history." <http://www.cr.nps.gov/nr/travel/Charleston/intro.htm> (accessed June 15, 2006).

National Public Radio. "Split Ruling on Affirmative Action." June 23, 2003 <http://www.npr.org/news/special/michigan> (accessed June 14, 2006).

Neal, David. *The Rule of Law in a Penal Colony: Law and Politics in Early New South Wales.* Cambridge, U.K.: Cambridge University Press, 1992.

Neff, John R. *Honoring the Civil War Dead: Commemoration and the Problem of Reconciliation.* Lawrence: University Press of Kansas, 2005.

Nevins, Joseph. *Operation Gatekeeper: The rise of the illegal alien and the making of the U.S.-Mexico boundary.* New York; Routledge, 2002.

New Zealand Government. "History of Immigration." <http://www.teara.govt.nz/NewZealanders/NewZealandPeoples/HistoryOfImmigration/2/e> (accessed June 15, 2006).

Ngai, Mae M. *Impossible Subjects: Illegal Aliens and the Making of Modern America.* Princeton, N.J.: Princeton University Press, 2005.

Ngai, Mae M. *Impossible Subjects: Illegal Aliens and the Making of Modern America.* Princeton, N.J.: Princeton University Press, 2005.

NICHD - National Institute of Child Health and Human Development. "NICHD - National Institute of Child Health and Human Development." <http://www.nichd.nih.gov> (accessed on June 24, 2006).

Niven, Bill. *Facing the Nazi Past: United Germany and the Legacy of the Third Reich.* London and New York: Routledge, 2002.

Northern California Media Workers Guild/Typographical Union. "Agreement 2004–2006, Northern California Media Workers Guild/Typographical Union-CWA, Local 39521 and McClatchy Newspapers, Inc., Publisher of the Sacramento Bee." <http://www.mediaworkers.org/sacbee/sacbeecontract.html> (accessed June 26, 2006).

Northwest Regional Education Laboratory. "Improving Education for Immigrant Students." September 6, 2001 <http://www.nwrel.org/cnorse/booklets/immigration/5.html> (accessed July 1, 2006).

Norton Poets Online. "Eavan Boland." <http://www.wwnorton.com/trade/external/nortonpoets/bolande. htm> (accessed July 15, 2006).

Nowlan, Kevin B. and Maurice, R. O'Connell. *Daniel O'Connell, Portrait of a Radical.* New York: Fordham University Press, 1985.

O'Halloran, Kerry. *The Politics of Adoption: International Perspectives on Law, Policy & Practice.* Dordrecht, The Netherlands: Springer, 2006.

O'Harrow, Robert. *No Place to Hide: Behind the Scenes of Our Emerging Surveillance Society*. New York: Free Press, 2005.

O'Neill, William L. *A Democracy at War. America's Fight at Home and Abroad in World War II*. New York: The Free Press, 1993.

Office of Global Health Affairs. "Office of Global Health Affairs." <http://www.globalhealth.gov> (accessed on June 24, 2006).

Office of the Secretary, U.S. Department of Labor. "President George W. Bush and Secretary of Labor Elaine L. Chao Celebrating Asian Pacific American Heritage Month, East Room, The White House, Washington, D.C., May 17, 2002." <http://www.dol.gov/_sec/media/speeches/20020517_POTUS_APA.htm> (accessed June 28, 2006).

O'Harrow, Robert. *No Place to Hide: Behind the Scenes of Our Emerging Surveillance Society*. New York: Free Press, 2005.

Ojito, Mirta A. *Finding Manana: A Memoir of a Cuban Exodus*. New York: Penguin Press, 2005.

Oni, Kent A., and John M. Sloop. *Shifting Borders: Rhetoric, Immigration, and CaliforIorna's Proposition 187*. Philadelphia: Temple University Press, 2002.

Pérez Y Gonzìlez, María E. *Puerto Ricans in the United States*. Westport, Conn.: Greenwood Press, 2000.

Padilla, Amado M., Halford H. Fairchild, and Concepcion M. Valdez. *Bilingual Education: Issues and Strategies*. Newbury Park, CA: Sage, 1990.

Padilla, Elena. *Up from Puerto Rico*. New York: Columbia University Press, 1958.

Paine, Albert Bigelow. *Thomas Nast: His Period and his Pictures*. Gloucester, Mass.: P. Smith, 1967.

Paul, Kathleen. *Whitewashing Britain: Race and Citizenship in the Postwar Era*. Ithaca, N.Y.: Cornell University Press, 1997.

PBS Online Newshour. "The Elian Gonzalez Case." <http://www.pbs.org/newshour/bb/law/elian/> (accessed June 28, 2006).

PBS.org. "Freedom: A History of Us." 2002. <http://www.pbs.org/wnet/historyofus/web08/segment5.html> (accessed June 20, 2006).

PBS.org. "Online News Hour: Angel Island." September 5, 2000. <http://www.pbs.org/newshour/bb/entertainment/july-dec00/Angel_8-5.html> (accessed June 29, 2006).

PBS. "Becoming American: The Chinese Experience." <http://www.pbs.org/becominganamerican/> (accessed June 5, 2006).

PBS. "History's Great Escapes." <http://www.pbs.org/wgbh/nova/greatescape/history.html> (accessed June 13, 2006).

PBS. "The Great War and the Shaping of the 20th Century." <http://www.pbs.org/greatwar/> (accessed June 7, 2006).

Pedraza-Bailey, Silvia. *Political and Economic Migrants in America: Cubans and Mexicans*. Austin, Tex.: University of Texas Press, 1985.

Perez, Louis A., Jr. *Cuba: Between Reform and Revolution*. New York: Oxford University Press, 1995.

Perry, Barbara. *In the Name of Hate: Understanding Hate Crimes*. New York: Routledge, 2001.

Pertman, Adam. *Adoption Nation: How the Adoption Revolution is Transforming America*. New York: Basic Books, 2000.

Pham, John-Peter. *Boston Liberia: Portrait of a Failed State*. New York: Reed Press, 2004.

Phillips, Kevin. *William McKinley*. New York; Times Books, 2003.

Pitti, Stephen J. *The Devil in Silicon Valley: Northern California, Race and Mexican Americans*. Princeton, New Jersey; Princeton University Press, 2003.

Porter, Elisabeth J. *Researching Conflict in Africa: Insights and Experiences*. New York: United Nations University Press, 2005.

Portes, Alejandro, and Ruben G. Rumbaut. *Immigrant America: A Portrait*. Second Edition, Revised, Expanded, and Updated. Los Angeles: University of California Press, 1997.

Potter, George W. *To the Golden Door: The Story of the Irish in Ireland and America*. Boston: Little, Brown, 1960.

Powell, Enoch, and Rex Collings. *Reflections of a Statesman: The Selected Writings and Speeches of Enoch Powell*. London: Bellew Publishing, 1992.

Provoyeur, Paul, and June Ellen Hargrove, eds. *Liberty: The French-American Statue in Art and History*. New York: Perennial Library, 1986.

Puzzanghera, Jim. "Amendment Would Drop Requirement for President to be U.S.-Born." *Seattle Times*, September 16, 2004. <http://seattletimes.nwsource.com/html/nationworld/2002036961_amendment16.html> (accessed June 12, 2006).

Rabin, Yitzhak. *Major Knesset Debates: 1948–1981*. Lanham, Md: University Press of America, 1975.

Rauchway, Eric. *Murdering McKinley; The Making of Theodore Roosevelt*. New York; Hill and Wang, 2003.

Reimers, David M. *Unwelcome Strangers: American Identity and the Turn against Immigration*. New York: Columbia University Press, 1998.

Rethinking Schools Online. "History of Bilingual Education." <http://www.rethinkingschools.org/special_reports/bilingual/langhst.shtml> (accessed June 7, 2006).

Riis, Jacob A. *The Making of an American*. Honolulu, Hawaii: University Press of the Pacific, 2003.

Riley, Edward Miles, ed. *The Journal of John Harrower: an indentured servant in the Colony of Virginia, 1773–1776*. Williamsburg, VA: Colonial Williamsburg Foundation, 1963.

Robson, Lloyd. *A History of Tasmania*. Melbourne, Australia: Oxford University Press, 1983.

Rockaway, Robert A. *Words of the Uprooted: Jewish Immigrants in Early Twentieth-Century America*. Ithaca, N.Y.: Cornell University Press, 1998.

Roediger, David R. *Working Toward Whiteness: How America's Immigrants Become White: The Strange Journey from Ellis Island to the Suburbs*. New York: Basic Books, 2005.

Roots World. "World Music." 2006 <http://www.rootsworld.com/rw/> (accessed June 25, 2006).

Rosales, F. Arturo. *Chicano! The History of the Mexican American Civil Rights Movement*. Houston, Tex.: Arte Publico Press, 1996.

Rose, Tricia. *Black Noise: Rap Music and Black Culture in Contemporary America*. Wesleyan University Press, 1994.

Rosen, Ellen. *Making Sweatshop: The Globalization of the U.S. Apparel Industry*. Berkeley, Calif.: University of California Press, 2002.

Ross, Robert J.S. *Slaves to Fashion: Poverty and Abuse in the New Sweatshops*. Ann Arbor, Mich.: University of Michigan Press, 2004.

Rossi, Renzo. *A History of Powered Ships*. San Diego, Calif.: Blackbird Press, 2005.

Rudanko, Martti Juhani. *James Madison and Freedom of Speech: Major Debates in the Early Republic*. Dallas, TX: University Press of America, 2004.

Sánchez Korrol, Virginia E. *From Colonia to Community: The History of Puerto Ricans in New York City, 1917–1948*. Westport, Conn.: Greenwood Press, 1983.

Sacher, Howard M. *A History of Israel*. New York: Alfred Knopf, 1979.

Salomone, Frank A. *Italians in Rochester, New York, 1900–1940*. Lewiston, N.Y.: Edwin Mellen Press, 2000.

Sanger, Margaret. *The Selected papers of Margaret Sanger*. Champaign, IL: University of Illinois Press, 2002.

Satel, Sally. *P.C., M.D.: How Political Correctness is Corrupting Medicine*. New York: Basic Books, 2000.

Schmemann, Serge. *When the Wall Came Down: The Berlin Wall and the Fall of Soviet Communism*. New York: KingFisher, 1989.

Schmidt, Regin. *Red Scare: FBI and the Origins of Anticommunism in the U.S., 1919–1943*. Copenhagen: University of Copenhagen, 2000.

Schunck, Peter H. *Diversity in America: Keeping Government at a Safe Distance*. Cambridge, Mass.: Harvard University Press, 2003.

Segal, Uma A. *A Framework for Immigration: Asians in the United States*. New York: Columbia University Press, 2002.

Shakira. <http://www.shakira.com> (accessed June 22, 2006).

Shotwell, Louisa R. *The Harvesters: The Story of the Migrant People*. New York: Octagon Books, 1979.

Simon Wiesenthal Center. "Simon Wiesenthal Center." <http://www.wiesenthal.com> (accessed on June 24, 2006).

Skelton, George. "GOP's Prop. 187 Wounds Healing, But Dems Are Bleeding." *Los Angeles Times*, May 11, 2006. <http://www.latimes.com/news/local/la-me-cap11may11,1,6088958.column?coll=la-util-politics-cal> (accessed June 7, 2006).

Slotsky, Susan. *Losing Our Language*. New York: The Free Press, 1999.

Smith, James Morton. *Freedom's Fetters: The Alien and Sedition Laws and American Civil Liberties*. Ithaca, NY: Cornell University Press, 1966.

Sollors Werner. *Beyond Ethnicity: Consent and Descent in American Culture*. Oxford and New York: Oxford University Press, 1986.

Somerville, A. *Letters from Ireland during the Famine of 1847*. Edited by K. D. M. Snell. Dublin: Irish Academic Press, 1995.

Somerville, A., *Letters from Ireland during the Famine of 1847*. Edited by K.D.M. Snell. Dublin: Irish Academic Press, 1995.

South Caroline State Government. "A Brief History of South Carolina." <http://www.state.sc.us/scdah/history.htm> (accessed June 15, 2006).

Southern Poverty Law Center. "Southern Poverty Law Center." <http://www.splcenter.org/> (accessed on June 24, 2006).

Southern Poverty Law Center: Intelligence Report. "Blood on the Border." 2001. http://www.splcenter.org/intel/intel report/article.jsp?aid=230 (accessed July 25, 2006).

Spencer, Ian R.G. *British Immigration Policy since 1939: The Making of Multi Racial Britain*. London and New York: Routledge, 1997.

State Records Office of Western Australia. "Convict Records." <http://www.sro.wa.gov.au/collection/convict.asp> (accessed June 19, 2006).

Statue of Liberty-Ellis Island Foundation, Inc. "Statue History." <http://www.statueofliberty.org/Statue_History.html> (accessed June 24, 2006).

Steinberg, Salme. *Reformer in the Marketplace: Edward W. Bok and the Ladies' Home Journal*. Baton Rouge: Louisiana State University, 1979.

Steiner, Henry, and Philip Alston. *International Human Rights in Context: Law, Politics, Morals*. Oxford and New York: Oxford University Press, 2000.

Steiner, Henry, and Philip Alston. *International Human Rights in Context: Law, Politics, Morals*. Oxford: Oxford University Press, 2000.

Stone, Scott C.S. and John E. McGowan. *Wrapped in the Wind's Shawl: Refugees of Southeast Asia and the Western World*. San Rafael, CA: Presidio, 1980.

Suarez-Orozco, Carola, and Marcelo Suarez-Orozco. *Children of Immigration*. Cambridge, Mass.: Harvard University Press, 2001.

Summers, Judith. *Soho: A History of London's Most Colourful Neighborhoods*. London: Bloomsbury, 1989.

Szatmary, David. *Rockin' in Time: A Social History of Rock and Roll*. Prentice Hall Press, 2006.

Taylor, Ronald B. *Chávez and the Farm Workers*. Boston: Beacon Press, 1975.

Taylor, Ronald B. *Sweatshops in the Sun: Child Labor on the Farm*. Boston: Beacon Press, 1973.

Tenement Museum. <http://www.thirteen.org/tenement/eagle. html> (accessed June 28, 2006).

Tennessee Immigration and Refugee Rights Coalition. "Tennessee Immigration and Refugee Rights Coalition." <http:// www.tnimmigrant.org/> (accessed June 21, 2006).

ThomasNast.com. "The World of Thomas Nast." <http:// www.thomasnast.com> (accessed June 28, 2006).

Tichenor, Daniel J. *Dividing Lines: The Politics of Immigration Control in America*. Princeton, N.J.: Princeton University Press, 2002.

TimesOnLine. "Points system will favor skilled immigrant workers, says Clarke." March 8, 2006 <http:// www.timesonline.co.uk/article/0,,2–2075110,00.html> (accessed June 28, 2006).

Trommler, Frank, and Joseph McVeigh, editors. *America and the Germans: An Assessment of a Three-Hundred Year History*. Philadelphia: University of Pennsylvania Press, 1985.

Truett, Samuel and Elliot Young, ed. *Continental Cross-roads: Remapping U.S.-Mexico Borderlands History*. Raleigh, North Carolina: Duke University Press, 2004.

Truman Presidential Museum and Library. "George L. Warren Papers." <http://www.trumanlibrary.org/hstpaper/ warren.htm> (accessed June 7, 2006).

Truman Presidential Museum and Library. "Statement by the President upon Signing the Displaced Persons Act." June 25, 1948 <http://trumanlibrary.org/publicpapers/ viewpapers.php?pid=1688> (accessed June 15, 2006).

Tsesis, Alexander. *The Thirteenth Amendment and American Freedom: A Legal History*. New York: New York University Press, 2004.

Tucker, Nancy Bernkoft, editor. *China Confidential: American Diplomats and Sino-American Relations 1945– 1996*. New York: Columbia University Press, 2001.

U.S. Army Judge Advocate General's Corps. "Naturalization Information for Military Personnel." <http://www.jagcnet. army.mil/JAGCNETInternet/Homepages/AC/Legal%20 Assistance%20Home%20Page.nsf/0/6d81833c6d5d6df58 5256a05005d39c0/$FILE/MilitaryBrochurev77.pdf> (accessed June 13, 2006).

U.S. Bureau of the Census. "Historical Statistics of the Foreign Born Population of the United States, 1850–1990." <http://www. census.gov/population/www/documentation/twps0029/ twps0029. html> (accessed June 20, 2006).

U.S. Centers for Disease Control and Prevention. "Cholera." <http:// www.cdc.gov/ncidod/dbmd/diseaseinfo/cholera_g.htm> (accessed June 12, 2006).

U.S. Citizenship and Immigration Services. "Elian Gonzalez." <http://www.uscis.gov/graphics/publicaffairs/ElianG.htm> (accessed June 28, 2006).

U.S. Citizenship and Immigration Services. "This Month in Immigration History: December 1943." <http:// www.uscis.gov/graphics/aboutus/history/dec43.htm> (accessed June 12, 2006).

U.S. Conference of Catholic Bishops. "Bishops' Conference Chairmen Support Farm Worker Proposal." November 7, 2003. <http://216.239.51.104/search?q=cache:blvMS MjutmkJ:www.nccbuscc.org/comm/archives/> (accessed July 15, 2006).

U.S. Congress. House. Constitutional Amendment to Allow Foreign-Born Citizens to be President. HJR 88, 106th Congress, 2nd session. Available at: <http://comm docs.house.gov/ committees/judiciary/hju67306.000/hju67306_0f.htm> (accessed June 10, 2006).

U.S. Department of Health and Human Services. *Proposed Refugee Admission for Fiscal Year 2005*. Report to the Congress. Department of State. Department of Homeland Security. Washington, D.C.: U.S. Department of Health and Human Services, 2004.

U.S. Department of Homeland Security. "Injured Soldier Naturalized at Walter Reed by USCIS Director." <http://uscis.gov/graphics/publicaffairs/newsrels/Walter ReedNatz03_08_05.pdf> (accessed June 13, 2006).

U.S. Department of Homeland Security. "United States Citizenship and Immigration Services." June 23, 2006 <http://www.uscis.gov/graphics/index.htm> (accessed June 28, 2006).

U.S. Department of State: Outline of U.S. History. "Chapter 3: The Road to Independence." November 2005 <http:// usinfo.state.gov/products/pubs/histryotln/road.htm> (accessed July 17, 2006).

U.S. Department of State. "International Adoption." <http:// travel.state.gov/family/adoption/notices/notices_473. html> (accessed June 25, 2006).

U.S. Holocaust Memorial Museum. "Emigration." <http:// www.ushmm.org/museum/exhibit/online/dp//emigrate. htm> (accessed June 15, 2006).

U.S. Homeland Security. "U.S. Citizenship and Immigration Services." June 23, 2006 <http://www.uscis.gov/ graphics/index.htm> (accessed June 26, 2006).

U.S. Office of Citizenship and Immigration Services. "Office of Citizenship." <http://www.uscis.gov/graphics/citizen ship/index.htm> (accessed June 13, 2006).

U.S. State Department. "The New Colossus." <http:// usinfo.state.gov/usa/infousa/facts/democrac/63.htm> (accessed June 22, 2006).

UCLA Department of Epidemiology. "John Snow." <http://www. ph.ucla.edu/epi/snow.html> (accessed June 12, 2006).

Ueda, Reed, ed. *A Companion to American Immigration.* Boston: Blackwell Publishing, 2006.

Umutesi, Marie B. *Surviving the Slaughter: The Ordeal of a Rwandan Refugee in Zaire.* Madison: University of Wisconsin Press , 2004.

UNAIDS. "UNAIDS Research." <http://www.unaids.org/ en/Issues/Research/default.asp> (accessed on June 24, 2006).

United Nation's Educational, Scientific, and Cultural Organization (UNESCO). "UNESCO Universal Declaration on Cultural Diversity—2001." <http://portal.unesco.org/ culture/en/> (accessed June 26, 2006).

United Nations High Commissioner for Refugees. *The State of the World's Refugees: Human Displacement in the New Millennium.* New York: Oxford University Press, 2006.

United Nations Office of the High Commissioner for Human Rights. "United Nations." <http://www.ohchr.org/ english/> (accessed on June 24, 2006).

United Nations. *Universal Declaration of Human Rights, Articles 13–15.* New York: United Nations, 1948.

United Nations. "Human Rights." <http://www.un.org/ rights/> (accessed June 11, 2006).

United Nations. "World Day for Cultural Diversity for Dialogue and Development: May 21." <http://www. un.org/depts/dhl/cultural_diversity/> (accessed June 26, 2006).

United States Census Bureau. "United States Census Bureau." <http://www.census.gov> (accessed on June 24, 2006).

United States House of Representatives. "The United States House of Representatives." <http://www.house.gov/> (accessed on June 24, 2006).

United States Senate. "The United States Senate." <http:// www.senate.gov/> (accessed on June 24, 2006).

University of Buffalo. "McKinley Assassination." 2004 <http:// www.ublib.buffalo.edu/libraries/exhibits/panam/law/ assassination.html> (accessed June 13, 2006).

University of California at Berkeley. "Emma Goldman." June 2003 <http://www.sunrite.berkeley.edu/Goldman/Exhi bition/assassination.html> (accessed).

University of Dayton. "Asian Pacific Americans and Immigration Law." <http://academic.udayton.edu/ race/02rights/immigr05.htm> (accessed June 8, 2006).

University of Houston: Digital History. "A Chronology of World War I." <http://www.digitalhistory.uh.edu/ historyonline/ww1_chron.cfm> (accessed June 8, 2006).

University of Missouri. Department of Sociology. "A Historical Look at U.S. Immigration Policy." <http://web. missouri.edu/~socbrent/immigr.htm> (accessed June 7, 2006).

University of Oklahoma College of Law. "The Sedition Act of 1798." <http://www.law.ou.edu/ushistory/sedact.shtml> (accessed June 26, 2006).

University of Pennsylvania. African Studies Center. "Liberia Page." <http://www.africa.upenn.edu/Country_Specific/ Liberia.html> (accessed June 7, 2006).

University of Pittsburgh Law School. "Learning from Living: The University of Michigan Affirmative Action Cases." September 5, 2003 <http://www.jurist.law.pitt.edu/forum/ symposium-aa/bell.php> (accessed June 13, 2006).

University of Pittsburgh Law School. "Some Observations on Grutter." September 5, 2003 <http://www.jurist. law. pitt.edu/forum/symposium-aa/shields.php> (accessed June 13, 2006).

University of Texas: Reagan Archive. "Remarks at the Opening Ceremonies of the Statue of Liberty Centennial Celebration in New York, New York," July 3, 1986 <http:// www.reagan.utexas.edu/archives/speeches/1986/70386d. htm> (accessed June 24, 2006).

University of Virginia. "Jazz Roots, 1890–1935 <http:// xroads.virginia.edu/~ASI/musi212/brandi/bmain.html> (accessed June 25, 2006).

Uschan, Michael V. *The Iraq War: Life of an American Soldier in Iraq.* New York: Lucent Books, 2004.

Vidal, Gore. *Inventing a Nation: Washington, Adams, Jefferson.* New Haven, Conn.: Yale University Press, 2003.

Vo, Nghia M. *The Vietnamese Boat People, 1954 and 1975–1992.* Jefferson, NC: McFarland, 2006.

Voss-Hubbard, Mark. *Beyond Party: Cultures of Anti-partisanship in Northern Politics before the Civil War.* Baltimore, Md.: Johns Hopkins University Press, 2002.

Wald, Lillian. *The House on Henry Street.* New York: Henry Holt and Company, 1915.

Waldinger, Roger. *Strangers at the Gates: New Immigrants in Urban America.* Berkeley, Calif.: University of California Press, 2001.

Walker, Juliet E. K. *Encyclopedia of African American Business History.* Westport, Conn.: Greenwood Press, 1999.

Walker, Juliet E. K. *The History of Black Business in America: Capitalism, Race, Entrepreneurship.* New York: Macmillan Press, 1998.

Weinbaum, Paul Owen. *Statue of Liberty: The Story Behind the Scenery.* Haddonfield, NJ: K.C. Publishing, 1988.

Weinberg, Sydney Stahl. *The World of Our Mothers: The Lives of Jewish Immigrant Women.* Chapel Hill: University of North Carolina Press, 1988.

Weiss, Bernard J., ed. *American Education and the European Immigrant, 1840–1940.* Urbana: University of Illinois Press, 1982.

Weissbrodt, David S., and Laura Danielson. *Immigration Law and Procedure in a Nutshell.* St. Paul, Minn: Thomson/West Group Publishing, 2005.

Wheeler, Rebecca. *The Workings of Language: From Prescriptions to Perspectives.* Westport, Conn., and London: Praeger Publishers, 1999.

White House. "Comprehensive Immigration Reform." <http://www.whitehouse.gov/infocus/immigration/> (accessed June 13, 2006).

White House. "President Attends Naturalization Ceremony." March 2006. <http://www.whitehouse.gov/news/releases/2006/03/20060327.html> (accessed June 13, 2006).

White House. "President Bush Proposes New Temporary Worker Program." January 2004. <http://www.whitehouse.gov/news/releases/2004/01/20040107-3.html> (accessed June 7, 2006).

White House. "White House Office of Communications." <http://www.whitehouse.gov/news/> (accessed on June 24, 2006).

White House. "Thomas Jefferson." <http://www.whitehouse.gov/history/presidents/tj3.html> (accessed June 26, 2006).

Wilkes, Stephen. *Ellis Island: Ghosts of Freedom.* New York: W.W. Norton & Company, 2006.

Williams, Mary E., ed. *Immigration: Opposing Viewpoints.* Chicago: Greenhaven Press, 2003.

Willis, Deborah. *Reflections in Black: A History of Black Photographers, 1840 to the Present.* New York: W. W. Norton, 2000.

Wisconsin Historical Society. "Turning Points in Wisconsin History." <http://content.wisconsinhistory.org/cdm4/> (accessed July 10, 2006).

Wong, K. Scott (ed.) and Sucheng Chan. *Claiming America: Constructing Chinese Identities During the Exclusion Era.* Philadelphia, Pennsylvania: Temple University Press, 1998.

World Health Organization. "WHO Bulletin." <http://www.who.int/bulletin/en> (accessed on June 24, 2006).

Wyman, David S. *Paper Walls: America and the Refugee Crisis, 1938–1941.* Amherst: University of Massachusetts Press, 1968.

Wyman, Mark. *Europe's Displaced Persons 1945–1951.* New York: Associated University Presses, 1989.

Yang, Philip Q. *Post–1965 Immigration to the United States: Structural Determinants.* Westport, Conn.: Praeger, 1995.

Yezierska, Anzia. *Bread Givers: A Struggle between a Father of the Old World and a Daughter of the New.* New York: G. Braziller, 1975.

Yoshida, Chisa To and Alan Woodland. *The Economics of Illegal Immigration.* New York: Palgrave MacMillan, 2005.

Yoshida, Chisato, and Alan Woodland. *The Economics of Illegal Immigration.* New York: Palgrave MacMillan, 2005.

Zangwill, Israel. *Melting Pot, Drama in Four Acts.* New York: The Macmillan Company, 1909.

Ziglar, James W. "International Adoptions." *GPO/USCIS,* May 22, 2002 <http://www.uscis.gov/graphics/aboutus/congress/testimonies/2002/1ZIGHOUS.pdf> (accessed July 14, 2006).

Zucker, Bat-Ami. *In Search of Refuge: Jews and US Consuls in Nazi Germany, 1933–1941.* London: Vallentine Mitchell, 2001.

Zucker, Naomi Flink and Zucker, Norman L. *Desperate Crossings: Seeking Refuge in America.* Armonk, New York: M.E. Sharpe, 1996.

Index

Boldface indicates a primary source.
Italics indicates an illustration on the page.